ORDNANCE SU

GW01179442

STREET ATLAS
Berkshire

Contents

IV   *Key to maps*

VI   *Administrative boundaries*

1   *Street maps*

154   *Index explanation and abbreviations*

155   *Index of towns, villages and rural localities*

156   *Index of street names*

PHILIP'S

First edition published 1990
Third edition published 1994 by

Ordnance Survey   and   Philip's
Romsey Road   an imprint of Reed Consumer Books Limited
Maybush   Michelin House, 81 Fulham Road, London, SW3 6RB
Southampton SO16 4GU   and Auckland, Melbourne, Singapore and Toronto

ISBN 0-540-05992-7 (Philip's, hardback)
ISBN 0-540-05993-5 (Philip's, softback)
ISBN 0-319-00475-9 (Ordnance Survey, hardback)
ISBN 0-319-00476-7 (Ordnance Survey, softback)

To the best of the Publishers' knowledge, the information in this atlas was correct at the
time of going to press. No responsibility can be accepted for any errors or their
consequences.

The representation in this atlas of a road, track or path is no evidence of the existence of
a right of way.

Printed and bound in Great Britain by
Butler & Tanner Ltd, Frome and London

Key to map symbols

⇌	**British Rail station**
⊖	**London transport station**
🚂	**Private railway station**
◆	**Bus or coach station**
Ⓗ	**Heliport**
◆	**Police station** (may not be open 24 hours)
✚	**Hospital with casualty facilities** (may not be open 24 hours)
☐	**Post office**
+	**Place of worship**
◼	**Important building**
P	**Parking**
120	**Adjoining page indicator**
═══	**Motorway or dual carriageway**
A27(T)	**Main or through road** (with Department of Transport number)
──┬──	**Gate or obstruction to traffic** (restrictions may not apply at all times or to all vehicles)
- - - - -	**Footpath**
— — —	**Bridleway**
─ ─ ─	**Path**
═══	**Track**

The representation in this atlas of a road, track or path is no evidence of the existence of a right of way

Amb Sta	**Ambulance station**	LC	**Level crossing**
Coll	**College**	Liby	**Library**
FB	**Footbridge**	Mus	**Museum**
F Sta	**Fire station**	Sch	**School**
Hospl	**Hospital**	TH	**Town hall**

0	¼	½	¾	1 mile
0	250m	500m	250m	1 Kilometre

The scale of the maps is 3½ inches to 1 mile (1:18103)

The small numbers around the edges of the maps identify the 1 kilometre National Grid lines

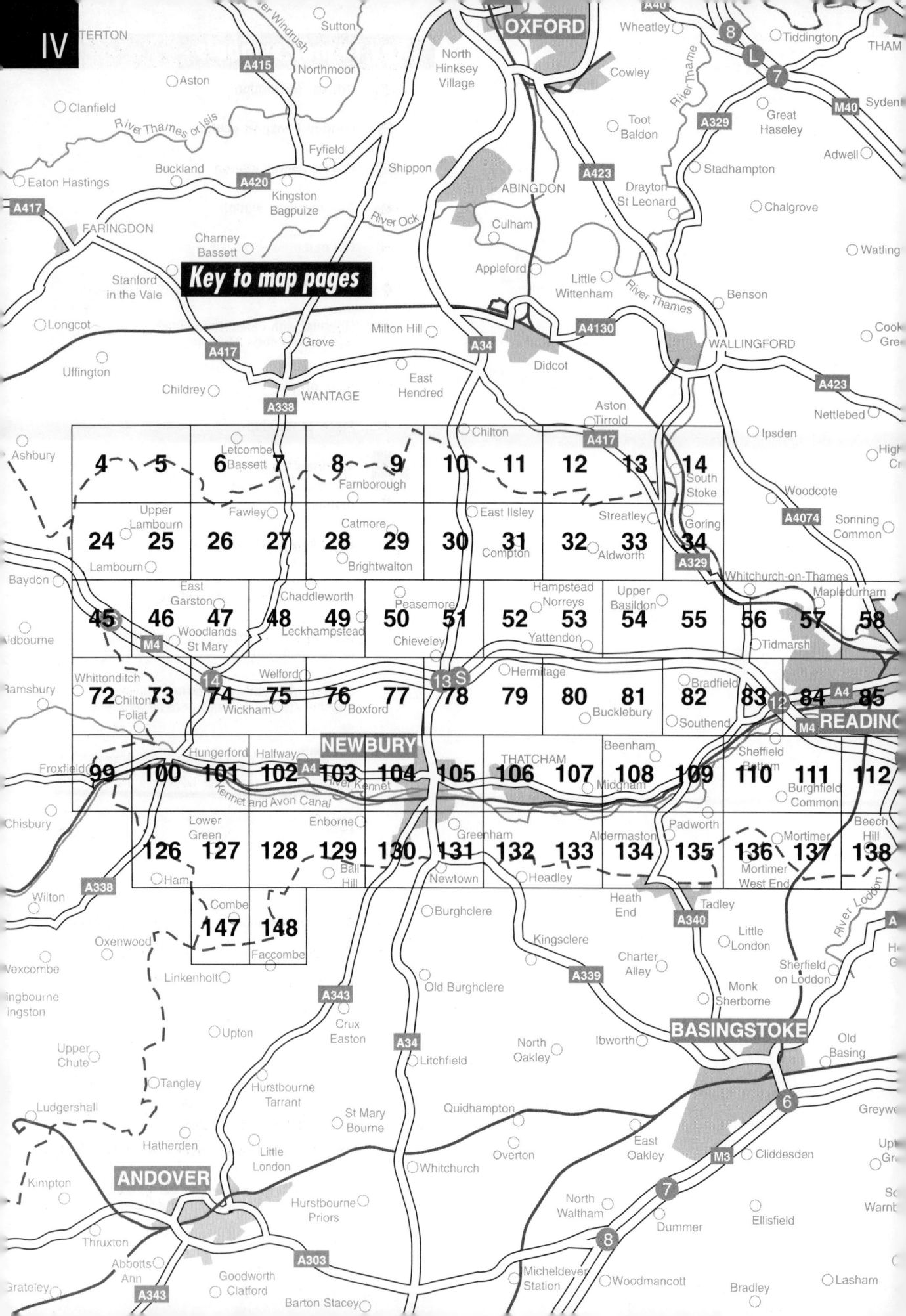

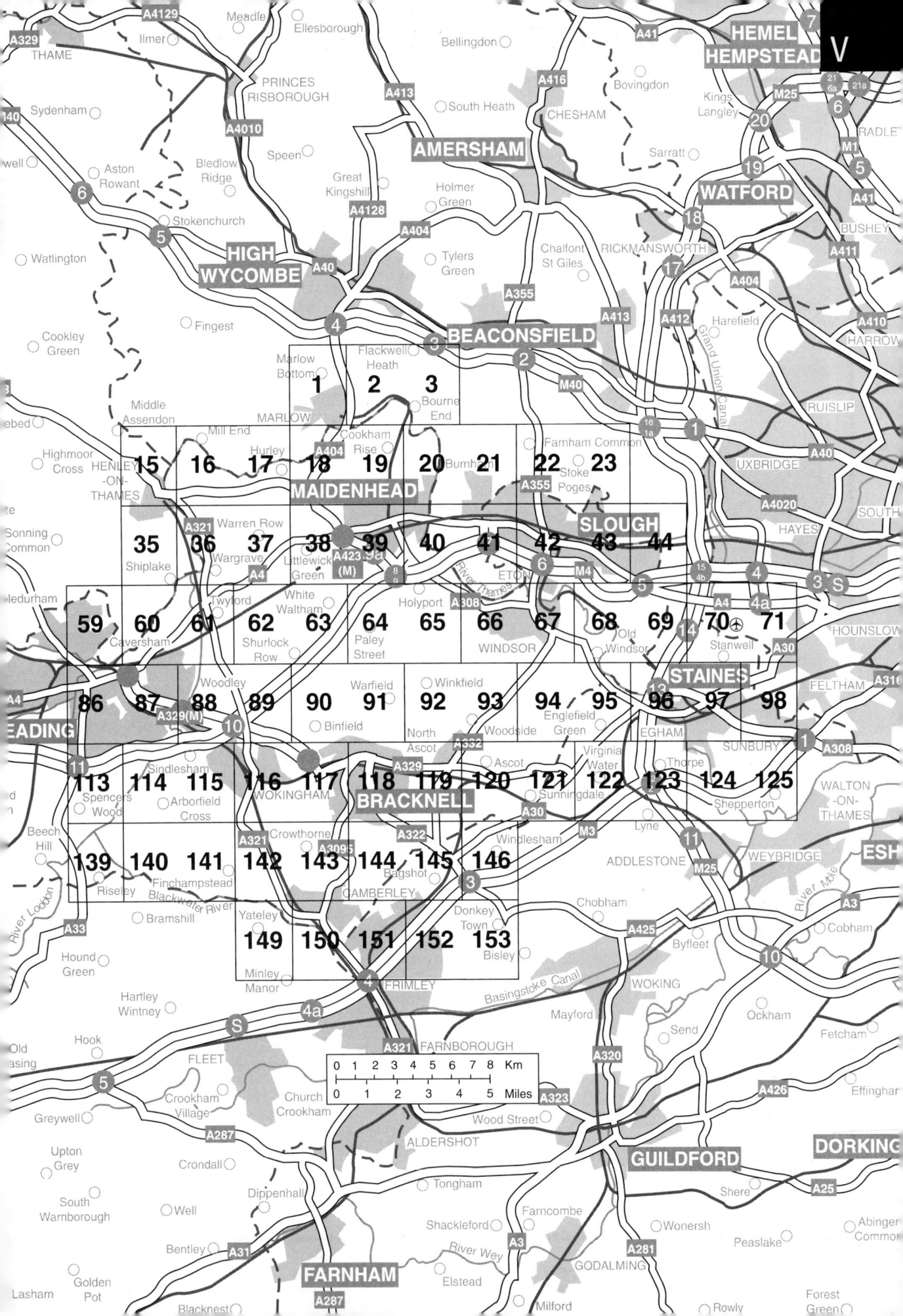

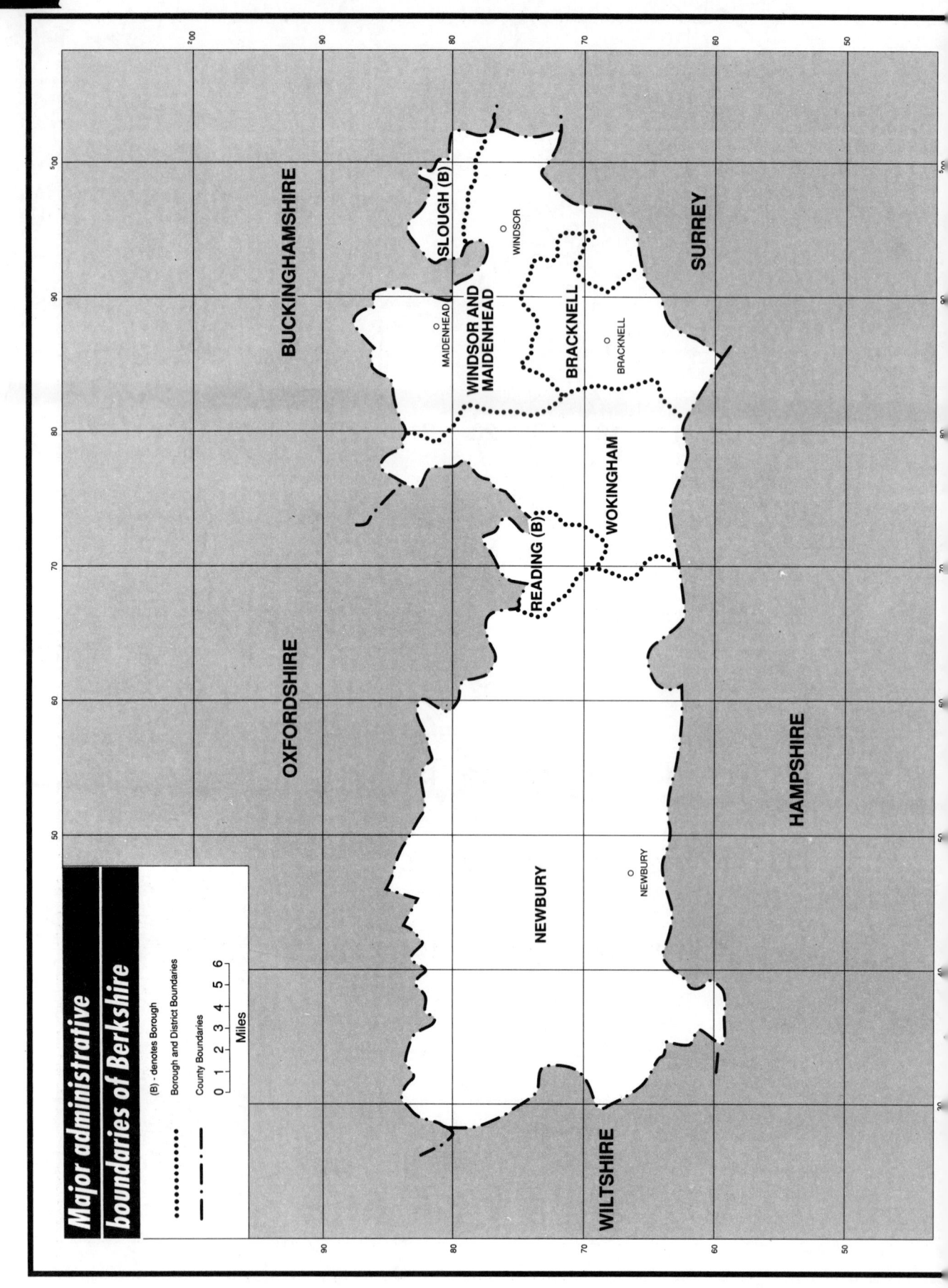

Major administrative boundaries of Berkshire

(B) - denotes Borough

•••••• Borough and District Boundaries

—·—·— County Boundaries

0 1 2 3 4 5 6
Miles

BUCKINGHAMSHIRE

SLOUGH (B)

WINDSOR
○ WINDSOR

WINDSOR AND MAIDENHEAD

MAIDENHEAD ○

BRACKNELL

BRACKNELL ○

SURREY

READING (B)

WOKINGHAM

OXFORDSHIRE

NEWBURY

NEWBURY ○

HAMPSHIRE

WILTSHIRE

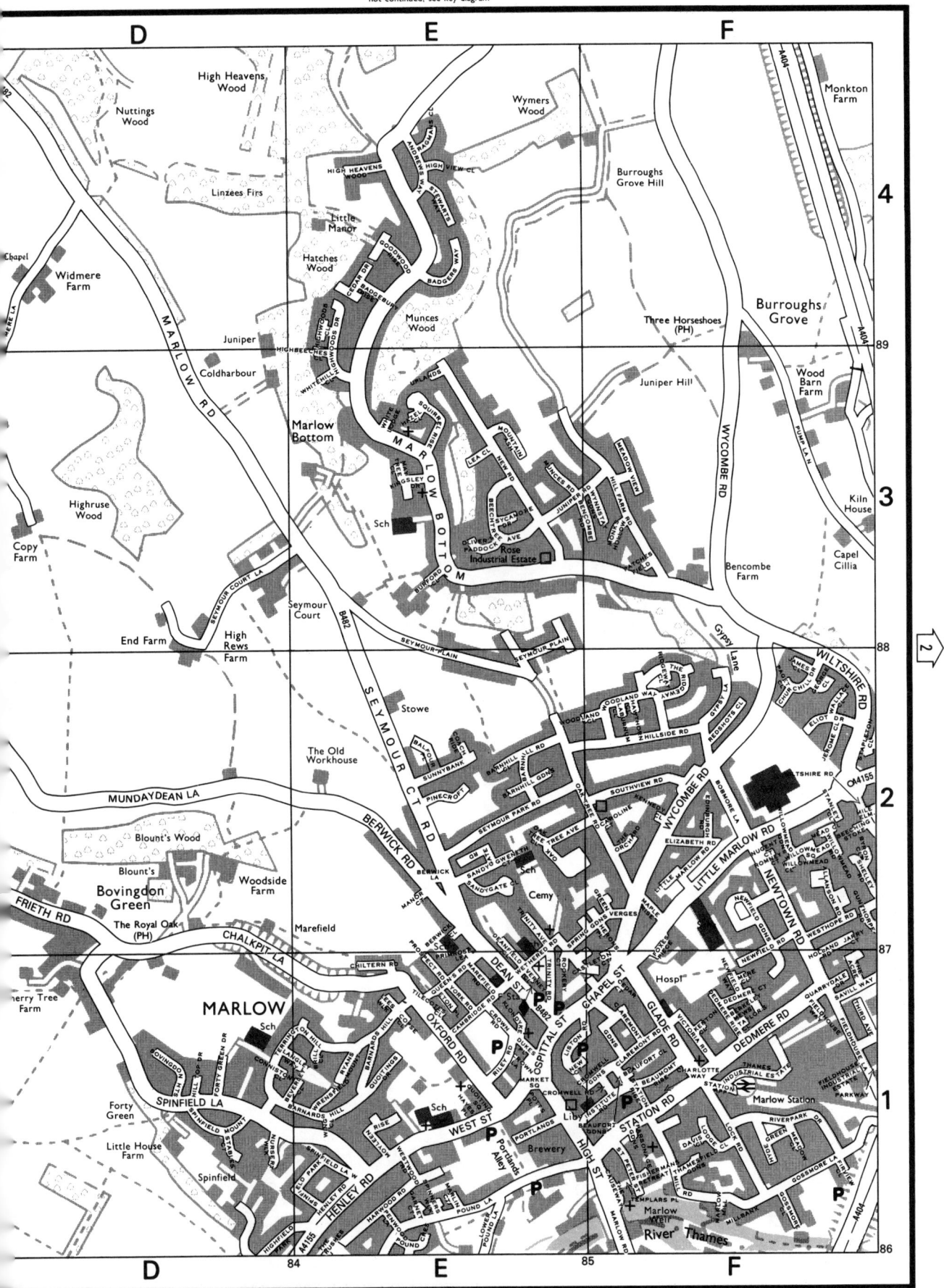

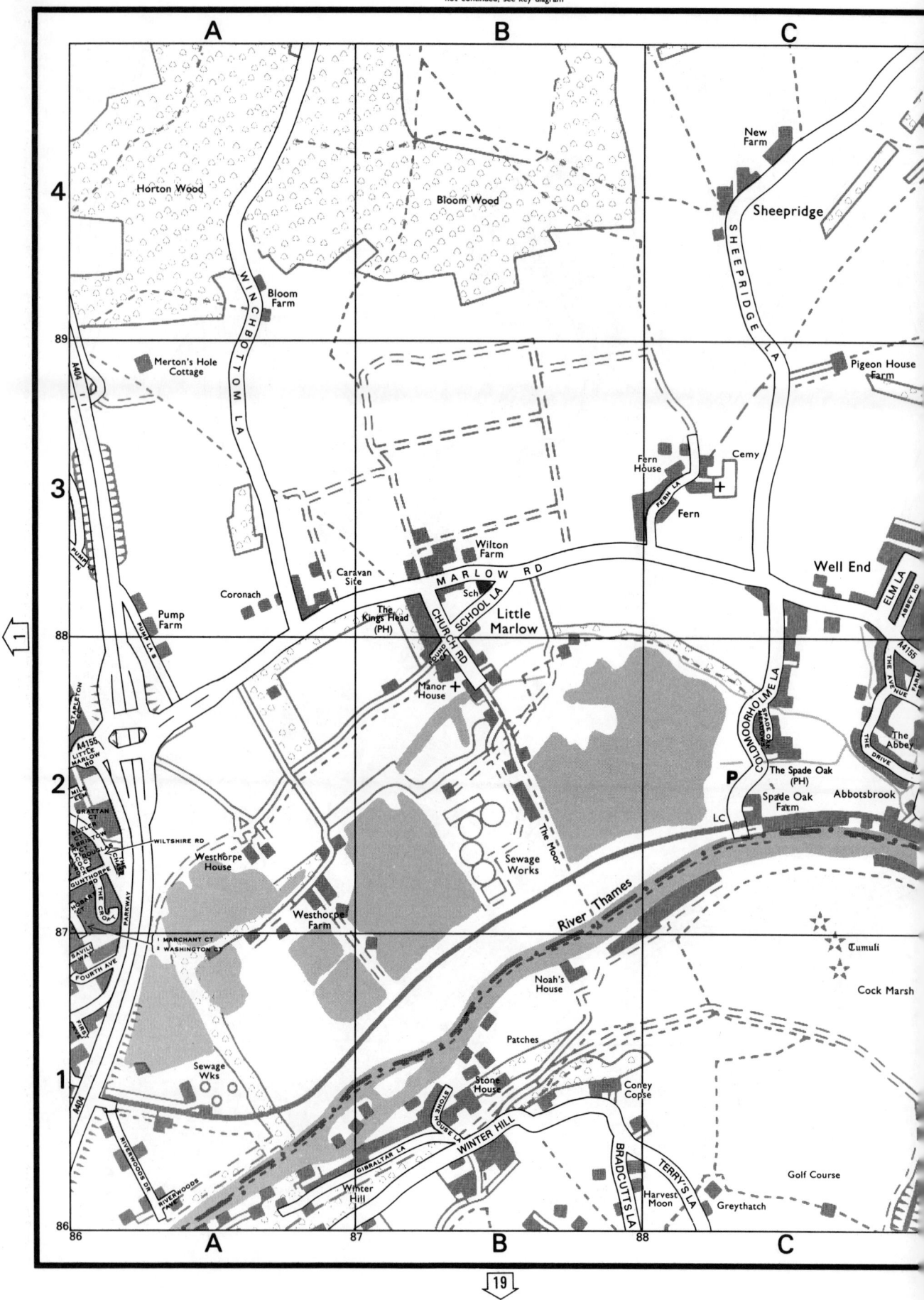

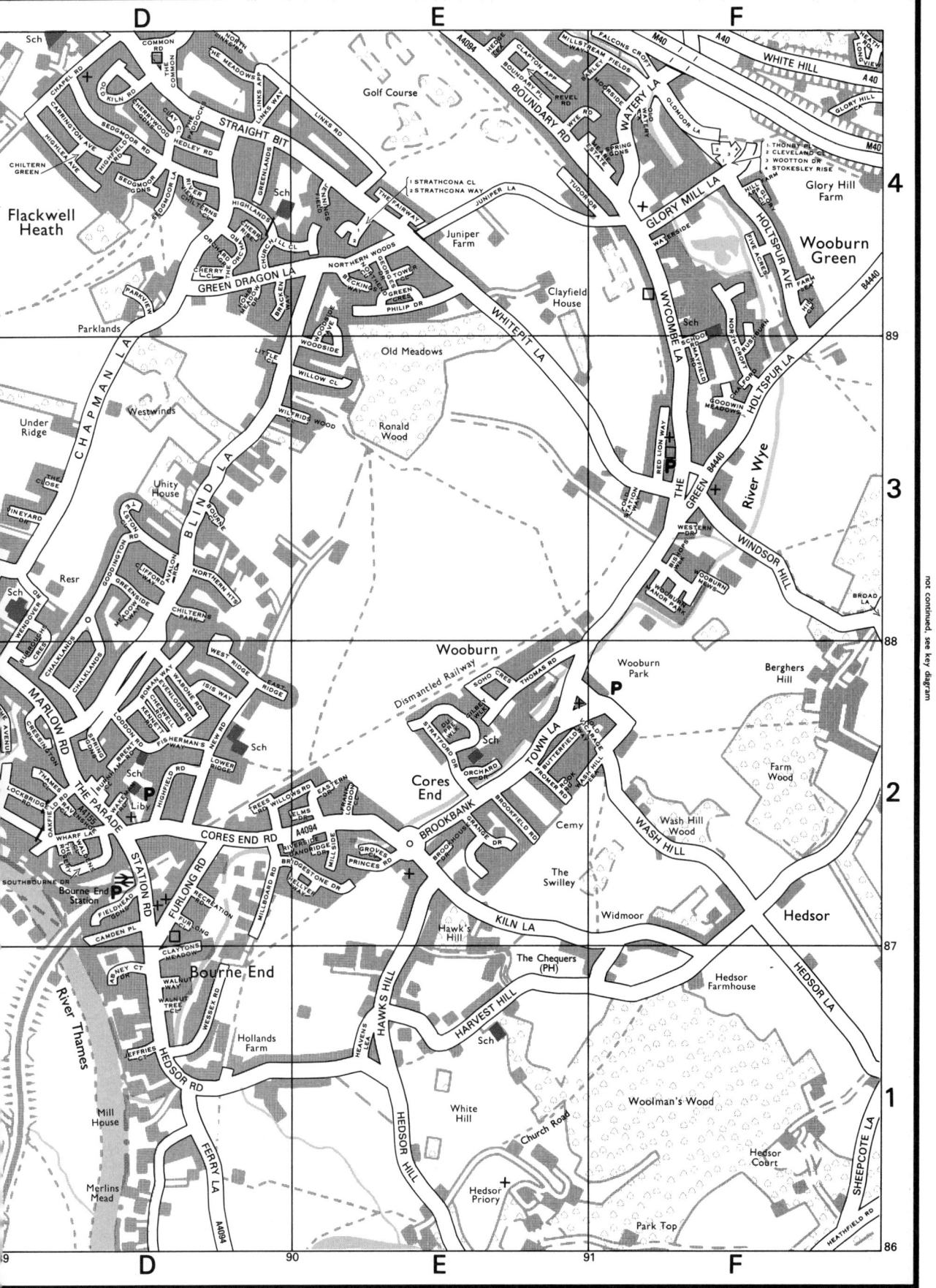

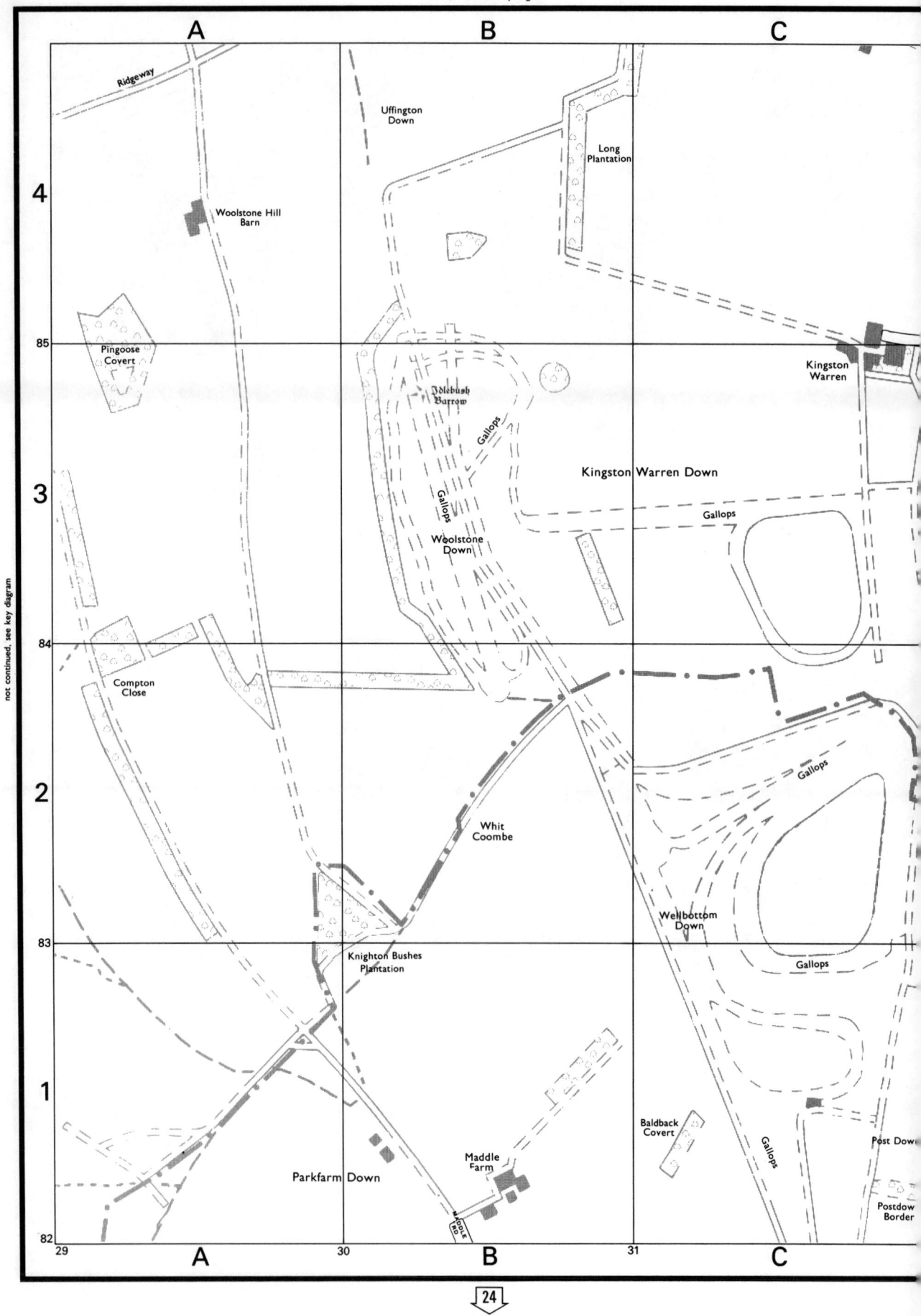

A   B   C

Ridgeway

Uffington
Down

Long
Plantation

4

Woolstone Hill
Barn

85

Pingoose
Covert

Idlebush
Barrow

Kingston
Warren

Gallops

Kingston Warren Down

3

Gallops

Gallops

Woolstone
Down

84

Compton
Close

Gallops

2

Whit
Coombe

Wellbottom
Down

Gallops

83

Knighton Bushes
Plantation

Gallops

1

Baldback
Covert

Post Down

Maddle
Farm

Parkfarm Down

MIDDLE ROD

Postdown
Border

82 29   30   31

A   B   C

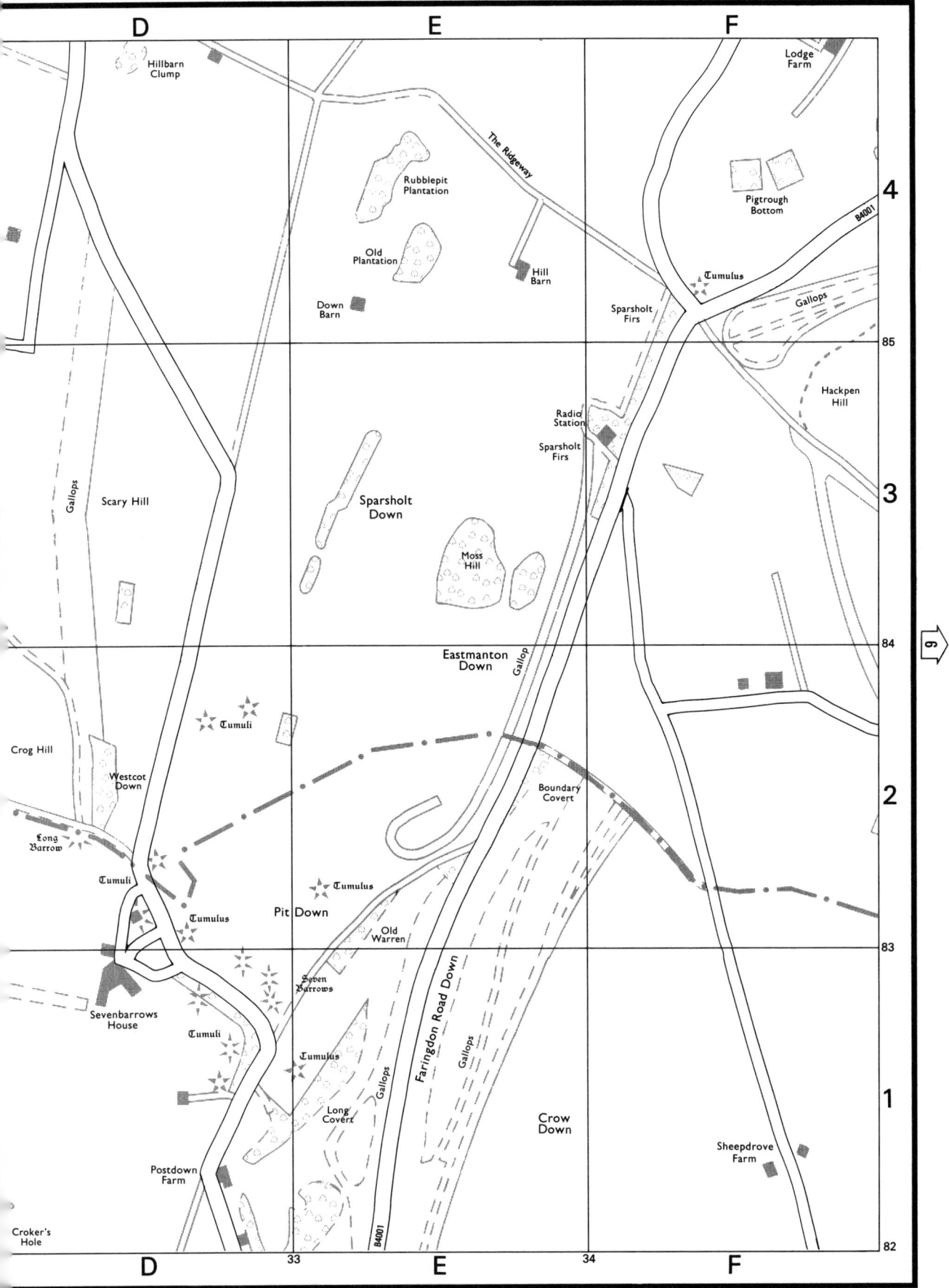

5

D E F

Hillbarn Clump

The Ridgeway

Rubblepit Plantation

Old Plantation

Down Barn

Hill Barn

Lodge Farm

Pigtrough Bottom

B4001

4

Tumulus

Sparsholt Firs

Gallops

85

Radio Station

Sparsholt Firs

Hackpen Hill

Gallops

Scary Hill

Sparsholt Down

Moss Hill

3

Eastmanton Down

Gallop

84

Crog Hill

Westcot Down

Tumuli

Boundary Covert

2

Long Barrow

Tumuli

Tumulus

Tumulus

Pit Down

Old Warren

83

Seven Barrows

Sevenbarrows House

Tumuli

Tumulus

Faringdon Road Down

Gallops

Gallops

Crow Down

1

Long Covert

Postdown Farm

B4001

Sheepdrove Farm

Croker's Hole

82

D 33 E 34 F

6

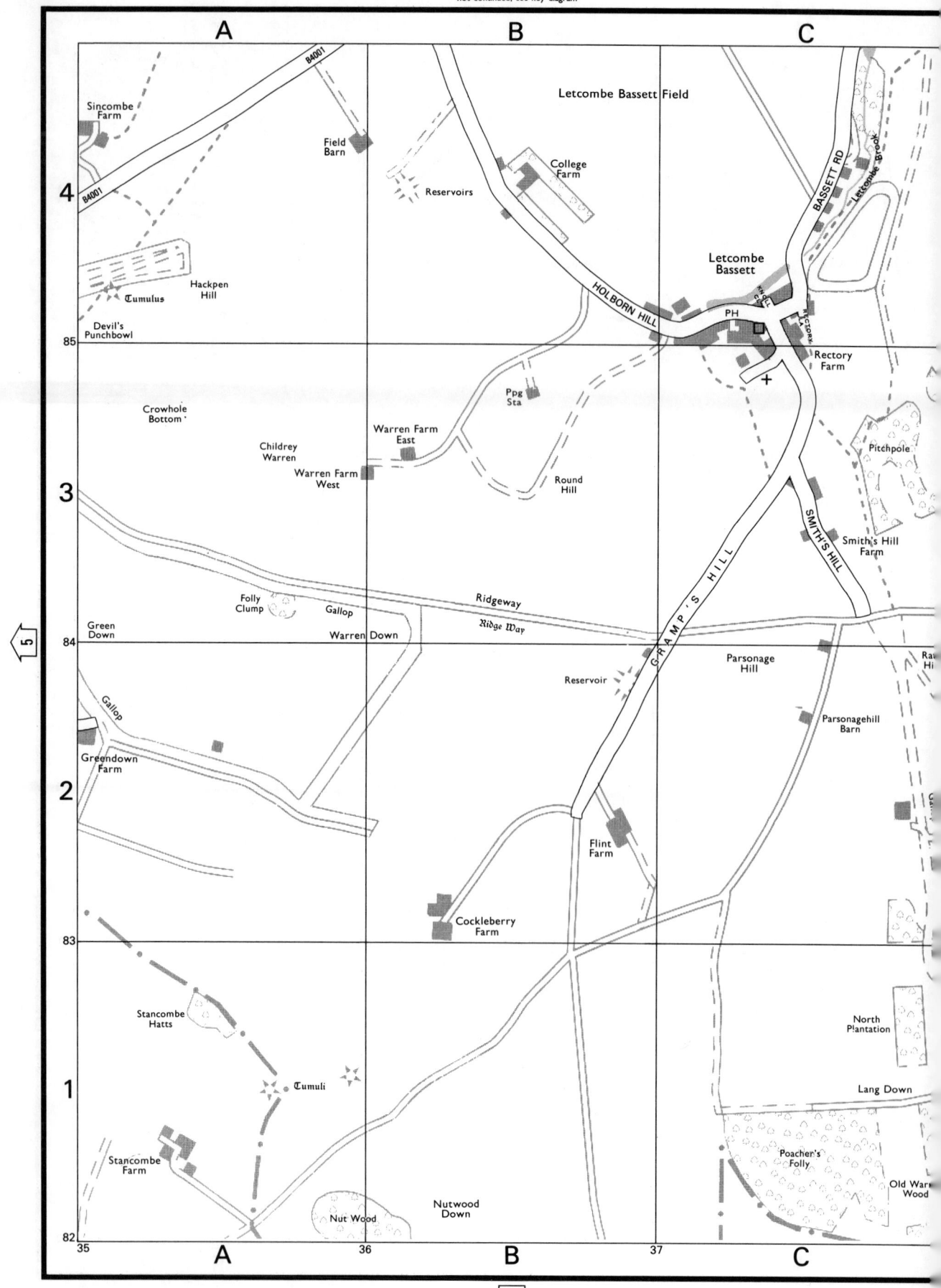

A   B   C

B4001

Sincombe Farm

Field Barn

Letcombe Bassett Field

BASSETT RD

Letcombe Brook

4

Reservoirs

College Farm

B4001

Letcombe Bassett

Hackpen Hill

Tumulus

85

Devil's Punchbowl

HOLBORN HILL

CH

PH

RECTORY LA

Rectory Farm

Crowhole Bottom

Ppg Sta

Round Hill

Pitchpole

Childrey Warren

Warren Farm East

Warren Farm West

SMITH'S HILL

Smith's Hill Farm

3

Folly Clump

Gallop

Ridgeway

GRAMP'S HILL

Green Down

Ridge Way

84

Warren Down

Reservoir

Parsonage Hill

Raf Hi

Gallop

Parsonagehill Barn

Greendown Farm

2

Flint Farm

Cockleberry Farm

83

Stancombe Hatts

North Plantation

1

Tumuli

Lang Down

Stancombe Farm

Poacher's Folly

Old War Wood

82

Nut Wood

Nutwood Down

35   A   36   B   37   C

5

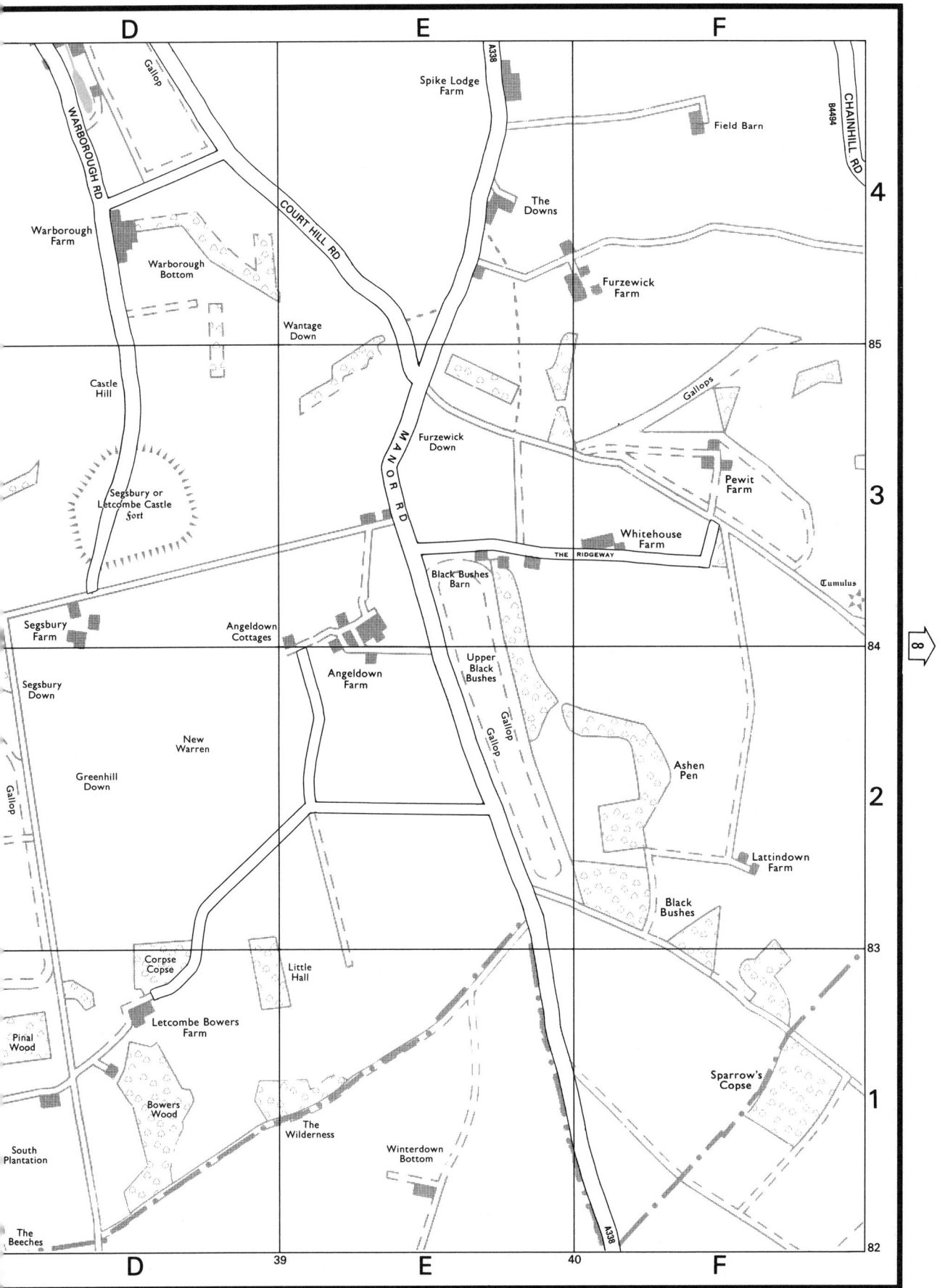

D   E   F

Gallop

WARBOROUGH RD

COURT HILL RD

A338

Spike Lodge Farm

CHAINHILL RD

B4494

Field Barn

The Downs

4

Warborough Farm

Warborough Bottom

Wantage Down

Furzewick Farm

85

Castle Hill

Furzewick Down

MANOR RD

Gallops

Pewit Farm

3

Segsbury or Letcombe Castle Fort

Whitehouse Farm

THE RIDGEWAY

Black Bushes Barn

Tumulus

Segsbury Farm

Angeldown Cottages

Upper Black Bushes

84

⟨∞⟩8

Segsbury Down

Angeldown Farm

Gallop

New Warren

Greenhill Down

Gallop

Ashen Pen

2

Gallop

Lattindown Farm

Black Bushes

Corpse Copse

Little Hall

83

Pinal Wood

Letcombe Bowers Farm

Sparrow's Copse

Bowers Wood

1

South Plantation

The Wilderness

Winterdown Bottom

A338

The Beeches

82

D   39   E   40   F

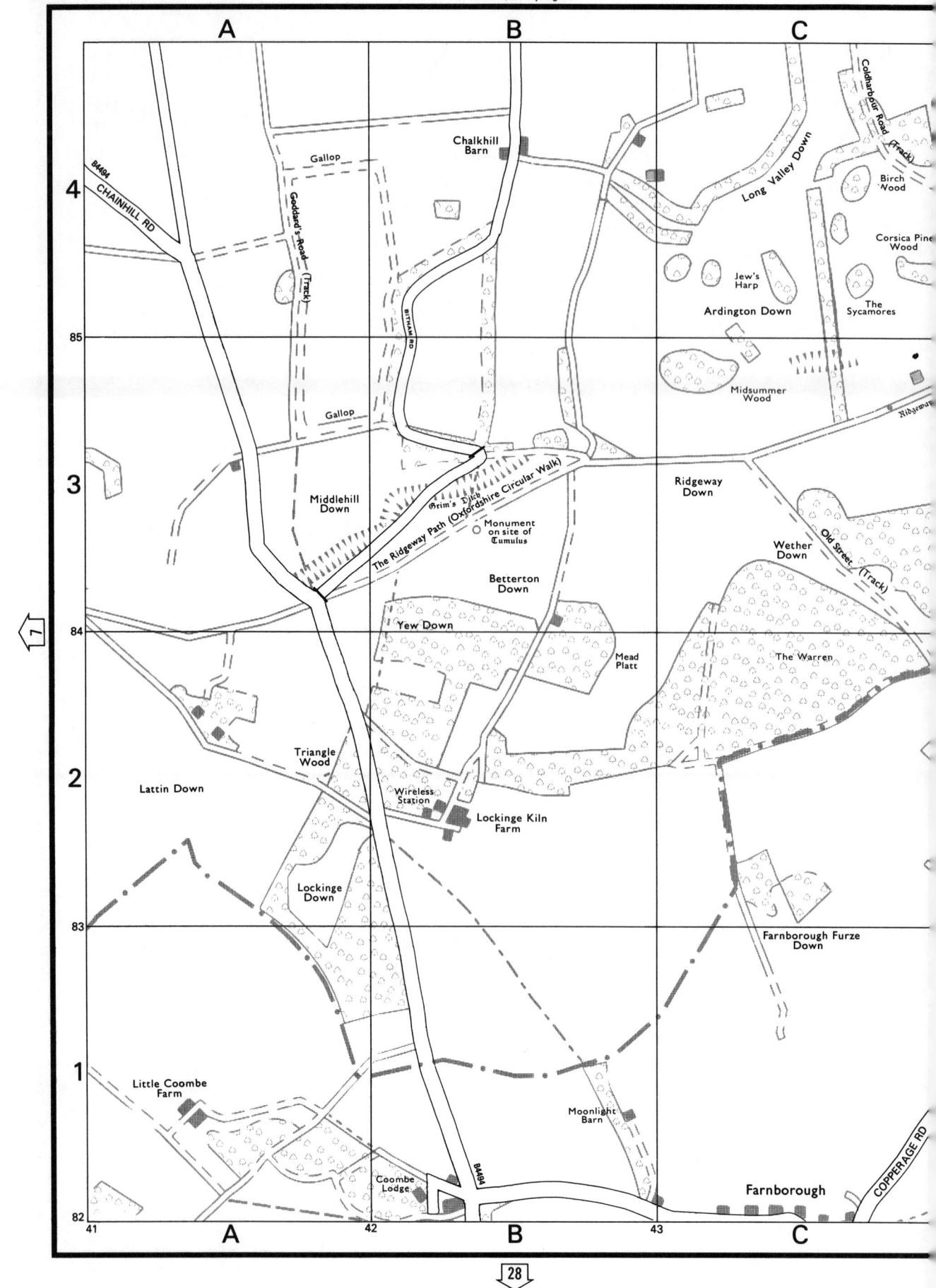

A   B   C

B4494

CHAINHILL RD

Gallop

Chalkhill
Barn

Goddard's Road (Track)

Long Valley Down

Coldharbour Road (Track)

Birch
Wood

4

Corsica Pine
Wood

BITHAM RD

85

Gallop

Jew's
Harp

Ardington Down

The
Sycamores

Midsummer
Wood

Ridgeway

Middlehill
Down

Grim's Ditch

The Ridgeway Path (Oxfordshire Circular Walk)

Ridgeway
Down

3

Monument
on site of
Tumulus

Betterton
Down

Wether
Down

Old Street (Track)

84

Yew Down

Mead
Platt

The Warren

Triangle
Wood

2

Lattin Down

Wireless
Station

Lockinge Kiln
Farm

Lockinge
Down

83

Farnborough Furze
Down

7

1

Little Coombe
Farm

Moonlight
Barn

COPPERAGE RD

82

Coombe
Lodge

B4494

Farnborough

41   A   42   B   43   C

28

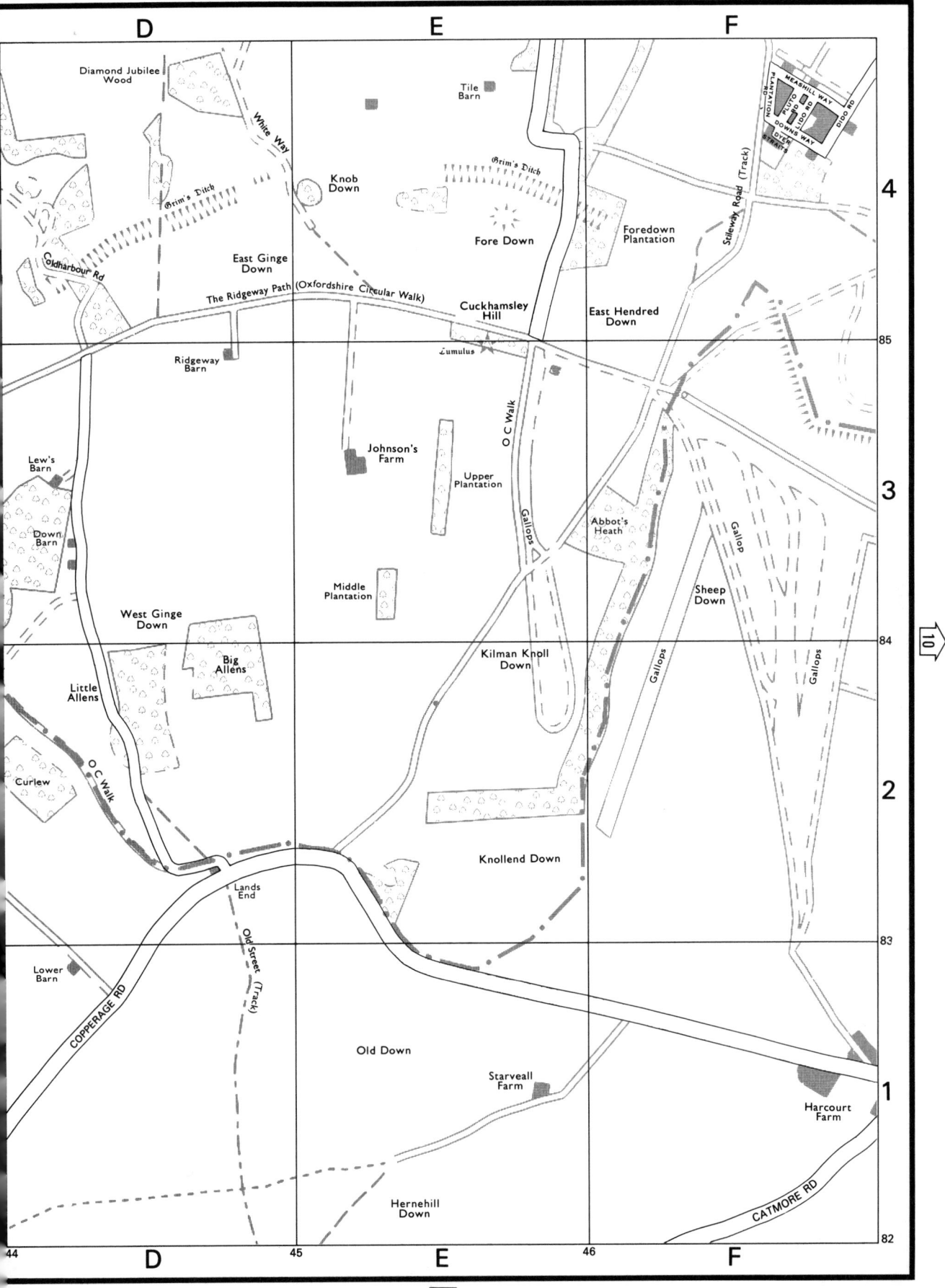

D

E

F

Diamond Jubilee
Wood

White Way

Tile
Barn

Grim's Ditch

Grim's Ditch

Knob
Down

Fore Down

Foredown
Plantation

Stileway Road (Track)

MEASHILL WAY

PLANTATION RD

DOWNS WAY

FLUTE RD

LIDO RD

DIDO RD

DYER

STRAITS

4

Coldharbour Rd

East Ginge
Down

The Ridgeway Path (Oxfordshire Circular Walk)

Cuckhamsley
Hill

East Hendred
Down

85

Tumulus

Ridgeway
Barn

O C Walk

Johnson's
Farm

Upper
Plantation

Gallops

Abbot's
Heath

Lew's
Barn

3

Down
Barn

Middle
Plantation

Gallop

Sheep
Down

Gallops

West Ginge
Down

84

Little
Allens

Big
Allens

Kilman Knoll
Down

Gallops

Gallops

Curlew

O C Walk

Knollend Down

2

Lands
End

83

Old Street (Track)

COPPERAGE RD

Lower
Barn

Old Down

Starveall
Farm

Harcourt
Farm

1

Hernehill
Down

CATMORE RD

82

44

D

45

E

46

F

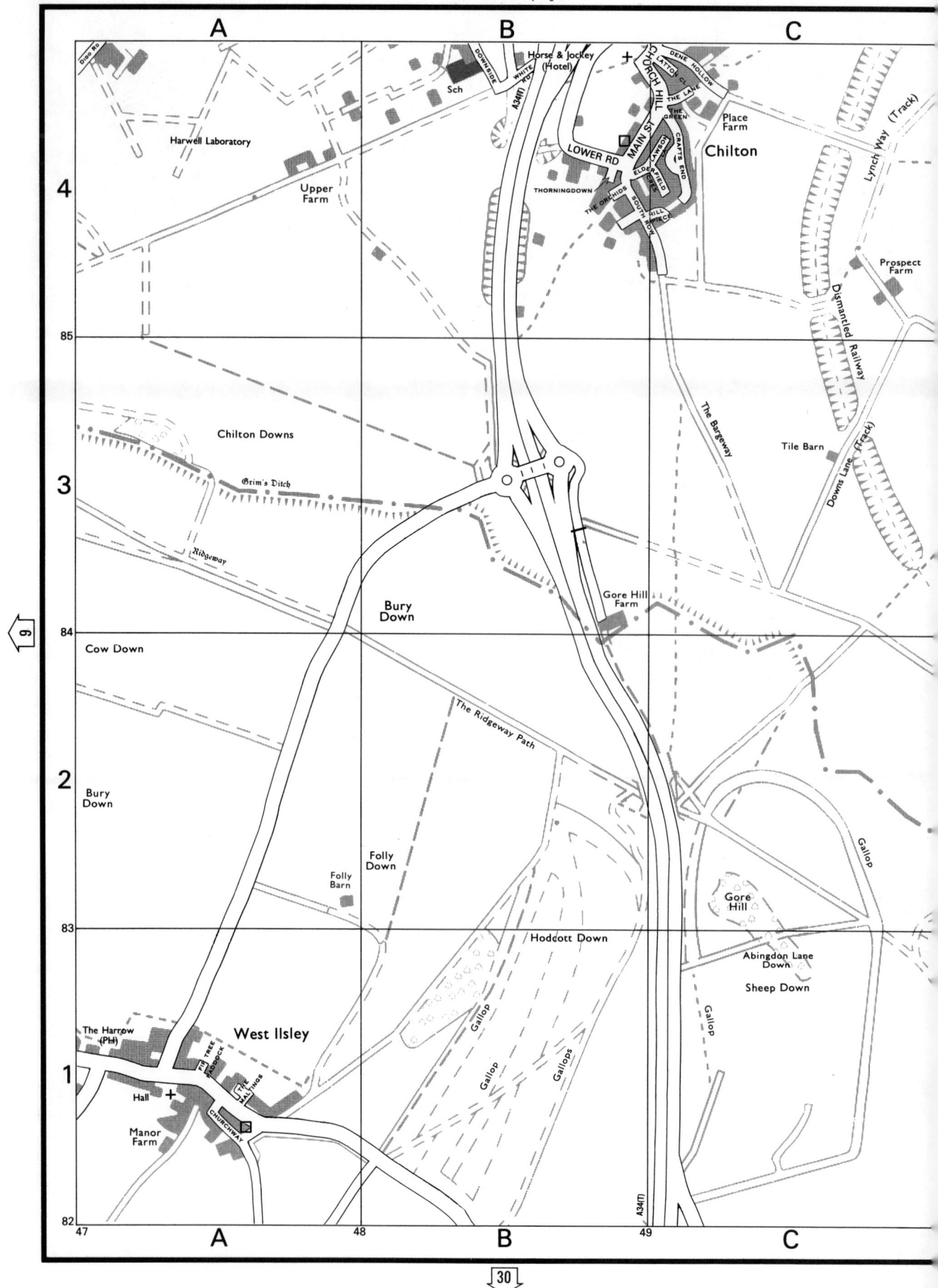

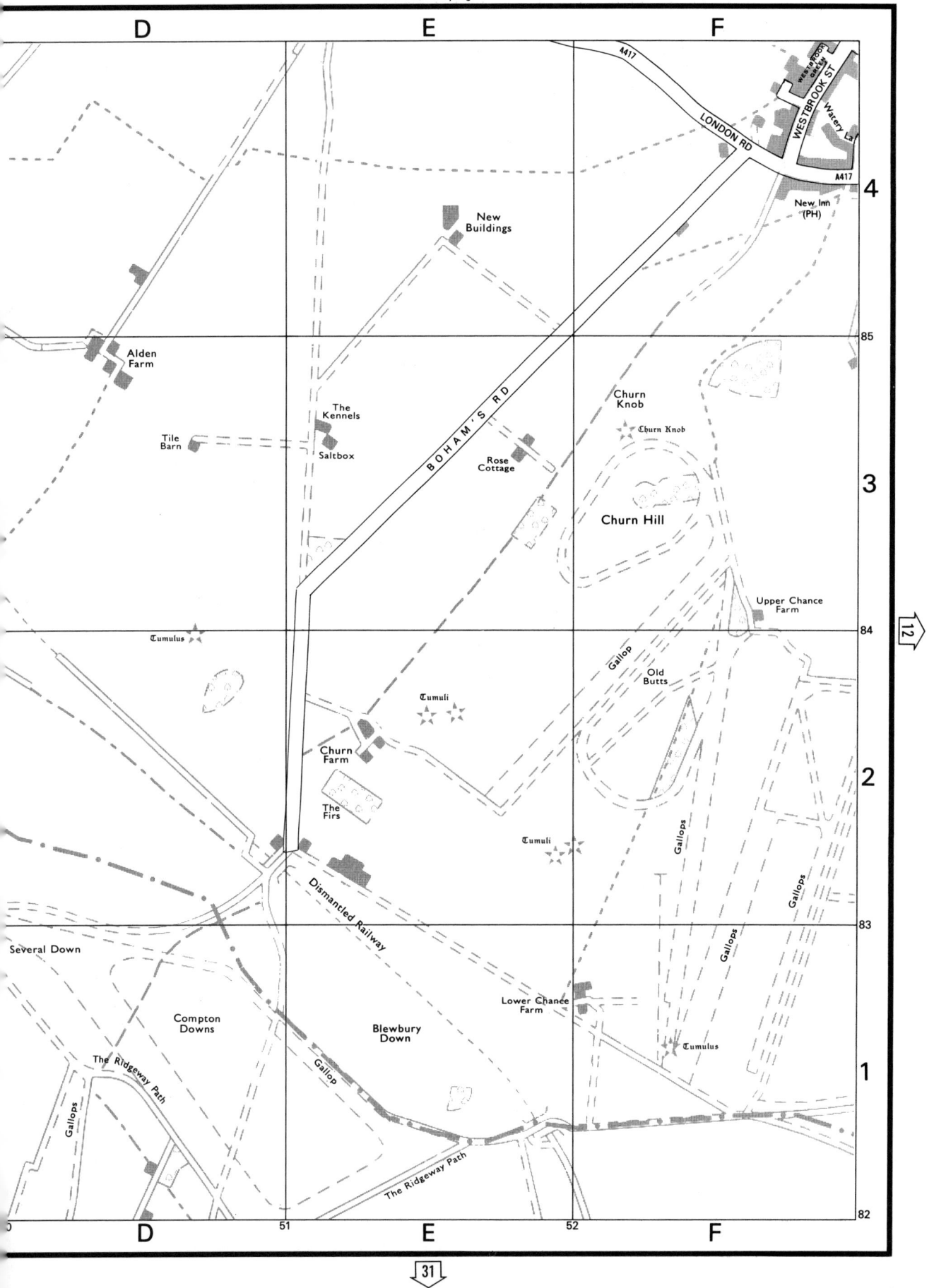

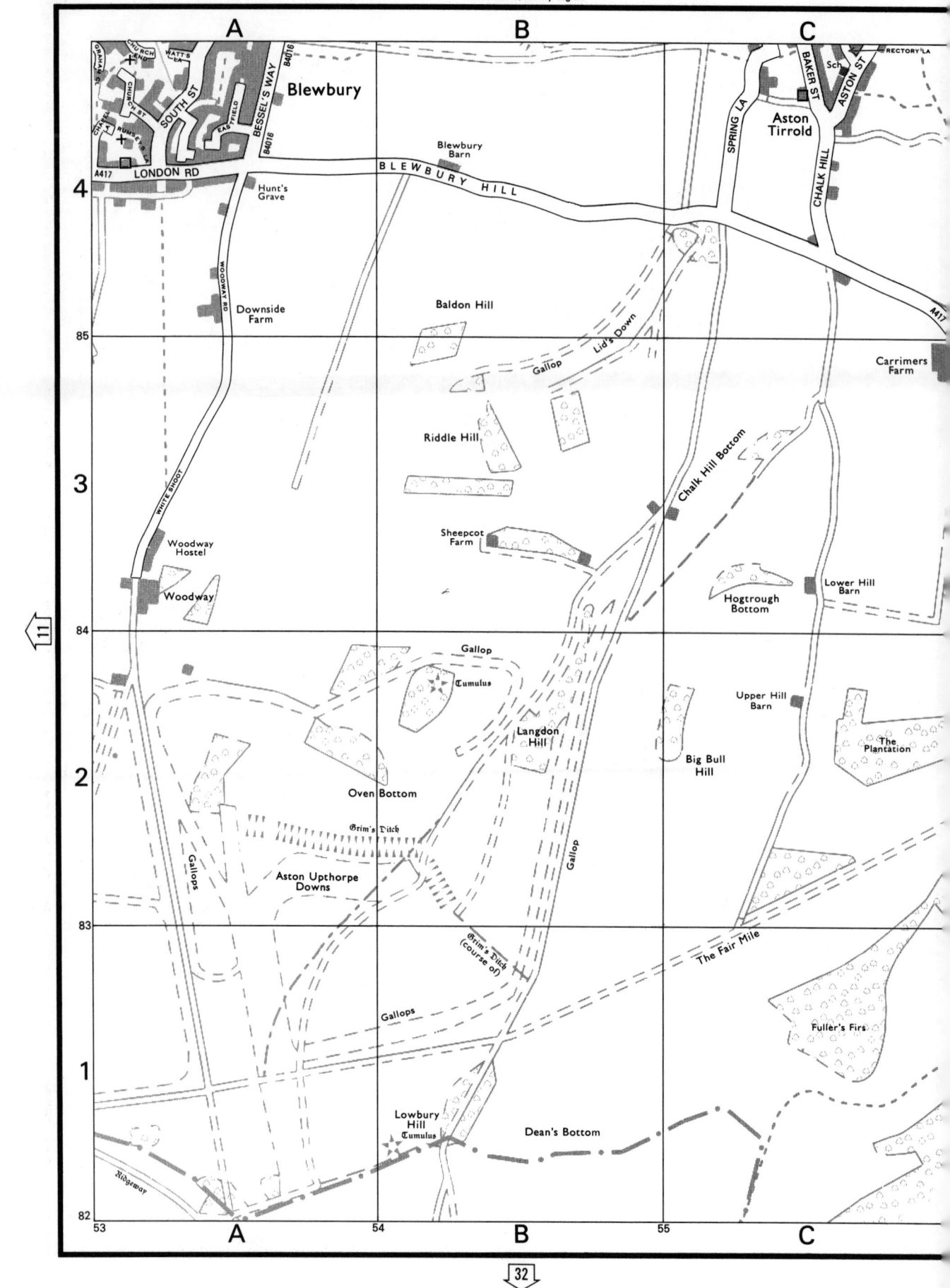

Blewbury

Aston Tirrold

CHURCH LANE
GRAHAM'S
WATT'S LA
CHAPEL ST
CHURCH ST
RUMSEY'S
SOUTH ST
EASTFIELD
BESSEL'S WAY
B4016
B4016
A417
LONDON RD
WOODWAY RD
WHITE SHOOT

Blewbury Barn

BLEWBURY HILL

Hunt's Grave

Downside Farm

Baldon Hill

Lid's Down

Gallop

Riddle Hill

Chalk Hill Bottom

Carrimers Farm

SPRING LA
BAKER ST
ASTON ST
RECTORY LA
Sch
CHALK HILL
A417

Woodway Hostel

Woodway

Sheepcot Farm

Hogtrough Bottom

Lower Hill Barn

Gallop

Tumulus

Langdon Hill

Upper Hill Barn

The Plantation

Oven Bottom

Big Bull Hill

Grim's Ditch

Aston Upthorpe Downs

Gallops

Grim's Ditch (course of)

The Fair Mile

Gallops

Fuller's Firs

Lowbury Hill Tumulus

Dean's Bottom

Ridgeway

◁ 11

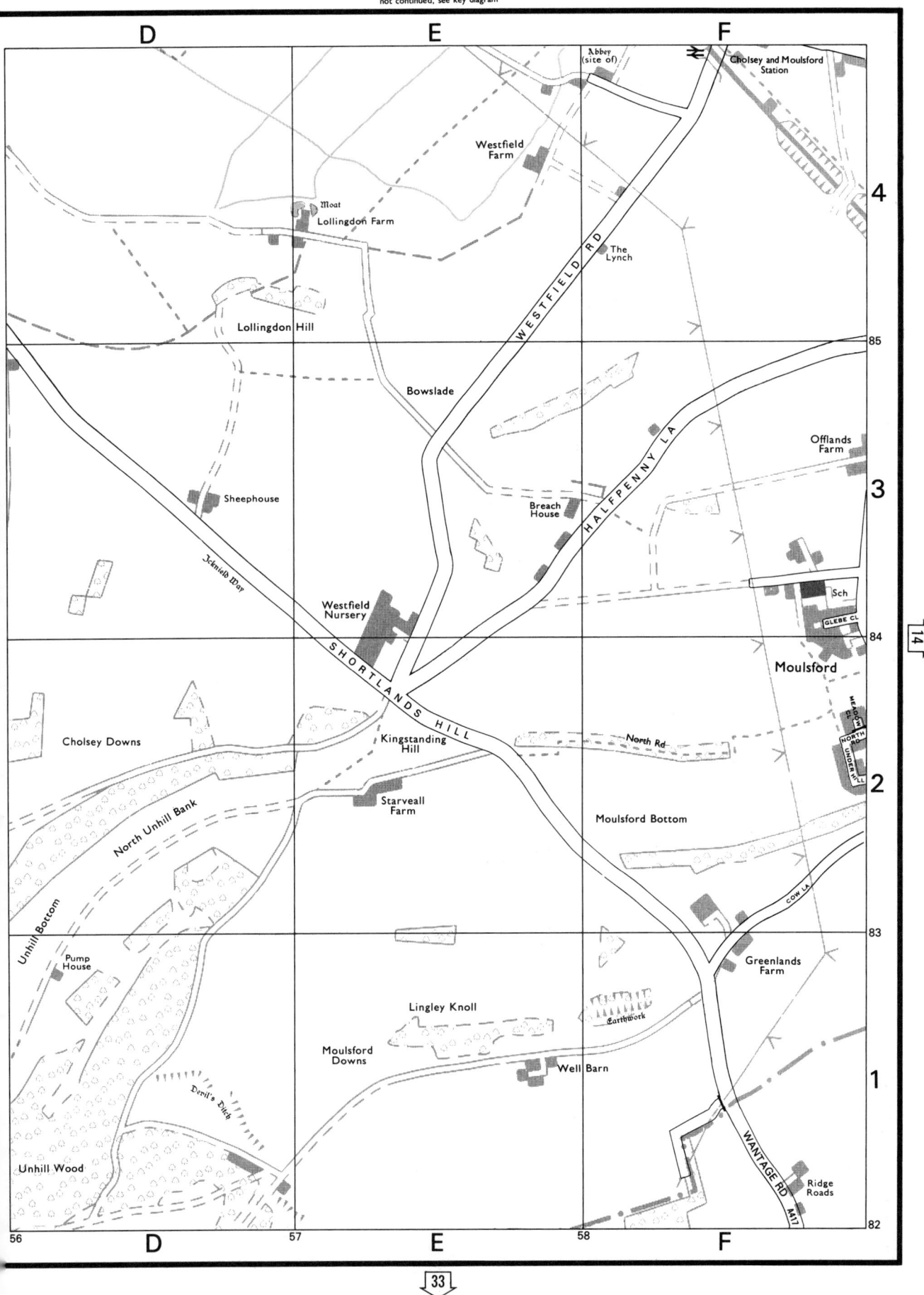

D   E   F

Abbey (site of)

Cholsey and Moulsford Station

Westfield Farm

4

Moat
Lollingdon Farm

The Lynch

WESTFIELD RD

Lollingdon Hill

85

Bowslade

Offlands Farm

HALFPENNY LA

3

Sheephouse

Breach House

Ichnield Way

Sch

Westfield Nursery

GLEBE CL

84

14

Moulsford

SHORTLANDS HILL

Cholsey Downs

North Rd

MEADOW CL

NORTH RD UNDER HILL

Kingstanding Hill

2

North Unhill Bank

Starveall Farm

Moulsford Bottom

Unhill Bottom

COW LA

83

Pump House

Greenlands Farm

Lingley Knoll

Earthwork

Moulsford Downs

Well Barn

1

Devil's Ditch

Unhill Wood

WANTAGE RD

Ridge Roads

M17

82

56   D   57   E   58   F

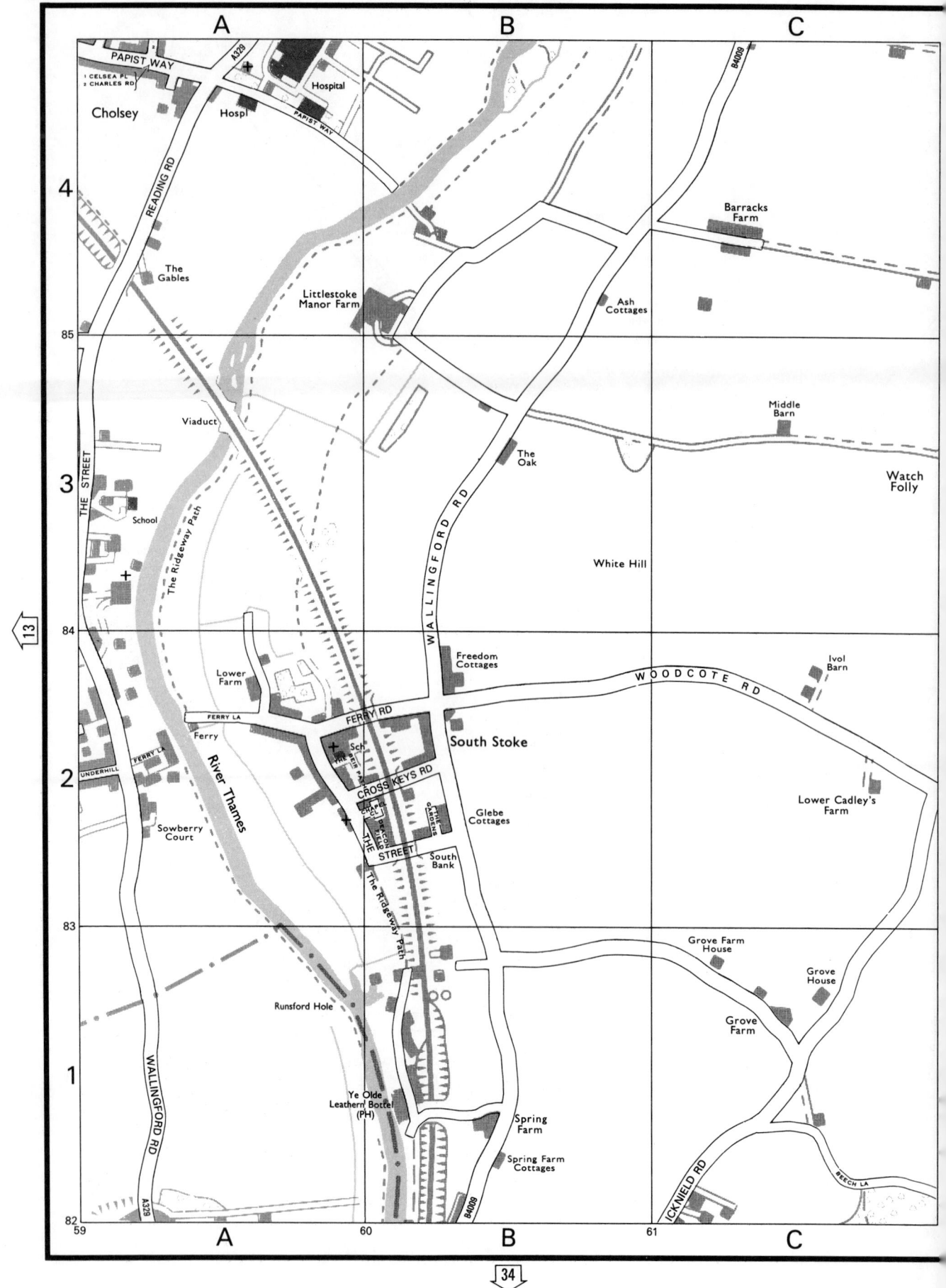

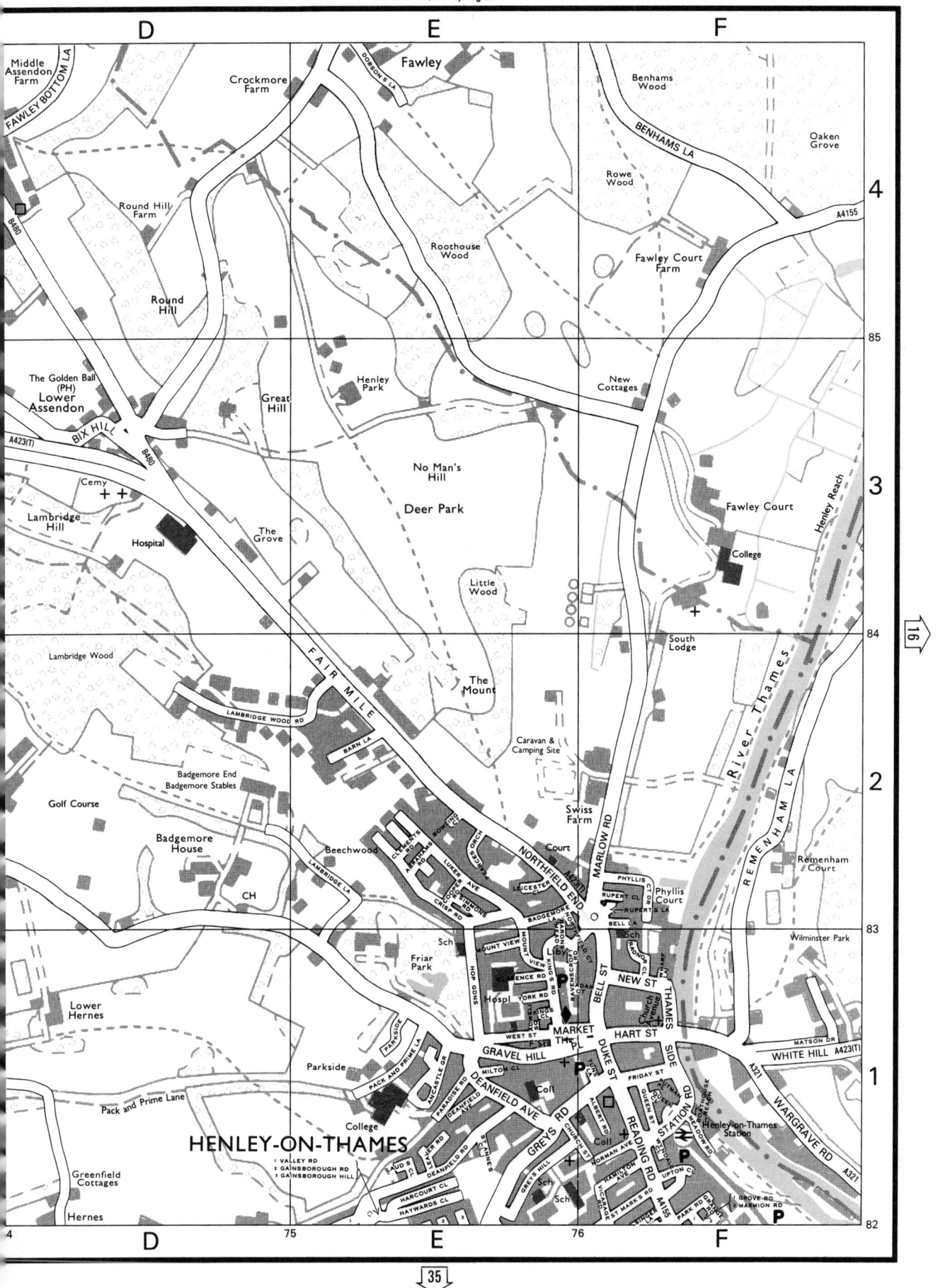

HENLEY-ON-THAMES

1 VALLEY RD
2 GAINSBOROUGH RD
3 GAINSBOROUGH HILL

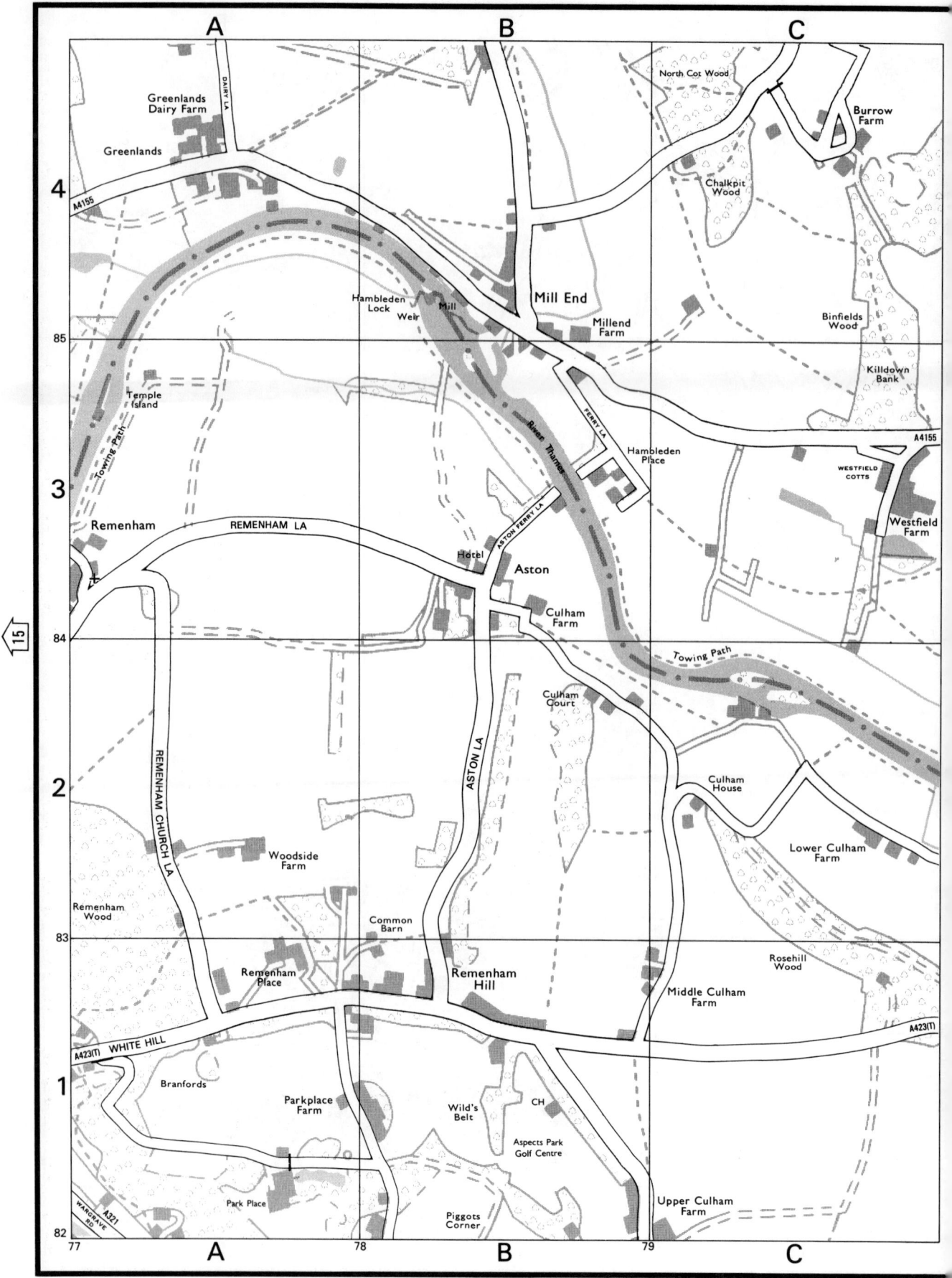

A • B • C

Greenlands
Dairy Farm

DAIRY LA

Greenlands

4

A4155

Hambleden
Lock
Weir

Mill

Temple
Island

Towing Path

85

3

Remenham

REMENHAM LA

Hotel

ASTON FERRY LA

Aston

Culham
Farm

84

15

REMENHAM CHURCH LA

Woodside
Farm

ASTON LA

Culham
Court

2

Remenham
Wood

Common
Barn

83

Remenham
Place

Remenham
Hill

Middle Culham
Farm

A423(T)

WHITE HILL

A423(T)

Branfords

1

Parkplace
Farm

Wild's
Belt

CH

Aspects Park
Golf Centre

WARGRAVE RD

A321

Park Place

Piggots
Corner

Upper Culham
Farm

82

77 • A • 78 • B • 79 • C

Mill End

Millend
Farm

River Thames

FERRY LA

Hambleden
Place

North Cot Wood

Burrow
Farm

Chalkpit
Wood

Binfields
Wood

Killdown
Bank

A4155

WESTFIELD
COTTS

Westfield
Farm

Towing Path

Culham
House

Lower Culham
Farm

Rosehill
Wood

not continued, see key diagram

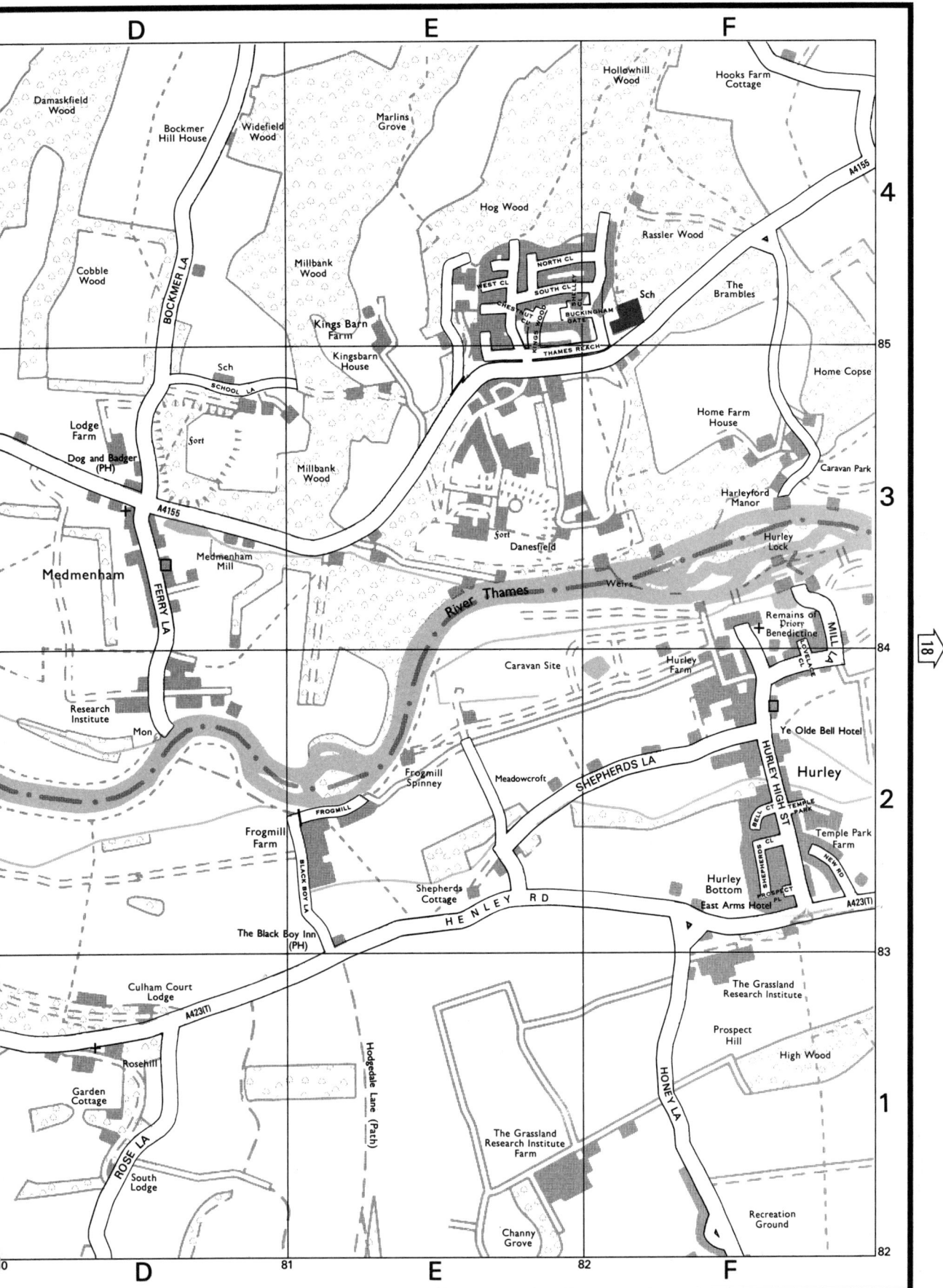

D **E** **F**

4

Damaskfield Wood

Hollowhill Wood

Hooks Farm Cottage

A4155

Bockmer Hill House

Widefield Wood

Marlins Grove

Hog Wood

Rassler Wood

Cobble Wood

Millbank Wood

NORTH CL
WEST CL
SOUTH CL
CHESTNUT WOOD
BUCKINGHAM GATE
KINGS ROAD
THAMES REACH

The Brambles

Sch

85

BOCKMER LA

Kings Barn Farm

Kingsbarn House

Sch

Home Copse

SCHOOL LA

Home Farm House

Lodge Farm

Dog and Badger (PH)

A4155

Fort

Millbank Wood

Caravan Park

Harleyford Manor

3

Medmenham

FERRY LA

Medmenham Mill

Fort

Danesfield

River Thames

Weirs

Hurley Lock

Remains of Benedictine Priory

MILL LA

COTTAGE LANE

84

Research Institute

Mon

Caravan Site

Hurley Farm

Ye Olde Bell Hotel

Hurley

SHEPHERDS LA

HURLEY HIGH ST

Frogmill Spinney

Meadowcroft

BELL CT
TEMPLE PARK
SOMERIES CL
NEW RD

Temple Park Farm

2

FROGMILL

Frogmill Farm

BLACK BOY LA

Shepherds Cottage

HENLEY RD

Hurley Bottom

East Arms Hotel

PROSPECT PL

A423(T)

The Black Boy Inn (PH)

83

Culham Court Lodge

A423(T)

The Grassland Research Institute

Rosehill

Hodgedale Lane (Path)

Prospect Hill

High Wood

HONEY LA

1

Garden Cottage

The Grassland Research Institute Farm

ROSE LA

South Lodge

Channy Grove

Recreation Ground

82

D **E** **F**

0 81 82

18

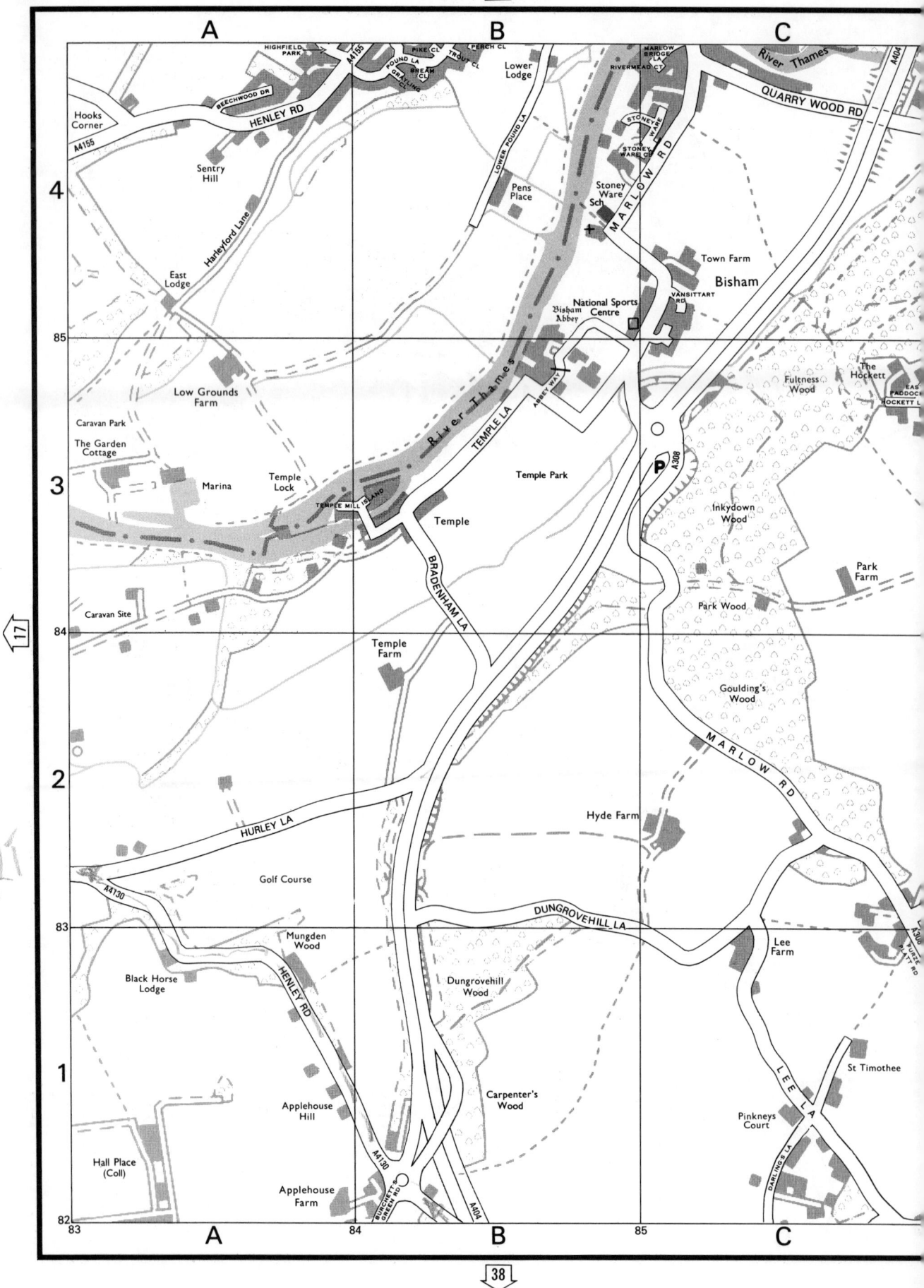

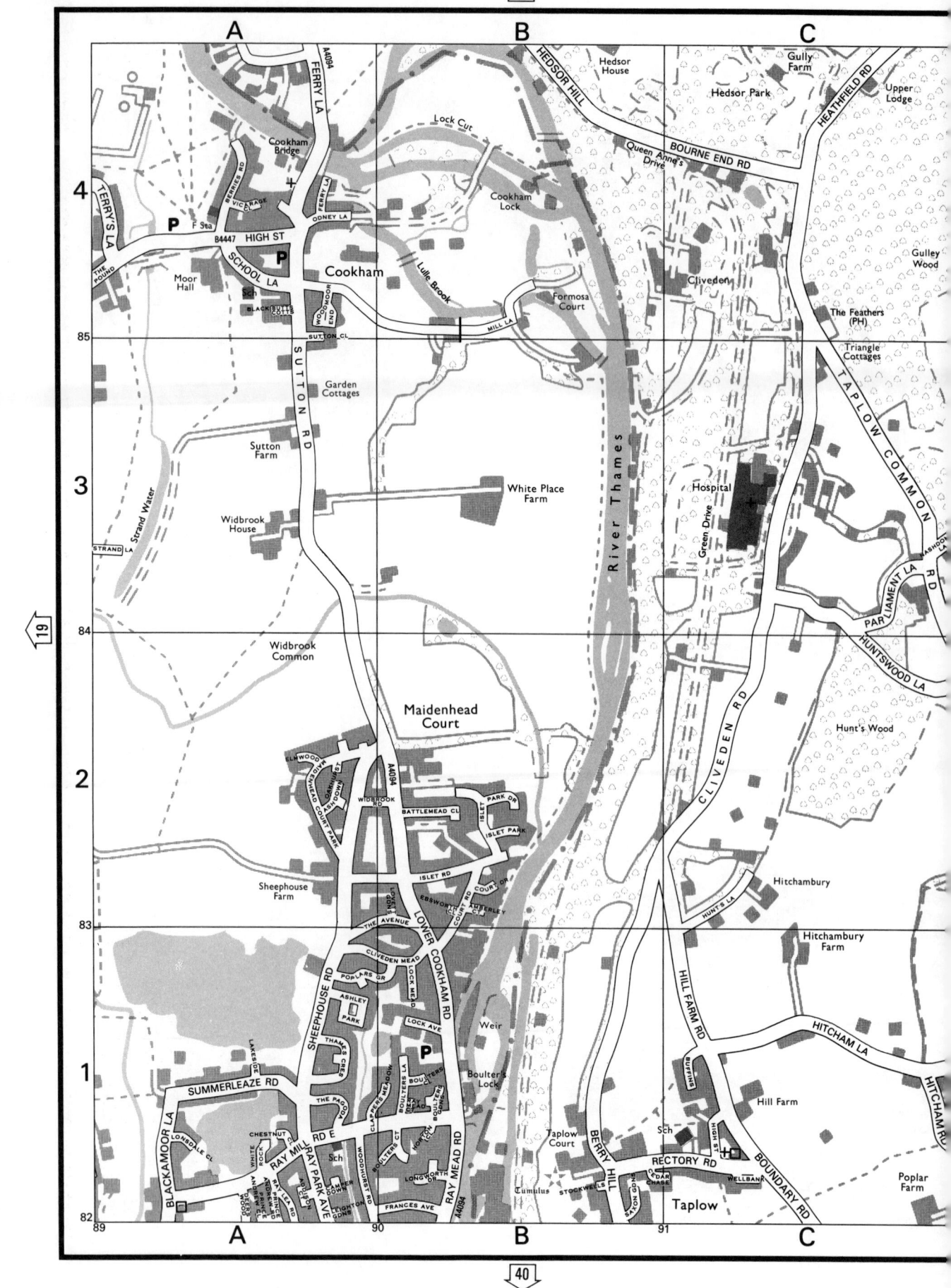

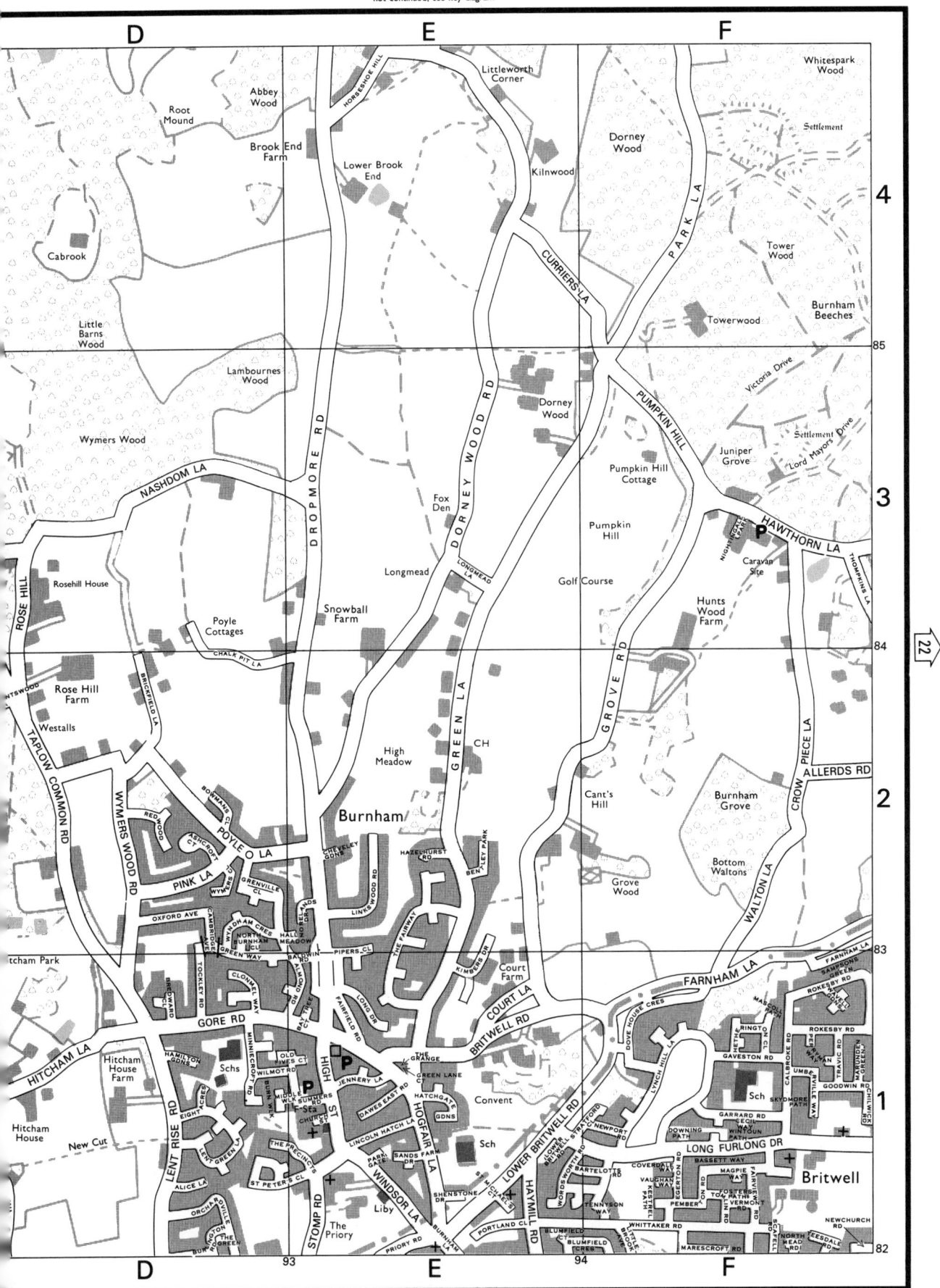

Whitespark
Wood

Abbey Wood

Root
Mound

Settlement

Dorney
Wood

Brook End
Farm

Tower
Wood

Lower Brook
End

Littleworth
Corner

Kilnwood

4

Cabrook

Burnham
Beeches

Towerwood

Little
Barns
Wood

85

Victoria Drive

Lambournes
Wood

Dorney
Wood

Settlement Drive

Lord Mayors' Drive

NASHDOM LA

Fox
Den

Pumpkin Hill
Cottage

Juniper
Grove

Wymers Wood

3

Rosehill House

Pumpkin
Hill

Hawthorn La

P

Longmead

Caravan
Site

Poyle
Cottages

Snowball
Farm

Longmead

Golf Course

Hunts
Wood
Farm

84

22

Rose Hill
Farm

CHALK PIT LA

High
Meadow

CH

2

Westalls

Cant's
Hill

Burnham
Grove

Burnham

Grove
Wood

Bottom
Waltons

ALLERDS RD

PINK LA

OXFORD AVE

High
Meadow

Court
Farm

83

Farnham La

FARNHAM LA

tcham Park

Court La

Britwell Rd

HITCHAM LA

Hitcham
House
Farm

GORE RD

Convent

Sch

1

P

P

The
Grange

Green Lane

Hitcham
House

New Cut

Sch

Britwell

LENT RISE RD

STOMP RD

WINDSOR LA

Liby

The
Priory

LOWER BRITWELL RD

HAYMILL RD

LONG FURLONG DR

82

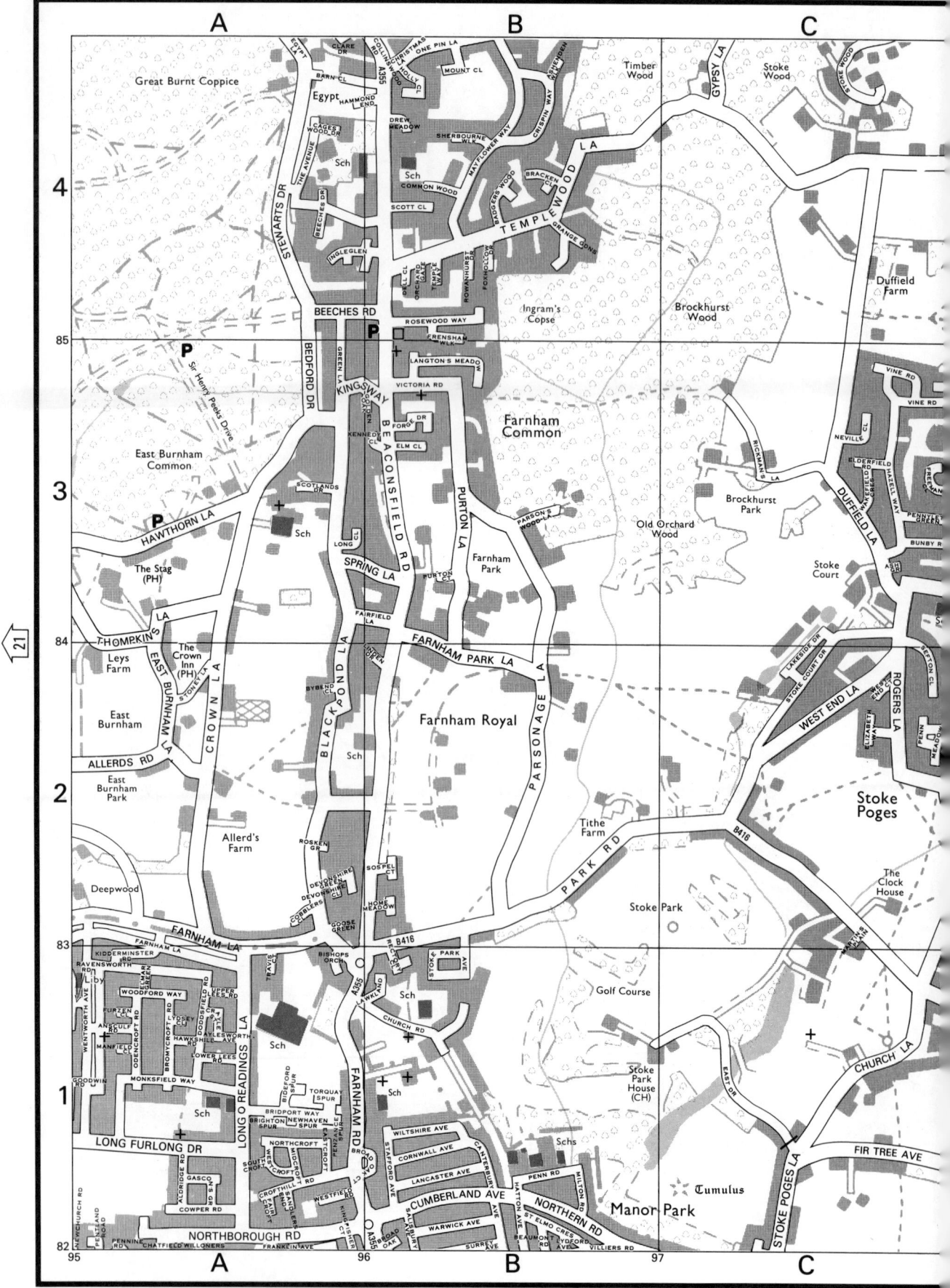

A B C

4

Great Burnt Coppice

EGYPT RD
CLARE DR
BARN CL
Egypt
HAMMOND END
CAGES WOOD DR
Sch

A355
COLUMBINE RD
CHRISTMAS LA
ONE PIN LA
HOLLY LA
MOUNT CL
DREW MEADOW
SHERBOURNE WLK
CRISPIN WAY
ASPEN
MAYFLOWER WAY
COMMON WOOD
BADGERS WOOD
BRACKEN
SCOTT CL

Timber Wood

GYPSY LA
Stoke Wood
STOKES WOOD

STENARTS DR
THE AVENUE
BEECHES DR
INGLEGLEN

DELL CL
ORCHARD
TEMPLE WAY
ROWNHURST DR
FOXHOLLOW
GRANGE GDNS

TEMPLEWOOD LA

Brockhurst Wood

Duffield Farm

85

BEECHES RD
ROSEWOOD WAY

BEDFORD DR

P
FRENSHAM
LANGTON'S MEADOW

Ingram's Copse

P
Sir Henry Peak's Drive
KINGSWAY
GREEN LA
YORK
VICTORIA RD

FORGE DR
ELM CL

Farnham Common

VINE RD
VINE RD
NEVILLE CL
RICKMANS RD
ELDERFIELD
WAKEFIELD RD
HAZELL WAY
FREEMAN
PENNYFIELD
BUNBY R
ASH

East Burnham Common

P
HAWTHORN LA
SCOTLANDS DR
Sch
LONG LA
JG

BEACONSFIELD RD
KENNEDY CL

PURTON LA
PURTON CL
SPRING LA
Farnham Park

Old Orchard Wood

Brockhurst Park

DUFFIELD LA

Stoke Court

3

The Stag (PH)

LA
T HOMPKINS LA

84

Leys Farm
The Crown Inn (PH)
STOVEY LA

EAST BURNHAM LA

CROWN LA

FAIRFIELD LA
BLACKPOND LA
BYBEND CL
GREEN
FARNHAM PARK LA

Farnham Royal

Stoke Court DR
LAKESIDE DR
WEST END LA
ELIZABETH END
PENN

ROGERS LA
SEFTON CL
PENN MEADOW

East Burnham
ALLERDS RD
East Burnham Park

Sch

PARSONAGE LA

Stoke Poges

B416
The Clock House

2

Deepwood
Allerd's Farm
ROSKEN GR
DEVONSHIRE GREEN
DEVONSHIRE
COBBLERS
GOOSE GREEN
SOSPEL CT
HOME MEADOW

Tithe Farm

PARK RD

Stoke Park

FARNHAM LA
FARNHAM LA
KIDDERMINSTER RD
RAVENSWORTH RD
Liby

83

B416
BISHOPS ORCH
RECTORY
STOKE PARK AVE
Sch

Golf Course

CHURCH LA
FIR TREE AVE

WOODFORD WAY
UPPER LEES RD
DODDSFIELD RD
ANSCULF RD
FURZEN CL
HAWKSHILL RD
BROMCROFT RD
RYDEY CR
DAYLESWORTH
LOWER LEES RD

LONG O READINGS LA

TRAVIS GR
UPPER GREEN
STAFFORD SPUR
CHURCH RD

A355
OAK LA
LAWKLAND
Sch

Sch

STOKE PARK AVE

1

GOODWIN
WENTWORTH AVE
ODENCROFT RD
MANFIELD
MONKSFIELD WAY
Sch

BRIDPORT WAY
NORTHCROFT
BRIGHTON SPUR
NEWHAVEN SPUR
TORQUAY SPUR
Sch

FARNHAM RD
BROAD CL

WILTSHIRE AVE
CORNWALL AVE
STAFFORD AVE
PENN RD

LANCASTER AVE
CANTERBURY
HATTON AVE
MILTON RD
Schs

Stoke Park House (CH)

EAST DR

MARTINS
STOKE POGES LA

LONG FURLONG DR

SOUTH WESTCROFT SPUR
MICROFT SPUR
WEST CROFT SPUR
CROFTHILL RD
WESTFIELD
SANDELS WAY
KINSHAM CT

WARWICK AVE
NORTHERN RD

Manor Park

Tumulus

82

MAW CHURCH RD
PENTLAND ROAD
ALDRIDGE RD
GASCO RD
COWPER RD
PENNINE
CHATFIELD
WILLONERS

NORTHBOROUGH RD

FRANKLIN AVE

BEAUMONT
RYDFORD
VILLIERS RD
SURREY
OAK
A355
ST ELMO CRES
CUMBERLAND AVE

95 A 96 B 97 C

21
42

not continued, see key diagram

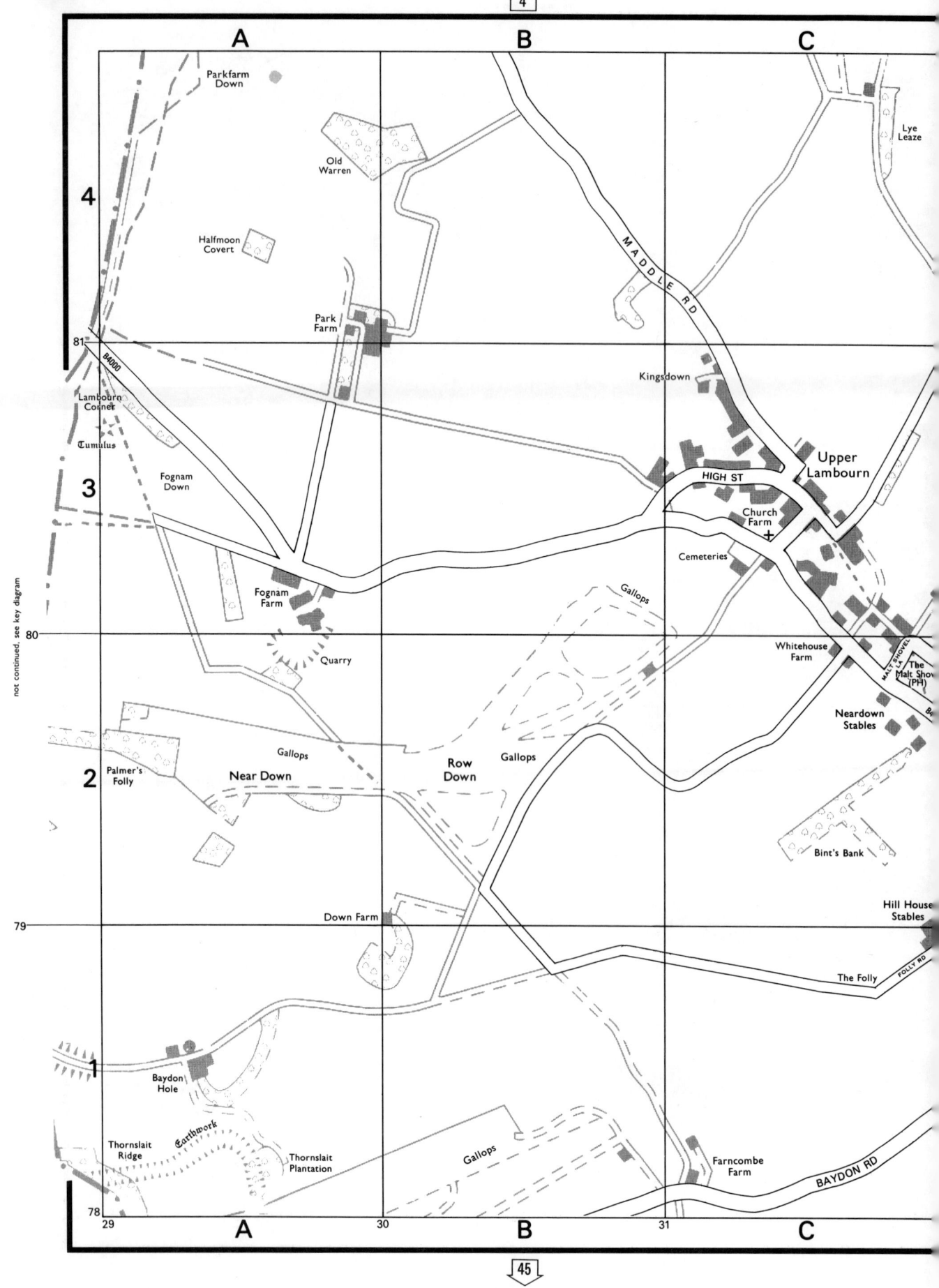

A   B   C

Parkfarm Down

Old Warren

Lye Leaze

4

Halfmoon Covert

MADDLE RD

Park Farm

Kingsdown

81

B4000

Lambourn Corner

HIGH ST

Upper Lambourn

Tumulus

Fognam Down

Church Farm

3

Cemeteries

Fognam Farm

Gallops

Whitehouse Farm

MALT SHOVEL LA

The Malt Shov (PH)

80

Quarry

Gallops

Neardown Stables

Gallops

Row Down

Gallops

Palmer's Folly

Near Down

Bint's Bank

2

Hill House Stables

79

Down Farm

The Folly

FOLLY RD

1

Baydon Hole

Farncombe Farm

BAYDON RD

Thornslait Ridge

Earthwork

Thornslait Plantation

Gallops

78

29   A   30   B   31   C

not continued, see key diagram

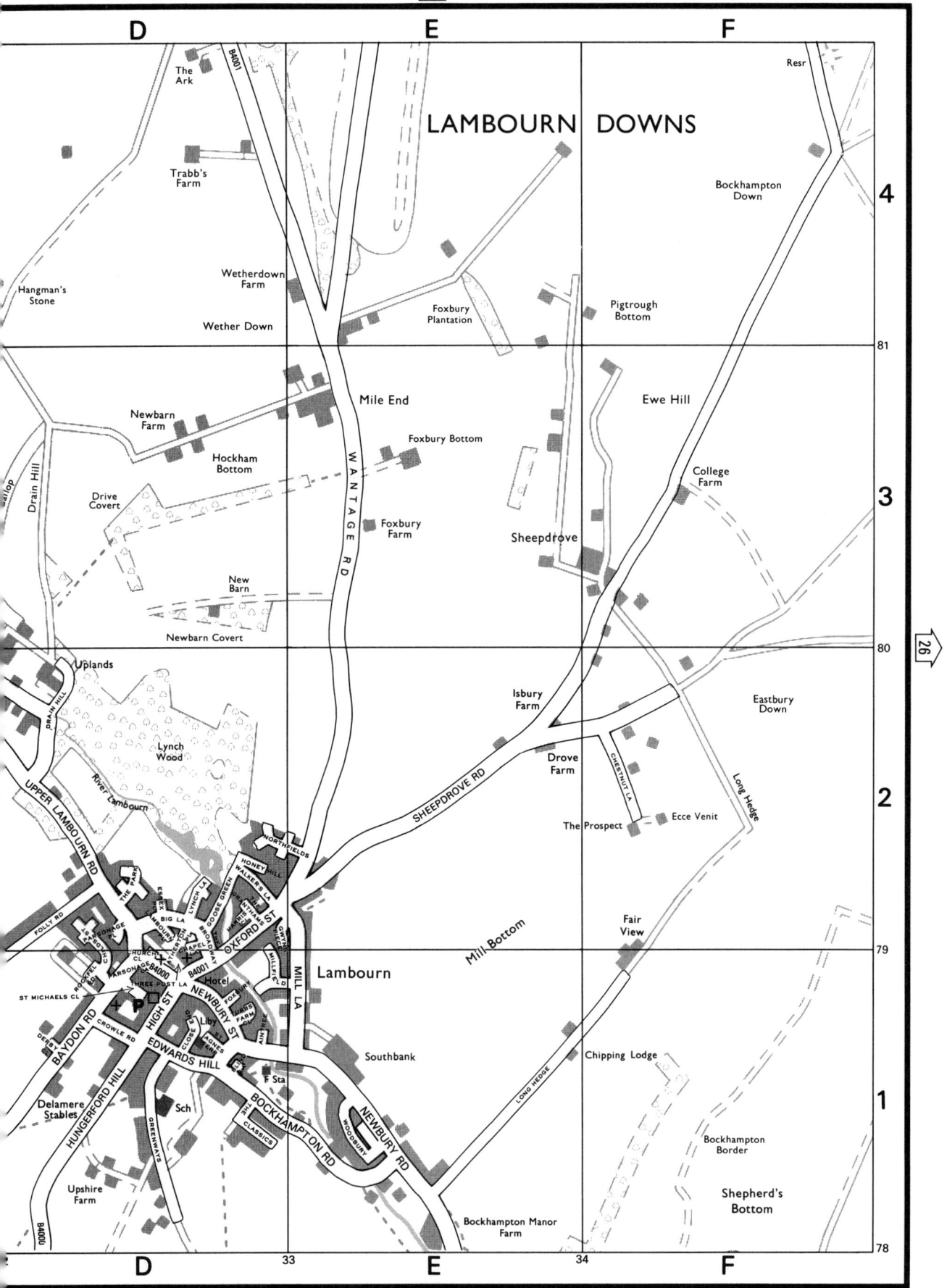

D   E   F

The Ark

B4001

LAMBOURN DOWNS

Resr

Trabb's Farm

Bockhampton Down

4

Hangman's Stone

Wetherdown Farm

Foxbury Plantation

Pigtrough Bottom

Wether Down

81

Newbarn Farm

Mile End

Foxbury Bottom

Ewe Hill

Drain Hill

Hockham Bottom

WANTAGE RD

College Farm

3

Drive Covert

Foxbury Farm

Sheepdrove

New Barn

Newbarn Covert

80

26

Uplands

Isbury Farm

Eastbury Down

Lynch Wood

DRAIN HILL

River Lambourn

SHEEPDROVE RD

Drove Farm

CHESTNUT LA

Long Hedge

2

UPPER LAMBOURN RD

THE PARKS

NORTHFIELDS

HONEY HILL

WALKERS LA

The Prospect

Ecce Venit

FOLLY RD

ESSEX

BIG RD

LYNCH LA

MALDURY

GOODE GREEN

GREENTHAMS

BROADWAY

OXFORD ST

Mill Bottom

Fair View

PARSONAGE

CHURCH CL

CHAPEL

MILLFIELD

MILL LA

Lambourn

79

ST MICHAELS CL

ROCKFEL

PARSONAGE

B4000

B4001

Hotel

FOXBURY

THREE POST LA

NEWBURY ST

FOX

BAYDON RD

CROWLE RD

HIGH ST

AGNES

TUBBS FARM

Southbank

Chipping Lodge

DERBY

CLOSE

LONG HEDGE

Delamere Stables

HUNGERFORD HILL

EDWARDS HILL

F Sta

BOCKHAMPTON RD

Sch

GREENWAYS

NEWBURY RD

WOODBURY

CLASSICS

Bockhampton Border

1

Upshire Farm

B4000

Bockhampton Manor Farm

Shepherd's Bottom

78

D   33   E   34   F

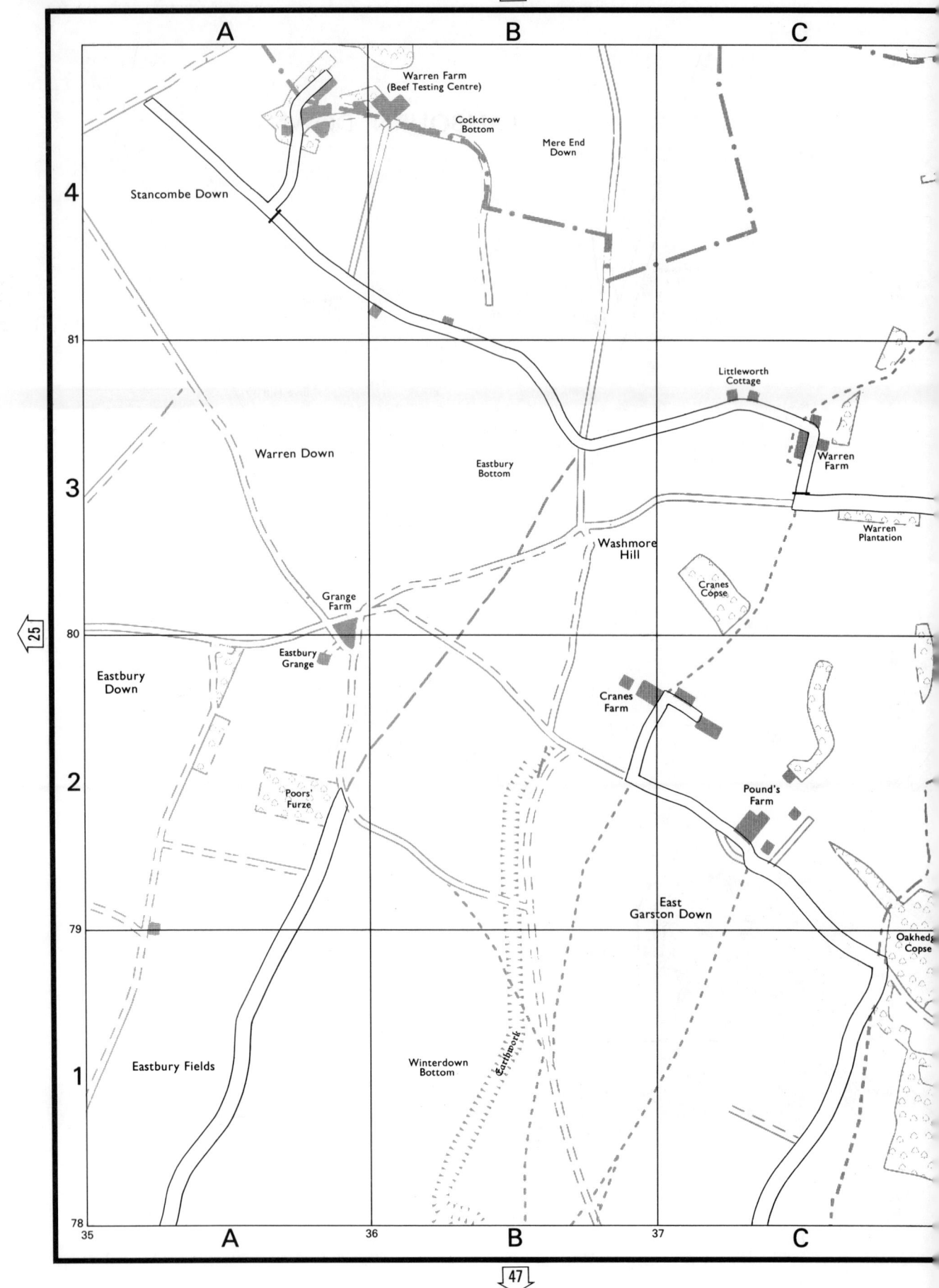

A   B   C

Warren Farm
(Beef Testing Centre)

Cockcrow
Bottom

Mere End
Down

4

Stancombe Down

81

Littleworth
Cottage

Warren Down

Eastbury
Bottom

Warren
Farm

3

Washmore
Hill

Warren
Plantation

Cranes
Copse

Grange
Farm

80

Eastbury
Grange

Eastbury
Down

Cranes
Farm

Pound's
Farm

2

Poors'
Furze

East
Garston Down

79

Oakhedge
Copse

Winterdown
Bottom

Earthwork

1

Eastbury Fields

78

35   A   36   B   37   C

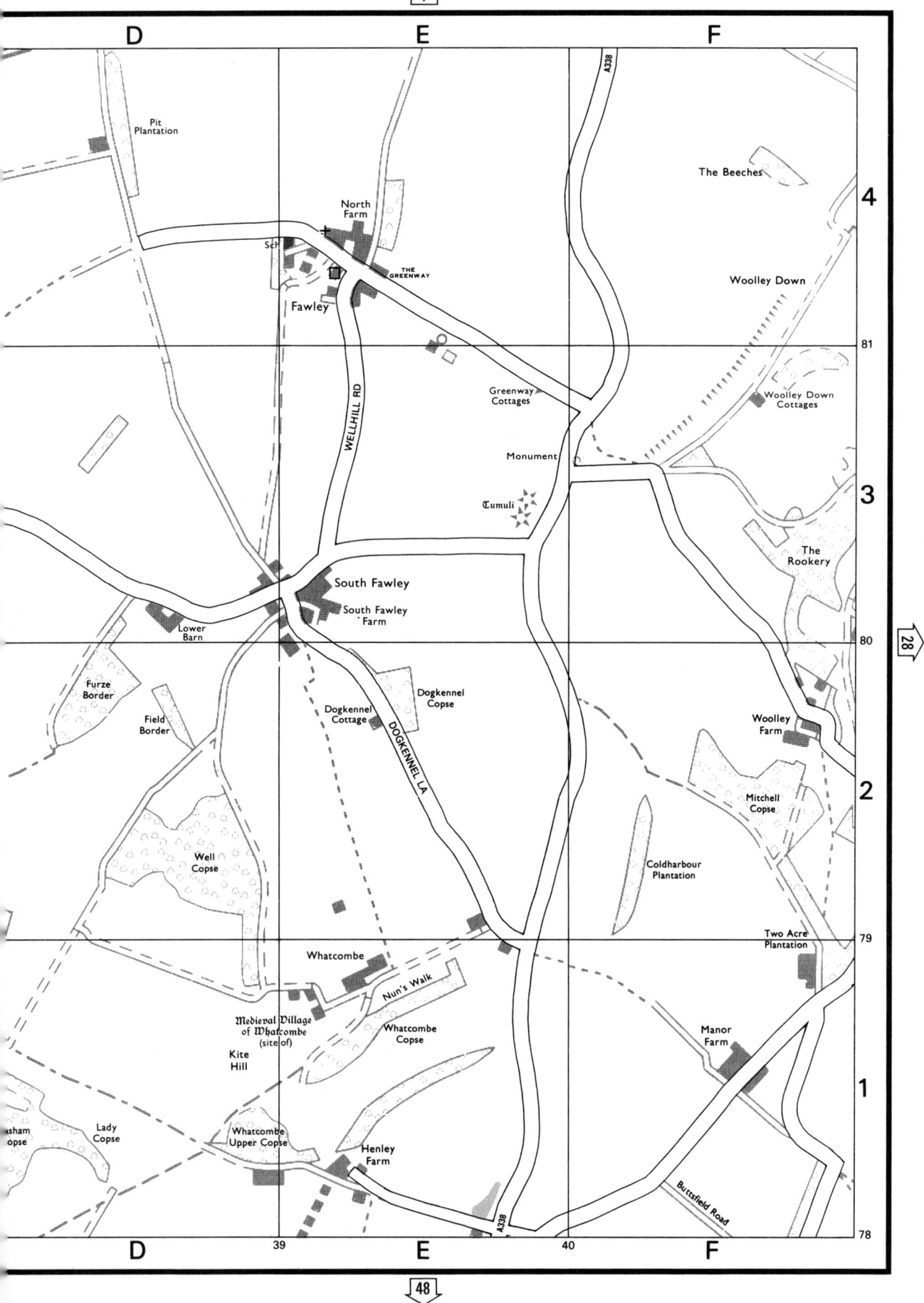

28

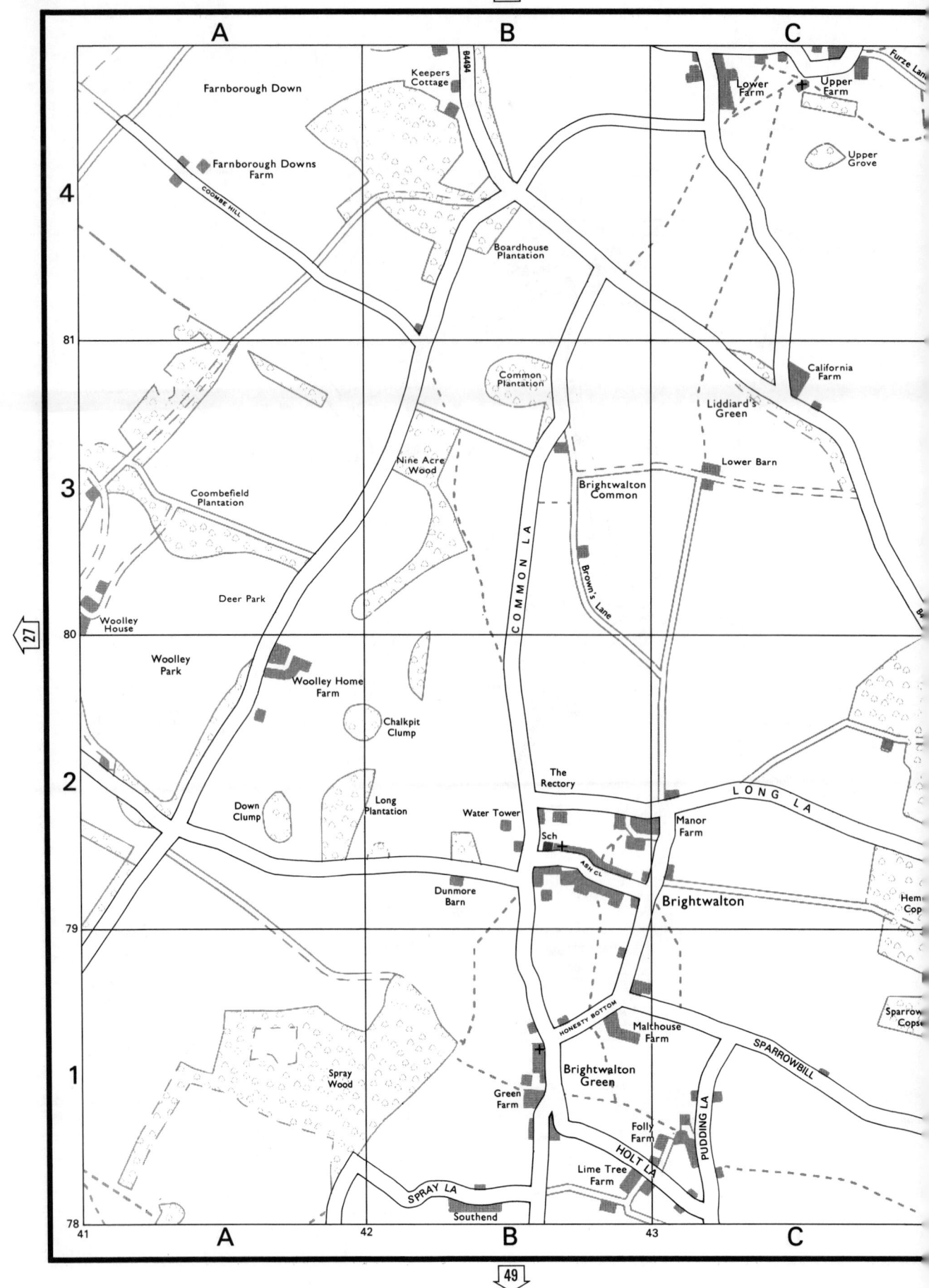

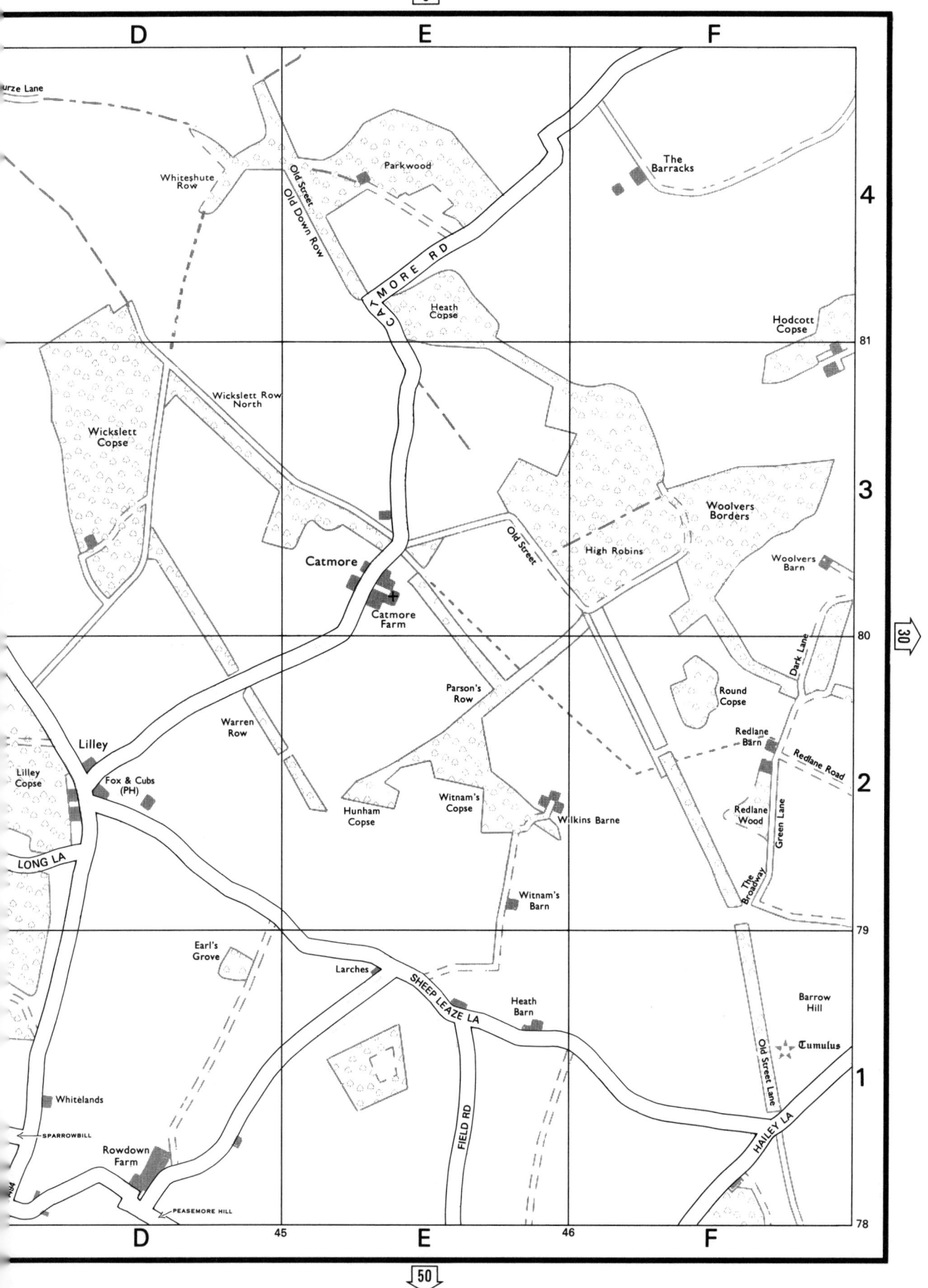

D E F

urze Lane
Whiteshute Row
Old Street
Old Down Row
Parkwood
The Barracks
CATMORE RD
Heath Copse
Hodcott Copse
4
81
Wickslett Row North
Wickslett Copse
Woolvers Borders
High Robins
Old Street
Woolvers Barn
3
Catmore
Catmore Farm
80
Parson's Row
Round Copse
Dark Lane
Warren Row
Redlane Barn
Redlane Road
Lilley
Lilley Copse
Fox & Cubs (PH)
Hunham Copse
Witnam's Copse
Wilkins Barne
Redlane Wood
Green Lane
2
LONG LA
Witnam's Barn
The Broadway
79
Earl's Grove
Larches
SHEEP LEAZE LA
Heath Barn
Barrow Hill
Old Street Lane
Tumulus
1
Whitelands
FIELD RD
SPARROWBILL
Rowdown Farm
HAILEY LA
PEASEMORE HILL
78
D 45 E 46 F

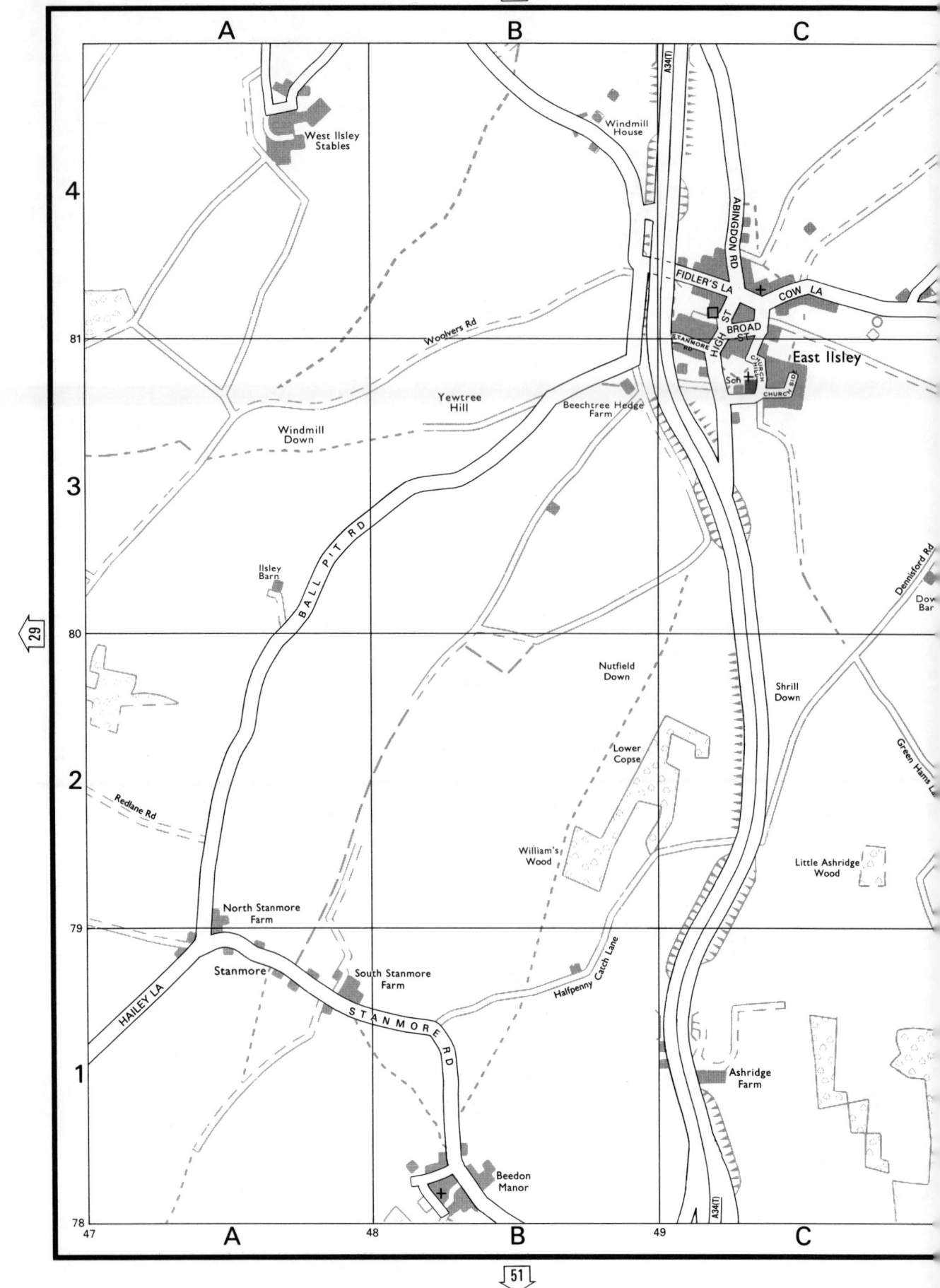

West Ilsley
Stables

Windmill
House

A34(T)

ABINGDON RD

FIDLER'S LA

COW LA

HIGH ST

BROAD ST

STANMORE RD

CHURCH HILL

Sch

CHURCHSIDE

East Ilsley

Woolvers Rd

Yewtree
Hill

Beechtree Hedge
Farm

Windmill
Down

BALL PIT RD

Ilsley
Barn

Dennisford Rd

Dow
Bar

Nutfield
Down

Shrill
Down

Green Hams La

Lower
Copse

Redlane Rd

William's
Wood

Little Ashridge
Wood

North Stanmore
Farm

Stanmore

South Stanmore
Farm

Catch Lane

Halfpenny

HAILEY LA

STANMORE RD

Ashridge
Farm

Beedon
Manor

A34(T)

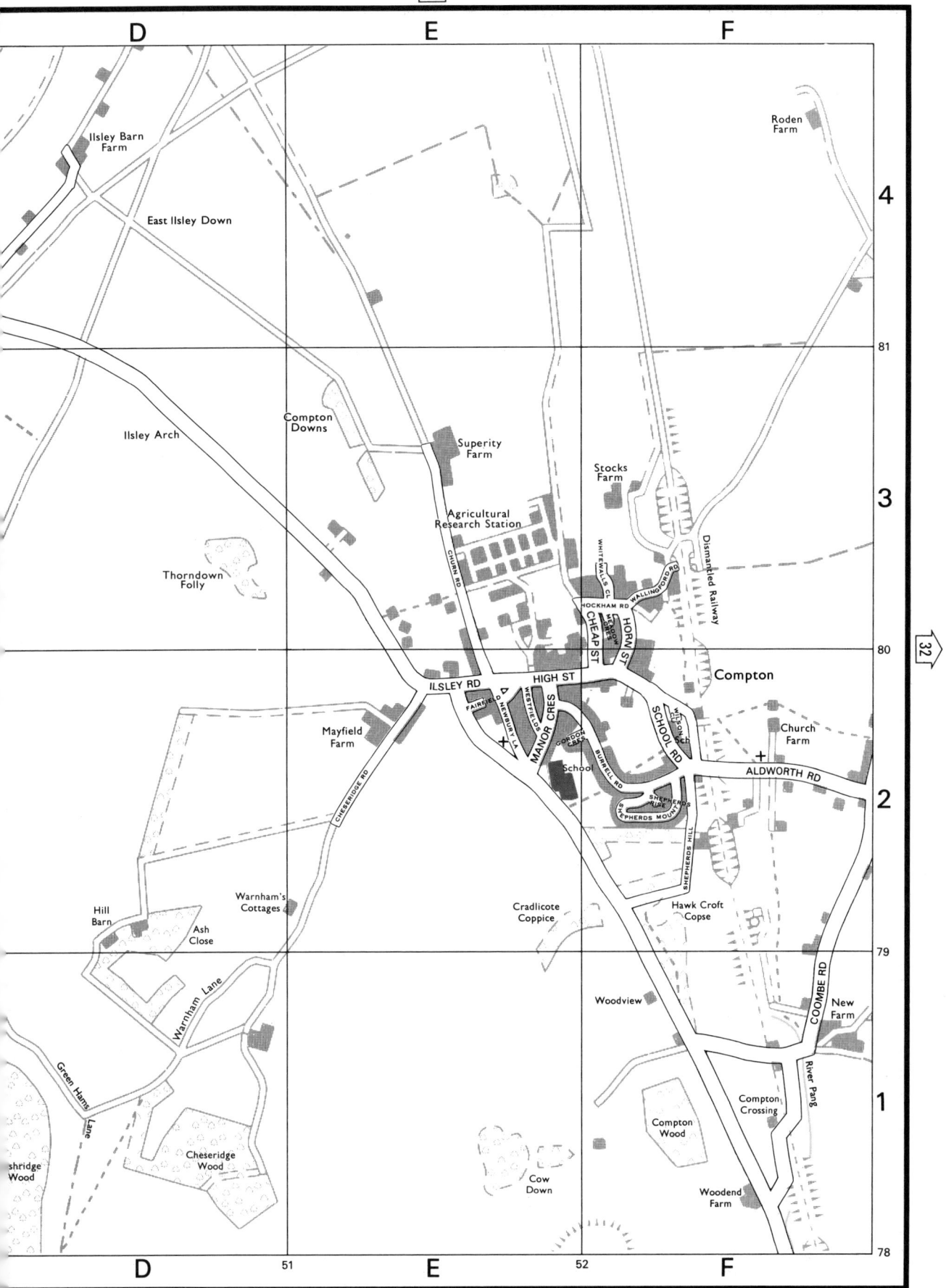

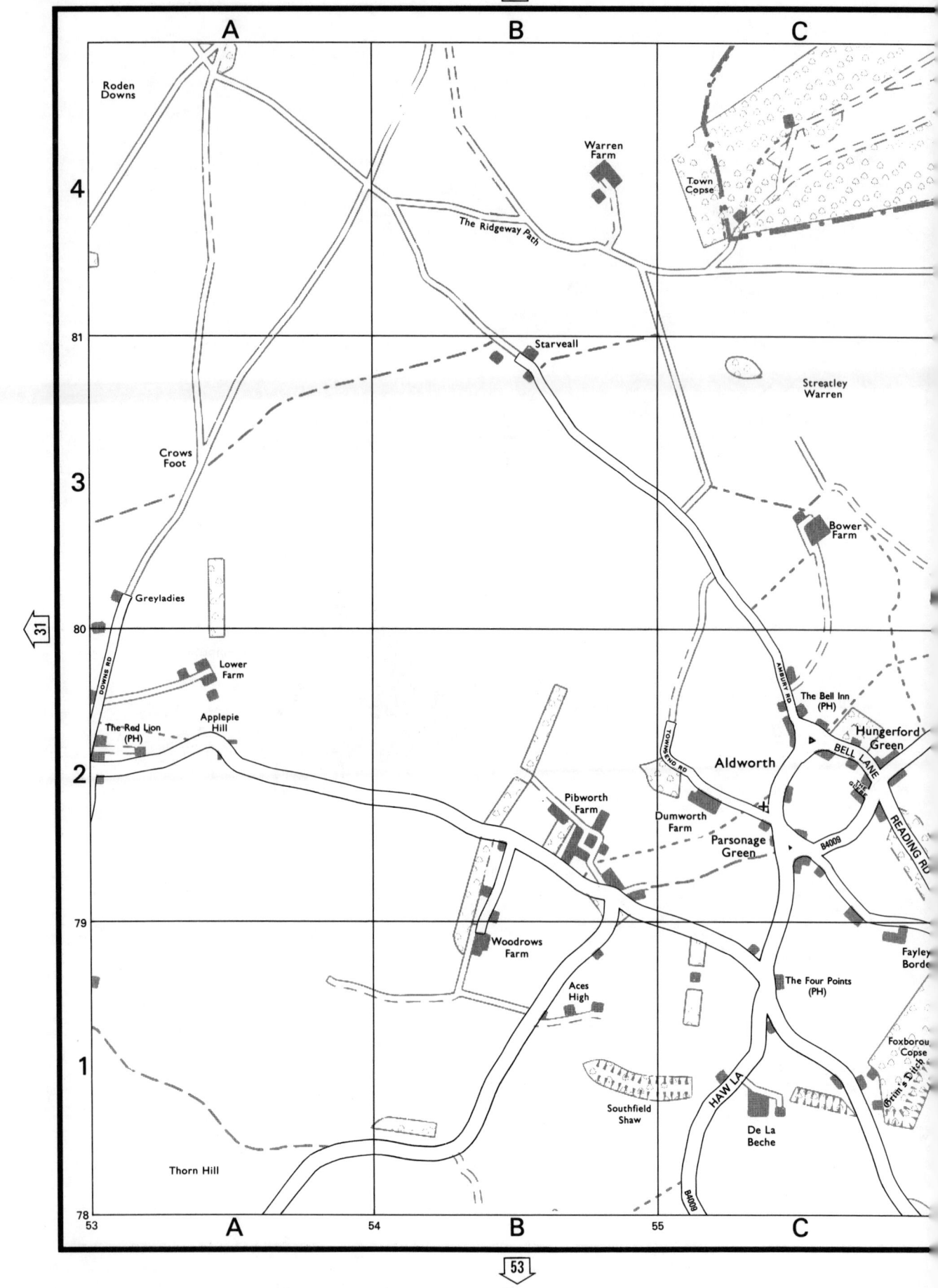

A   B   C

Roden
Downs

Warren
Farm

Town
Copse

4

The Ridgeway Path

Starveall

81

Streatley
Warren

Crows
Foot

3

Bower
Farm

Greyladies

80

Lower
Farm

The Bell Inn
(PH)

DOWNS RD

ASBURY RD

The Red Lion
(PH)

Applepie
Hill

Hungerford
Green

TOWNSEND RD

Aldworth

BELL LANE

2

Pibworth
Farm

Dumworth
Farm

READING RD

Parsonage
Green

B4009

79

Woodrows
Farm

Fayley
Borde

The Four Points
(PH)

Aces
High

Foxborou
Copse

Grim's Ditch

1

HAW LA

Southfield
Shaw

De La
Beche

Thorn Hill

B4009

78

53   A   54   B   55   C

13

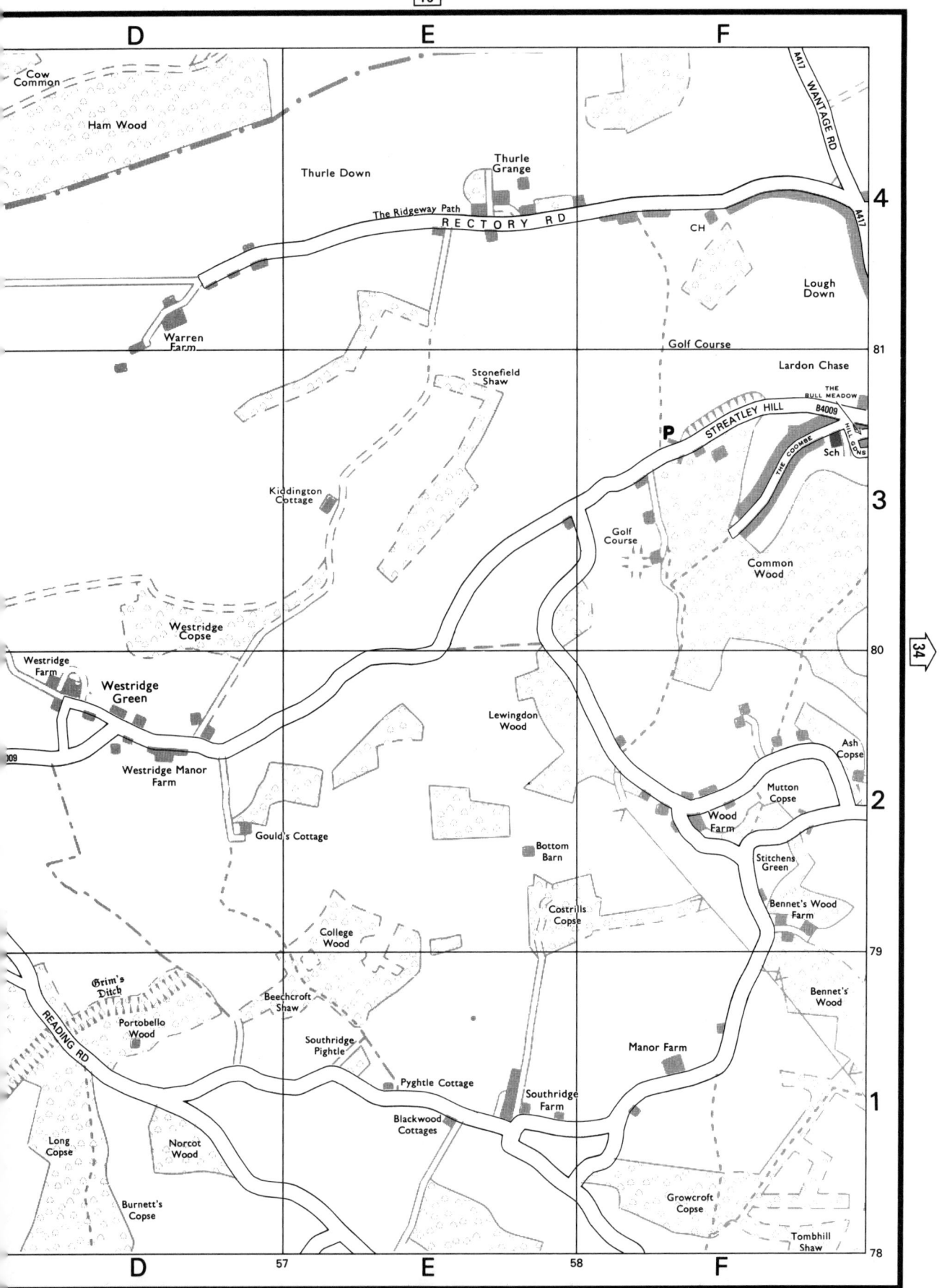

D E F

Cow
Common

Ham Wood

Thurle Down

Thurle
Grange

The Ridgeway Path

R E C T O R Y   R D

CH

4

Lough
Down

Warren
Farm

Golf Course

81

Stonefield
Shaw

Lardon Chase

THE
BULL MEADOW

B4009

P

STREATLEY HILL

HILL GDNS

Sch

Kiddington
Cottage

Golf
Course

THE COOMBE

Common
Wood

3

Westridge
Copse

80

Westridge
Farm

Westridge
Green

Lewingdon
Wood

Ash
Copse

009

Westridge Manor
Farm

Mutton
Copse

Wood
Farm

2

Gould's Cottage

Bottom
Barn

Stitchens
Green

Bennet's Wood
Farm

College
Wood

Costrills
Copse

79

Grim's
Ditch

Beechcroft
Shaw

Bennet's
Wood

Portobello
Wood

Southridge
Pightle

Manor Farm

READING RD

Pyghtle Cottage

Southridge
Farm

1

Blackwood
Cottages

Long
Copse

Norcot
Wood

Growcroft
Copse

Burnett's
Copse

Tombhill
Shaw

78

D 57 E 58 F

34

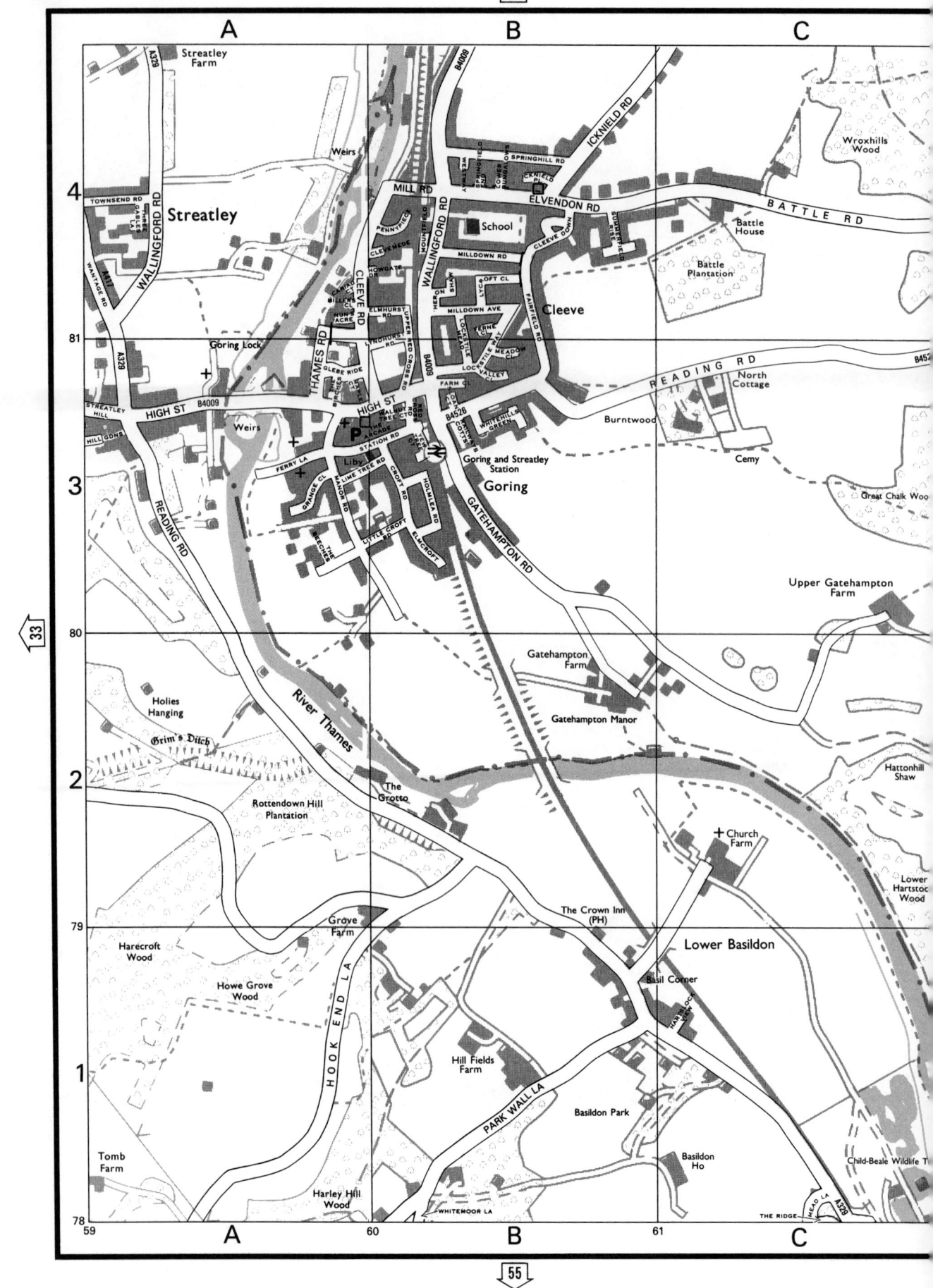

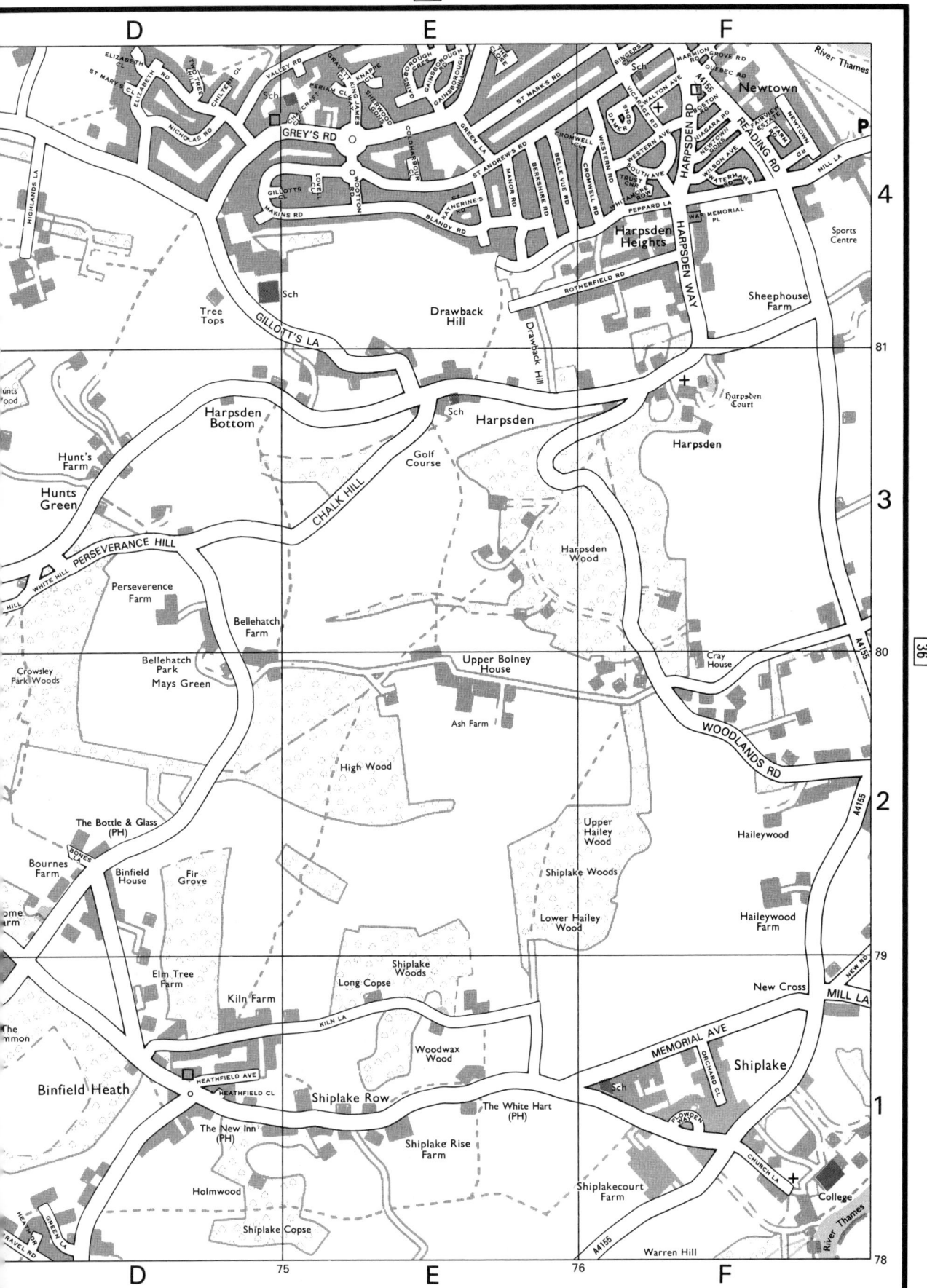

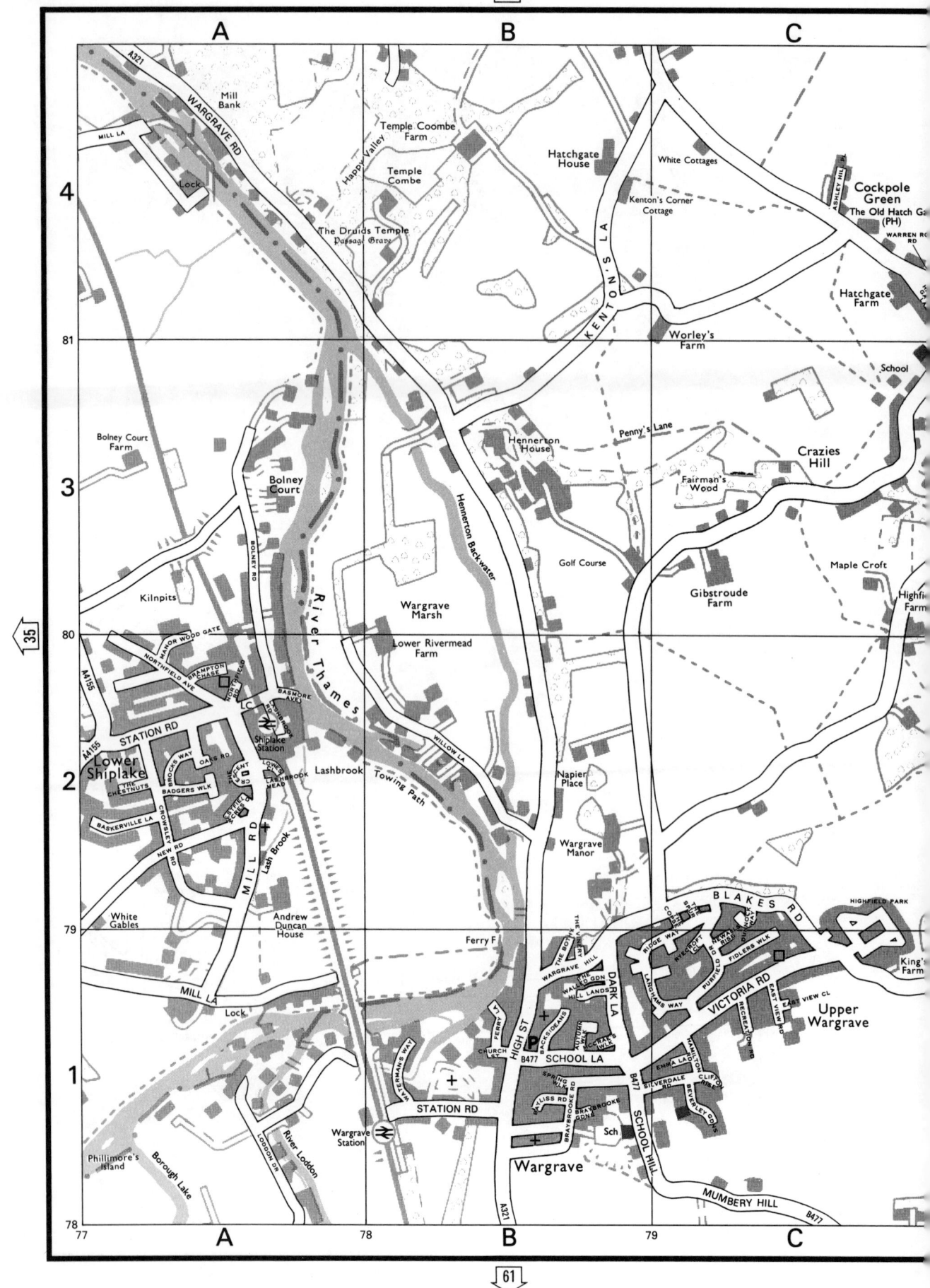

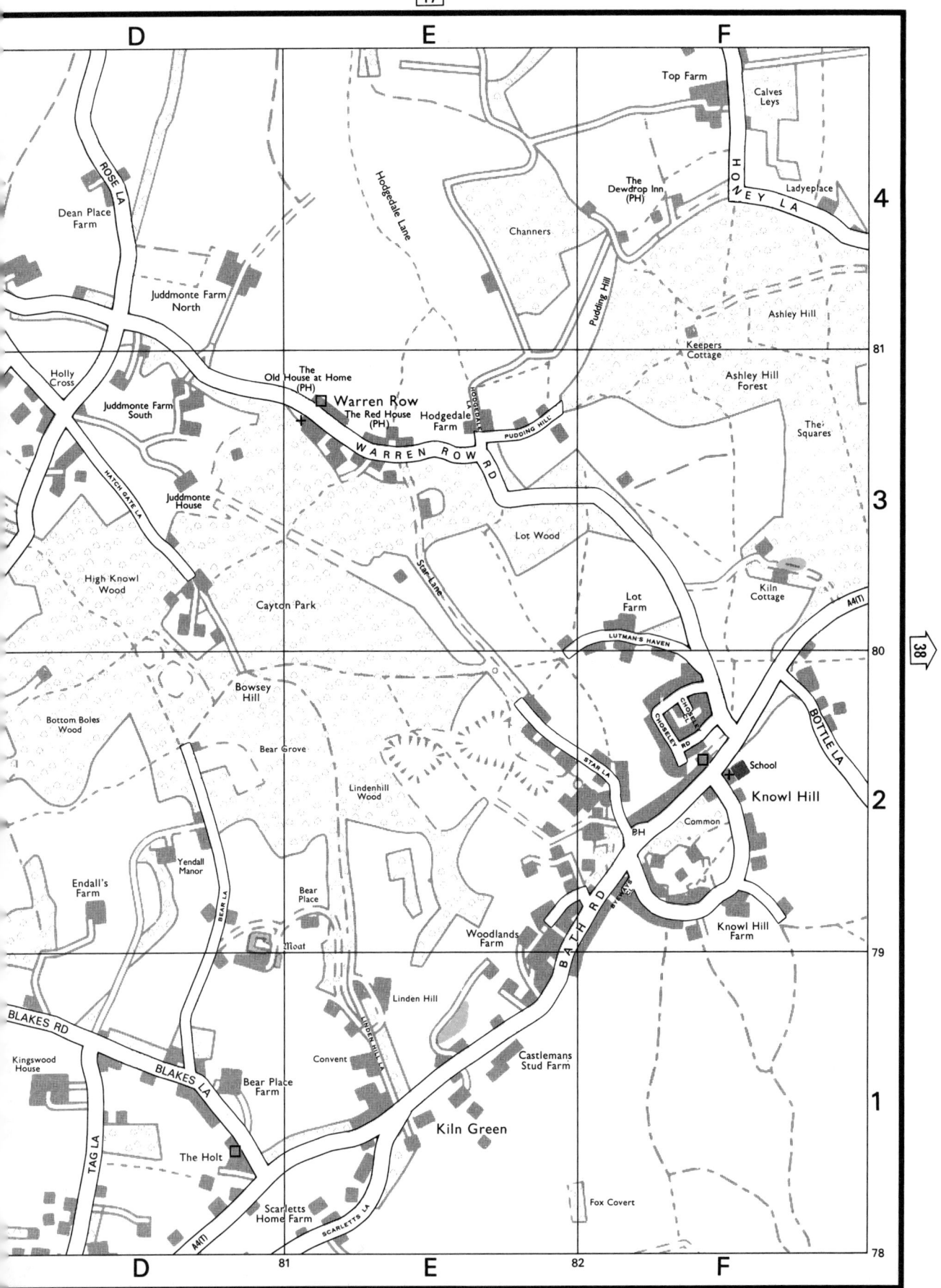

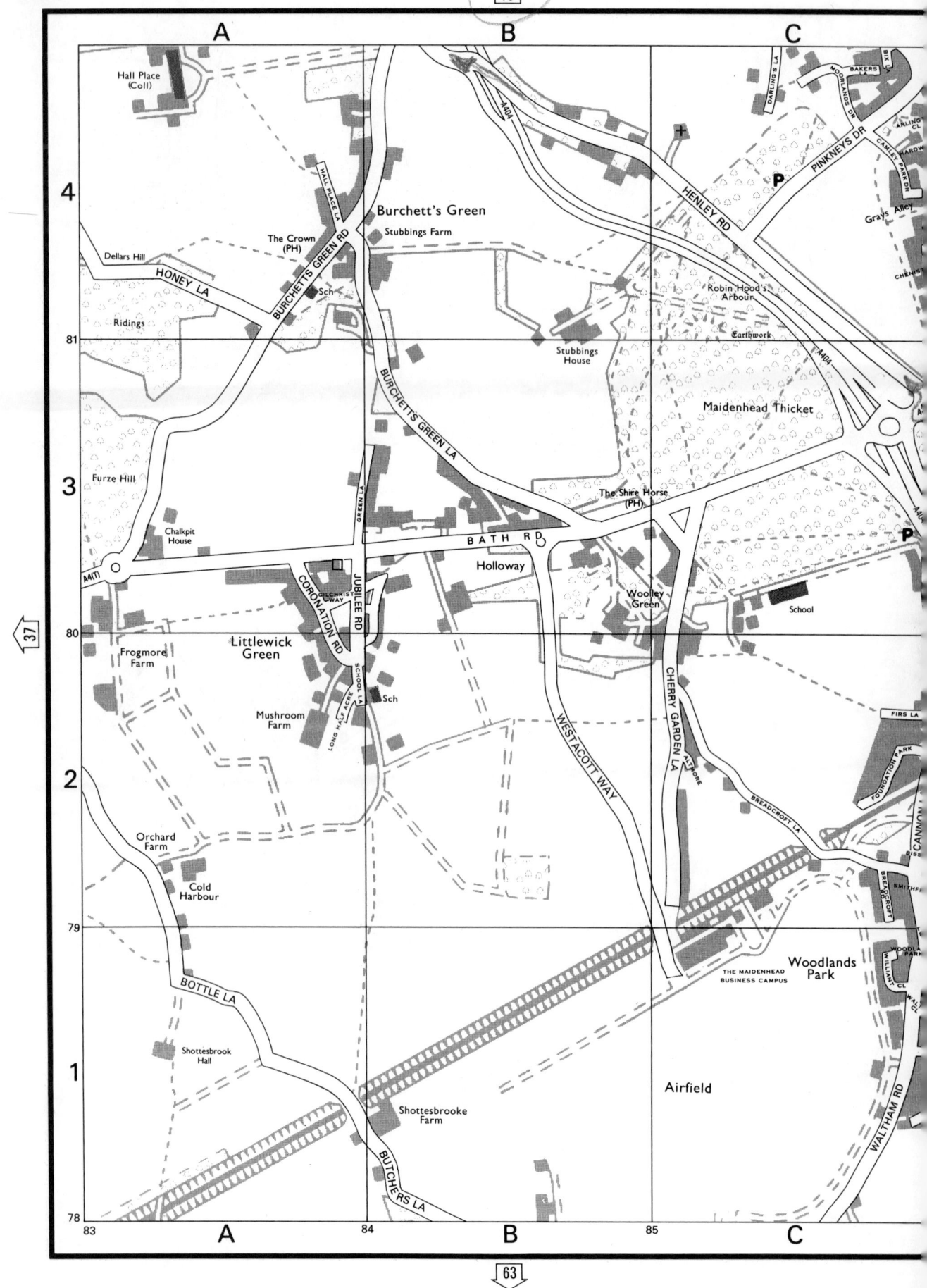

38

18

A   B   C

4

Hall Place (Coll)

Dellars Hill

HONEY LA

Ridings

HALL PLACE LA

BURCHETTS GREEN RD

The Crown (PH)

Burchett's Green

Stubbings Farm

Sch

81

Stubbings House

Robin Hood's Arbour

Earthwork

Maidenhead Thicket

BURCHETT'S GREEN LA

PINKNEYS DR

HENLEY RD

BAKERS

MOORLANDS DR

DARLING'S LA

ARLING CL

CAMLEY PARK DR

Grays Alley

P

3

Furze Hill

GREEN LA

Chalkpit House

A4(T)

A404

BATH RD

Holloway

The Shire Horse (PH)

Woolley Green

School

P

A404

80

CORONATION RD

JUBILEE RD

GILCHRIST WAY

Littlewick Green

Frogmore Farm

SCHOOL LA

Sch

LONG HALF ACRE

Mushroom Farm

CHERRY GARDEN LA

ALTMORE

FIRS LA

FOUNDATION PARK

2

Orchard Farm

Cold Harbour

WESTACOTT WAY

BREADCROFT LA

BREADCROFT

SMITHFI

CANNON

79

BOTTLE LA

THE MAIDENHEAD BUSINESS CAMPUS

Woodlands Park

WOODLA PARK

WILLIAM CL

WALTHAM RD

1

Shottesbrook Hall

Shottesbrooke Farm

Airfield

78

83

A

84

B

85

C

37

63

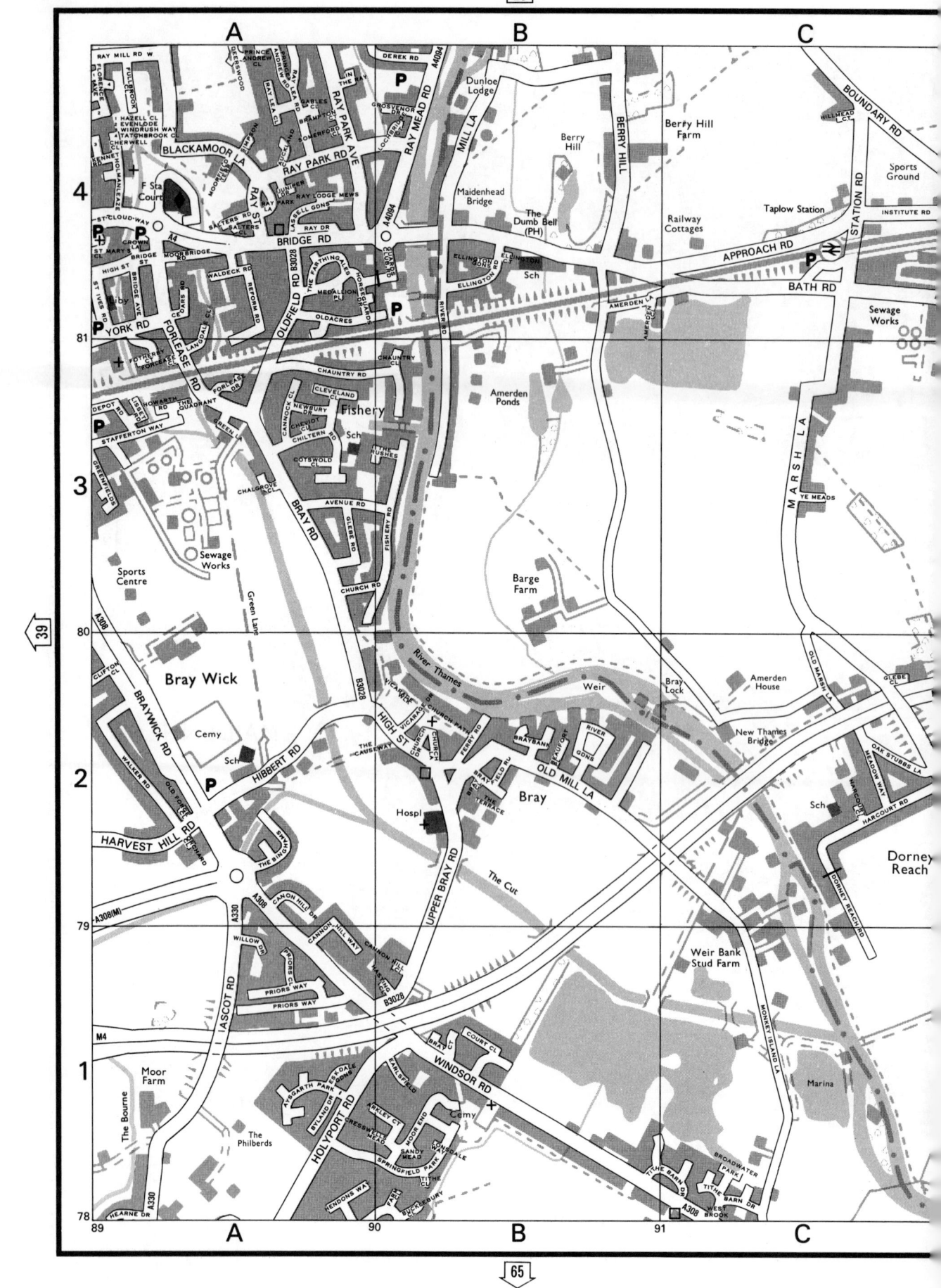

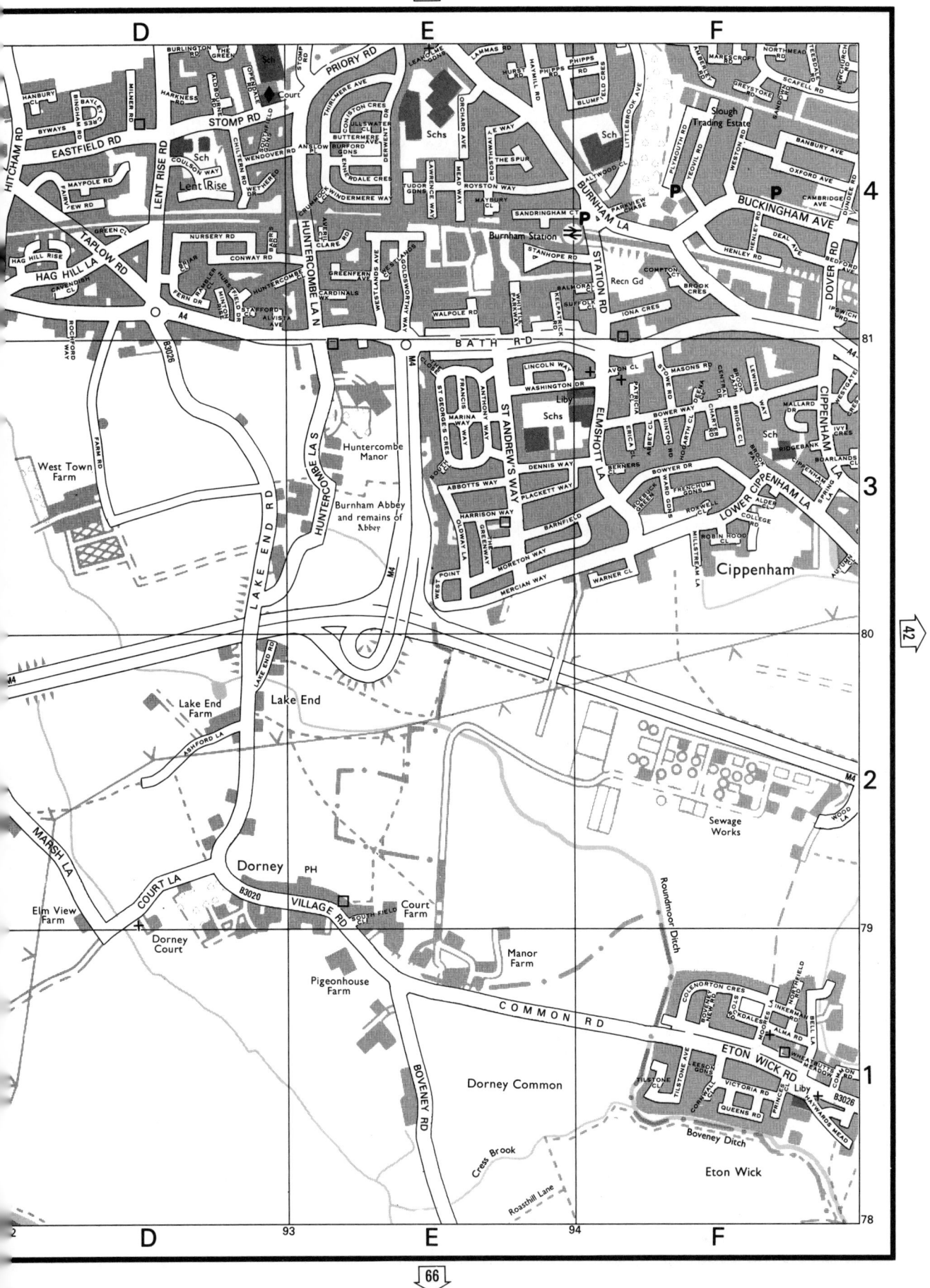

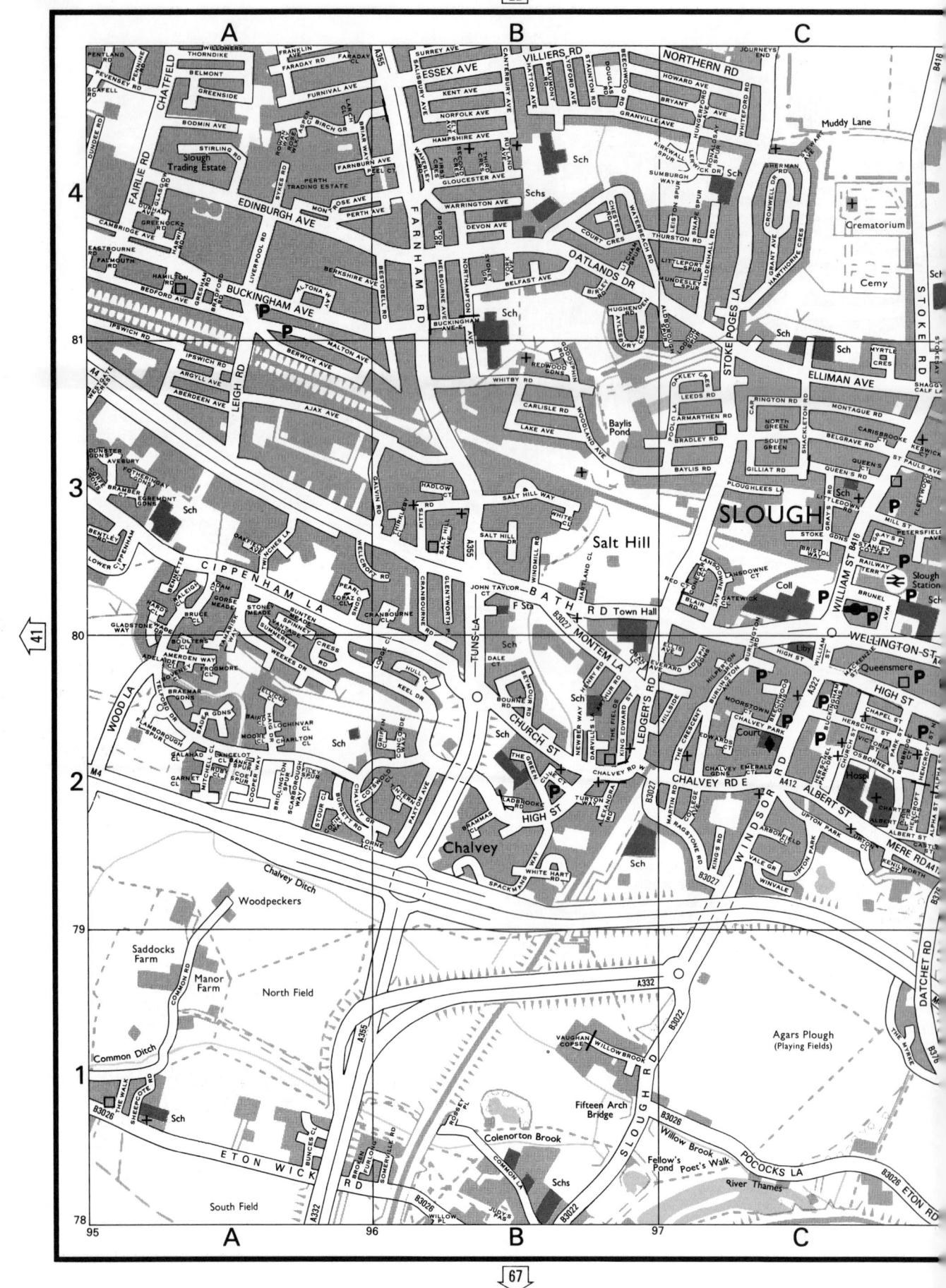

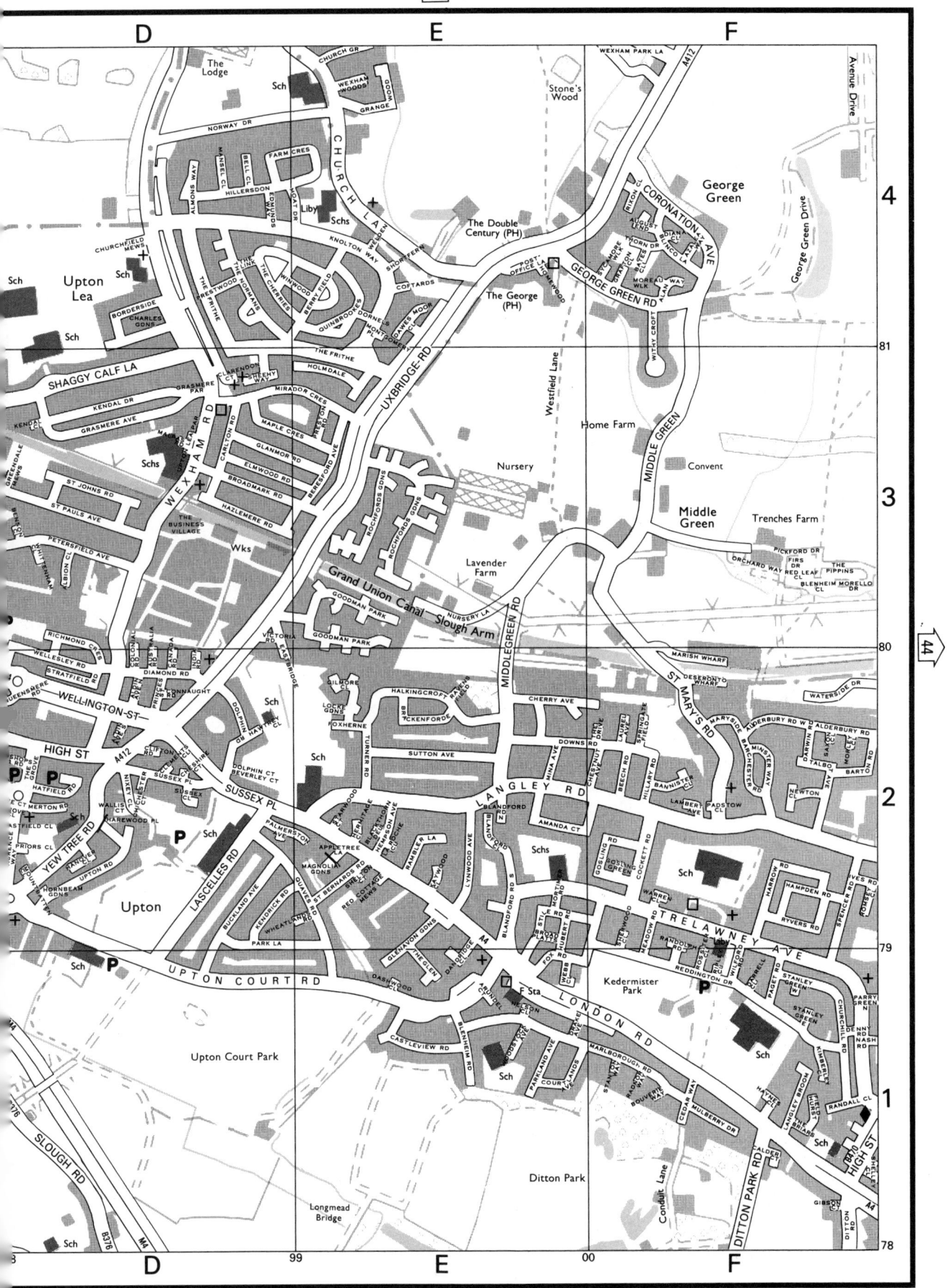

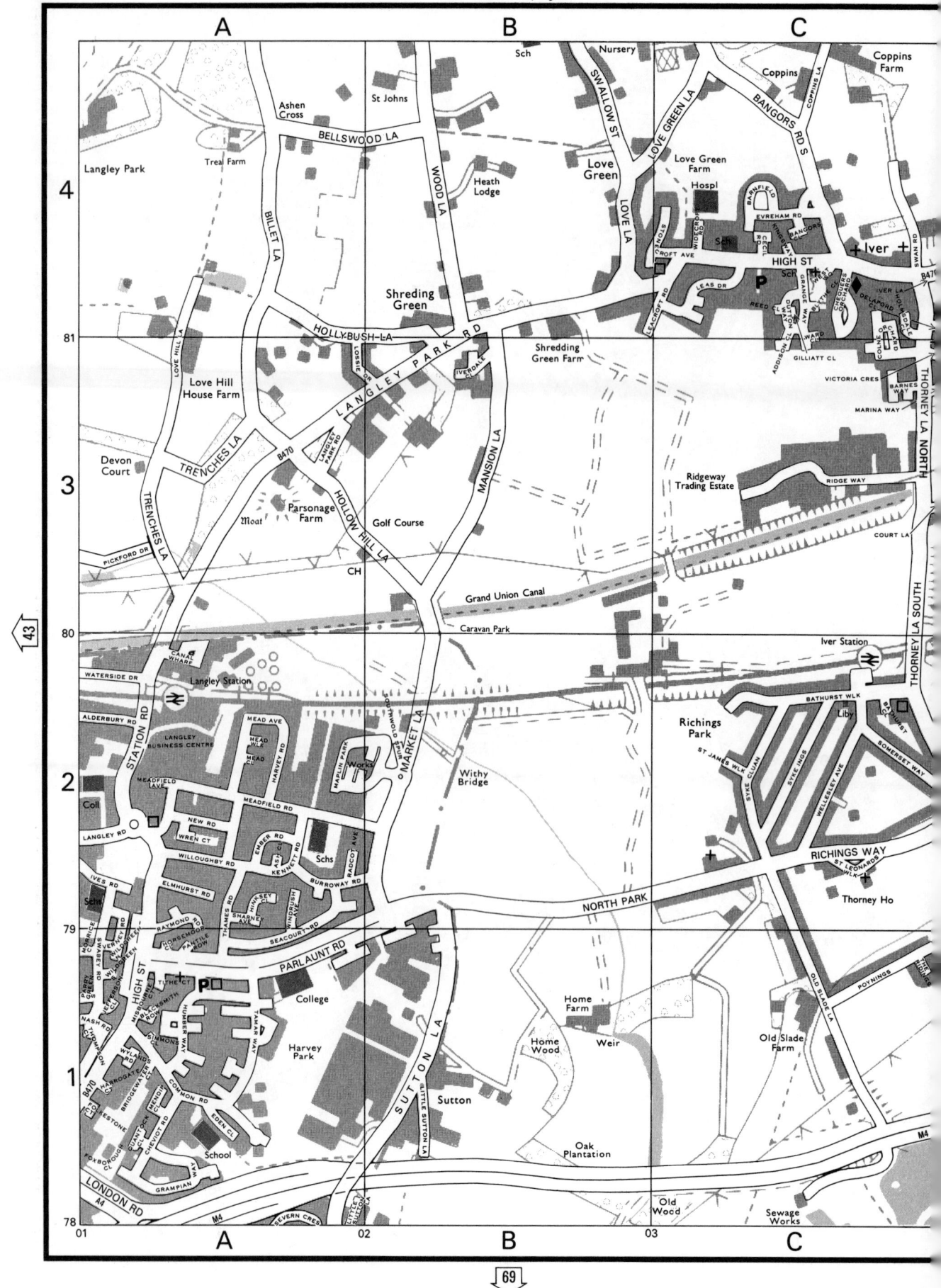

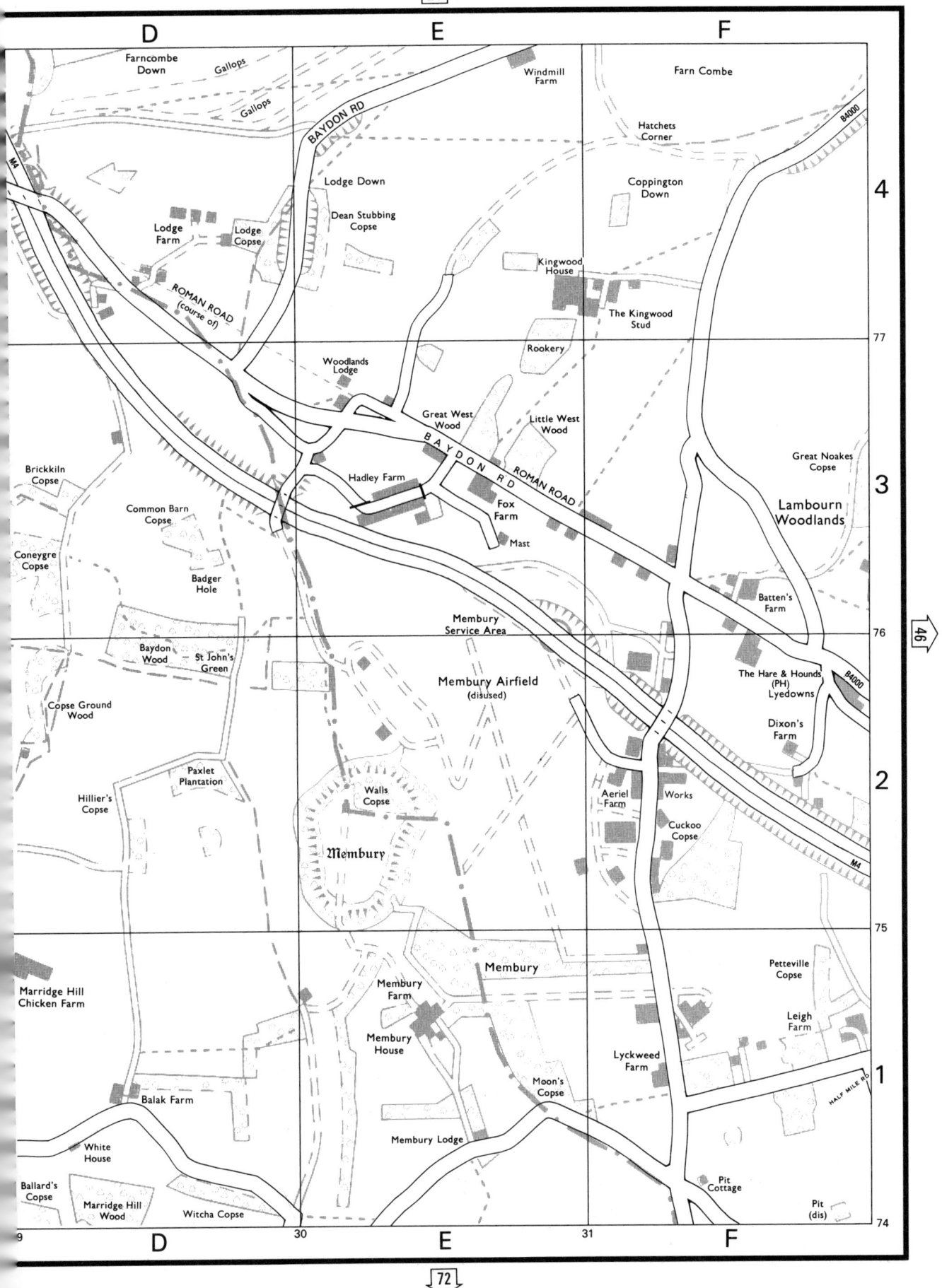

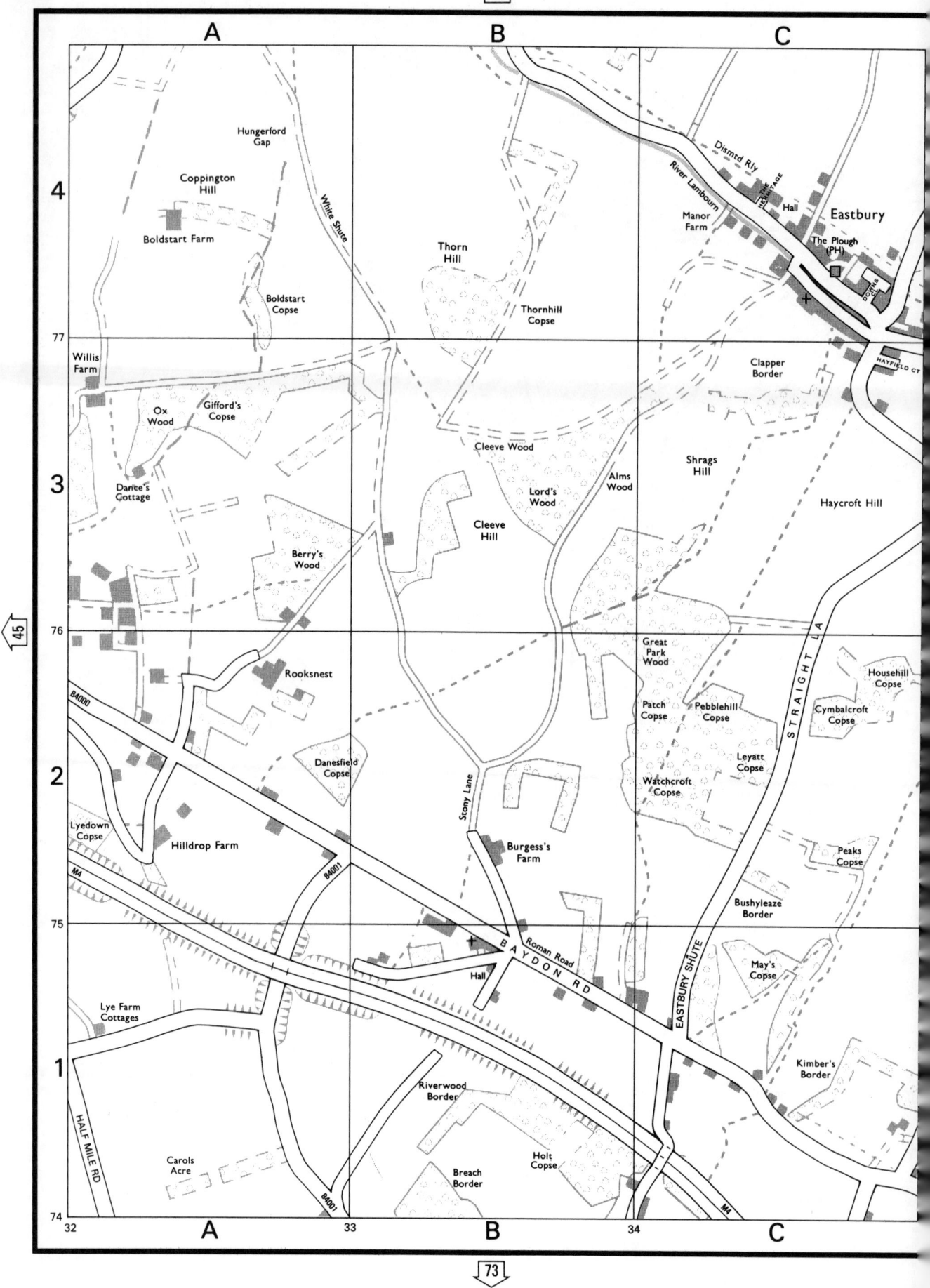

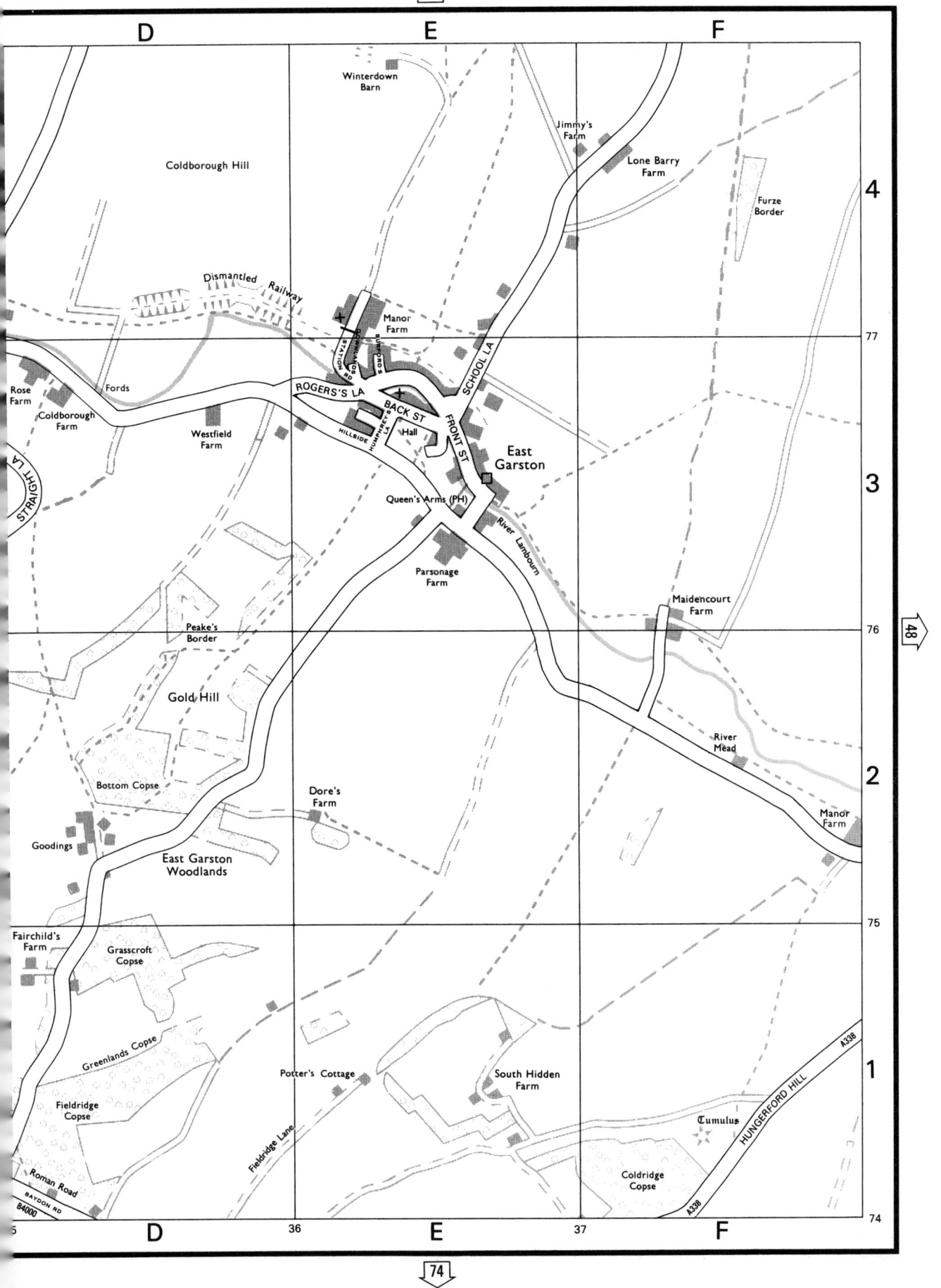

D   E   F

Winterdown Barn

Jimmy's Farm

Lone Barry Farm

Coldborough Hill

Furze Border

4

Dismantled Railway

Manor Farm

STATION RD

HUMPHREY'S

SCHOOL LA

Rose Farm

Fords

ROGERS'S LA

Coldborough Farm

Westfield Farm

BACK ST

HILLSIDE

HUMPHREY'S LA

Hall

FRONT ST

East Garston

STRAIGHT LA

77

Queen's Arms (PH)

River Lambourn

3

Parsonage Farm

Maidencourt Farm

48

Peake's Border

76

Gold Hill

River Mead

Bottom Copse

Dore's Farm

Manor Farm

2

Goodings

East Garston Woodlands

75

Fairchild's Farm

Grasscroft Copse

Greenlands Copse

Potter's Cottage

South Hidden Farm

1

Fieldridge Copse

Tumulus

A338

HUNGERFORD HILL

Roman Road

Fieldridge Lane

Coldridge Copse

A338

BAYDON RD

B4000

74

D   36   E   37   F

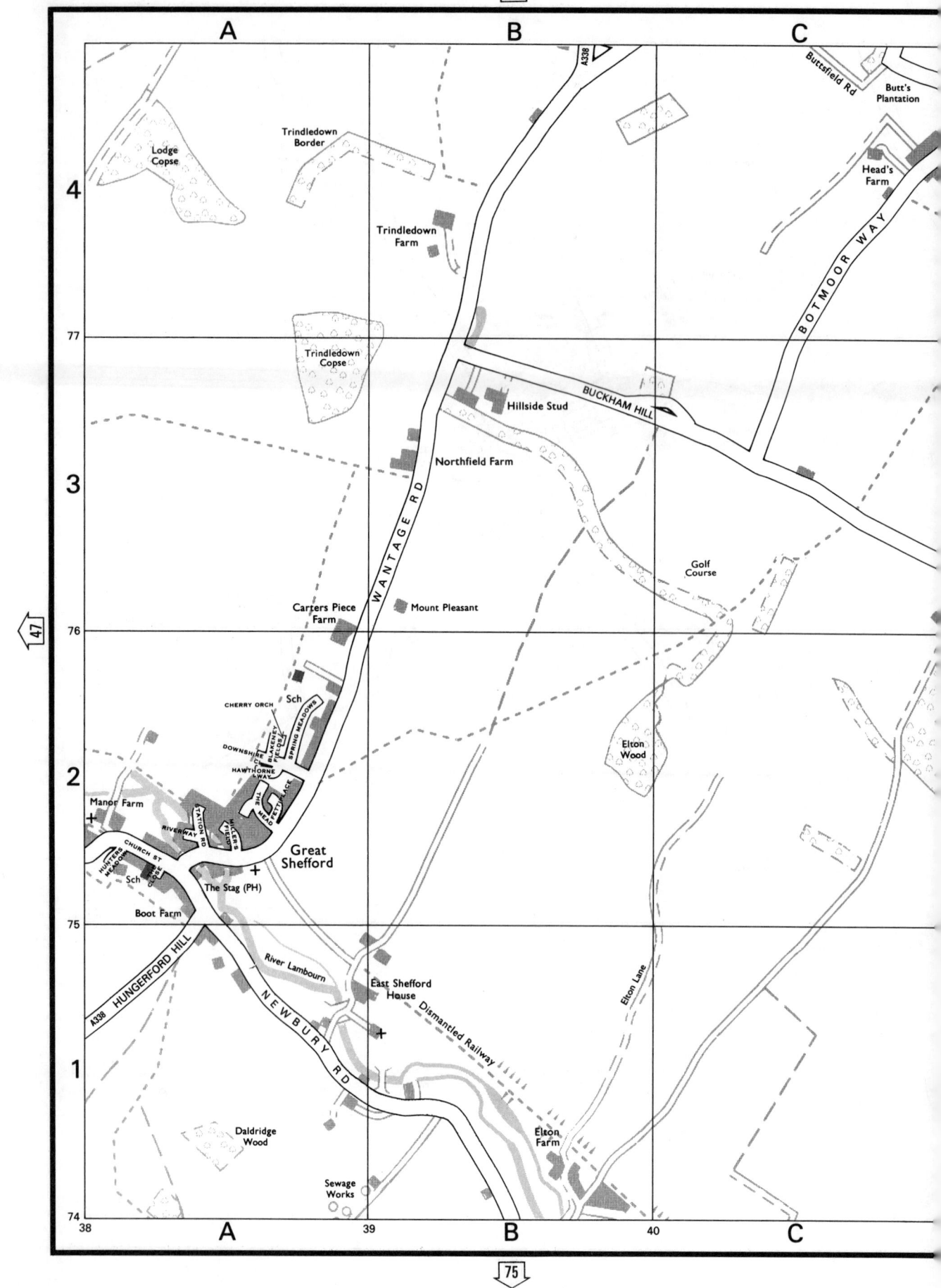

Lodge Copse

Trindledown Border

Trindledown Farm

A338

Buttsfield Rd

Butt's Plantation

Head's Farm

BOTMOOR WAY

Trindledown Copse

BUCKHAM HILL

Hillside Stud

WANTAGE RD

Northfield Farm

Golf Course

Carters Piece Farm

Mount Pleasant

Elton Wood

CHERRY ORCH

Sch

SPRING MEADOWS

DOWNSHIRE

BLAKENEY FIELDS

HAWTHORNE WAY

THE MEAD

PETTY PLACE

Manor Farm

STATION RD

MILLER'S FIELDS

RIVERWAY

Great Shefford

CHURCH ST

HUNTERS MEADOW

Sch

The Stag (PH)

Boot Farm

HUNGERFORD HILL

A338

River Lambourn

NEWBURY RD

East Shefford House

Elton Lane

Dismantled Railway

Daldridge Wood

Elton Farm

Sewage Works

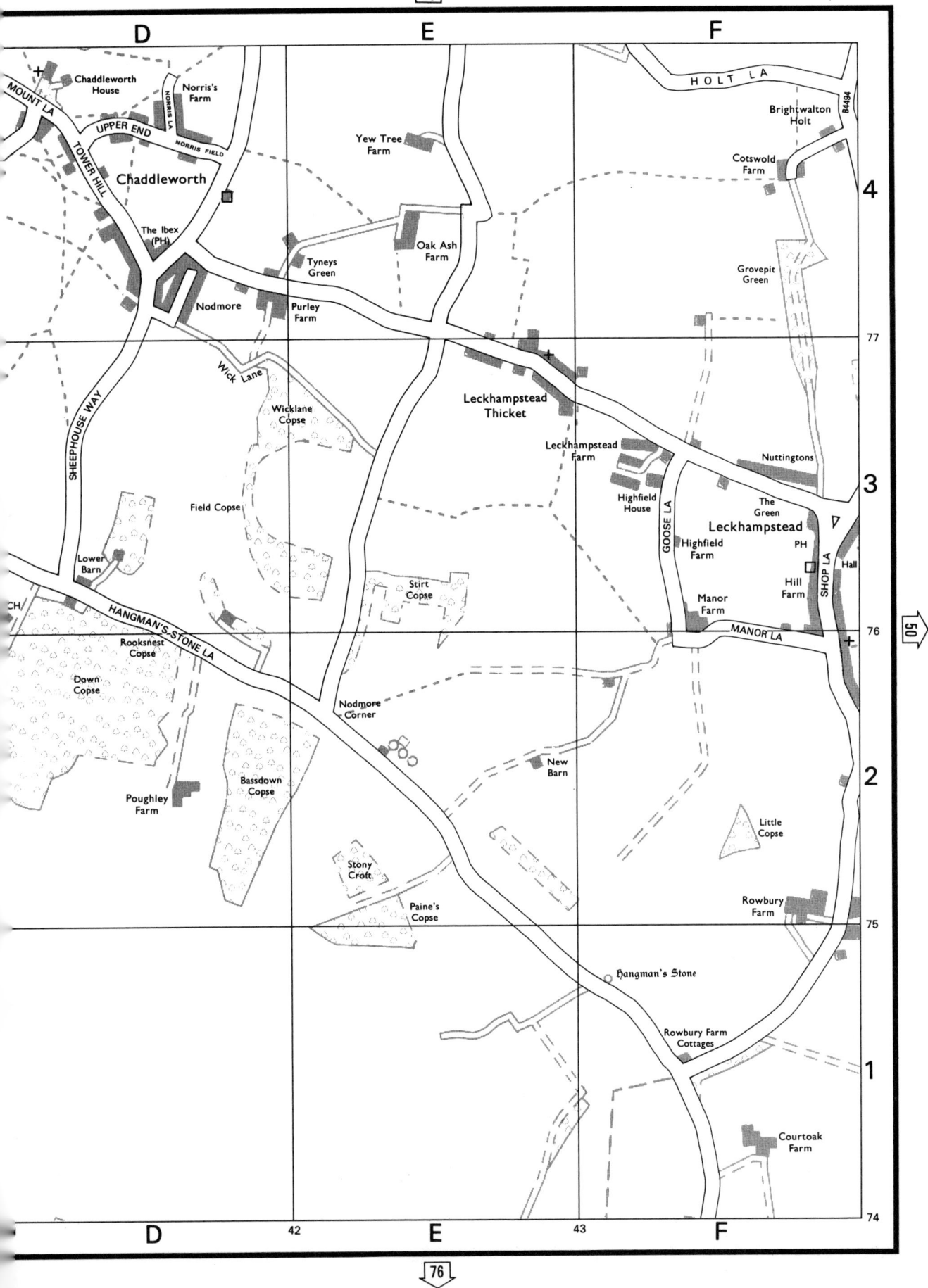

28

D E F

HOLT LA

MOUNT LA

Chaddleworth House

Norris's Farm

B4494

Brightwalton Holt

UPPER END

NORRIS LA

NORRIS FIELD

Cotswold Farm

TOWER HILL

Chaddleworth

Yew Tree Farm

4

The Ibex (PH)

Tyneys Green

Oak Ash Farm

Grovepit Green

Nodmore

Purley Farm

77

Wick Lane

SHEEPHOUSE WAY

Wicklane Copse

Leckhampstead Thicket

Nuttingtons

Leckhampstead Farm

3

Field Copse

Highfield House

GOOSE LA

The Green

Leckhampstead

Lower Barn

Highfield Farm

PH

SHOP LA

Hall

Stirt Copse

Manor Farm

Hill Farm

HANGMAN'S-STONE LA

Rooksnest Copse

MANOR LA

76

50

Down Copse

Nodmore Corner

Bassdown Copse

New Barn

Little Copse

2

Poughley Farm

Stony Croft

Rowbury Farm

Paine's Copse

75

Hangman's Stone

Rowbury Farm Cottages

1

Courtoak Farm

74

D 42 E 43 F

76

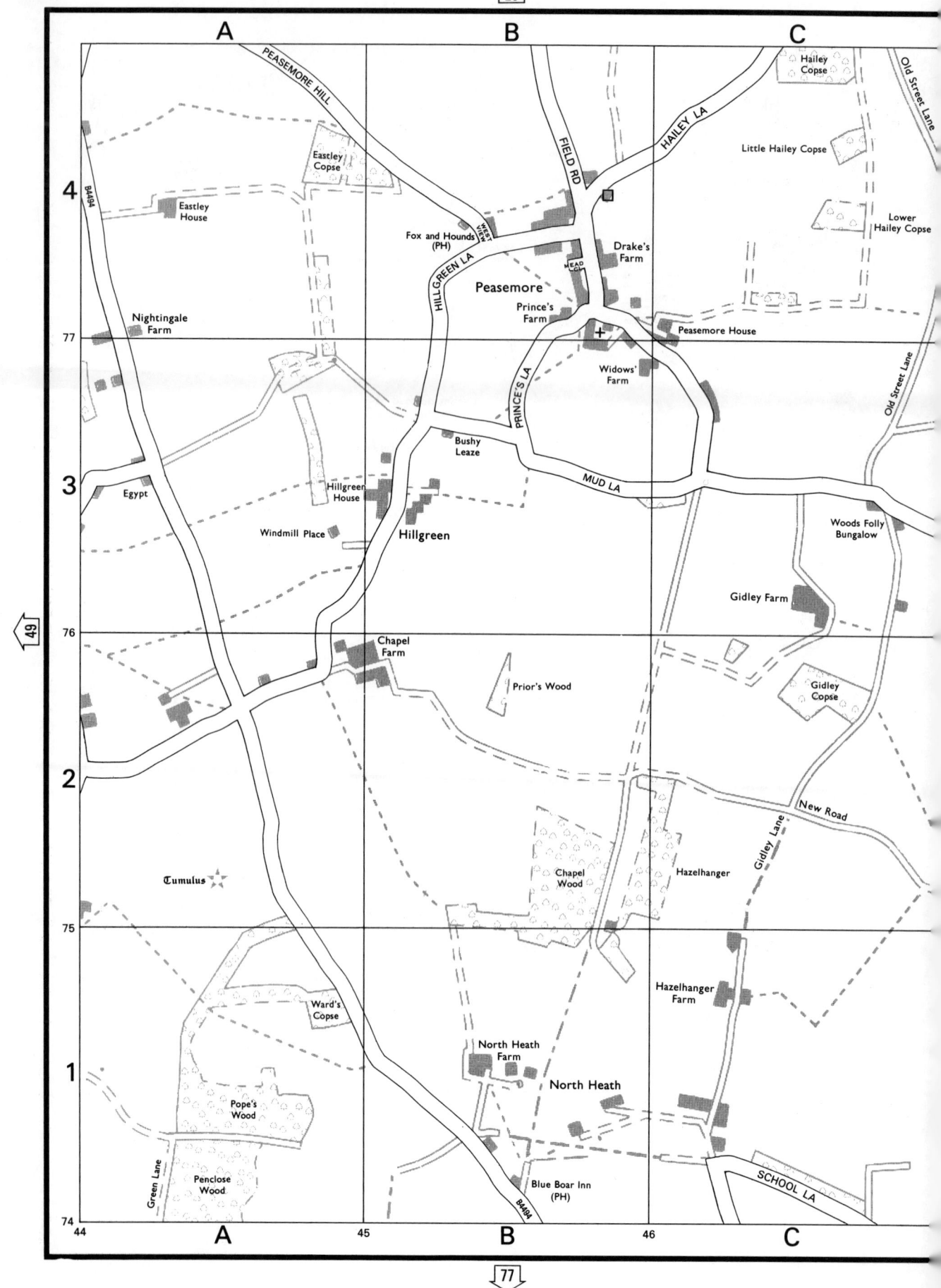

A   B   C

PEASEMORE HILL

Eastley
Copse

FIELD RD

HAILEY LA

Old Street Lane

Hailey
Copse

Little Hailey Copse

Lower
Hailey Copse

B4494

4

Eastley
House

Fox and Hounds
(PH)

HILLGREEN LA

WEST VIEW

MEAD LA

Drake's
Farm

Peasemore

77

Nightingale
Farm

Prince's
Farm

Peasemore House

PRINCE'S LA

Widows'
Farm

Street Lane

3

Egypt

Hillgreen
House

Windmill Place

Bushy
Leaze

Hillgreen

MUD LA

Woods Folly
Bungalow

Gidley Farm

76

Chapel
Farm

Prior's Wood

Gidley
Copse

2

Tumulus

Chapel
Wood

Hazelhanger

Gidley Lane

New Road

75

Ward's
Copse

Hazelhanger
Farm

1

Pope's
Wood

North Heath
Farm

North Heath

Green Lane

Penclose
Wood

Blue Boar Inn
(PH)

B4494

SCHOOL LA

74

44   A   45   B   46   C

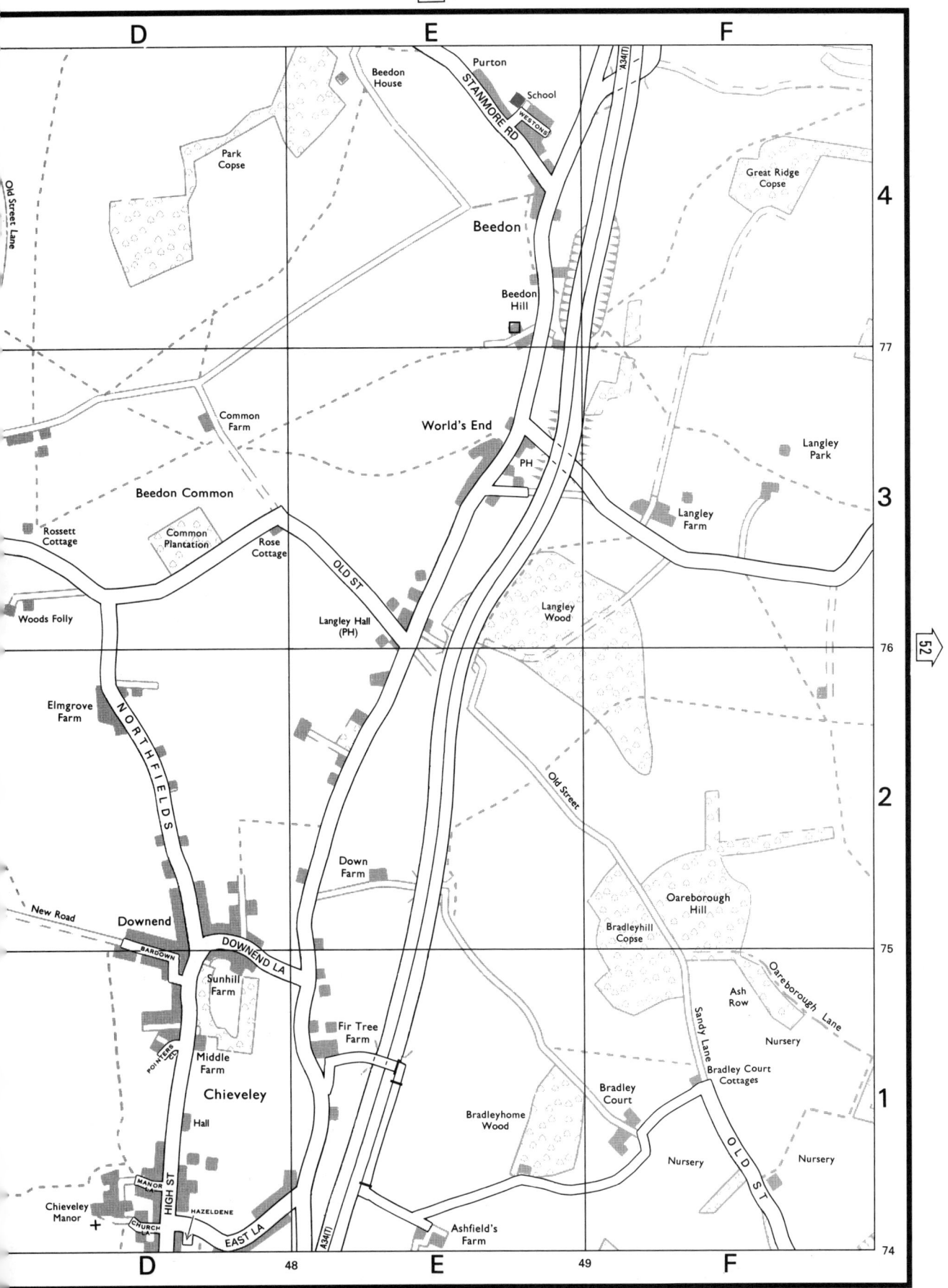

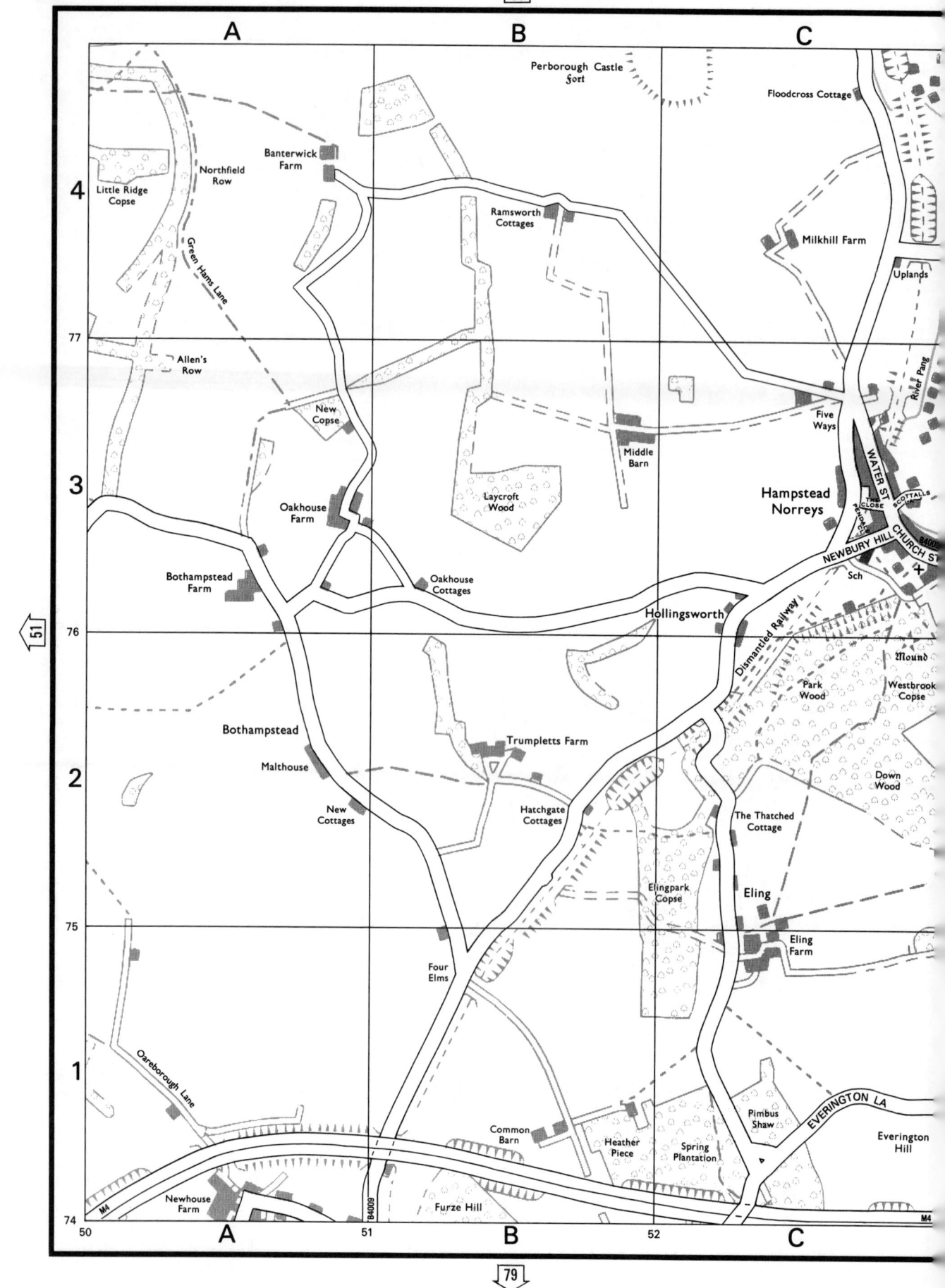

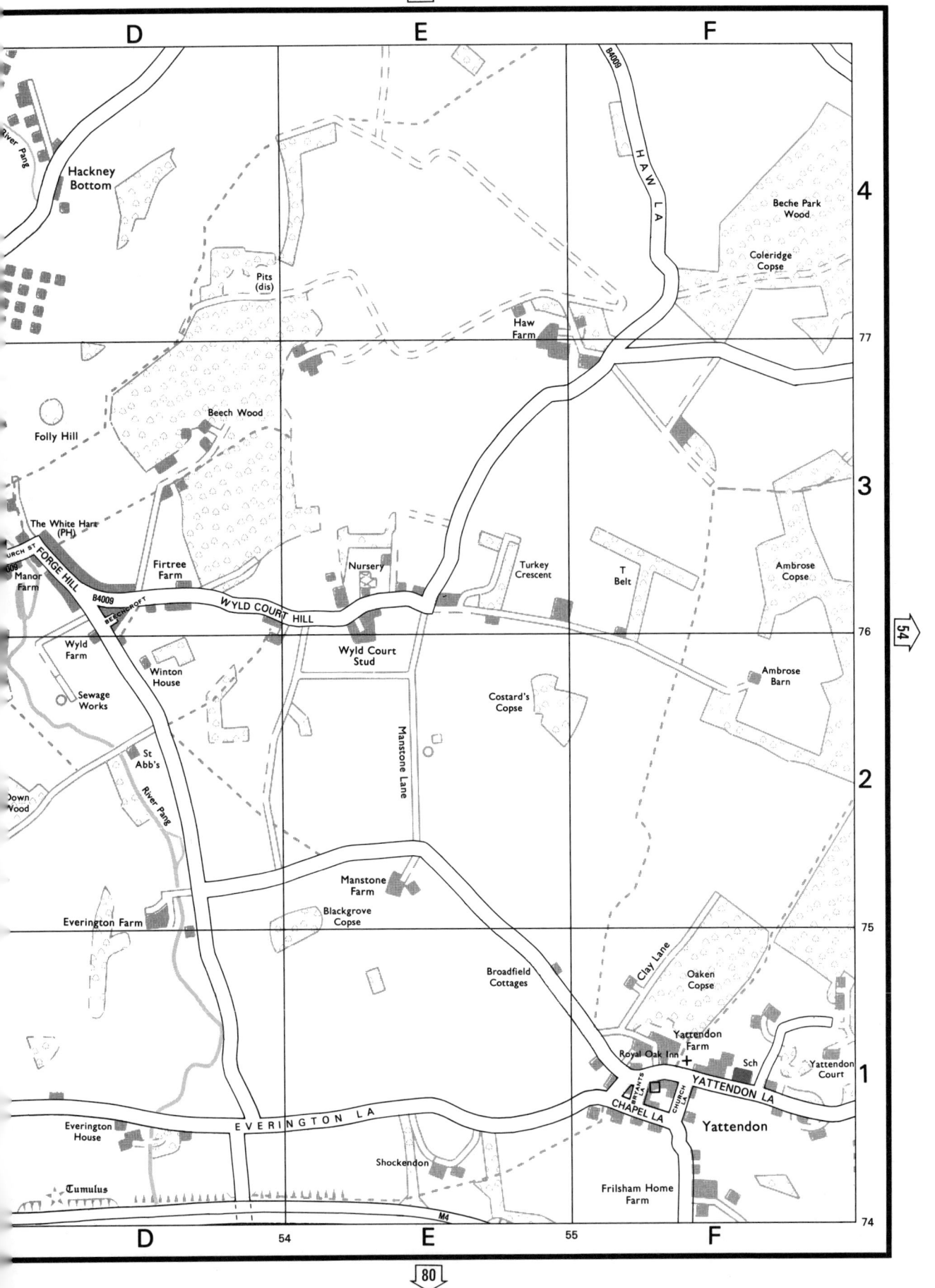

D E F

4

Hackney
Bottom

Beche Park
Wood

Coleridge
Copse

HAW LA

B4009

River Pang

Pits
(dis)

77

Haw
Farm

Beech Wood

Folly Hill

3

The White Hart
(PH)

URCH ST

FORGE HILL

Firtree
Farm

Nursery

Turkey
Crescent

T
Belt

Ambrose
Copse

54

Manor
Farm

009

B4009

BEECHCROFT

WYLD COURT HILL

76

Wyld Court
Stud

Ambrose
Barn

Wyld
Farm

Winton
House

Costard's
Copse

Sewage
Works

Manstone Lane

2

St
Abb's

River Pang

Down
Wood

Manstone
Farm

Everington Farm

Blackgrove
Copse

75

Broadfield
Cottages

Clay Lane

Oaken
Copse

Yattendon
Farm

Royal Oak Inn

PEASANTS

CHURCH LA

Sch

Yattendon
Court

YATTENDON LA

1

CHAPEL LA

Yattendon

Everington
House

EVERINGTON LA

Shockendon

Frilsham Home
Farm

Tumulus

M4

74

D 54 E 55 F

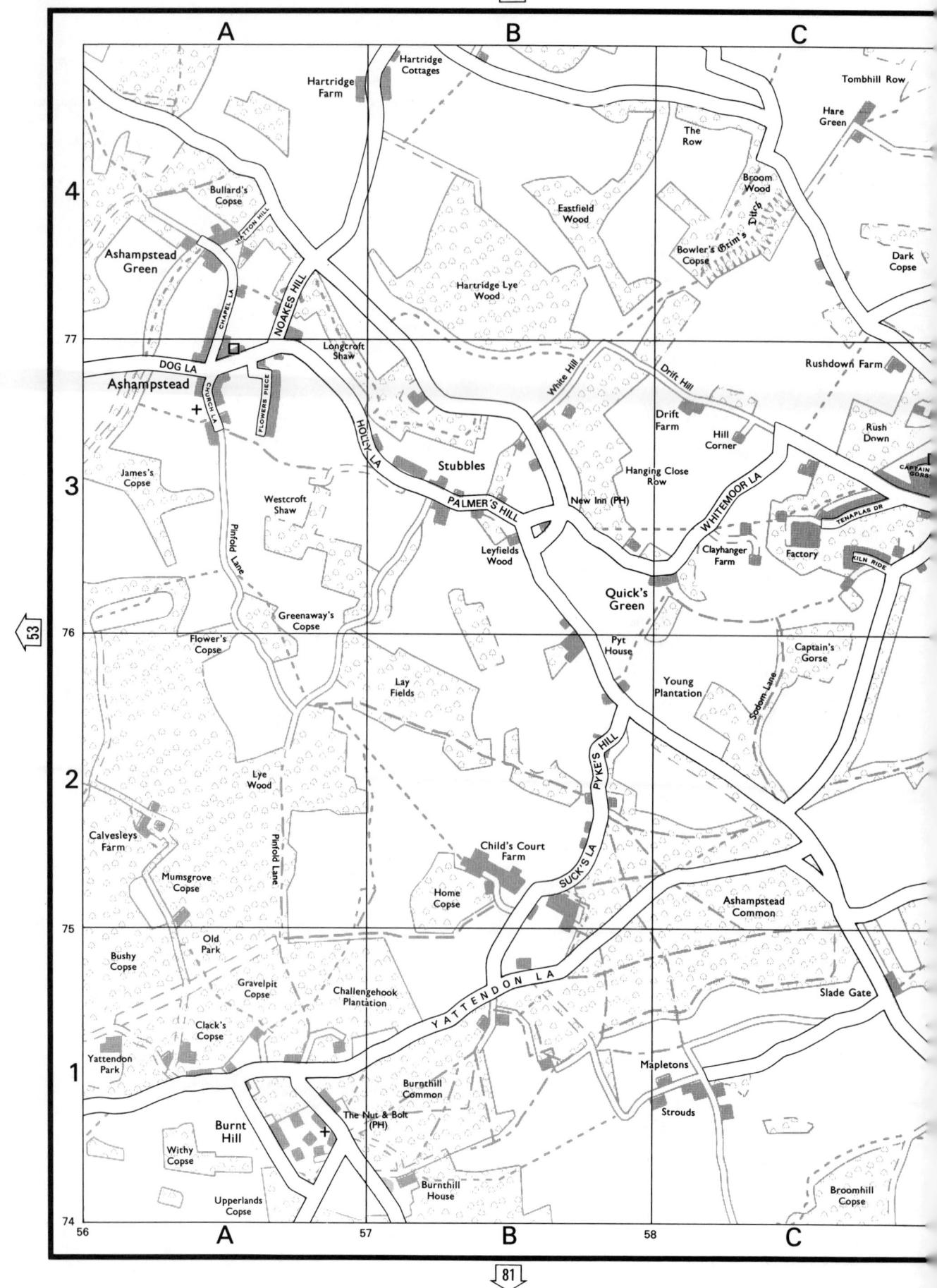

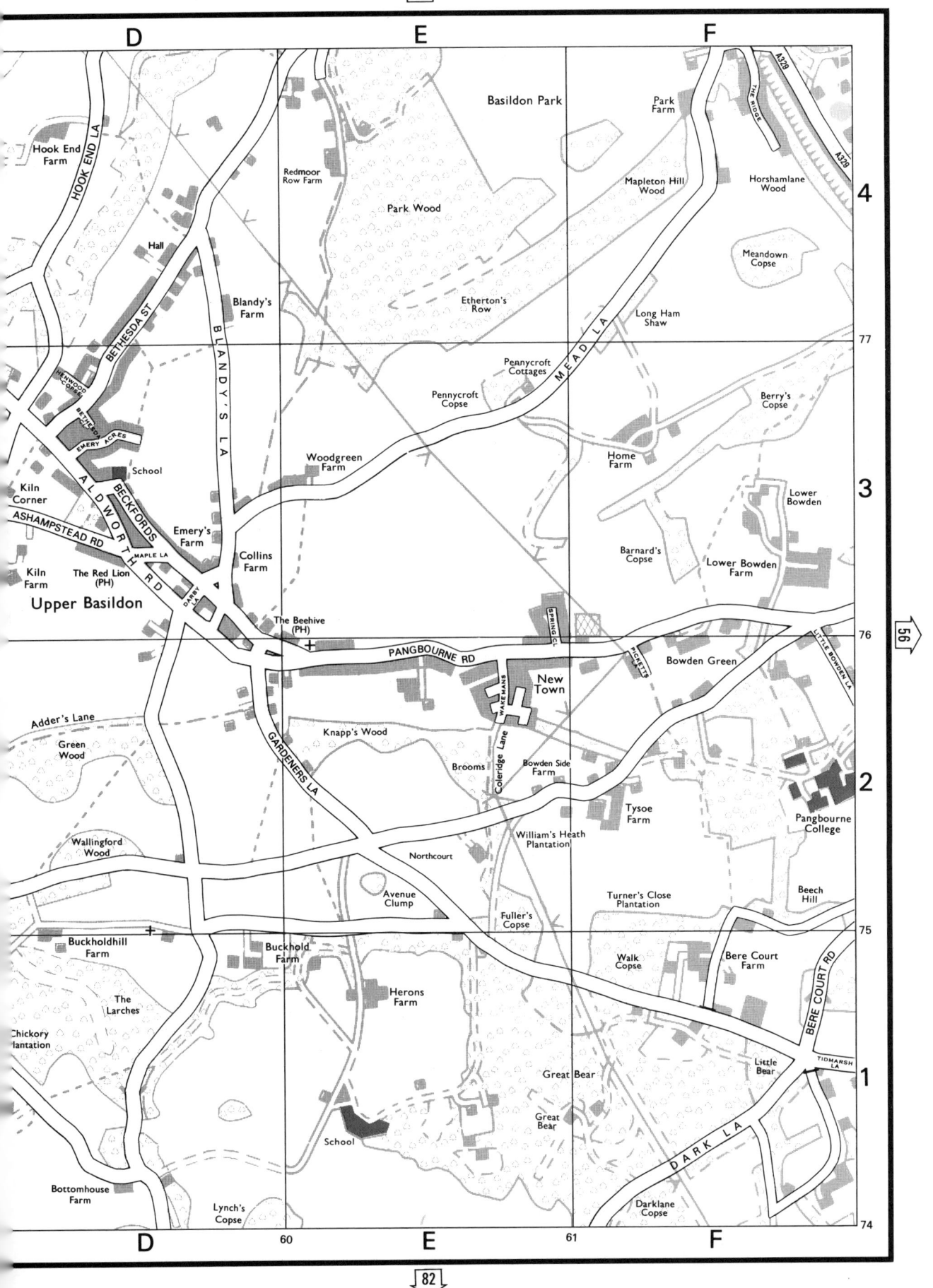

D E F

Hook End Farm

HOOK END LA

Basildon Park

Park Farm

Redmoor Row Farm

THE RIDGE

A329

A329

Mapleton Hill Wood

Horshamlane Wood

4

Park Wood

Hall

BETHESDA ST

Blandy's Farm

Meandown Copse

Etherton's Row

BLANDY'S LA

MEAD LA

Long Ham Shaw

77

MENWOOD COPSE

BETHESDA

EMERY ACRES

School

ALDWORTH RD

Kiln Corner

BECKFORDS

Emery's Farm

ASHAMPSTEAD RD

MAPLE LA

DARBY LA

Collins Farm

Pennycroft Cottages

Pennycroft Copse

Woodgreen Farm

Berry's Copse

Home Farm

Lower Bowden

3

Barnard's Copse

Lower Bowden Farm

Kiln Farm

The Red Lion (PH)

Upper Basildon

The Beehive (PH)

PANGBOURNE RD

New Town

WAKEMANS

SPRING CL

PICKETTS

Bowden Green

LITTLE BOWDEN LA

76

56

Adder's Lane

Green Wood

GARDENERS LA

Knapp's Wood

Coleridge Lane

Brooms

Bowden Side Farm

Tysoe Farm

Pangbourne College

2

Wallingford Wood

Northcourt

William's Heath Plantation

Avenue Clump

Fuller's Copse

Turner's Close Plantation

Beech Hill

75

Buckholdhill Farm

Buckhold Farm

Walk Copse

Bere Court Farm

BERE COURT RD

The Larches

Herons Farm

Chickory Plantation

Great Bear

Little Bear

TIDMARSH LA

1

Great Bear

School

DARK LA

Bottomhouse Farm

Lynch's Copse

Darklane Copse

74

D 60 E 61 F

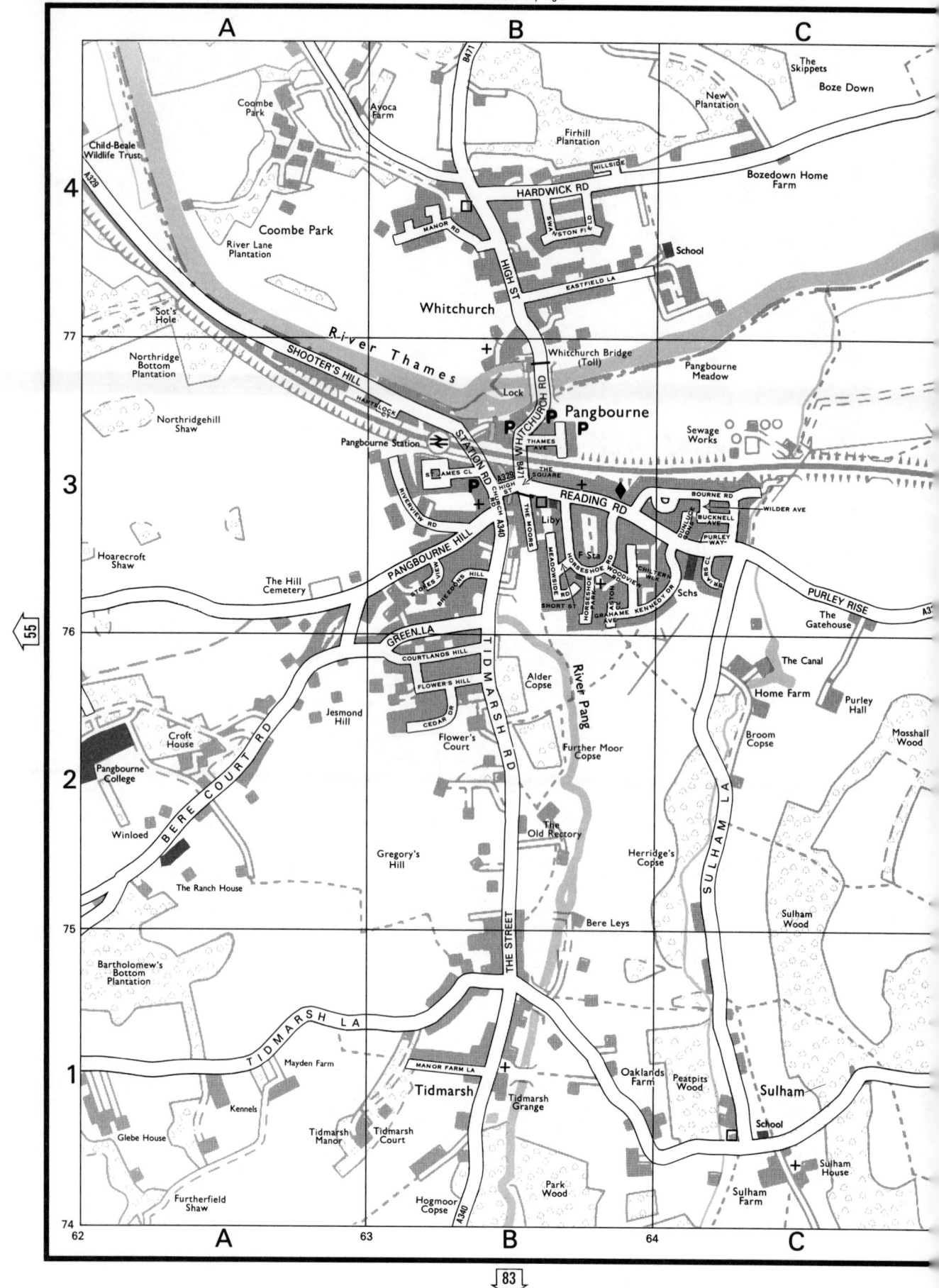

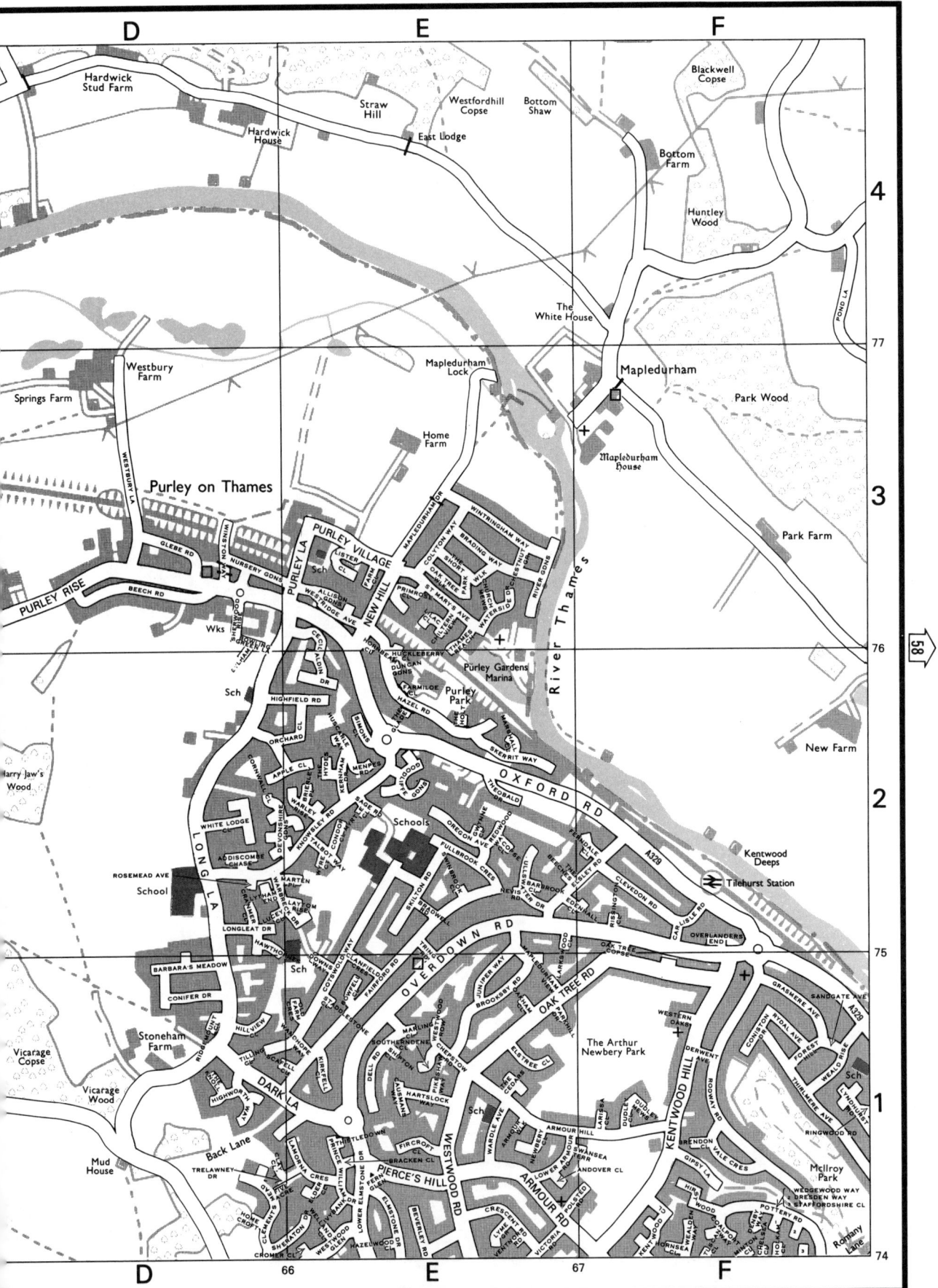

58

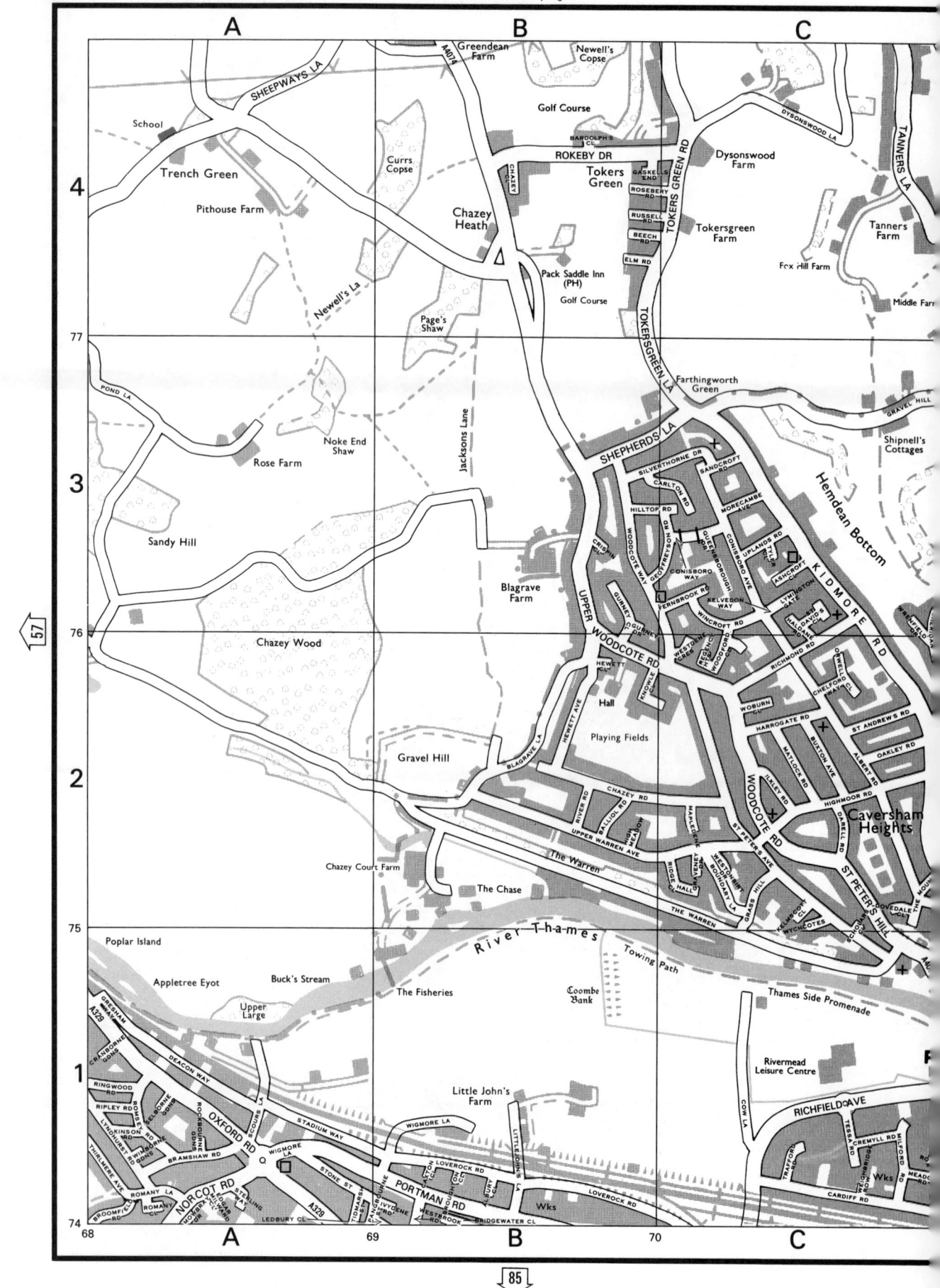

not continued, see key diagram

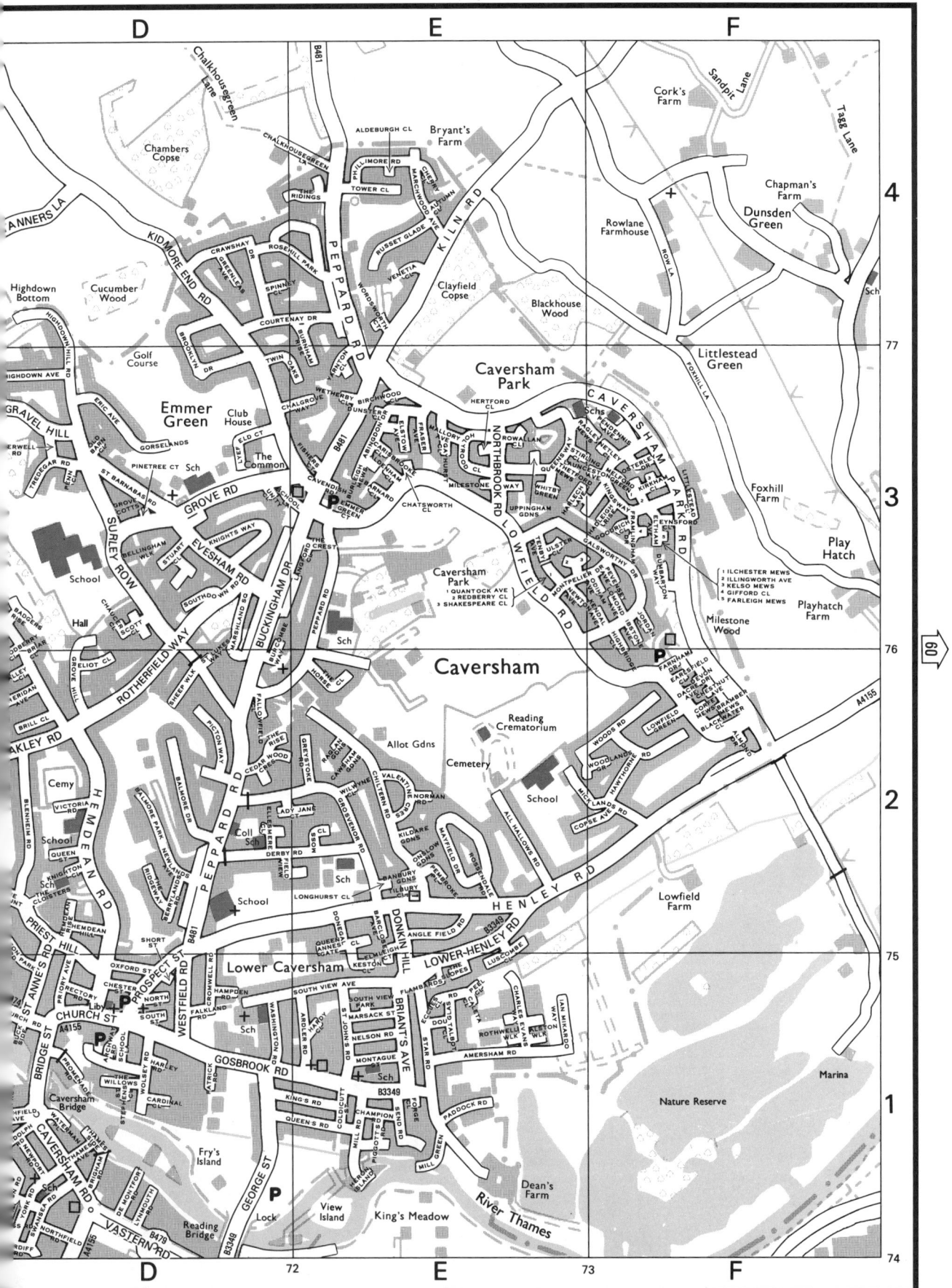

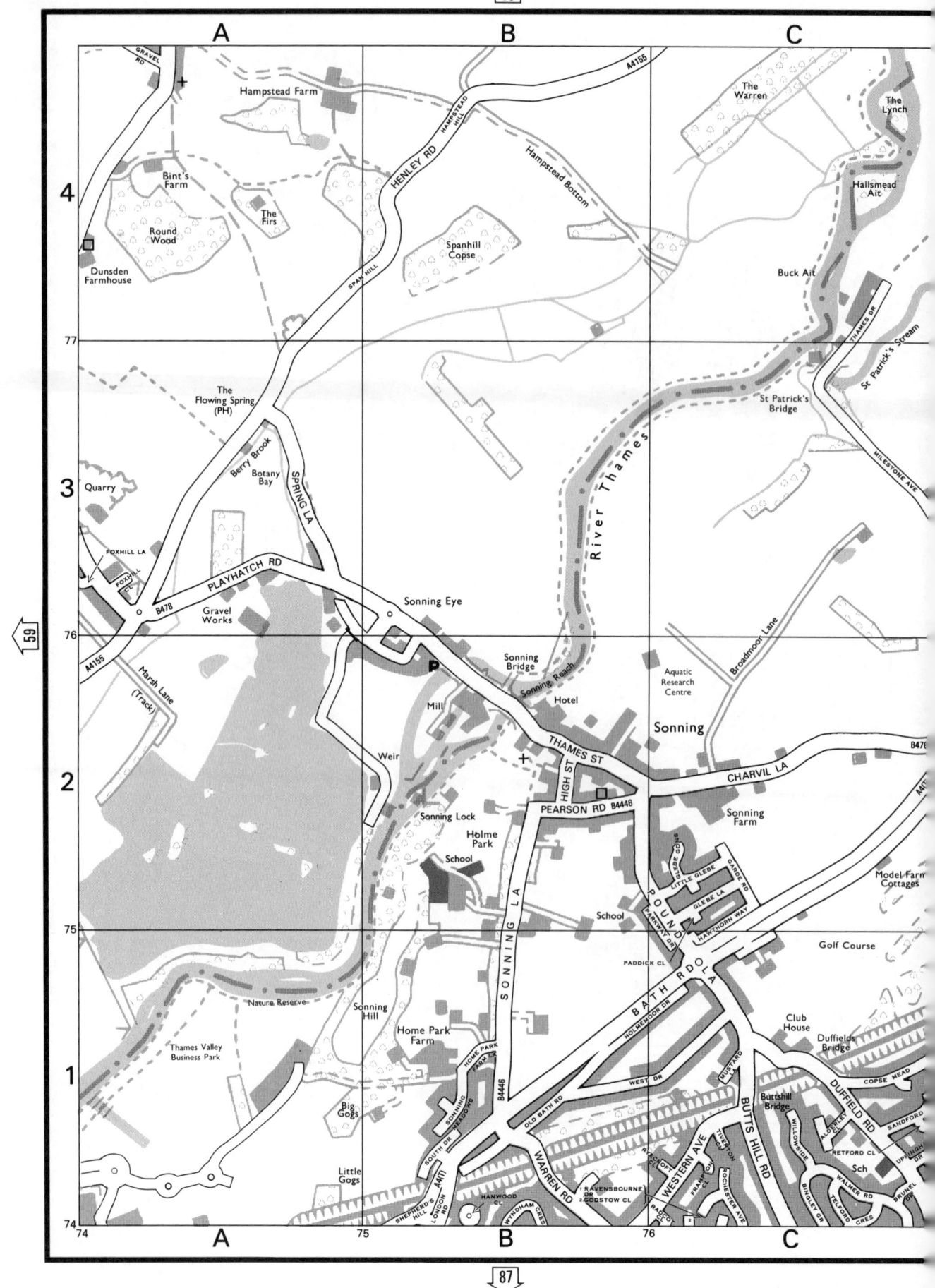

59

A
B
C

4

77

3

76

2

75

1

74

74
A
75
B
76
C

Hampstead Farm

The Warren

The Lynch

Bint's Farm

The Firs

Round Wood

Dunsden Farmhouse

HENLEY RD

HAMPSTEAD HILL

Hampstead Bottom

Spanhill Copse

SPAN HILL

Hallsmead Ait

Buck Ait

THAMES DR

St Patrick's Stream

St Patrick's Bridge

MILESTONE AVE

The Flowing Spring (PH)

Berry Brook

Botany Bay

SPRING LA

Quarry

River Thames

FOXHILL LA

FOXHILL CL

PLAYHATCH RD

B478

Gravel Works

Sonning Eye

Broadmoor Lane

A4155

Marsh Lane (Track)

Mill

Weir

Sonning Bridge

Sonning Reach

Hotel

Aquatic Research Centre

Sonning

CHARVIL LA

B478

THAMES ST

HIGH ST

PEARSON RD   B4446

Sonning Lock

Holme Park

School

Sonning Farm

Model Farm Cottages

LITTLE GLEBE

GLEBE GDNS

GARDE RD

GLEBE LA

HAWTHORN WAY

School

POUND LA

LARKWAY DR

Nature Reserve

Sonning Hill

Home Park Farm

Golf Course

PADDICK CL

BATH RD

OLD LA

Club House

Duffields Bridge

Thames Valley Business Park

Big Gogs

HOME PARK FARM LA

HOLMEMOOR DR

WEST DR

MUSTARD

Buttshill Bridge

COPSE MEAD

DUFFIELD RD

Little Gogs

Home Park Farm

B4446

SONNING MEADOWS

SOUTH DR

LONDON RD

A4(T)

WARREN RD

OLD BATH RD

WEST DR

RECTORY

BUTTS HILL RD

WESTERN AVE

TIVERTON CL

FRAMPTON

ROCHESTER AVE

WILLOWSIDE

ALDERLEY

RETFORD CL

WALMER RD

BINGLEY DR

TELFORD

Sch

SANDFORD

UPPHALL

BRUNEL CL

CRES

SHEPHERD'S HILL

HANWOOD CL

WYNDHAM CRES

RAVENSBOURNE DR

GODSTOW CL

RADCOT

2

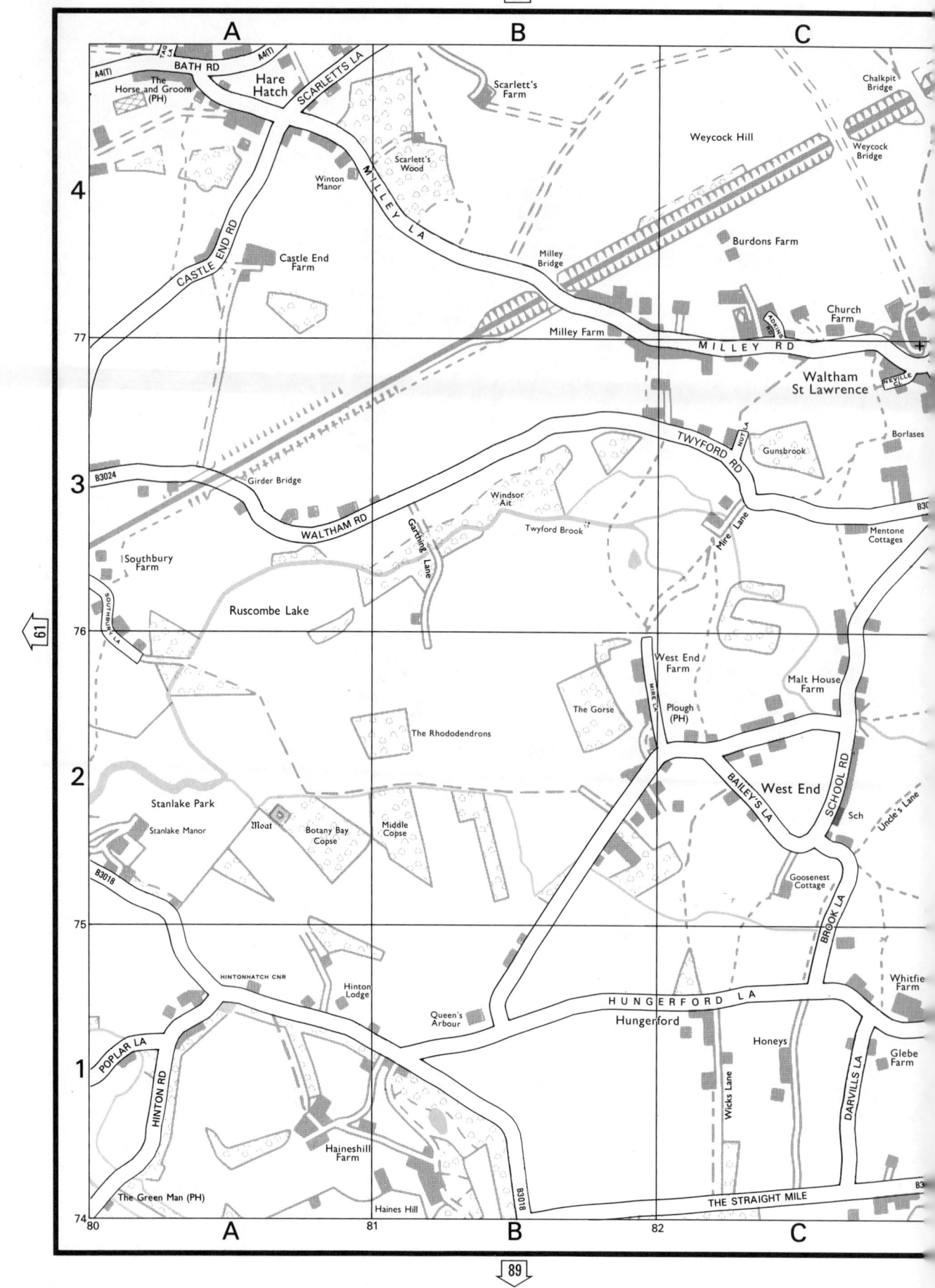

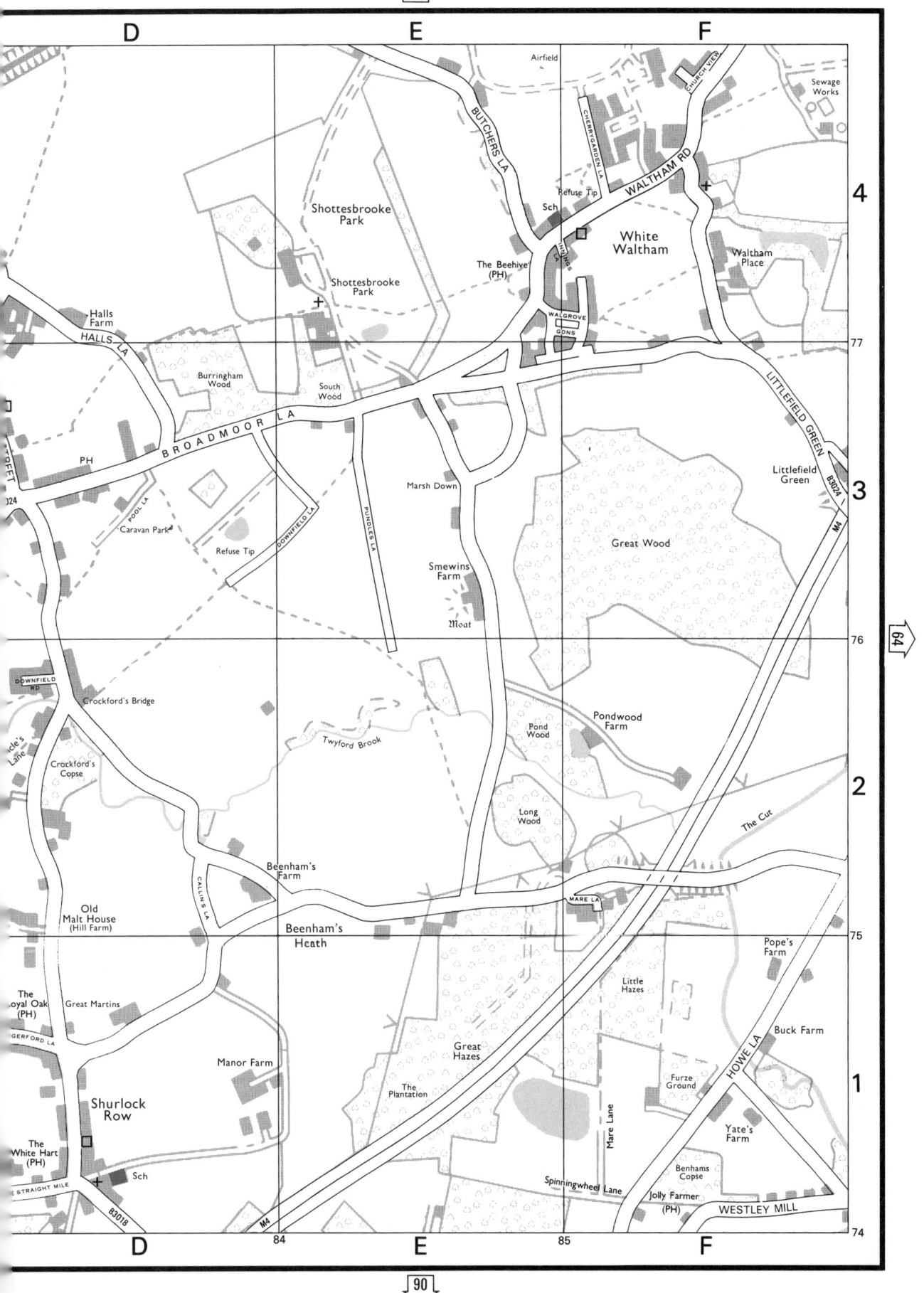

39

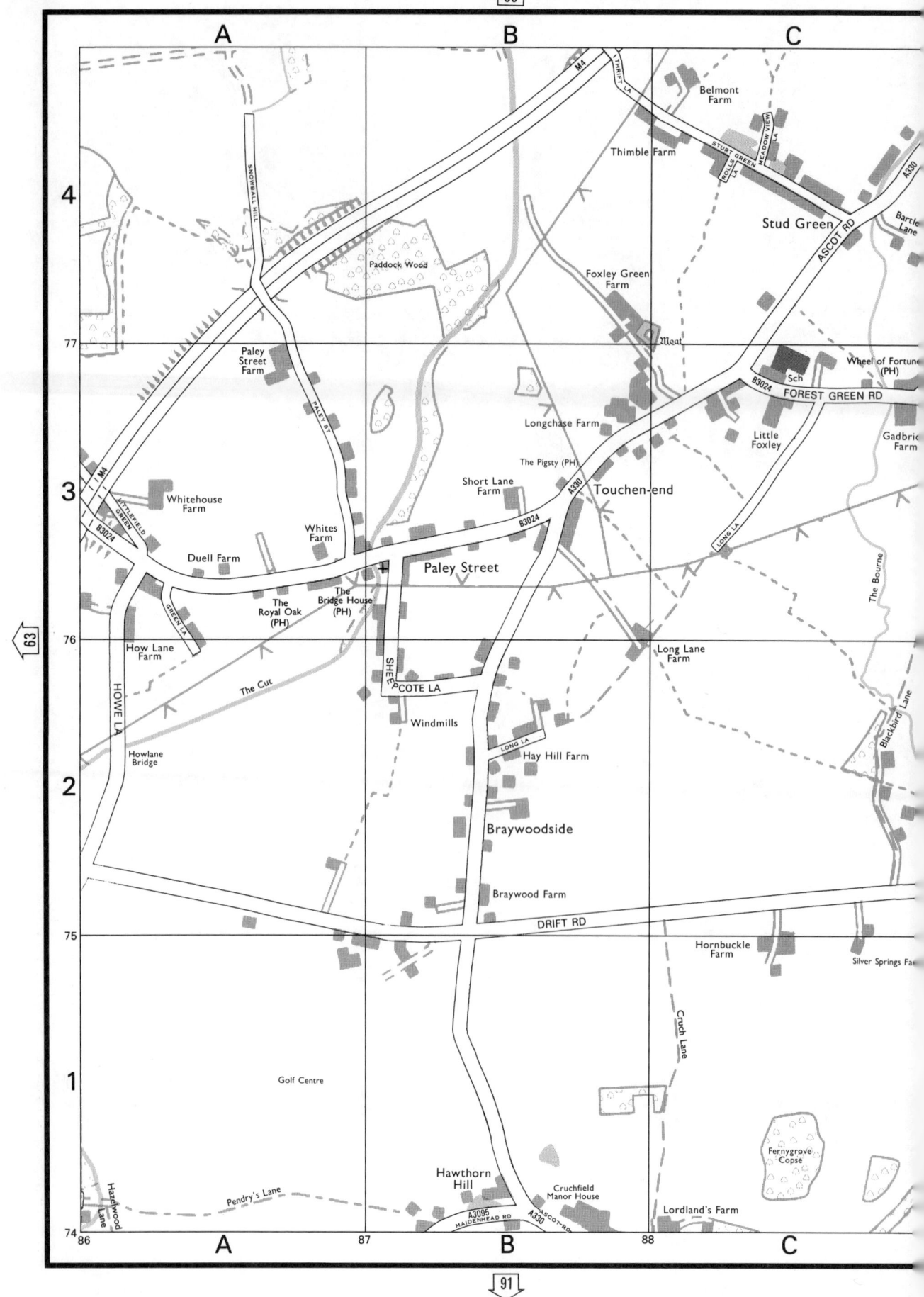

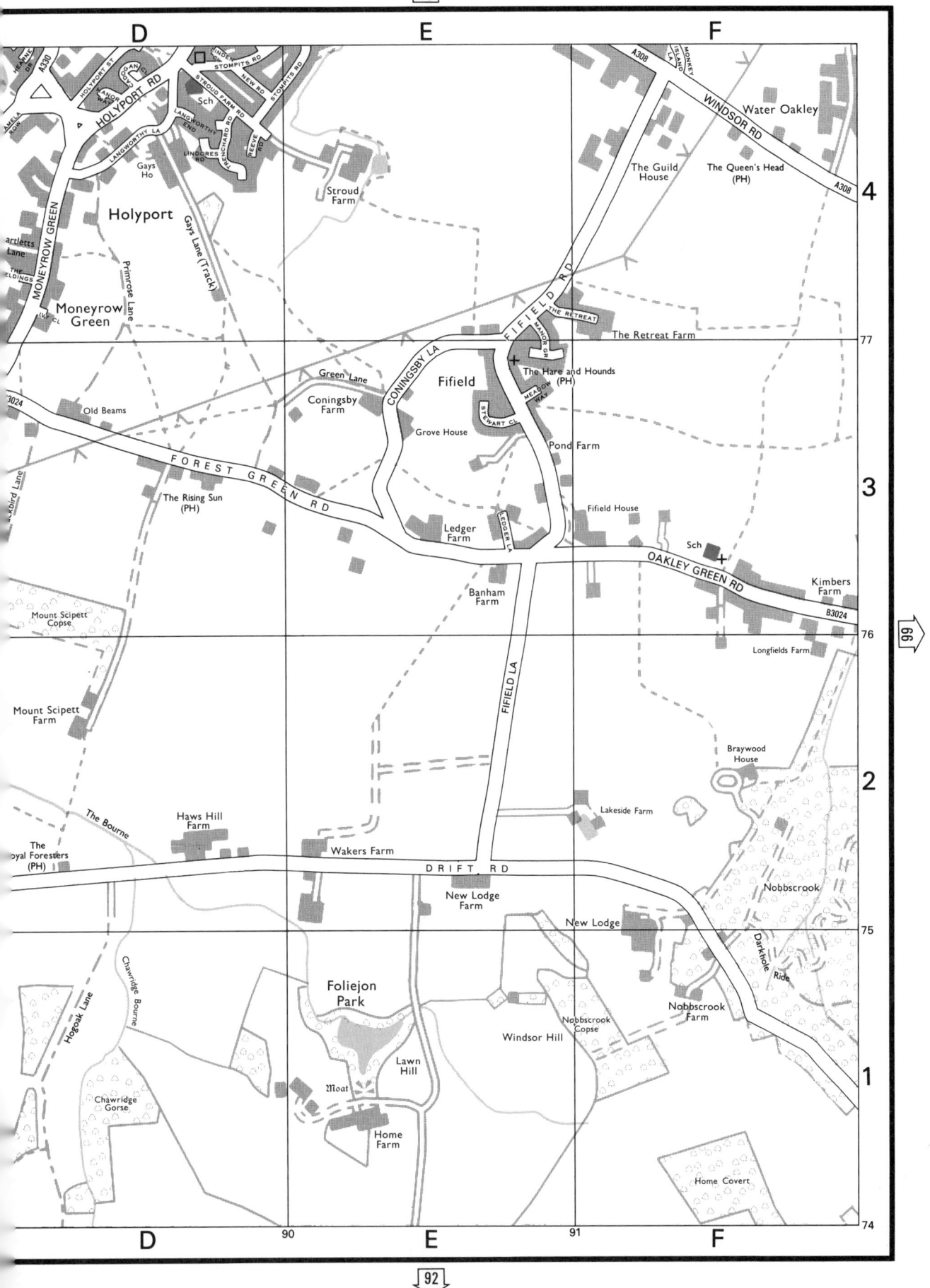

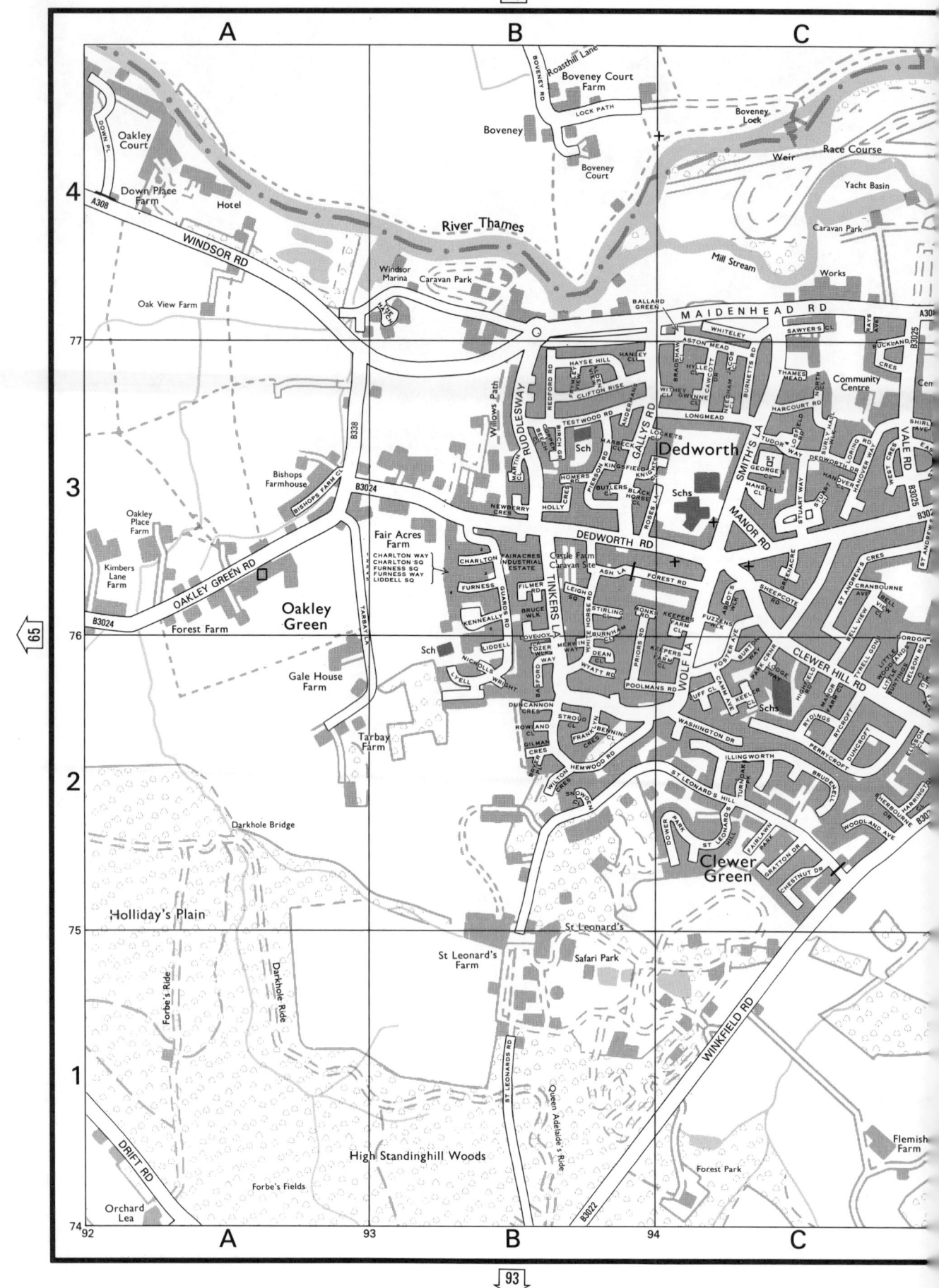

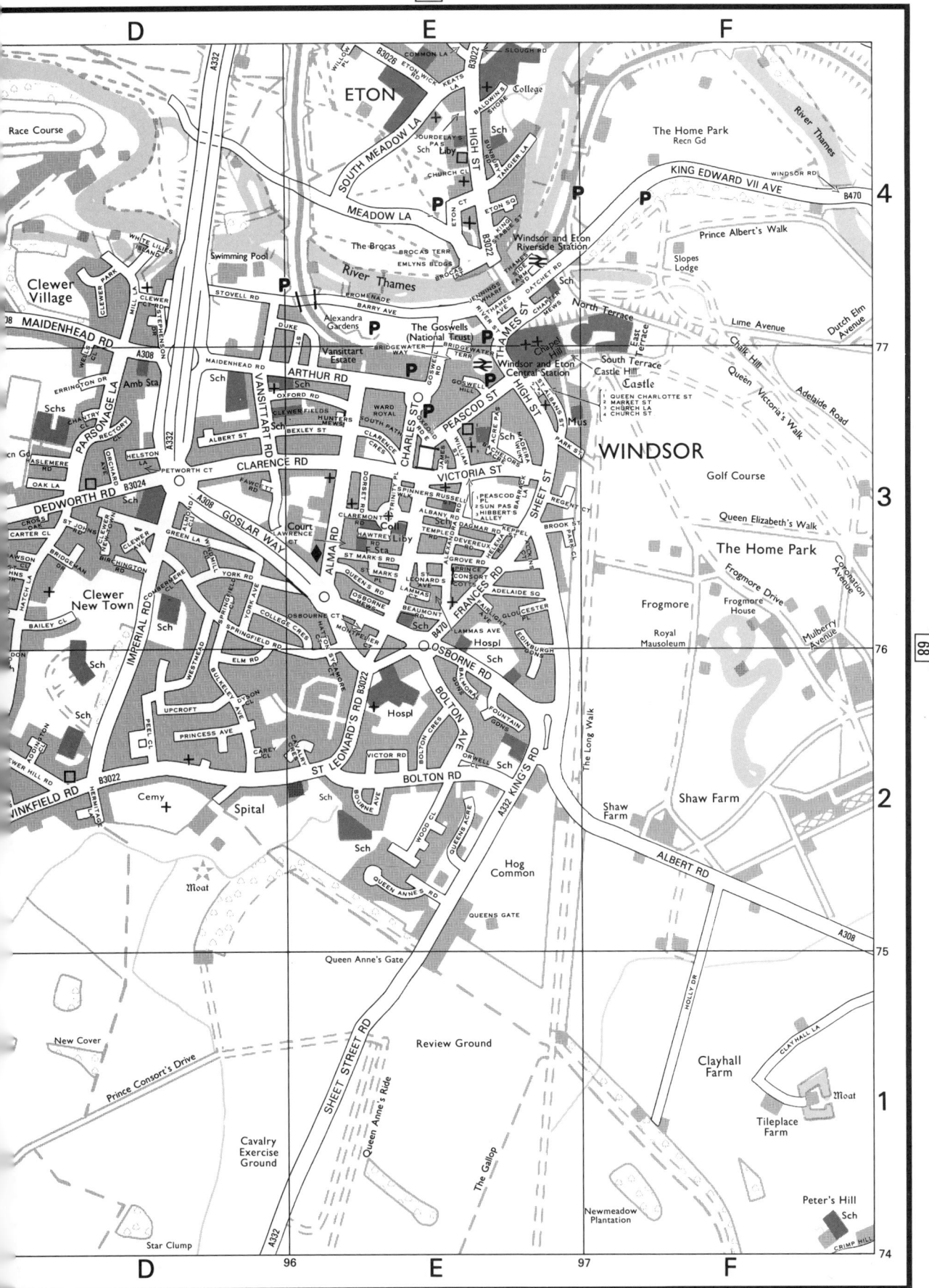

42

D E F

Race Course

ETON

EXONWICK
WILLOW PL
COMMON LA
B3026
B3022
SLOUGH RD
KEATS LA
BALDWIN'S SHORE
College
Sch
The Home Park
Recn Gd
River Thames

SOUTH MEADOW LA
JOURDELAY'S PAS
Sch
Liby
CHURCH CT
HIGH ST
BURNING BUSH LA
TANGIER LA
KING EDWARD VII AVE
WINDSOR RD
B470

4

MEADOW LA
ETON CT
ETON SQ
KING STABLE ST
Windsor and Eton
Riverside Station
Prince Albert's Walk

Clewer
Village
WHITE LILIES ISLAND
Swimming Pool
The Brocas
BROCAS TERR
EMLYNS BLDGS
BROCAS ST
River Thames
Datchet Rd
JENNINGS WHARF
Sch
Slopes
Lodge

CLEWER PARK
MILL LA
CLEWER CT RD
STOVELL RD
PROMENADE
BARRY AVE
THAMES SIDE
ROMNEY LOCK RD
North Terrace
Lime Avenue
Dutch Elm Avenue

MAIDENHEAD RD
08
Alexandra
Gardens
The Goswells
(National Trust)
East Terrace
77

ERRINGTON DR
A308
Amb Sta
MAIDENHEAD RD
ARTHUR RD
Sch
Vansittart
Estate
BRIDGEWATER WAY
GOSWELL HILL
BRIDGEWATER TERR
THAMES ST
Chapel
South Terrace
Castle Hill
Castle
1 QUEEN CHARLOTTE ST
2 MARKET ST
3 CHURCH LA
4 CHURCH ST
Queen Victoria's Walk
Chalk Hill
Adelaide Road

Schs
PARSONAGE LA
Oxford RD
CLEWER FIELDS
HUNTERS MEWS
SOUTH PATH
P
PEASCOD ST
GOSWELL HILL
HIGH ST
ST ALBANS ST
PARK ST
Mus
WINDSOR
Golf Course
Queen Victoria's Walk

CHANTRY LA
RECTORY LA
HELSTON LA
ORCHARD
ALBERT ST
BEXLEY ST
CLARENCE CRES
WILLIAM ST
ACRE PAS
Sch
VICTORIA ST
CASTLE LINK
HIGH ST
REGENT CT

CASLEMERE AVE
OAK LA
B3024
Sch
DEDWORTH RD
A308
PETWORTH CT
FAWCETT RD
CLAREMONT RD
DORSET RD
TRINITY PL
SPINNERS
RUSSELL ST
PEASCOD ST
SUN PAS
HIBBERT'S ALLEY
DEVEREUX RD
BROOK ST
Queen Elizabeth's Walk

CROSS RD
ST JOHNS RD
CLEWER
GOSLAR WAY
A308
Court
Coll
Liby
HAWTREY RD
ST MARKS RD
MARKS
TEMPLE RD
GROVE RD
PRINCE CONSORT RD
REPPEL ST
The Home Park

LAWSON RD
BRIDGMAN
BIRCHINGTON RD
Lawrence Ct
ST MARKS RD
ALBANY RD
DAGMAR RD
FROGMORE
Frogmore Drive

HATCH LA
Clewer
New Town
DEVIL
YORK AVE
ST MARKS
ST LEONARDS RD
ADELAIDE SQ
GLOUCESTER PL
Frogmore
Frogmore
House

BAILEY CL
Sch
SPRINGFIELD RD
COLLEGE CRES
OSBOURNE CT
QUEEN'S RD
OSBORNE MEWS
BEAUMONT
LAMMAS AVE
Sch
FRANCES RD
EDINBURGH GDNS
76
Royal
Mausoleum
Mulberry Avenue

Sch
IMPERIAL RD
CONWAY RD
WESTMEAD
ELM RD
MONTPELIER
HILTON ST
B3022
8470
Osborne RD
Hospl
Sch
CORONATION AVENUE

UPCROFT
PEEL CL
BULKELEY AVE
DYSON CL
PRINCESS AVE
Hospl
BOLTON AVE
BOLTON CRES
BALMORAL
FOUNTAIN GDNS
The Long Walk

CLEWER HILL RD
B3022
CAREY CL
VICTOR RD
ORWELL CL
Sch
Shaw
Farm
Shaw Farm

WINKFIELD RD
HERMITAGE LA
Cemy
Spital
Sch
BOURNE RD
BOLTON RD
QUEENS ACRE
KING'S RD
A332
ALBERT RD
2

Sch
QUEEN ANNE'S RD
Sch
Hog
Common
A308

Moat
WOOD CL
QUEENS GATE

Queen Anne's Gate
75

New Cover
Review Ground
HOLLY DR
Clayhall
Farm
CLAYHALL LA
Moat

Prince Consort's Drive
SHEET STREET RD
QUEEN ANNE'S RIDE
Tileplace
Farm
1

Cavalry
Exercise
Ground
The Gallop
Newmeadow
Plantation
Peter's Hill
Sch

Star Clump
A332
CRIMP HILL
74

D 96 E 97 F

94

68

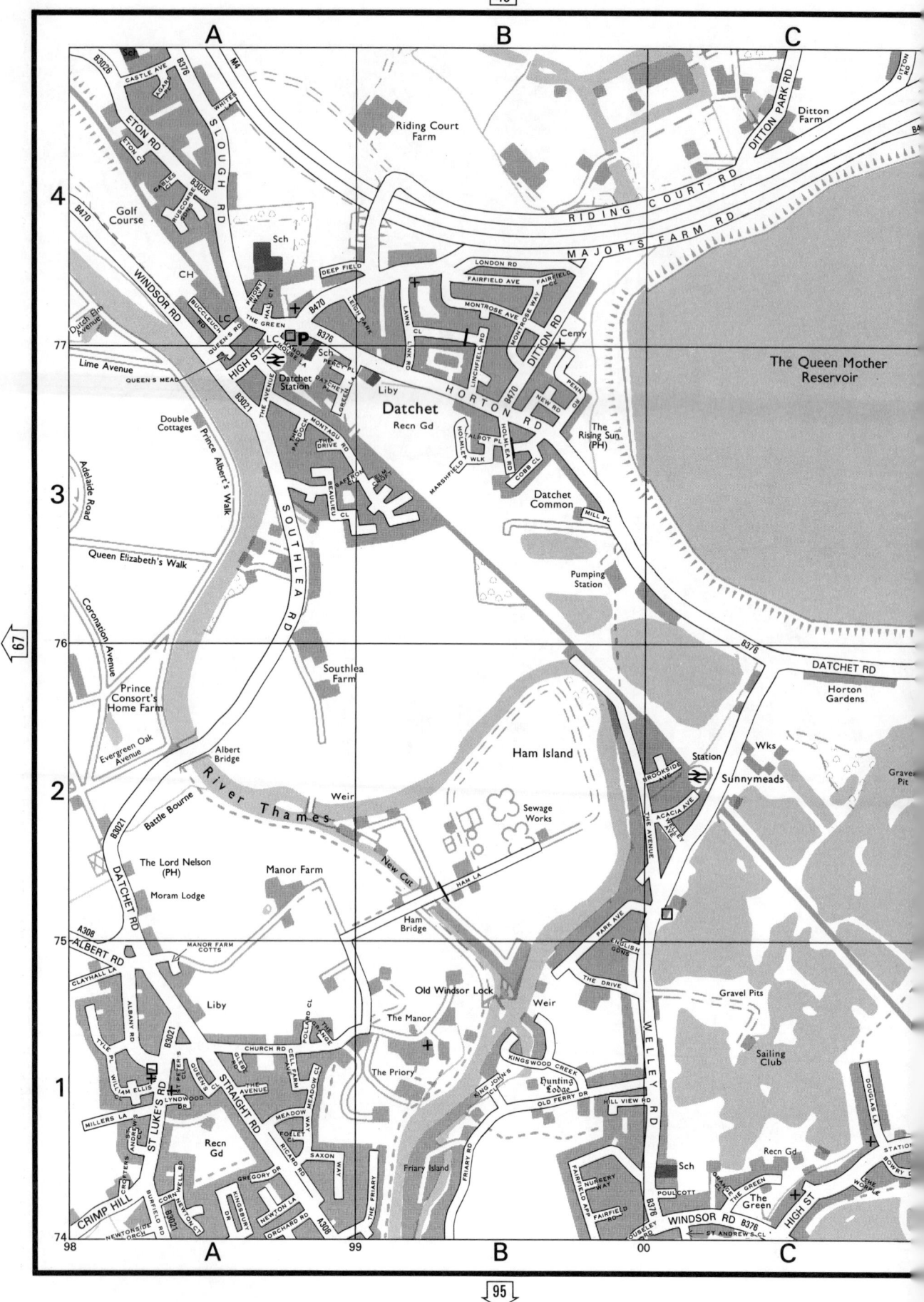

The Queen Mother
Reservoir

Riding Court
Farm

Ditton
Farm

RIDING COURT RD

MAJOR'S FARM RD

DITTON PARK RD

LONDON RD
FAIRFIELD AVE
FAIRFIELD
MONTROSE AVE
MONTROSE WAY
DEEP FIELD
LEIGH PARK
LAWN CL
LINCHFIELD RD
DITTON RD
Cemy

Datchet

CASTLE AVE
POACH
B3026
ETON RD
B376
ETON CT
WHITES
SLOUGH RD
BUSCOMBE
GABLES
B3026
M4

Golf
Course

B470

Sch

CH

WINDSOR RD

Dutch Elm Avenue

LC
LC
HIGH ST
QUEEN'S RD
BUCCLEUCH RD
PRIORY
HALL CT
THE GREEN
Datchet
Station
P
Sch
PERCY PL
DATCHET
GREEN
Liby
HORTON RD
NEW RD
PENN CL
B470
The Rising Sun
(PH)

Datchet
Recn Gd

HOLMLEA
TALBOT PL
MARSHFIELD
HOLMLEY
WLK
COBB CL
MILL PL

Datchet
Common

Lime Avenue

Queen's Mead

Adelaide Road

Double
Cottages

Prince Albert's Walk

THE AVENUE
B3021
SOUTHLEA RD
PADDOCK
MONTAGU RD
THE DRIVE
BEAULIEU CL
SAFFRON
ELM CROFT

Queen Elizabeth's Walk

Coronation Avenue

Southlea
Farm

Pumping
Station

B376

DATCHET RD

Horton
Gardens

Prince
Consort's
Home Farm

Evergreen Oak
Avenue

Albert
Bridge

River Thames

Weir

Ham Island

Sewage
Works

Station
Sunnymeads
BROOKSIDE AVE
ACACIA AVE
SUSSEX AVE
THE AVENUE

Wks

Gravel
Pit

Battle Bourne

The Lord Nelson
(PH)

Moram Lodge

Manor Farm

New Cut

HAM LA

Ham
Bridge

PARK AVE
ENGLISH
GDNS

DATCHET RD
B3021
A308

ALBERT RD

MANOR FARM
COTTS

Old Windsor Lock

Weir

THE DRIVE

Gravel Pits

CLAYHALL LA
ALBANY RD
TYLE PL
WILLIAM ELLIS
B3021
ST PETER'S
QUEEN'S CL
LYNDWOOD
DR
Liby

Church RD
POLLARD CL
THE THORPE
CELL FARM CL
MEADOW CL

The Manor

The Priory

KINGSWOOD CREEK
Hunting
Lodge
KING JOHN'S CL
OLD FERRY DR

HILL VIEW RD

WELLEY RD

Sailing
Club

MILLERS LA
ST ANDREW'S
CRES
STRAIGHT RD
THE AVENUE
MEADOW
FOLLET
AVE
RICARD RD
SAXON WAY

Recn
Gd

CRIMP HILL
NEWTON'S
ORCH
B3021
CORN WELL RD
BUFFELD RD
KINGSBURY DR
NEWTON LA
ORCHARD RD
A308
GREGORY DR
THE FRIARY

Friary Island

FRIARY RD

Fairfield
NURSERY
WAY
FAIRFIELD APP
FAIRFIELD
RD
B376
POULCOTT
OUSELEY
WINDSOR RD B376
St Andrew's CL

Sch

Recn Gd

The Green

HIGH ST

Station
BOWRY DR
THE WELL

44

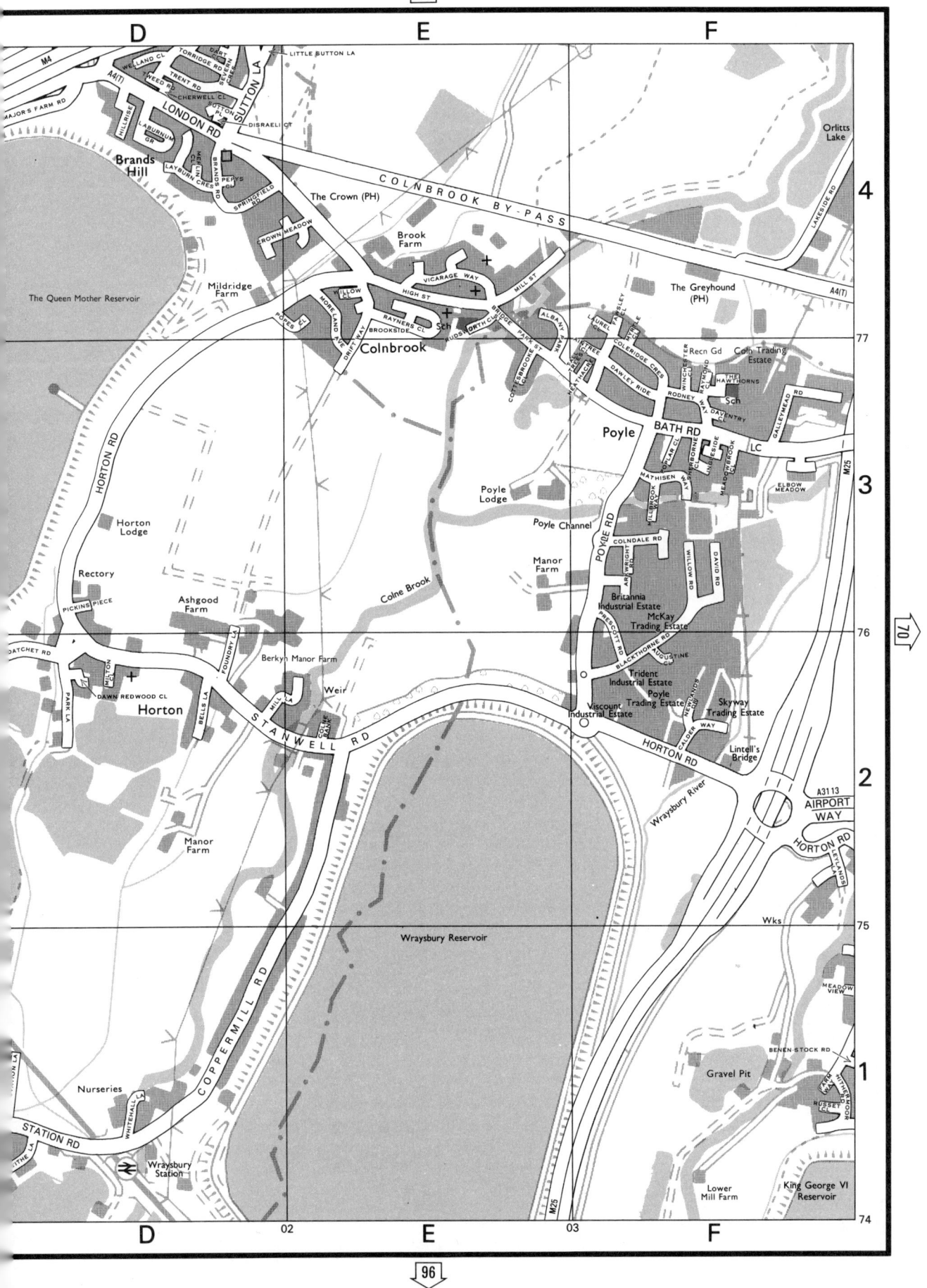

D   **E**   **F**

M4

A4(T)

MAJORS FARM RD

WELLAND CL
TORRIDGE RD
TRENT RD
DART
SEVERN
LITTLE BUTTON LA
CHERWELL CL
COLNE
SUTTON

HILLRIDGE
LABURNUM GR
LONDON RD
A4(T)
TWEED RD
DISRAELI CT

Brands Hill

MERLIN
BRANDS RD
SPRINGFIELD
CROWN MEADOW
LAYBURN CRES
PEPYS

The Crown (PH)

COLNBROOK BY-PASS

Mildridge Farm

Brook Farm

The Queen Mother Reservoir

VICARAGE WAY

MILL ST

4

A4(T)

The Greyhound (PH)

WILLOW
MORELAND
HIGH ST
DRIFT WAY
POYES CL
RAYNERS CL
BROOKSIDE
Sch
WORDSWORTH CLOSE
BRIDGE
PARK ST
ALBANY
WAY
COTTSBROOKE
LIME TREE
NETTLE LA
LAUREL
PAISLEY
COLERIDGE CRES
WINCHESTER
RAYMOND
RD
Coln Trading Estate
Recn Gd

Colnbrook

DAWLEY RIDE
RODNEY
DAVENTRY
THE HAWTHORNS
Sch
GALLEYMEAD RD

Poyle

BATH RD

LC

HORTON RD

Horton Lodge

POPLAR CL
SEABORNE
WAY
MATHISEN
WAY
LINESIDE
MEADOWBROOK
ELBOW MEADOW

M25

3

77

Rectory

PICKINS PIECE

Ashgood Farm

Poyle Lodge

Poyle Channel

POYLE RD

COLNDALE RD
ARKWRIGHT RD
WILLOW RD
DAVID RD

Manor Farm

Colne Brook

Britannia Industrial Estate

McKay Trading Estate

76

70

DATCHET RD

MILTON
DAWN REDWOOD CL
PARK LA
BELLS LA
FOUNDRY LA

Berkyn Manor Farm

Weir

MILL LA
STANWELL RD
COLNE BANK

PRESCOTT RD
BLACKTHORNE RD
AUGUSTINE
NEWLANDS

Trident Industrial Estate

Poyle Trading Estate

Skyway Trading Estate

Horton

Viscount Industrial Estate

CALDER WAY

Lintell's Bridge

HORTON RD

A3113

AIRPORT WAY

HORTON RD

LETLANDS

2

75

Manor Farm

COPPERMILL RD

WHITEHALL

Wraysbury River

Wks

Wraysbury Reservoir

MEADOW VIEW

BENEN-STOCK RD

Nurseries

STATION RD

Wraysbury Station

Gravel Pit

WITHEROW
RUSSET

King George VI Reservoir

Lower Mill Farm

M25

1

74

D   02   **E**   03   **F**

not continued, see key diagram

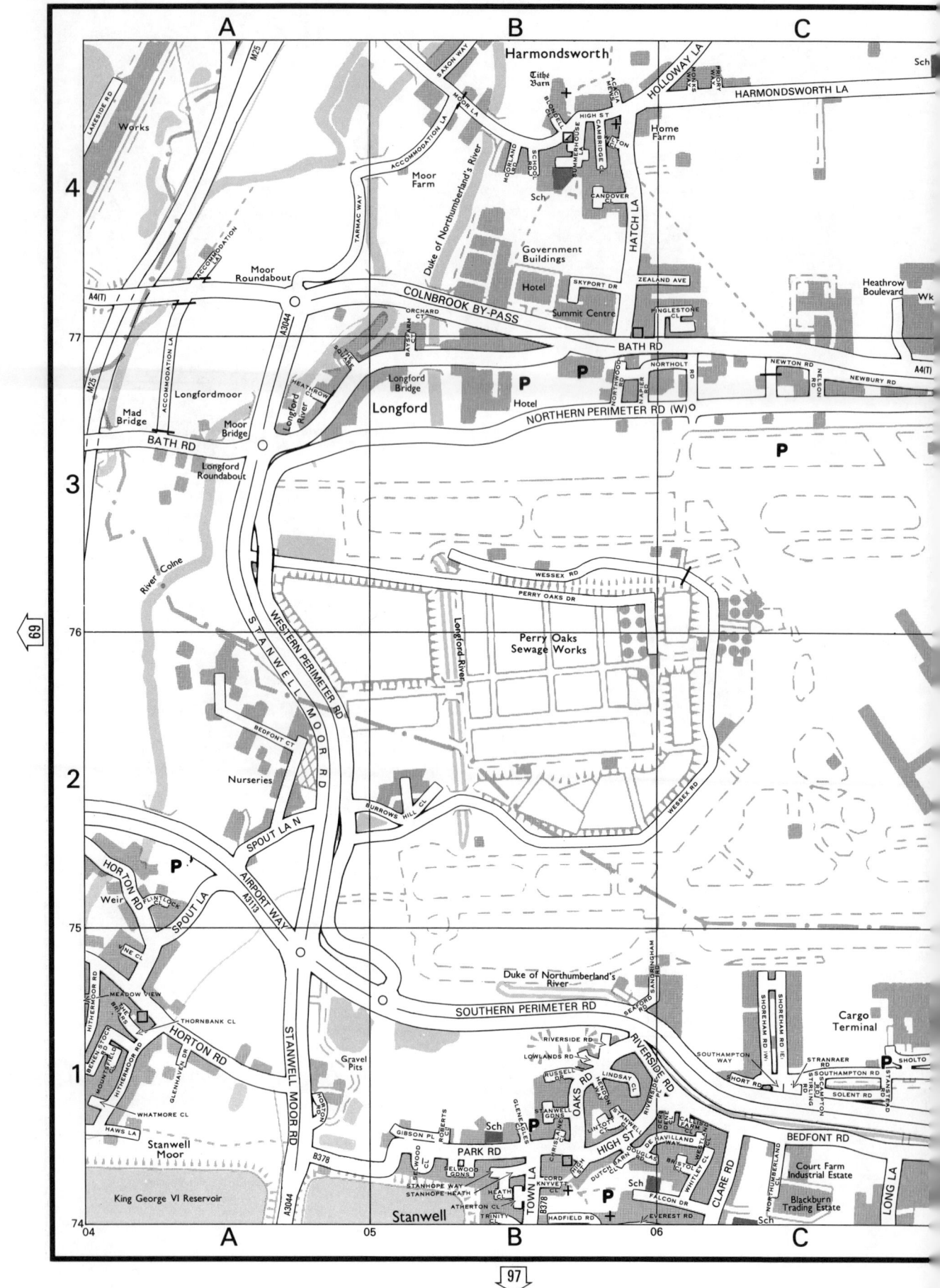

97

not continued, see key diagram

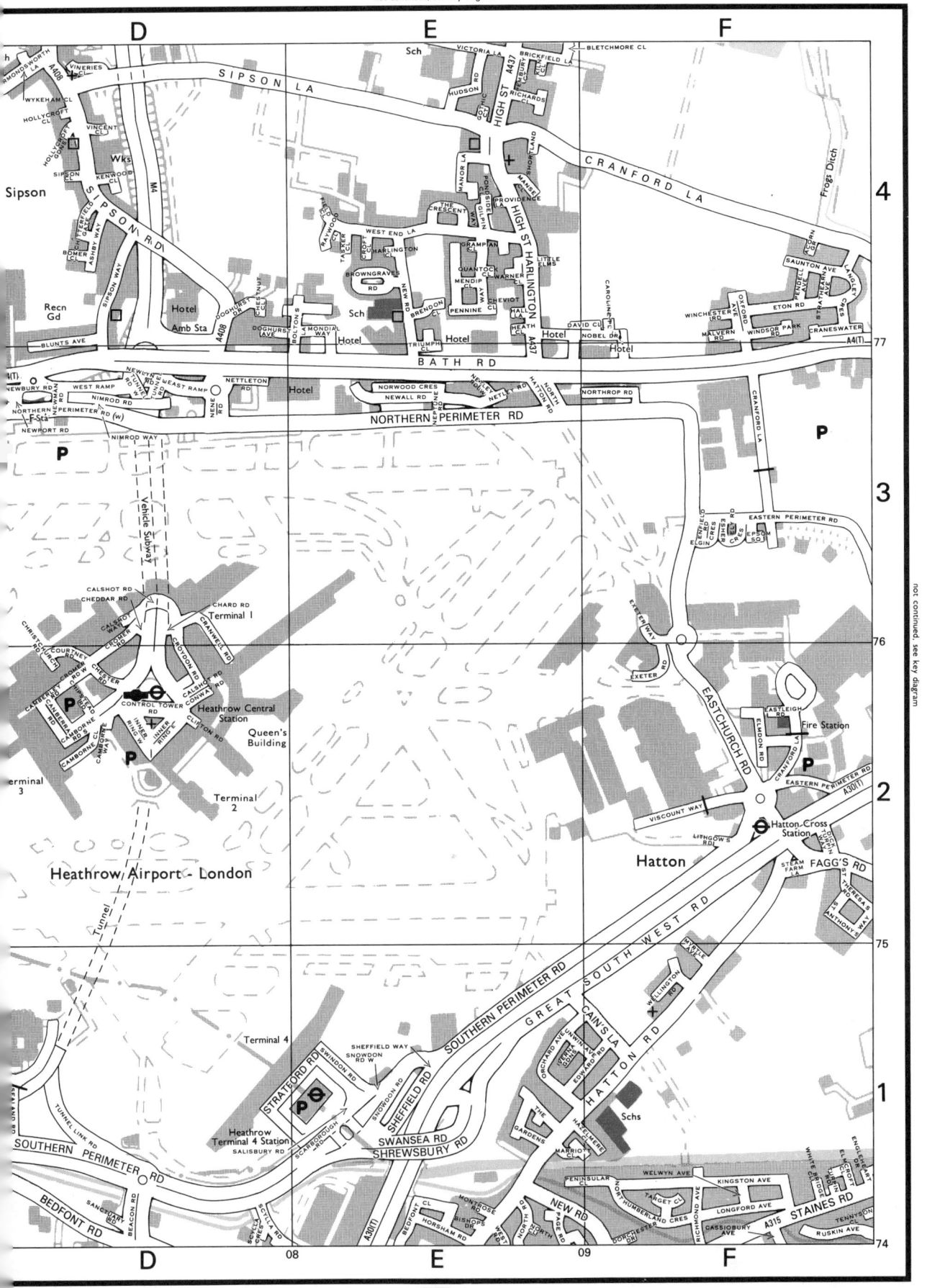

not continued, see key diagram

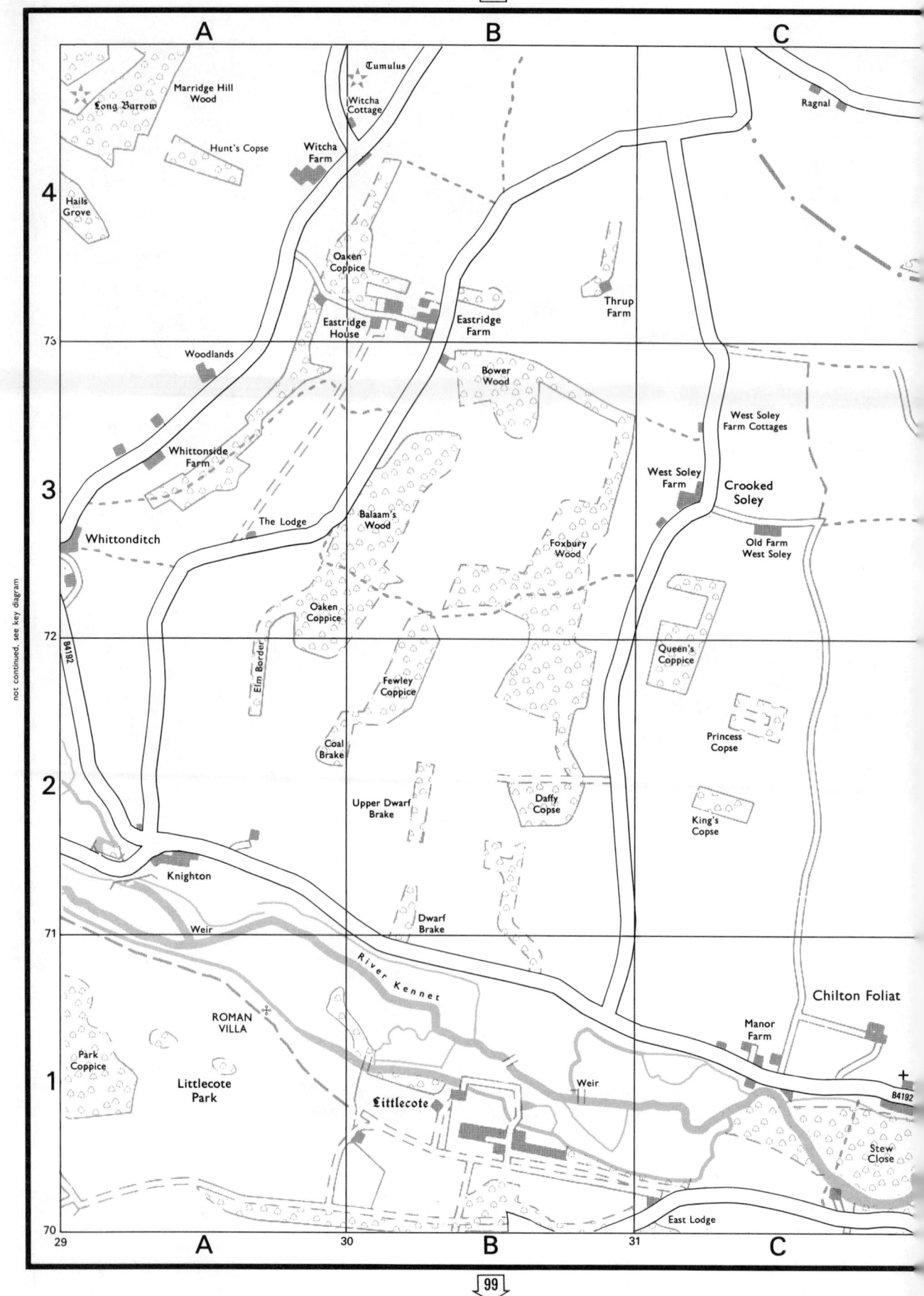

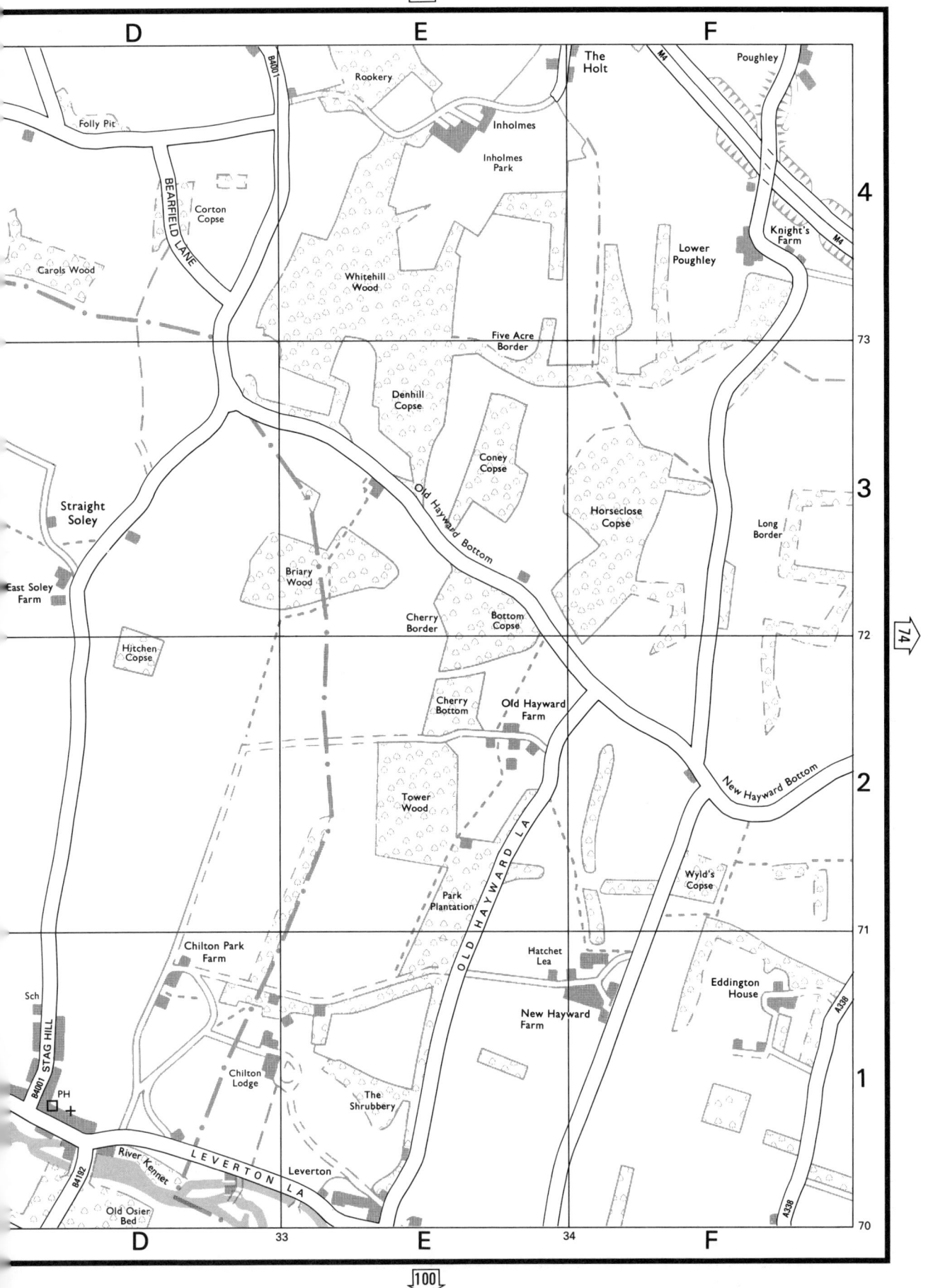

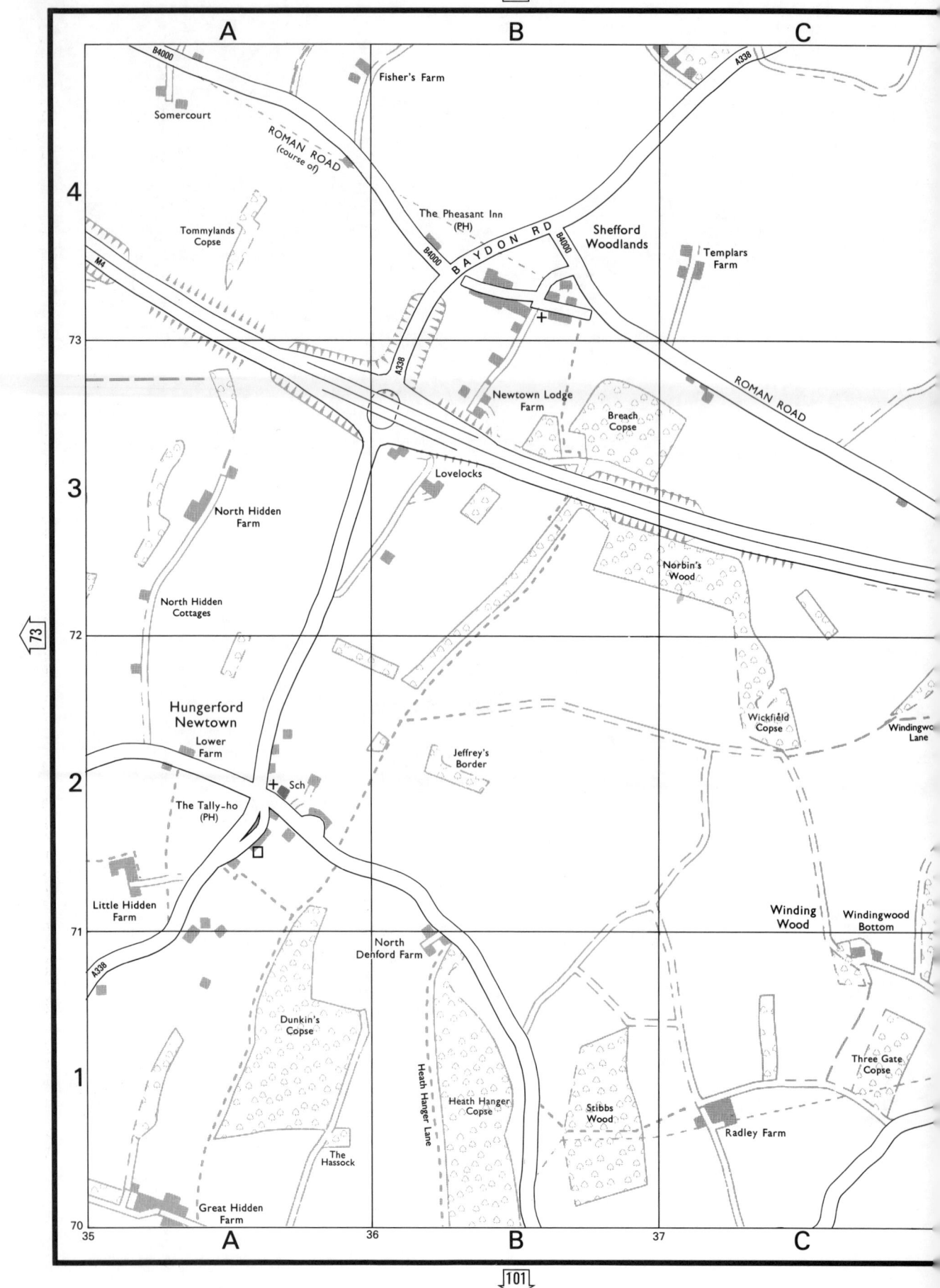

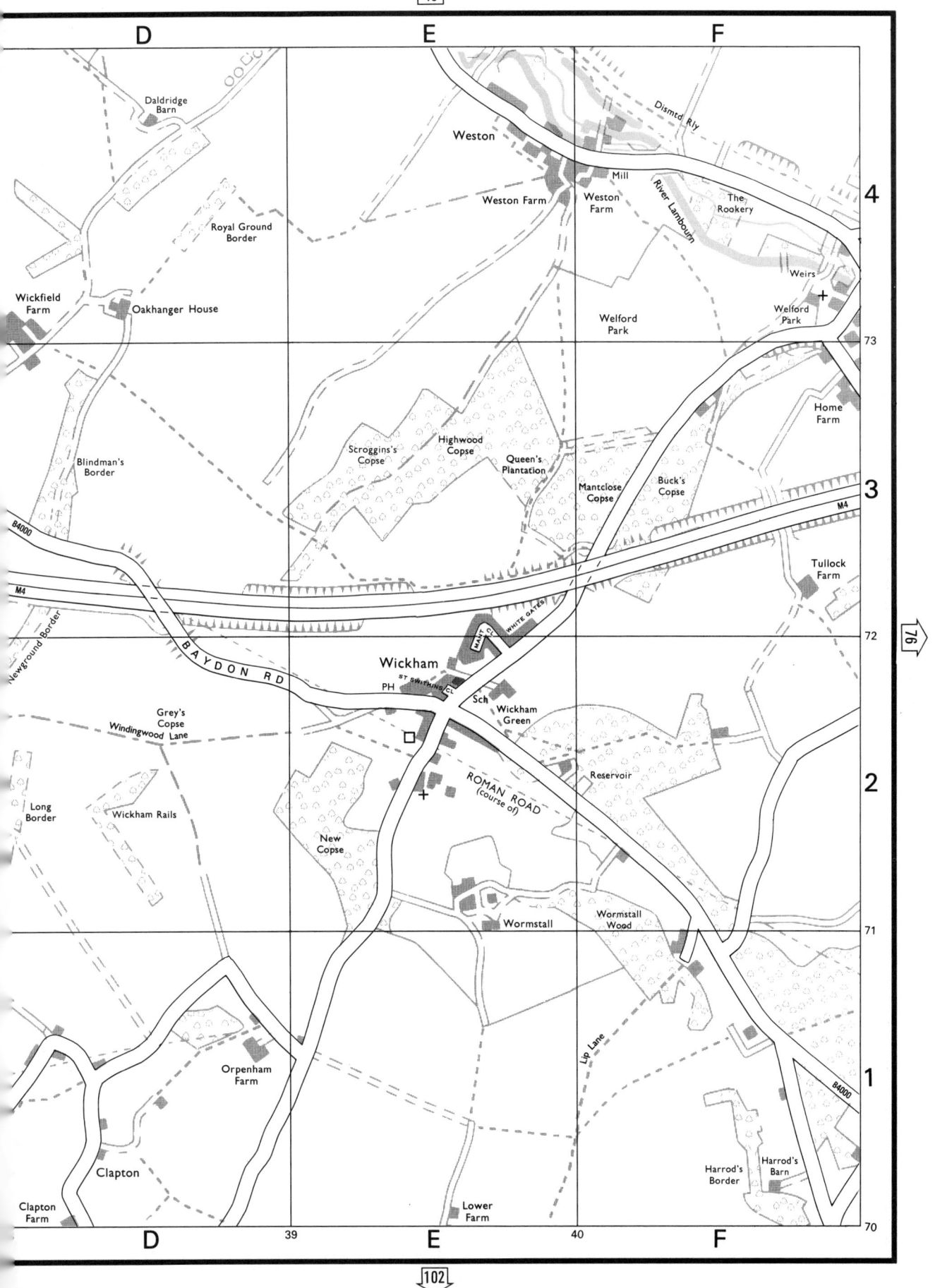

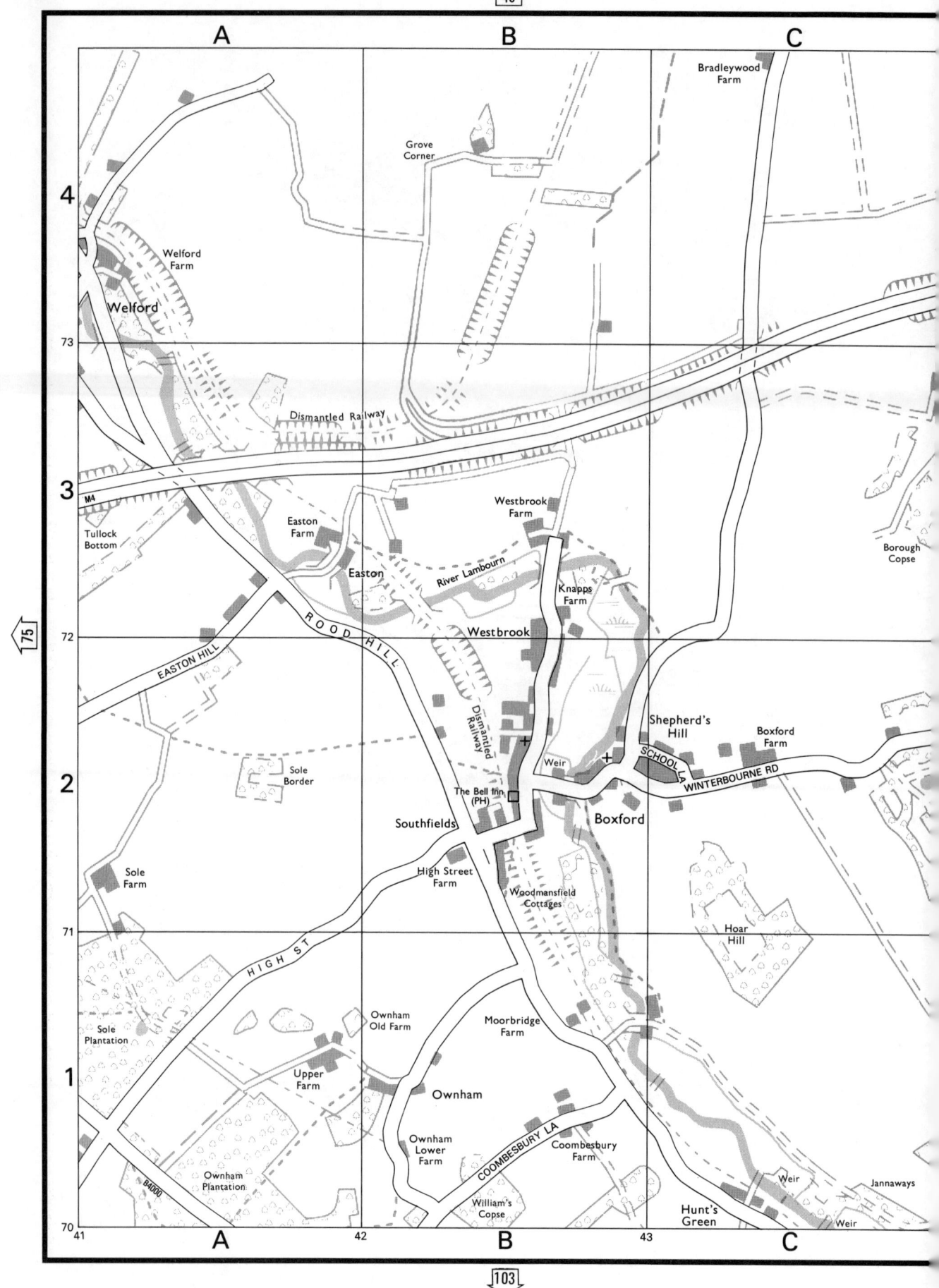

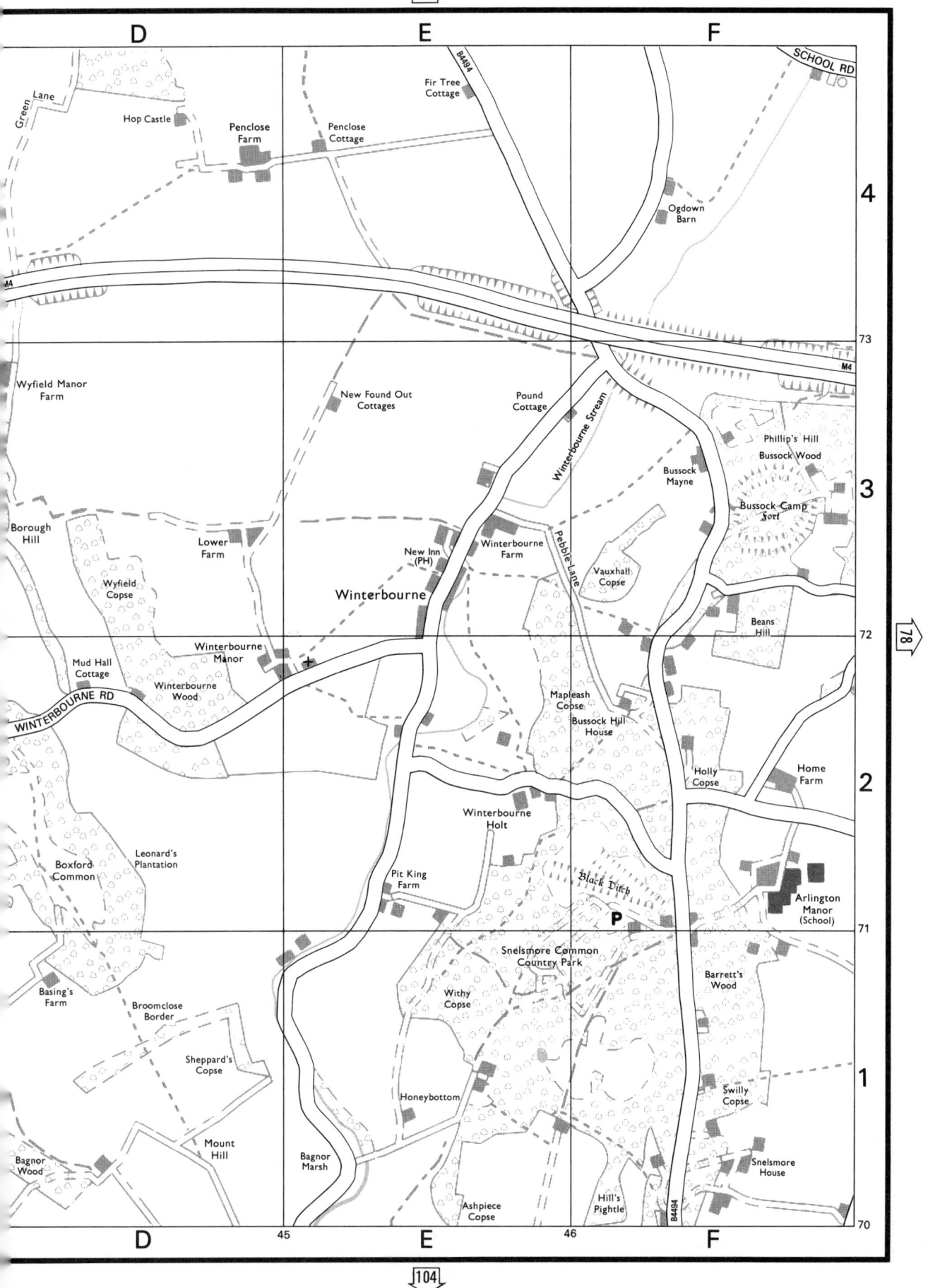

D E F

SCHOOL RD

Green Lane

Hop Castle

Penclose Farm

Penclose Cottage

Fir Tree Cottage

B4494

Ogdown Barn

4

M4

73

M4

Wyfield Manor Farm

New Found Out Cottages

Pound Cottage

Winterbourne Stream

Phillip's Hill

Bussock Wood

Bussock Mayne

Bussock Camp Fort

3

Borough Hill

Lower Farm

New Inn (PH)

Winterbourne Farm

Pebble Lane

Vauxhall Copse

Winterbourne

Wyfield Copse

Winterbourne Manor

Beans Hill

72

78

Mud Hall Cottage

Winterbourne Wood

Mapleash Copse

WINTERBOURNE RD

Bussock Hill House

Holly Copse

Home Farm

2

Winterbourne Holt

Boxford Common

Leonard's Plantation

Pit King Farm

Black Ditch

P

Arlington Manor (School)

71

Basing's Farm

Broomclose Border

Snelsmore Common Country Park

Withy Copse

Barrett's Wood

Sheppard's Copse

Honeybottom

Swilly Copse

1

Bagnor Wood

Mount Hill

Bagnor Marsh

Ashpiece Copse

Hill's Pightle

B4494

Snelsmore House

70

D

45

E

46

F

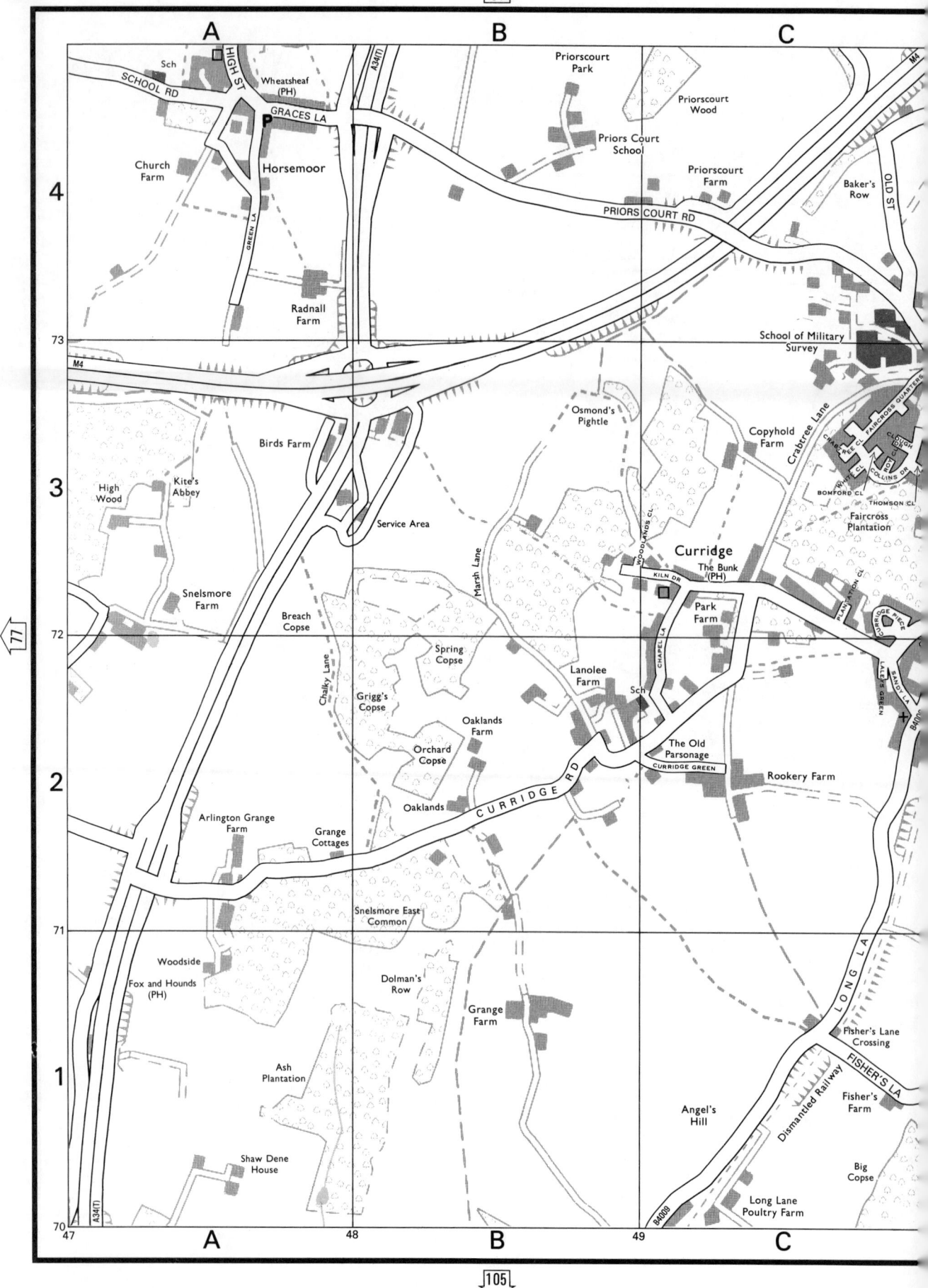

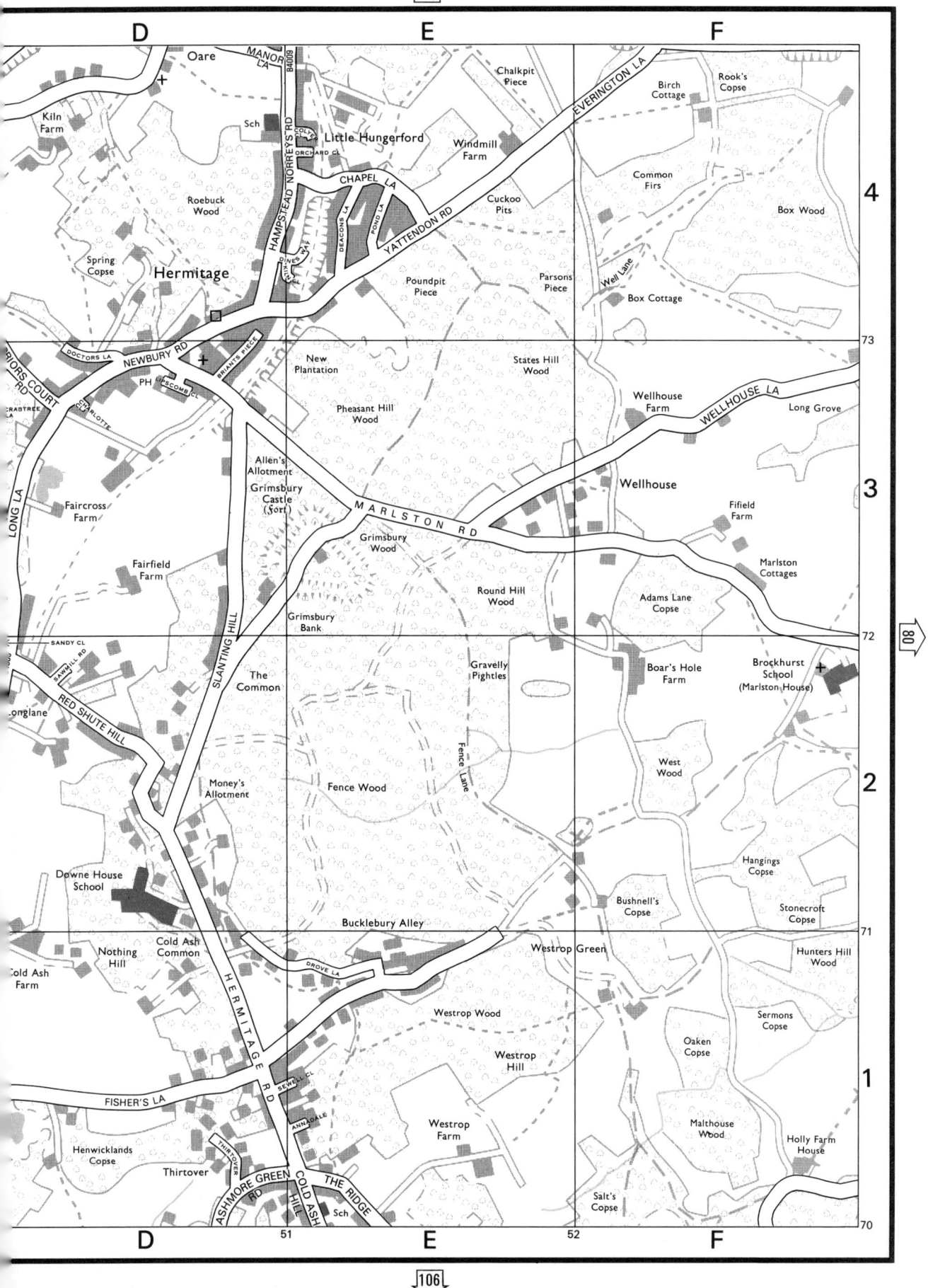

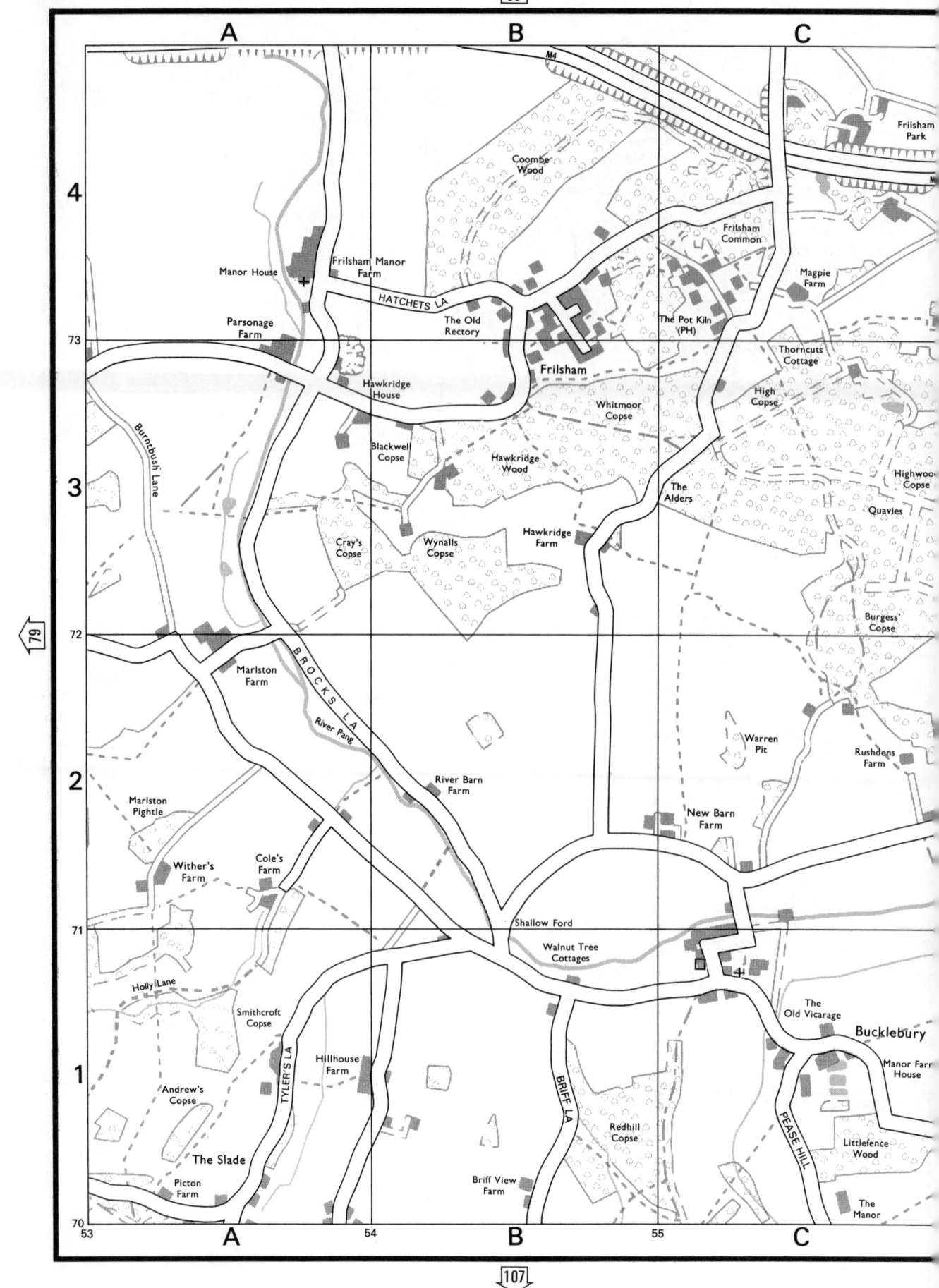

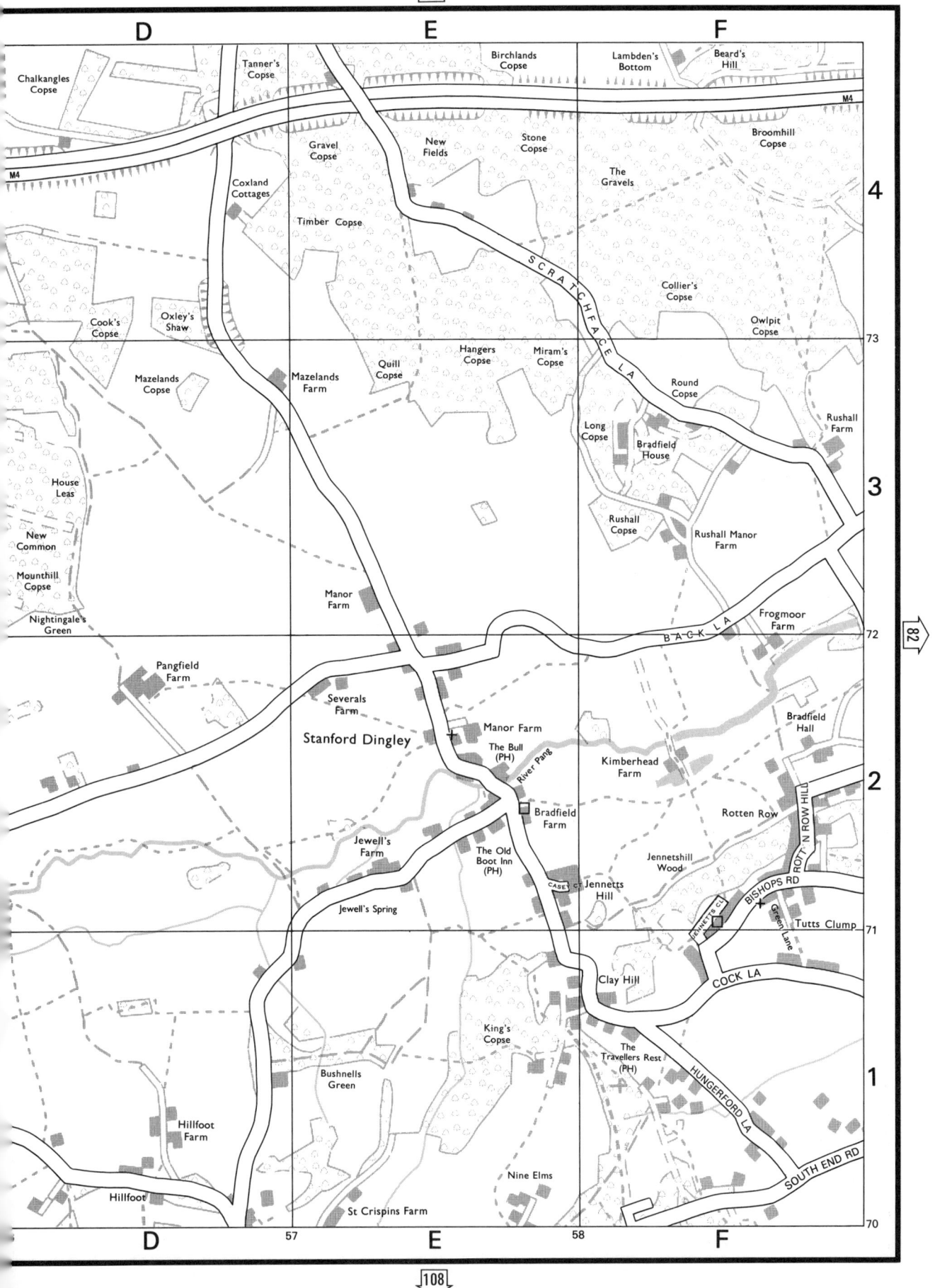

54

D · E · F

Chalkangles Copse

Tanner's Copse

Birchlands Copse

Lambden's Bottom

Beard's Hill

M4

Gravel Copse

New Fields

Stone Copse

Broomhill Copse

Coxland Cottages

The Gravels

4

M4

Timber Copse

Collier's Copse

SCRATCHFACE LA

Owlpit Copse

73

Cook's Copse

Oxley's Shaw

Mazelands Copse

Mazelands Farm

Quill Copse

Hangers Copse

Miram's Copse

Round Copse

Rushall Farm

House Leas

Long Copse

Bradfield House

3

New Common

Rushall Copse

Rushall Manor Farm

Mounthill Copse

Manor Farm

Nightingale's Green

BACK LA

Frogmoor Farm

72

Pangfield Farm

Severals Farm

Bradfield Hall

Stanford Dingley

Manor Farm

The Bull (PH)

Kimberhead Farm

Rotten Row

ROTT'N ROW HILL

2

River Pang

Bradfield Farm

BISHOPS RD

Jewell's Farm

The Old Boot Inn (PH)

Jennetshill Wood

Jennetts Hill

Green Lane

Tutts Clump

Jewell's Spring

CASE CT

JENNETTS CL

71

Clay Hill

COCK LA

King's Copse

The Travellers Rest (PH)

Bushnells Green

1

Hillfoot Farm

HUNGERFORD LA

Nine Elms

SOUTH END RD

Hillfoot

St Crispins Farm

70

D · 57 · E · 58 · F

82

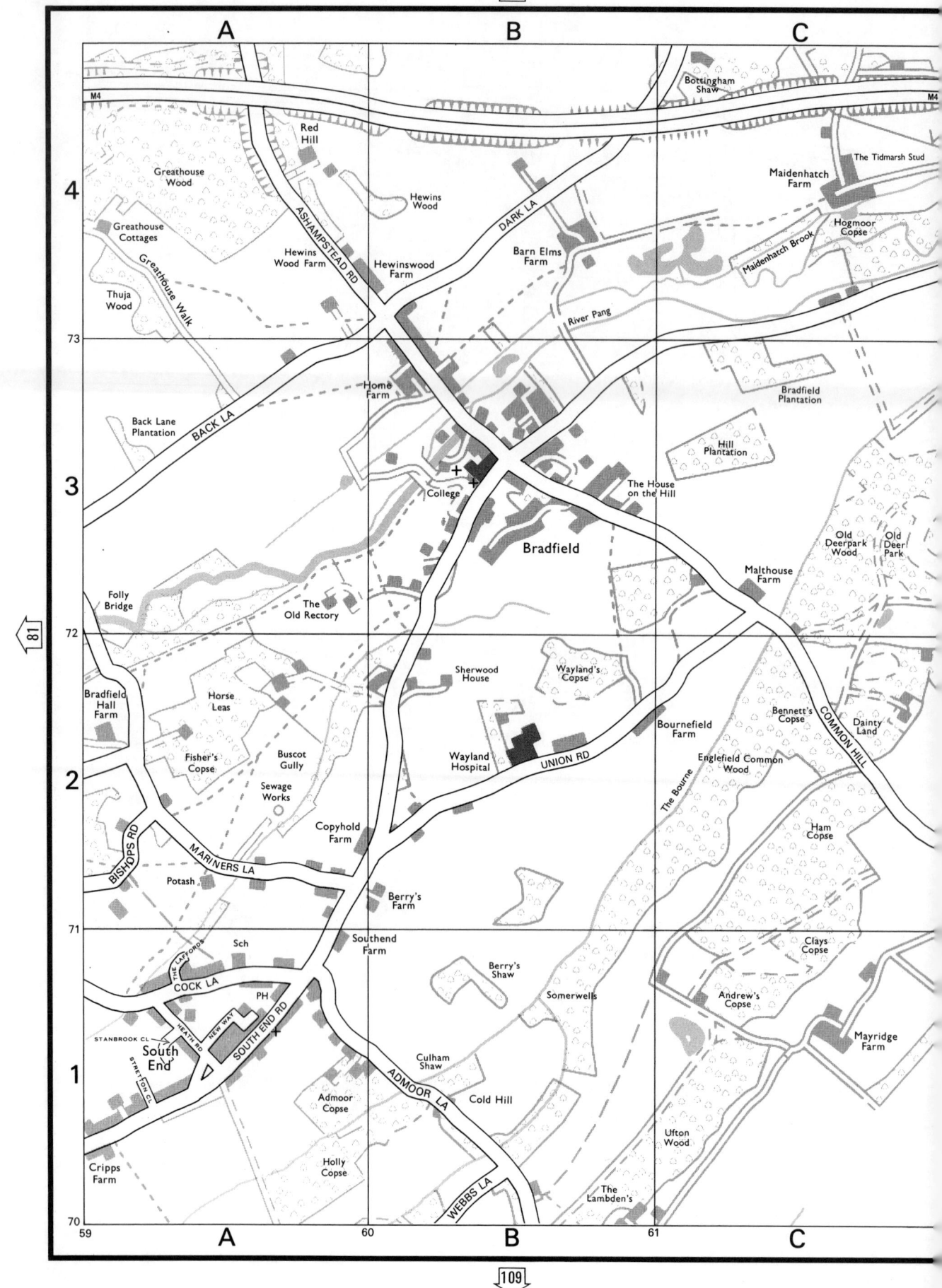

A B C

M4 M4

Bottingham Shaw

Red Hill

Greathouse Wood

Hewins Wood

The Tidmarsh Stud

Maidenhatch Farm

4

Greathouse Cottages

Hewins Wood Farm

Hewinswood Farm

Barn Elms Farm

Hogmoor Copse

Thuja Wood

DARK LA

Maidenhatch Brook

ASHAMPSTEAD RD

Greathouse Walk

River Pang

73

Home Farm

Bradfield Plantation

Back Lane Plantation

BACK LA

Hill Plantation

3

College

Bradfield

The House on the Hill

Old Deerpark Wood

Old Deer Park

Folly Bridge

The Old Rectory

Malthouse Farm

72

Sherwood House

Wayland's Copse

Bennett's Copse

Dainty Land

Bradfield Hall Farm

Horse Leas

Bournefield Farm

COMMON HILL

Fisher's Copse

Buscot Gully

Wayland Hospital

UNION RD

Englefield Common Wood

2

BISHOPS RD

Sewage Works

The Bourne

Ham Copse

Potash

MARINERS LA

Copyhold Farm

Berry's Farm

71

Sch

Southend Farm

Berry's Shaw

Clays Copse

COCK LA

THE LAYFORDS

PH

Somerwells

Andrew's Copse

Stanbrook CL

NEW WAY

HEATH RD

SOUTH END RD

Mayridge Farm

1

South End

STRETTON CL

Culham Shaw

ADMOOR LA

Cold Hill

Ufton Wood

Admoor Copse

Cripps Farm

Holly Copse

WEBBS LA

The Lambden's

70

59 A 60 B 61 C

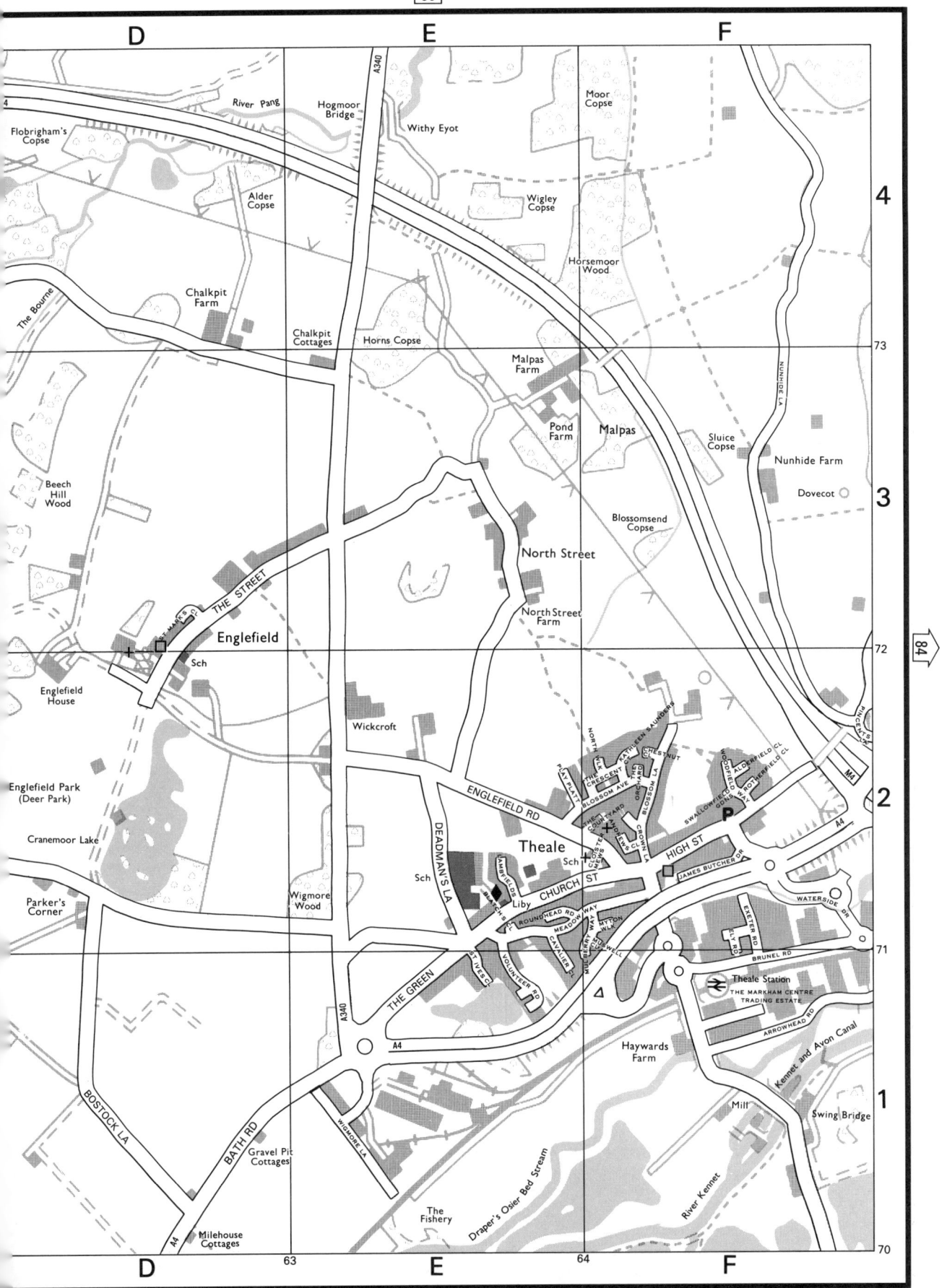

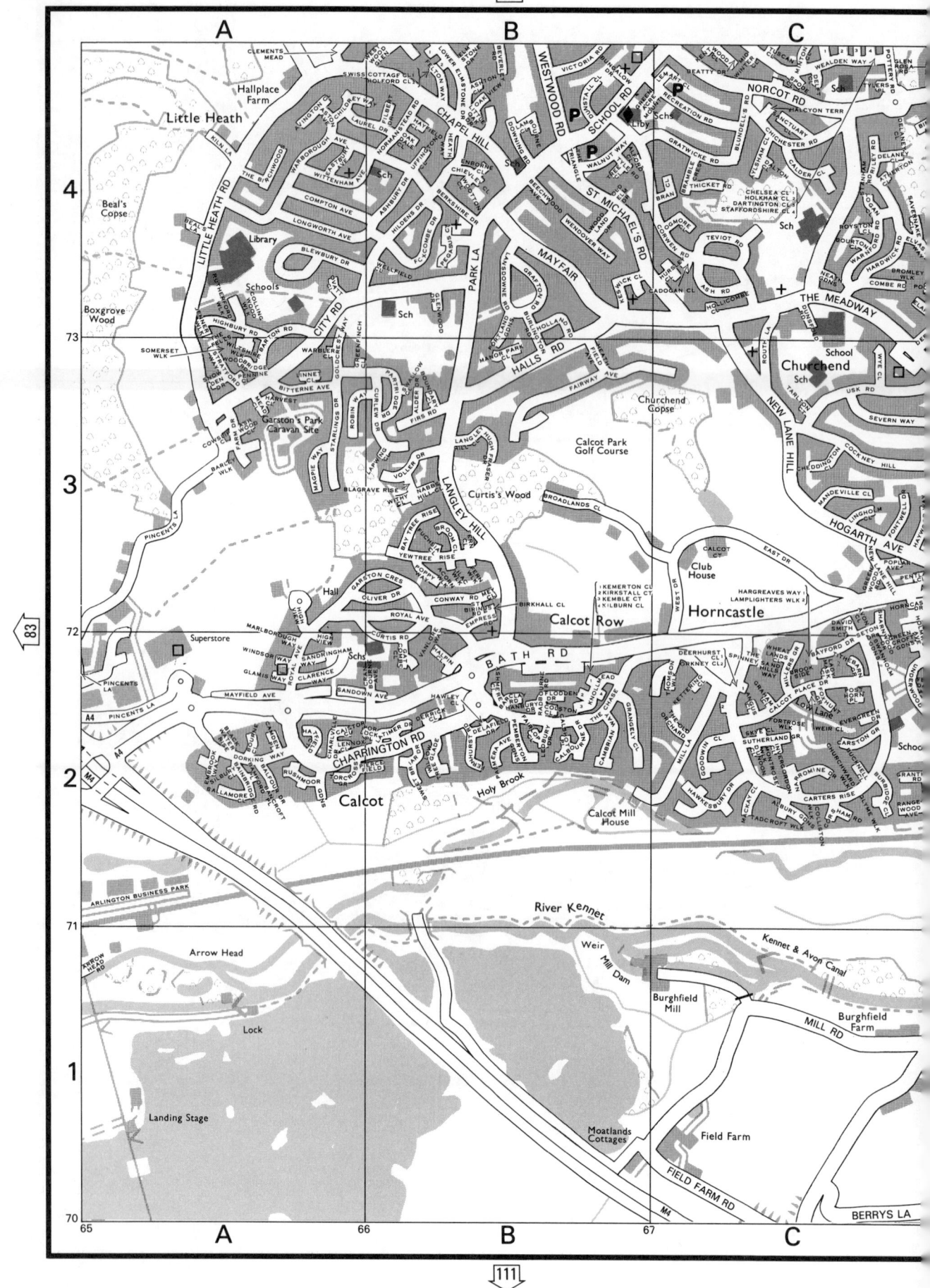

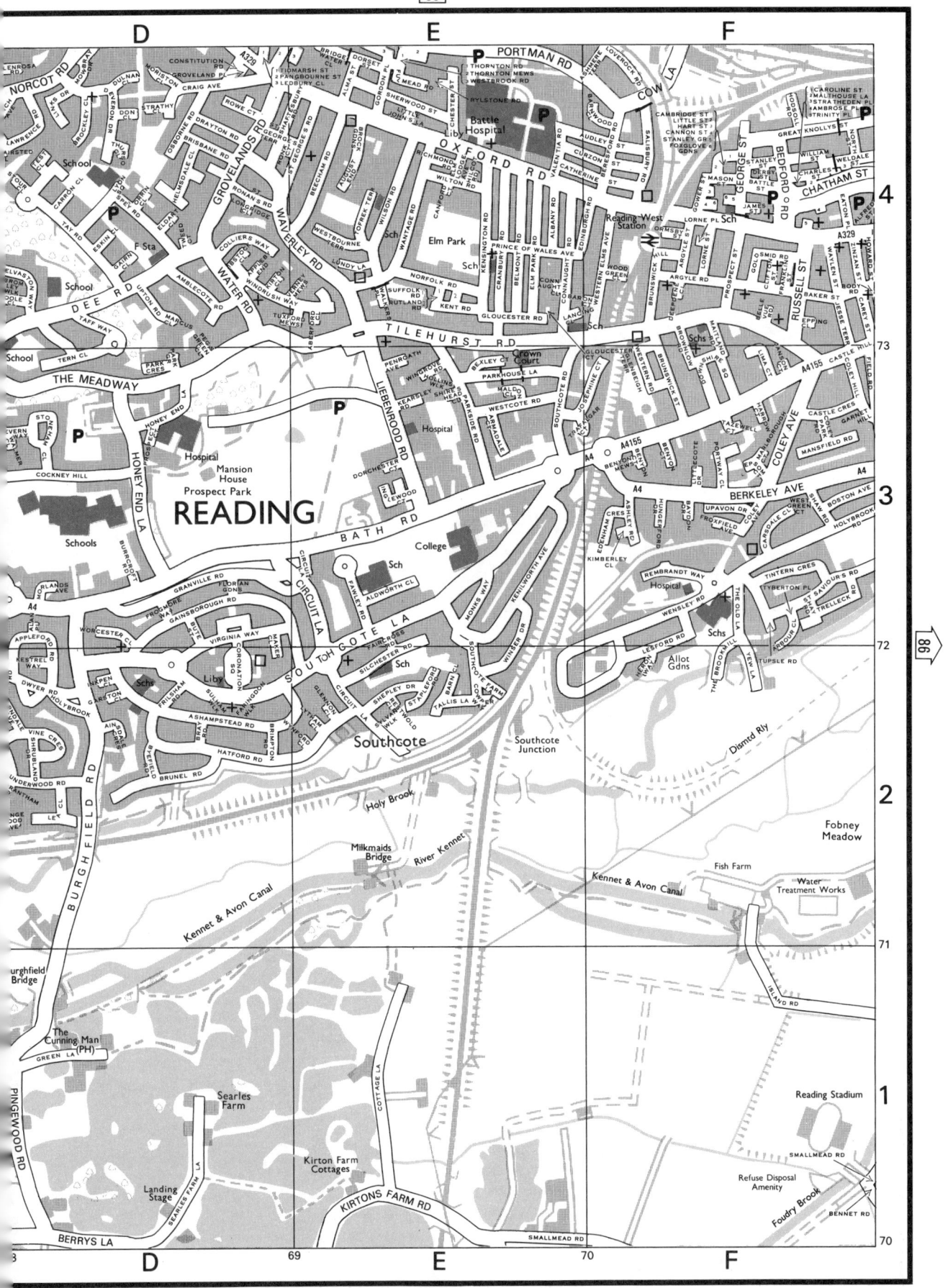

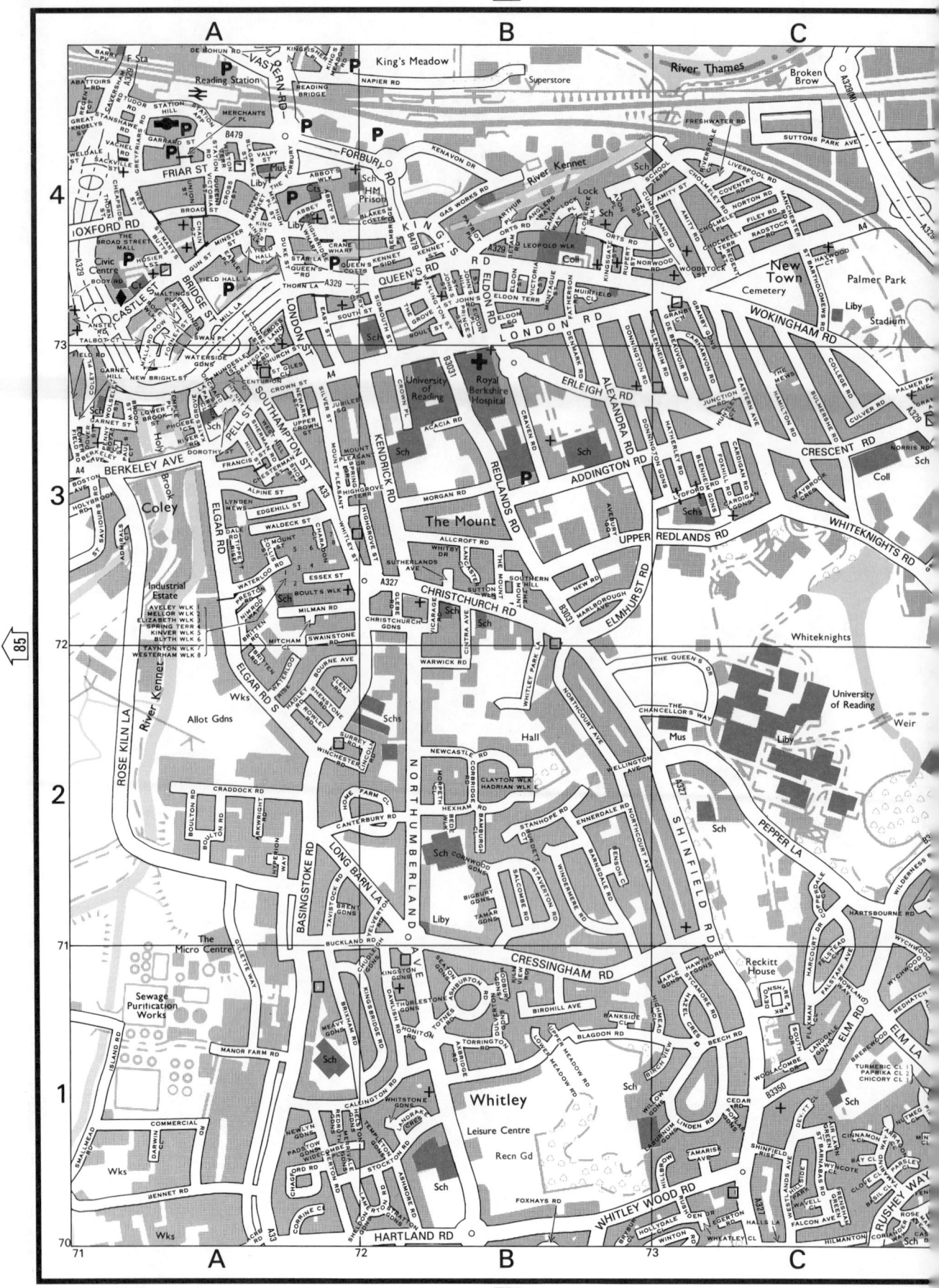

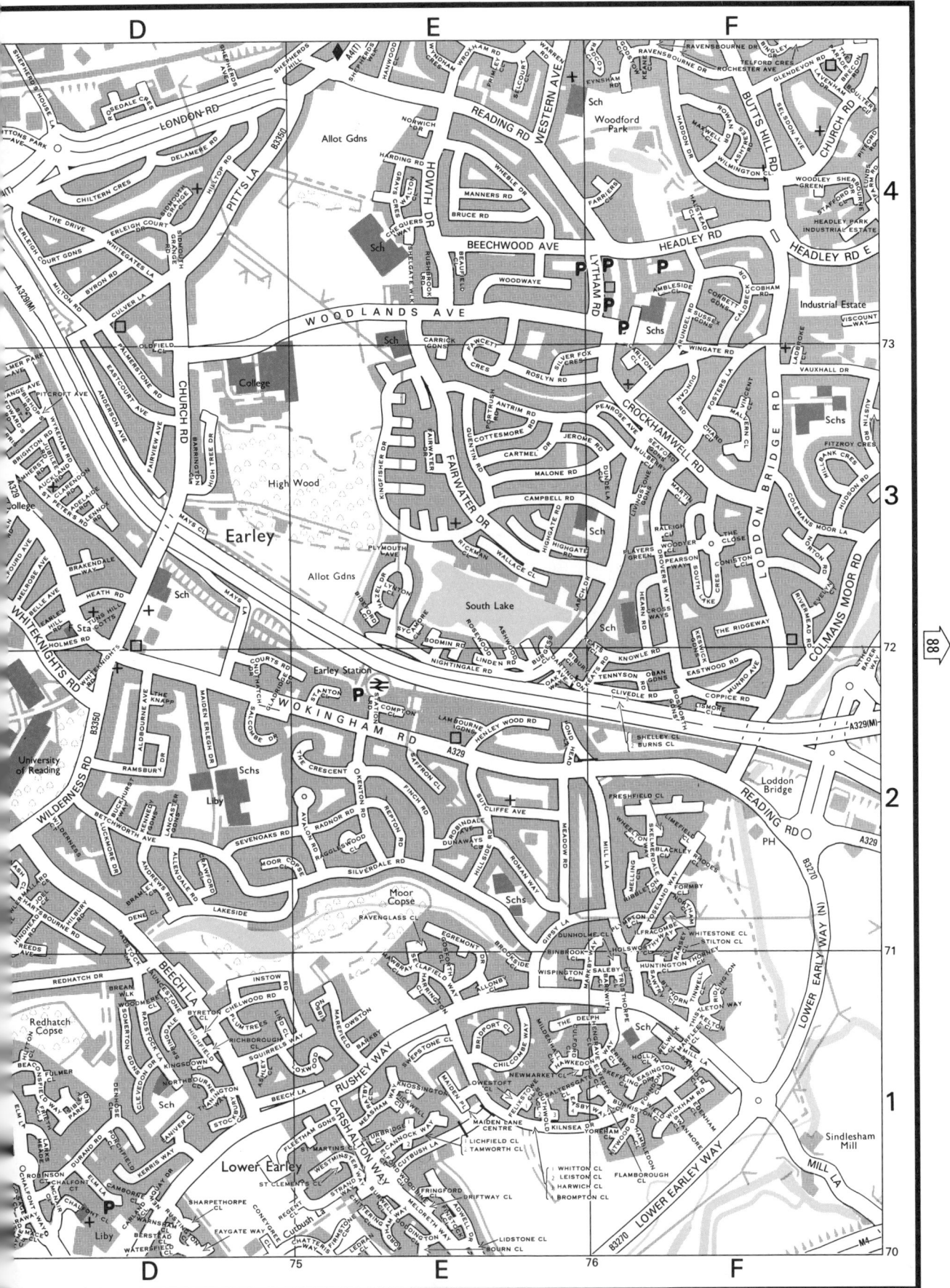

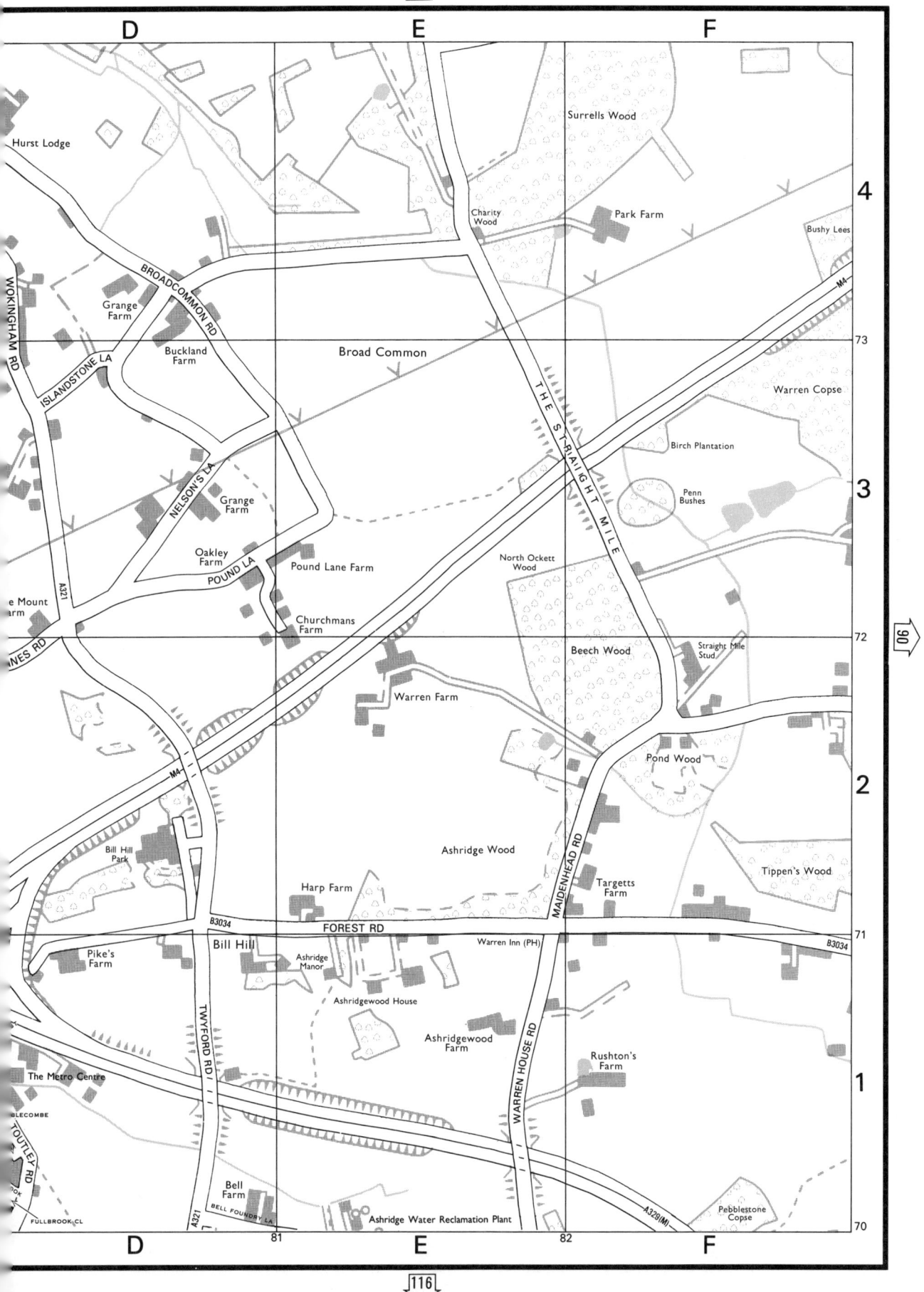

D E F

Hurst Lodge

Surrells Wood

Charity Wood

Park Farm

Bushy Lees

4

BROADCOMMON RD

WOKINGHAM RD

Grange Farm

M4

73

Buckland Farm

Broad Common

Warren Copse

ISLANDSTONE LA

Birch Plantation

THE STRAIGHT MILE

Penn Bushes

3

NELSON'S LA

Grange Farm

A321

Oakley Farm

POUND LA

Pound Lane Farm

North Ockett Wood

e Mount arm

Churchmans Farm

MAIDENHEAD RD

Straight Mile Stud

72

NES RD

Beech Wood

90

Warren Farm

Pond Wood

M4

2

Bill Hill Park

Ashridge Wood

Tippen's Wood

Harp Farm

Targetts Farm

B3034

FOREST RD

71

Pike's Farm

Bill Hill

Warren Inn (PH)

B3034

TWYFORD RD

Ashridge Manor

Ashridgewood House

WARREN HOUSE RD

Rushton's Farm

Ashridgewood Farm

The Metro Centre

1

BLECOMBE

TOUTLEY RD

Bell Farm

A321

BELL FOUNDRY LA

Ashridge Water Reclamation Plant

A329(M)

Pebblestone Copse

FULLBROOK CL

70

D E F

81 82

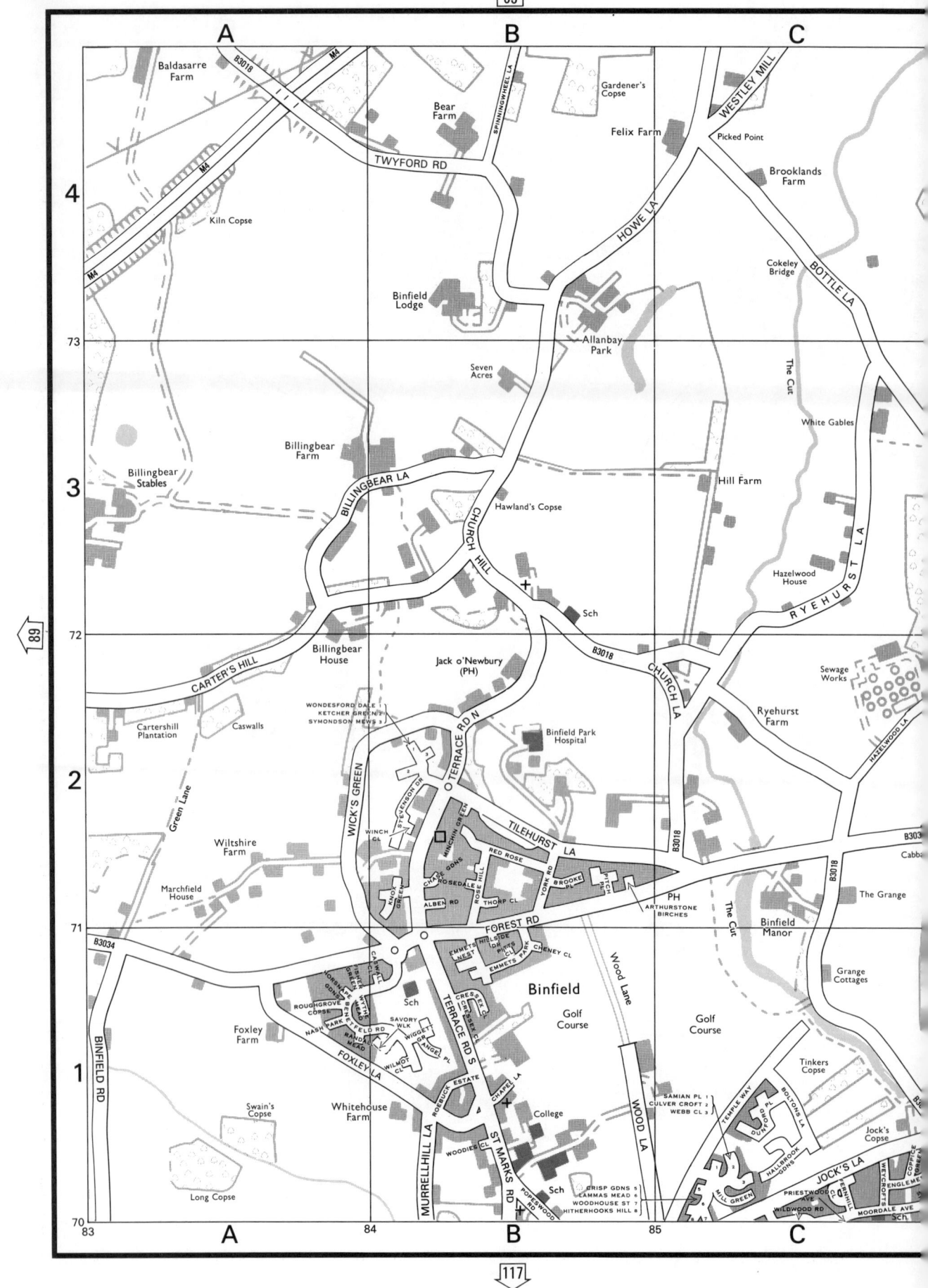

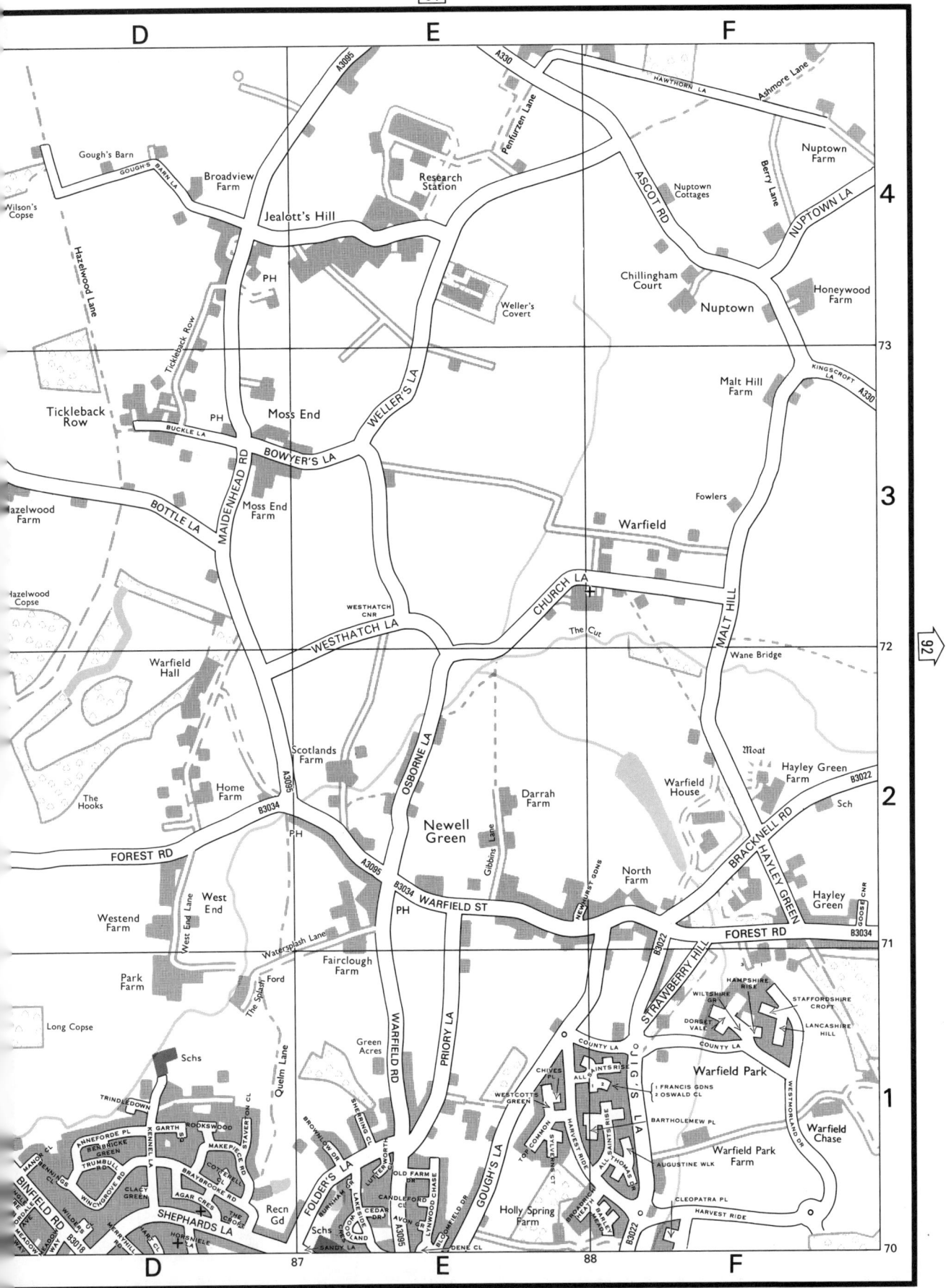

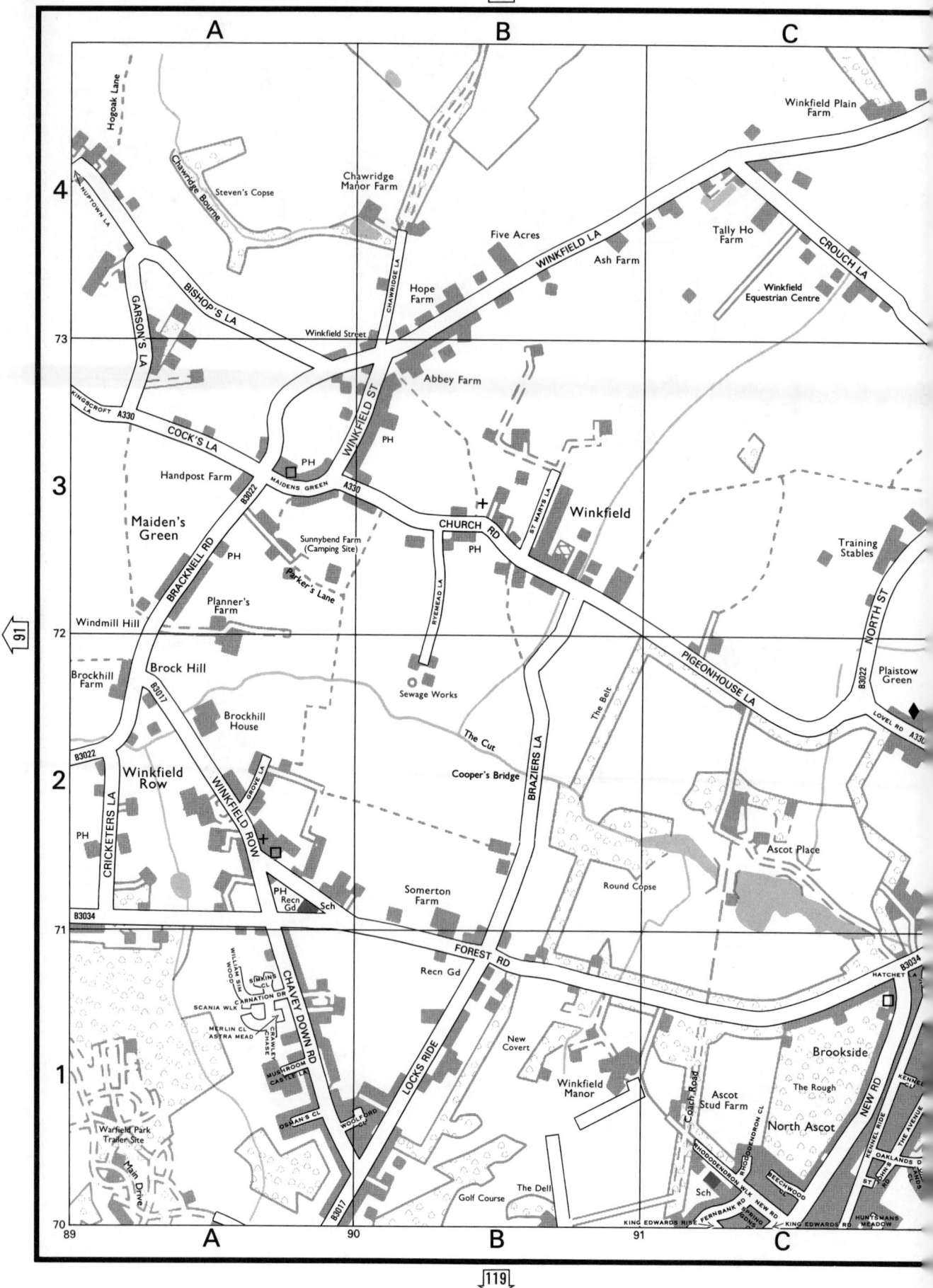

A   B   C

Hogoak Lane

Chawridge Bourne

Steven's Copse

Chawridge Manor Farm

Winkfield Plain Farm

4

NUPTOWN LA

BISHOP'S LA

GARSON'S LA

Five Acres

WINKFIELD LA

Ash Farm

Hope Farm

CHAWRIDGE LA

Tally Ho Farm

CROUCH LA

Winkfield Equestrian Centre

Winkfield Street

73

KINGSCROFT LA

A330

COCK'S LA

Handpost Farm

Abbey Farm

PH

PH

Winkfield

WINKFIELD ST

ST MARYS LA

3

Maiden's Green

MAIDENS GREEN

PH

A330

CHURCH RD

Sunnybend Farm
(Camping Site)

PH

Training Stables

BRACKNELL RD

PH

Parker's Lane

RYEMEAD LA

NORTH ST

B3022

Planner's Farm

Windmill Hill

72

Brockhill Farm

Brock Hill

Sewage Works

PIGEONHOUSE LA

B3022

Plaistow Green

LOVEL RD A330

B3017

Brockhill House

The Cut

The Belt

91

B3022

Winkfield Row

CRICKETERS LA

WINKFIELD ROW

GROVE LA

Cooper's Bridge

BRAZIERS LA

Ascot Place

2

PH

PH
Recn
Gd

Sch

Somerton Farm

Round Copse

B3034

71

CHAVEY DOWN RD

WILLIAM SIM WOOD DR

SIMKINS CL

CARNATION DR

SCANIA WLK

MERLIN CL
ASTRA MEAD

CRAWLEY CHASE

MUSHROOM CASTLE LA

OSMAN'S CL

WOOLFORD CL

FOREST RD

Recn Gd

LOCKS RIDE

New Covert

Winkfield Manor

Coach Road

Ascot Stud Farm

HATCHET LA

B3034

The Rough

Brookside

North Ascot

NEW RD

KENNEL RIDE

KENNEL CL

1

Warfield Park
Trailer Site

Main Drive

B3017

Golf Course

The Dell

Sch

RHODODENDRON WLK

RIDGEMOUNT CL

NEW RD

BEECHWOOD

OAKLANDS D

THE AVENUE

JOHN CL

70

KING EDWARDS RISE FERNBANK RD SPRING GDNS

KING EDWARDS RD

HUNT'SMANS MEADOW

89   A   90   B   91   C

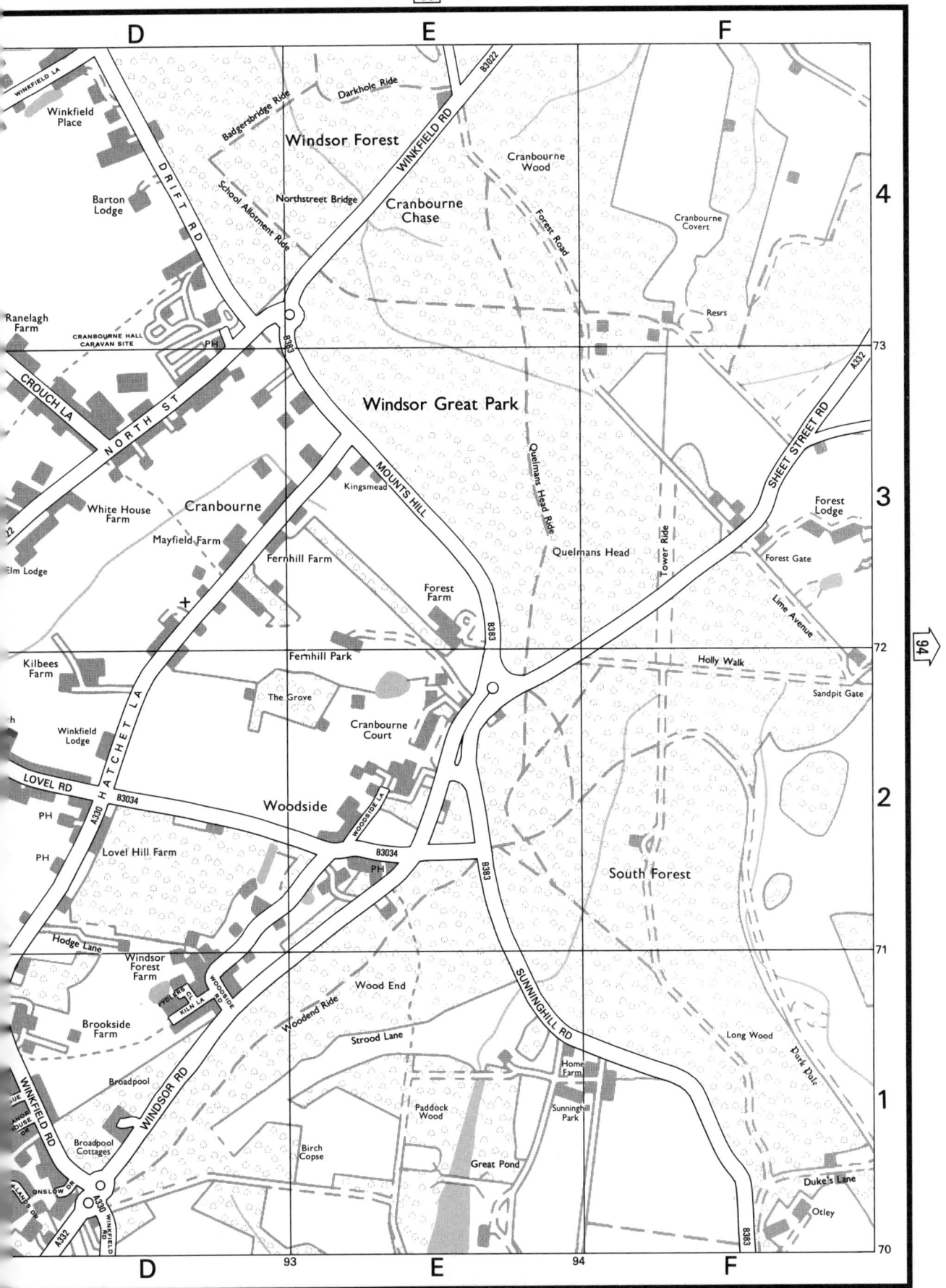

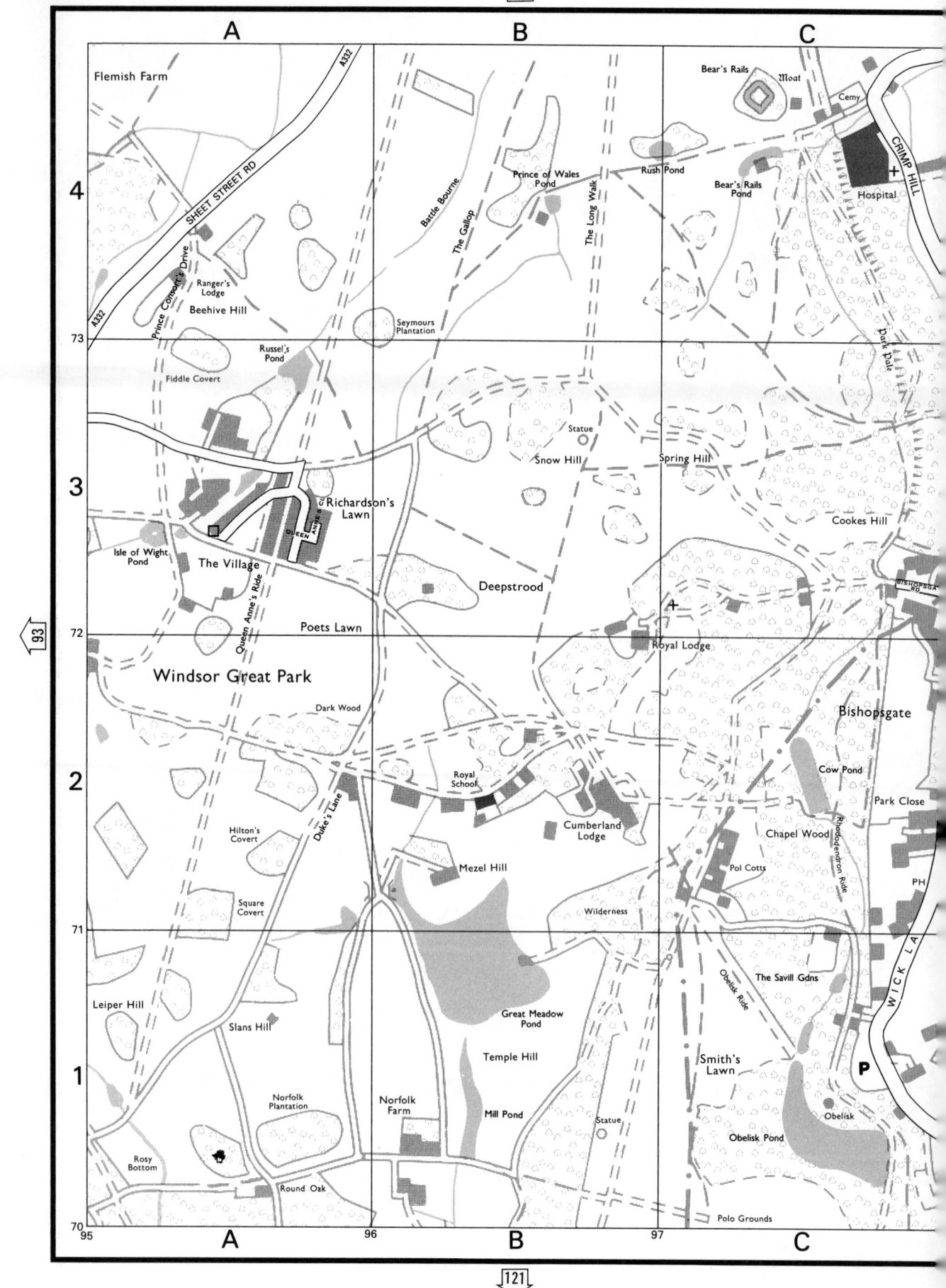

A B C

Flemish Farm

SHEET STREET RD

A332

Prince Consort's Drive

Ranger's
Lodge

Beehive Hill

A332

Bardle Bourne

The Gallop

The Long Walk

Prince of Wales
Pond

Rush Pond

Bear's Rails

Moat

Cemy

Hospital

CRIMP HILL

Bear's Rails
Pond

73

Russel's
Pond

Seymours
Plantation

Park Dale

Fiddle Covert

Statue

Snow Hill

Spring Hill

QUEEN ANNE'S CL

Richardson's
Lawn

Cookes Hill

3

Isle of Wight
Pond

The Village

Queen Anne's Ride

Deepstrood

BISHOPSGATE RD

72

Poets Lawn

Royal Lodge

Windsor Great Park

Dark Wood

Bishopsgate

Hilton's
Covert

Duke's Lane

Royal
School

Cow Pond

Park Close

2

Cumberland
Lodge

Chapel Wood

Rhododendron Ride

PH

Square
Covert

Mezel Hill

Pol Cotts

Wilderness

WICK LA

71

Leiper Hill

Obelisk Ride

The Savill Gdns

Slans Hill

Great Meadow
Pond

Smith's
Lawn

P

1

Norfolk
Plantation

Norfolk
Farm

Temple Hill

Mill Pond

Statue

Obelisk

Rosy
Bottom

Obelisk Pond

Round Oak

Polo Grounds

70
95 A 96 B 97 C

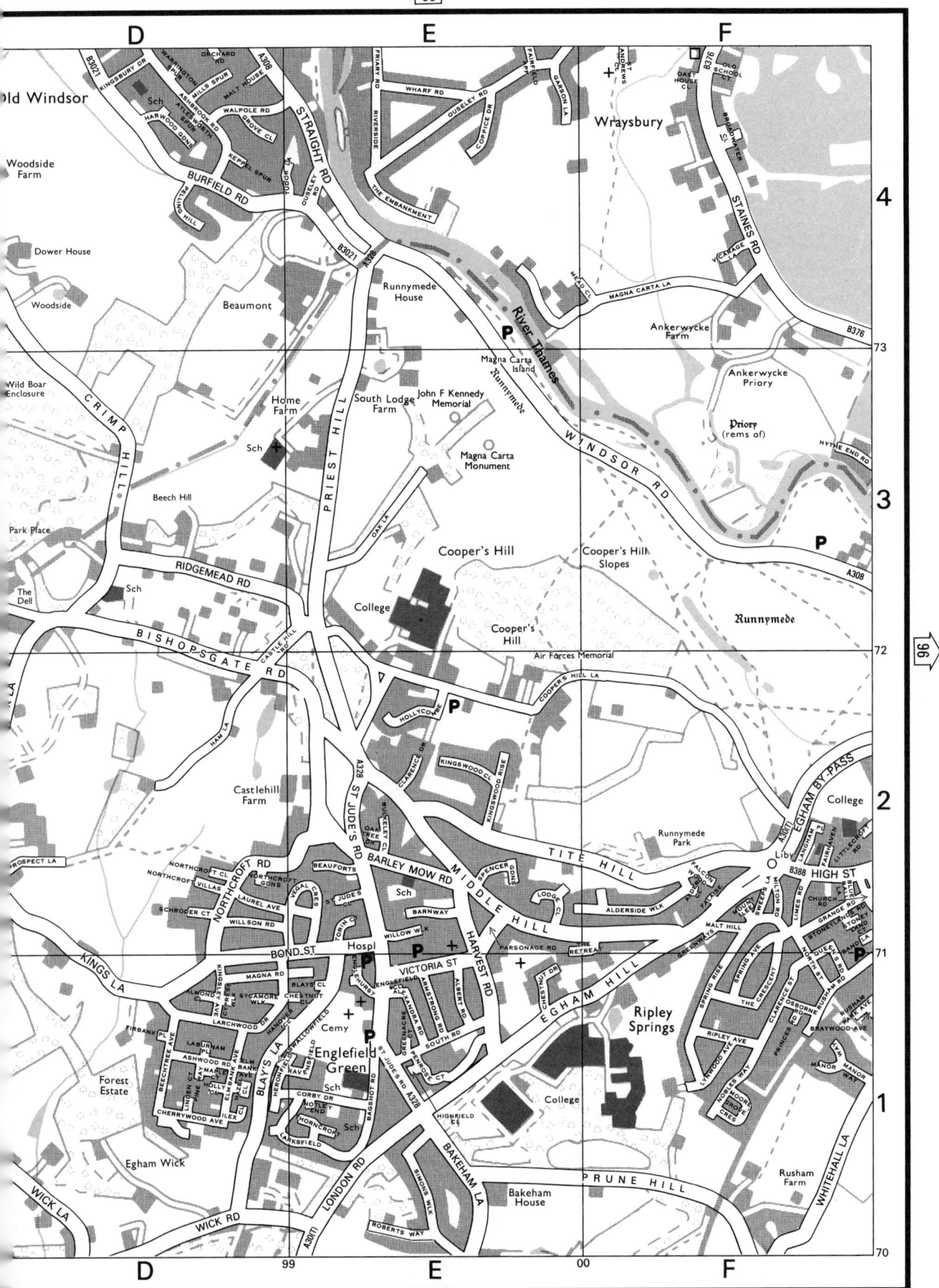

D   E   F

Old Windsor

Woodside
Farm

Woodside

Dower House

Wild Boar
Enclosure

Park Place

The
Dell

Beaumont

Beech Hill

RIDGEMEAD RD

Sch

BISHOPSGATE RD

CRIMP HILL

PRIEST HILL

STRAIGHT RD

BURFIELD RD

B3021

A308

B3021

A328

Runnymede
House

Home
Farm

South Lodge
Farm

John F Kennedy
Memorial

Magna Carta
Island

Magna Carta
Monument

Cooper's Hill

College

Cooper's
Hill

Air Forces Memorial

THE EMBANKMENT

River Thames

WINDSOR RD

Runnymede

Wraysbury

Ankerwycke
Farm

Ankerwycke
Priory

Priory
(rems of)

Cooper's Hill
Slopes

Runnymede

STAINES RD

B376

HYTHE END RD

A308

96

73

72

71

70

4

3

2

1

Castlehill
Farm

HAM LA

HOLLYCOMBE

CLARENCE DR

A328

ST JUDE'S RD

OAK TREE CL

BARLEY MOW RD

MIDDLE HILL

KINGSWOOD DR

KINGSWOOD RISE

SPENCER GDNS

TITE HILL

Runnymede
Park

Lib

College

EGHAM BY-PASS

A308(T)

B388 HIGH ST

Sch

LODGE CL

ALDERSIDE WLK

Hospl

BOND ST

Sch

NORTHCROFT RD

NORTHCROFT CL

NORTHCROFT GDNS

NORTHCROFT VILLAS

LAUREL AVE

SCHRODER CT

WILLSON RD

BEAUFORTS

VIGAR CRES

ST JUDE'S

WILLOW WLK

BARNWAY

PARSONAGE RD

THE RETREAT

MALT HILL

CHURCH RD

GRANGE RD

VICTORIA ST

HARVEST RD

ALBERT RD

ALEXANDRA RD

ARMSTRONG RD

SOUTH RD

EGHAM HILL

Ripley
Springs

SPRING RISE

THE CRESCENT

RIPLEY AVE

OSBORNE

CLARENCE RD

PRINCES RD

BRAYWOOD AVE

MANOR WAY

KINGS LA

BLAY'S LA

LONDON RD

BAKEHAM LA

WICK LA

WICK RD

A30(T)

Englefield
Green

Cemy

Forest
Estate

Egham Wick

BEECHTREE AVE

LABURNUM PL

ASHWOOD RD

ELM BANK

CHERRYWOOD AVE

LARKSFIELD

HORNCROFT

Sch

Sch

HIGHFIELD CL

College

PRUNE HILL

Bakeham
House

ROBERTS WAY

SIMONS WLK

Rusham
Farm

WHITEHALL LA

D   99   E   00   F

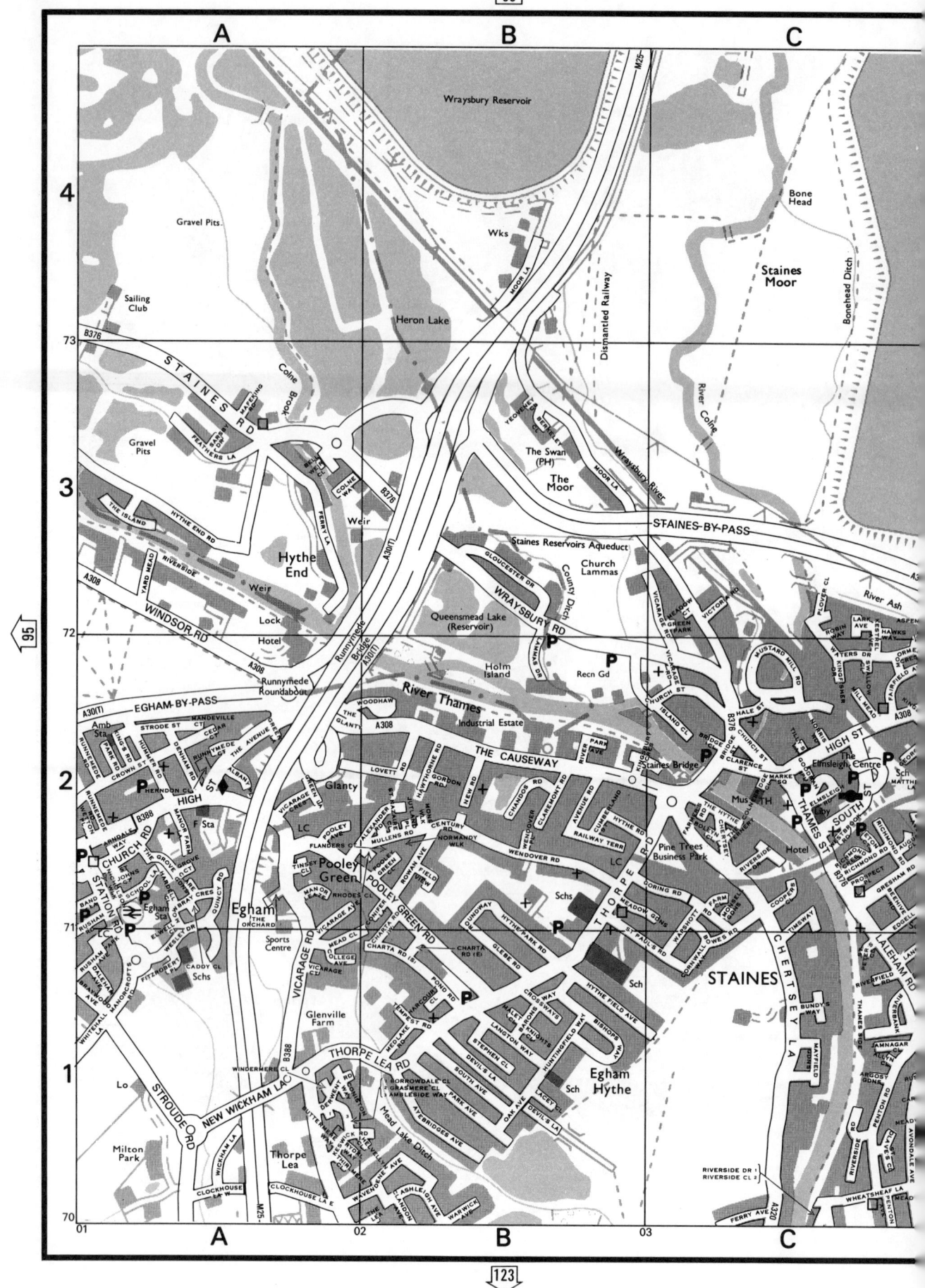

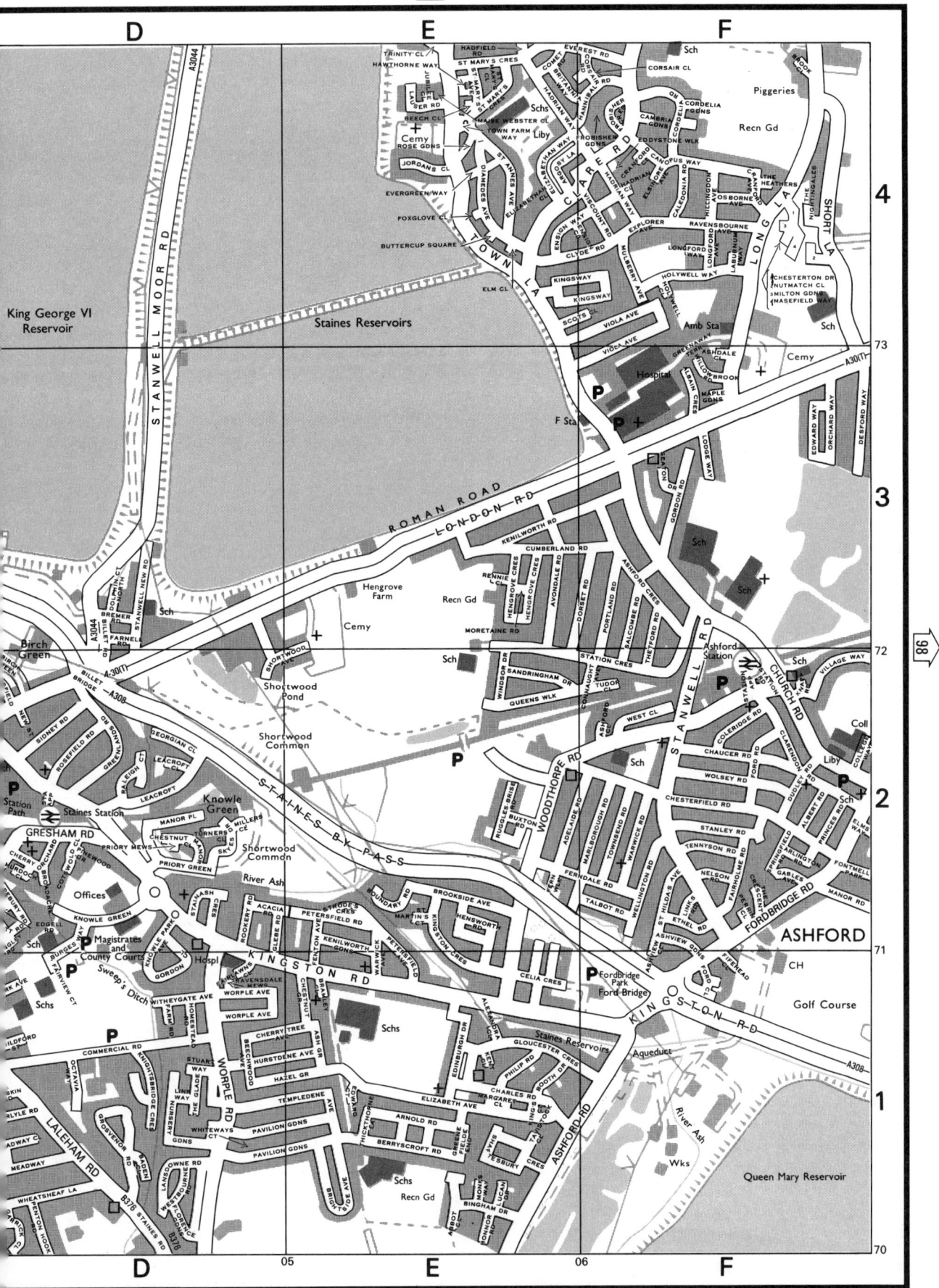

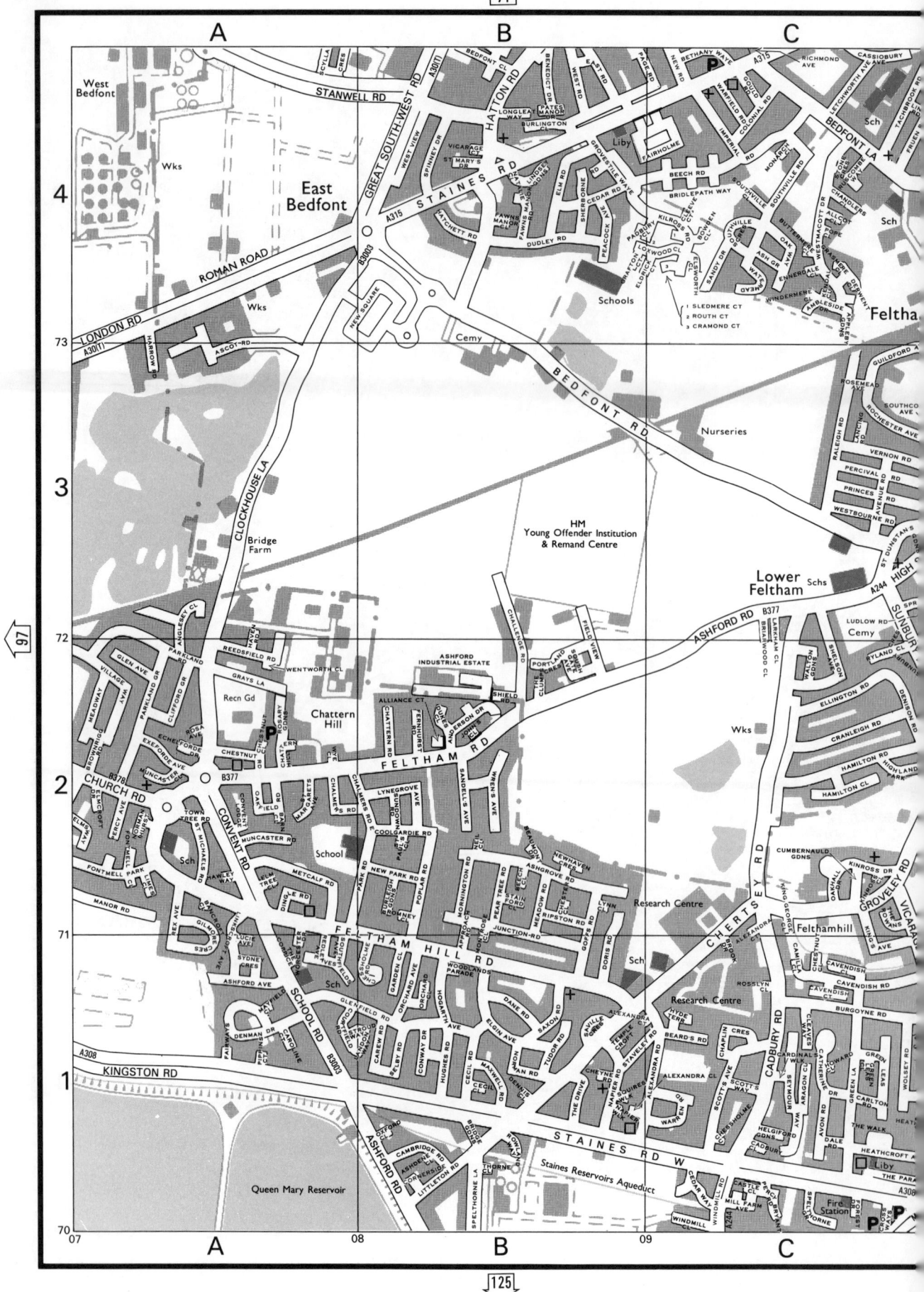

97

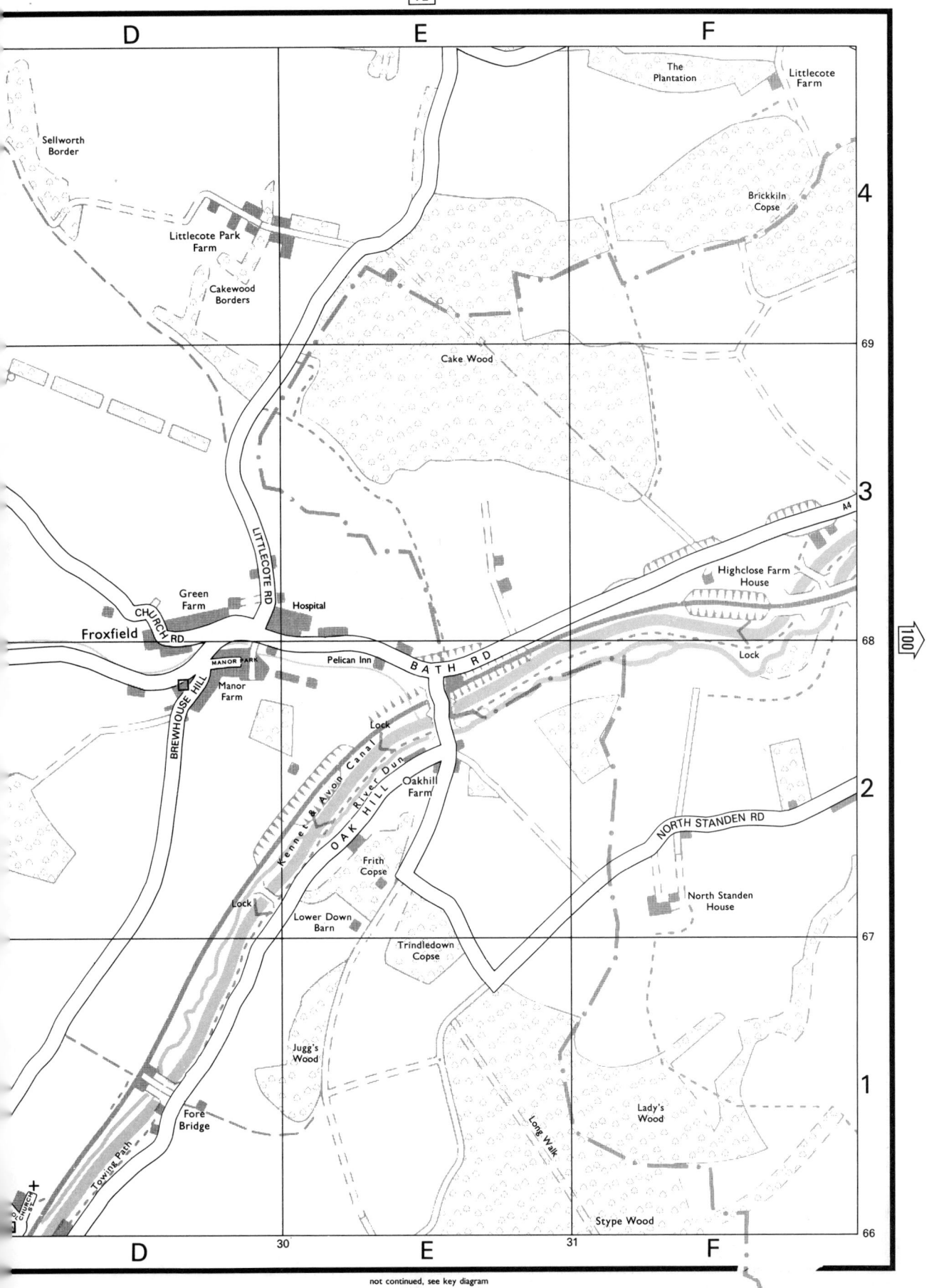

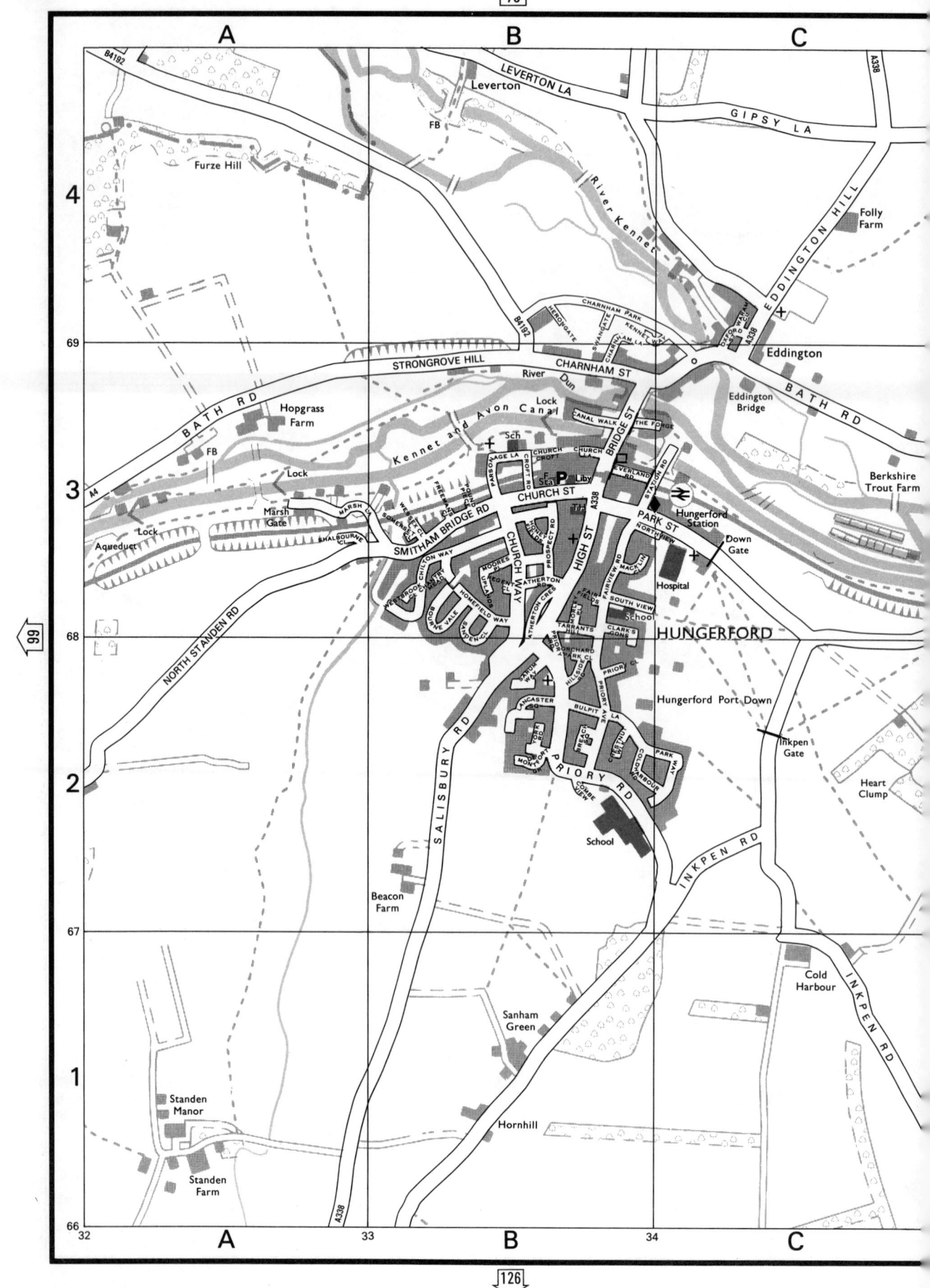

A **B** **C**

4

69

3

68

67

2

1

66

99

B4192

Furze Hill

Leverton

LEVERTON LA

FB

GIPSY LA

River Kennet

EDDINGTON HILL

Folly Farm

A338

Eddington

BATH RD

Eddington Bridge

Berkshire Trout Farm

CHARNHAM PARK

CHARNHAM ST

STRONGROVE HILL

River Dun

Lock

Canal Walk

BRIDGE ST

THE FORGE

BATH RD

B4192

HERONGATE

STYANGATE

KENNET CL

OXFORD WAY

A4

Hopgrass Farm

FB

Lock

Kennet and Avon Canal

Lock

Sch

PARSONAGE LA

CHURCH CROFT

CHURCH

CHURCH

EVERLAND RD

STATION RD

Hungerford Station

Down Gate

Hospital

Aqueduct

Lock

Marsh Gate

MARSH LA

CHALBOURNE CL

SMITHAM BRIDGE RD

CHURCH ST

CHURCH WAY

HIGH ST

PARK ST

NORTH VIEW

MAGDLN

FAIRVIEW RD

WESTBROOK

CHILTON WAY

BRIDGE CL

CROFT

FREEMANS

PRIORY

MOORES

REGENT

HOMEFIELD WAY

ATHERTON CRES

ATHERTON RD

HONEY FIELDS

PROSPECT RD

SOUTH VIEW

School

TARRANTS

CLARK'S GDNS

HUNGERFORD

DALE

HYDE VALE

MAYTHORN CL

HILLSIDE

ORCHARD PARK CL

PRIORY CL

PRIORY LA

Hungerford Port Down

Inkpen Gate

BATH RD

NORTH STANDEN RD

SALISBURY RD

LANCASTER

OXFORD

MONK

COMBE VIEW

PRIORY RD

BREACH

CHESTNUT

BULPIT LA

COLDHARBOUR

PARK WAY

School

INKPEN RD

Heart Clump

Beacon Farm

Cold Harbour

INKPEN RD

Sanham Green

Standen Manor

Hornhill

Standen Farm

A338

32

33

34

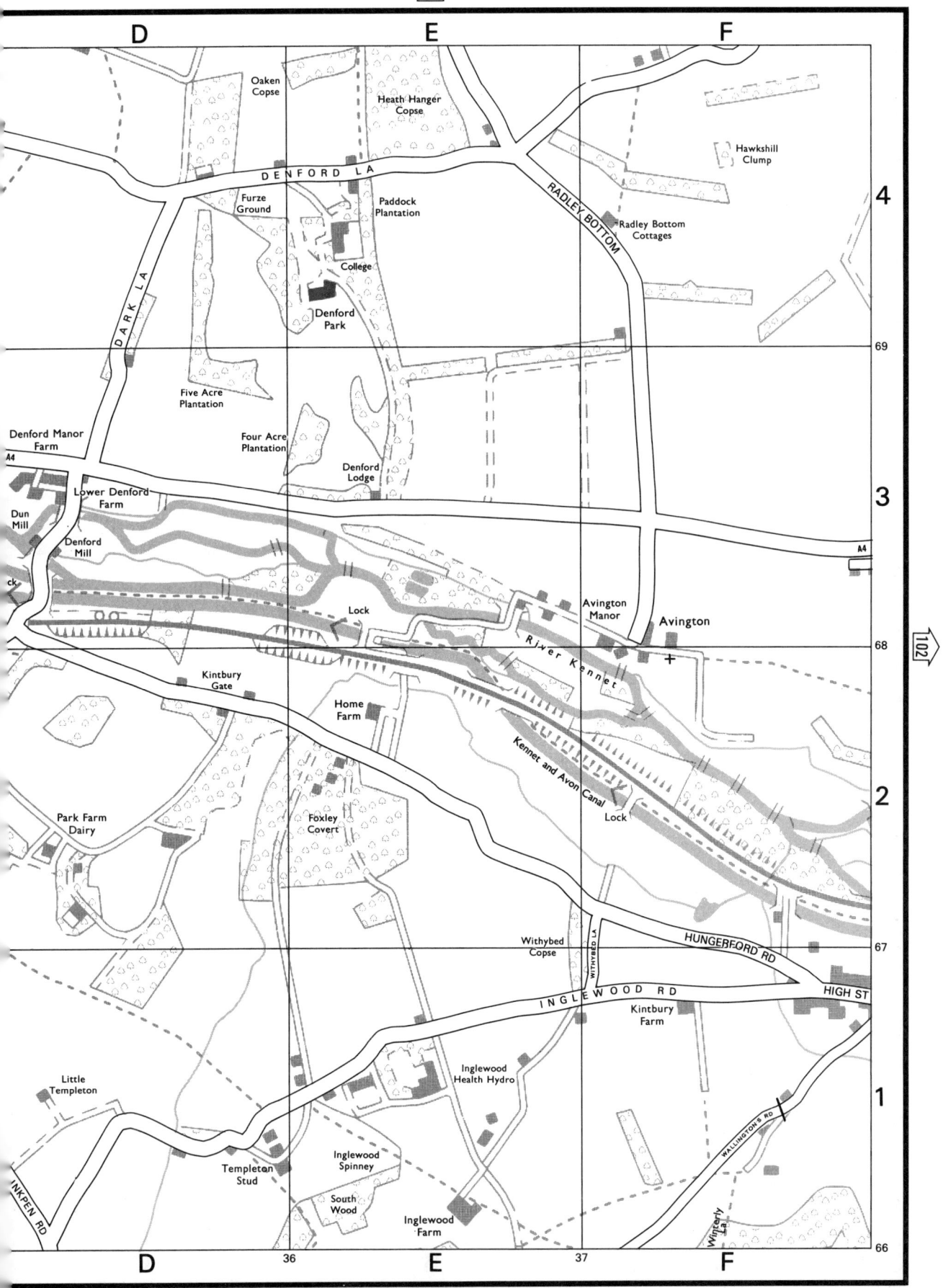

D E F

4

Oaken
Copse

Heath Hanger
Copse

Hawkshill
Clump

DENFORD LA

RADLEY BOTTOM

Furze
Ground

Paddock
Plantation

Radley Bottom
Cottages

DARK LA

College

69

Denford
Park

Five Acre
Plantation

Four Acre
Plantation

Denford Manor
Farm

Denford
Lodge

A4

Lower Denford
Farm

3

Dun
Mill

A4

Denford
Mill

Lock

Avington
Manor

Avington

River Kennet

68

102

ck

Kintbury
Gate

Home
Farm

Kennet and Avon Canal

Lock

Park Farm
Dairy

Foxley
Covert

2

Withybed
Copse

WITHYBED LA

HUNGERFORD RD

67

HIGH ST

INGLEWOOD RD

Kintbury
Farm

Little
Templeton

Inglewood
Health Hydro

WALLINGTON'S RD

1

INKPEN RD

Templeton
Stud

Inglewood
Spinney

South
Wood

Inglewood
Farm

Winterly
La

66

D 36 E 37 F

75

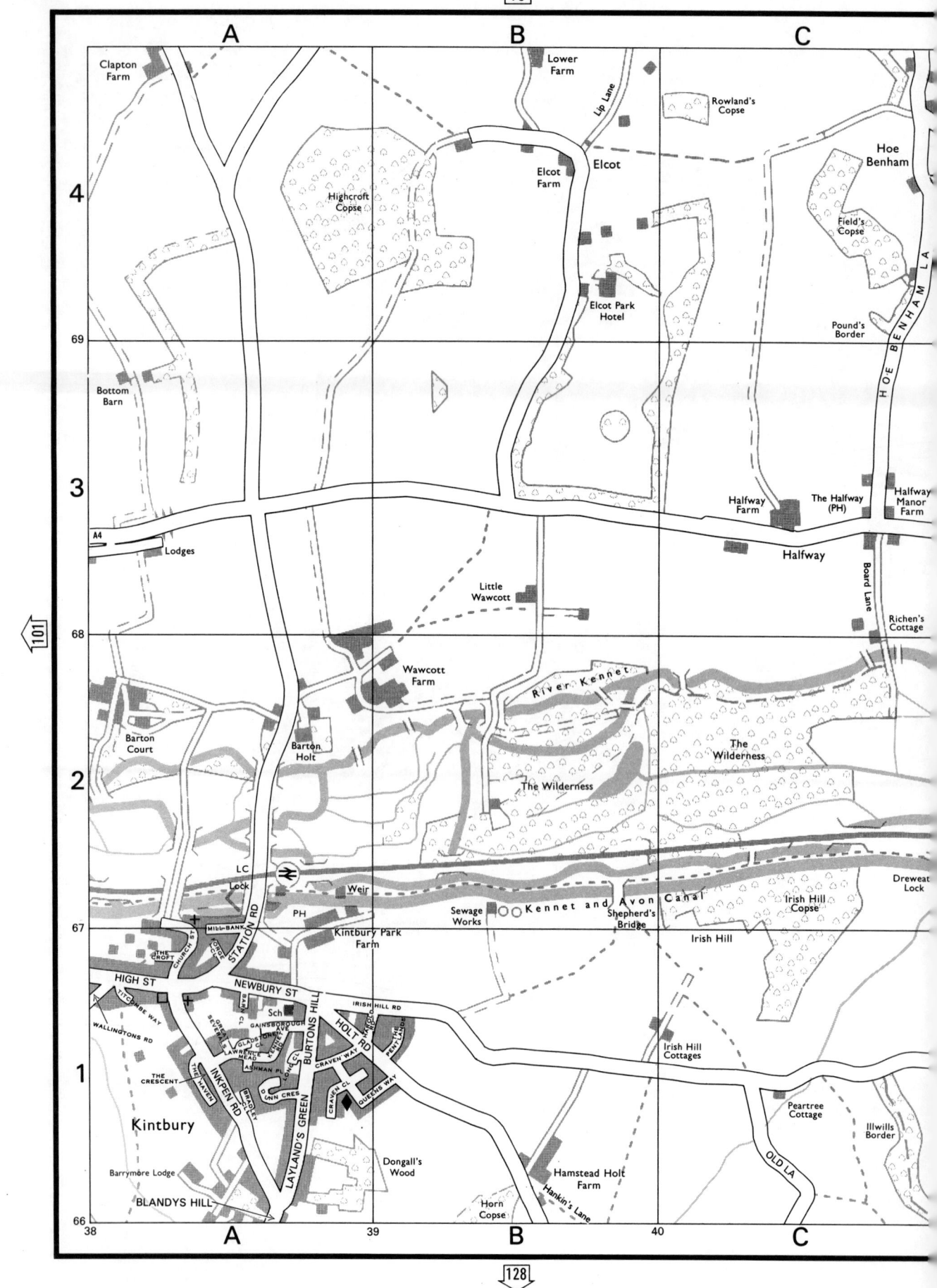

101

A   B   C

Clapton Farm
Lower Farm
Rowland's Copse
Hoe Benham
Elcot Farm
Elcot
Lip Lane
HOE BENHAM LA
Highcroft Copse
Field's Copse
4
Elcot Park Hotel
Pound's Border
69
Bottom Barn
Halfway Farm
The Halfway (PH)
Halfway Manor Farm
3
A4
Lodges
Halfway
Board Lane
Little Wawcott
Richen's Cottage
68
Wawcott Farm
River Kennet
The Wilderness
Barton Court
Barton Holt
The Wilderness
2
LC
Lock
Weir
Drewait Lock
Kennet and Avon Canal
Irish Hill Copse
67
Sewage Works
Shepherd's Bridge
Irish Hill
MILL BANK
Kintbury Park Farm
THE CROFT
CHURCH ST
STATION RD
PH
HIGH ST
NEWBURY ST
BURTONS HILL
IRISH HILL RD
HOLT RD
Sch
Irish Hill Cottages
GAINSBOROUGH
TITCOMBE WAY
WALLINGTONS RD
LAWRENCE MEAD
ASHMAN PL
CRAVEN WAY
QUEENS WAY
PENFLANE
1
THE CRESCENT
THE HAVEN
INKPEN RD
LANN CRES
CRAVEN CL
Peartree Cottage
Illwills Border
Kintbury
LAYLAND'S GREEN
Dongall's Wood
Hamstead Holt Farm
OLD LA
Barrymore Lodge
BLANDYS HILL
Horn Copse
Hankin's Lane
66
38   A   39   B   40   C

128

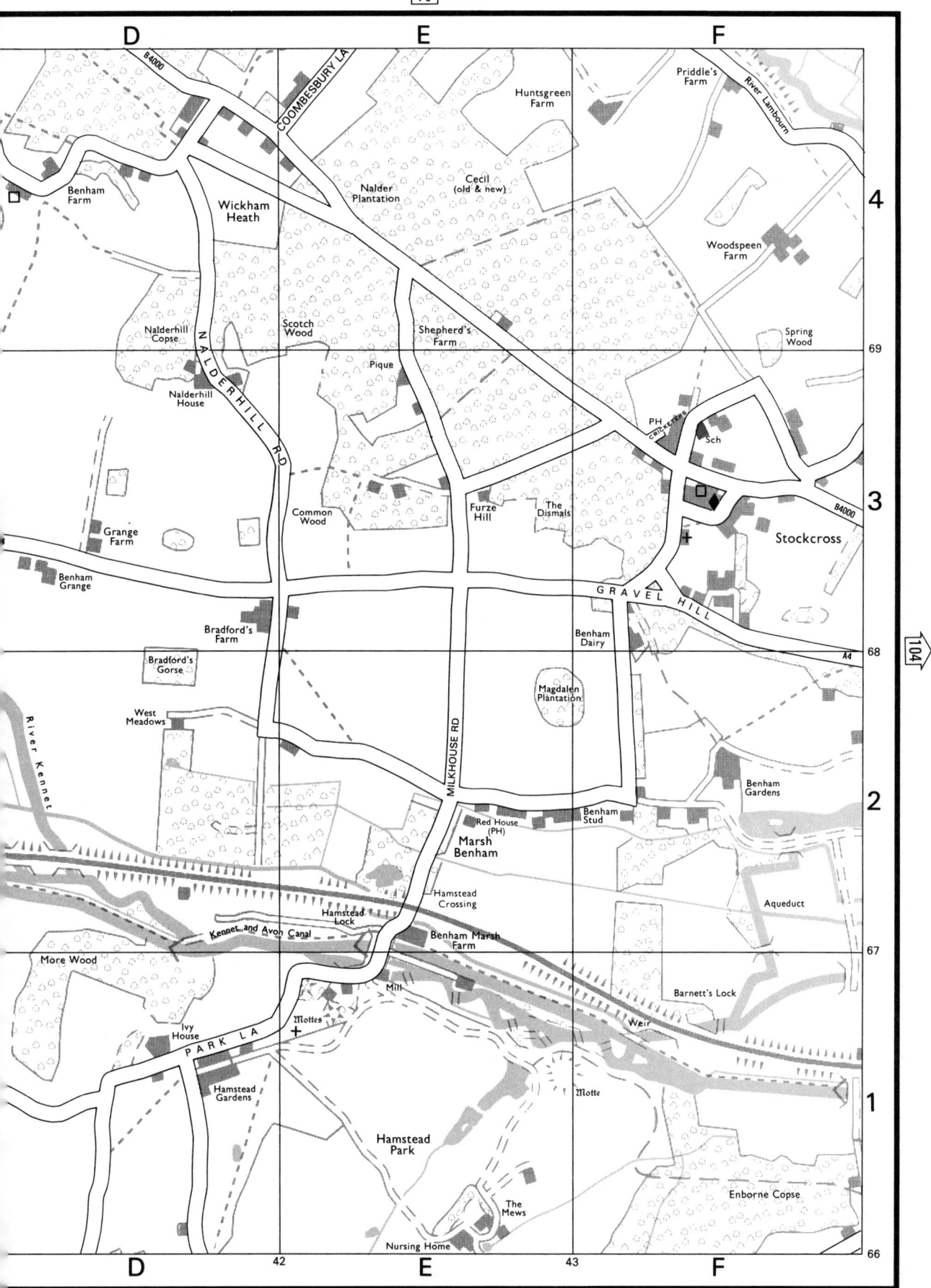

D E F

104

B4000
COOMBESBURY LA

Benham
Farm

Wickham
Heath

Huntsgreen
Farm

Priddle's
Farm

River Lambourn

Nalder
Plantation

Cecil
(old & new)

4

Woodspeen
Farm

Nalderhill
Copse

Scotch
Wood

Shepherd's
Farm

Spring
Wood

69

NALDERHILL RD

Nalderhill
House

Pique

PH
CRICKETERS

Sch

Common
Wood

Furze
Hill

The
Dismals

B4000

3

Grange
Farm

Stockcross

Benham
Grange

GRAVEL HILL

Bradford's
Farm

Benham
Dairy

A4

68

Bradford's
Gorse

Magdalen
Plantation

West
Meadows

Benham
Gardens

MILKHOUSE RD

River Kennet

Red House
(PH)

Benham
Stud

2

Aqueduct

Marsh
Benham

Hamstead
Crossing

Hamstead
Lock

Benham Marsh
Farm

Kennet and Avon Canal

67

More Wood

Mill

Barnett's Lock

Ivy
House

Mottes

Weir

PARK LA

Hamstead
Gardens

Motte

1

Hamstead
Park

Enborne Copse

The
Mews

Nursing Home

D 42 E 43 F 66

77

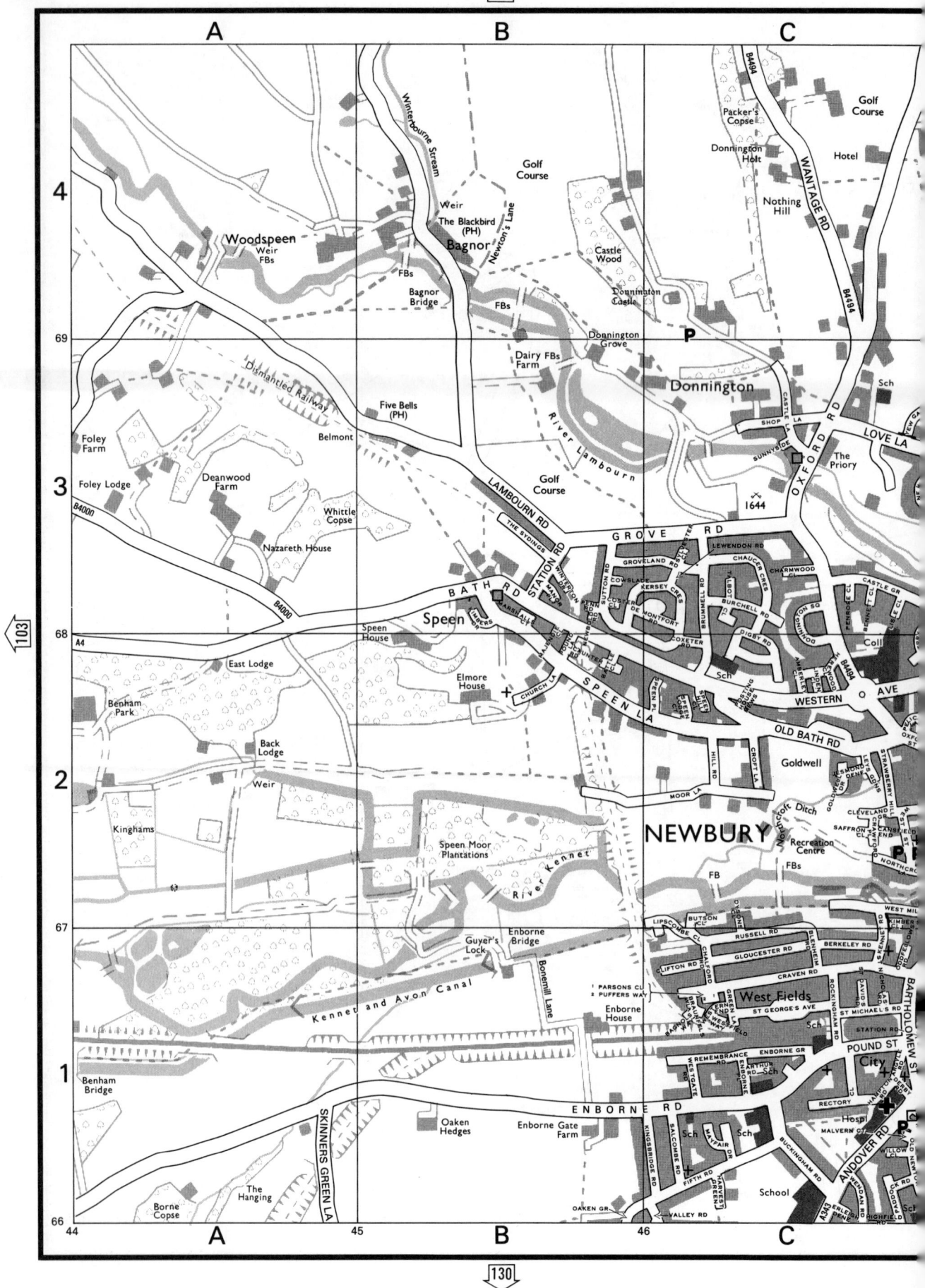

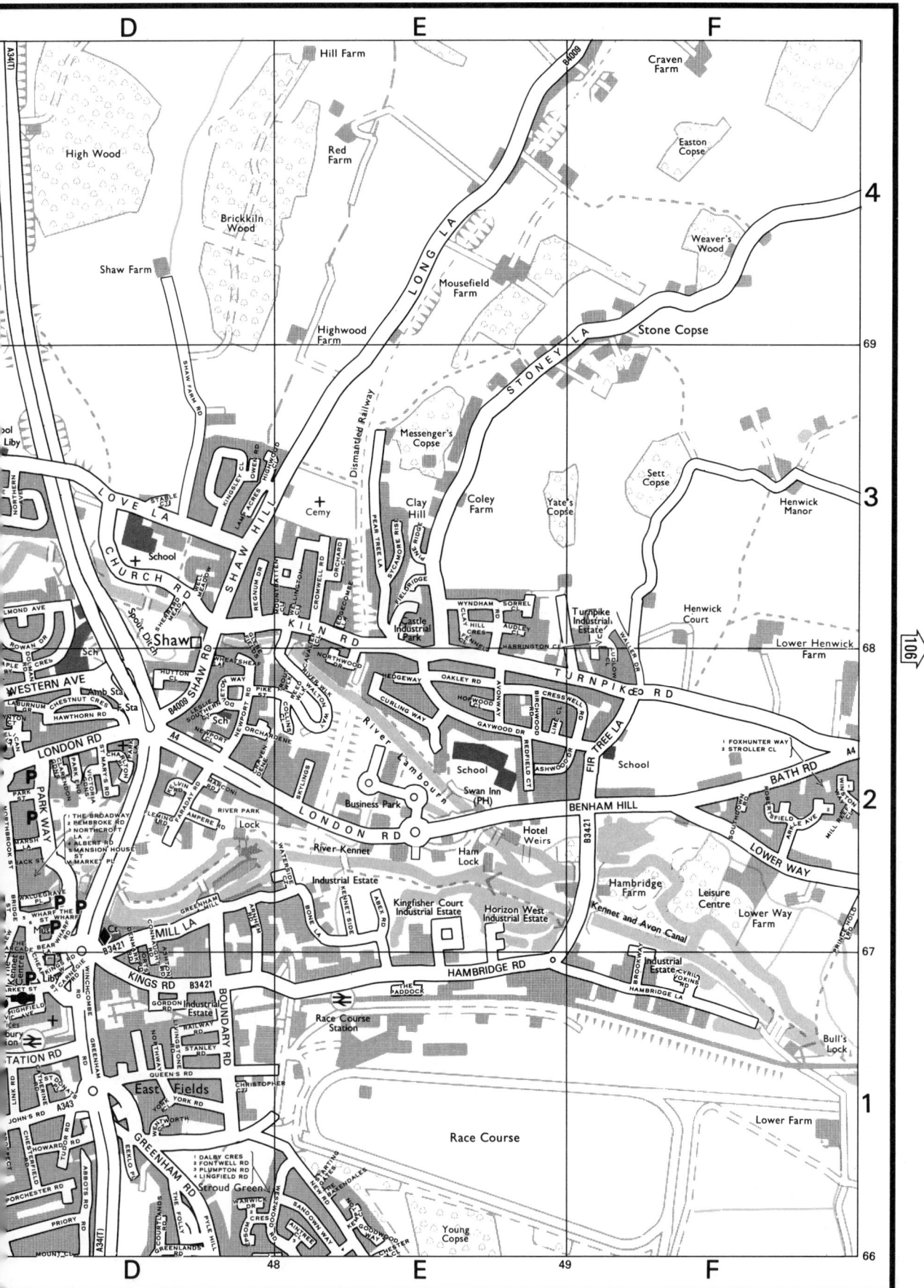

78

106

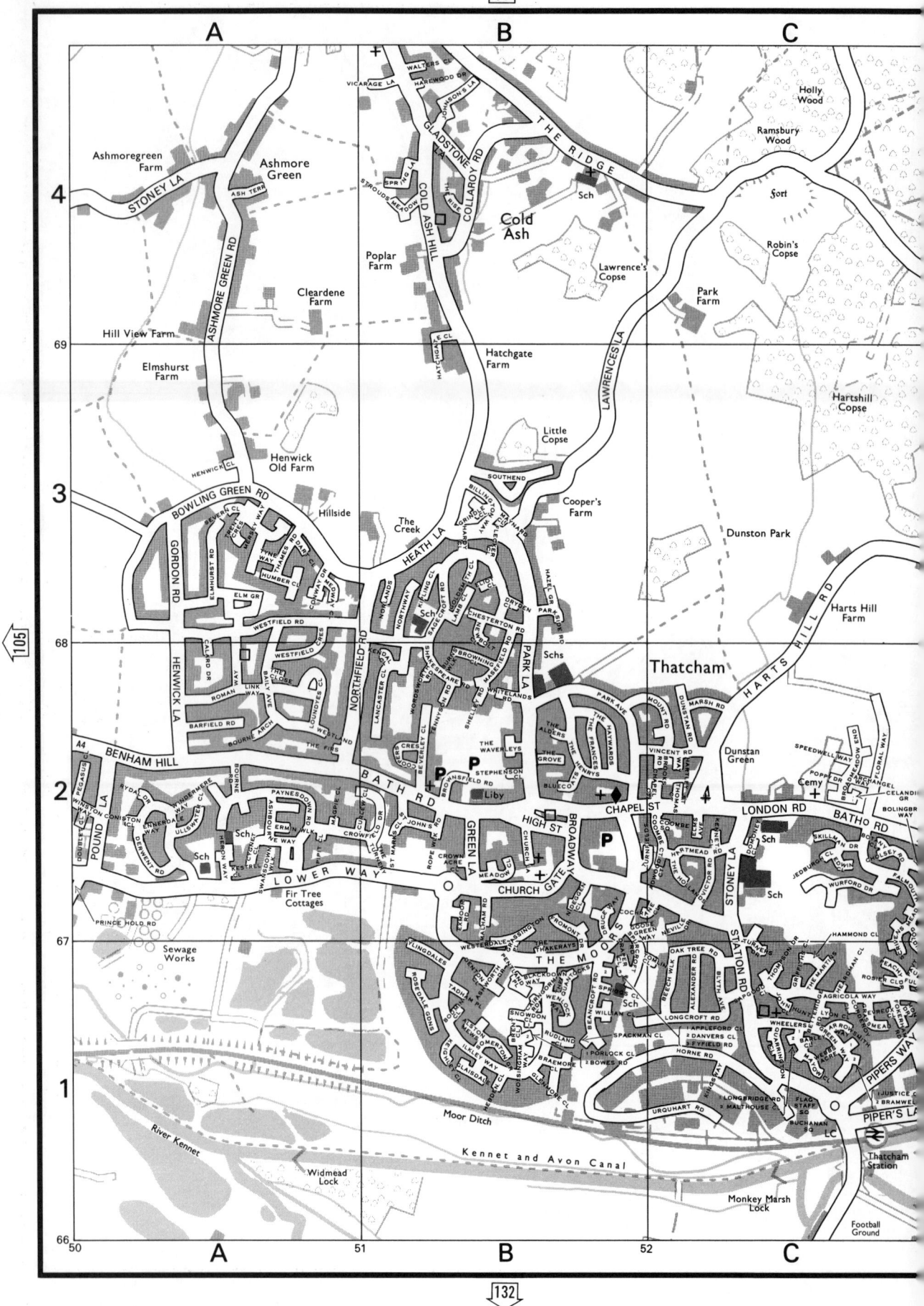

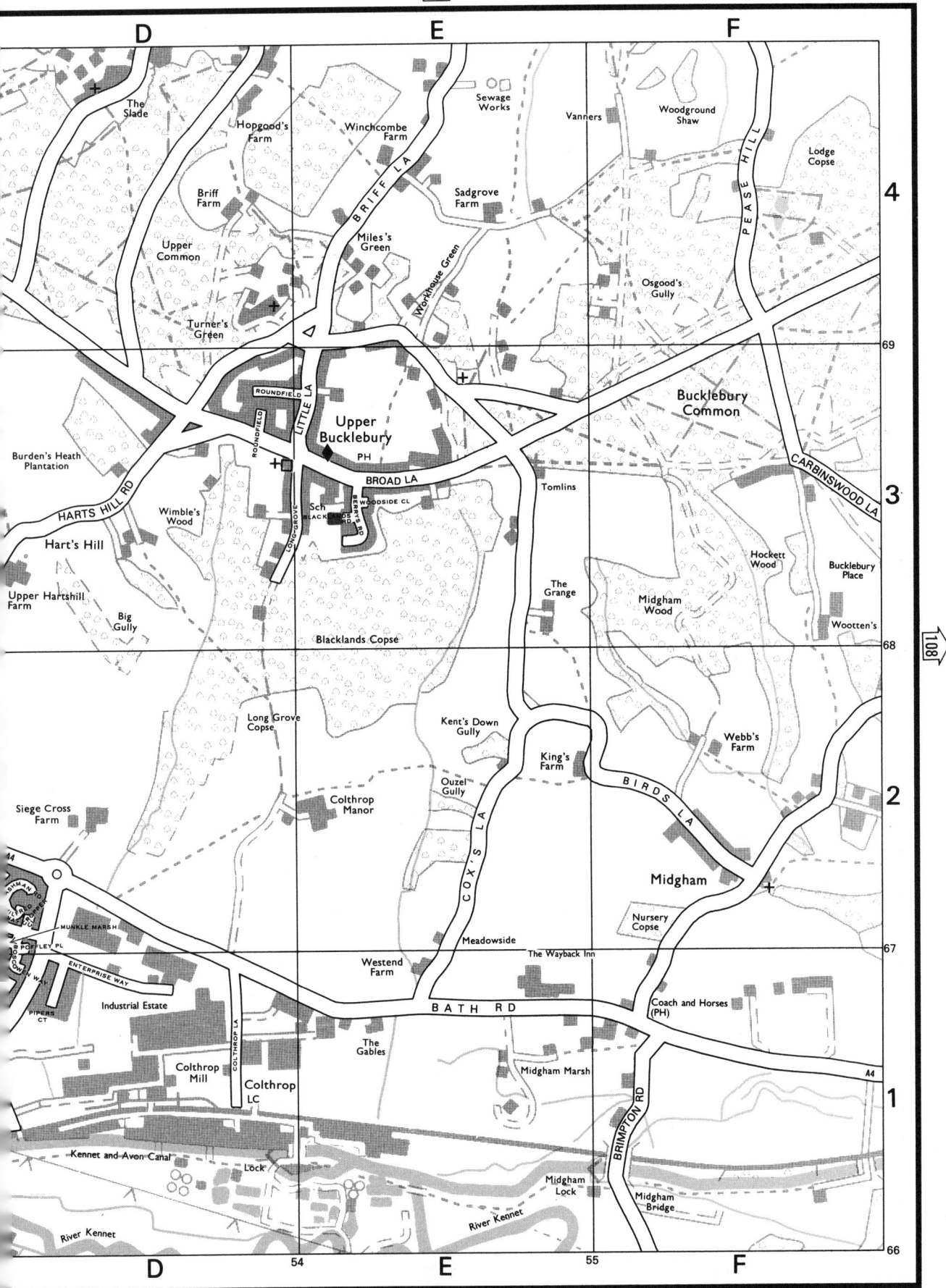

D   E   F

The Slade

Hopgood's Farm

Winchcombe Farm

Sewage Works

Vanners

Woodground Shaw

Lodge Copse

Briff Farm

Upper Common

Miles's Green

Sadgrove Farm

Workhouse Green

4

PEASE HILL

Osgood's Gully

Turner's Green

69

Burden's Heath Plantation

ROUNDFIELD

LITTLE LA

Upper Bucklebury

PH

Bucklebury Common

CARBINSWOOD LA

3

HARTS HILL RD

ROUNDFIELD

LONGGROVE

Wimble's Wood

BROAD LA

Sch
BLACKLANDS

WOODSIDE CL

BERRY'S RD

Tomlins

Hart's Hill

Upper Hartshill Farm

Big Gully

Blacklands Copse

The Grange

Midgham Wood

Hockett Wood

Bucklebury Place

Wootten's

68

Long Grove Copse

Kent's Down Gully

Webb's Farm

Siege Cross Farm

Colthrop Manor

Ouzel Gully

King's Farm

BIRDS LA

2

COX'S LA

Midgham

MUNKLE MARSH

POPLEY PL

ENTERPRISE WAY

Meadowside

Nursery Copse

The Wayback Inn

67

PIPERS CT

Industrial Estate

COLTHROP LA

Westend Farm

B A T H   R D

Coach and Horses (PH)

BRIMPTON RD

A4

The Gables

Colthrop Mill

Colthrop LC

Midgham Marsh

1

Kennet and Avon Canal

Lock

Midgham Lock

Midgham Bridge

River Kennet

River Kennet

66

D   54   E   55   F

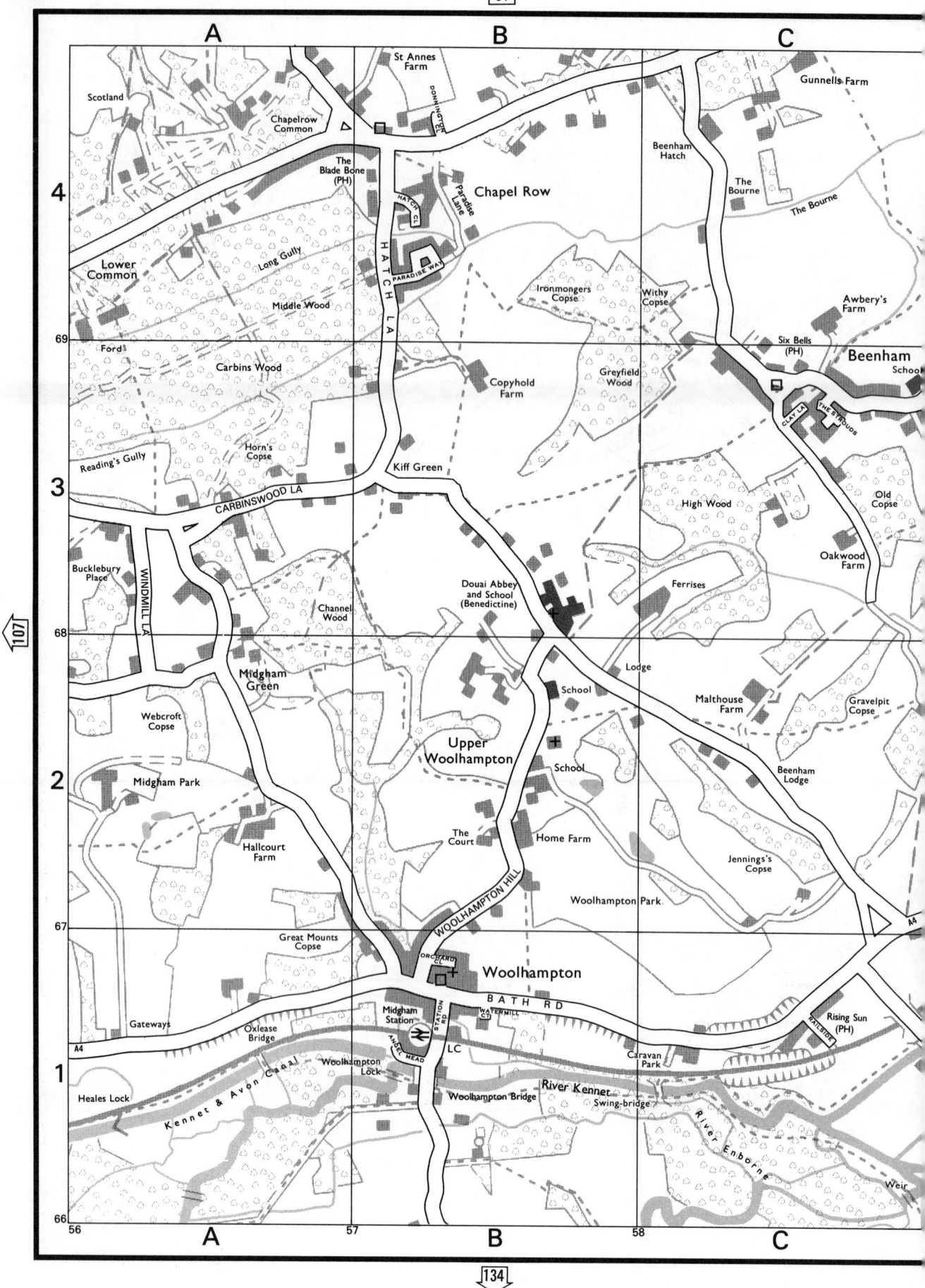

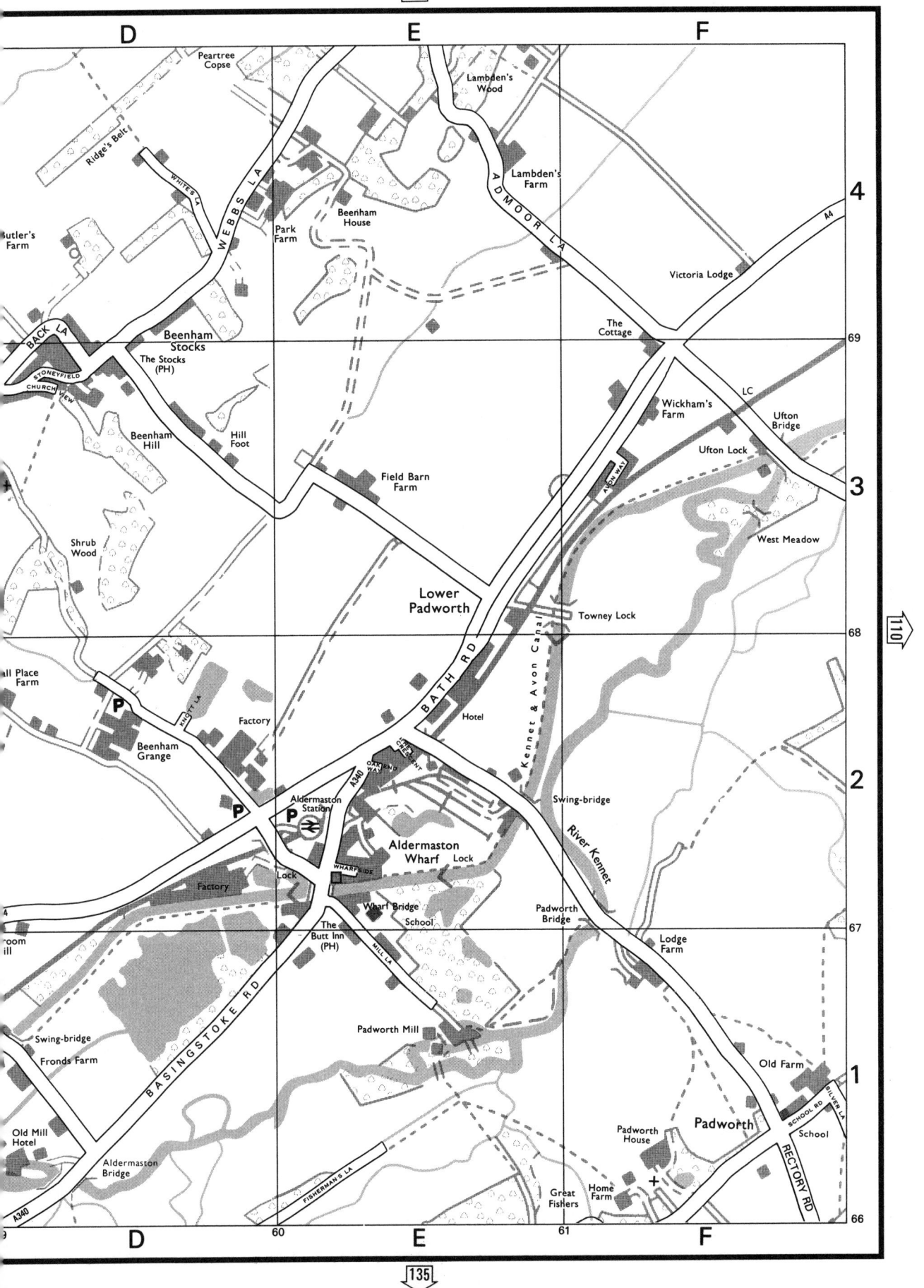

109

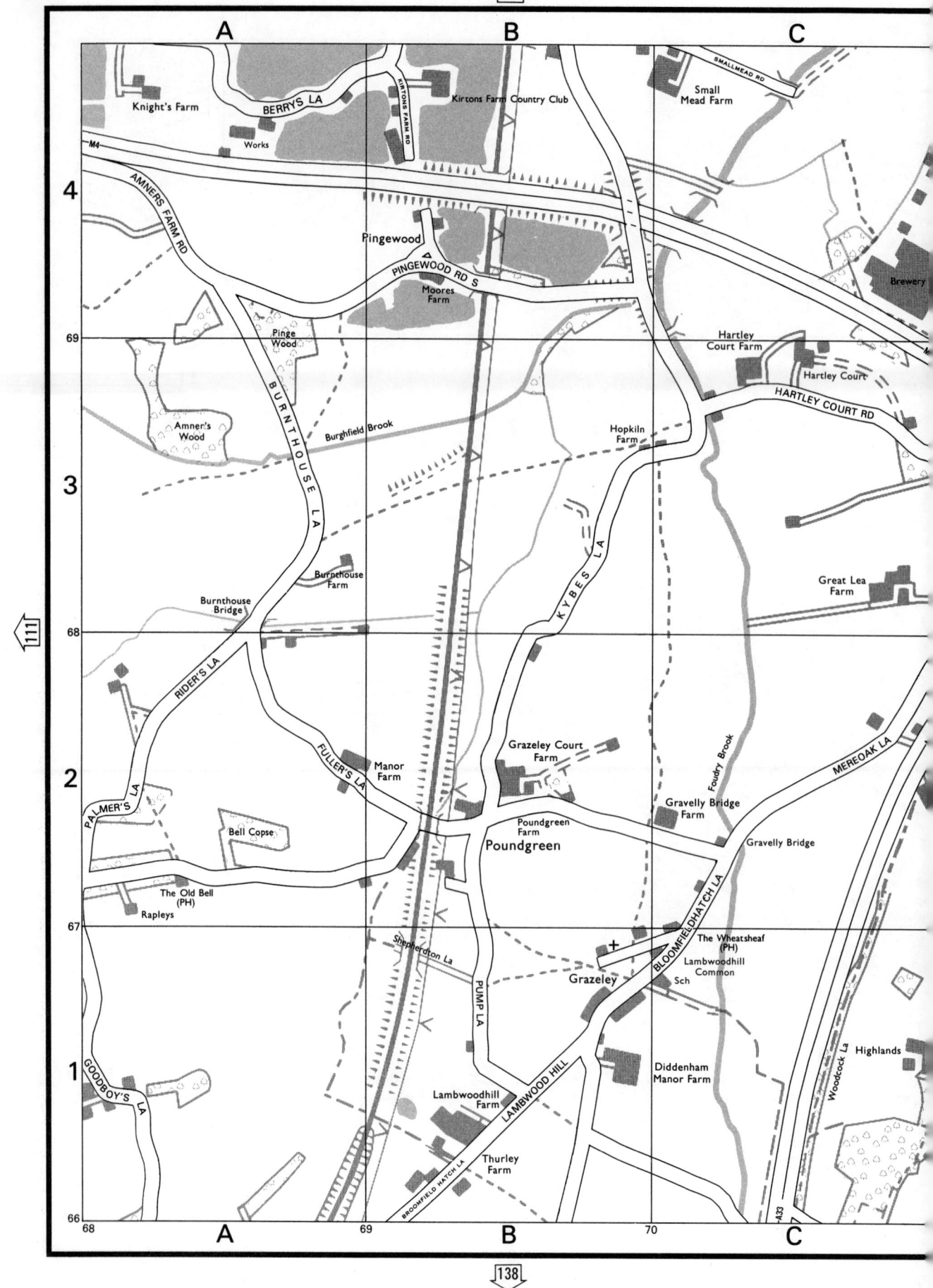

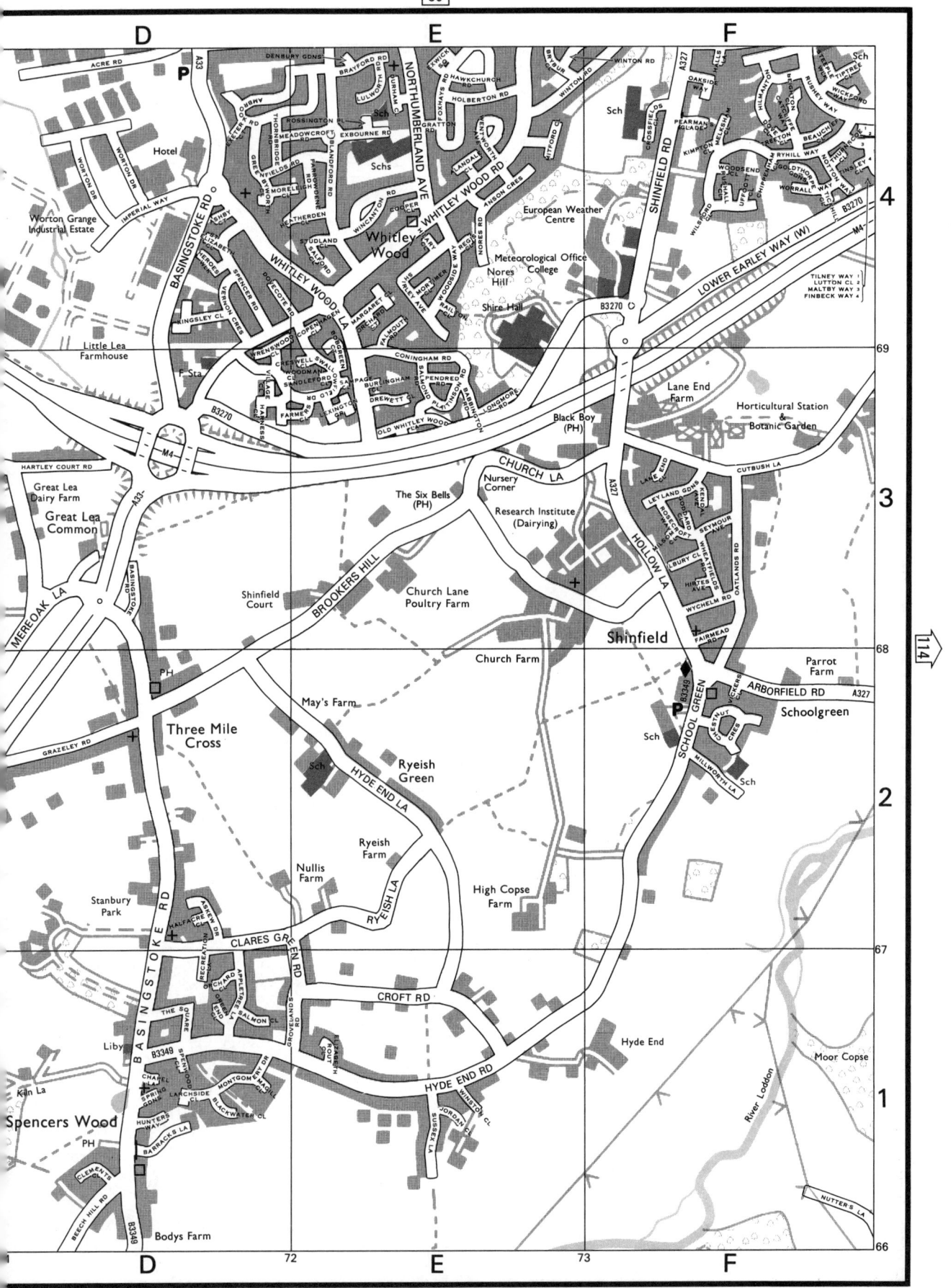

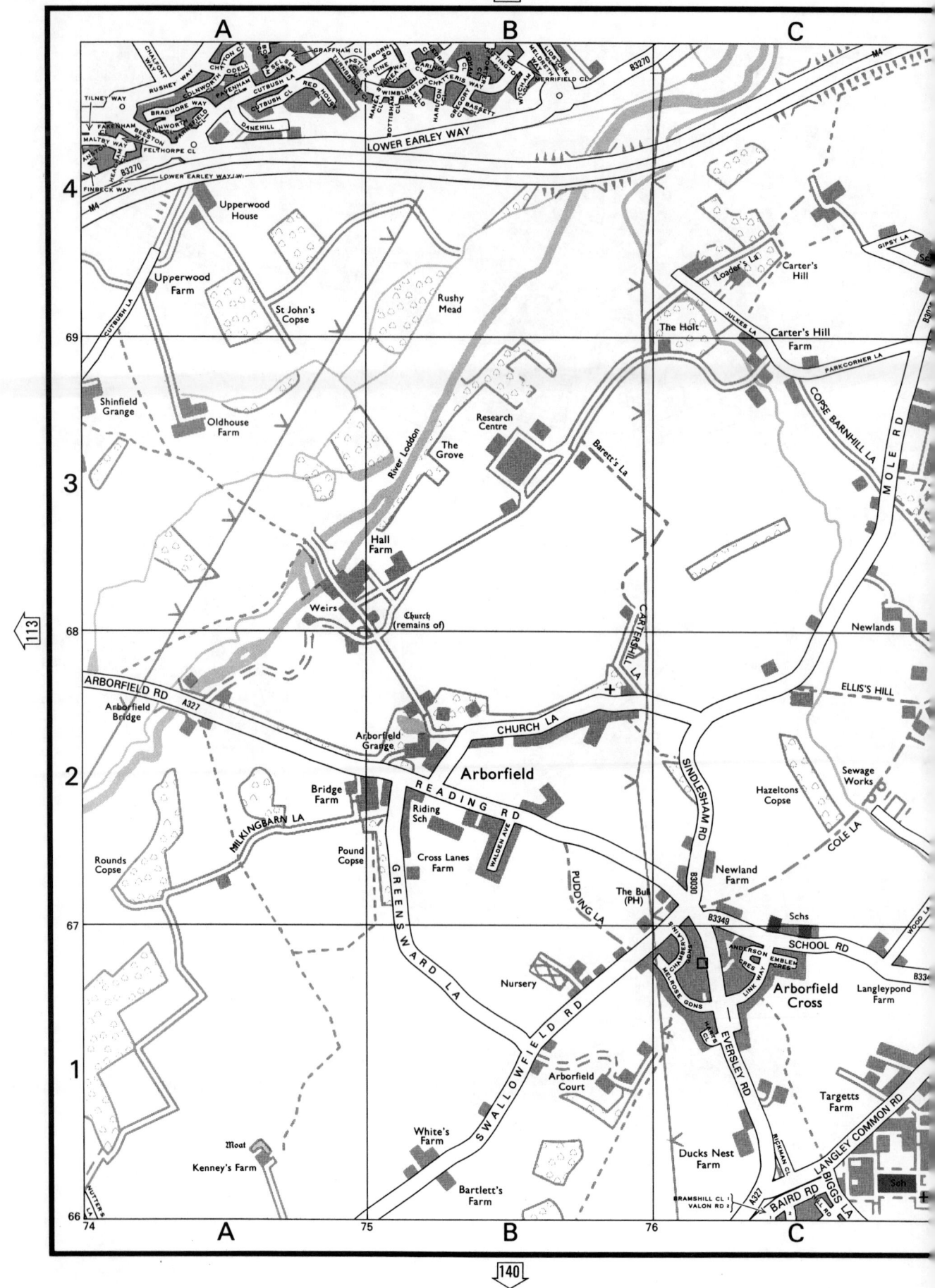

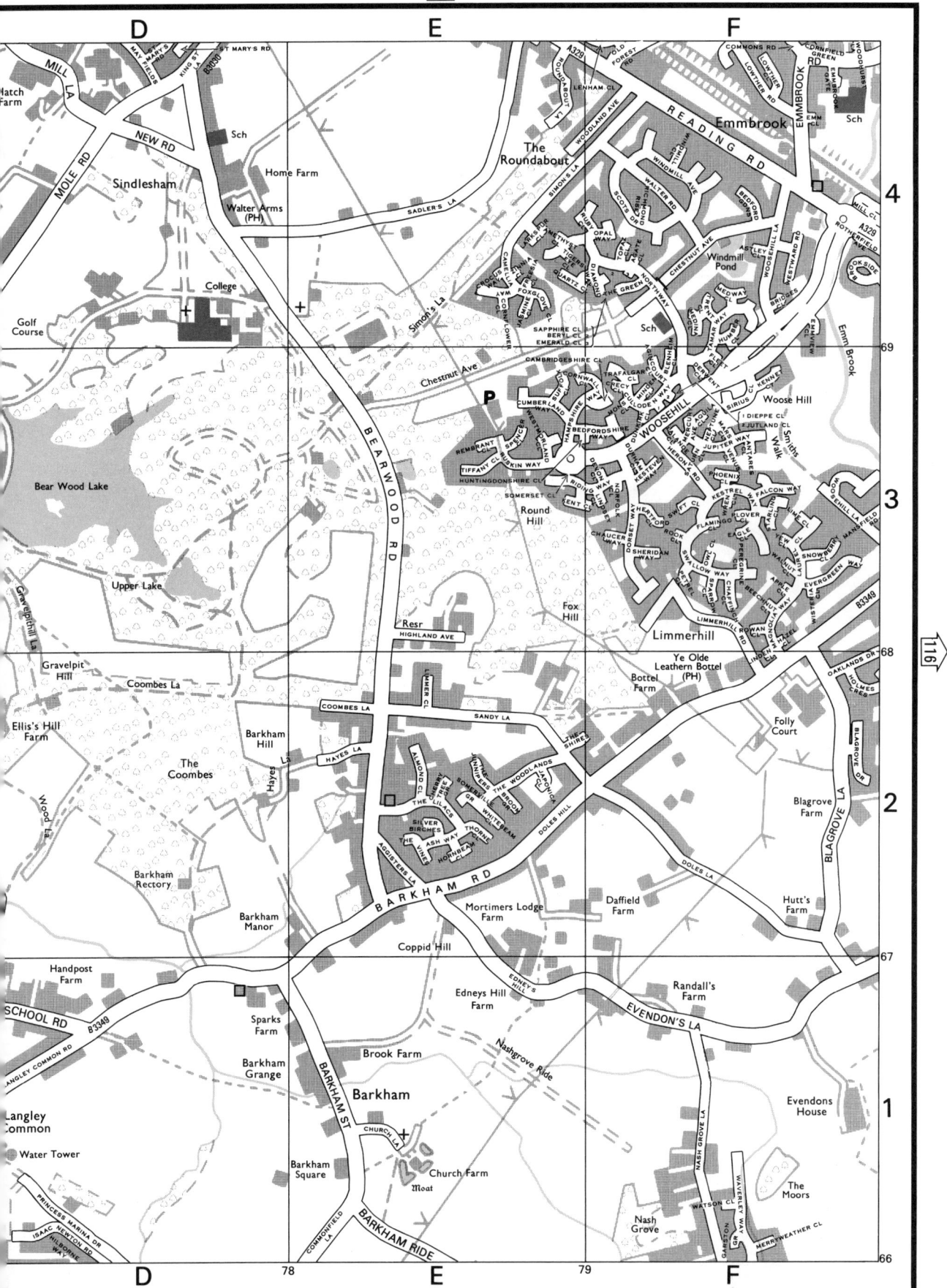

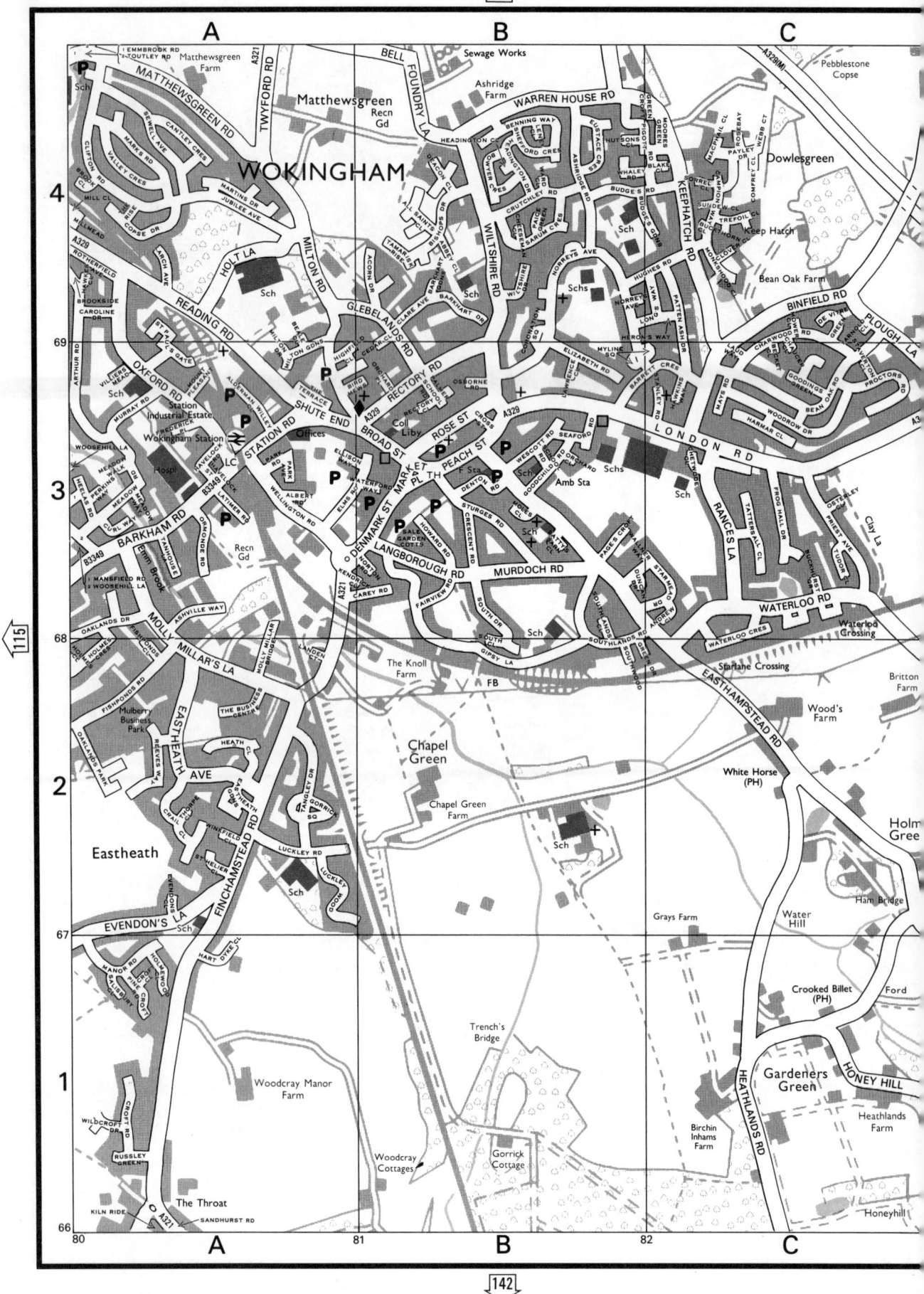

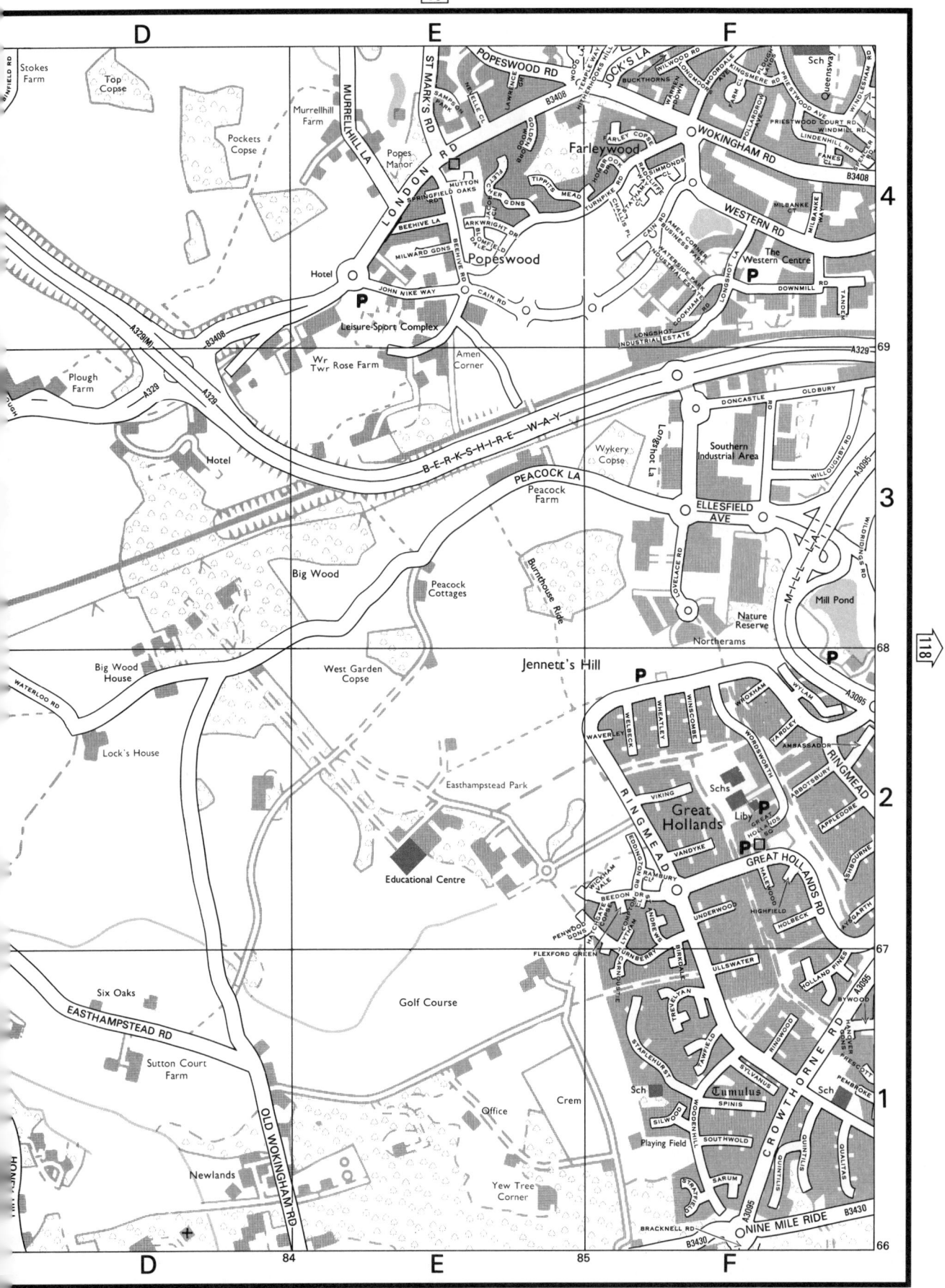

D E F

Stokes Farm

Top Copse

Pockets Copse

MURRELLHILL LA
Murrellhill Farm

ST MARK'S RD

POPESWOOD RD

JOCK'S LA

Buckthorns

Sch

Queensway

WINDLESHAM RD

Farleywood

WOKINGHAM RD
B3408

Popes Manor

SAMPSON PARK

NEVELLE CL

LAWRENCE GRN

WOOD LA

TEMPLE WAY

WILWOOD RD

LONGMOOR LA

MOORDALE

KINGSMERE

PRIESTWOOD AVE

PRIESTWOOD COURT RD

LINDENHILL RD

WINDMILL RD

FANES

4

LONDON RD

Springfield Oaks

BEEHIVE LA

Popeswood

GOLDEN ORB

FLEETS HILL

TIPPITS MEAD

FARLEY COPSE

HOGBROOK

TURNPIKE RD

SIMMONDS

RECTORY

CHALIS PL

AMEN CORNER

Milward Gdns

BEEHIVE RD

WESTERN RD

MILBANKE CT

MILBANKE WA

Hotel

P

JOHN NIKE WAY

CAIN RD

The Western Centre

LONGSHOT LA

P

DOWNMILL RD

TANDEM

Leisure Sport Complex

Wr Twr Rose Farm

Amen Corner

COOKHAM RD

LONGSHOT INDUSTRIAL ESTATE

A329

69

Plough Farm

A329

A329

B3408

BERKSHIRE WAY

Wykery Copse

Southern Industrial Area

DONCASTLE RD

OLDBURY

WILLOUGHBY RD

A3095

Hotel

PEACOCK LA

Peacock Farm

Longshot La

ELLESSFIELD AVE

MILL LANE

WILDRIDINGS RD

3

Big Wood

Peacock Cottages

Burndhouse Ride

COVELACE RD

Nature Reserve

Mill Pond

Northerams

68

Big Wood House

WATERLOO RD

West Garden Copse

Jennett's Hill

P

WOXHAM

WYLAM

A3095

RINGMEAD

118

Lock's House

Easthampstead Park

WAVERLEY

WELBECK

WHEATLEY

WINSCOMBE

VIKING

Schs

Great Hollands

Liby

WORDSWORTH

YARDLEY

ABBOTSBURY

AMBASSADOR

APPLEDORE

ASHBOURNE

P

P

2

RINGMEAD

Educational Centre

WICKHAM VALE

EDDINGTON

VANDYKE

RAMBURY

GREAT HOLLANDS

GREAT HOLLANDS RD

HALLWOOD

HIGHFIELD

HOLBECK

AXGARTH

BEEDON DR

ANDREWS

UNDERWOOD

67

PENWOOD GDNS

FLEXFORD GREEN

HATCHGATE

CHARLTON

TURNBERRY

BIRKDALE

CARNOUSTIE

ULLSWATER

HOLLAND PINES

BYWOOD

A3095

Six Oaks

EASTHAMPSTEAD RD

Golf Course

TREVELYAN

TANFIELD

RINGWOOD

CROWTHORNE RD

HANOVER GDNS

PRESCOTT

1

Sutton Court Farm

Office

Crem

Sch

Tumulus

SPINIS

SARUM

Sch

PEMBROKE

QUALITAS

OLD WOKINGHAM RD

STAPLEHURST

SYLVANUS

SILWOOD

WOODENHILL

SOUTHWOLD

QUINTILIS

Newlands

Playing Field

Yew Tree Corner

BRACKNELL RD

NINE MILE RIDE

B3430

B3430

SARAFIELD

A3095

66

D 84 E 85 F

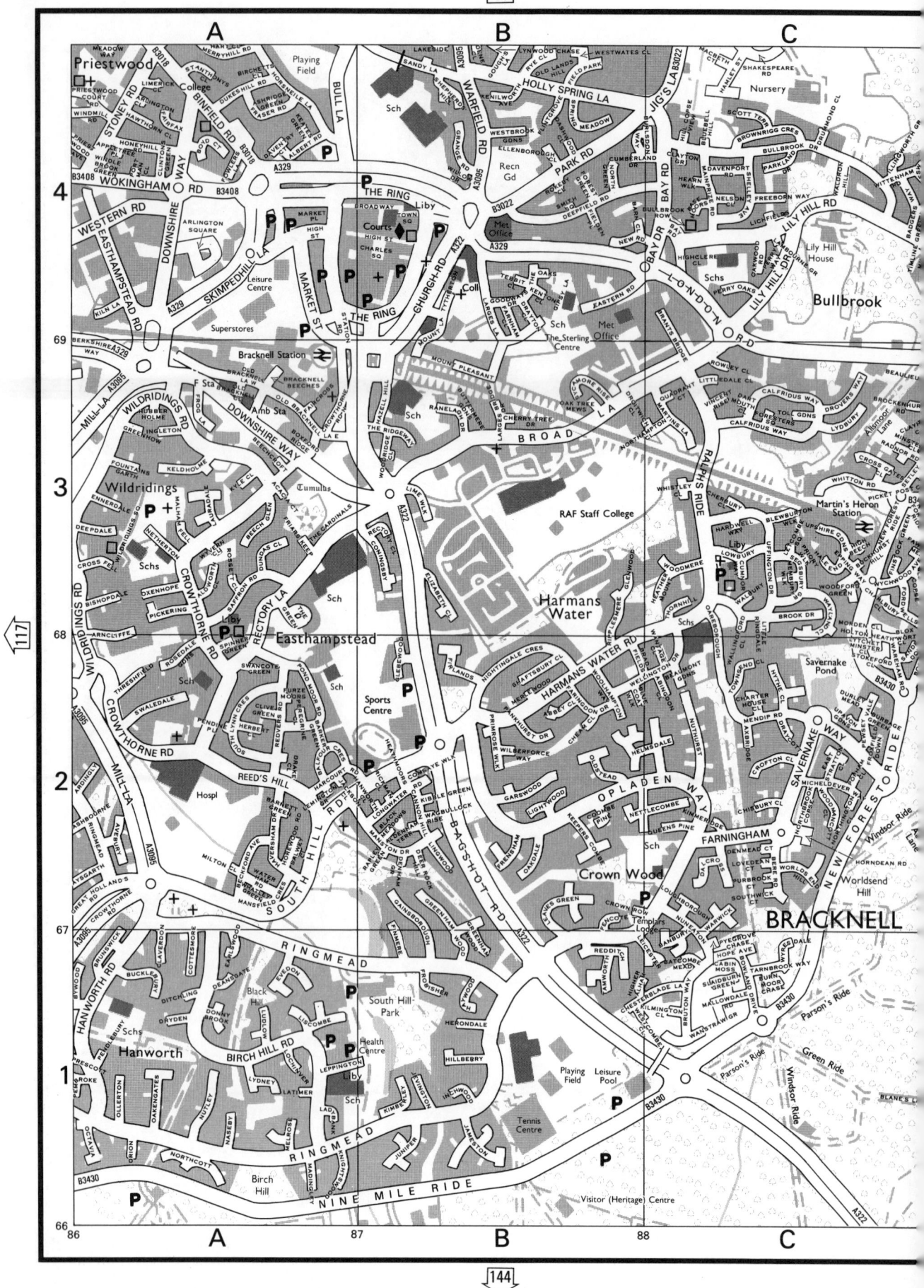

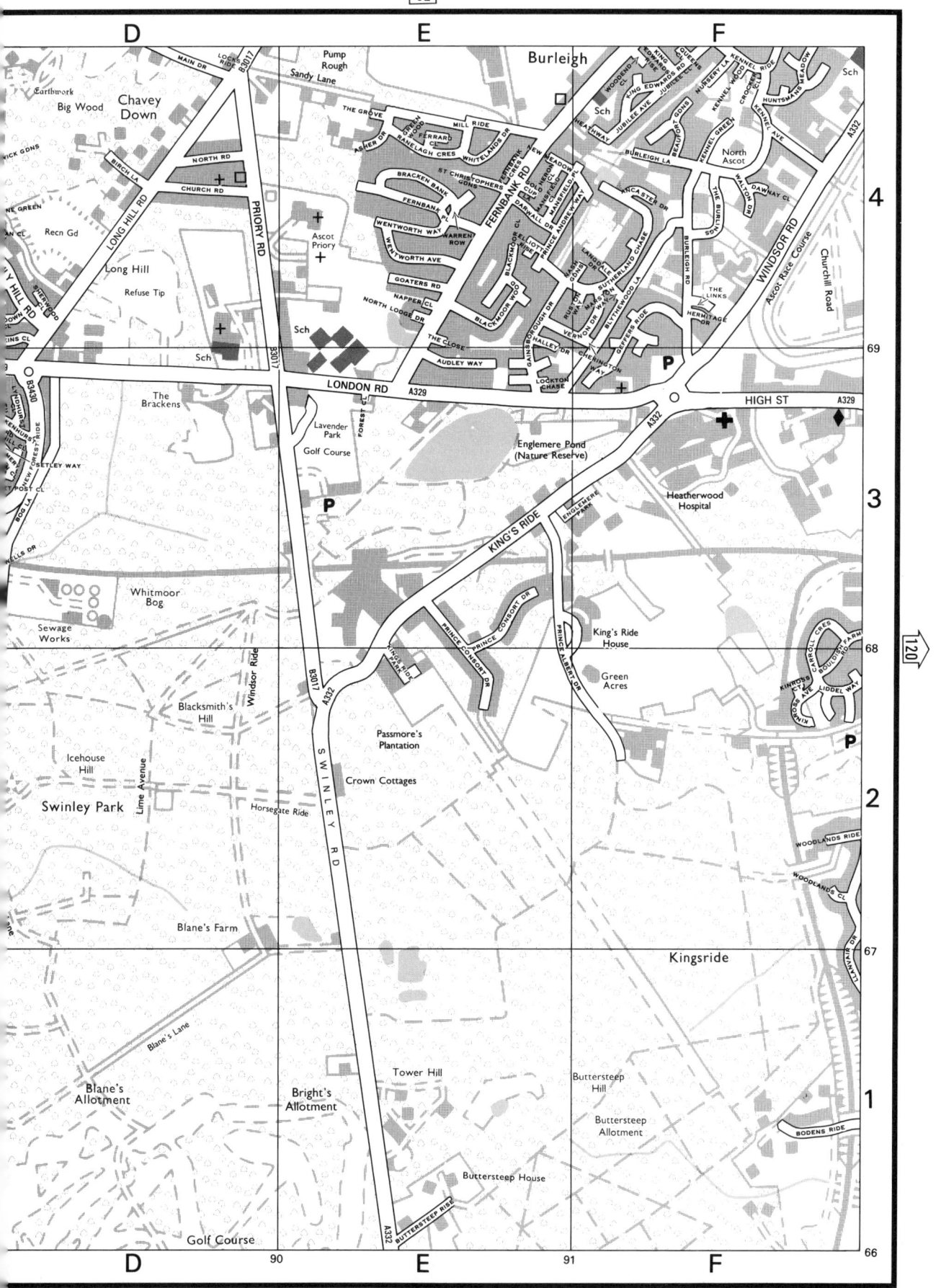

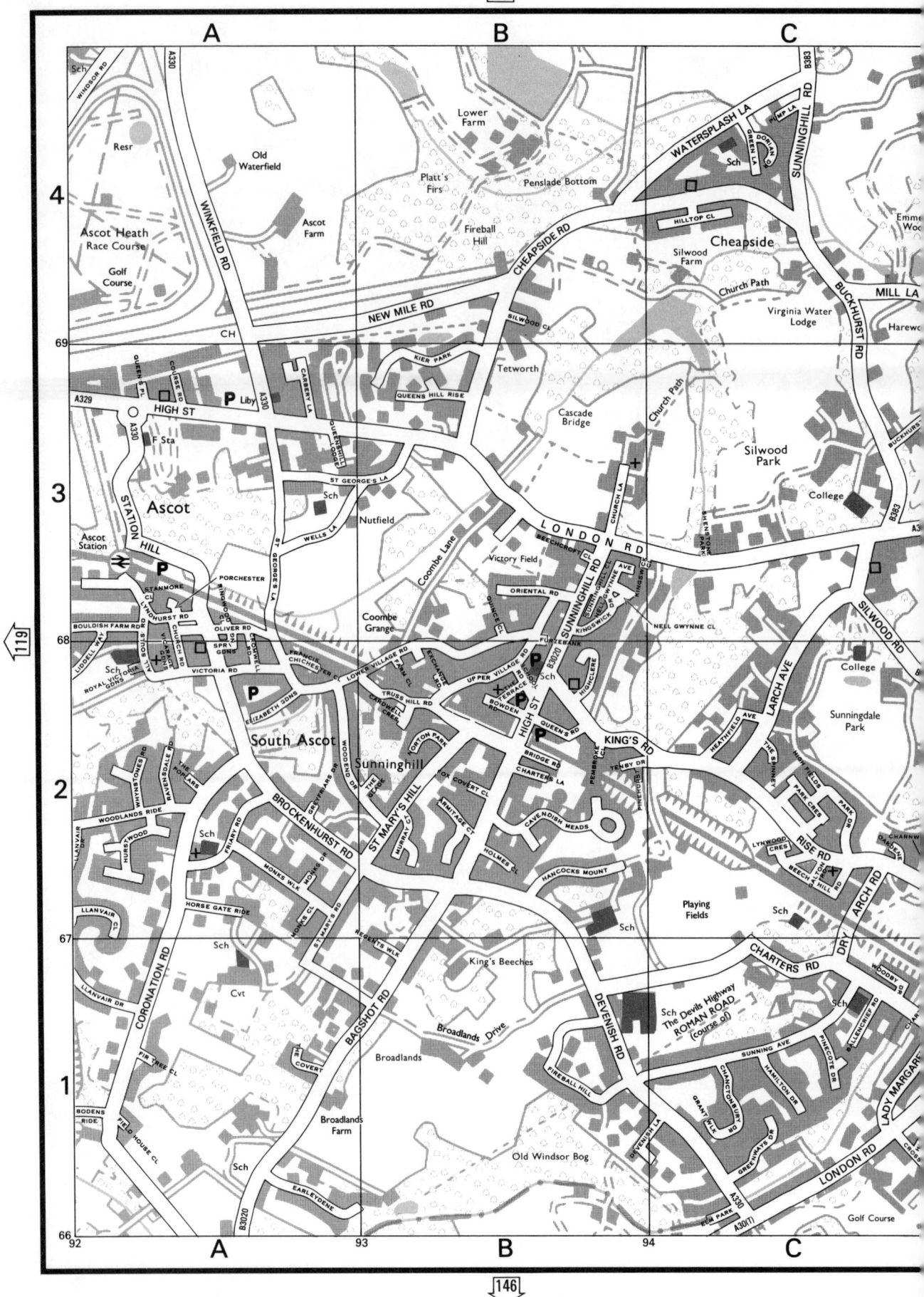

119

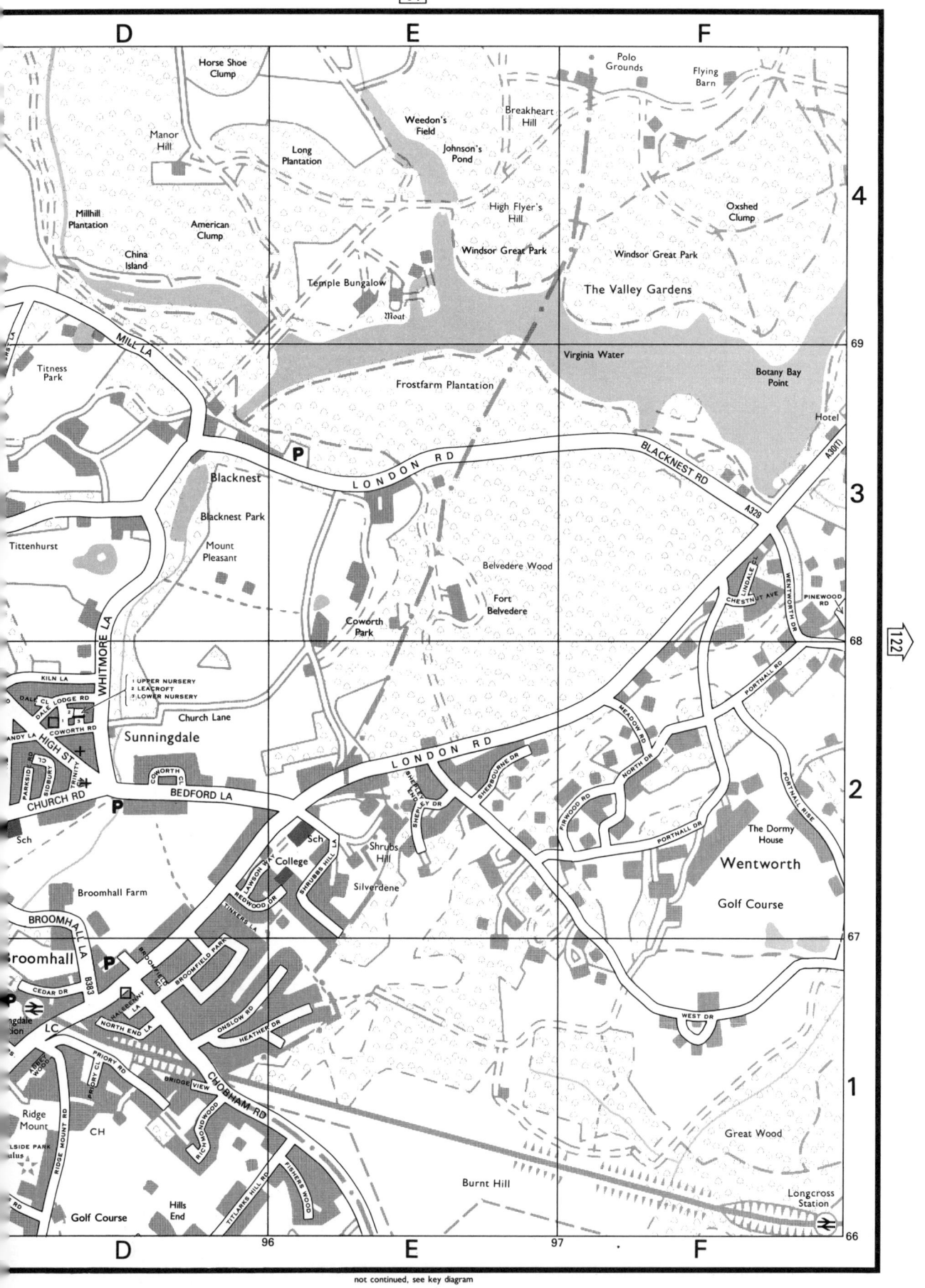

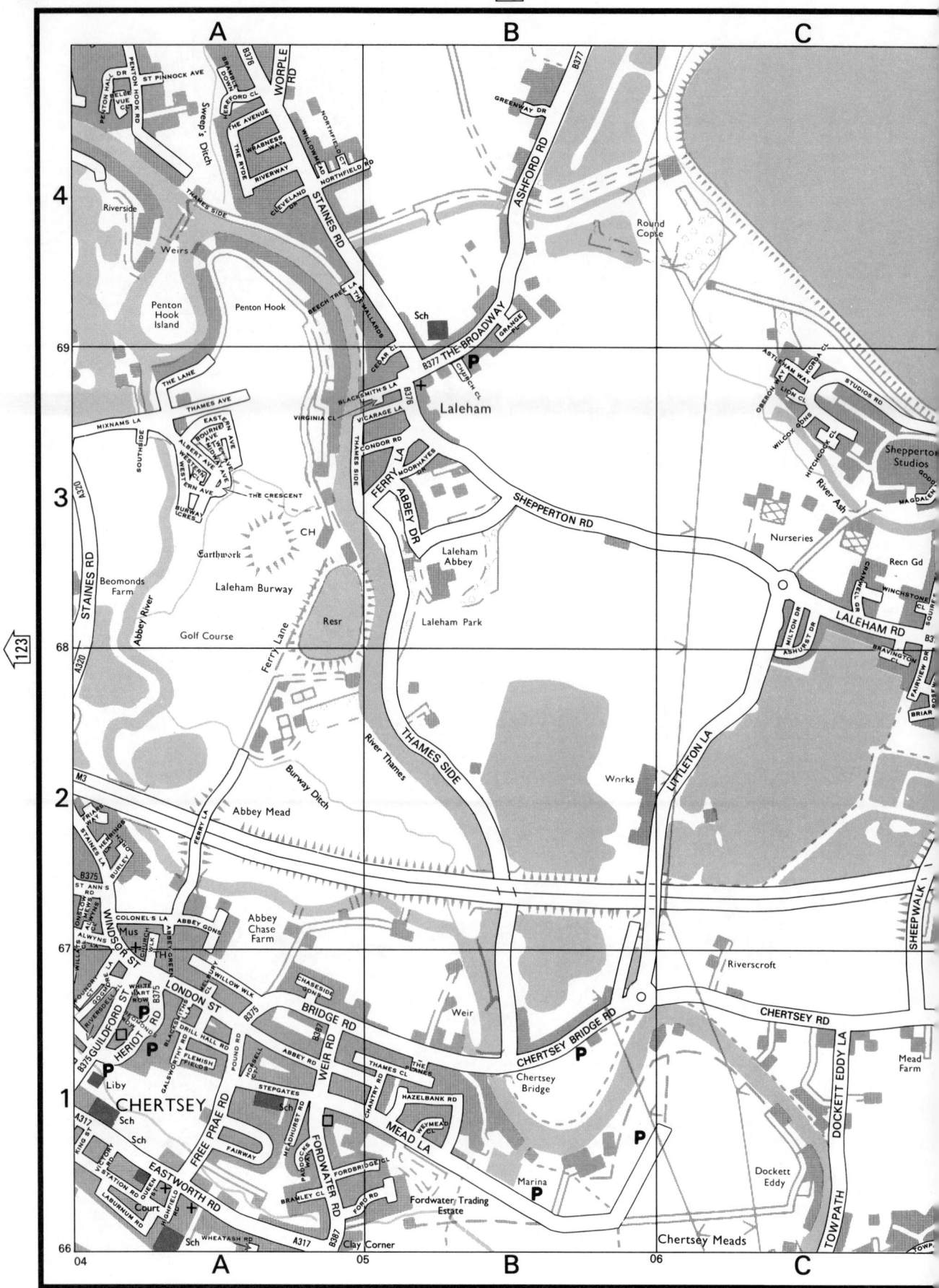

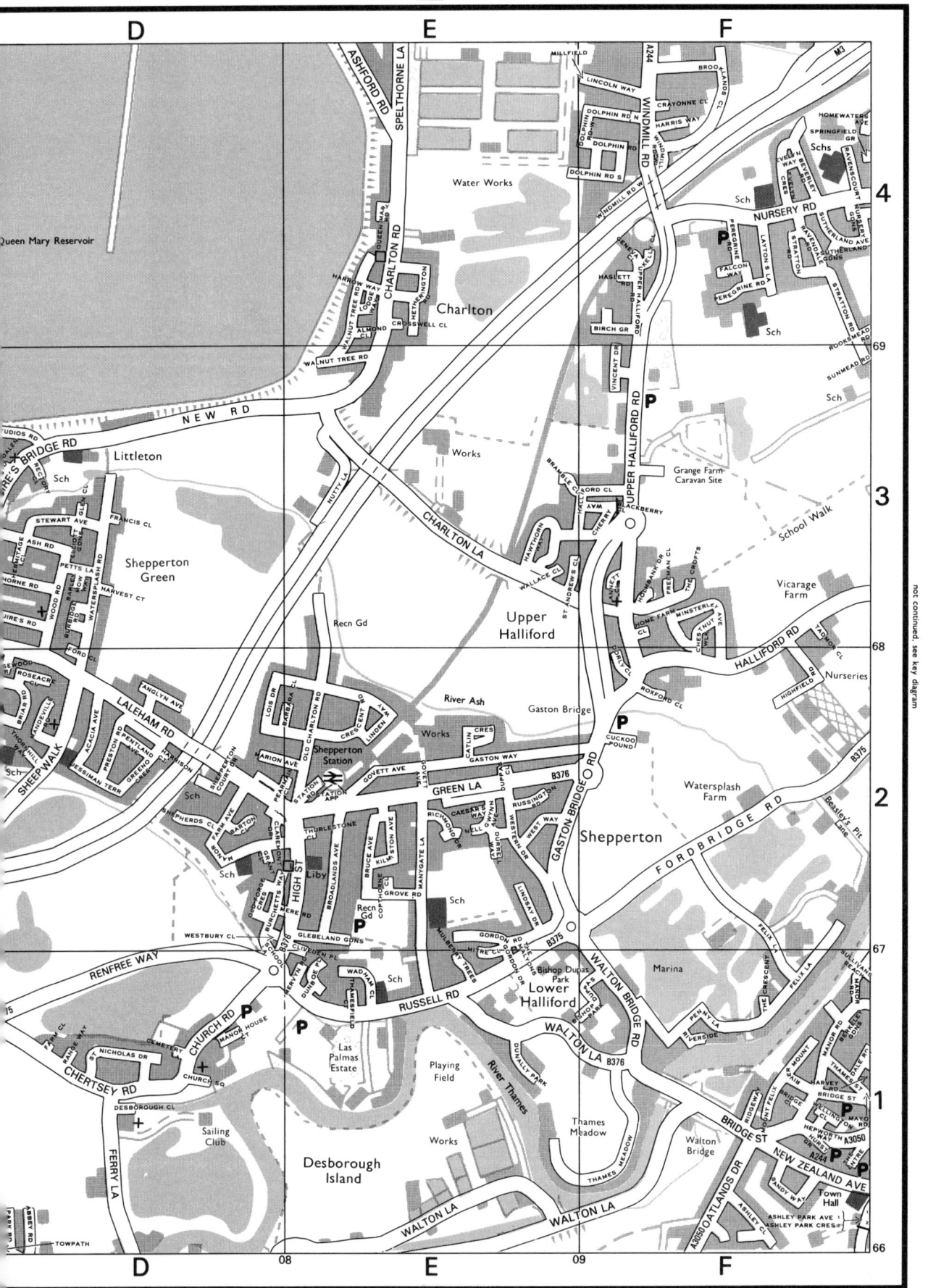

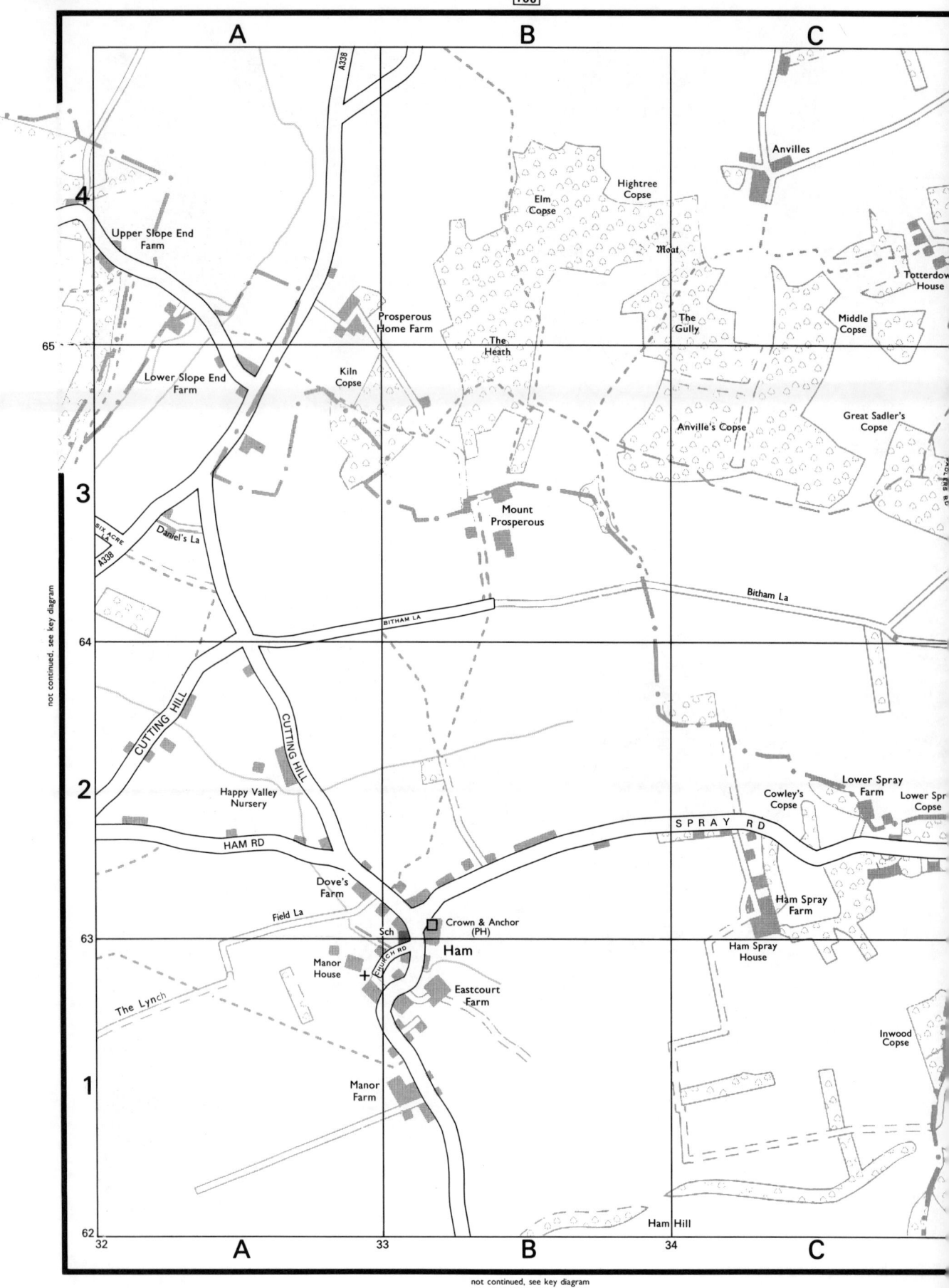

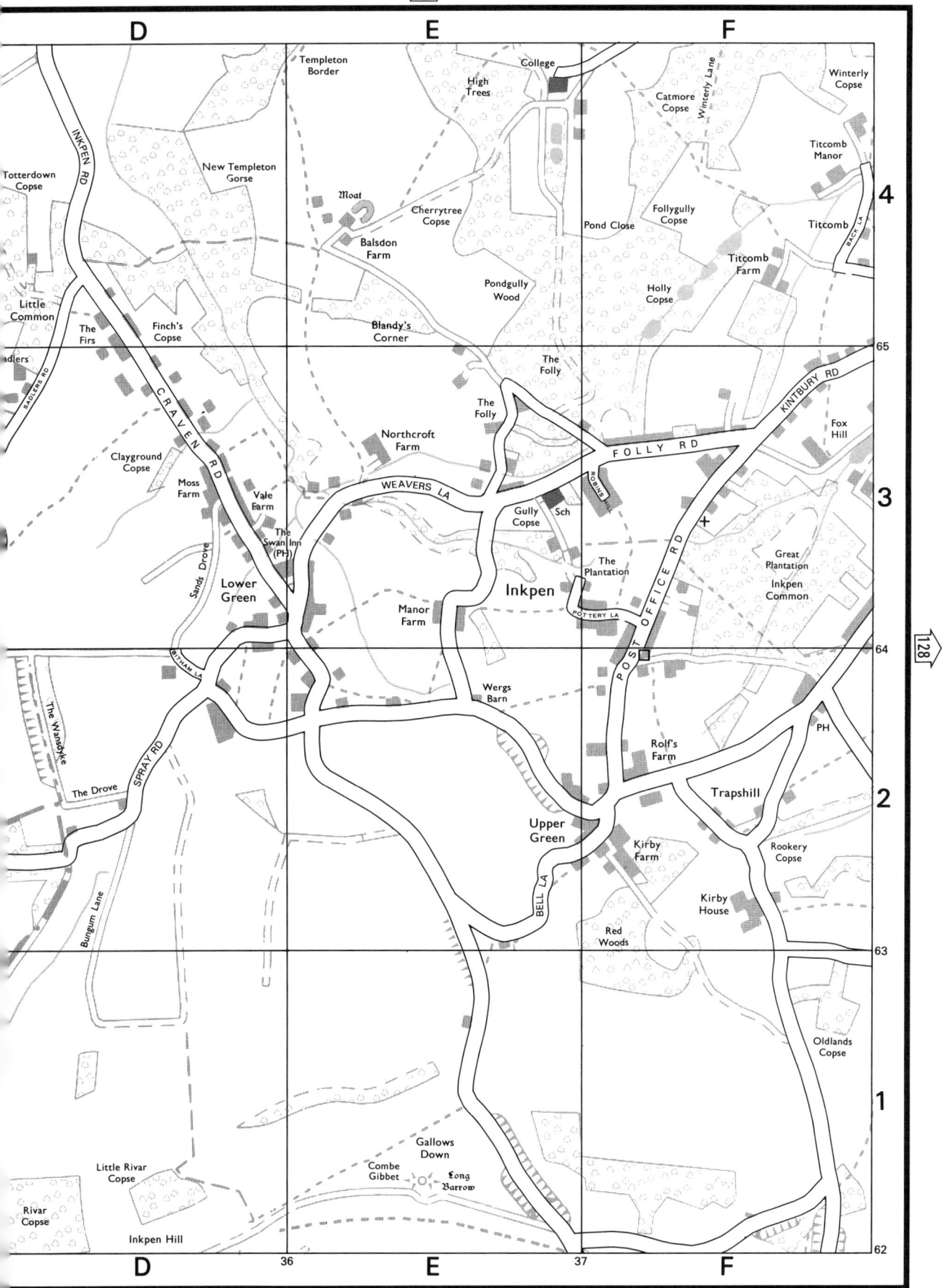

D   E   F

Templeton Border

College

High Trees

Winterly Lane

Catmore Copse

Winterly Copse

Totterdown Copse

INKPEN RD

New Templeton Gorse

Moat

Cherrytree Copse

Pond Close

Follygully Copse

Titcomb Manor

4

BACK LA

Titcomb

Balsdon Farm

Pondgully Wood

Titcomb Farm

Little Common

Blandy's Corner

Holly Copse

The Firs

Finch's Copse

The Folly

65

SADLERS RD

adlers

CRAVEN RD

Clayground Copse

Northcroft Farm

The Folly

The Folly

FOLLY RD

KINTBURY RD

Fox Hill

Moss Farm

Vale Farm

WEAVERS LA

Gully Copse

ROBINS Hill

Sch

3

The Swan Inn (PH)

Sands Drove

Lower Green

Manor Farm

Inkpen

The Plantation

POTTERY LA

POST OFFICE RD

Great Plantation

Inkpen Common

+

BITHAM LA

Wergs Barn

64

128

The Wansdyke

SPRAY RD

The Drove

Rolf's Farm

PH

Trapshill

2

Bungum Lane

Upper Green

BELL LA

Kirby Farm

Kirby House

Rookery Copse

Red Woods

63

Oldlands Copse

1

Little Rivar Copse

Gallows Down

Combe Gibbet

Long Barrow

Rivar Copse

Inkpen Hill

62

D   36   E   37   F

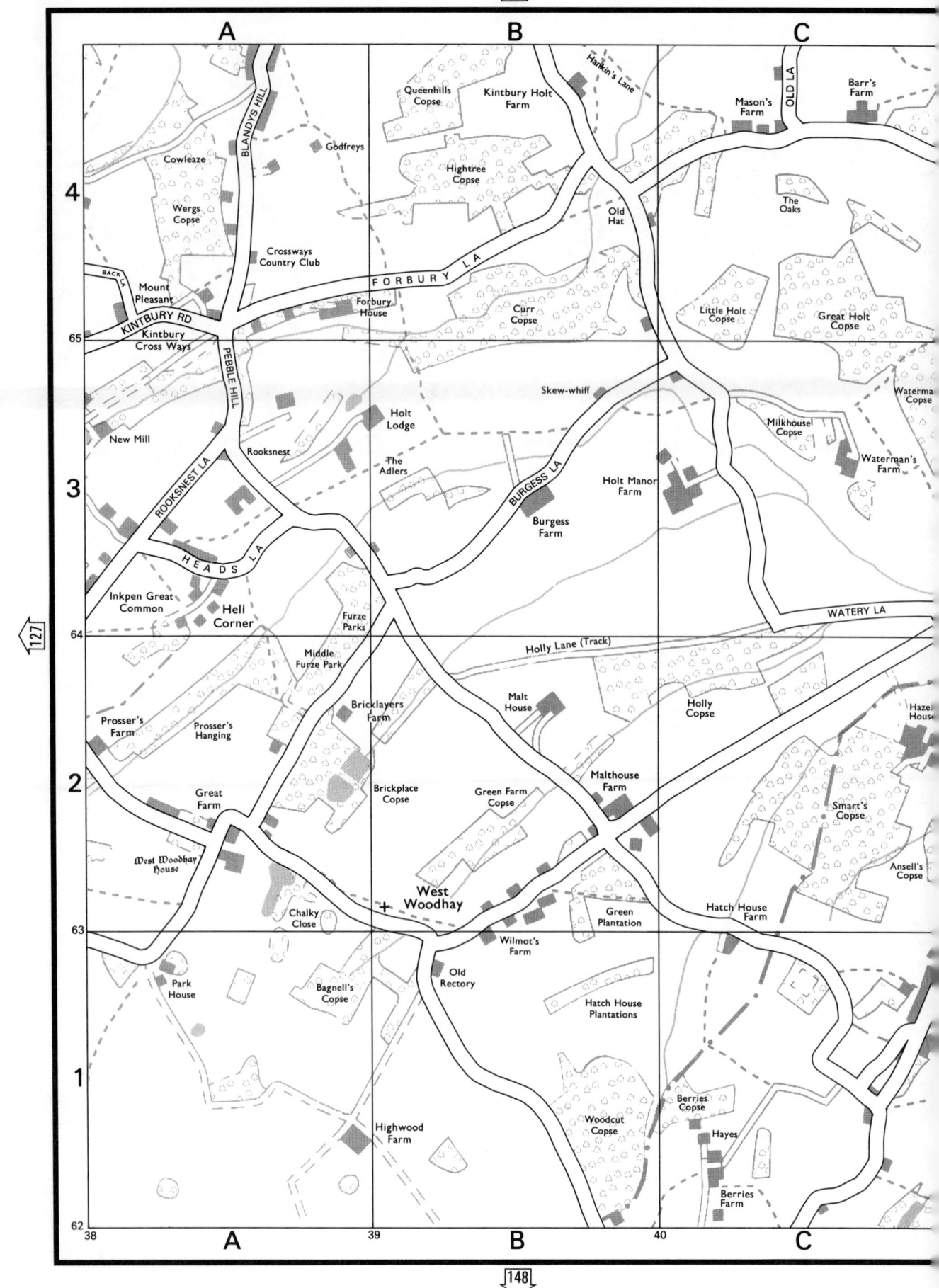

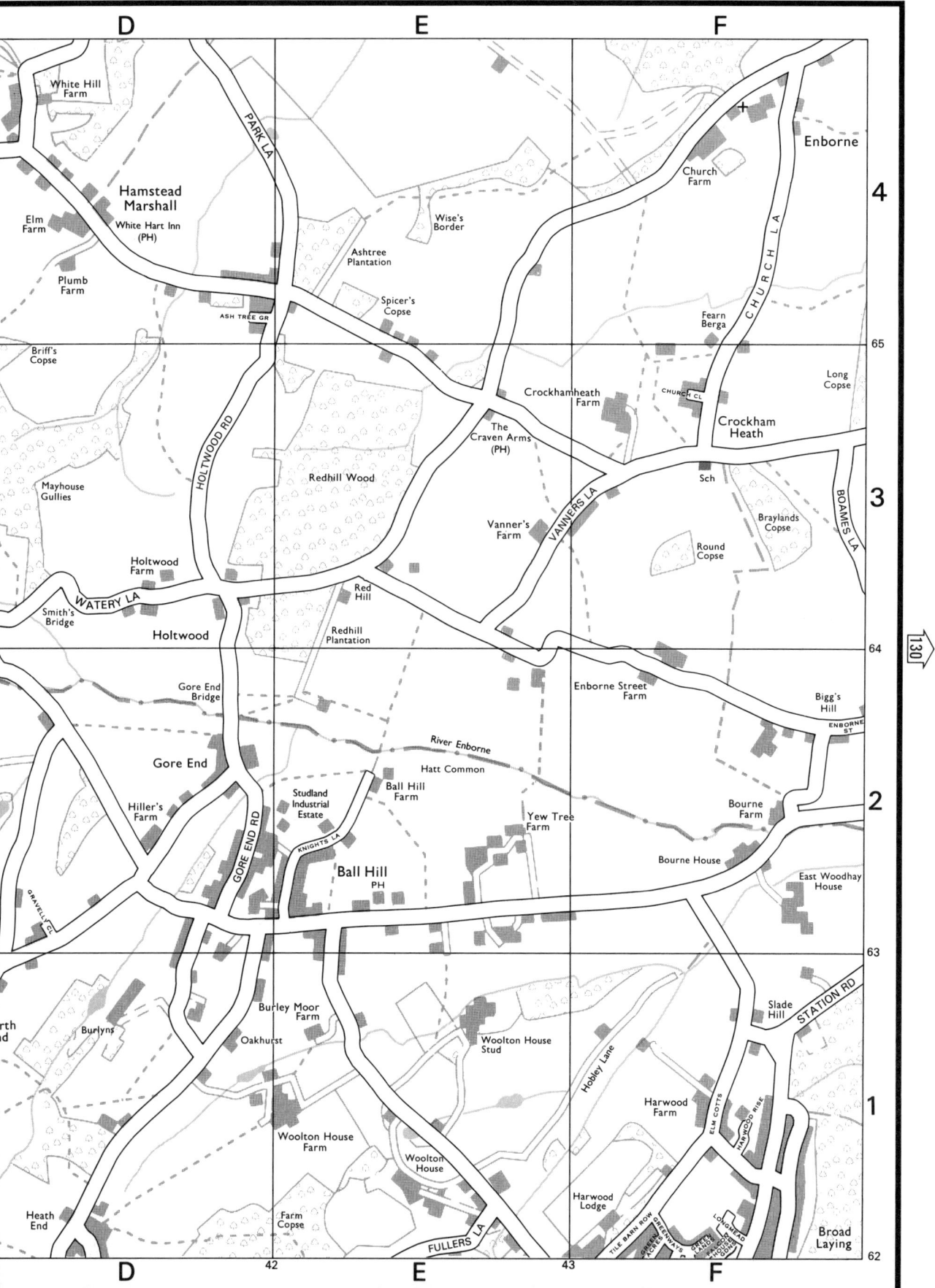

D   E   F

White Hill Farm

Hamstead Marshall

White Hart Inn (PH)

Elm Farm

Plumb Farm

PARK LA

ASH TREE GR

Ashtree Plantation

Wise's Border

Spicer's Copse

Church Farm

Enborne

4

Fearn Berga

CHURCH LA

Briff's Copse

65

Crockhamheath Farm

CHURCH CL

Long Copse

Crockham Heath

HOLTWOOD RD

Mayhouse Gullies

Redhill Wood

The Craven Arms (PH)

Vanner's Farm

VANNERS LA

Sch

Round Copse

Braylands Copse

BOAMES LA

3

Holtwood Farm

WATERY LA

Smith's Bridge

Holtwood

Red Hill

Redhill Plantation

64

130

Gore End Bridge

Enborne Street Farm

Bigg's Hill

ENBORNE ST

Gore End

Hiller's Farm

GORE END RD

GRAVELLY CL

Studland Industrial Estate

KNIGHTS LA

Ball Hill

PH

River Enborne

Hatt Common

Ball Hill Farm

Yew Tree Farm

Bourne House

Bourne Farm

East Woodhay House

2

63

Burley Moor Farm

Oakhurst

Burlyns

rth nd

Woolton House Stud

Hobley Lane

Slade Hill

STATION RD

Harwood Farm

ELM COTTS

HARWOOD RISE

1

Woolton House Farm

Woolton House

Harwood Lodge

TILE BARN ROW
GREENWAYS
DRIVEWAYS C
ACRES E
CARTER
LONGMEAD
GREEN
PADDOCK
CLOSE

Broad Laying

Heath End

Farm Copse

FULLERS LA

62

D   42   E   43   F

not continued, see key diagram

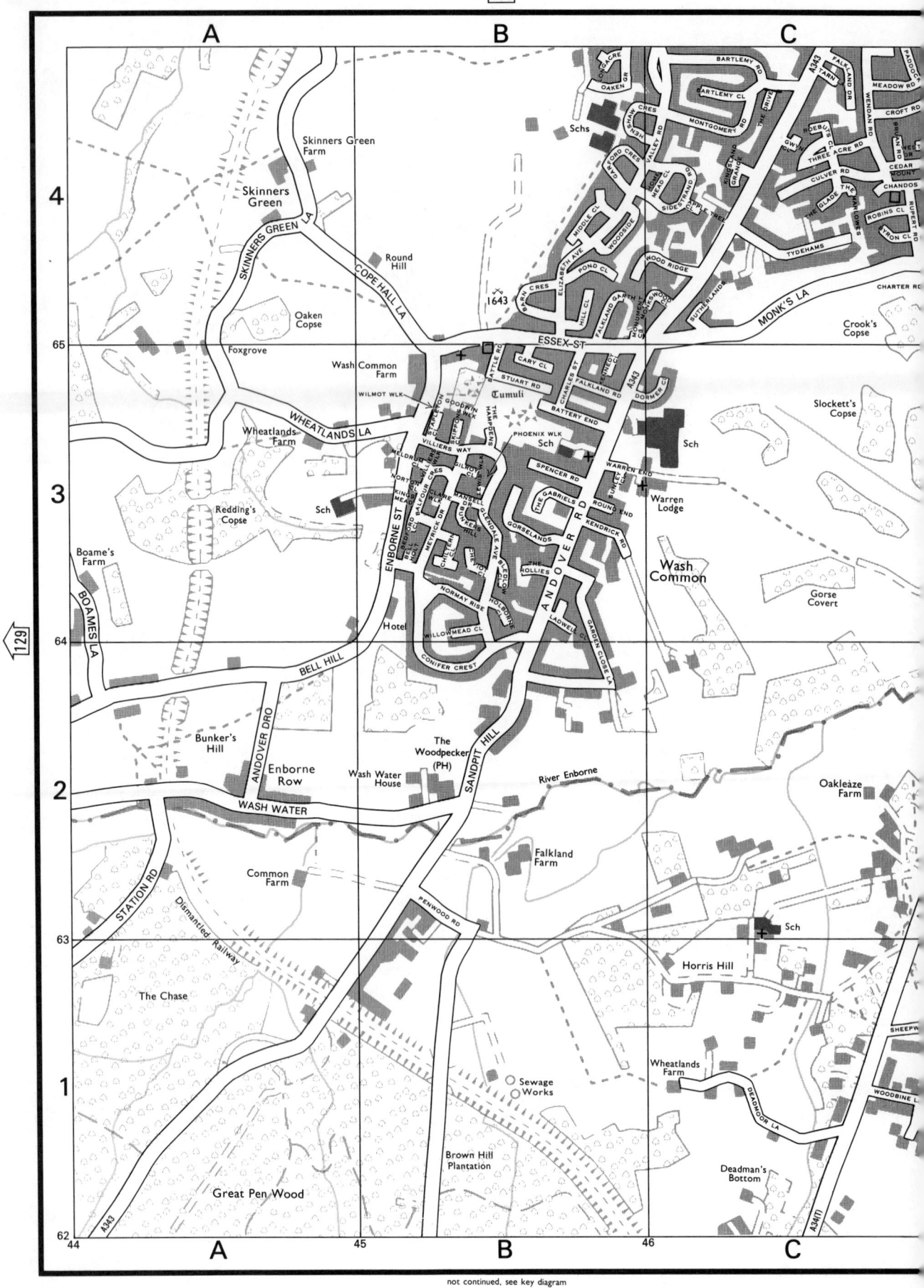

105

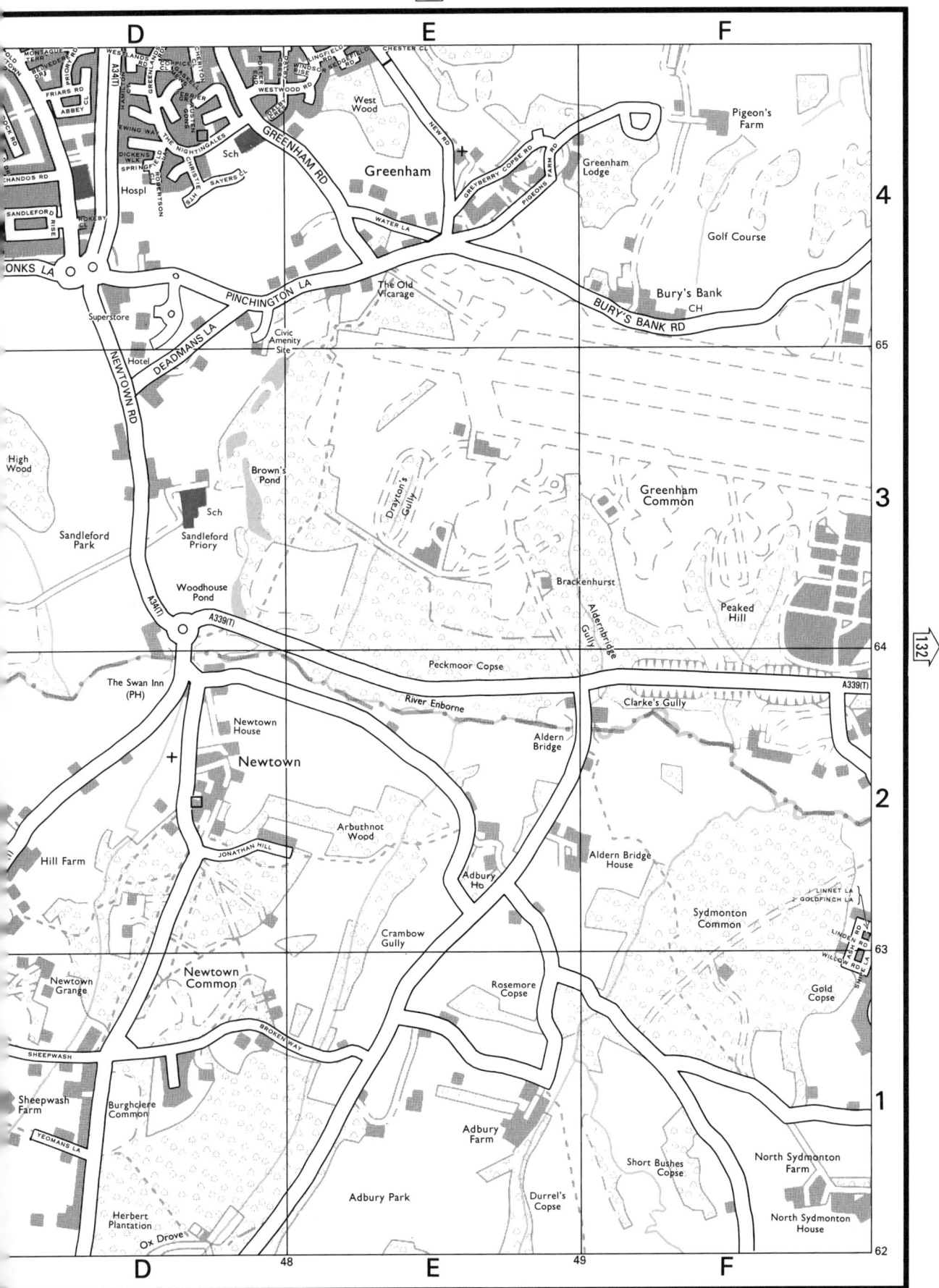

132

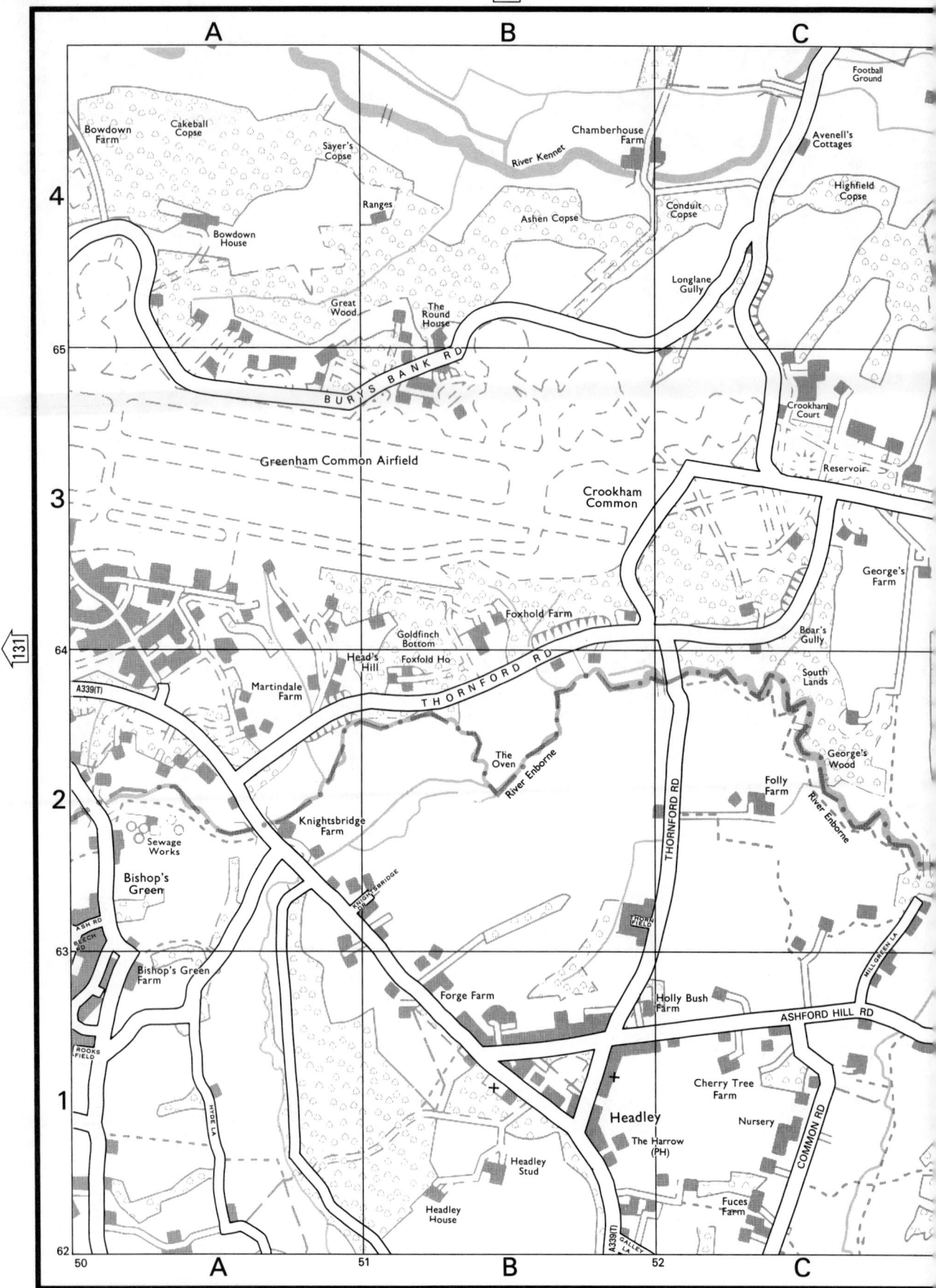

A   **B**   **C**

Football
Ground

Bowdown
Farm

Cakeball
Copse

Sayer's
Copse

Chamberhouse
Farm

River Kennet

Avenell's
Cottages

4

Ranges

Ashen Copse

Conduit
Copse

Highfield
Copse

Bowdown
House

Great
Wood

The
Round
House

Longlane
Gully

65

BURYS BANK RD

Crookham
Court

Greenham Common Airfield

Crookham
Common

Reservoir

3

George's
Farm

Foxhold Farm

Boar's
Gully

64

Goldfinch
Bottom

Head's
Hill

Foxfold Ho

THORNFORD RD

South
Lands

A339(T)

Martindale
Farm

George's
Wood

The
Oven

River Enborne

Folly
Farm

River Enborne

2

Knightsbridge
Farm

THORNFORD RD

Sewage
Works

Bishop's
Green

KNIGHTSBRIDGE

THORN
FIELD

ASH RD

BEECH
RD

63

Bishop's Green
Farm

Forge Farm

Holly Bush
Farm

ASHFORD HILL RD

MILL GREEN LA

ROOKS
FIELD

HYDE LA

+

+

Cherry Tree
Farm

COMMON RD

1

Headley

Nursery

The Harrow
(PH)

Headley
Stud

Fuces
Farm

Headley
House

A339(T)

GALLEY
LA

62

50   51   52

A   **B**   **C**

not continued, see key diagram

107

D   E   F

River Kennet
Crookham Manor

Prior's Moor Ditch

Brimpton Mill

King's Bridge

Roman Road (course of)

4

BRIMPTON RD

Waterside Copse

Hanging Lands Gully

The Lynch

Manor Farm

New Gully

Bond's Gully

East Field Copse

65

Limberlost Farm

Manor Lane

Stone House

Burnell's Farm

ghfield m

White Lodge

Holdaway's Farm

CHURCH ST

ENBORNE WAY

BANNISTER PL

Brimpton

Sch

3

The Travellers Friend (PH)

Caravan Park

Crookham

Manor Farm

Upper Hyde End Farm

HYDE END LA

Little Park House

Little Park Farm

64

Oak Cottage

134

Kenton's Wood

Park Copse

Hyde End Wood

Hyde End

Hyde End Farm

2

River Enborne

Park Gully Bridge

Park Lane

Flaggy Copse

River Enborne

HOCKFORD LA

Stonylands Copse

Riddings Farm

WOODHOUSE LA

Oxford Bridge

63

ASHFORD HILL RD

Goose Hill

RIDDINGS LA

Stark House Farm

Woodhouse Farm

Hillhouse Lane

The Drove

Woodlands Farm

1

B3051

Huntsmoor Hill

Brook Farm

OLD LA

The Ship (PH)

HILLHOUSE

Old Farm

Chippings Gully

Ashford Hill

CHAPEL L

Sch

B3051

62

D   54   E   55   F

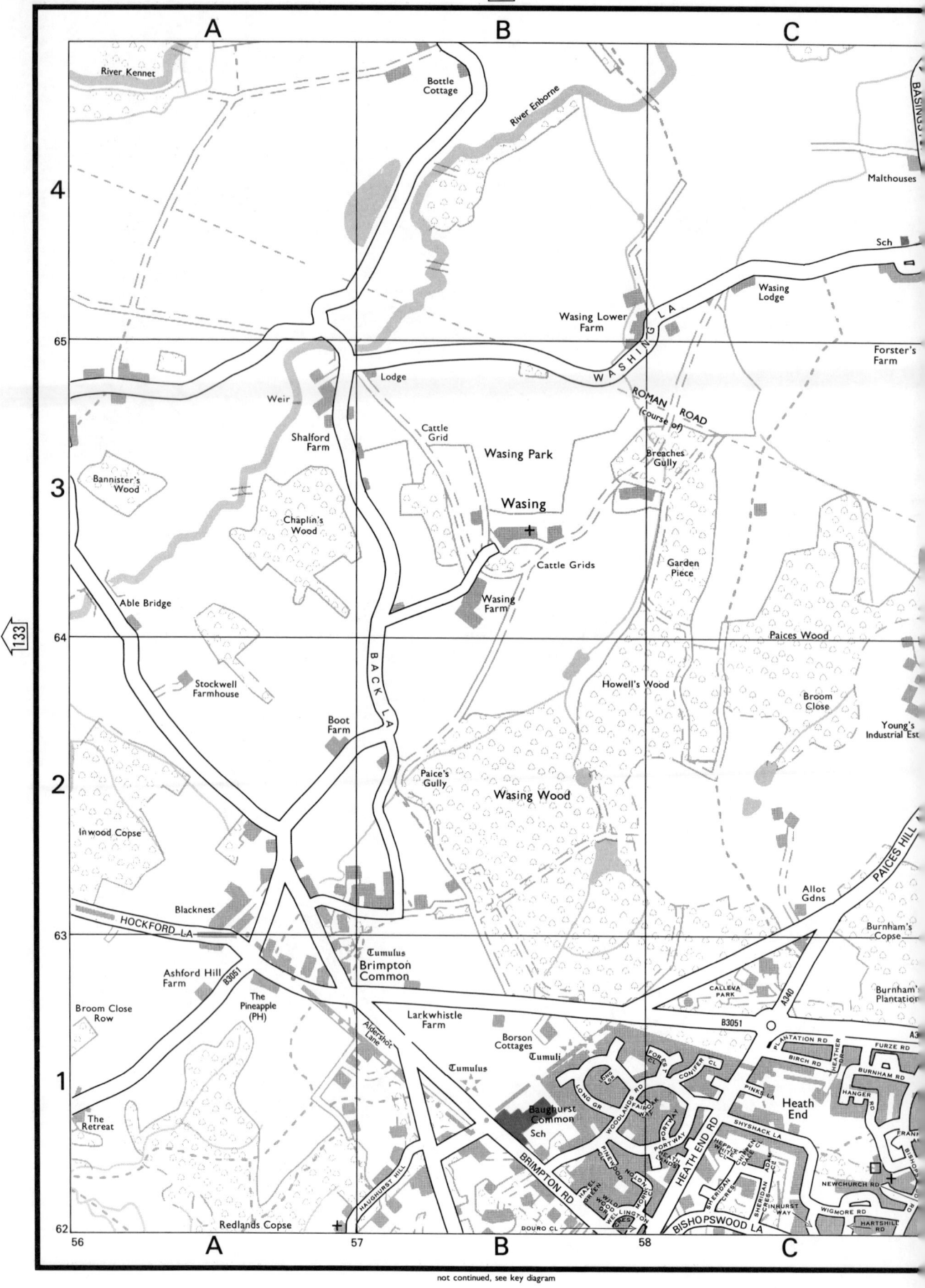

133

A   B   C

River Kennet

Bottle Cottage

River Enborne

BASING

4

Malthouses

Sch

Wasing Lodge

Wasing Lower Farm

WASHING LA

65

Forster's Farm

Lodge

Weir

ROMAN ROAD (course of)

Shalford Farm

Cattle Grid

Wasing Park

Breaches Gully

Bannister's Wood

3

Wasing

Chaplin's Wood

Cattle Grids

Garden Piece

Able Bridge

Wasing Farm

Paices Wood

64

Stockwell Farmhouse

Howell's Wood

Broom Close

BACK LA

Boot Farm

Young's Industrial Est

Paice's Gully

2

Inwood Copse

Wasing Wood

Allot Gdns

PAICES HILL

Blacknest

HOCKFORD LA

63

Burnham's Copse

Tumulus

CALLEVA PARK

Ashford Hill Farm

Brimpton Common

Burnham' Plantation

B3051

Broom Close Row

The Pineapple (PH)

Larkwhistle Farm

A340

B3051

A3

PLANTATION RD

Aldershot Lane

Borson Cottages

FURZE RD

BIRCH RD

HEATHER

Tumuli

BURNHAM RD

1

Tumulus

FORES

CONIFER CL

PINKS LA

HANGER

Baughurst Common Sch

LONG GR

WOODLANDS RD

FAIROAK

PORTWAY

SHYSHACK LA

Heath End

The Retreat

HEATH END RD

NEWCHURCH RD

HAIGHURST HILL

BRIMPTON RD

HAZEL

WIGMORE RD

Redlands Copse

DOURO CL

BISHOPSWOOD LA

HARTSHILL RD

62

56   A   57   B   58   C

not continued, see key diagram

109

D

E

F

Aqua Vitae
Copse

Fisherman's
Cottage

Padworth
Pig Farm

Upper
Lodge

The Old
Rectory

4

ewage
Works

Upper
Church Farm

Padworth Gully

RECTORY RD

FISHERMAN'S LA

Aldermaston

Church
Farm

Rays Farm

Springhill
Farm

65

STREET

A340

CONGREVE CL

CHURCH RD

SPRING LA

RAGHILL

The Birches

Court
Farm

REDLANE HILL

Foot
Bridge

Raghill
Farm

3

PAICES HILL

Harbourhill
Copse

RED LA

Black
Pightle

Grim's Bank

Old
Warren

CHAPEL LA

Aldermaston Park

WELSHMAN'S RD

64

136

Birch Copse

ROMAN ROAD

(course of)

Little Heath

Keeper's
Belt

2

Waterman's
Pightle

SOKE RD

Park Farm

63

Upper Moor's Gully

Soke
Pig Farm

The Falcon
(PH)

WINKWORTH LA

A340

FALCON FIELDS

PELICAN RD

1

SILCHESTER RD

PH

ALMSWOOD RD

SPENCER
CL

WAKEFORD

KNOLLYS

PRIORS RD

Liby

P

PAMBER HEATH RD

JUBILEE RD

OAKFIELD RD

SPRINGFIELD RD

ILEX CL

CLAPPS GATE RD

IMPSTONE RD

Pamber
Heath

SARUM RD

FRANKLIN AVE

BRACKENWOOD
DR

Stacey's
Industrial
Estate

P

CHURCH

VALLEY WAY

ROMANS
GATE

P

F Sta

BISHOPS CL

MULFORDS HILL A340

TADLEY COMMON RD

P

Tadley Court

WESTLYN
LAKE

EASTLYN
RD

THE GLEN

RS CL

Liby

P

Sch

NEWCHURCH RD

HUNTSMOOR
RD

SOUTHDOWN
RD

SILVERDALE RD

BROADHALFPENNY LA

BLAKE'S LA

GORSELANDS

Tadley
Common

GORDON
RD

ARNEWOOD
AVE

HEATH RD

BURNEY BIT

62

D

60

E

61

F

not continued, see key diagram

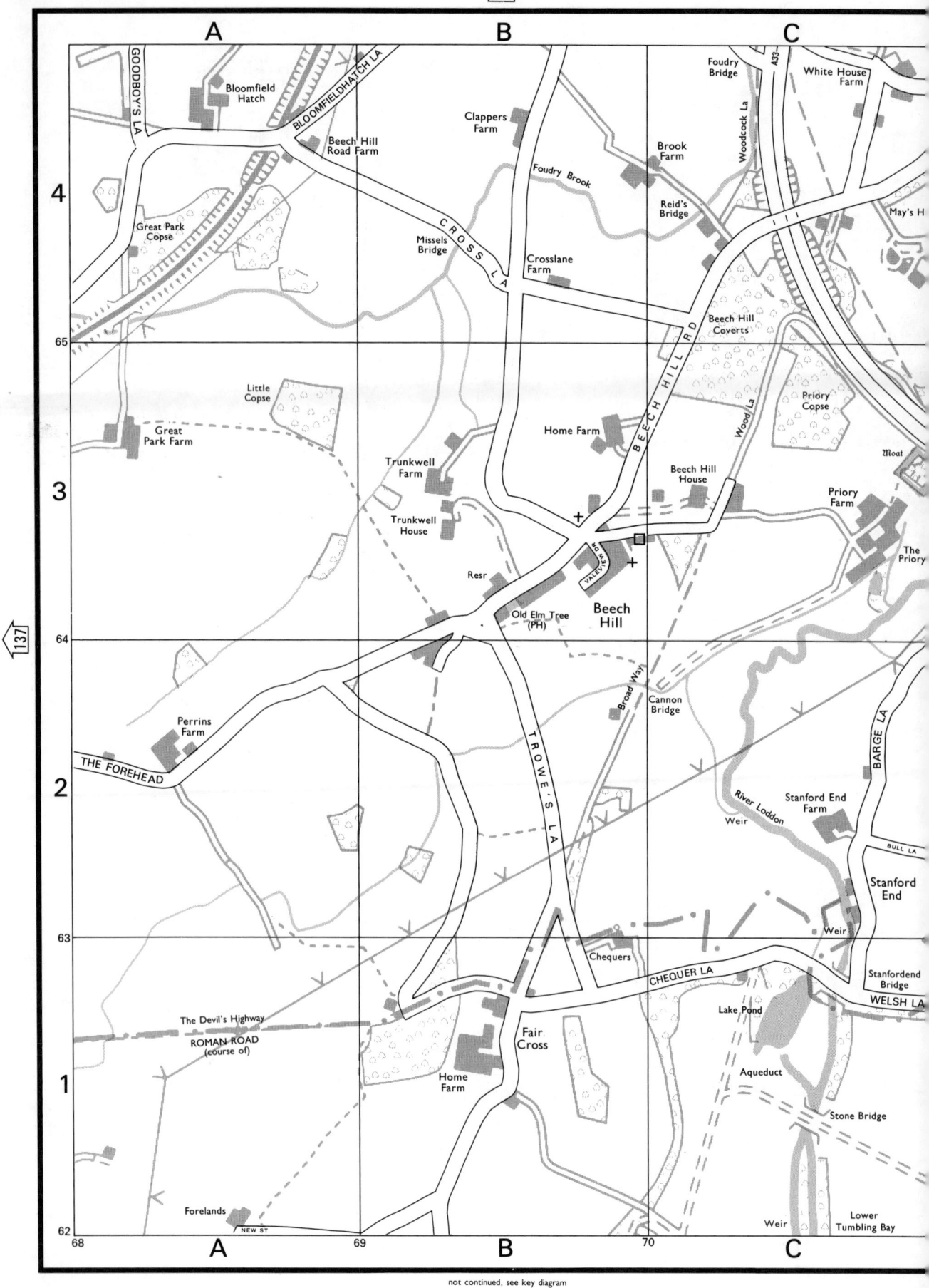

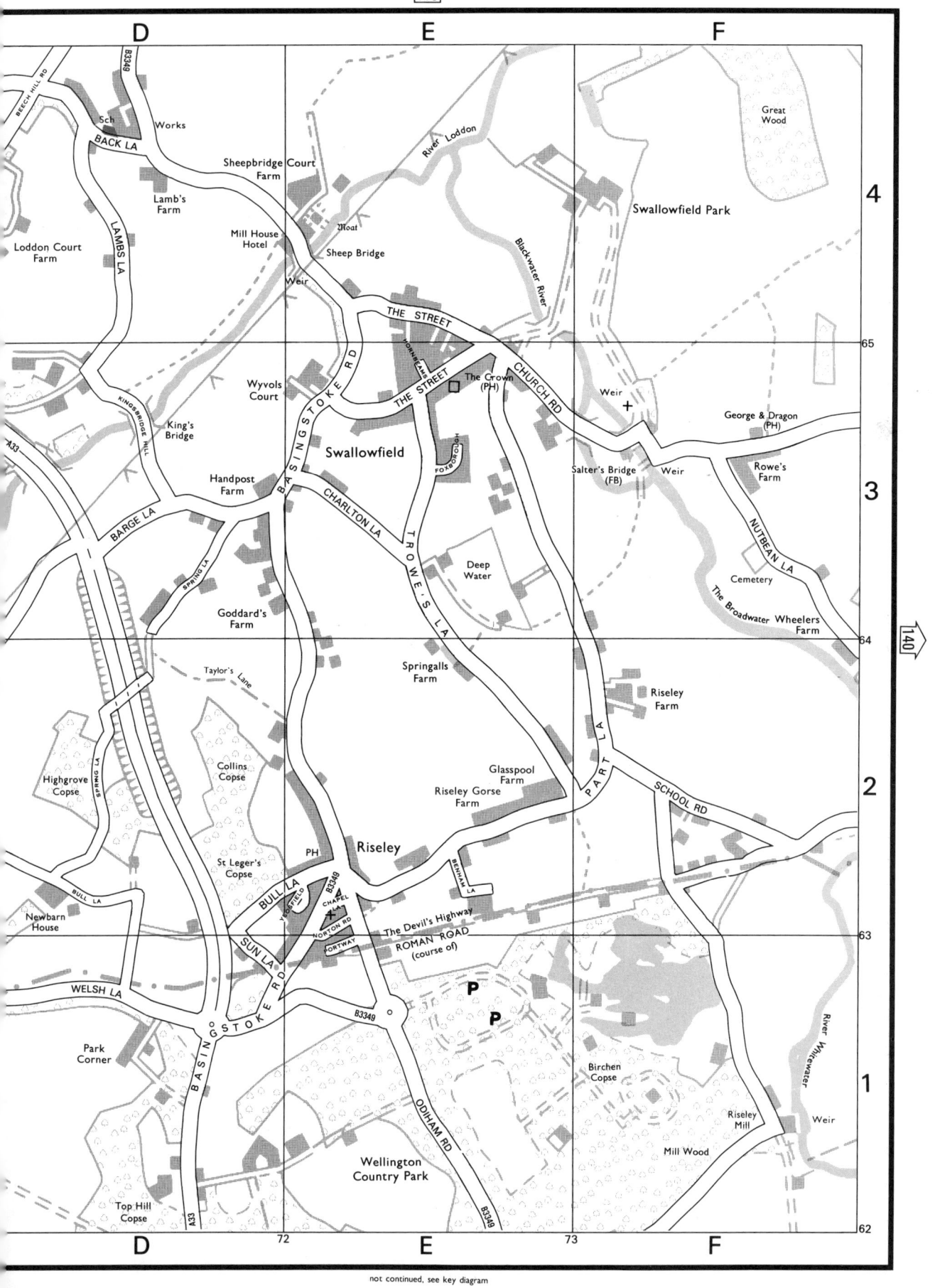

D   E   F

BEECH HILL RD

B3349

Sch

Works

BACK LA

Sheepbridge Court Farm

Lamb's Farm

LAMBS LA

Mill House Hotel

Loddon Court Farm

Moat

Sheep Bridge

Weir

River Loddon

4

Swallowfield Park

Great Wood

THE STREET

Blackwater River

65

KINGSBRIDGE HILL

King's Bridge

Wyvols Court

The Crown (PH)

CHURCH RD

Weir

George & Dragon (PH)

A33

BASINGSTOKE RD

Handpost Farm

THE STREET

JORDNEANS

HOLROYD

FOXBORO

Swallowfield

Salter's Bridge (FB)

Weir

Rowe's Farm

3

BARGE LA

CHARLTON LA

NUTBEAN LA

Cemetery

SPRING LA

Goddard's Farm

TROWE'S LA

Deep Water

The Broadwater Wheelers Farm

64

Taylor's Lane

Springalls Farm

Riseley Farm

Highgrove Copse

SPRING LA

Collins Copse

Glasspool Farm

PART LA

SCHOOL RD

2

Newbarn House

BULL LA

St Leger's Copse

PH

Riseley Gorse Farm

Riseley

PH

BULL LA

VESTFIELD

B3349

CHAPEL

NORTON RD

BENHAM LA

WELSH LA

SUN LA

PORTWAY

The Devil's Highway
ROMAN ROAD (course of)

63

BASINGSTOKE RD

Park Corner

B3349

P

P

Birchen Copse

River Whitewater

1

ODIHAM RD

Wellington Country Park

Riseley Mill

Weir

Mill Wood

Top Hill Copse

A33

B3349

62

D   72   E   73   F

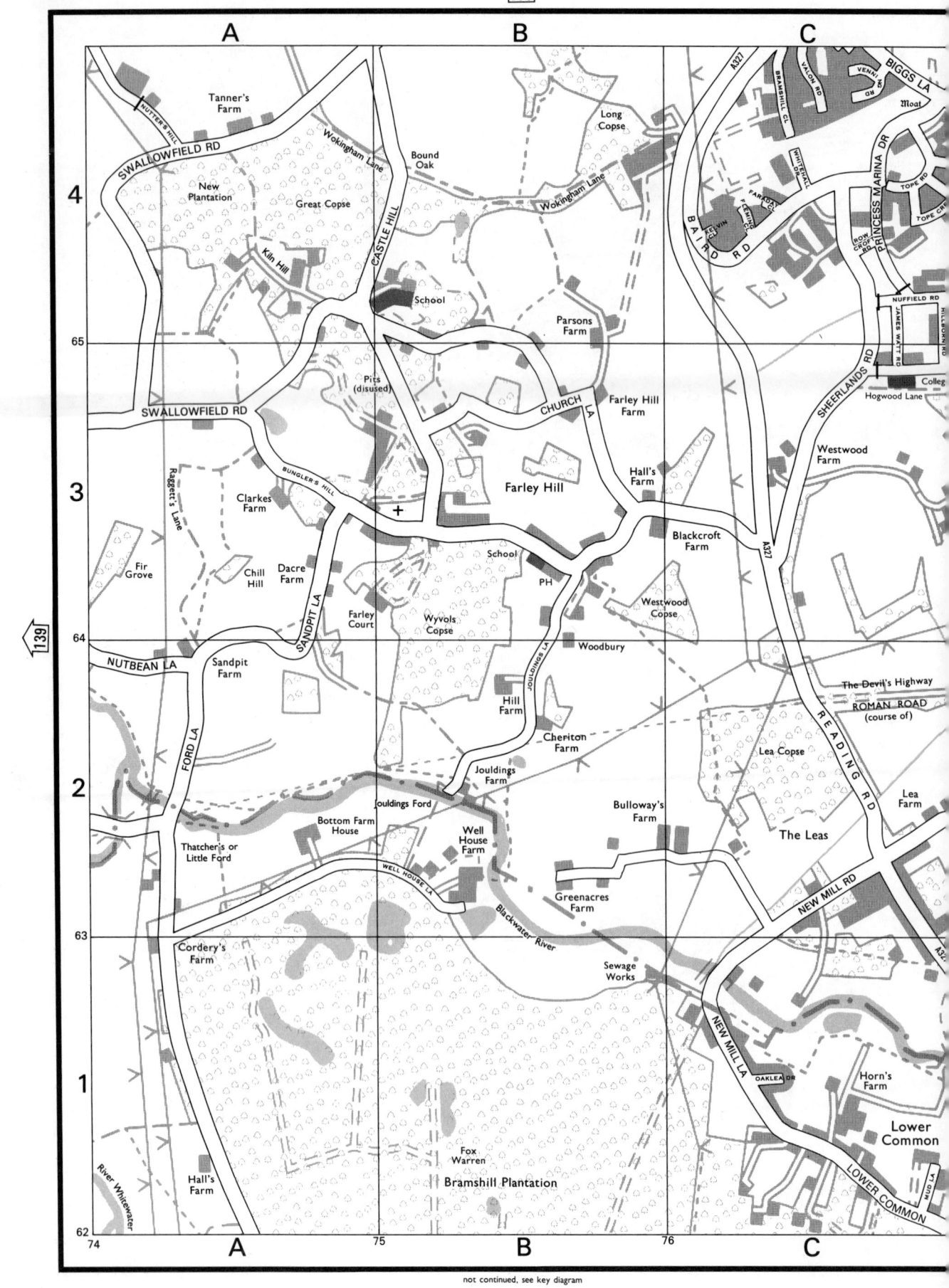

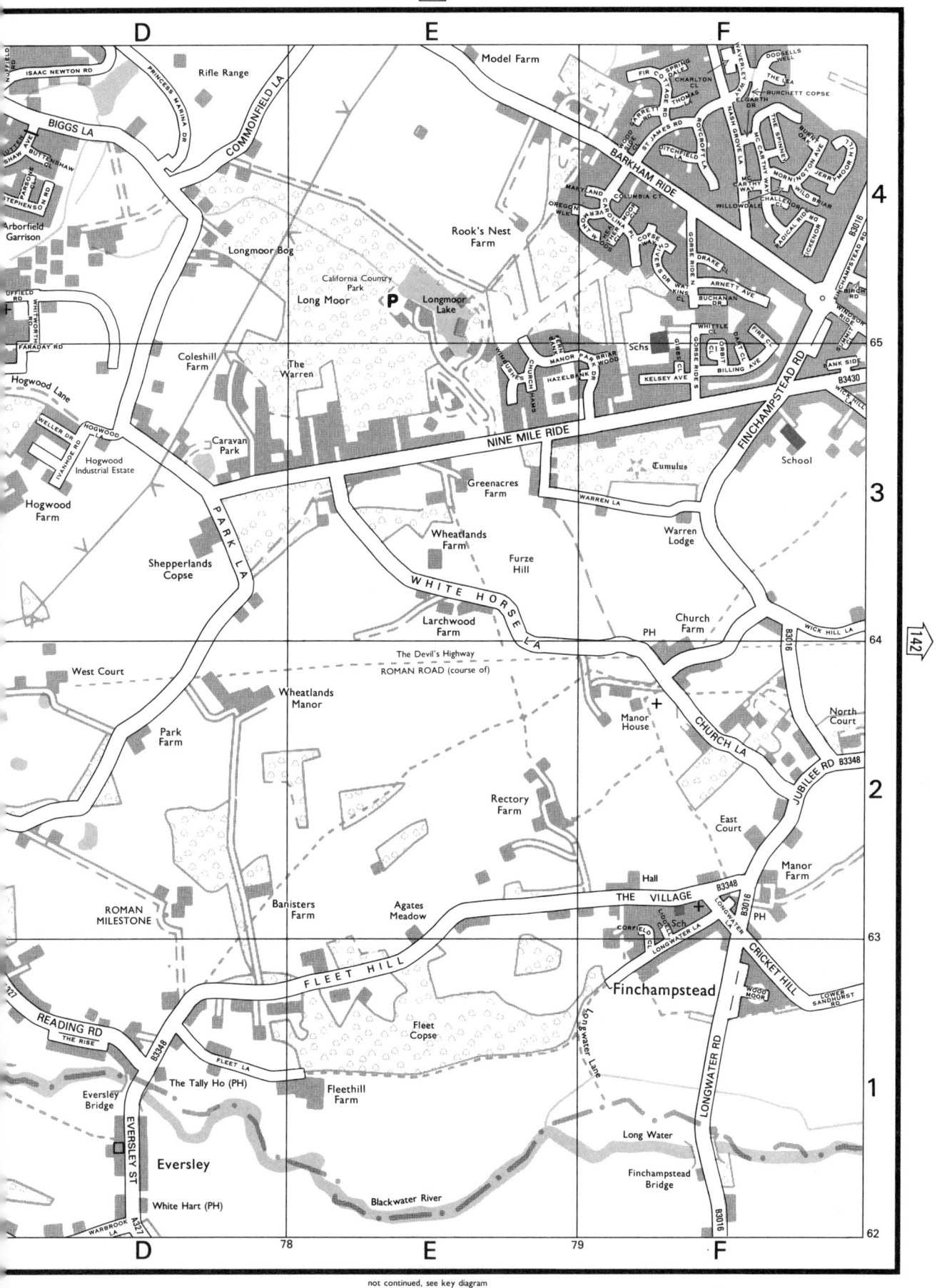

116

141

A **B** **C**

4

65

3

64

2

63

1

62

80 **A** 81 **B** 82 **C**

FINCHAMPSTEAD RD
B3016
SHEN STONE CL
A321
CAMBRIAN WAY
TINTAGEL RD
CYPRESS CL
WELLINGTON GDNS
INGLE GLEN
TANGLE WOOD
FOXCOTE
KILN RIDE
PINE DR
BIRCH RD
FOXCOTE
TOMLINSON DR
RANGE RD
WINDSOR RIDE
B3430

SANDHURST RD

Pickeridge House

Silverstock Bog

Queen's Mere

Gorrick Plantation

HEATHLANDS RD
HATCH RIDE

NINE MILE RIDE
KINGSBRIDGE COTTS
ST SEBASTIAN CL
GROVE CL

B3430

A321
SOLDIERS RISE

Pineridge Farm

St Andrews CL
OLEANDER CL
MARIGOLD
MERRYMAN DR
GREEN CL
HEATHER
MOUNT DR

Wick Hill
WICK HILL LA
WICK HILL EXTENSION
KILN RIDE EXTENSION

King's Mere

ASHDALE PARK
LITTLE FRITH
HOLLYBUSH RIDE
HEATH RIDE

THE BRAMBLES
BRAMLEY

LOWER WOKINGHAM RD

Ravenswood Village Settlement

Golf Course

GREENSIDE
BADGERS SETT
SQUIRREL DRI
BIRCH

Wick Hill Lane

Ridge Farm

The Devil's Highway
Roman Road (course of)

HOUSTON WAY
ROMAN RIDE

Talisman CL
PRIORS WOOD

CH

The Devil's Highway
LINKWAY
RAVENSWOOD AVE
KNOWLES AVE

WICK HILL LA

North Court Farm

B3348

The Ridges

DELL RD

Finchampstead Ridges

P

WELLINGTONIA AVE

B3348

A321

WOKINGHAM RD

Sch
FEATHERDENE
WELLESLEY DR
ST MONICA
SHEPHERDS

DUKE'S RIDE
FINCHAM END DR
BOWMAN CT
Sports Centre
Crowthorne Station
WELLINGTON BUSINESS PARK
Derby Field
Pollock Bridge
CONYNGHAM CL

ROWELL CL
KNOWLES AVE
WOOD END
BENSON RD
COPPICE
CORFE

Poultry Farm

P
Moor Green Farm

Hall Farm

Sandhurst Lodge

Beech Hill

Coalpit Copse

LOWER SANDHURST RD
AMBARROW LA

Ambarrow Farm

Perry's Bridge

CHURCH RD
AMBARROW CRES
MAYBRICK
WYLD
COTS...
COLT...
PILLOW
WILLOW WAY
PERRYHILL DR
SAND...
FIRTREE
A321
HIGH ST
LOWER CHURCH RD
MILL LA
CHELWOOD DR
High St
Sch

118
143
151

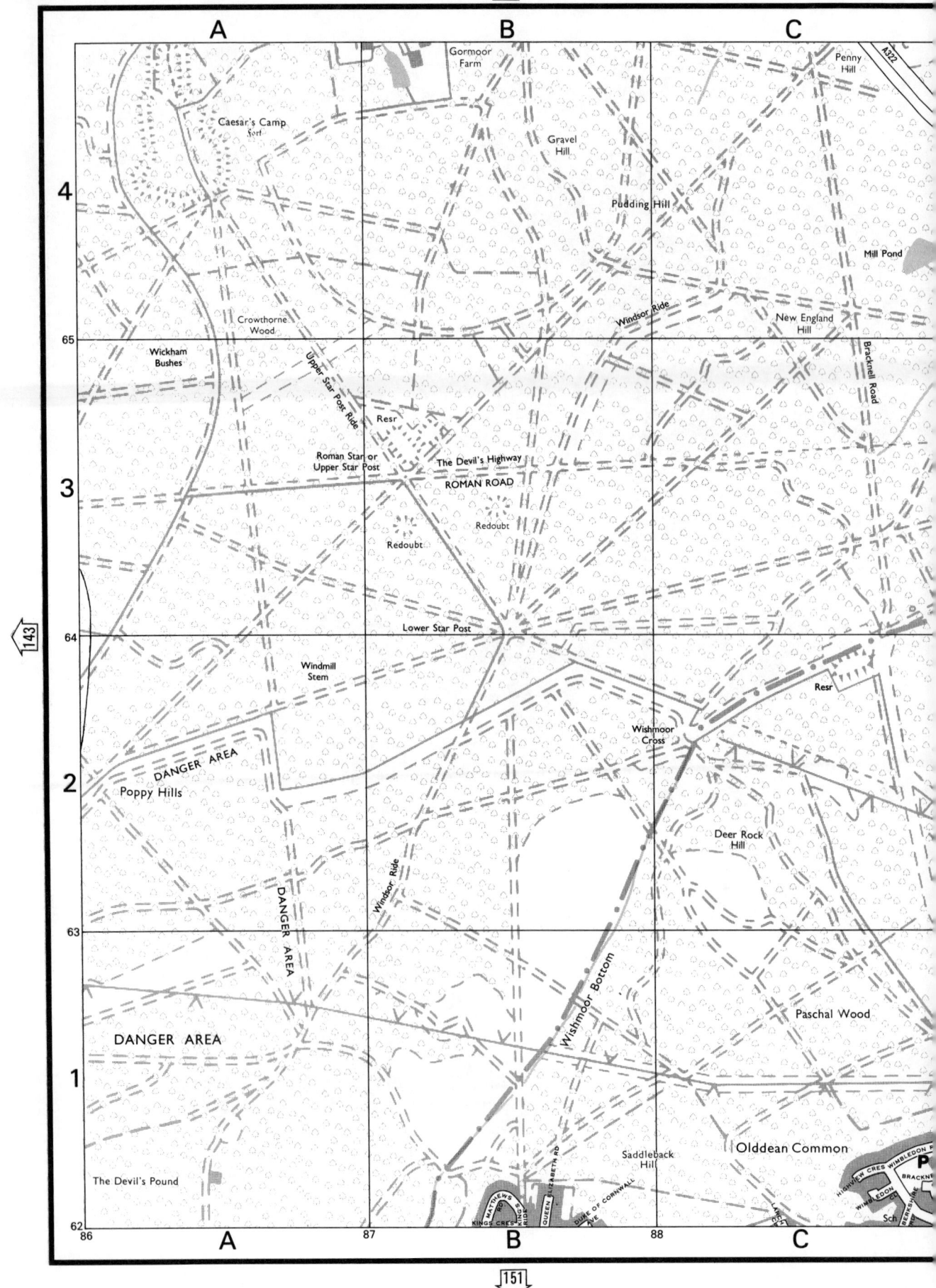

A   B   C

Gormoor Farm

Caesar's Camp
Fort

Gravel Hill

Penny Hill

A322

Pudding Hill

Mill Pond

Crowthorne Wood

Windsor Ride

New England Hill

65

Wickham Bushes

Upper Star Post Ride

Bracknell Road

Resr

Roman Star or Upper Star Post

The Devil's Highway
ROMAN ROAD

Redoubt

Redoubt

3

Lower Star Post

64

Windmill Stem

Resr

Wishmoor Cross

2

DANGER AREA
Poppy Hills

Deer Rock Hill

DANGER AREA

Windsor Ride

63

Wishmoor Bottom

Paschal Wood

DANGER AREA

1

Olddean Common

Saddleback Hill

MATTHEWS RD
KINGS CRES
KING'S RIDE
QUEEN ELIZABETH RD
DUKE OF CORNWALL AVE

The Devil's Pound

HIGHVIEW CRES
WIMBLEDON
BRACKNE
WIMBLEDON
BERKSHIRE
Sch
P

62

86   A   87   B   88   C

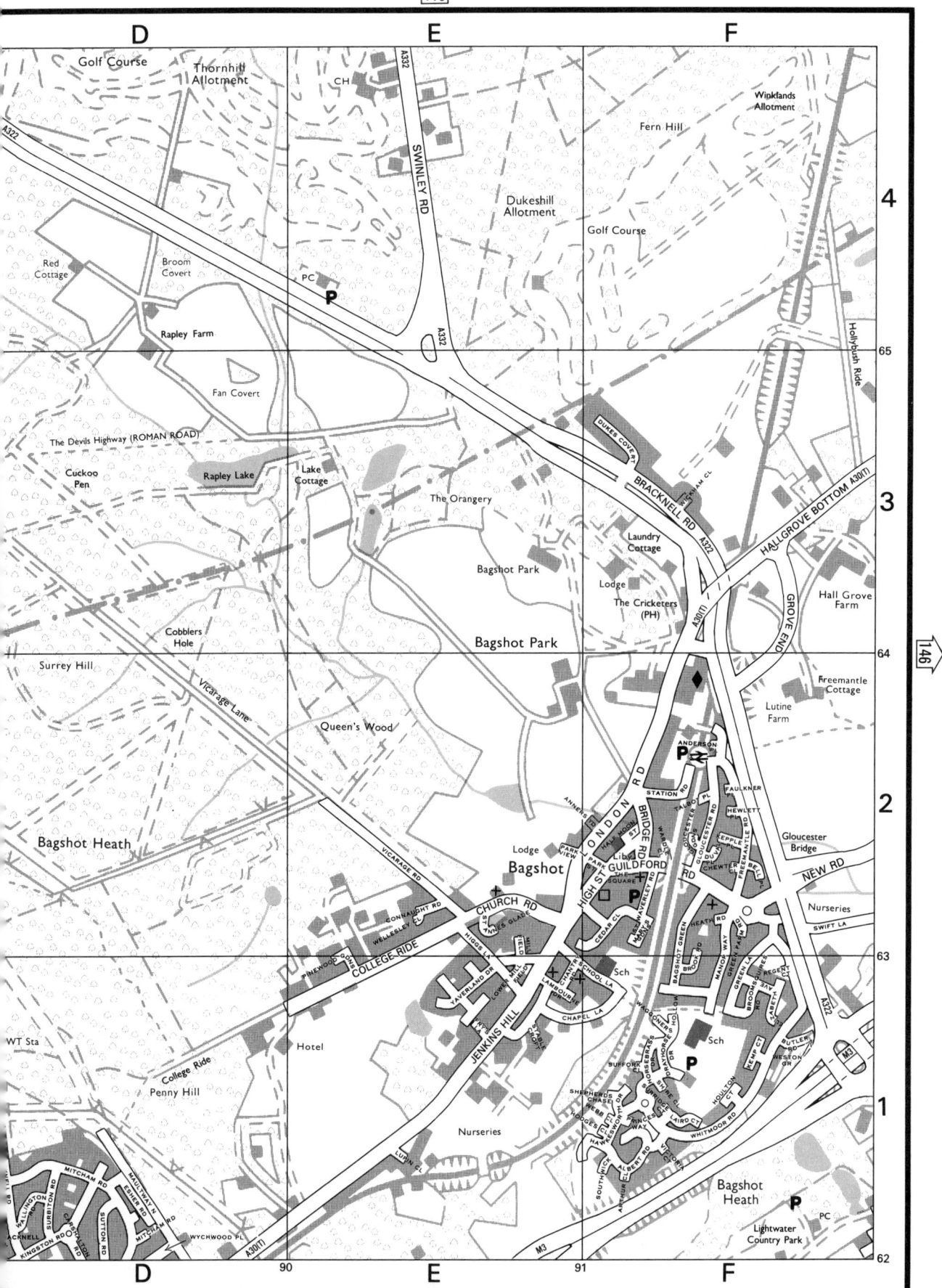

145

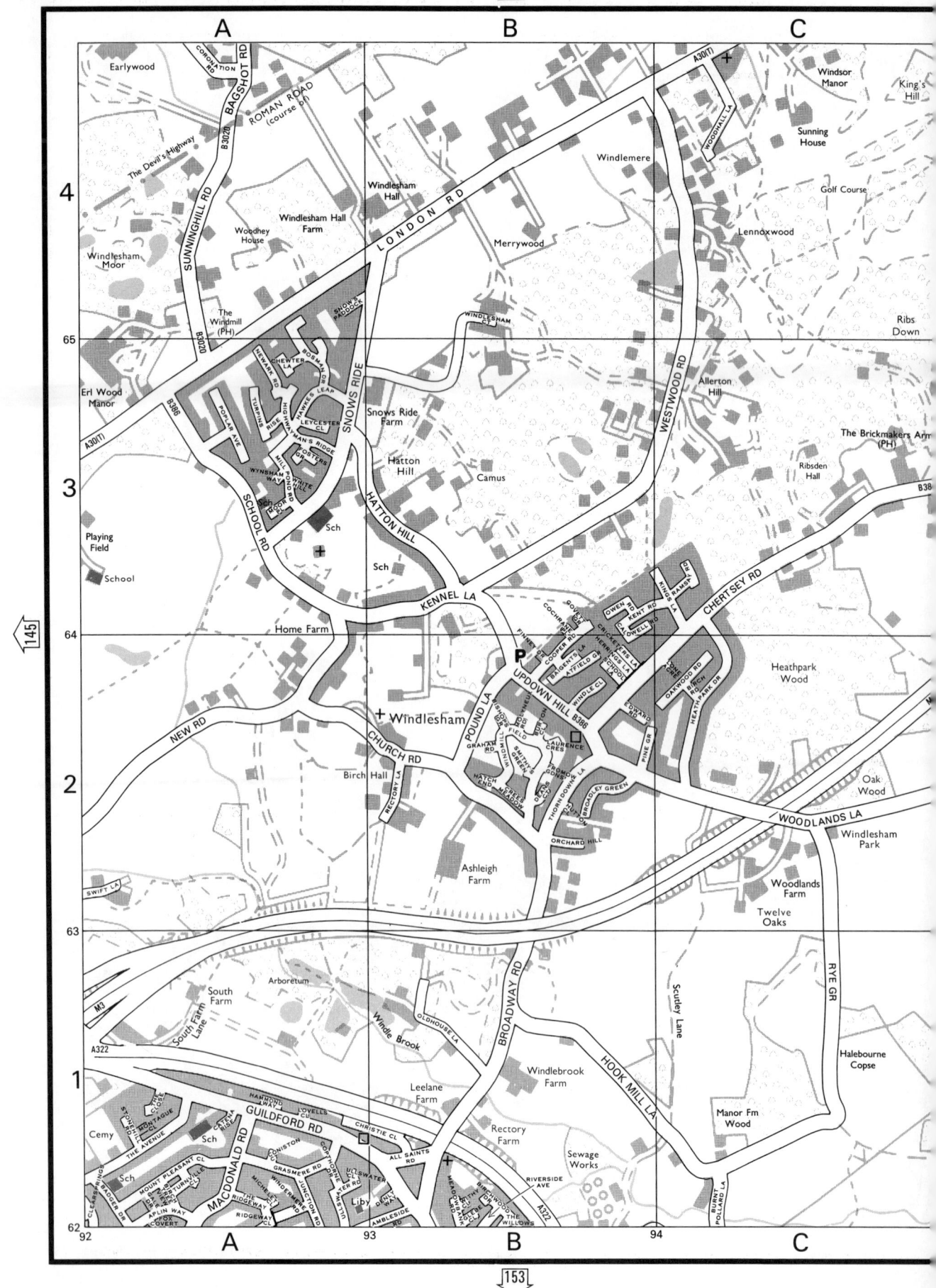

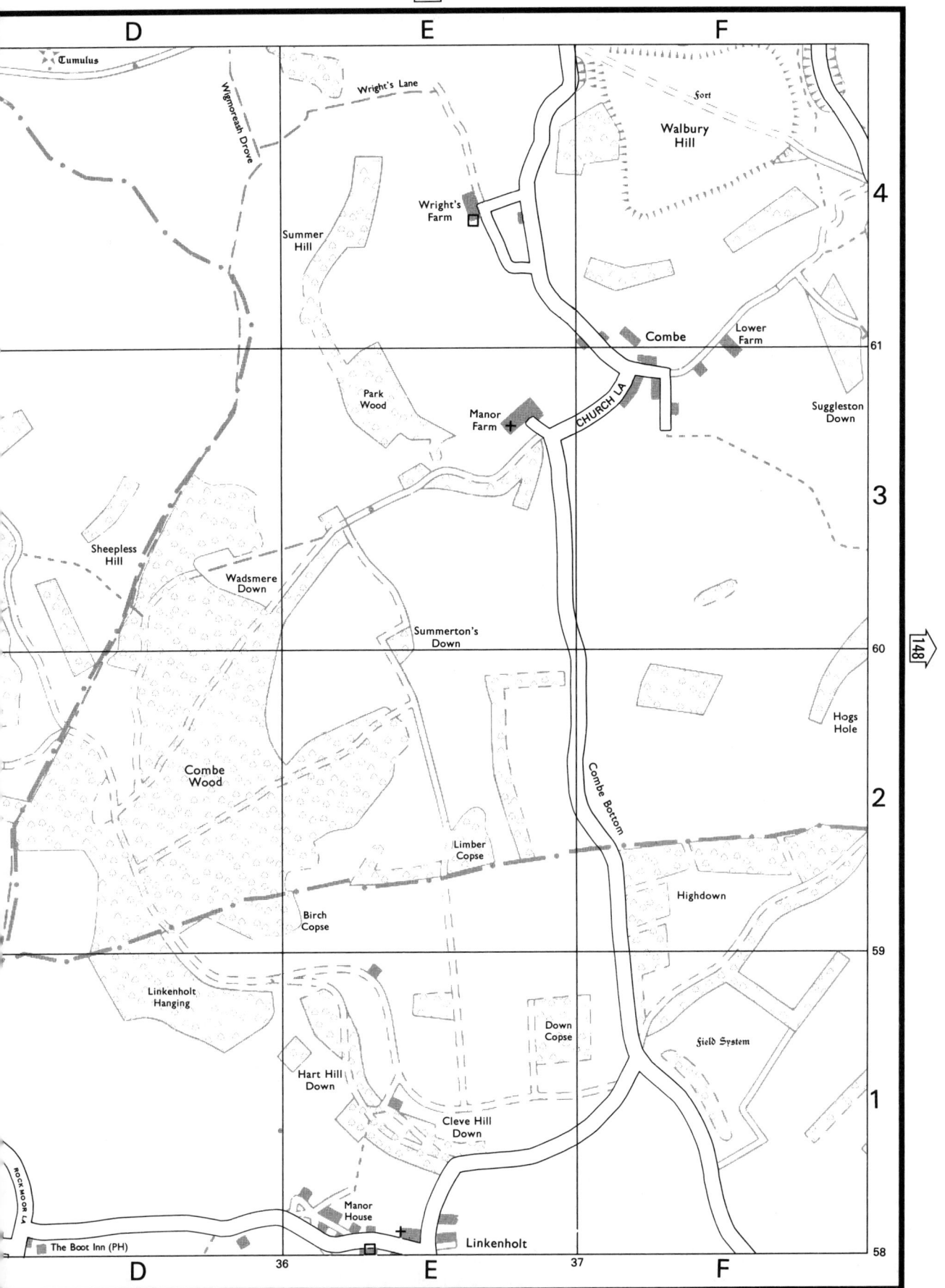

D   E   F

Tumulus

Wigmoreash Drove

Wright's Lane

Fort

Walbury Hill

Wright's Farm

Summer Hill

4

Combe

Lower Farm

61

Suggleston Down

Park Wood

Manor Farm

CHURCH LA

Sheepless Hill

Wadsmere Down

3

Summerton's Down

60

Hogs Hole

Combe Wood

Combe Bottom

2

Limber Copse

Highdown

Birch Copse

59

Linkenholt Hanging

Down Copse

Field System

Hart Hill Down

1

Cleve Hill Down

ROCK MOOR LA

Manor House

The Boot Inn (PH)

Linkenholt

36   37

58

D   E   F

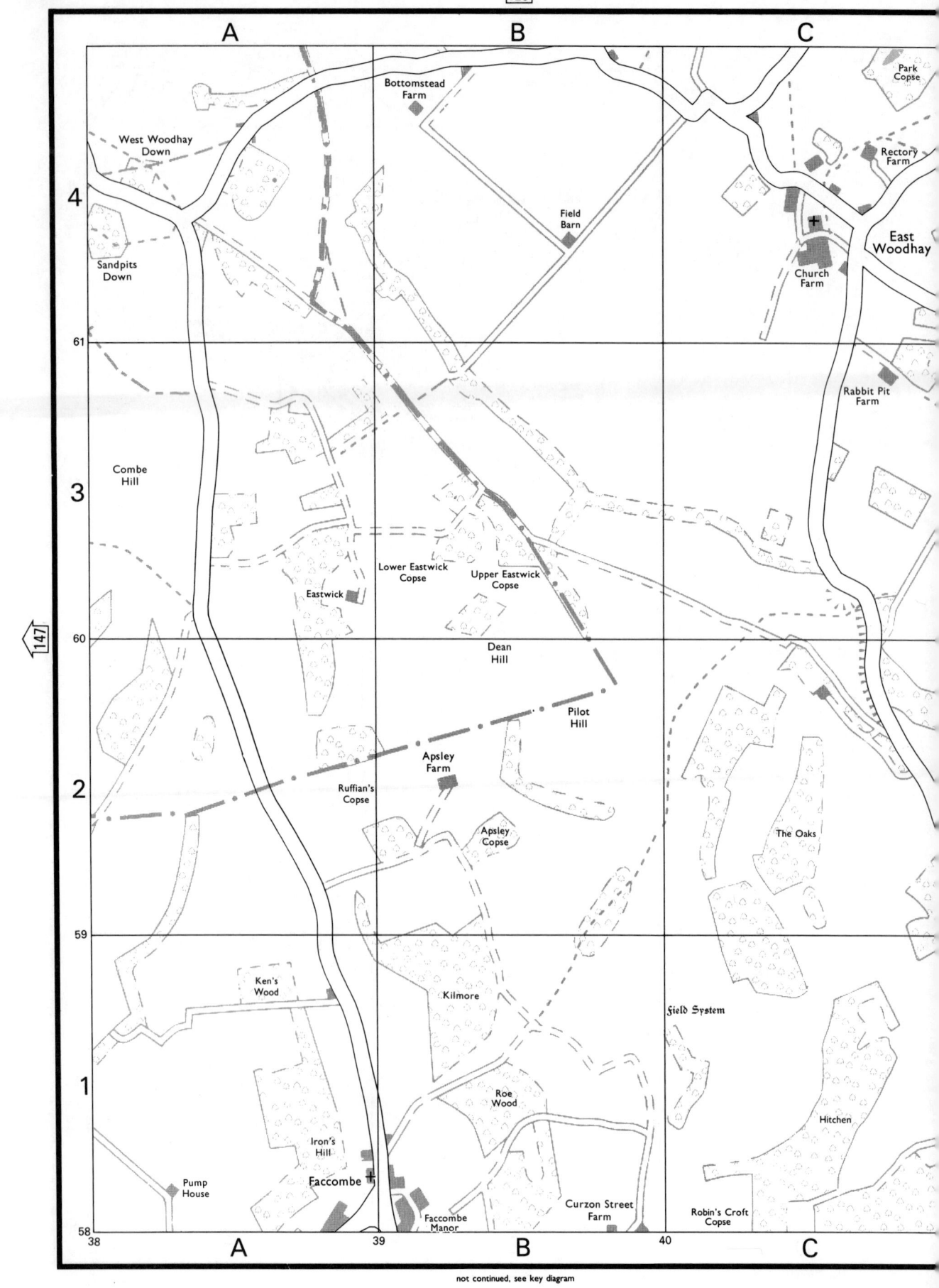

128

A B C

147

Park Copse

Bottomstead Farm

West Woodhay Down

Field Barn

Rectory Farm

East Woodhay

Sandpits Down

Church Farm

61

Rabbit Pit Farm

Combe Hill

3

Lower Eastwick Copse

Upper Eastwick Copse

Eastwick

60

Dean Hill

Pilot Hill

The Oaks

Ruffian's Copse

Apsley Farm

2

Apsley Copse

59

Ken's Wood

Kilmore

Field System

1

Roe Wood

Hitchen

Iron's Hill

Pump House

Faccombe

Faccombe Manor

Curzon Street Farm

Robin's Croft Copse

58

38 A 39 B 40 C

142

D E F

150

Mill Farm
Pavilion
Blackwater River
Church Farm
Lower Church Rd
Sch
Firtree Cl
High St
A321
Moulsham Green
Copse Lane
Watmore Farm
Canberra
Moulsham La
The Yateley Lakes
Yateley Rd
A321

4

Vicarage La
Chandlers La
Vicarage Rd
Crondall End
White House Gdns
White Lion La
Mill La
Coronation Rd
Plough Rd
Kevins Dr
Weybridge Mead
Sandhurst Rd

Love Lane
Celandine
The Link
Firgrove Rd
Yateley Green
READING RD
Oaklands
Yateley
Schs
Pond Croft
61

Honeysuckle Cl
Rokes Pl
Holbeche Cl
School La
Hall La
Liby Schools
Lawford Cres
Cranford Park Dr
Home Park
Somerville Cres
Manor Park Dr
Old Welmore
Quarry La
Potley Hill Rd
Round Cl
Ashfield Green
B3272
Jesse Cl
Sch

3

Oldcorne Hollow
Huddington Glade
Arnet Field
Catesby Gdns
Throgmorton Rd
Monteagle La
Vigo La
Hilltop View
Byways
The Dell
Farm View
Hall Farm Cres
Denham
Beaver La
Cricket Hill
Stevens Hill
Corbett's La

Silver Fox Farm
Handford La
Dickens
Wordsworth Ave
Byron Cl
Christie
Hardy Ave
Sch
Cricket Hill La
Cemetery
Hill Farm
60

P
The Anchor (PH)
Little Vigo
Gorselands
Woodlands
Works
Yateley Common
Cottage Farm

2

Vigo La
Blackbush Market
Blackbushe Airport
A30
59

Hartford Bridge Flats
B3013
A327
Blackwater Tumulus Lodge

Forest Lodge
Yateley Drive
Barracks
Minley Rd
Hornley Common

1

West Minley Farm
B3013
Minley Manor
Minley
A327
Clapperoak Cottage
58

D 81 E 82 F

not continued, see key diagram

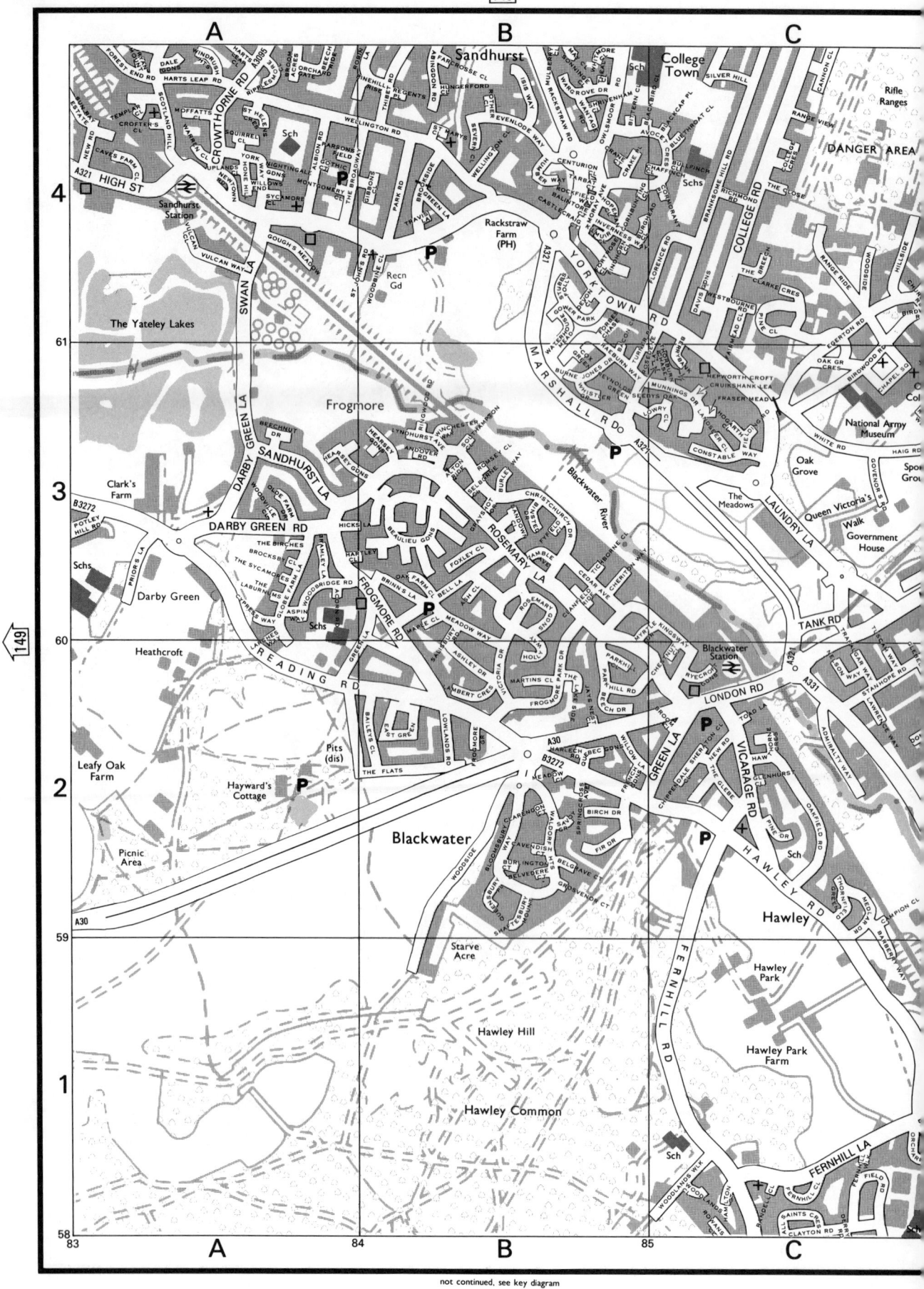

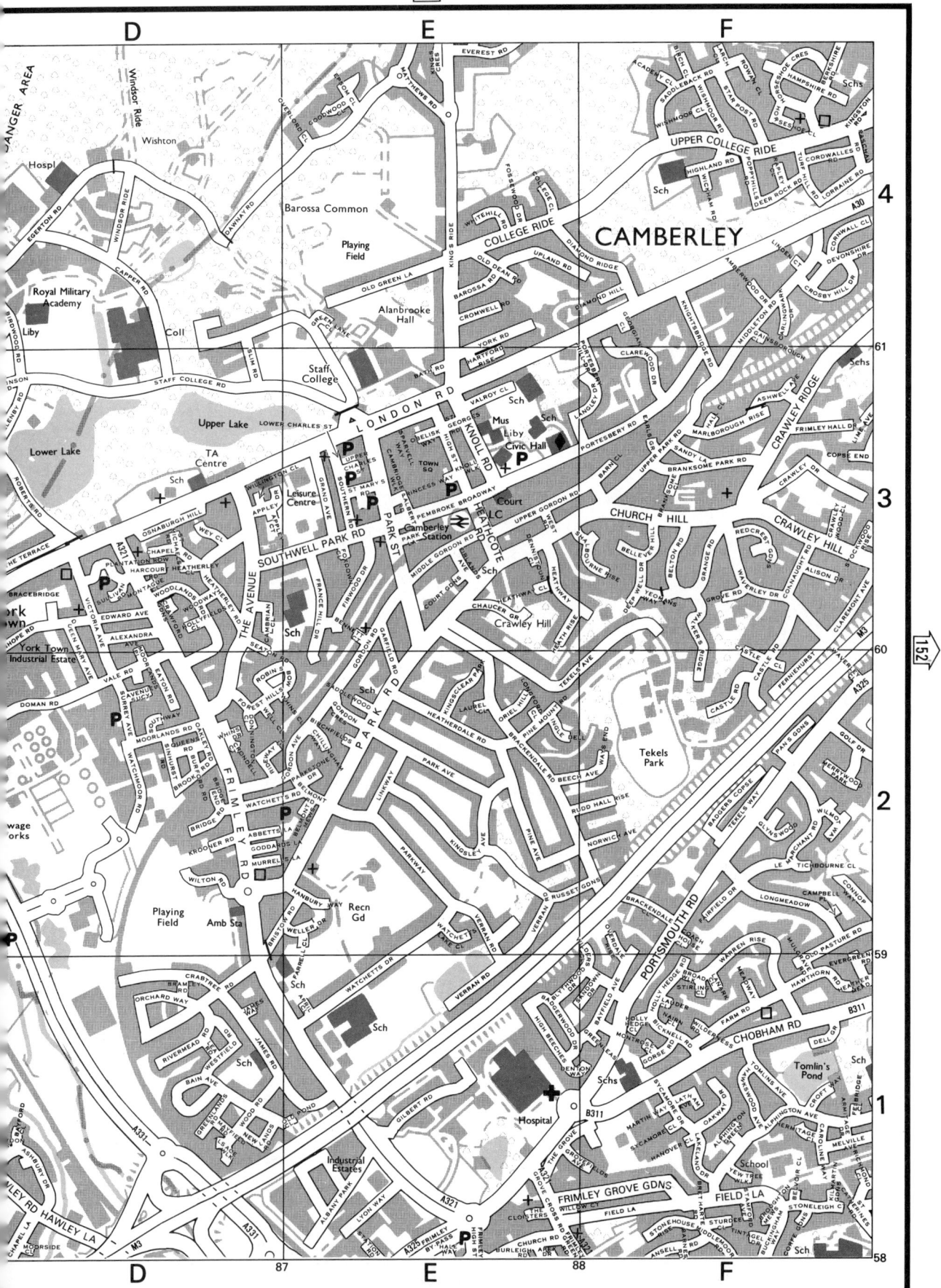

CAMBERLEY

D

DANGER AREA

Windsor Ride

Wishton

Hospl

Royal Military Academy

Liby

Coll

Barossa Common

Playing Field

Alanbrooke Hall

Staff College

Upper Lake

Lower Lake

Lower Charles St

TA Centre

LONDON RD

E

EVEREST RD

Matthews Rd

College Ride

College Ride

Old Dean Rd

Old Green La

Barossa Rd

York Rd

Hartford Rise

Valroy Cl

Mus

Liby

Civic Hall

Court

Pembroke Broadway

Camberley Station

LC

Upper Gordon Rd

Crawley Hill

F

Schs

UPPER COLLEGE RIDE

Sch

A30

CAMBERLEY

Schs

CHURCH HILL

CRAWLEY HILL

Crawley Ridge

Frimley Hall Dr

Tekels Park

GOLF DR

Kerrywood

Portsmouth Rd

A325

M3

Playing Field

Amb Sta

Recn Gd

Hospital

Industrial Estates

CHOBHAM RD

Tomlin's Pond

Sch

B311

FRIMLEY GROVE GDNS

FIELD LA

School

Yew Tree

A321

Frimley

not continued, see key diagram

87
88
58
59
60
61
1
2
3
4

D
E
F

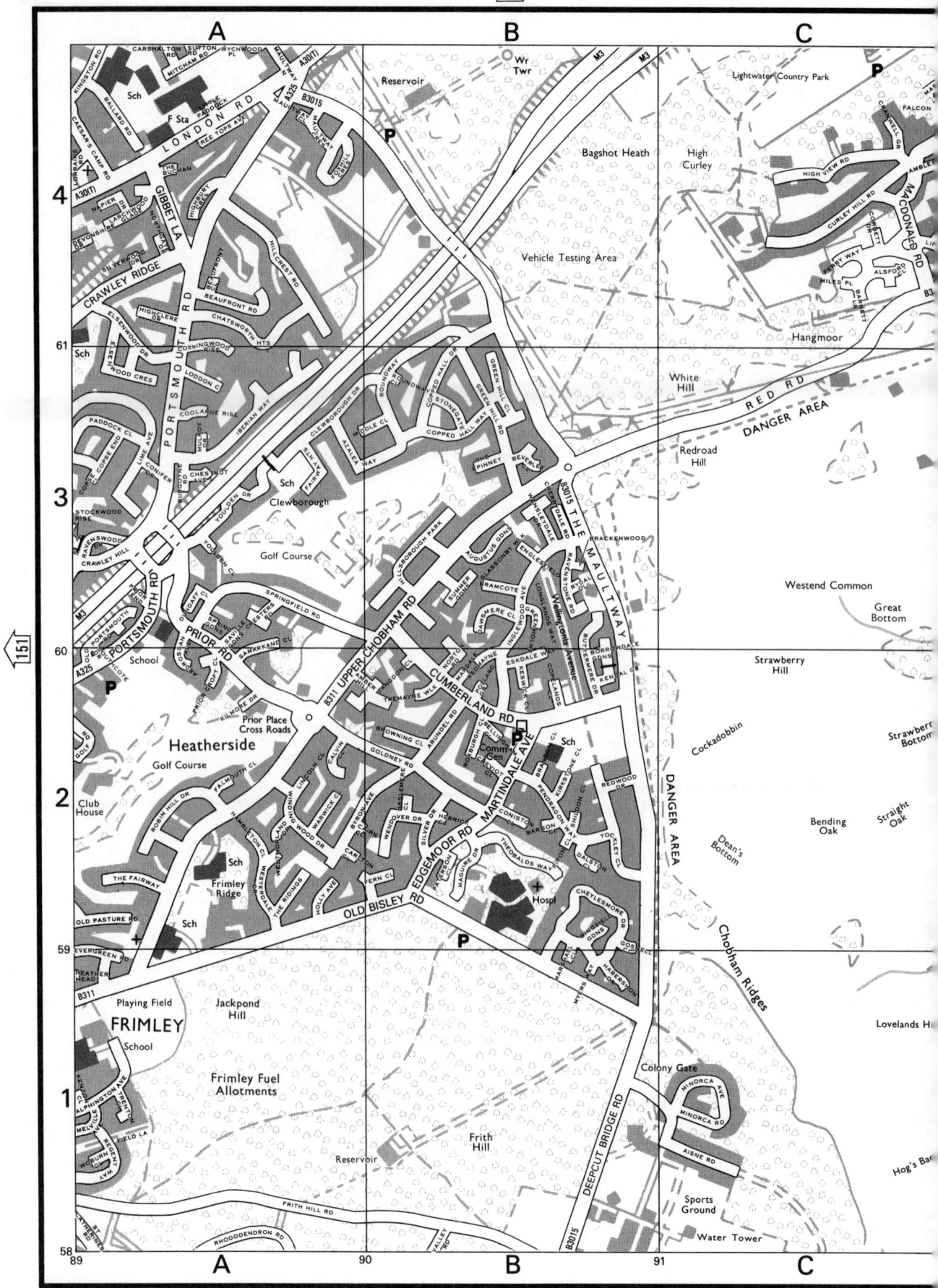

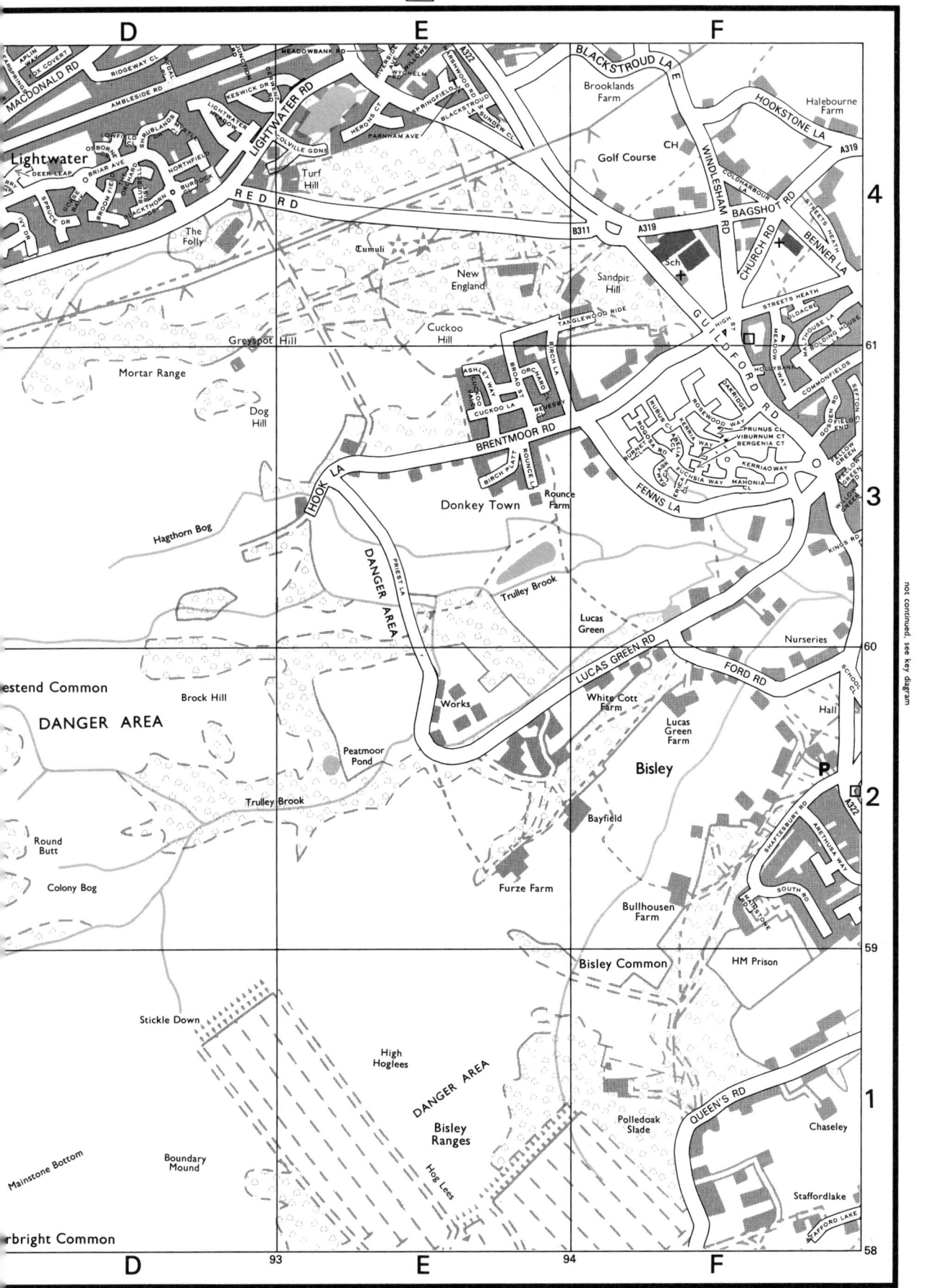

D E F

Lightwater

MACDONALD RD

APLIN WAY
FOX COVERT
RIDGEWAY CL
AMBLESIDE RD
KESWICK DR
LIGHTWATER MEADOW
LONFIELD
SHRUBLANDS
NORTHFIELD
DEER LEAP
GORSE
BRIAR AVE
SPRUCE DR
BLUEBELL
BLACKTHORN
BURDOCK

MEADOWBANK RD

LIGHTWATER RD
COLVILLE GDNS
HERONS CT
HIGH AVE
WINDLE WY
WILLOW CL
SPRINGFIELD
BLACKSTROUD LA W
SUNDEW CL
PARNHAM AVE

A322
FRENWOOD RD
BLACKSTROUD LA E

BLACKSTROUD LANE

Brooklands Farm

HOOKSTONE LA

Halebourne Farm

CH

Golf Course

A319

WINDLESHAM RD
COLDHARBOUR LA

BAGSHOT RD

CHURCH RD

BENNER LA

TEETS HEATH

RED RD

B311

A319

Turf Hill

Tumuli

New England

Cuckoo Hill

Greyspot Hill

Sandpit Hill

The Folly

Sch
+
+

HIGH ST
STREETS HEATH
OLDACRE
MEADOW WAY
MATTHOUSE LA
BOLDING HOUSE

GUILDFORD RD

HOLLYBANK
COMMONFIELDS
GOSDEN RD
SEFTON CL
GOSDEN RD END

61

Mortar Range

Dog Hill

BRENTMOOR RD

ASHLEY WAY
CUCKOO LA
BROAD ST
ORCHARD END
REVESBY
ROUNCE LA
BIRCH PLATT
PINE VIEW

BIRCH LA

Donkey Town

Rounce Farm

ROSEWOOD WAY
PATRIDGE LA
CHAPEL
RUBUS CL
MOROSS
TURRET CT
TANSY CL
XENIA WAY
FUCHSIA WAY
PRUNUS CL
VIBURNUM CT
BERGENIA CT
KERRIA WAY
MAHONIA CL

FENNS LA

WILLOW GREEN
KINGS RD
FELTON GREEN

3

HOOK LA

Hagthorn Bog

DANGER AREA

PRIEST LA

Trulley Brook

Lucas Green

LUCAS GREEN RD

FORD RD

Nurseries

SCHOOL CL

60

stend Common

DANGER AREA

Brock Hill

Peatmoor Pond

Works

White Cott Farm

Lucas Green Farm

Bisley

Hall

P

A322

2

Round Butt

Trulley Brook

Bayfield

SHAFTESBURY RD
ARETHUSA WAY
SOUTH RD
HEATHMOOR

Colony Bog

Furze Farm

Bullhousen Farm

59

Stickle Down

Bisley Common

HM Prison

1

Mainstone Bottom

Boundary Mound

High Hoglees

DANGER AREA

Bisley Ranges

Hog Lees

Polledoak Slade

QUEEN'S RD

Chaseley

rbright Common

Staffordlake

STAFFORD LAKE

58

D 93 E 94 F

4

not continued, see key diagram

INDEX

EXPLANATION OF THE STREET INDEX REFERENCE SYSTEM

Street names are listed alphabetically and show the locality, the page number and a reference to the square in which the name falls on the map page.

Example:	Rushey Way. Read...87 E1

Rushey Way	This is the full street name, which may have been abbreviated on the map.
Read	This is the abbreviation for the town, village or locality in which the street falls.
87	This is the page number of the map on which the street name appears.
E1	The letter and figure indicate the square on the map in which the centre of the street falls. The square can be found at the junction of the vertical column carrying the appropriate letter and the horizontal row carrying the appropriate figure.

ABBREVIATIONS USED IN THE INDEX
Road Names

Approach	App	Lane	La
Avenue	Ave	North	N
Boulevard	Bvd	Orchard	Orch
Broadway	Bwy	Parade	Par
By-Pass	By-Ps	Passage	Pas
Causeway	Cswy	Place	Pl
Common	Comm	Pleasant	Plea
Corner	Cnr	Precinct	Prec
Cottages	Cotts	Promenade	Prom
Court	Ct	Road	Rd
Crescent	Cres	South	S
Drive	Dr	Square	Sq
Drove	Dro	Street,Saint	St
East	E	Terrace	Terr
Gardens	Gdns	Walk	Wlk
Grove	Gr	West	W
Heights	Hts	Yard	Yd

dermaston	Alde	135	D4	Cold Ash	Cold A	106	B4	Iver	Iver	44	C4	Stanwell	Stan	70	B1

Aldermaston ..... Alde 135 D4
dworth ..... Aldw 32 C2
oorfield ..... Arbo 114 B2
scot ..... Ascot 120 A3
hampstead ..... Asham 54 A4
hford ..... Ashf 97 F2
ton Tirrold ..... Ast T 12 C4
gshot ..... Bags 145 E2
ll Hill ..... Ball H 129 E2
rkham ..... Bark 115 E1
ech Hill ..... Bee H 138 B3
edon ..... Beed 51 E4
enham ..... Been 108 C3
nfield ..... Binf 90 B1
sham ..... Bish 18 C4
sley ..... Bis 153 F2
ackwater ..... Black 150 B2
ewbury ..... Blew 12 A4
urne End ..... Bou E 3 D1
xford ..... Box 76 B2
acknell ..... Brac 118 C2
adfield ..... Brad 82 B3
ghtwalton ..... Brig 28 C2
mpton ..... Brim 133 F3
cklebury ..... Buck 80 C1
rchett's Green ..... Bur G 38 B4
rghfield Common ..... Bur C 110 C1
rleigh ..... Burl 119 E4
rnham ..... Burn 21 E2
mberley ..... Camb 151 F4
versham ..... Caver 59 E2
addleworth ..... Chadd 49 D4
arvil ..... Char 61 D3
ertsey ..... Chert 124 A1
ieveley ..... Chiev 51 D1
ilton ..... Chil 10 C4
ilton Foliat ..... Chil F 72 C1
olsey ..... Chol 14 A4

Cold Ash ..... Cold A 106 B4
Combe ..... Combe 147 F4
Compton ..... Comp 31 F2
Cookham ..... Cook 20 A4
Crowthorne ..... Crow 143 D2
Datchet ..... Datch 68 B3
Dorney ..... Dorn 41 D2
East Garston ..... East G 47 E3
East Isley ..... East I 30 C3
Englefield ..... Eng G 95 E1
Eton ..... Eton 67 E4
Farnborough ..... Farn 8 C1
Farnham Common ..... Far C 22 B3
Fawley ..... Fawl 27 E4
Fawley (Bucks) ..... Faw (Bu) 15 E4
Feltham ..... Felt 98 C4
Finchampstead ..... Finch 141 F1
Flackwell Heath ..... Fla H 3 D4
Froxfield ..... Frox 99 D3
Fulmer ..... Fulm 23 E4
Goring ..... Gori 34 B3
Great Shefford ..... Gr She 48 A2
Greenham ..... Gree 131 E4
Ham ..... Ham 126 B1
Hambledon ..... Hamb 16 B4
Hampstead Norreys ..... Hamp N 52 C3
Hamstead Marshall ..... Ham M 129 D4
Harlington ..... Harl 71 E4
Harmonsworth ..... Harm 70 B4
Headley ..... Head 132 B1
Henley-on-Thames ..... Hen-O-T 15 E1
Hermitage ..... Herm 79 D4
Holyport ..... Holy 65 D4
Horton ..... Hort 69 D2
Hungerford ..... Hung 100 C3
Hurley ..... Hurl 17 F2
Hurst ..... Hurst 88 C3
Inkpen ..... Ink 127 E3

Iver ..... Iver 44 C4
Iver Heath ..... Iver H 23 F2
Kintbury ..... Kint 102 A1
Knowle Hill ..... Know H 37 F2
Lambourn ..... Lamb 25 E1
Leckhampstead ..... Leckh 50 A3
Letcombe Bassett ..... Let B 6 C4
Lightwater ..... Light 153 D4
Linkenholt ..... Link 147 E1
Little Marlow ..... Lit M 2 B3
Maidenhead ..... Maid 39 F2
Mapledurham ..... Maple 57 F3
Marlow ..... Mar 1 A1
Marlow Bottom ..... Mar B 1 B3
Medmenham ..... Medm 17 D3
Mortimer ..... Mort 137 D3
Moulsford ..... Moul 13 F2
Newbury ..... Newb 104 C2
Newell Green ..... New G 91 E2
Newtown ..... Newt 131 D2
Oakley Green ..... Oak G 66 A3
Old Windsor ..... Old W 95 D4
Padworth ..... Padw 109 F1
Pangbourne ..... Pang 56 A3
Peasemore ..... Pease 50 C4
Purley on Thames ..... Pur O T 57 D3
Reading ..... Read 85 D3
Remenham Hill ..... Rem H 16 B1
Sandhurst ..... Sand 150 B4
Shepperton ..... Shepp 125 F2
Shinfield ..... Shin 113 F3
Shiplake ..... Shipl 35 F1
Silchester ..... Silc 136 B1
Slough ..... Slough 42 C3
Sonning ..... Sonn 60 C2
South Stoke ..... Sou S 14 B2
Staines ..... Stai 96 C1
Stanford Dingley ..... Stan D 81 E2

Stanwell ..... Stan 70 B1
Stoke Poges ..... Sto P 22 C2
Streatley ..... Stre 34 A4
Sulham ..... Sulh 56 C1
Sulhamstead ..... Sulhd 110 B3
Swallowfield ..... Swal 139 E3
Tadley ..... Tad 134 C1
Taplow ..... Tapl 20 C1
Thatcham ..... That 106 C2
Theale ..... Thea 83 E2
Tidmarsh ..... Tidm 56 B1
Twyford ..... Twyf 61 E3
Upper Basildon ..... Upp B 55 D3
Virginia Water ..... Vir W 122 B3
Waltham St Lawrence ..... W St L 62 C3
Wargrave ..... Warg 36 B1
Wentworth ..... Went 121 F2
West End ..... West E 153 F3
West Isley ..... West I 10 A1
West Woodhay ..... West W 128 B2
Whitchurch-on-Thames ..... Whi-O-T 56 B4
White Waltham ..... Whi Wa 63 F4
Wickham ..... Wick 75 E2
Windlesham ..... Windl 146 B2
Windsor ..... Wind 67 F3
Winkfield ..... Wink 92 B3
Winnersh ..... Winn 88 A2
Winterbourne ..... Wint 77 E3
Wokingham ..... Woki 116 A4
Woodburn Green ..... Woo G 3 F4
Woodley ..... Wood 88 A4
Woolhampton ..... Wool 108 B1
Wraysbury ..... Wray 95 F4
Yateley ..... Yate 149 E3
Yattendon ..... Yatt 53 F1

Abattoirs Rd. Read

Abattoirs Rd. Read ... 86 A4
Abbetts La. Camb ... 151 D2
Abbey Cl. Brac ... 118 B2
Abbey Cl. Newb ... 131 D4
Abbey Cl. Slough ... 41 F3
Abbey Cl. Woki ... 116 B4
Abbey Gdns. Chert ... 124 A2
Abbey Green. Chert ... 124 A2
Abbey Park. Bur C ... 110 C2
Abbey Rd. Bou E ... 2 C3
Abbey Rd. Chert ... 124 A1
Abbey Rd. Shepp ... 125 D1
Abbey Rd. Vir W ... 122 B3
Abbey Rd. Went ... 121 D1
Abbey Sq. Read ... 86 A4
Abbey St. Read ... 86 A4
Abbey Way. Bish ... 18 B3
Abbot Cl. Stai ... 97 E1
Abbot's Rd. Bur C ... 110 C1
Abbot's Wlk. Read ... 86 A4
Abbot's Wlk. Wind ... 66 C3
Abbots Dr. Vir W ... 122 B3
Abbots Rd. Newb ... 105 D1
Abbotsbury. Brac ... 117 F2
Abbotts Way. Slough ... 41 E3
Abelia Cl. Camb ... 153 F3
Aberford Cl. Read ... 85 E4
Abex Rd. Newb ... 105 E2
Abingdon Cl. Brac ... 118 C2
Abingdon Dr. Caver ... 59 E3
Abingdon Rd. East I ... 30 C4
Abingdon Rd. Sand ... 143 E1
Abingdon Wlk. Maid ... 19 F2
Abney Ct Dr. Bou E ... 3 D1
Aborfield Cl. Slough ... 42 C2
Abrahams Rd. Hen-O-T ... 15 E2
Acacia Ave. Crow ... 143 E1
Acacia Ave. Stai ... 125 D2
Acacia Ave. Wray ... 68 C3
Acacia Ct. Brac ... 118 A3
Acacia Mews. Harm ... 70 B4
Acacia Rd. Read ... 86 B3
Acacia Rd. Stai ... 97 D2
Academy Cl. Camb ... 151 F4
Accommodation La. Harm ... 70 A4
Ackrells Mead. Sand ... 142 C1
Acorn Dr. Woki ... 116 B4
Acorn Gr. Harl ... 71 F4
Acorn Rd. Black ... 150 A3
Acre Pas. Wind ... 67 E3
Acre Rd. Read ... 113 D4
Acre The. Mar ... 1 C1
Adam Cl. Slough ... 42 A3
Adam Cl. Tad ... 134 C1
Adam Ct. Hen-O-T ... 15 F1
Adams Way. Read ... 86 C1
Addington Cl. Wind ... 67 D2
Addington Rd. Read ... 86 B3
Addiscombe Chase. Sulh ... 57 D2
Addiscombe Rd. Crow ... 143 E2
Addison Cl. Iver ... 44 C4
Addison Ct. Maid ... 20 A1
Addison Rd. Read ... 59 D1
Adelaide Cl. Slough ... 42 A2
Adelaide Rd. Ashf ... 97 E2
Adelaide Rd. Read ... 87 D3
Adelaide Sq. Wind ... 67 E3
Adelphi Gdns. Slough ... 42 C2
Adkins Rd. W St L ... 62 C4
Admirals Ct. Read ... 86 A3
Admiralty Way. Sand ... 150 C2
Admoor La. Been ... 109 E4
Adwell Dr. Winn ... 87 E1
Adwell Sq. Hen-O-T ... 15 E1
Adwood Ct. That ... 106 C2
Agar Cres. Brac ... 91 D1
Agars Pl. Datch ... 68 A4
Agate Cl. Woki ... 115 F4
Aggisters La. Woki ... 115 E2
Agincourt Cl. Woki ... 115 F3
Agricola Way. That ... 106 C1
Ainsdale Cres. Read ... 85 D2
Aintree Cl. Newb ... 105 E1
Aintree Cl. Stan ... 69 F3
Aintree. Lamb ... 25 D1
Airport Way. Stan ... 70 A2
Aisne Rd. Camb ... 152 C1
Ajax Ave. Slough ... 42 A3
Alan Pl. Read ... 85 D3
Alan Way. Slough ... 43 F4
Alandale Cl. Read ... 113 E4
Albain Cres. Stan ... 97 F3
Albany Park Dr. Winn ... 88 A2
Albany Park. Camb ... 151 E1
Albany Park. Stan ... 69 E4
Albany Pl. Eng G ... 96 A2
Albany Rd. Old W ... 68 A1
Albany Rd. Read ... 85 E4
Albany Rd. Wind ... 67 E3
Alben Rd. Binf ... 90 B2
Albert Ave. Chert ... 124 A3
Albert Cl. Slough ... 42 C2
Albert Rd. Ashf ... 97 F2
Albert Rd. Bags ... 145 F1
Albert Rd. Brac ... 118 A4
Albert Rd. Camb ... 151 E3
Albert Rd. Caver ... 58 C2
Albert Rd. Crow ... 143 D3
Albert Rd. Eng G ... 95 E1

Albert Rd. Hen-O-T ... 15 F1
Albert Rd. Newb ... 105 D2
Albert Rd. Old W ... 68 A1
Albert Rd. Wind ... 67 F2
Albert Rd. Woki ... 116 A3
Albert St. Maid ... 39 F4
Albert St. Slough ... 42 C2
Albert St. Wind ... 67 D3
Albion Cl. Slough ... 43 D3
Albion Rd. Sand ... 150 A4
Albion Terr. Read ... 86 B4
Albury Cl. Read ... 58 B1
Albury Gdns. Read ... 84 C2
Alcot Cl. Crow ... 143 D2
Aldborough Spur. Slough ... 42 C4
Aldbourne Ave. Read ... 87 D2
Aldbourne Rd. Burn ... 41 D4
Aldebury Cl. Caver ... 59 E4
Aldenham Cl. Caver ... 59 E3
Aldenham Terr. Brac ... 118 B2
Alder Cl. Eng G ... 95 F2
Alder Cl. Slough ... 41 F3
Alder Dr. Read ... 84 B3
Alder Gr. Yate ... 149 E3
Alderbourne La. Fulm ... 23 F4
Alderbrook Cl. Finch ... 142 C3
Alderbury Rd W. Slough ... 43 F2
Alderbury Rd. Slough ... 43 F2
Alderfield Cl. Thea ... 83 F2
Alderley Cl. Wood ... 60 C1
Alderman Willey Cl. Woki ... 116 A3
Alders The. That ... 106 B2
Alderside Wlk. Eng G ... 95 F2
Aldin Ave S. Slough ... 43 D2
Aldridge Rd. Slough ... 22 A1
Aldwick Dr. Maid ... 39 E3
Aldworth Cl. Brac ... 118 A3
Aldworth Cl. Read ... 85 E3
Aldworth Gdns. Crow ... 143 D3
Aldworth Rd. Comp ... 31 F2
Aldworth Rd. Upp B ... 55 D3
Alexander Rd. Stai ... 96 B2
Alexander Rd. That ... 106 C1
Alexandra Ave. Camb ... 151 D3
Alexandra Cl. Ashf ... 98 B1
Alexandra Cl. Stai ... 97 E1
Alexandra Cl. Ashf ... 98 B1
Alexandra Ct. Ashf ... 98 C2
Alexandra Rd. Ashf ... 98 C1
Alexandra Rd. Eng G ... 95 E1
Alexandra Rd. Maid ... 39 E4
Alexandra Rd. Read ... 86 B3
Alexandra Rd. Slough ... 42 B2
Alexandra Rd. Wind ... 67 E3
Alford Cl. Read ... 84 B4
Alfred St. Read ... 85 F4
Alice La. Burn ... 21 D1
Alison Cl. Bur C ... 110 C1
Alison Dr. Camb ... 151 F3
All Hallows Rd. Caver ... 59 E2
All Saints Cl. Woki ... 116 B4
All Saints Cres. Black ... 150 C1
All Saints Rise. New G ... 91 F1
All Saints' Ave. Maid ... 39 E4
All Saints' Rd. Light ... 146 B1
All Souls' Rd. Ascot ... 120 A3
Allanson Rd. Mar ... 1 C2
Allcot Cl. Felt ... 98 C4
Allcroft Rd. Read ... 86 B3
Allenby Rd. Camb ... 151 D3
Allenby Rd. Maid ... 39 D4
Allendale Cl. Sand ... 143 D1
Allendale Rd. Read ... 87 D2
Allerds Rd. Burn ... 22 A2
Alleyns La. Cook ... 19 E4
Allhusen Gdns. Fulm ... 23 F4
Alliance Ct. Ashf ... 98 B2
Allison Gdns. Pur O T ... 57 E3
Allkins Ct. Wind ... 67 E3
Allnatt Ave. Winn ... 88 B1
Allonby Cl. Wood ... 87 E1
Allsmoor La. Brac ... 118 C3
Allyn Cl. Stai ... 96 C1
Alma Rd. Eton ... 41 F1
Alma Rd. Wind ... 67 E3
Alma St. Read ... 85 E4
Almners Rd. Chert ... 123 D1
Almond Ave. Newb ... 105 D3
Almond Cl. Eng G ... 95 D1
Almond Cl. Stai ... 125 E4
Almond Cl. Wind ... 67 D3
Almond Cl. Woki ... 115 E2
Almond Dr. Caver ... 59 F2
Almond Rd. Burn ... 21 E1
Almons Way. Slough ... 43 D4
Almswood Rd. Tad ... 135 D1
Alpha St N. Slough ... 42 C2
Alpha St S. Slough ... 42 C2
Alphington Ave. Camb ... 151 F1
Alphington Green. Camb ... 151 F1
Alpine St. Read ... 86 A3
Alsace Wlk. Camb ... 151 D1
Alsford Cl. Camb ... 152 C4
Alston Mews. That ... 106 B1
Alston Wlk. Caver ... 59 E1
Altmore. Bur G ... 38 C2
Alton Ct. Stai ... 123 F4

Alton Ride. Black ... 150 B3
Altona Way. Slough ... 42 A4
Altwood Bailey. Maid ... 39 D3
Altwood Cl. Burn ... 41 F4
Altwood Cl. Maid ... 39 D3
Altwood Dr. Maid ... 39 D3
Altwood Rd. Maid ... 39 D3
Alvista Ave. Burn ... 41 D4
Alwyn Rd. Maid ... 39 D4
Alwyns Cl. Chert ... 124 A2
Alwyns La. Chert ... 123 F2
Amanda Ct. Slough ... 43 E2
Ambarrow Cres. Sand ... 142 C1
Ambarrow La. Sand ... 142 C1
Ambassador. Brac ... 117 F2
Amber Hill. Camb ... 152 A2
Amberley Cl. Newb ... 104 C2
Amberley Cl. Maid ... 20 B2
Amberley Dr. Twyf ... 61 E3
Amberley Rd. Burn ... 41 F4
Amberwood Dr. Camb ... 151 F4
Amblecote Rd. Read ... 85 D4
Ambleside Cl. Wood ... 87 F4
Ambleside Dr. Felt ... 98 C4
Ambleside Dr. Felt ... 98 C4
Ambleside Rd. Light ... 153 D4
Ambleside Way. Stai ... 96 A1
Ambrook Road. Read ... 113 D4
Ambrose Pl. Read ... 85 F4
Ambury Rd. Comp ... 32 C2
Amen Corner Bsns Park. Brac 117 F2
Amerden Cl. Tapl ... 40 B4
Amerden La. Tapl ... 40 B4
Amerden La. Tapl ... 40 C2
Amerden Way. Slough ... 42 A2
Amersham Rd. Caver ... 59 E1
Amethyst Cl. Woki ... 115 E4
Amherst Rd. Read ... 87 D3
Amity Rd. Read ... 86 C4
Amity St. Read ... 86 C4
Amners Farm Rd. Bur C ... 112 A4
Ampere Rd. Newb ... 105 D2
Ancaster Dr. Ascot ... 119 F4
Ancastle Gr. Hen-O-T ... 15 E1
Andermans. Wind ... 66 B3
Anderson Ave. Read ... 87 D3
Anderson Cres. Arbo ... 114 C1
Anderwood Dr. Ashf ... 98 B2
Anderson Pl. Bags ... 145 F2
Andover Cl. Read ... 57 E1
Andover Dro. Ham M ... 130 A2
Andover Rd. Ball H ... 130 B3
Andover Rd. Black ... 150 B3
Andover Rd. Newb ... 130 B3
Andrew Cl. Woki ... 116 C3
Andrews Cl. Thea ... 83 F2
Andrews Rd. Read ... 87 D2
Andrews Way. Mar B ... 1 B4
Angel Ct. Newb ... 105 D2
Angel Mead. Wool ... 108 B1
Angel Pl. Binf ... 90 B1
Angle Field Rd. Caver ... 59 E2
Anglers Way. Read ... 86 B4
Anglesey Cl. Ashf ... 98 A3
Angus Cl. Read ... 84 C2
Annadale. Cold A ... 79 E1
Anne Cl. Maid ... 19 F1
Anneforde Pl. Brac ... 91 D1
Anners Cl. Stai ... 123 E3
Annesley Gdns. Winn ... 88 B2
Annett Cl. Shepp ... 125 F3
Anscult Rd. Slough ... 22 A1
Ansell Rd. Camb ... 151 F1
Anslow Pl. Slough ... 41 E4
Anson Cres. Read ... 113 E4
Anstey Pl. Bur C ... 111 D2
Anstey Rd. Read ... 86 A4
Anston Cl. Read ... 114 A4
Antares Cl. Woki ... 115 F3
Anthony Way. Slough ... 41 E3
Antrim Rd. Wood ... 87 E3
Apex Dr. Camb ... 151 E1
Aplin Way. Light ... 146 A1
Apple Cl. Pur O T ... 57 D2
Apple Cl. Woki ... 115 F3
Apple Tree Cl. Newb ... 130 C4
Apple Tree Way. Sand ... 143 E1
Appleby End. Read ... 85 D4
Appleby Gdns. Felt ... 98 C4
Applecroft. Maid ... 39 E2
Appledore. Brac ... 117 F2
Appleford Cl. That ... 106 B1
Appleford Rd. Read ... 85 D3
Appletree La. Shin ... 113 D1
Appletree La. Slough ... 43 E2
Appletree Pl. Brac ... 118 A4
Appley Ct. Camb ... 151 D3
Appley Dr. Camb ... 151 D3
Approach Rd. Ashf ... 98 B1
Approach Rd. Tapl ... 40 C4
April Cl. Camb ... 151 E1
Aquila Cl. Woki ... 115 F3
Aragon Cl. Ashf ... 98 C1
Arbor La. Winn ... 88 A2
Arbor Meadows. Winn ... 88 A2
Arborfield Rd. Shin ... 113 F2
Arbour Cl. Read ... 85 F3
Arcade The. Gori ... 34 B3
Arcade The. Newb ... 105 D2

Archangel Way. That ... 106 C2
Archer Cl. Maid ... 39 E4
Archway Rd. Caver ... 59 D1
Arden Cl. Brac ... 119 D4
Ardingly. Brac ... 118 A2
Ardler Rd. Caver ... 59 E1
Ardrossan Ave. Camb ... 152 A3
Arenal Dr. Crow ... 143 E2
Arethusa Way. Bis ... 153 F2
Argosy Gdns. Stai ... 96 C1
Argosy La. Stan ... 97 E4
Argyle Rd. Newb ... 104 C1
Argyle Rd. Read ... 85 F4
Argyle St. Read ... 85 F4
Arkle Ave. That ... 105 F2
Arkley Ct. Holy ... 40 B1
Arkwright Dr. Brac ... 117 E4
Arkwright Rd. Read ... 86 A2
Arkwright Rd. Stan ... 69 F3
Arlington Bsns Park. Read ... 84 A2
Arlington Cl. Brac ... 118 A4
Arlington Cl. Maid ... 38 C4
Arlington Rd. Ashf ... 97 F2
Arlington Square. Brac ... 118 A4
Armadale Ct. Read ... 85 E3
Armitage Ct. Ascot ... 120 B2
Armitage Dr. Camb ... 151 F1
Armour Hill. Read ... 57 E1
Armour Rd. Read ... 57 E1
Armour Wlk. Pur O T ... 57 E1
Armstrong Rd. Eng G ... 95 E1
Armstrong Way. Wood ... 88 A4
Arncliffe. Brac ... 118 A2
Arndale Way. Eng G ... 96 A2
Arnett Ave. Woki ... 141 F4
Arnewood Ave. Tad ... 135 E1
Arnhem Rd. Newb ... 105 D2
Arnold Rd. Stai ... 97 E1
Arnside Cl. Twyf ... 61 E4
Arrowhead Rd. Thea ... 83 F1
Arrowsmith Way. That ... 106 C1
Arthur Cl. Bags ... 145 F1
Arthur Pl. Read ... 86 B4
Arthur Rd. Newb ... 104 C1
Arthur Rd. Slough ... 42 B2
Arthur Rd. Wind ... 67 D3
Arthur Rd. Woki ... 116 A3
Arthurstone Birches. Binf ... 90 B2
Arun Cl. Winn ... 88 A1
Arundel Cl. Maid ... 39 D4
Arundel Ct. Slough ... 43 E1
Arundel Rd. Camb ... 152 B2
Arundel Rd. Wood ... 87 F4
Ascot Rd. Felt ... 98 A3
Ascot Rd. Holy ... 40 A1
Ascot Rd. Holy ... 64 C1
Ascot Rd. New G ... 91 F4
Ash Cl. Brig ... 28 B2
Ash Cl. Sand ... 150 B3
Ash Cl. Slough ... 44 A2
Ash Gr. Felt ... 98 C4
Ash Gr. Stai ... 97 E1
Ash Gr. Sto P ... 22 C3
Ash La. Bur C ... 111 D2
Ash La. Wind ... 66 B3
Ash Rd. Newt ... 131 F2
Ash Rd. Newt ... 132 A2
Ash Rd. Read ... 84 C4
Ash Rd. Stai ... 125 D3
Ash Terr. Cold A ... 106 A4
Ash Tree Gr. Ham M ... 129 D4
Ash Way. Woki ... 115 E2
Ashampstead Rd. Brad ... 82 A4
Ashampstead Rd. Read ... 85 D2
Ashampstead Rd. Upp B ... 55 D3
Ashbourne Gr. Maid ... 39 E2
Ashbourne Way. That ... 106 A2
Ashbourne. Brac ... 117 F2
Ashbrook Rd. Old W ... 95 D4
Ashburton Rd. Read ... 86 B1
Ashbury Dr. Camb ... 151 D1
Ashbury Dr. Read ... 84 B4
Ashby Ct. Read ... 113 D4
Ashby Way. Harm ... 71 D4
Ashcroft Cl. Caver ... 58 C3
Ashcroft Cl. Burn ... 21 D2
Ashcroft Rd. Maid ... 39 E4
Ashdale Cl. Stan ... 97 F3
Ashdale Park. Brac ... 142 B3
Ashdene Cl. Stai ... 98 B1
Ashdown Cl. Brac ... 119 D4
Ashdown. Maid ... 20 A2
Ashen Cross. Slough ... 44 A4
Ashenden Wlk. Far C ... 22 B4
Asher Dr. Burl ... 119 E4
Ashfield Green. Yate ... 149 F3
Ashford Ave. Ashf ... 98 A1
Ashford Cl. Ashf ... 97 F2
Ashford Cres. Ashf ... 97 F3
Ashford Hill Rd. Head ... 132 C1
Ashford Ind Est. Felt ... 98 B2
Ashford La. Dorn ... 41 D2
Ashford Rd. Felt ... 98 C3
Ashford Rd. Stai ... 97 E1
Ashford Rd. Stai ... 98 B1
Ashgrove Rd. Ashf ... 98 B2
Ashleigh Ave. Stai ... 96 B1
Ashley Cl. Read ... 87 D1

Ashley Cl. Shepp ... 125
Ashley Dr. Black ... 150
Ashley Hill Pl. Know H ... 36
Ashley Park Ave. Shepp ... 125
Ashley Park Cres. Shepp ... 125
Ashley Park. Maid ... 20
Ashley Rd. Read ... 85
Ashley Way. West E ... 153
Ashman Pl. Kint ... 102
Ashman Rd. That ... 107
Ashmere Cl. Bur C ... 84
Ashmere Terr. Read ... 85
Ashmore Green Rd. Cold A ... 106
Ashmore Rd. Read ... 86
Ashridge Green. Brac ... 118
Ashridge Rd. Woki ... 116
Ashton Cl. Read ... 84
Ashton Pl. Maid ... 39
Ashton Rd. Newb ... 105
Ashton Rd. Woki ... 88
Ashtrees Rd. Wood ... 87
Ashurst Dr. Stai ... 124
Ashview Cl. Ashf ... 97
Ashview Gdns. Ashf ... 97
Ashville Way. Woki ... 116
Ashwell Ave. Camb ... 84
Ashwood Cl. Read ... 84
Ashwood Dr. Newb ... 105
Ashwood Pl. Eng G ... 95
Ashwood. Wood ... 87
Ashworth Dr. That ... 106
Askew Dr. Shin ... 113
Aspen Cl. Slough ... 42
Aspen Cl. Stai ... 96
Aspin Way. Black ... 150
Astleham Way. Stai ... 124
Astley Cl. Woki ... 115
Aston Ave. Read ... 57
Aston Cl. Pangb ... 56
Aston Ferry La. Rem H ... 16
Aston La. Rem H ... 16
Aston Mead. Wind ... 66
Aston St. Ast T ... 12
Astor Cl. Winn ... 88
Astra Mead. Burl ... 92
Atfield Gr. Windl ... 146
Atherton Cl. Read ... 84
Atherton Cl. Stan ... 70
Atherton Cres. Hung ... 100
Atherton Pl. Lamb ... 25
Atherton Rd. Hung ... 100
Athlone Cl. Maid ... 39
Atrebatti Rd. Sand ... 143
Auckland Cl. Maid ... 39
Auckland Rd. Read ... 87
Auclum Cl. Bur C ... 111
Auclum La. Bur C ... 111
Audley Cl. Newb ... 105
Audley Dr. Maid ... 39
Audley St. Read ... 85
Audley Way. Burl ... 119
Augur Cl. Stai ... 96
August End. Read ... 85
August End. Slough ... 43
Augustine Cl. Stan ... 69
Augustine Wlk. New G ... 91
Augustus Gdns. Camb ... 152
Austen Gdns. Newb ... 131
Austin Rd. Wood ... 87
Australia Ave. Maid ... 39
Australia Rd. Slough ... 42
Autumn Cl. Caver ... 59
Autumn Cl. Slough ... 41
Autumn Wlk. Maid ... 39
Autumn Wlk. Warg ... 36
Avalon Rd. Bou E ... 3
Avalon Rd. Read ... 87
Avebury Sq. Read ... 86
Avebury. Brac ... 118
Avebury. Slough ... 98
Avenue Rd. Felt ... 98
Avenue Rd. Maid ... 40
Avenue Rd. Stai ... 96
Avenue Sucy. Camb ... 151
Avenue The. Ascot ... 92
Avenue The. Bou E ... 3
Avenue The. Camb ... 151
Avenue The. Crow ... 143
Avenue The. Eng G ... 96
Avenue The. Far C ... 22
Avenue The. Light ... 146
Avenue The. Maid ... 20
Avenue The. Mort ... 137
Avenue The. Old W ... 68
Avenue The. Slough ... 68
Avenue The. Stai ... 124
Avenue The. Wray ... 68
Averil Cl. Slough ... 41
Avington Cl. Read ... 86
Avocet Cres. Sand ... 150
Avon Cl. Read ... 86
Avon Cl. Slough ... 41
Avon Gr. Brac ... 91
Avon Pl. Read ... 86
Avon Rd. Ashf ... 98
Avon Way. Padw ... 109
Avondale Ave. Stai ... 96
Avondale Rd. Ashf ... 98
Avondale. Maid ... 19

...ridge Rd. Read ...86 B1
...ridge. Brac ...118 C2
...bridges Ave. Stai ...96 B1
...sbury Cres. Slough ...42 B3
...sham Way. Yate ...149 D3
...esworth Ave. Slough ...22 A1
...esworth Spur. Old W ...95 D4
...sham Cl. Read ...84 C4
...ner Cl. Stai ...123 F4
...ner Dr. Stai ...123 F4
...garth Park. Holy ...40 A1
...garth. Brac ...118 A2
...lea Way. Camb ...152 A3
...lea Way. Slough ...43 F4
...bington Rd. Read ...113 E3
...chelors Acre. Wind ...67 E3
...k La. Been ...109 D4
...k La. Brad ...81 F2
...k La. Brim ...134 B2
...k La. Kint ...127 F4
...k La. Shin ...139 D4
...k La. Stan D ...81 F2
...k St. East G ...47 E3
...ksideans. Warg ...36 B1
...on Cl. Sand ...150 B3
...l Godesberg Way. Maid ...39 F4
...en Cl. Stai ...97 D1
...er Gdns. Slough ...42 A2
...er Way The. Wood ...88 A3
...gebury Rise. Mar B ...1 B4
...gemore La. Hen-O-T ...15 E2
...ger Cl. Maid ...39 E2
...ger Dr. Light ...146 A1
...ger Dr. Twyf ...61 E4
...gers Copse. Camb ...151 F2
...gers Croft. Mort ...137 D3
...gers Hill. Vir W ...122 B2
...gers Holt. Yate ...149 D3
...gers Rise. Caver ...59 D3
...gers Sett. Crow ...142 C3
...gers Way. Brac ...118 C4
...gers Way. Mar B ...1 B4
...gers Wlk. Shipl ...36 A2
...gers Wood. Far C ...22 B4
...gerwood Dr. Camb ...151 E1
...minton Rd. Maid ...39 D3
...nols Way. Newb ...104 C1
...shot Green. Bags ...145 F2
...shot Rd. Ascot ...120 A1
...shot Rd. Brac ...118 B2
...shot Rd. Eng G ...95 E1
...shot Rd. Sunn ...120 A1
...shot Rd. West E ...153 F4
...ents La. Windl ...146 B2
...ey Cl. Maid ...39 F4
...ey Cl. Wind ...67 D3
...ey's La. Hurst ...62 C2
...eys Cl. Black ...150 B2
...y Ave. That ...106 A2
... Ave. Camb ...151 D1
...bridge Rd. Bur C ...84 A2
...d Cl. Slough ...42 A2
...d Rd. Arbo ...140 C4
...d Rd. Bark ...140 C4
...eham La. Eng G ...95 E1
...er St. Ast T ...12 C4
...er St. Read ...85 F4
...ers La. Maid ...38 C2
...dwin Rd. Burn ...21 E1
...dwin's Shore. Eton ...67 E4
...our Cres. Brac ...118 A2
...our Cres. Newb ...130 B3
...our Dr. Bur C ...84 A2
...our Rd. Mar ...1 B2
...ntore Ct. Sand ...150 B4
... Pit Rd. Beed ...30 A3
... Pit Rd. East I ...30 A3
...amore Cl. Bur C ...84 A2
...ard Green. Wind ...66 C4
...ard. Camb ...152 A4
...encrief Rd. Sunn ...120 C1
...ol Rd. Caver ...58 B2
...ol Way. Crow ...143 F1
...moral Cl. Slough ...41 F4
...moral Gdns. Wind ...67 E2
...moral. Maid ...19 D1
...nor Dr. Caver ...59 D2
...burgh Cl. Read ...86 B2
...bury Ave. Slough ...41 F4
...bury Gdns. Caver ...59 E2
...bury. Brac ...118 C1
...croft Cl. Ashf ...98 A2
...croft Rd. Bur C ...84 A2
...d La. Eng G ...96 A2
...gors Cl. Iver ...44 C4
...gors Rd S. Iver ...44 C4
...k Side. Woki ...141 F3
...ks Spur. Slough ...42 A2
...kside Rd. Read ...86 B1
...nard Rd. Maid ...39 D3
...nister Cl. Slough ...43 F2
...nister Gdns. Yate ...149 D1
...nister Pl. Brim ...133 F3
...nister Rd. Bur C ...110 C2
...bara Cl. Shepp ...125 D2
...bara's Meadow. Sulh ...57 D1

Barber Cl. Hurst ...88 C4
Barberry Way. Black ...150 C1
Barbon Cl. Camb ...152 B2
Barbrook Cl. Read ...57 E2
Barchester Rd. Slough ...43 F2
Barclay Rd. Bur C ...84 B2
Barclose Ave. Caver ...59 E2
Bardney Cl. Maid ...39 E2
Bardolph's Cl. Maple ...58 B4
Bardown. Chiev ...51 D1
Barfield Rd. That ...106 A2
Barge La. Swal ...139 D3
Bargeman Rd. Maid ...39 F2
Bargeman Rd. Maid ...39 F3
Barholm Cl. Winn ...87 F1
Barkby. Read ...87 E1
Barker Ct. Hurst ...88 C4
Barker Green. Brac ...118 A2
Barker Rd. Chert ...123 F1
Barkham Rd. Bark ...115 E2
Barkham Rd. Woki ...115 E2
Barkham Ride. Bark ...141 F4
Barkham Ride. Woki ...141 F4
Barkham St. Bark ...115 E1
Barkhart Dr. Woki ...116 B4
Barkhart Gdns. Woki ...116 B4
Barkwith Cl. Winn ...87 F1
Barley Cl. That ...106 C3
Barley Fields. Woo G ...3 F4
Barley Mead. New G ...91 F1
Barley Mow Rd. Eng G ...95 E2
Barley Mow Way. Stai ...125 D3
Barley Wlk. Read ...84 A3
Barn Cl. Ashf ...98 A2
Barn Cl. Brac ...118 B4
Barn Cl. Camb ...151 F3
Barn Cl. Far C ...22 A4
Barn Cl. Kint ...102 A1
Barn Cl. Maid ...19 F1
Barn Cl. Read ...85 E2
Barn Cres. Newb ...130 B4
Barn Dr. Maid ...39 D2
Barn La. Hen-O-T ...15 E2
Barn Owl Way. Bur C ...111 D2
Barnard Cl. Caver ...59 E3
Barnards Hill. Mar ...1 B1
Barnes Rd. Camb ...151 F1
Barnes Way. Iver ...44 C3
Barnett Green. Brac ...118 A2
Barnett La. Camb ...152 C4
Barnfield. Iver ...44 C4
Barnfield. Slough ...41 E3
Barnhill Cl. Mar ...1 B2
Barnhill Gdns. Mar ...1 B2
Barnhill Rd. Mar ...1 B2
Barnsdale Rd. Read ...86 B2
Barnway. Eng G ...95 E2
Barnwood Cl. Read ...85 F4
Baron Ct. Read ...85 F4
Barons Mead. Hen-O-T ...15 E1
Barons Way. Stai ...96 B1
Barossa Rd. Camb ...151 E4
Barr's Rd. Burn ...41 D4
Barracane Dr. Crow ...143 D3
Barrack La. Wind ...67 E3
Barracks La. Shin ...113 D1
Barrett Cres. Woki ...116 C3
Barrington Cl. Read ...87 D3
Barris Head. Crow ...143 F1
Barry Ave. Wind ...67 E4
Barry Pl. Read ...86 A4
Bartelotts Rd. Slough ...21 F1
Bartholemew Pl. New G ...91 F1
Bartholomew St. Newb ...104 C1
Bartlemy Cl. Newb ...130 C4
Bartlemy Rd. Newb ...130 C4
Barton Cl. Shepp ...125 D2
Barton Rd. Read ...84 A4
Barton Rd. Slough ...43 F2
Bartons Dr. Yate ...149 E2
Barwell Cl. Crow ...142 C2
Basemoors. Brac ...118 C4
Basford Way. Wind ...66 B2
Basil Cl. Read ...86 C1
Basingstoke Rd. Alde ...109 D1
Basingstoke Rd. Read ...86 A2
Basingstoke Rd. Shin ...139 E3
Basingstoke Rd. Swal ...139 E3
Baskerville La. Shipl ...36 A2
Baslow Rd. Winn ...88 A1
Bass Mead. Cook ...19 F3
Bassett Cl. Winn ...114 B4
Bassett Rd. Let B ...6 C4
Bassett Way. Slough ...21 F1
Batcombe Mead. Brac ...118 C1
Bates Cl. Slough ...43 F4
Bath Rd. Been ...108 B1
Bath Rd. Brad ...108 B1
Bath Rd. Bur G ...38 B3
Bath Rd. Burn ...41 E4
Bath Rd. Camb ...151 E3
Bath Rd. Frox ...99 D2
Bath Rd. Harl ...71 E3
Bath Rd. Harm ...70 B3
Bath Rd. Hung ...100 C4
Bath Rd. Know H ...38 B3
Bath Rd. Maid ...38 B3
Bath Rd. Newb ...104 B3

Bath Rd. Padw ...108 B1
Bath Rd. Read ...85 E3
Bath Rd. Slough ...41 E4
Bath Rd. Sonn ...60 C1
Bath Rd. That ...108 B1
Bath Rd. Thea ...108 B1
Bath Rd. Warg ...62 A4
Bath Rd. Wool ...108 B1
Bathurst Cl. Iver ...44 C2
Bathurst Rd. Winn ...88 A1
Bathurst Wlk. Iver ...44 C2
Battery End. Newb ...130 B3
Battle Cl. Newb ...104 B2
Battle Rd. Gori ...34 C4
Battle Rd. Newb ...130 B3
Battle St. Read ...85 F4
Battlemead Cl. Maid ...20 B2
Batty's Barn Cl. Woki ...116 B3
Baxendales The. Newb ...105 E1
Bay Cl. Read ...86 C1
Bay Dr. Brac ...118 C4
Bay Rd. Brac ...118 C4
Bay Tree Ct. Burn ...21 E1
Bay Tree Rise. Read ...84 B3
Baydon Dr. Read ...85 F3
Baydon Rd. East G ...46 B2
Baydon Rd. Gr She ...46 B2
Baydon Rd. Lamb ...46 B2
Bayfield Ave. Camb ...151 F1
Bayford Cl. Camb ...151 D1
Bayford Dr. Read ...84 C2
Bayley Cres. Burn ...41 D4
Bayley Ct. Winn ...88 A1
Baylis Rd. Slough ...42 C3
Bayliss Rd. Warg ...36 B1
Baysfarm Ct. Harm ...70 B3
Beacon Rd. Felt ...71 D1
Beaconsfield Rd. Far C ...22 B3
Beaconsfield Way. Read ...87 D1
Beal's La. Sulh ...84 A4
Beale Cl. Woki ...116 A4
Bean Oak Rd. Woki ...116 C3
Beancroft Rd. That ...106 B1
Bear La. Newb ...105 D2
Bear La. Warg ...37 D2
Beard's Rd. Ashf ...98 C1
Bearwood Path. Winn ...88 A1
Bearwood Rd. Woki ...115 E3
Beatty Dr. Read ...84 C4
Beauchief Cl. Read ...113 F4
Beaufield Cl. Wood ...87 E4
Beaufort Cl. Mar ...1 C1
Beaufort Gdns. Ascot ...119 F4
Beaufort Gdns. Mar ...1 C1
Beaufort Pl. Maid ...40 B2
Beauforts. Eng G ...95 E2
Beaufront Cl. Camb ...152 A4
Beaufront Rd. Camb ...152 A4
Beaulieu Cl. Brac ...119 D3
Beaulieu Cl. Datch ...68 A3
Beaulieu Gdns. Sand ...150 B3
Beaumont Cl. Maid ...39 D2
Beaumont Dr. Ashf ...98 B2
Beaumont Gdns. Brac ...118 C2
Beaumont Rd. Slough ...42 B4
Beaumont Rd. Wind ...67 E3
Beaumont Rise. Mar ...1 C1
Beaver La. Yate ...149 F3
Beaver Way. Wood ...88 A4
Beavers Cl. Tad ...135 D1
Becket Cl. Woki ...116 C3
Beckford Ave. Brac ...118 A2
Beckford Cl. Woki ...88 C1
Beckfords. Upp B ...55 D3
Beckings Way. Fla H ...3 E4
Bede Wlk. Read ...86 B2
Bedfont Cl. Felt ...71 E1
Bedfont Cl. Stan ...70 A2
Bedfont La. Felt ...98 C4
Bedfont Rd. Felt ...98 B3
Bedfont Rd. Stan ...70 C1
Bedford Ave. Slough ...42 A4
Bedford Cl. Maid ...39 D2
Bedford Dr. Far C ...22 A3
Bedford Gdns. Woki ...115 F4
Bedford La. Sunn ...121 D2
Bedford Rd. Read ...85 F4
Bedfordshire Way. Woki ...115 F3
Bedwins Way. Cook ...19 D3
Beech Ave. Camb ...151 E2
Beech Cl. Ashf ...98 B2
Beech Cl. Bur C ...111 D2
Beech Cl. Stan ...97 E4
Beech Dr. Black ...150 B2
Beech Glen. Brac ...118 A3
Beech Hill Rd. Bee H ...138 C3
Beech Hill Rd. Sunn ...120 C2
Beech La. Gori ...14 C1
Beech La. Read ...87 D1
Beech Rd. Felt ...98 C4
Beech Rd. Maple ...58 B4
Beech Rd. Newt ...132 A2
Beech Rd. Pur O T ...57 D3
Beech Rd. Read ...86 C1
Beech Rd. Slough ...43 F2
Beech Ride. Sand ...143 D1
Beech Tree La. Stai ...124 A4
Beech Wlk. That ...106 C1

Beecham Rd. Read ...85 E4
Beechbrook Ave. Yate ...149 F3
Beechcroft Cl. Ascot ...120 B3
Beechcroft. Brac ...118 A3
Beechcroft. Hamp N ...53 D3
Beeches Dr. Far C ...22 A4
Beeches Rd. Far C ...22 A4
Beeches The. Gori ...34 A3
Beeches The. Read ...57 E2
Beechingstoke. Mar ...1 C2
Beechmont Ave. Went ...122 B2
Beechnut Cl. Woki ...115 F3
Beechnut Dr. Black ...150 A3
Beechtree Ave. Eng G ...95 D1
Beechtree Ave. Mar B ...1 B3
Beechwood Ave. Read ...84 B4
Beechwood Ave. Stai ...97 D1
Beechwood Ave. Wood ...87 E4
Beechwood Cl. Burl ...92 C1
Beechwood Dr. Maid ...39 D3
Beechwood Dr. Mar ...18 A4
Beechwood Gdns. Slough ...42 C2
Beechwood Rd. Slough ...42 B4
Beechwood Rd. Went ...122 A1
Beedon Dr. Brac ...117 F2
Beehive La. Brac ...117 E4
Beehive Rd. Brac ...117 E4
Beehive Rd. Stai ...96 C2
Beeston Way. Read ...114 A4
Beggars Hill Rd. Char ...61 D1
Beighton Cl. Read ...113 F4
Beir Path The. Sou S ...14 A2
Belfast Ave. Slough ...42 B4
Belgrave Ct. Black ...150 B3
Belgrave Rd. Slough ...42 C3
Bell Cl. Slough ...43 D4
Bell Corner. Chert ...123 F1
Bell Ct. Hurl ...17 F2
Bell Foundary La. Woki ...116 B4
Bell Foundry La. Woki ...116 B4
Bell Hill. Ham M ...130 A2
Bell Hill. Newb ...130 A2
Bell Holt. Newb ...130 B3
Bell La. Comp ...32 C2
Bell La. Eton ...41 F1
Bell La. Hen-O-T ...15 E2
Bell La. Ink ...127 E2
Bell La. Sand ...150 B3
Bell Pl. Bags ...145 F2
Bell St. Hen-O-T ...15 F1
Bell St. Maid ...39 F3
Bell View Cl. Wind ...66 C3
Bell View. Wind ...66 C3
Bell Weir Cl. Wray ...96 A3
Belle Ave. Read ...87 D3
Belle Vue Cl. Stai ...124 A4
Belle Vue Rd. Hen-O-T ...35 E4
Belle Vue Rd. Read ...85 F4
Bellever Hill. Camb ...151 F3
Bellingham Cl. Camb ...152 B2
Bellingham Wlk. Caver ...59 D3
Bells Hill Green. Sto P ...23 D3
Bells Hill. Sto P ...23 D3
Bells La. Hort ...69 D2
Bellswood La. Iver ...44 A4
Belmont Cres. Maid ...39 E4
Belmont Dr. Maid ...39 E4
Belmont Mews. Camb ...151 E2
Belmont Park Ave. Maid ...39 E4
Belmont Park Rd. Maid ...39 E4
Belmont Rd. Camb ...151 E2
Belmont Rd. Crow ...143 D3
Belmont Rd. Maid ...39 E4
Belmont Rd. Read ...85 E4
Belmont Vale. Maid ...39 E4
Belmont. Slough ...42 A4
Belton Rd. Camb ...151 F3
Belvedere Ct. Black ...150 B2
Belvedere Dr. Newb ...131 D4
Belvedere Wlk. Winn ...88 A2
Belvoir Cl. Camb ...151 F1
Bembridge Ct. Slough ...42 C2
Bembridge Pl. Read ...86 B4
Benbricke Green. Brac ...91 D1
Bence The. Stai ...123 D3
Bencombe Rd. Mar B ...1 C3
Benedict Dr. Felt ...98 C4
Benedict Green. New G ...91 F1
Benen-stock Rd. Stan ...70 A1
Benetfeld Rd. Binf ...90 A1
Benham Hill. Newb ...105 F2
Benham Hill. That ...105 F2
Benham La. Swal ...139 E2
Benhams La. Faw (Bu) ...15 F4
Benner La. West E ...153 F4
Bennet Rd. Read ...86 A1
Bennett Cl. Newb ...104 C3
Bennett Ct. Camb ...151 E3
Bennett's Hill. Bur C ...111 E4
Bennetts Cl. Slough ...42 A3
Benning Cl. Wind ...66 B2
Benning Way. Woki ...116 B3
Bennings Cl. Brac ...91 D1
Benson Cl. Read ...86 B2
Benson Cl. Slough ...43 D3
Benson Rd. Crow ...142 C3
Bentley Park. Burn ...21 E2
Bentley Rd. Slough ...42 A3
Benyon Ct. Read ...85 F3

Benyon Mews. Read ...85 F3
Beomonds Row. Chert ...124 A1
Bere Court Rd. Pangb ...56 A2
Bere Rd. Brac ...118 C2
Beresford Ave. Slough ...43 E3
Beresford Rd. Read ...85 F4
Bergenia Ct. Camb ...153 F3
Berkeley Ave. Read ...85 F3
Berkeley Cl. Stan ...96 B3
Berkeley Gdns. Shepp ...125 F1
Berkeley Mews. Mar ...1 C1
Berkeley Rd. Newb ...104 C1
Berkley Cl. Maid ...39 D4
Berkshire Ave. Slough ...42 A4
Berkshire Dr. Read ...84 B4
Berkshire Rd. Camb ...151 F4
Berkshire Rd. Hen-O-T ...35 E4
Berkshire Way. Brac ...117 E3
Berners Cl. Slough ...41 F3
Bernersh Cl. Sand ...143 E1
Berries Rd. Cook ...20 A4
Berry Field. Slough ...43 E4
Berry Hill. Tapl ...40 B4
Berrybank. Sand ...150 C3
Berrylands Rd. Caver ...59 D2
Berrys La. Bur C ...85 D1
Berrys Rd. Buck ...107 E3
Berryscroft Rd. Stai ...97 E1
Berstead Cl. Read ...87 D1
Berwick Ave. Slough ...42 A3
Berwick Cl. Mar ...1 B2
Berwick La. Mar ...1 B2
Berwick Rd. Mar ...1 B2
Beryl Cl. Woki ...115 F4
Bessel's Way. Blew ...12 A4
Bestobell Rd. Slough ...42 B4
Betam Rd. Read ...86 B4
Betchworth Ave. Read ...87 D2
Bethany Waye. Felt ...98 C4
Bethesda Cl. Upp B ...55 D3
Bethesda St. Upp B ...55 D4
Betjeman Way. Yate ...149 D2
Betteridge Rd. That ...106 C1
Beverley Cl. Camb ...152 B3
Beverley Cl. Mar ...1 C1
Beverley Cl. That ...106 B2
Beverley Ct. Slough ...43 D2
Beverley Gdns. Maid ...19 D1
Beverley Gdns. Warg ...36 C1
Beverley Rd. Read ...57 E1
Beverley Rd. Shepp ...125 F4
Bevers The. Mort ...137 D3
Bexley Ct. Read ...85 E3
Bexley St. Wind ...67 E3
Bibury Cl. Wood ...87 E2
Bicknell Rd. Camb ...151 F1
Bideford Cl. Wood ...87 E3
Bideford Spur. Slough ...22 A1
Big La. Lamb ...25 D2
Bigbury Gdns. Read ...86 B2
Bigfrith La. Cook ...19 D3
Biggs La. Bark ...141 D4
Billet Bridge. Stai ...97 D2
Billet La. Slough ...44 A4
Billet Rd. Stan ...97 D3
Billing Ave. Woki ...141 F3
Billingbear La. Binf ...90 A3
Billington Rd. Cold A ...106 B3
Binbrook Cl. Winn ...87 E1
Binfield Rd. Binf ...116 C4
Binfield Rd. Brac ...118 A4
Binfield Rd. Woki ...116 C4
Bingham Dr. Stai ...97 E1
Bingham Rd. Burn ...41 D4
Binghams The. Maid ...40 A2
Bingley Gr. Wood ...60 C1
Binsted Dr. Black ...150 B3
Birch Ave. Read ...85 D4
Birch Cl. Camb ...151 F4
Birch Dr. Black ...150 B2
Birch Gr. Shepp ...125 F4
Birch Gr. Slough ...42 A4
Birch Gr. Wind ...66 B3
Birch Hill Rd. Brac ...118 A1
Birch La. Burl ...119 D4
Birch La. Silc ...136 C3
Birch La. West E ...153 E3
Birch Platt. West E ...153 E3
Birch Rd. Bur C ...111 D2
Birch Rd. Tad ...134 C1
Birch Rd. Windl ...146 C2
Birch Rd. Woki ...142 A4
Birch Side. Crow ...142 C3
Birch Tree View. Light ...146 A1
Birch View. Read ...86 C1
Birches The. Black ...150 A3
Birches The. Gori ...34 A3
Birchetts Cl. Brac ...118 A4
Birchfields. Camb ...151 E2
Birchington Rd. Wind ...67 D3
Birchland Cl. Silc ...136 C3
Birchmead. Winn ...88 B1
Birchview Cl. Yate ...149 E2
Birchwood Cl. Caver ...59 E3
Birchwood Dr. Light ...146 B1
Birchwood Rd. Newb ...105 D2
Birchwood The. Read ...57 D3
Bird Mews. Woki ...116 A3
Birdhill Ave. Read ...86 B1

Birds La. Wool 107 F2
Birdwood Rd. Maid 39 D4
Birdwood Rd. Sand 151 D4
Birkdale. Brac 117 F1
Birkhall Cl. Read 84 B3
Birley Rd. Slough 42 B4
Bishop Ct. Maid 39 E3
Bishop Duppas Park. Shepp . 125 F1
Bishop's La. New G 92 A4
Bishop's La. Wink 92 A4
Bishop's Rd. Brad 87 D3
Bishopdale. Brac 118 A3
Bishops Cl. Tad 135 D1
Bishops Dr. Felt 71 E1
Bishops Dr. Woki 116 B4
Bishops Farm Cl. Oak G 66 A3
Bishops Gr. Windl 146 B2
Bishops Orch. Far C 22 A1
Bishops Rd. Brad 81 F2
Bishops Rd. Slough 43 D2
Bishops Way. Stai 96 B1
Bishops Wlk. Bou E 3 F3
Bishopsgate Rd. Eng G 95 D2
Bishopswood La. Tad 134 C1
Bishopswood Rd. Tad 134 C1
Bissley Dr. Maid 39 D2
Bitham La. Ham 126 B3
Bitham La. Ink 127 D2
Bitham Rd. Farn 8 B4
Bittern Cl. Sand 150 B4
Bix Hill. Faw (Bu) 15 D3
Bix La. Maid 38 C4
Black Boy La. Hurl 17 E2
Black Butts Cotts. Cook 20 A4
Black Horse Cl. Wind 66 B3
Black Park Rd. Fulm 23 F2
Black Park Rd. Iver H 23 F2
Blackamoor La. Maid 40 A4
Blackberry Cl. Shepp 125 F3
Blackbird Cl. Bur C 111 D2
Blackbird Cl. Sand 150 B4
Blackcap Pl. Sand 150 C4
Blackdown Way. That 106 B1
Blackett Cl. Stai 123 F4
Blacklands Rd. Buck 107 E3
Blackley Cl. Winn 87 F2
Blackmeadows. Brac 118 B2
Blackmoor Cl. Burl 119 E4
Blackmoor Wood. Burl 119 E4
Blacknest Rd. Went 121 F3
Blacksmith Row. Slough 44 A1
Blacksmith's La. Stai 124 B3
Blacksmiths La. Chert 124 A1
Blackstroud La E. Light 146 B1
Blackstroud La W. Light 153 E4
Blackthorn Dell. Slough 43 E2
Blackthorn Dr. Light 153 D4
Blackthorne Rd. Stan 69 F2
Blackwater Cl. Caver 59 F2
Blackwater Cl. Shin 113 D1
Blackwater Rise. Bur C 84 A2
Blagdon Rd. Read 86 B1
Blagrave La. Caver 58 B2
Blagrave St. Read 86 A4
Blagrove Rise. Read 84 B3
Blagrove La. Woki 115 F2
Blagrove La. Woki 115 F2
Blair Rd. Slough 42 C3
Blaire Park. Yate 149 D4
Blake Cl. Crow 143 E2
Blake Cl. Woki 116 C4
Blake's La. Tad 135 E1
Blakeney Fields. Gr She 48 A2
Blakes Cotts. Read 86 B4
Blakes La. Warg 37 D1
Blakes Rd. Warg 36 C2
Blakes Ride. Yate 149 D3
Blanchard Cl. Wood 88 A4
Bland's Cl. Bur C 110 C1
Blandford Cl. Slough 43 E2
Blandford Rd N. Slough 43 E2
Blandford Rd S. Slough 43 E2
Blandford Rd. Read 113 E4
Blandy Rd. Hen-O-T 35 E4
Blandy's La. Upp B 55 D3
Blandys Hill. Kint 128 A4
Blatch's Cl. Thea 83 E2
Blay's La. Eng G 95 D1
Blays Cl. Eng G 95 E1
Bledlow La. Newb 130 B3
Blenheim Cl. Slough 43 F3
Blenheim Cl. Woki 115 F3
Blenheim Gdns. Read 86 C3
Blenheim Rd. Caver 59 D2
Blenheim Rd. Maid 39 D4
Blenheim Rd. Newb 104 C1
Blenheim Rd. Read 86 C3
Blenheim Rd. Slough 43 E1
Bletchmore Cl. Harl 71 E4
Blewburton Wlk. Brac 118 C3
Blewbury Dr. Read 84 A4
Blewbury Hill. Blew 12 B4
Blinco La. Slough 43 F4
Blind La. Bou E 3 D3
Blind La. Fla H 3 D3
Blind La. Lamb 25 D1

Blomfield Dale. Brac 117 E4
Blomfield Dr. Brac 91 E1
Blondell Cl. Harm 70 B4
Bloomfield Rd. Maid 39 D3
Bloomfieldhatch La. Bee H ... 138 A4
Bloomfieldhatch La. Shin 112 C2
Bloomsbury Way. Black 150 B2
Blossom Ave. Thea 83 F2
Blossom La. Thea 83 F2
Bloxworth Cl. Brac 118 C3
Blue Ball La. Eng G 95 F2
Blue Coat Wlk. Brac 118 B2
Bluebell Dr. Bur C 110 C2
Bluebell Hill. Brac 118 C4
Bluebell Meadow. Winn 88 B2
Bluebell Rise. Light 153 D4
Bluecoats. That 106 B2
Bluethroat Cl. Sand 150 C4
Blumfield Cres. Burn 41 F4
Blumfield Cl. Slough 21 E1
Blundell's Rd. Read 84 C4
Blyth Ave. Harm 71 D4
Blythe Cl. Iver 44 C4
Blythewood La. Ascot 119 F4
Blythwood Dr. Camb 151 E1
Boames La. Ham M 129 F3
Boarlands Cl. Slough 41 F3
Boathouse Reach. Hen-O-T .. 15 F1
Bobgreen Ct. Read 113 E4
Bobmore La. Mar 1 C2
Bockhampton Rd. Lamb 25 E1
Bockmer La. Medm 17 D4
Bodens Ride. Brac 119 F1
Bodmin Ave. Slough 42 A4
Bodmin Cl. That 106 B1
Bodmin Rd. Wood 87 D3
Body Rd. Read 85 F4
Bog La. Brac 119 D3
Boham's Rd. Blew 11 E3
Bolding House La. West E 153 F4
Boldrewood. Bur C 110 C1
Boleyn Cl. Stai 96 C2
Bolingbroke Way. That 106 C2
Bolney Rd. Shipl 36 A3
Bolton Ave. Wind 67 E2
Bolton Cres. Wind 67 E2
Bolton Rd. Wind 67 E2
Bolton's La. Harl 71 E4
Bolwell Cl. Twyf 61 F2
Bomer Cl. Harm 71 D4
Bomford Cl. Herm 78 C3
Bond St. Eng G 95 E2
Bone La. Newb 105 E2
Bones La. Shipl 35 D2
Booth Dr. Stai 97 E1
Borderside. Slough 43 D4
Borderside. Yate 149 D3
Borrowdale Cl. Stai 96 A1
Borrowdale Gdns. Camb 152 B2
Borrowdale Rd. Winn 88 A2
Boscombe Cl. Stai 123 E4
Boscowen Way. That 107 D1
Bosham Cl. Road 114 A4
Bosman Dr. Windl 146 A3
Bostock La. Thea 83 D1
Boston Ave. Read 85 F3
Boston Gr. Slough 42 B4
Boston Rd. Hen-O-T 35 F4
Bosworth Gdns. Wood 87 F2
Botany Cl. That 106 C2
Bothy The. Warg 36 B1
Botmoor Way. Chadd 48 C4
Bottisham Cl. Winn 114 B4
Bottle La. Binf 91 D3
Bottle La. Know H 38 A2
Bottle La. New G 91 D3
Bottom La. Sulhd 110 B4
Bouldish Farm Rd. Ascot 119 F3
Boult Rd. Read 86 B4
Boult's Wlk. Read 86 A3
Boulters Cl. Maid 20 B1
Boulters Cl. Slough 42 A2
Boulters Ct. Wood 87 F4
Boulters Ct. Maid 20 B1
Boulters Gdns. Maid 20 B1
Boulters La. Maid 20 B1
Boulton Rd. Read 86 A2
Boultons La. Binf 90 C1
Boundary Cl. Read 84 B3
Boundary La. Caver 58 C2
Boundary Pl. Woo G 3 E4
Boundary Rd. Newb 105 D1
Boundary Rd. Stai 97 E2
Boundary Rd. Tapl 40 C4
Boundary Rd. Woo G 3 E4
Bourn Cl. Winn 87 E1
Bourne Arch. That 106 A2
Bourne Ave. Chert 124 A3
Bourne Ave. Read 86 A2
Bourne Ave. Wind 67 E2
Bourne Cl. Bou E 3 D3
Bourne Cl. Bur C 84 A2
Bourne End Rd. Bou E 20 C4
Bourne End Rd. Tapl 20 C4
Bourne Meadow. Stai 123 D3
Bourne Rd. Pangb 56 C3
Bourne Rd. Slough 42 B2
Bourne Rd. That 106 A2

Bourne Rd. Went 122 B2
Bourne Vale. Hung 100 B3
Bourneside. Went 122 A1
Bourton Cl. Read 84 C4
Bouverie Way. Slough 43 F1
Boveney Cl. Slough 42 A2
Boveney New Rd. Eton 41 F1
Boveney Rd. Dorn 41 E1
Bovingdon Hts. Mar 1 C1
Bowden Cl. Felt 98 C4
Bowden Rd. Ascot 120 B2
Bower Way. Slough 41 F3
Bowes Rd. Stai 96 C1
Bowes Rd. That 106 B1
Bowfell Cl. Read 57 E1
Bowland Drive. Brac 118 C1
Bowling Ct. Hen-O-T 15 E2
Bowling Green La. Pur O T 57 D3
Bowling Green Rd. That 106 A3
Bowman Ct. Woki 142 C2
Bowmans Cl. Burn 21 D2
Bowry Dr. Wray 68 C1
Bowyer Cres. Woki 116 B4
Bowyer Dr. Slough 41 F3
Bowyer's La. New G 91 E3
Boxford Ridge. Brac 118 A3
Boyd Ct. Brac 118 A4
Boyn Hill Ave. Maid 39 E3
Boyn Hill Cl. Maid 39 E3
Boyn Hill Rd. Maid 39 E3
Boyn Valley Rd. Maid 39 E3
Boynden Rd. Maid 39 E4
Bracebridge. Camb 151 D3
Bracken Bank. Burl 119 E4
Bracken Cl. Far C 22 B4
Bracken Cl. Read 57 E1
Bracken La. Yate 149 D3
Bracken Rd. Maid 39 E2
Bracken Way. Bur C 111 D1
Brackendale Cl. Camb 151 F2
Brackendale Rd. Camb 151 E2
Brackenforde. Slough 43 E2
Brackens The. Brac 143 D4
Brackenwood Dr. Tad 135 D1
Brackenwood. Bur C 110 C1
Brackenwood. Camb 152 B3
Bracknell Beeches. Brac 118 A3
Bracknell Cl. Camb 144 C1
Bracknell Rd. Bags 145 F3
Bracknell Rd. Brac 143 F4
Bracknell Rd. Camb 145 D1
Bracknell Rd. New G 91 F2
Bracknell Rd. New G 92 A3
Bracknell Rd. Wink 92 A3
Bradcutts La. Cook 19 F4
Bradenham La. Bish 18 B3
Bradfields. Brac 118 B2
Bradford Rd. Slough 42 A4
Brading Way. Pur O T 57 E3
Bradley Cl. Kint 102 A1
Bradley Rd. Slough 42 C3
Bradmore Way. Read 114 A4
Bradshaw Cl. Wind 66 C3
Bradwell Rd. Read 57 E2
Braemar Gdns. Slough 42 A2
Braemore Cl. That 106 B1
Brakendale Way. Read 87 D3
Bramber Cl. Slough 42 A3
Bramber Mews. Caver 59 F2
Bramble Cl. Shepp 125 E3
Bramble Cres. Read 84 C4
Bramble Dr. Maid 91 D1
Brambledown. Stai 124 A4
Bramblegate. Crow 143 D3
Brambles The. Brac 142 B3
Bramcote. Camb 152 B3
Bramley Cl. Chert 124 A1
Bramley Cl. Maid 39 E2
Bramley Cl. Read 87 D2
Bramley Cl. Stai 97 E1
Bramley Gr. Brac 142 B3
Bramley La. Black 150 A3
Bramley Rd. Camb 151 D1
Bramley Rd. Silc 136 A1
Bramling Ave. Yate 149 D3
Brammas Cl. Slough 42 B2
Brampton Chase. Shipl 36 A2
Bramshaw Rd. Read 58 A1
Bramshill Cl. Arbo 140 C4
Bramwell Cl. That 106 C1
Bran Cl. Read 84 C4
Brandon Ave. Wood 88 A4
Brandon Cl. Camb 152 B2
Brands Rd. Slough 69 D4
Branksome Cl. Camb 151 F3
Branksome Hill Rd. Sand 150 C4
Branksome Park Rd. Camb .. 151 F3
Brants Bridge. Brac 118 C3
Braunfels Wlk. Newb 104 C1
Bravington Cl. Stai 124 C2
Bray Cl. Maid 40 B2
Bray Cl. Holy 40 B1
Bray Rd. Maid 40 A3
Bray Rd. Read 85 D2
Braybank. Maid 40 B2
Braybrooke Gdns. Warg 36 B1
Braybrooke Rd. Brac 91 D1
Braybrooke Rd. Warg 36 B1

Braye Cl. Sand 143 E1
Brayfield Rd. Maid 40 B2
Brayford Rd. Read 113 E4
Braywick Rd. Maid 40 A3
Braywood Ave. Eng G 96 A1
Braziers La. Wink 92 B2
Breach Sq. Hung 100 B2
Breadcroft La. Bur G 38 C2
Breadcroft Rd. Whi Wa 38 C2
Bream Cl. Mar 18 B4
Brecon Rd. Wood 87 F4
Bredon Rd. Woki 88 C1
Bredward Cl. Burn 21 D1
Breech The. Sand 150 B4
Breedons Hill. Pangb 56 B3
Bremer Rd. Stan 97 D3
Brendon Cl. Harl 71 E4
Brendon Cl. Read 57 F1
Brent Cl. That 106 B1
Brent Gdns. Read 86 A2
Brent Rd. Bou E 3 D2
Brentmoor Rd. West E 153 E3
Brerewood. Read 86 C1
Bret Harte Rd. Camb 151 F1
Brewery Comm. Mort 137 D4
Brewhouse Hill. Frox 99 D2
Briant's Ave. Caver 59 E1
Briants Piece. Herm 79 D3
Briar Ave. Light 153 D4
Briar Cl. Burn 41 D4
Briar Cl. Caver 59 D3
Briar Dene. Maid 19 E1
Briar Glen. Cook 19 F3
Briar Rd. Stai 125 D2
Briar Way. Slough 42 A4
Briarlea Rd. Mort 136 C3
Briars Cl. Pangb 56 C3
Briars The. Slough 43 F1
Briars The. Stan 70 A1
Briarwood Cl. Felt 98 C3
Briarwood. Woki 141 F3
Brickfield La. Burn 21 D2
Brickfield La. Harl 71 E4
Bridge Ave. Cook 19 F3
Bridge Cl. Shepp 125 F1
Bridge Cl. Slough 41 F3
Bridge Cl. Stai 96 C2
Bridge End. Camb 151 D2
Bridge Gdns. Stai 98 B1
Bridge La. Went 122 C2
Bridge Rd. Ascot 120 B2
Bridge Rd. Bags 145 F2
Bridge Rd. Camb 151 D2
Bridge Rd. Chert 124 A1
Bridge Rd. Maid 40 A4
Bridge St. Caver 59 D1
Bridge St. Hung 100 B3
Bridge St. Iver 69 E4
Bridge St. Maid 40 A4
Bridge St. Newb 105 D2
Bridge St. Read 86 A4
Bridge St. Shepp 125 F1
Bridge St. Stai 96 C2
Bridge View. Went 121 D1
Bridge Walk. Yate 149 E4
Bridgeman Dr. Wind 67 D3
Bridges Cl. Woki 115 F4
Bridges The. Silc 136 B3
Bridgestone Dr. Bou E 3 E2
Bridgewater Cl. Read 58 B1
Bridgewater Ct. Slough 44 A1
Bridgewater Terr. Wind 67 E3
Bridgewater Way. Wind 67 E3
Bridle Cl. Maid 19 F1
Bridle Rd. Maid 19 F1
Bridlepath Way. Felt 98 C4
Bridlington Spur. Slough 42 A2
Bridport Cl. Read 87 E1
Bridport Way. Slough 22 A1
Brierley Pl. Pur O T 57 E2
Briff La. Buck 107 E4
Brigham Rd. Read 59 D1
Brighton Rd. Read 87 D3
Brighton Spur. Slough 22 A1
Brightside Ave. Stai 97 E1
Brill Cl. Caver 59 D2
Brill Cl. Maid 39 E2
Brill Cl. Mar 1 B1
Brimblecombe Cl. Woki 89 D1
Brimpton Rd. Brim 133 F4
Brimpton Rd. Read 85 D2
Brimpton Rd. Tad 134 B1
Brimpton Rd. Wool 133 F4
Brinn's La. Sand 150 B3
Brisbane Rd. Read 85 D4
Bristol Cl. Stan 70 C1
Bristol Way. Slough 42 C3
Bristow Cres. Camb 151 E2
Bristow Cl. Mar 2 A2
Bristow Rd. Camb 151 D2
Britannia Way. Stan 97 E4
Britten Rd. Read 86 A3
Britwell Rd. Burn 21 E1
Brixham Rd. Read 86 A1
Broad Hinton. Twyf 61 F2
Broad La. Bou E 3 F3
Broad La. Brac 118 B3
Broad La. Buck 107 E3
Broad Oak Ct. Slough 22 B1

Broad Oak. Slough 22
Broad Platts. Slough 43
Broad St. East I 30
Broad St. Read 86
Broad St. West E 153
Broad St. Woki 116
Broad Street Mall The. Read .. 86
Broad Wlk. Camb 151
Broadacre. Stai 97
Broadcommon Rd. Hurst 89
Broadhalfpenny La. Tad 135
Broadlands Ave. Shepp 125
Broadlands Cl. Read 84
Broadlands Dr. Sunn 120
Broadley Green. Windl ....
Broadmark Rd. Slough 43
Broadmeadow End. That 106
Broadmoor La. W St L 63
Broadmoor La. Whi Wa 63
Broadrich Heath. New G 91
Broadwater Cl. Wray 95
Broadwater La. Hurst 61
Broadwater Park. Holy 40
Broadwater Park. Holy 40
Broadwater Rd. Twyf 61
Broadway Rd. Light 146
Broadway The. Lamb 25
Broadway The. Newb 105
Broadway The. Sand 150
Broadway The. Stai 124
Broadway. Brac ....
Broadway. Maid 39
Broadway. That 106
Brocas Rd. Bur C 110
Brocas St. Eton 67
Brocas Terr. Eton 67
Brock Gdns. Read 85
Brock La. Maid 39
Brock Way. Vir W 122
Brockenhurst Dr. Yate 149
Brockenhurst Rd. Ascot 120
Brockenhurst Rd. Brac 119
Brocklands. Yate 149
Brockley Cl. Read 85
Brocks La. Buck 80
Brocks Way. Shipl 36
Brocksby Cl. Black 150
Broken Furlong. Eton 42
Broken Way. Newt 131
Bromley Wlk. Read 84
Brompton Cl. Winn 87
Brompton Dr. Maid 39
Bromycroft Rd. Slough 22
Brook Cl. Sand 143
Brook Cl. Stan 97
Brook Cl. Woki 116
Brook Cres. Slough 41
Brook Dr. Ashf 98
Brook Dr. Brac 118
Brook La. Hurst 62
Brook Path. Slough 41
Brook Path. Slough 41
Brook Rd. Bags 145
Brook Rd. Camb 151
Brook St W. Read 86
Brook St. Twyf 61
Brook St. Wind 67
Brookbank. Bou E 3
Brookdene Cl. Maid 19
Brooke Pl. Binf 90
Brookers Cnr. Crow 143
Brookers Hill. Read 113
Brookers Row. Brac 143
Brookfield Rd. Bou E 3
Brookhouse Dr. Bou E 3
Brooklands Cl. Stai 125
Brooklyn Dr. Caver 59
Brookmill The. Read 85
Brooks Rd. That 106
Brooksby Rd. Read 85
Brookside Ave. Stai 97
Brookside Ave. Wray 68
Brookside Cl. Read 87
Brookside. Chert 123
Brookside. Iver 44
Brookside. Read 84
Brookside. Sand 150
Brookside. Woki 115
Brookway. Newb 105
Broom Acres. Sand 143
Broom Cl. Black 150
Broom Cl. Read 84
Broom Field. Light 153
Broom Gr. Woki 115
Broom Hill. Cook 19
Broom Hill. Sto P 23
Broome Cl. Yate 149
Broomfield Cl. Went 121
Broomfield Park. Went 119
Broomfield Rd. Read 58
Broomfield Rd. Read 85
Broomhall La. Sunn 121
Broomsquire Rd. Bags 145
Broughton Cl. Read 58
Broughton Mews. Camb 151
Brownfields Gdns. Maid 19
Browngraves Rd. Harl 71
Browning Cl. Camb 151
Browning Cl. That 106

ownlow Dr. Brac ... 91 E1
wnlow Rd. Read ... 85 F4
wnrigg Cres. Brac ... 118 C4
wnrigg Rd. Ashf ... 98 A2
wnsfield Rd. That ... 106 B2
an Rd. Newb ... 130 C4
ce Ave. Shepp ... 125 E2
ce Cl. Slough ... 42 A3
ce Rd. Wood ... 87 E4
ce Wlk. Wind ... 66 B3
tenell. Wind ... 66 C2
nel Cl. Maid ... 39 F3
nel Dr. Wood ... 60 C1
nel Rd. Maid ... 39 E3
nel Rd. Read ... 85 D2
nel Rd. Thea ... 83 F1
nel Way. Slough ... 42 C3
nswick Hill. Read ... 85 F4
nswick St. Read ... 85 F3
swick. Brac ... 118 A1
ison Way. Brac ... 118 C1
ant Ave. Slough ... 42 C4
er Pl. Wind ... 66 B2
caneer Cl. Wood ... 88 A4
cleuch Rd. Datch ... 68 A4
han The. Camb ... 152 A4
hanan Dr. Woki ... 141 F4
hanan Sq. That ... 106 C1
k Side. Caver ... 59 D1
kden Cl. Wood ... 88 A3
kham Hill. Chadd ... 48 B3
khurst Gr. Woki ... 116 C3
khurst Hill. Brac ... 118 C3
khurst La. Ascot ... 121 D3
khurst Rd. Ascot ... 120 C4
kle La. New G ... 91 D3
klebury Cl. Holy ... 40 B1
klebury. Brac ... 118 A1
knell Ave. Pangb ... 56 C3
knell Cl. Read ... 84 C2
kthorn Cl. Woki ... 116 C4
ebury Rd. Read ... 97 D2
ge's Gdns. Woki ... 116 C4
ge's Rd. Woki ... 116 B4
ins. Tapl ... 20 B1
eley Ave. Wind ... 67 D2
eley Cl. Eng G ... 95 E2
La. Brac ... 118 A4
La. Swal ... 139 D2
Meadow The. Stre ... 33 F3
orook Dr. Brac ... 118 C4
orook Row. Brac ... 118 C4
finch Cl. Sand ... 150 C4
nershe Rd. Read ... 86 C3
it La. Hung ... 100 B2
ry Rd. Sto P ... 22 C3
ces Cl. Eton ... 42 A1
ces La. Bur C ... 111 D1
dy's Way. Stai ... 96 C1
galow Dr. Read ... 84 B4
gler's Hill. Swal ... 140 A3
kers Hill. Newb ... 130 B3
ten Meade. Slough ... 42 A3
bage Green. Brac ... 118 C2
oidge Cl. Read ... 84 C2
oidge Rd. Stai ... 125 D3
chell Rd. Newb ... 104 C3
chett Copse. Woki ... 141 F4
chetts Green La. Bur G ... 38 B3
chetts Green Rd. Bur G ... 38 A4
chetts Way. Shepp ... 125 D2
combe Way. Caver ... 59 D2
cot Gdns. Maid ... 19 F2
dock Cl. Read ... 86 B2
dock Cl. Light ... 153 D4
dock Rd. Old W ... 95 D4
ord Cl. Mar B ... 1 B3
ord Gdns. Slough ... 41 E4
ord Rd. Camb ... 151 D2
ord's. East G ... 47 E3
ges Way. Stan ... 97 D1
gess Cl. Wood ... 87 E2
gess La. Kint ... 128 B3
ett Rd. Slough ... 42 A2
ghead Cl. Sand ... 150 B4
ghfield Rd. Read ... 85 D2
goyne Rd. Ashf ... 98 C1
goyne Rd. Camb ... 152 A4
eigh Gdns. Ashf ... 98 B2
eigh Rd. Ascot ... 119 F4
eigh Mews. Caver ... 59 E3
eigh Rd. Ascot ... 119 F4
eigh Rd. Camb ... 151 E1
ey Orch. Chert ... 124 A2

Burley Way. Black ... 150 B3
Burlingham Cl. Read ... 113 E3
Burlings The. Ascot ... 119 F4
Burlington Ave. Slough ... 42 C2
Burlington Cl. Felt ... 98 B4
Burlington Ct. Black ... 150 B2
Burlington Rd. Burn ... 41 D4
Burlington Rd. Read ... 84 B4
Burlington Rd. Slough ... 42 C2
Burlsdon Way. Brac ... 118 C4
Burn Moor Chase. Brac ... 118 C1
Burn Wlk. Burn ... 21 D1
Burne-Jones Dr. Sand ... 150 B3
Burnet Cl. Camb ... 153 F3
Burnetts Rd. Wind ... 66 C3
Burney Bit. Silc ... 135 F1
Burnham Cl. Bou E ... 3 D2
Burnham Cl. Wind ... 66 B3
Burnham Gr. Brac ... 91 E1
Burnham La. Slough ... 41 F4
Burnham Rd. Tad ... 134 C1
Burnham Rise. Caver ... 59 E3
Burniston Cl. Winn ... 87 F1
Burns Cl. Wood ... 87 F2
Burns Wlk. That ... 106 B2
Burnt Cl. Camb ... 153 F3
Burnt Oak. Cook ... 19 F4
Burnt Oak. Woki ... 141 F4
Burnt Pollard La. West E ... 146 C1
Burnthouse La. Bur C ... 112 A3
Burrcroft Rd. Read ... 85 D3
Burrell Rd. Comp ... 31 F2
Burroughs Cres. Bou E ... 3 D2
Burroway Rd. Slough ... 44 A2
Burrows Hill Cl. Stan ... 70 C1
Burton Cl. Windl ... 146 B2
Burton Way. Wind ... 66 C2
Burtons Hill. Kint ... 102 A1
Burway Cres. Chert ... 124 A3
Burwell Cl. Winn ... 87 E1
Burys Bank Rd. Gree ... 132 A3
Burys Bank Rd. That ... 132 A3
Bush Rd. Stai ... 125 D2
Business Centre The. Woki ... 116 A2
Business Village The. Slough ... 43 D3
Butchers La. Whi Wa ... 63 E4
Bute St. Read ... 85 D3
Butler Ct. Mar ... 2 A2
Butler Rd. Bags ... 145 F1
Butler Rd. Crow ... 143 D3
Butlers Cl. Wind ... 66 B3
Butson Cl. Newb ... 104 C2
Buttenshaw Ave. Bark ... 141 D4
Buttenshaw Cl. Bark ... 141 D4
Butter Market. Read ... 86 A4
Butterfield. Bou E ... 3 E2
Buttercup Square. Stan ... 97 E4
Buttermere Ave. Slough ... 41 E4
Buttermere Cl. Felt ... 98 C4
Buttermere Dr. Camb ... 152 B3
Buttermere Gdns. Brac ... 118 B3
Buttermere Way. Stai ... 96 A1
Buttersteep Rise. Brac ... 119 E1
Butts Hill Rd. Wood ... 87 F4
Buxton Ave. Caver ... 58 C2
Buxton Rd. Ashf ... 97 E2
Bybend Cl. Far C ... 22 A2
Byefield Rd. Read ... 85 D2
Byeways. Warg ... 37 F2
Byland Dr. Holy ... 40 A1
Byreton Cl. Read ... 87 D1
Byron Ave. Camb ... 152 A2
Byron Cl. Mar ... 1 C2
Byron Cl. Newb ... 130 C4
Byron Cl. Twyf ... 61 F2
Byron Cl. Yate ... 149 D2
Byron Dr. Crow ... 143 D2
Byron Rd. Read ... 87 D4
Byron Rd. Twyf ... 61 F2
Bythorn Cl. Winn ... 87 F1
Byways. Burn ... 41 D4
Byways. Yate ... 149 D3
Bywood. Brac ... 118 A1
Byworth Cl. Read ... 113 D4

Cabin Moss. Brac ... 118 C1
Cabrera Ave. Went ... 122 B2
Cabrera Cl. Went ... 122 B2
Cadbury Cl. Ashf ... 98 C1
Cadbury Rd. Ashf ... 98 C1
Caddy Cl. Eng G ... 96 A2
Cadogan Cl. Holy ... 65 D4
Cadogan Rd. Read ... 84 C4
Cadwell Dr. Maid ... 39 E2
Caesar's Camp Rd. Camb ... 152 A4
Caesar's Way. Shepp ... 125 E2
Cages Wood Dr. Far C ... 22 A4
Cain Rd. Binf ... 117 E4
Cain Rd. Brac ... 117 F4
Cain's La. Harm ... 71 F1
Cairn Cl. Camb ... 152 A4
Cairngorm Rd. That ... 106 B1
Caistor Cl. That ... 84 C2
Calard Dr. That ... 106 A3
Calbourne Dr. Bur C ... 84 B2
Calbroke Rd. Slough ... 21 F1
Calcot Cl. Read ... 84 C3
Calcot Place Dr. Read ... 84 C2
Caldbeck Dr. Wood ... 87 F4
Calder Cl. Maid ... 19 F1

Calder Cl. Read ... 84 C4
Calder Cl. Read ... 19 E1
Calder Ct. Slough ... 43 F1
Calder Way. Stan ... 69 F2
Caldwell Rd. Windl ... 146 B3
Caledonia Rd. Stan ... 97 F4
Caleta Ct. Caver ... 59 E1
Calfridus Way. Brac ... 118 C3
Calleva Park. Alde ... 134 C1
Callin's La. W St L ... 63 D2
Callington Rd. Read ... 86 B1
Callis Farm Cl. Stan ... 70 C1
Callow Hill. Vir W ... 122 B4
Calshot Pl. Bur C ... 84 B2
Calshot Rd. Harm ... 71 D3
Calshot Way. Harm ... 71 D3
Calvin Cl. Camb ... 152 A2
Camberley Rd. Harm ... 71 D2
Camborne Cl. Crow ... 143 D1
Camborne Cl. Harm ... 71 D1
Camborne Cl. Read ... 87 D1
Camborne Rd S. Harm ... 71 D2
Camborne Way. Harm ... 71 D2
Cambria Gdns. Stan ... 97 F4
Cambrian Cl. Camb ... 151 D3
Cambrian Way. Camb ... 142 A4
Cambrian Way. Bur C ... 84 B2
Cambridge Ave. Burn ... 21 D2
Cambridge Ave. Slough ... 42 A4
Cambridge Cl. Harm ... 70 B4
Cambridge Rd. Crow ... 143 E2
Cambridge Rd. Mar ... 1 B1
Cambridge Rd. Sand ... 143 F1
Cambridge Rd. Stai ... 98 B1
Cambridge St. Read ... 85 F4
Cambridge Wlk. Camb ... 151 E3
Cambridgeshire Cl. Woki ... 115 F3
Camden Pl. Bou E ... 3 D2
Camden Pl. Bur C ... 84 A2
Camden Rd. Maid ... 19 E1
Camellia Way. Woki ... 115 E4
Camilla Cl. Ashf ... 98 C1
Camley Gdns. Maid ... 39 D4
Camley Park Dr. Maid ... 38 C4
Camm Ave. Wind ... 66 C2
Campbell Cl. Yate ... 149 F3
Campbell Pl. Camb ... 151 F2
Campbell Rd. Wood ... 87 E3
Camperdown. Maid ... 20 A1
Campion Cl. Black ... 150 C2
Campion Way. Woki ... 116 C4
Canada Rd. Slough ... 43 D2
Canal Walk. Hung ... 100 B3
Canal Way. Read ... 86 B4
Canal Wharf. Slough ... 44 A2
Canberra Cl. Yate ... 149 D4
Canberra Rd. Harm ... 71 D2
Candleford Cl. Brac ... 91 E1
Candover Cl. Harm ... 70 B4
Canford Ct. Read ... 85 E4
Cannock Cl. Maid ... 40 A3
Cannock Way. Wood ... 87 E1
Cannon Cl. Sand ... 150 C4
Cannon Court Rd. Cook ... 19 E2
Cannon Court Rd. Maid ... 19 E2
Cannon Hill Cl. Maid ... 40 B1
Cannon Hill. Brac ... 118 B2
Cannon La. Maid ... 38 C2
Cannon La. Whi Wa ... 38 C2
Cannon St. Read ... 85 F4
Cannondown Rd. Cook ... 19 F3
Canon Hill Dr. Maid ... 40 A2
Canopus Way. Stan ... 97 F4
Cansfield End. Newb ... 104 C2
Canterbury Ave. Slough ... 22 B1
Canterbury Rd. Read ... 86 B2
Cantley Cres. Woki ... 116 A4
Capper Rd. Camb ... 151 D4
Captains Gorse. Upp B ... 54 C3
Caraway Rd. Read ... 87 D1
Carbery La. Ascot ... 120 A3
Carbinswood La. Buck ... 108 A3
Cardiff Rd. Read ... 58 C1
Cardigan Gdns. Read ... 86 C3
Cardigan Rd. Read ... 86 C3
Cardinal Cl. Caver ... 59 D1
Cardinal's Wlk. Ashf ... 98 C1
Cardinals The. Brac ... 118 A3
Cardinals Wlk. Slough ... 41 E4
Cardwell Cres. Ascot ... 120 B2
Carew Rd. Ashf ... 98 B1
Carey Cl. Wind ... 67 D2
Carey Rd. Woki ... 116 B3
Carey St. Read ... 85 F4
Cariad Ct. Gori ... 34 A4
Carisbrooke Ct. Caver ... 59 E3
Carisbrooke Ct. Maid ... 39 E3
Carisbrooke Ct. Slough ... 42 C3
Carland Cl. Read ... 87 D1
Carlile Gdns. Twyf ... 61 E3
Carlinwork Dr. Camb ... 151 F4
Carlisle Rd. Read ... 57 F2
Carlisle Rd. Slough ... 42 B3
Carlton Cl. Camb ... 152 A2
Carlton Cl. Wood ... 87 F3
Carlton Rd. Ashf ... 98 C1
Carlton Rd. Caver ... 58 C3
Carlton Rd. Slough ... 43 D3

Carlyle Rd. Stai ... 97 D1
Carmarthen Rd. Slough ... 42 C3
Carnarvon Rd. Read ... 86 C3
Carnation Dr. Burl ... 92 A1
Carnegie Rd. Newb ... 105 D1
Carnoustie. Brac ... 117 F1
Carolina Rd. Woki ... 141 F4
Caroline Ct. Ashf ... 98 A1
Caroline Ct. Mar ... 1 C2
Caroline Dr. Woki ... 116 A4
Caroline Pl. Stan ... 71 F4
Caroline St. Read ... 85 F4
Caroline Way. Camb ... 151 F1
Carrick Gdns. Wood ... 87 E4
Carrick La. Yate ... 149 F3
Carrington Ave. Fla H ... 3 C2
Carrington Rd. Slough ... 42 C3
Carroll Cres. Ascot ... 119 F3
Carron Cl. Read ... 85 D4
Carsdale Cl. Read ... 85 F3
Carshalton Rd. Camb ... 145 D1
Carshalton Way. Wood ... 87 E1
Carston Gr. Read ... 84 C2
Carter Cl. Wind ... 67 D3
Carter's Hill. Binf ... 90 A2
Carters Rise. Read ... 84 C2
Cartmel Dr. Wood ... 87 E3
Cary Cl. Newb ... 130 B3
Casey Ct. Stan D ... 81 E2
Cassia Dr. Read ... 86 C1
Cassiobury Ave. Felt ... 98 C4
Castle Ave. Datch ... 68 A4
Castie Cl. Camb ... 151 F2
Castle Cl. Stai ... 98 C1
Castle Cres. Read ... 85 F4
Castle Dr. Maid ... 39 E4
Castle End Rd. W St L ... 62 A4
Castle Gr. Newb ... 104 C3
Castle Hill Rd. Eng G ... 95 D3
Castle Hill. Eng G ... 95 E3
Castle Hill Terr. Maid ... 39 F4
Castle Hill. Maid ... 39 F4
Castle Hill. Read ... 85 F3
Castle Hill. Swal ... 140 B4
Castle La. Wint ... 104 C3
Castle Mews. Maid ... 39 F4
Castle Rd. Camb ... 151 F2
Castle St. Read ... 86 A4
Castle St. Slough ... 42 C2
Castlecraig Ct. Sand ... 150 B4
Castleton Ct. Mar ... 1 C1
Castleview Rd. Slough ... 43 E1
Castor Ct. Yate ... 149 D4
Caswall Cl. Binf ... 90 B1
Caswall Ride. Yate ... 149 F3
Catalina Cl. Wood ... 88 A4
Catcliffe Way. Read ... 113 F4
Catena Rise. Light ... 146 A1
Catesby Gdns. Yate ... 149 D3
Catherine Dr. Ashf ... 98 C1
Catherine Rd. Newb ... 105 D1
Catherine St. Read ... 85 F4
Catlin Cres. Shepp ... 125 E2
Catmore Rd. Farn ... 29 E4
Catmore Rd. West I ... 29 E4
Caunter Rd. Newb ... 104 B2
Causeway The. Maid ... 40 B2
Causeway The. Mar ... 1 C1
Causeway The. Stai ... 96 B2
Causmans Way. Read ... 57 E1
Cavalier Cl. Newb ... 105 E3
Cavalier Cl. Thea ... 83 E1
Cavalry Cres. Wind ... 67 E2
Cavendish Cl. Ashf ... 98 C1
Cavendish Cl. Burn ... 41 D4
Cavendish Ct. Ashf ... 98 C1
Cavendish Ct. Black ... 150 B2
Cavendish Gdns. Winn ... 88 A2
Cavendish Meads. Ascot ... 120 B2
Cavendish Rd. Ashf ... 98 C1
Cavendish Rd. Caver ... 59 E3
Caversham Park Rd. Caver ... 59 F3
Caversham Rd. Caver ... 59 D1
Caves Farm Cl. Sand ... 150 A4
Cawcott Dr. Wind ... 66 C3
Cawsham Gdns. Caver ... 59 E2
Caxton Cl. Read ... 58 B1
Cecil Aldin Dr. Pur O T ... 57 E2
Cecil Cl. Ashf ... 98 B1
Cecil Rd. Ashf ... 98 B1
Cecil Rd. Iver ... 44 C4
Cecil Way. Slough ... 21 F1
Cedar Ave. Black ... 150 B3
Cedar Chase. Tapl ... 20 B1
Cedar Cl. Bags ... 145 F2
Cedar Cl. Stai ... 124 B3
Cedar Cl. Woki ... 116 B3
Cedar Dr. Eng G ... 96 A2
Cedar Dr. Mar ... 1 C1
Cedar Dr. Brac ... 91 E1
Cedar Dr. Mar B ... 1 B4
Cedar Dr. Pangb ... 56 B2
Cedar Dr. Windl ... 121 D1
Cedar Mount. Newb ... 130 C4
Cedar Rd. Felt ... 98 B4
Cedar Rd. Read ... 86 C1
Cedar Way. Slough ... 43 F1
Cedar Way. Stai ... 98 C1

Cedar Wood Cres. Caver ... 59 D2
Cedars Cl. Sand ... 149 F4
Cedars Rd. Maid ... 40 A4
Cedars The. Read ... 57 E1
Celandine Cl. Crow ... 143 E3
Celandine Ct. Yate ... 149 D4
Celandine Gr. That ... 106 C2
Celia Cres. Stai ... 97 E1
Cell Farm Ave. Old W ... 68 A1
Celsea Pl. Chol ... 14 A4
Cemetery La. Shepp ... 125 D1
Central Dr. Slough ... 41 F3
Centre The. Shepp ... 125 F1
Centurion Cl. Read ... 86 A3
Centurion Cl. Sand ... 150 B4
Century Rd. Stai ... 96 B2
Cerotus Pl. Chert ... 123 F2
Ceviot Rd. Sand ... 142 C1
Chaffinch Cl. Sand ... 150 B4
Chaffinch Cl. Woki ... 115 F3
Chagford Rd. Read ... 86 A1
Chain St. Read ... 86 A4
Chainhill Rd. Farn ... 8 A4
Chalcraft Cl. Hen-O-T ... 35 E4
Chalfont Cl. Read ... 87 D1
Chalfont Ct. Read ... 87 D1
Chalfont Way. Read ... 87 D1
Chalford Rd. Newb ... 104 C1
Chalford. Woo G ... 3 F3
Chalgrove Cl. Maid ... 40 A3
Chalgrove Way. Caver ... 59 E3
Chalk Hill. Ast T ... 12 C4
Chalk Hill. Shipl ... 35 E3
Chalk Pit La. Burn ... 21 D2
Chalkhousegreen La. Maples ... 59 D4
Chalklands. Bou E ... 3 D2
Chalkpit La. Mar ... 1 A2
Challenge Rd. Felt ... 98 C4
Challenor Cl. Woki ... 141 F4
Challis Pl. Brac ... 117 E4
Challow Ct. Maid ... 19 E1
Chalmers Rd E. Ashf ... 98 B2
Chalmers Rd. Ashf ... 98 A2
Chalvey Gdns. Slough ... 42 C2
Chalvey Gr. Slough ... 42 A2
Chalvey Park. Slough ... 42 C2
Chalvey Rd E. Slough ... 42 C2
Chalvey Rd W. Slough ... 42 B2
Chamberlain's Gdns. Arbo ... 114 C1
Champion Rd. Caver ... 59 E1
Chancellor's Way The. Read ... 86 C2
Chanctonbury Dr. Sunn ... 120 C1
Chandlers Cl. Felt ... 98 C4
Chandlers La. Yate ... 149 E4
Chandos Rd. Newb ... 131 D4
Chandos Rd. Stai ... 96 B2
Chantry Cl. Wind ... 67 D3
Chantry Mead. Hung ... 100 B3
Chantry Rd. Bags ... 145 E1
Chantry Rd. Chert ... 124 B1
Chapel Cl. Sou S ... 14 B2
Chapel Cl. That ... 106 C2
Chapel Hill. Read ... 84 B4
Chapel La. Asham ... 54 A4
Chapel La. Bags ... 145 E1
Chapel La. Binf ... 90 B1
Chapel La. Blew ... 12 A4
Chapel La. Camb ... 151 D1
Chapel La. Head ... 133 F1
Chapel La. Herm ... 78 C2
Chapel La. Herm ... 79 E4
Chapel La. Lamb ... 25 D2
Chapel La. Shin ... 113 D1
Chapel La. Silc ... 135 D1
Chapel La. Sto P ... 23 D3
Chapel La. Swal ... 139 E2
Chapel La. Yatt ... 53 F1
Chapel Rd. Camb ... 151 D3
Chapel Rd. Fla H ... 3 D3
Chapel Row. Twyf ... 61 E3
Chapel Sq. Sand ... 150 C3
Chapel St. Mar ... 1 C1
Chapel St. Slough ... 42 C2
Chapel St. That ... 106 B2
Chaplain's Hill. Crow ... 143 E2
Chaplin Cres. Sunn ... 120 C1
Chapman La. Bou E ... 3 D3
Chapman La. Fla H ... 3 D3
Chapter Mews. Wind ... 67 E4
Charadon Cl. Read ... 86 A3
Chard Cl. Wood ... 87 F3
Chard Rd. Harm ... 71 D3
Charlbury Cl. Brac ... 118 C3
Charles Evans Way. Caver ... 59 E1
Charles Gdns. Slough ... 43 D4
Charles Rd. Chol ... 14 A4
Charles Rd. Stai ... 97 D1
Charles Sq. Brac ... 118 B4
Charles St. Chert ... 123 F1
Charles St. Newb ... 130 B3
Charles St. Read ... 85 F4
Charles St. Wind ... 67 D3
Charlotte Cl. Herm ... 79 D3
Charlotte Way. Mar ... 1 C1
Charlton Cl. Slough ... 42 A2
Charlton Cl. Woki ... 141 F4
Charlton Ct. Sand ... 143 D1
Charlton La. Shepp ... 125 E3
Charlton La. Swal ... 139 E3

Charlton Pl. Newb 105 D2
Charlton Rd. Stai 125 E4
Charlton Sq. Oak G 66 B3
Charlton Way. Oak G 66 B3
Charlton. Oak G 66 B3
Charlville Dr. Bur C 84 A2
Charmwood Cl. Newb 104 C3
Charnham La. Hung 100 B4
Charnham Park. Hello 100 B4
Charnham St. Hung 100 B3
Charnwood. Ascot 120 C2
Charrington Rd. Bur C 84 B2
Charta Rd (E). Stai 96 B1
Charta Rd (S). Stai 96 B1
Charta Rd (W). Stai 96 B2
Charter Cl. Slough 42 C2
Charter Rd. Newb 131 D4
Charter Rd. Slough 41 F3
Charterhouse Cl. Brac 118 C2
Charters La. Ascot 120 B2
Charters Rd. Sun 120 C1
Charters Rd. Windl 120 C1
Charters Way. Windl 120 C1
Charvil House Rd. Char 61 D3
Charvil La. Sonn 60 C2
Charwood Rd. Woki 116 C4
Chase Gdns. Binf 90 B2
Chase The. Bur C 84 B2
Chase The. Crow 143 D3
Chase The. Mar 2 A2
Chaseside Ave. Twyf 61 E4
Chaseside Gdns. Chert 124 A1
Chatfield. Slough 42 A4
Chatham St. Read 85 F4
Chatsworth Ave. Winn 88 A1
Chatsworth Cl. Caver 59 E3
Chatsworth Cl. Maid 39 E3
Chatsworth Hts. Camb 152 A4
Chatteris Way. Winn 114 B4
Chattern Hill. Ashf 98 A2
Chattern Rd. Ashf 98 B2
Chatton Cl. Read 114 A4
Chaucer Cl. Caver 59 D3
Chaucer Cl. Woki 116 C3
Chaucer Cres. Newb 104 C3
Chaucer Gr. Camb 151 E3
Chaucer Rd. Ashf 97 F2
Chaucer Rd. Crow 143 D2
Chaucer Way. Woki 115 F3
Chauntry Cl. Maid 40 B3
Chauntry Rd. Maid 40 A3
Chavey Down Rd. Burl 92 A1
Chawridge La. Wink 92 B4
Chazey Cl. Maple 58 B4
Chazey Rd. Caver 58 B2
Cheam St. Comp 31 F3
Cheap St. Newb 105 D1
Cheapside Rd. Ascot 120 B4
Cheapside. Read 86 A4
Cheddar Rd. Harm 71 D3
Cheddington Cl. Read 84 C3
Cheeseman Cl. Woki 116 B4
Chelford Way. Caver 58 C2
Chelsea Cl. Read 57 F1
Chelwood Dr. Sand 142 C1
Chelwood Rd. Read 87 D1
Cheney Cl. Binf 90 B1
Cheniston Gr. Maid 38 C4
Chepstow Rd. Read 57 E1
Chequer La. Bee H 138 C1
Chequers Orch. Iver 44 C4
Chequers Way. Wood 87 E4
Cherbury Cl. Brac 118 C3
Cherington Gate. Maid 19 D1
Cherington Way. Ascot 119 F4
Cheriton Ave. Twyf 61 E3
Cheriton Cl. Newb 131 D4
Cheriton Way. Black 150 B3
Cherries The. Slough 43 D4
Cherry Ave. Slough 43 E2
Cherry Cl. Caver 59 E4
Cherry Cl. Fla H 3 D4
Cherry Cl. Newb 104 C2
Cherry Garden La. Bur G 38 C2
Cherry Orch. Gr She 48 A2
Cherry Orch. Stai 97 D2
Cherry Orch. Sto P 23 D3
Cherry Rise. Fla H 3 D4
Cherry Tree Ave. Stai 97 D1
Cherry Tree Cl. Sand 143 E1
Cherry Tree Dr. Brac 118 B3
Cherry Tree Gr. Woki 115 E2
Cherry Tree La. Fulm 23 F3
Cherry Tree Rd. Far C 22 B3
Cherry Way. Shepp 125 F3
Cherrydale Rd. Camb 152 B3
Cherrygarden La. Whi Wa ... 63 F4
Cherrywood Ave. Eng G 95 D1
Cherrywood Gdns. Fla H 3 D4
Chertsey Bridge Rd. Shepp . 124 B1
Chertsey La. Stai 96 C1
Chertsey Rd. Felt 98 C2
Chertsey Rd. Shepp 124 B1
Chertsey Rd. Windl 146 C3
Chervil Way. Bur C 111 D1
Cherwell Cl. Maid 40 A4
Cherwell Cl. Slough 69 D4
Cherwell Rd. Bou E 3 D2

Cherwell Rd. Caver 59 D3
Cheseridge Rd. Comp 31 E2
Cheshire Ct. Slough 43 D2
Chessholme Ct. Ashf 98 C1
Chessholme Rd. Ashf 98 B1
Chester Cl. Ashf 98 B2
Chester Cl. Newb 105 E1
Chester Rd. Harm 71 D2
Chester Rd. Slough 42 B4
Chester St. Caver 59 D1
Chester St. Read 85 E4
Chesterblade La. Brac 118 C1
Chesterfield Rd. Ashf 97 F2
Chesterfield Rd. Newb 105 D1
Chesterman St. Read 86 A3
Chesters Rd. Camb 152 A3
Chesterton Dr. Stan 97 D1
Chesterton Rd. That 106 B3
Chestnut Ave. Camb 152 A3
Chestnut Ave. Caver 59 F2
Chestnut Ave. Slough 43 F2
Chestnut Ave. Went 121 F3
Chestnut Cl. Ashf 98 A2
Chestnut Cl. Ashf 98 C1
Chestnut Cl. Black 150 C3
Chestnut Cl. Eng G 95 E1
Chestnut Cl. Harl 71 D4
Chestnut Cl. Maid 20 A1
Chestnut Cl. Medm 17 E4
Chestnut Cl. Thea 83 F2
Chestnut Cres. Newb 105 D2
Chestnut Cres. Shin 113 F2
Chestnut Dr. Bur C 111 D2
Chestnut Dr. Eng G 95 E1
Chestnut Dr. Wind 66 C2
Chestnut Gr. Pur O T 57 E3
Chestnut Gr. Stai 97 E1
Chestnut La. Lamb 25 F2
Chestnut Manor Cl. Stai 97 D2
Chestnut Rd. Ashf 98 A2
Chestnut Wlk. Hung 100 B2
Chestnut Wlk. Shepp 125 F3
Chestnuts The. Shipl 36 A2
Chetwode Cl. Woki 116 C3
Cheveley Gdns. Burn 21 E2
Cheviot Cl. Camb 152 B2
Cheviot Cl. Hart 71 E4
Cheviot Cl. Maid 40 A3
Cheviot Cl. Newb 130 B3
Cheviot Dr. Char 61 D2
Cheviot Rd. Slough 44 A1
Chewter Cl. Bags 145 F2
Chewter La. Windl 146 A3
Cheylesmore Dr. Camb 152 B2
Cheyne Rd. Ashf 98 B1
Chichester Ct. Slough 43 D2
Chichester Rd. Read 84 C4
Chicory Cl. Read 86 C1
Chievley Cl. Read 84 B4
Chilcombe Way. Read 87 E1
Child St. Lamb 25 D1
Childrey Way. Read 84 B4
Chillingham Way. Camb ... 151 E2
Chilsey Green Rd. Chert ... 123 F1
Chiltern Cl. Hen-O-T 35 D4
Chiltern Cl. Newb 130 B3
Chiltern Cres. Read 87 D4
Chiltern Dr. Char 61 D2
Chiltern Green. Fla H 3 D4
Chiltern Rd. Burn 41 D4
Chiltern Rd. Caver 59 E2
Chiltern Rd. Maid 40 A3
Chiltern Rd. Mar 1 B1
Chiltern Rd. Sand 142 C1
Chiltern View. Pur O T 57 E3
Chiltern Wlk. Pangb 56 C3
Chilterns Cl. Fla H 3 D4
Chilterns Park. Bou E 3 D3
Chilton Way. Hung 100 B3
Chilwick Rd. Slough 21 F1
Chippendale Cl. Black 150 C2
Chippendale Cl. Tad 134 C1
Chippenham Cl. Read 113 F4
Chipstead Rd. Harm 71 D2
Chisbury Cl. Brac 118 C2
Chitterfield Gate. Harm 71 D4
Chittering Cl. Winn 87 E1
Chive Rd. Read 87 D1
Chivers Dr. Woki 141 F4
Chives Pl. New G 91 F1
Chobham La. Went 122 A1
Chobham Rd. Camb 151 F1
Chobham Rd. Went 121 D1
Choke La. Cook 19 D2
Cholmeley Pl. Read 86 C4
Cholmeley Rd. Read 86 C4
Cholmeley Terr. Read 86 C4
Cholsey Rd. That 106 C2
Choseley Rd. Know H 37 F2
Choseley Rd. Know H 37 F2
Chrislaine Cl. Stan 70 B1
Christchurch Dr. Black 150 B3
Christchurch Gdns. Read ... 86 B3
Christchurch Rd. Harm 71 D2
Christchurch Rd. Read 86 B3
Christchurch Rd. Vir W 122 B3
Christie Cl. Light 146 B1
Christie Hts. Newb 131 D4
Christie Wlk. Yate 149 E2

Christmas La. Far C 22 B4
Christopher Ct. Newb 105 D1
Chudleigh Gdns. Read 86 B1
Church App. Stai 123 E3
Church Cl. Eton 67 E4
Church Cl. Ham M 129 F3
Church Cl. Lamb 25 D2
Church Cl. Maid 39 E3
Church Cl. Stai 124 B3
Church Cl. Winn 88 B1
Church Croft. Hung 100 B3
Church Dr. Maid 40 B2
Church End La. Read 84 C4
Church Farmbarns. Mort .. 137 E3
Church Gate. That 106 B2
Church Gr. Slough 43 E4
Church Hams. Woki 141 E3
Church Hill. Binf 90 B3
Church Hill. Camb 151 F3
Church Hill. Chil 10 B4
Church Hill. East I 30 C3
Church Hill. Hurst 88 C3
Church La. Arbo 114 B2
Church La. Ascot 120 B3
Church La. Asham 54 A3
Church La. Bark 115 E1
Church La. Binf 90 B2
Church La. Brim 133 F3
Church La. Bur C 111 F3
Church La. Chiev 51 D1
Church La. Combe 147 D3
Church La. Finch 141 F2
Church La. Ham M 129 F4
Church La. Hung 100 B3
Church La. Maid 40 B2
Church La. New G 91 B3
Church La. Newb 104 B2
Church La. Padw 110 B2
Church La. Read 113 E3
Church La. Shipl 35 F1
Church La. Silc 136 C1
Church La. Slough 43 E4
Church La. Sto P 22 C1
Church La. Swal 140 B3
Church La. That 106 B2
Church La. Twyf 61 F3
Church La. Wind 67 E3
Church La. Yatt 53 F1
Church Mews. Pur O T 57 E3
Church Path. Maid 40 B2
Church Rd E. Crow 143 D3
Church Rd W. Crow 143 D3
Church Rd. Alde 135 D4
Church Rd. Ascot 120 A3
Church Rd. Ashf 97 F2
Church Rd. Bags 145 E2
Church Rd. Brac 118 A2
Church Rd. Burl 119 D4
Church Rd. Camb 151 E1
Church Rd. Caver 59 D1
Church Rd. Cook 19 D3
Church Rd. Eng G 96 A2
Church Rd. Far C 22 B1
Church Rd. Frox 99 D3
Church Rd. Ham 126 A1
Church Rd. Lit M 2 B1
Church Rd. Maid 40 A3
Church Rd. Newb 105 D3
Church Rd. Pangb 56 B3
Church Rd. Read 87 D3
Church Rd. Sand 143 F1
Church Rd. Sand 150 C4
Church Rd. Shepp 125 D1
Church Rd. Silc 135 F1
Church Rd. Sunn 121 D2
Church Rd. Swal 139 E3
Church Rd. West E 153 F4
Church Rd. Windl 146 B2
Church Rd. Wink 92 B3
Church Rd. Wood 87 F4
Church Side. East I 30 C3
Church Sq. Shepp 125 D1
Church St. Blew 12 A1
Church St. Burn 21 E1
Church St. Caver 59 D1
Church St. Crow 143 D3
Church St. Frox 99 D1
Church St. Gr She 48 A2
Church St. Hamp N 52 C3
Church St. Hen-O-T 15 E1
Church St. Hung 100 B3
Church St. Kint 102 A1
Church St. Read 86 A3
Church St. Slough 42 B2
Church St. Slough 42 C2
Church St. Stai 96 C2
Church St. Thea 83 F2
Church St. Twyf 61 E2
Church St. Warg 36 B1
Church St. Wind 67 E3
Church View. Been 109 D3
Church View. Whi Wa 63 F4
Church View. Yate 149 E3
Church Views. Maid 39 F4
Church Way. Hung 100 B3
Church Wlk. Chert 124 A2
Churchfield Mews. Slough ... 43 D4
Churchill Cl. Fla H 3 D4
Churchill Cl. Fla H 3 E4

Churchill Cres. Yate 149 E3
Churchill Dr. Mar 1 C2
Churchill Dr. Winn 88 A1
Churchill Rd. Slough 43 F1
Churchward Wlk. Read 84 C2
Churchway. West I 10 A1
Churn Rd. Comp 31 E3
Cinnamon Cl. Read 86 C1
Cintra Ave. Read 86 B3
Cippenham Cl. Slough 41 F3
Cippenham La. Slough 42 A3
Circle Hill Rd. Crow 143 E3
Circuit La. Read 85 E3
City Rd. Read 84 A4
Clacy Green. Brac 91 D1
Clandon Ave. Stai 96 B1
Clanfield Cres. Read 57 E1
Clanfield Ride. Black 150 B3
Clappers Meadow. Maid 20 B1
Clapps Gate Rd. Silc 135 F1
Clapton App. Woo G 3 E4
Clare Ave. Woki 116 B4
Clare Dr. Far C 22 A4
Clare Gdns. Eng G 96 A2
Clare Rd. Maid 39 E3
Clare Rd. Slough 41 E4
Clare Rd. Stan 70 C1
Clare Rd. Stan 97 F4
Clare Wlk. Newb 130 B3
Claredon Cl. Winn 88 B1
Clarefield Cl. Maid 19 D1
Clarefield Dr. Maid 19 D1
Clarefield Rd. Maid 19 D1
Claremont Ave. Camb 151 F3
Claremont Dr. Shepp 125 D2
Claremont Gdns. Mar 1 C1
Claremont Rd. Mar 1 C1
Claremont Rd. Stai 96 B2
Claremont Rd. Wind 67 E3
Clarence Cres. Wind 67 E3
Clarence Dr. Eng G 95 E2
Clarence Rd. Hen-O-T 15 E1
Clarence Rd. Wind 67 D3
Clarence St. Eng G 95 F1
Clarence St. Stai 96 C2
Clarence Way. Read 84 A2
Clarendon Ct. Black 150 B2
Clarendon Cl. Slough 43 D3
Clarendon Gdns. Newb 105 D2
Clarendon Rd. Ashf 97 F2
Clarendon Rd. Read 87 D3
Clares Green Rd. Shin 113 D2
Clarewood Dr. Camb 151 F3
Clark's Gdns. Hung 100 B3
Clarke Cres. Sand 150 C4
Classics The. Lamb 25 D1
Claverdon. Brac 118 A1
Clay Cl. Fla H 3 D4
Clay Cl. Pur O T 57 D1
Clay Hill Cres. Newb 105 E3
Clay La. Been 108 C3
Claydon Gdns. Camb 151 D1
Clayhall La. Old Wind 67 F1
Clayhill Cl. Brac 119 D3
Clayton Gr. Brac 118 C4
Clayton Rd. Black 150 C1
Clayton Wlk. Read 86 B2
Claytons Meadow. Bou E 3 D2
Clearsprings. Camb 153 D4
Clearsprings. Light 146 A1
Cleaves Way. Ashf 98 C1
Cleeve Ct. Felt 98 C4
Cleeve Down. Gori 34 B4
Cleeve Rd. Gori 34 A4
Clements Cl. Read 113 D1
Clements Cl. Slough 43 D2
Clements Mead. Sulh 57 D1
Clements Rd. Hen-O-T 15 E2
Clent Rd. Read 86 A2
Cleopatra Pl. New G 91 F1
Cleve Ct. Wind 66 C2
Clevedon Dr. Read 87 D1
Clevedon Rd. Read 57 F2
Clevehurst Cl. Sto P 23 D3
Cleveland Cl. Maid 40 A3
Cleveland Cl. Woo G 3 F4
Cleveland Dr. Stai 124 A4
Cleveland Gr. Newb 104 C2
Cleveland. Char 61 D2
Clevemede. Gori 34 B4
Clewborough Dr. Camb 152 A3
Clewer Ave. Wind 67 D3
Clewer Ct Rd. Wind 67 D3
Clewer Fields. Wind 67 D3
Clewer Hill Rd. Wind 66 C2
Clewer New Town. Wind 67 D3
Clewer Park. Wind 67 D4
Clifford Gr. Ashf 98 A2
Clifford Way. Bou E 3 D3
Clifton Cl. Maid 40 A2
Clifton Rd. Harm 71 D2
Clifton Rd. Newb 104 C1
Clifton Rd. Slough 43 D2
Clifton Rd. Woki 116 A4
Clifton Rise. Warg 36 C1
Clifton Rise. Wind 66 B3
Clifton St. Read 85 F4
Clintons Green. Brac 118 A4
Clive Ct. Slough 42 B2

Clive Green. Brac 118
Clivedale Rd. Wood 87
Cliveden Mead. Maid 20
Cliveden Pl. Shepp 125
Cliveden Rd. Tapl 20
Clivemont Rd. Maid 39
Clockhouse La E. Stai 96
Clockhouse La W. Eng G 96
Clockhouse La. Ashf 98
Clockhouse La. Felt 98
Cloister Mews. Thea 83
Cloisters The. Camb 151
Cloisters The. Caver 59
Clonmel Way. Burn 21
Close End. Lamb 25
Close The. Bou E 3
Close The. Bur C 111
Close The. Burl 119
Close The. Gr She 48
Close The. Hamp N 52
Close The. Hen-O-T 35
Close The. Light 146
Close The. Sand 150
Close The. Slough 41
Close The. That 106
Close The. Vir W 122
Close The. Wood 87
Clough Dr. Herm 78
Clove Cl. Read 86
Clover Cl. Woki 116
Clover La. Yate 149
Club La. Crow 143
Clumps The. Felt 98
Clyde Rd. Stan 97
Clyve Way. Stai 123
Coach House Cl. Camb 151
Coach Ride. Mar 1
Coalport Way. Read 57
Cobb Cl. Datch 68
Cobbett's La. Yate 149
Cobblers Cl. Far C 22
Cobham Rd. Wood 87
Cochrane Cl. That 106
Cochrane Pl. Windl 146
Cock La. Brad 82
Cock's La. New G 92
Cock's La. Wink 92
Cock-a-Dobby. Sand 143
Cockett Rd. Slough 43
Cockney Hill. Read 84
Cody Cl. Read 88
Coe Spur. Slough 42
Coftards. Slough 43
Cold Ash Hill. Cold A 106
Coldharbour Cl. Hen-O-T 35
Coldharbour Cl. Stai 123
Coldharbour La. Stai 123
Coldharbour La. West E 153
Coldharbour Rd. Hung 100
Coldicutt St. Caver 59
Coldmoorholme La. Bou E 2
Colemans Moor La. Wood ... 87
Colemans Moor Rd. Wood .. 88
Colenorton Cres. Eton 41
Coleridge Ave. Yate 149
Coleridge Cl. Crow 143
Coleridge Cl. Twyf 61
Coleridge Cres. Stan 69
Coleridge Rd. Ashf 98
Coley Ave. Read 85
Coley Hill. Read 85
Coley Park Rd. Read 85
Coley Pl. Read 86
Colin Way. Slough 42
Collaroy Rd. Cold A 106
College Ave. Maid 39
College Ave. Slough 42
College Ave. Stai 96
College Cl. Camb 151
College Cres. Sand 150
College Cres. Wind 67
College Glen. Maid 39
College Piece. Mort 136
College Rd. Maid 39
College Rd. Read 86
College Rd. Slough 41
College Ride. Bags 145
College Ride. Camb 151
College Rise. Maid 39
College Way. Ashf 97
Colleton Dr. Twyf 61
Collier Cl. Maid 19
Colliers Way. Read 85
Collingwood Rise. Camb ... 152
Collingwood Wlk. Read 84
Collins Cl. Newb 105
Collins Dr. Herm 78
Collinswood Rd. Far C 22
Collis St. Read 86
Colliston Wlk. Read 84
Collum Green Rd. Sto P 22
Coln Cl. Maid 39
Colnbrook By-Pass. Iver 69
Colnbrook By-Pass. Slough . 69
Colndale Rd. Stan 69
Colne Bank. Hort 69
Colne Orchard. Iver 44
Colne Way. Wray 96
Colnebridge Cl. Stai 96

worth Cl. Read 114 A4
nel's La. Chert 124 A2
nial Rd. Felt 98 C4
nial Rd. Slough 43 D2
ton Cl. Bur C 84 B2
rop La. That 107 D1
mbia Ct. Woki 141 F4
ille Gdns. Light 153 E4
yn Cl. Yate 149 E3
er Cl. Herm 79 E4
ton Way. Pur O T 57 E3
be Rd. Read 84 C4
be View. Hung 100 B2
bermere Cl. Wind 67 D3
et Rd. Stan 97 E4
et Way. Wood 88 A4
frey Cl. Woki 116 C4
mercial Rd. Read 86 A1
mercial Rd. Stai 97 D1
mon Hill. Brad 82 C2
mon La. Brig 28 B3
mon La. Eton 42 B1
mon Rd. Dorn 41 E1
mon Rd. Eton 42 A1
mon Rd. Fla H 3 D4
mon Rd. Head 132 C1
mon Rd. Slough 44 A1
mon The. Fla H 3 D4
mon Wood. Far C 22 B4
monfield La. Bark 141 D4
monfields. West E 153 F3
mons Rd. Woki 88 C1
mpton Ave. Read 57 D3
pton Cl. Brac 117 F2
pton Cl. Read 87 E2
pton Cl. Sand 143 E1
pton Ct. Slough 41 F4
pton Dr. Maid 39 D4
saye Wlk. Brac 118 B2
corde Way. Slough 42 B2
corde Way. Wood 88 A4
dor Cl. Sulh 57 E2
dor Rd. Stai 124 B3
egar Ct. Slough 42 C3
eygore Cl. Read 87 D1
greve Cl. Alde 135 D4
er Cl. Tad 134 C1
fer Crest. Newb 130 B2
fer Dr. Camb 152 A3
fer Dr. Sulh 57 D1
fer La. Stai 96 B2
fers The. Brac 143 D4
ingham Rd. Read 113 E3
ngsby Cl. Maid 39 E2
ngsby La. Holy 65 E3
ngsby. Brac 118 B3
sboro Ave. Caver 58 C3
sboro Way. Caver 58 C3
ston Cl. Camb 152 B2
ston Cl. That 106 A2
ston Cl. Wood 87 F3
ston Cres. Slough 41 E4
ston Ct. Light 146 A1
ston Dr. Read 57 F1
ston Way. Stai 96 A1
naught Cl. Ashf 97 F2
naught Cl. Crow 142 C2
naught Cl. Maid 19 F1
naught Cl. Read 85 E4
naught Cl. Yate 149 D3
naught Rd. Bags 145 E2
naught Rd. Camb 151 F3
naught Rd. Newb 105 D2
naught Rd. Read 85 E4
naught Rd. Slough 43 D2
niston Cl. Mar 1 A1
oop Way. Camb 151 F2
stable Way. Sand 150 C3
stitution Rd. Read 85 D4
sul Cl. Wood 88 A3
rol Tower Rd. Harm 71 D2
vent Lodge. Ashf 98 A2
vent Rd. Ashf 98 A2
vent Rd. Wind 67 D3
way Dr. Ashf 98 B1
way Dr. That 106 A3
way Rd. Burn 41 D4
way Rd. Harm 71 D2
way Rd. Read 84 B3
way Rd. Slough 41 D4
cham Cl. Sand 143 E1
cham Dean Bottom La. Cook
.... 19 D4
cham Rd. Brac 117 F4
cham Rd. Maid 19 F1
cham Rd. Maid 19 F2
arne Rise. Camb 152 A3
gardie Rd. Ashf 98 B2
er Cl. That 106 C2
nbe Hill. Farn 28 A4
nbe Pine. Brac 118 B2
nbe Rd. Comp 31 F2
nbe Rd. Yate 149 D4
nbe Gdns. Camb 152 A3
nbe Sq. That 106 C2
nbe The. Stre 33 F3
nbes La. Woki 115 E2
nbesbury La. Box 76 B1
er Cl. Read 113 E4
er Rd. Hen-O-T 15 E2

Cooper Rd. Windl 146 B2
Cooper Way. Slough 42 A2
Cooper's Hill La. Eng G 95 E2
Coopers Cl. Stai 96 C2
Coopers Cres. That 106 B2
Cope Hall La. Ham M 130 B4
Copeland's Cl. Camb 152 B2
Copenhagen Cl. Read 113 E4
Copped Hall Dr. Camb 152 B3
Copped Hall Way. Camb 152 B3
Copper Beech Cl. Wind 66 B3
Copperage Rd. Farn 9 D1
Copperdale Cl. Read 86 C2
Coppermill Rd. Hort 69 D1
Coppermill Rd. Wray 69 D1
Coppice Cl. Newb 131 D4
Coppice Dr. Wray 95 E4
Coppice Gdns. Crow 142 C3
Coppice Gdns. Yate 149 E3
Coppice Green. Brac 90 C1
Coppice Rd. Wood 87 F2
Coppice The. Ashf 98 A1
Coppins La. Iver 44 C4
Copse Ave. Caver 59 F2
Copse Cl. Camb 152 A3
Copse Cl. Mar 1 B1
Copse Cl. Read 57 E2
Copse Dr. Woki 116 A4
Copse End. Camb 152 A3
Copse Mead. Wood 60 C1
Copse The. Warg 36 C2
Copse Way. Woki 141 F4
Copthorn Cl. Maid 39 D2
Copthorne Cl. Shepp 125 E2
Copthorne Dr. Light 146 A1
Corbett Dr. Camb 152 C4
Corbett Gdns. Wood 87 F4
Corbridge Rd. Read 86 B2
Corby Cl. Wood 61 D1
Corby Dr. Eng G 95 E1
Cordelia Gdns. Stan 97 F4
Cordelia Rd. Stan 97 F4
Corderoy Cl. That 106 C1
Corderoy Pl. Chert 123 F2
Cordwalles Rd. Camb 151 F2
Cordwallis Rd. Maid 39 F4
Cordwallis St. Maid 39 F4
Cores End Rd. Bou E 3 D2
Corfe Gdns. Camb 151 F1
Corfe Gdns. Slough 42 A3
Corfe Mews. Caver 59 F2
Corfe Pl. Maid 39 E4
Corfield Cl. Finch 141 F2
Coriander Way. Read 86 C1
Cormorant Pl. Sand 150 C4
Cornbunting Cl. Sand 150 B4
Cornerside. Ashf 98 B1
Cornfield Green. Woki 115 F4
Cornfield Rd. Wood 88 A4
Cornfields. Yate 149 D2
Cornflower Cl. Woki 115 E4
Cornwall Ave. Slough 22 B1
Cornwall Cl. Camb 151 F4
Cornwall Cl. Eton 41 F1
Cornwall Cl. Maid 19 F1
Cornwall Cl. Pur O T 57 D2
Cornwall Cl. Woki 115 E3
Cornwall Way. Stai 96 C1
Cornwell Rd. Old W 68 A1
Cornwood Gdns. Read 86 B2
Coronation Ave. Slough 43 F4
Coronation Rd. Ascot 120 A1
Coronation Rd. Bish 38 A3
Coronation Rd. Brac 120 A1
Coronation Rd. Yate 149 F4
Coronation Sq. Read 85 D2
Coronation Sq. Woki 116 B4
Corrie Gdns. Went 122 B1
Corrine Cl. Read 86 A1
Corsair Cl. Stan 97 F4
Corsair Rd. Stan 97 F4
Corsham Rd. Read 84 C2
Corsham Way. Crow 143 D3
Corwen Rd. Read 84 C4
Coster Cl. Newb 104 B3
Cotswold Cl. Maid 40 A3
Cotswold Cl. Slough 42 B2
Cotswold Cl. Stai 97 D2
Cotswold Rd. Sand 142 C1
Cotswold Way. Read 57 E1
Cottage Farm Way. Stai 123 E3
Cottage La. Bur C 85 E1
Cotterell Cl. Brac 91 D1
Cottesbrooke Cl. Stan 69 E3
Cottesmore Rd. Wood 87 E3
Cottesmore. Brac 118 A4
Coulson Way. Burn 41 D4
County La. New G 91 F1
Course Rd. Ascot 120 A3
Court Cl. Holy 40 B1
Court Cres. Slough 42 B4
Court Dr. Maid 20 B2
Court Gdns. Camb 151 E3
Court Hill Rd. Farn 7 D4
Court Hill Rd. Let B 7 D4
Court La. Burn 21 E1
Court La. Iver 44 C3
Court La. Slough 41 D2
Court Rd. Maid 20 B2

Courtenay Dr. Caver 59 D4
Courtfield Rd. Ashf 98 A1
Courtfields Dr. Maid 39 E3
Courthouse Rd. Maid 39 E4
Courtlands Ave. Slough 43 E1
Courtlands Hill. Pangb 56 B2
Courtlands Rd. Newb 105 D1
Courtlands. Maid 39 F3
Courtney Rd. Harm 71 D2
Courts Rd. Read 87 D2
Coventry Rd. Read 86 C4
Coverdale Way. Slough 21 F1
Covert The. Sunn 120 A1
Cow La. East I 30 C4
Cow La. Moul 13 F2
Cow La. Read 58 C1
Cowley Ave. Chert 123 F1
Cowley La. Chert 123 F1
Coworth Cl. Sunn 121 D2
Coworth Rd. Sunn 121 D2
Cowper Cl. Chert 123 F2
Cowper Rd. Slough 22 A1
Cowper Way. Read 85 D2
Cowslade. Newb 104 B3
Cowslip Cl. Read 84 A3
Cox Green La. Maid 39 E2
Cox Green Rd. Maid 39 E2
Cox Green. Sand 150 B4
Cox's La. Wool 107 E2
Coxborrow Cl. Cook 19 F4
Coxeter Rd. Newb 104 C2
Crabtree Cl. Herm 78 C3
Crabtree Rd. Camb 151 D1
Crabtree Rd. Stai 123 E4
Craddock Rd. Read 86 A2
Crafts End. Chil 10 C4
Craig Ave. Read 85 D4
Craigwell Cl. Stai 123 F4
Crail Cl. Woki 116 A2
Crake Pl. Sand 150 B4
Cramond Ct. Felt 98 C4
Cranborne Gdns. Read 58 A1
Cranbourne Ave. Bur C 84 B2
Cranbourne Ave. Wind 66 C3
Cranbourne Cl. Slough 42 B3
Cranbourne Hall Caravan Site. Wink
.... 93 D4
Cranbourne Rd. Slough 42 B3
Cranbrook Dr. Maid 19 E1
Cranbury Rd. Read 85 E4
Crane Ct. Sand 150 B4
Crane Wharf. Read 86 A4
Craneswater. Harl 71 F4
Cranford Ave. Stan 97 F4
Cranford Cl. Hurst 88 C4
Cranford Cl. Stan 97 F4
Cranford La. Harl 71 F4
Cranford La. Harm 71 F2
Cranford La. Harm 71 F3
Cranford Park Dr. Yate 149 E3
Cranleigh Rd. Felt 98 C2
Cranmer Cl. Sulh 57 D2
Cranwell Gr. Light 152 C4
Cranwell Gr. Stai 124 C3
Cranwell Rd. Harm 71 F2
Craufurd Rise. Maid 39 F4
Craven Cl. Kint 102 A1
Craven Dene. Newb 105 D2
Craven Rd. Ink 127 D3
Craven Rd. Newb 104 C1
Craven Rd. Read 86 B3
Craven Way. Kint 102 A1
Crawford Cl. Read 87 D2
Crawford Gdns. Camb 151 D3
Crawford Pl. Newb 104 C2
Crawley Chase. Burl 92 A1
Crawley Dr. Camb 151 F3
Crawley Hill. Camb 151 F3
Crawley Ridge. Camb 151 F3
Crawley Wood Cl. Camb 151 F3
Crawshay Dr. Caver 59 D4
Crayle St. Slough 22 A1
Crayonne Cl. Stai 125 F4
Crecy Cl. Woki 115 F3
Creden Cl. Maid 39 E4
Crediton Cl. Wood 88 A3
Crees Meadow. Windl 146 B2
Cremyll Rd. Read 58 C1
Crescent Ave. Read 86 C3
Crescent Dr. Maid 39 F4
Crescent Rd. Read 57 E1
Crescent Rd. Shepp 125 E2
Crescent Rd. Woki 116 B3
Crescent The. Ashf 97 F2
Crescent The. Chert 124 A3
Crescent The. Eng G 95 F1
Crescent The. Eng G 95 F1
Crescent The. Harl 71 E4
Crescent The. Kint 102 A1
Crescent The. Maid 39 F4
Crescent The. Mort 137 D3
Crescent The. Padw 109 E2
Crescent The. Read 87 E2
Crescent The. Shepp 125 F1
Crescent The. Shipl 36 A2
Crescent The. Slough 42 C2
Crescent The. Thea 83 F2
Cress Rd. Slough 42 A2

Cressex Cl. Binf 90 B1
Cressingham Rd. Read 86 B1
Cressington Pl. Bou E 3 D2
Cresswell Rd. Newb 105 E2
Cresswells Mead. Holy 40 B1
Crest Cl. Twyf 61 F3
Crest The. Caver 59 E3
Creswell Cl. Read 113 E3
Cricket Field Gr. Crow 143 E2
Cricket Hill La. Yate 149 F2
Cricket Hill. Finch 141 F1
Cricketers La. Burl 92 A2
Cricketers La. Windl 146 B2
Cricketers. Box 103 F3
Crimp Hill. Eng G 95 D3
Crimp Hill. Old W 95 D3
Crisp Gdns. Binf 90 C1
Crisp Rd. Hen-O-T 15 E2
Crispin Cl. Caver 58 B3
Crispin Way. Far C 22 B4
Crocker Cl. Ascot 119 F4
Crockhamwell Rd. Wood 87 F3
Crocus Way. Woki 115 E4
Croft Cl. Harl 71 E4
Croft Cl. Woki 116 A1
Croft La. Newb 104 C2
Croft La. Yate 149 E4
Croft Rd. Gori 34 B3
Croft Rd. Hung 100 B3
Croft Rd. Mort 136 C3
Croft Rd. Newb 130 C4
Croft Rd. Woki 116 A1
Croft Road. Shin 113 E1
Croft The. Brac 91 D1
Croft The. Kint 102 A1
Croft The. Maid 39 E3
Croft The. Mar 2 A2
Croft Way. Camb 151 F1
Crofter's Cl. Sand 150 A4
Crofters. Old W 68 A1
Crofthill Rd. Slough 22 A1
Crofton Cl. Brac 118 C2
Crofts The. Shepp 125 F3
Cromer Cl. Read 57 E1
Cromer Rd W. Harn 71 D2
Cromer Rd. Harm 71 D3
Cromwell Cl. Hen-O-T 35 F4
Cromwell Dr. Slough 42 C4
Cromwell Gdns. Mar 1 C1
Cromwell Rd. Ascot 120 A3
Cromwell Rd. Camb 151 E4
Cromwell Rd. Caver 59 D1
Cromwell Rd. Hen-O-T 35 F4
Cromwell Rd. Maid 39 E4
Cromwell Rd. Mar 1 C1
Cromwell Rd. Newb 105 E3
Crondall End. Yate 149 E4
Crondell Ct. Camb 151 D2
Cropper Cl. That 107 D2
Crosby Gdns. Yate 149 D4
Crosby Hill Dr. Camb 151 F4
Cross Fell. Brac 118 A3
Cross Gates Cl. Brac 118 C3
Cross Keys Rd. Sou S 14 B2
Cross La. Bee H 138 B4
Cross Oak. Wind 67 D3
Cross Rd. Windl 121 D1
Cross St. Read 86 A4
Cross St. Woki 116 B3
Crossfields Cl. Read 113 F4
Crossland Rd. Read 86 A4
Crossways. Stai 96 B1
Crossways. Stai 98 C1
Crossways. Wood 87 F3
Crosswell Cl. Stai 125 E4
Crosthwaite Way. Slough 41 E4
Crouch La. Wink 92 C4
Crow Piece La. Burn 21 F2
Crowfield Dr. That 106 A2
Crowle Rd. Lamb 25 D1
Crown Acre Cl. That 106 B2
Crown La. Burn 22 A2
Crown La. Maid 40 A4
Crown La. Mar 1 B1
Crown La. Thea 83 F2
Crown La. Went 122 B2
Crown Meadow. Iver 69 D4
Crown Pl. Read 86 B3
Crown Pl. Sand 143 F1
Crown Rd. Mar 1 B1
Crown Rd. Went 122 B2
Crown Row. Brac 118 B2
Crown St. Eng G 96 A2
Crown St. Read 86 A3
Crowthorne Rd N. Brac 118 A3
Crowthorne Rd. Brac 117 F1
Crowthorne Rd. Brac 118 A2
Crowthorne Rd. Sand 143 D1
Croxley Rise. Maid 39 E3
Croydon Rd. Harm 71 D2
Cruikshank Lea. Sand 150 C3
Crummock Cl. Slough 41 E4
Crutchley Rd. Woki 116 B4
Cuckoo La. West E 153 E3
Cuckoo Pound. Shepp 125 F2
Cuckoo Vale. West E 153 E3
Culford Cl. Winn 87 E1
Culham Dr. Maid 19 F1

Cullen Cl. Yate 149 E3
Cullen's Pas. Maid 39 F3
Culley Way. Maid 39 D2
Culloden Way. Woki 115 F3
Culver Croft. Binf 90 C1
Culver La. Read 87 D4
Culver Rd. Newb 130 C4
Culver Rd. Read 86 C3
Culver Rd. Sand 143 E1
Cumberland Ave. Slough 22 B1
Cumberland Dr. Brac 118 B4
Cumberland Rd. Ashf 97 D3
Cumberland Rd. Camb 152 B2
Cumberland Rd. Read 86 C4
Cumberland St. Stai 96 B2
Cumberland Way. Woki 115 E3
Cumbernauld Gdns. Ashf 98 C3
Cumbria Cl. Maid 39 E2
Cumnor Way. Brac 118 C3
Curl Way. Woki 116 A3
Curlew Cl. That 106 B2
Curlew Dr. Read 84 B3
Curley Hill Rd. Light 152 C4
Curling Way. Newb 105 E2
Curls Rd. Maid 39 E2
Curridge Green. Herm 78 C2
Curridge Piece. Herm 78 C3
Curridge Rd. Herm 78 B2
Curriers La. Burn 21 F4
Curtis Rd. Read 84 B2
Curzon St. Read 85 F2
Cutbush Cl. Read 114 A4
Cutbush La. Read 114 A4
Cutting Hill. Ham 126 A2
Cygnet Cl. That 106 A2
Cypress Cl. Brac 142 A4
Cypress Rd. Stai 125 F4
Cypress Rd. Wood 88 A3
Cypress Way. Black 150 A3
Cypress Wlk. Eng G 95 D1
Cyril Vokins Rd. Gree 105 F1

Dacre Ave. Caver 59 F2
Dagmar Rd. Wind 67 E3
Dairy La. Hamb 16 A4
Dalby Cres. Newb 131 D4
Dalby Cres. Newb 131 E4
Dalcross. Brac 118 C2
Dale Cl. Sunn 121 D2
Dale Ct. Slough 42 B2
Dale Gdns. Sand 150 A4
Dale Lodge Rd. Sunn 121 D2
Dale Rd. Ashf 98 C1
Dale Rd. Read 86 A3
Dale Rd. Shepp 125 F1
Daleham Ave. Eng G 96 A1
Dalston Cl. Camb 152 B2
Dalton Cl. Read 84 C4
Damar Gdns. Hen-O-T 35 F4
Damask Cl. Camb 153 F3
Dandridge Cl. Slough 43 E1
Dandridge Dr. Bou E 3 E2
Dane Rd. Ashf 98 B1
Danehill. Read 114 A4
Danvers Cl. That 106 B1
Danywern Dr. Winn 88 B1
Darby Green La. Black 150 A3
Darby Green Rd. Black 150 A3
Darby La. Upp B 55 D3
Darell Rd. Caver 58 C2
Dark La. Brad 82 B4
Dark La. Read 57 D1
Dark La. Warg 36 B1
Dark La. Wick 101 D4
Darleydale Cl. Crow 143 E1
Darling's La. Bish 18 C1
Darrell Cl. Slough 43 F1
Dart Cl. Slough 69 D4
Dart Cl. That 106 A3
Dart Cl. Woki 141 F3
Dartington Ave. Wood 87 E2
Dartmouth Cl. Brac 118 C3
Darvill's La. W St L 62 C1
Darwall Dr. Burl 119 E4
Darwin Cl. Read 86 A1
Darwin Rd. Slough 43 F2
Dashwood Cl. Brac 118 B4
Dashwood Cl. Slough 43 E1
Datchet Pl. Slough 68 A3
Datchet Rd. Datch 42 C1
Datchet Rd. Hort 68 C2
Datchet Rd. Old W 68 A3
Datchet Rd. Slough 42 C1
Datchet Rd. Wind 67 E4
Dauntless Rd. Bur C 111 D2
Davenport Rd. Brac 118 C4
Daventry Cl. Stan 69 F3
Daventry Ct. Brac 118 A4
David Cl. Harl 71 E4
David Rd. Stan 69 F3
David Smith Ct. Read 84 C3
Davis Cl. Mar 1 C1
Davis Cl. Winn 88 A1
Davis Gdns. Sand 150 C4
Davis St. Hurst 88 B3
Davis Way. Hurst 88 B3
Dawes East Rd. Burn 21 E1
Dawes Moor Cl. Slough 43 E4

Dawley Ride. Stan

Dawley Ride. Stan ... 69 F3
Dawlish Rd. Read ... 86 B1
Dawn Redwood Cl. Hort ... 69 D2
Dawnay Cl. Ascot ... 119 F4
Dawnay Rd. Sand ... 151 D4
Dawsmere Cl. Camb ... 152 B3
Dawson Cl. Wind ... 67 D3
De Beauvoir Rd. Read ... 86 C3
De Bohun Rd. Read ... 86 A4
De Havilland Way. Stan ... 70 C1
De Montfort Gr. Hung ... 100 B2
De Montfort Rd. Newb ... 104 C3
De Montfort Rd. Read ... 59 D1
De Vitre Green. Woki ... 116 C4
Deacon Cl. Woki ... 116 B4
Deacon Way. Read ... 58 A1
Deaconfield. Sou S ... 14 B2
Deacons La. Herm ... 79 E4
Deadman's La. Thea ... 83 E2
Deadmans La. Gree ... 131 D4
Deadmoor La. Ball H ... 130 C1
Deadmoor La. Newt ... 130 C1
Deal Ave. Slough ... 41 F4
Dean Cl. Wind ... 66 B2
Dean La. Cook ... 19 E4
Dean St. Mar ... 1 B1
Deanfield Ave. Hen-O-T ... 15 E1
Deanfield Cl. Mar ... 1 B2
Deanfield Rd. Hen-O-T ... 15 E1
Deans Cl. Sto P ... 23 D2
Deans Ct. Windl ... 146 B2
Deansgate Rd. Read ... 86 A3
Deansgate. Brac ... 118 A1
Decies Way. Sto P ... 23 D2
Dedmere Ct. Mar ... 1 C1
Dedmere Rd. Mar ... 1 C1
Dedmere Rise. Mar ... 1 C1
Dedworth Dr. Wind ... 66 C3
Dedworth Rd. Wind ... 66 B3
Dee Rd. Read ... 85 D4
Deena Cl. Slough ... 41 F3
Deep Field. Datch ... 68 A4
Deep Well Dr. Camb ... 151 F3
Deepcut Bridge Rd. Camb ... 152 B1
Deepdene Cl. Read ... 85 F4
Deepfield Rd. Brac ... 118 B4
Deer Leap. Camb ... 153 D4
Deer Rock Hill. Brac ... 118 B2
Deer Rock Rd. Camb ... 151 F4
Deerhurst Ave. Winn ... 88 B1
Deerhurst Cl. Read ... 84 C2
Deerswood. Maid ... 20 A1
Defford Cl. Woki ... 88 C1
Delafield Dr. Bur C ... 84 B2
Delaford Cl. Iver ... 44 C4
Delamere Rd. Read ... 87 D4
Delane Dr. Winn ... 88 A1
Delaney Cl. Read ... 84 C4
Delft Cl. Read ... 84 C4
Dell Cl. Far C ... 22 B4
Dell Gr. Camb ... 151 F4
Dell Rd. Finch ... 142 A2
Dell Rd. Read ... 57 E1
Dell The. Whi Wa ... 38 C2
Dell The. Yate ... 149 E3
Dellars Hill. Hurl ... 38 A4
Delph The. Winn ... 87 E1
Delta Way. Stai ... 123 E4
Denbury Gdns. Read ... 113 E4
Denby Way. Read ... 57 F1
Dene Cl. Brac ... 118 B4
Dene Cl. Read ... 87 D2
Dene Hollow. Chil ... 10 C4
Dene Way. Newb ... 105 D3
Denford La. Hung ... 101 D4
Denford La. Wick ... 101 D4
Denham Cl. Maid ... 39 E3
Denham Dr. Yate ... 149 F3
Denham Gr. Brac ... 118 B2
Denham Rd. Eng G ... 96 A2
Denhose Cl. Read ... 87 D1
Denison Rd. Felt ... 98 C2
Denly Way. Light ... 146 B1
Denman Dr. Ashf ... 98 A1
Denmark Ave. Wood ... 61 D1
Denmark Rd. Newb ... 105 D2
Denmark Rd. Read ... 86 B3
Denmark St. Maid ... 39 F4
Denmark St. Woki ... 116 B3
Denmead Ct. Brac ... 118 C2
Dennis Cl. Ashf ... 98 B1
Dennis Way. Slough ... 41 E3
Dennisford Rd. East I ... 31 D3
Dennistoun Cl. Camb ... 151 E3
Denny Rd. Slough ... 43 F1
Denton Cl. That ... 106 B1
Denton Rd. Woki ... 116 B3
Denton Way. Camb ... 151 E1
Depot Rd. Maid ... 40 A3
Deppdale. Brac ... 118 A3
Derby Cl. Lamb ... 25 D1
Derby Rd. Caver ... 59 D2
Derby Rd. Newb ... 104 C1
Derby St. Read ... 85 F4
Derek Rd. Maid ... 40 B4
Deri Dene Cl. Stan ... 70 C1
Derrick Cl. Bur C ... 84 B2
Derry Rd. Black ... 150 C1
Derwent Ave. Read ... 57 F1

Derwent Cl. Felt ... 98 C4
Derwent Cl. Woki ... 115 F3
Derwent Dr. Maid ... 39 E4
Derwent Dr. Slough ... 41 E4
Derwent Rd. Light ... 153 D4
Derwent Rd. Stai ... 96 A1
Derwent Rd. That ... 106 A2
Desborough Cl. Shepp ... 125 D1
Desborough Cres. Maid ... 39 E3
Deseronto Wharf. Slough ... 43 F2
Desford Way. Ashf ... 97 F3
Devenish La. Sunn ... 120 B1
Devenish Rd. Ascot ... 120 B1
Devenish Rd. Sunn ... 120 B1
Devereux Rd. Wind ... 67 E3
Deveron Dr. Read ... 85 D4
Devil's Highway The. Brac ... 142 C3
Devil's Highway The. Finch ... 142 C3
Devil's La. Stai ... 96 B1
Devitt Cl. Read ... 86 C1
Devon Ave. Slough ... 42 B4
Devon Cl. Sand ... 150 B4
Devon Cl. Woki ... 115 F3
Devon Dr. Caver ... 59 F2
Devonshire Cl. Slough ... 22 A2
Devonshire Dr. Camb ... 151 F4
Devonshire Gdns. Sulh ... 57 D2
Devonshire Green. Far C ... 22 A2
Devonshire Park. Read ... 86 C1
Dhoon Rise. Maid ... 39 F3
Diamedes Ave. Stan ... 97 E4
Diamond Hill. Camb ... 151 F4
Diamond Rd. Slough ... 43 D2
Diamond Ridge. Camb ... 151 F4
Diamond Way. Woki ... 115 F4
Diana Cl. Slough ... 43 F4
Dianthus Cl. Chert ... 123 F1
Dick Turpin Way. Harm ... 71 F2
Dickens Way. Yate ... 149 E3
Dickens Wlk. Newb ... 131 D4
Dido Rd. Chil ... 9 F4
Dieppe Cl. Woki ... 115 F3
Digby Rd. Newb ... 104 C2
Dines Way. Herm ... 79 E4
Dingle Rd. Ashf ... 98 A2
Disraeli Cl. Slough ... 69 D4
Ditchfield La. Woki ... 141 F4
Ditchling. Brac ... 118 A1
Ditton Park Rd. Datch ... 68 C4
Ditton Rd. Datch ... 68 B4
Ditton Rd. Slough ... 68 C4
Dobson's La. Faw (Bu) ... 15 E4
Dockett Eddy La. Shepp ... 124 C1
Doctors La. Herm ... 79 D3
Doddington Cl. Winn ... 87 E1
Doddsfield Rd. Slough ... 22 A1
Dodsells Well. Woki ... 141 F4
Dog La. Asham ... 54 A3
Doghurst Ave. Harl ... 71 D4
Doghurst Dr. Harl ... 71 D4
Dogkennel La. Fawl ... 27 E2
Doles Hill. Woki ... 115 E2
Doles La. Woki ... 115 F2
Dolman Rd. Newb ... 105 D2
Dolphin Ct N. Stai ... 97 D3
Dolphin Ct. Slough ... 43 D2
Dolphin Ct. Stan ... 97 D3
Dolphin Rd N. Stai ... 125 F4
Dolphin Rd S. Stai ... 125 F4
Dolphin Rd W. Stai ... 125 F4
Dolphin Rd. Slough ... 43 D2
Dolphin Rd. Stai ... 125 F4
Doman Rd. Camb ... 151 D2
Domoney Cl. That ... 106 C2
Don Cl. Read ... 85 D4
Donaldson Way. Read ... 88 A4
Doncastle Rd. Brac ... 117 F3
Donegal Cl. Caver ... 59 E2
Donkin Hill. Caver ... 59 E2
Donnington Cl. Buck ... 108 B4
Donnington Cl. Camb ... 151 D2
Donnington Gdns. Read ... 86 C3
Donnington Pl. Winn ... 88 B1
Donnington Rd. Read ... 86 B3
Donnington Sq. Newb ... 104 C3
Donnybrook. Brac ... 118 A1
Dorchester Cl. Maid ... 19 D1
Dorchester Ct. Read ... 85 E3
Dorchester Dr. Felt ... 71 F1
Dorian Dr. Ascot ... 120 C4
Doris Rd. Ashf ... 98 B1
Dorking Way. Bur C ... 84 A2
Dorly Cl. Shepp ... 125 F2
Dormer Cl. Crow ... 143 D3
Dormer Cl. Newb ... 130 C3
Dornels. Slough ... 43 E4
Dorney Reach Rd. Dorn ... 40 C2
Dorney Wood Rd. Burn ... 21 E3
Dorothy St. Read ... 86 A3
Dorset Rd. Ashf ... 97 E3
Dorset Rd. Wind ... 67 E3
Dorset St. Read ... 85 E4
Dorset Vale. New G ... 91 F1
Dorset Way. Woki ... 115 F3
Doublet Cl. That ... 106 A2
Douglas Cl. Mar ... 2 A2
Douglas Grange. Hurst ... 88 A2
Douglas La. Wray ... 68 C1
Douglas Rd. Caver ... 59 E1

Douglas Rd. Slough ... 42 B4
Douglas Rd. Stan ... 70 B1
Doultons The. Stan ... 97 D1
Douro Cl. Tad ... 134 B1
Dove Cl. Read ... 113 F4
Dove House Cres. Slough ... 21 F1
Dovecote Rd. Read ... 113 D4
Dovedale Cl. Caver ... 58 C2
Dovedale Cl. Crow ... 143 E1
Dover Rd. Slough ... 41 F4
Dover St. Read ... 86 A3
Doveton Way. Newb ... 105 D2
Dowding Cl. Wood ... 88 A4
Dower Park. Wind ... 66 C2
Down Pl. Oak G ... 66 A4
Downend La. Chiev ... 51 D1
Downfield La. W St L ... 63 D3
Downfield Rd. W St L ... 63 D2
Downing Path. Slough ... 21 F1
Downing Rd. Read ... 84 B4
Downlands. East G ... 47 E3
Downmill Rd. Brac ... 117 F4
Downs Cl. Lamb ... 46 C4
Downs Rd. Comp ... 32 A2
Downs Rd. Slough ... 43 E2
Downs Way. Chil ... 9 F4
Downs Way. Read ... 57 E1
Downshire Cl. Gr She ... 48 A2
Downshire Sq. Read ... 85 F3
Downshire Way. Brac ... 118 A3
Downside. Chert ... 123 F1
Downside. Chil ... 10 B4
Doyle Gdns. Yate ... 149 E2
Drake Ave. Slough ... 43 E1
Drake Ave. Stai ... 96 C2
Drake Cl. Brac ... 118 A2
Drake Cl. Woki ... 141 F4
Draper Cl. That ... 106 B1
Drawback Hill. Shipl ... 35 E3
Draycott. Brac ... 118 C2
Drayhorse Dr. Bags ... 145 F1
Drayton Cl. Brac ... 118 B4
Drayton Rd. Read ... 85 D4
Dresden Way. Read ... 57 F1
Drew Meadow. Far C ... 22 B4
Drewett Cl. Read ... 113 E3
Drift Rd. Holy ... 65 E2
Drift Rd. Wink ... 93 D4
Drift Way. Iver ... 69 E4
Driftway Cl. Winn ... 87 E1
Drill Hall Rd. Chert ... 124 A1
Drive The. Ashf ... 98 B1
Drive The. Bou E ... 2 C2
Drive The. Newb ... 130 C4
Drive The. Read ... 87 D4
Drive The. Slough ... 43 F2
Drive The. Slough ... 68 A3
Drive The. Vir W ... 122 C2
Drive The. Wray ... 68 B1
Droitwich Cl. Brac ... 118 C3
Dromepath. Winn ... 88 A2
Dropmore Rd. Burn ... 21 E3
Drove La. Herm ... 79 E1
Drovers Way. Brac ... 118 C3
Drovers Way. Wood ... 87 F3
Druce Way. That ... 106 B2
Drummond Cl. Brac ... 118 C4
Drury La. Mort ... 137 D2
Dry Arch Rd. Sunn ... 120 C2
Dryden Cl. That ... 106 B3
Dryden. Brac ... 118 A1
Du Pre Wlk. Bou E ... 3 E2
Dudley Cl. Read ... 57 F1
Dudley Mews. Read ... 57 F1
Dudley Rd. Ashf ... 97 F2
Dudley Rd. Felt ... 98 B4
Duffield La. Sto P ... 22 C3
Duffield Park. Sto P ... 23 D1
Duffield Rd. Wood ... 60 C1
Duke Of Cornwall Ave. Camb ... 144 B1
Duke St. Hen-O-T ... 15 F1
Duke St. Read ... 86 A4
Duke St. Wind ... 67 E4
Duke's Ride. Crow ... 143 D3
Duke's Ride. Finch ... 143 D3
Dukes Cl. Ashf ... 98 B2
Dukes Covert. Bags ... 145 F3
Dukes Pl. Mar ... 1 B1
Dukes Ride. Silc ... 136 A1
Dukes Wood. Crow ... 143 D3
Dukeshill Rd. Brac ... 118 A4
Dulnan Cl. Read ... 85 D4
Dulverton Gdns. Read ... 86 B1
Dumas Cl. Yate ... 149 E3
Dumbarton Way. Caver ... 59 F3
Dunally Park. Shepp ... 125 E1
Dunaways Cl. Read ... 87 E2
Dunbar Dr. Wood ... 88 A3
Dunboe Pl. Shepp ... 125 E1
Duncan Dr. Woki ... 116 C3
Duncan Gdns. Pur O T ... 57 E2
Duncan Rd. Wood ... 87 F3
Duncannon Cres. Wind ... 66 B2
Duncroft. Wind ... 66 C2
Dundaff Cl. Camb ... 152 A3
Dundas Cl. Brac ... 118 A3
Dundee Rd. Slough ... 42 A4
Dundela Cl. Wood ... 87 F3
Dunford Pl. Binf ... 90 C1

Dungells Farm Cl. Yate ... 149 E2
Dungells La. Yate ... 149 E2
Dungrovehill La. Bish ... 18 B2
Dunholme Cl. Winn ... 87 F1
Dunholme End. Maid ... 39 E2
Dunkirk Cl. Woki ... 115 F3
Dunluce Gdns. Pangb ... 56 C3
Dunn Cres. Kint ... 102 A1
Dunnock Way. Warg ... 36 C2
Dunoon Cl. Read ... 84 C2
Dunsfold Rd. Read ... 84 C4
Dunsmore Gdns. Yate ... 149 D3
Dunstall Cl. Read ... 84 B4
Dunstan Rd. That ... 106 C2
Dunster Cl. Caver ... 59 E3
Dunster Gdns. Slough ... 42 A3
Dunt Ave. Hurst ... 88 C2
Dunt La. Hurst ... 88 C2
Duppas Cl. Shepp ... 125 E2
Durand Rd. Read ... 87 D1
Durham Ave. Slough ... 42 A4
Durham Cl. Read ... 113 E4
Durham Cl. Woki ... 115 F3
Durham Rd. Sand ... 143 F1
Durley Mead. Brac ... 118 C2
Durrell Way. Shepp ... 125 E2
Dutch Barn Cl. Stan ... 70 B1
Dutton Way. Iver ... 44 C4
Duval Pl. Bags ... 145 F2
Dwyer Rd. Read ... 85 D2
Dyer Straits. Chil ... 9 F4
Dyson Cl. Wind ... 67 D2
Dysonswood La. Maple ... 58 C4

Eagle Cl. Brac ... 143 D4
Eagle Cl. Woki ... 115 F3
Eagles Nest. Crow ... 143 D1
Earley Hill Rd. Read ... 87 D3
Earley Pl. Read ... 86 A4
Earleydene. Sunn ... 120 A1
Earls Gr. Camb ... 151 F3
Earlsfield Cl. Caver ... 59 F2
Earlsfield. Holy ... 40 B1
Earlswood. Brac ... 118 A1
Easby La. Winn ... 87 E1
Easington Dr. Winn ... 87 F1
East Burnham La. Burn ... 22 A2
East Cres. Wind ... 66 C3
East Dr. Read ... 84 C3
East Dr. Sto P ... 22 C1
East Dr. Vir W ... 122 A2
East Green. Black ... 150 B2
East La. Chiev ... 51 D1
East Paddock. Bish ... 18 C3
East Ramp. Harm ... 71 D3
East Rd. Felt ... 98 B4
East Rd. Maid ... 39 F3
East Rd. Maid ... 39 F4
East Ridge. Bou E ... 3 D2
East St. Read ... 86 A4
East Stratton Cl. Brac ... 118 C2
East View. Warg ... 36 C1
East View Rd. Warg ... 36 C1
Eastbourne Rd. Slough ... 42 A4
Eastbridge. Slough ... 43 D3
Eastbury Ave. Read ... 57 D3
Eastbury Park. Winn ... 88 B1
Eastbury Shute. Lamb ... 46 C1
Eastchurch Rd. Harm ... 71 F2
Eastcourt Ave. Read ... 87 D3
Eastcroft. Slough ... 22 A1
Easterfield La. Whi-O-T ... 56 B4
Eastern Ave. Chert ... 124 A3
Eastern Ave. Read ... 86 C3
Eastern Dr. Bou E ... 3 E2
Eastern La. Crow ... 143 F2
Eastern Perimeter Rd. Harm ... 71 F3
Eastern Rd. Brac ... 118 B4
Eastfield Cl. Slough ... 43 D2
Eastfield La. White ... 56 B4
Eastfield Rd. Burn ... 41 D4
Eastfield. Blew ... 12 A4
Easthampstead Rd. Brac ... 116 C2
Easthampstead Rd. Brac ... 118 A4
Eastheath Ave. Woki ... 116 A2
Eastheath Gdns. Woki ... 116 A2
Eastleigh Rd. Harm ... 71 F2
Eastly Rd. Silc ... 135 F1
Easton Hill. Wick ... 76 A3
Eastwood Rd. Wood ... 87 F2
Eastworth Rd. Chert ... 124 A1
Eaton Pl. Read ... 85 F4
Eaton Rd. Camb ... 151 D2
Ebborn Sq. Winn ... 114 B4
Ebsworth Cl. Maid ... 20 B2
Eccles Cl. Caver ... 59 E1
Echelforde Dr. Ashf ... 98 A2
Eddington Hill. Hung ... 100 C4
Eddington Rd. Brac ... 117 F2
Eddystone Wlk. Stan ... 97 F4
Eden Cl. Slough ... 44 A1
Eden Way. Winn ... 88 A1
Edenhall Cl. Read ... 57 E2
Edenham Cl. Winn ... 87 F1
Edenham Cres. Read ... 85 F3
Edgar Milward Cl. Read ... 58 A1
Edgbarrow Rise. Sand ... 143 D1
Edgcumbe Park Dr. Crow ... 143 D3
Edgecombe La. Newb ... 105 E3

Elmhurst Rd. Re

Edgedale Cl. Crow ... 143
Edgehill St. Read ... 86
Edgell Cl. Vir W ... 122
Edgell Rd. Stai ... 96
Edgemoor Rd. Camb ... 152
Edgewood Cl. Brac ... 143
Edinburgh Ave. Slough ... 42
Edinburgh Dr. Stai ... 97
Edinburgh Gdns. Wind ... 67
Edinburgh Rd. Maid ... 19
Edinburgh Rd. Mar ... 1
Edinburgh Rd. Read ... 85
Edith Rd. Maid ... 39
Edmunds Way. Slough ... 43
Edney's Hill. Woki ... 115
Edward Ave. Camb ... 151
Edward Ct. Stai ... 97
Edward Rd. Harm ... 71
Edward Rd. Twyf ... 61
Edward Rd. Windl ... 146
Edward Way. Ashf ... 97
Edwards Ct. Slough ... 42
Edwards Hill. Lamb ... 25
Edwin Cl. That ... 106
Eeklo Pl. Newb ... 105
Egerton Rd. Read ... 86
Egerton Rd. Sand ... 150
Egerton Rd. Slough ... 21
Egham By-Pass. Eng G ... 96
Egham Hill. Eng G ... 95
Egremont Dr. Read ... 87
Egremont Gdns. Slough ... 42
Egypt La. Far C ... 22
Eight Acres. Burn ... 21
Elan Cl. Read ... 84
Elbow Meadow. Stan ... 69
Eldart Cl. Read ... 85
Elder Cl. Read ... 57
Elderfield Cres. Chil ... 10
Elderfield Rd. Sto P ... 22
Eldon Pl. Read ... 86
Eldon Rd. Read ... 86
Eldon Sq. Read ... 86
Eldon St. Read ... 86
Eldon Terr. Read ... 86
Eldrick Ct. Felt ... 98
Elford Cl. Wood ... 87
Elgar Ave. Crow ... 143
Elgar Rd. Read ... 86
Elgarth Dr. Woki ... 141
Elgin Ave. Ashf ...
Elgin Cres. Harm ... 71
Eliot Cl. Caver ... 59
Eliot Cl. That ... 106
Eliot Dr. Mar ... 1
Elizabeth Ave. Bags ... 145
Elizabeth Ave. Newb ... 130
Elizabeth Ave. Stai ... 97
Elizabeth Cl. Brac ... 118
Elizabeth Cl. Hen-O-T ... 35
Elizabeth Ct. Read ... 85
Elizabeth Gdns. Ascot ... 120
Elizabeth Rd. Hen-O-T ... 35
Elizabeth Rd. Mar ... 1
Elizabeth Rd. Woki ... 116
Elizabeth Rout Cl. Shin ... 113
Elizabeth Way. Sto P ... 23
Elizabethan Cl. Stan ... 97
Elizabethan Way. Stan ... 97
Ellesfield Ave. Brac ... 117
Ellesmere Cl. Caver ... 59
Elliman Ave. Slough ... 42
Ellington Cl. Tapl ... 40
Ellington Gdns. Tapl ... 40
Ellington Park. Maid ... 19
Ellington Rd. Felt ... 98
Ellington Rd. Tapl ... 40
Elliott Gdns. Stai ... 125
Elliott Rise. Burl ... 119
Ellis Ave. Slough ... 42
Ellis Rd. Crow ... 143
Ellison Cl. Wind ... 66
Ellison Way. Woki ... 116
Elm Bank. Yate ... 149
Elm Cl. Far C ... 22
Elm Cl. Stan ... 97
Elm Cotts. Ball H ... 129
Elm Croft. Datch ... 68
Elm Dr. Bur C ... 111
Elm Gr. Maid ... 39
Elm Gr. That ... 106
Elm La. Bou E ... 2
Elm La. Read ... 86
Elm Lodge Ave. Read ... 85
Elm Park Ave. Read ... 85
Elm Park. Windl ... 120
Elm Rd. Felt ... 98
Elm Rd. Maple ... 58
Elm Rd. Read ... 86
Elm Rd. Wind ... 67
Elm Tree Cl. Ashf ... 98
Elmar Green. Slough ...
Elmbank Ave. Eng G ... 7
Elmcroft Cl. Felt ... 7
Elmcroft Dr. Ashf ... 98
Elmcroft. Gori ... 34
Elmdon Rd. Harm ... 7
Elmhurst Rd. Gori ... 3
Elmhurst Rd. Read ... 86

mhurst Rd. Slough 44 A2	Eton Wick Rd. Eton 42 A1
hurst Rd. That 106 A3	Eustace Cres. Woki 116 B4
leigh Ct. Caver 59 E2	Evedon. Brac 118 A1
ley Cl. Woki 88 C1	Evelyn Cres. Shepp 125 F4
s Ave. That 106 C2	Evelyn Ct. Wood 87 F3
s Dr. Bou E 3 E2	Evelyn Way. Shepp 125 F4
s Rd. Woki 116 A3	Evendon's La. Bark 115 F1
shott La. Slough 41 F3	Evendons Cl. Woki 116 A2
sleigh Rd. Stai 96 C2	Evenlode Rd. Bou E 3 D2
stone Dr. Read 57 E1	Evenlode Way. Sand 150 B4
sway. Ashf 98 A2	Evenlode. Maid 39 F4
wood Rd. Slough 43 D3	Everard Ave. Slough 42 C2
wood. Maid 20 A2	Everest Rd. Camb 151 E4
enwood Cres. Camb 152 A3	Everest Rd. Crow 143 D3
enwood Dr. Camb 152 A4	Everest Rd. Stan 97 F4
nore Ave. Stan 97 F4	Evergreen Dr. Read 84 C2
ley Rd. Read 57 F2	Evergreen Rd. Camb 152 A1
ow Ave. Caver 59 E3	Evergreen Way. Stan 97 E4
tree Cl. Read 57 E1	Evergreen Way. Woki 115 F3
worth Cl. Felt 98 C4	Everington La. Yatt 53 D1
am Ave. Caver 59 F3	Everland Rd. Hung 100 B3
n Dr. Maid 39 E4	Eversley Rd. Arbo 114 C1
aston Way. Read 85 D4	Eversley St. Finch 141 D1
edon Cl. Winn 87 F1	Eversley Way. Stai 123 E4
endon Rd. Gori 34 B4	Evesham Rd. Caver 59 D3
ell Cl. Eng G 96 A1	Evesham Wlk. Crow 143 E1
Ave. Slough 42 B4	Evreham Rd. Iver 44 C4
Rd. Harm 71 F3	Evreux Cl. That 106 C1
ier Rd. Thea 83 F2	Ewing Way. Newb 131 D4
bankment The. Wray 95 E4	Exbourne Rd. Read 113 E4
brook Way. Read 84 A2	Exchange Rd. Ascot 120 B2
erald Cl. Woki 115 F4	Exeforde Ave. Ashf 98 A2
erald Ct. Slough 42 C2	Exeter Cl. Read 113 D4
ery Acres. Upp B 55 D3	Exeter Gdns. Yate 149 D4
ery Down Cl. Brac 119 D3	Exeter Rd. Stan 71 F2
lyns Bldgs. Eton 67 E4	Exeter Rd. Thea 83 F2
m Cl. Woki 115 F4	Exeter Way. Stan 71 F2
ma The. Warg 36 C1	Exmoor Rd. That 106 B2
mbrook Gate. Woki 115 F4	Explorer Ave. Stan 97 F4
mbrook Rd. Woki 115 F4	Exwick Sq. Read 113 E4
mbrook Vale. Woki 89 D1	Eylham. Pur O T 57 D3
mer Green Ct. Caver 59 E3	Eynsford Cl. Caver 59 F3
mets Nest. Binf 90 B1	Eynsham Rd. Wood 87 F4
mets Park. Binf 90 B1	
mview Cl. Woki 115 F4	Fagg's Rd. Harm 71 F2
press Rd. Read 84 B3	Fair Lawn Green. Read 86 C1
orne Cl. Read 84 B4	Fair Mile. Hen-O-T 15 E2
orne Gr. Newb 104 C1	Fairacre. Maid 39 E3
orne Pl. Newb 104 C1	Fairacres Ind Est. Wind 66 B3
orne Rd. Ham M 104 C1	Faircroft. Slough 22 A1
orne Rd. Newb 104 C1	Faircross Quarters. Herm 78 C3
orne St. Ham M 130 B3	Faircross Rd. Read 85 E3
orne St. Newb 130 B3	Faircross. Brac 118 A3
orne Way. Brim 133 F3	Fairfax. Brac 118 A4
ield Rd. Harm 71 F3	Fairfield App. Wray 68 B1
glefield Cl. Eng G 95 E1	Fairfield Ave. Datch 68 B4
glefield Rd. Thea 83 E2	Fairfield Ave. Stai 96 C2
gleheart Dr. Felt 71 F1	Fairfield Cl. Datch 68 B4
glehurst. Eng G 95 E1	Fairfield Cl. Camb 151 F2
glemere Park. Burl 119 F3	Fairfield La. Far C 22 A2
glemere Rd. Brac 90 C1	Fairfield Rd. Burn 21 E1
glesfield. Camb 152 B3	Fairfield Rd. Gori 34 B4
glish Gdns. Wray 68 B1	Fairfield Rd. Wray 68 B1
herdale Cl. Felt 98 C4	Fairfield. Comp 31 E2
herdale Cres. Slough 41 E4	Fairfields. Hung 100 B3
herdale Rd. Read 86 B2	Fairford Rd. Maid 39 F4
herdale Way. That 106 A2	Fairford Rd. Read 57 E1
herdale. Brac 118 A3	Fairhaven. Eng G 95 F2
sign Cl. Stan 97 E4	Fairholme Rd. Ashf 97 F2
sign Way. Stan 97 E4	Fairholme. Felt 98 C4
stone Rd. Wood 88 A4	Fairlawn Park. Wind 66 C2
erprise Way. That 107 D1	Fairlawns Cl. Stai 97 D1
ping Cl. Read 85 F4	Fairlea. Maid 39 D2
ping Way. Brac 118 C3	Fairlie Rd. Slough 42 A4
som Cl. Camb 151 E4	Fairlight Ave. Wind 67 E3
som Cres. Newb 105 D1	Fairlop Cl. Bur C 84 B2
som Cl. Read 85 F3	Fairmead Cl. Sand 150 C4
son Sq. Harm 71 F3	Fairmead Rd. Shin 113 F3
n Ave. Caver 59 D3	Fairoak Way. Tad 134 B1
ca Cl. Camb 153 F3	Fairsted Cl. Read 85 D4
ca Cl. Slough 41 F3	Fairview Ave. Read 87 D3
swell Cl. Winn 87 F1	Fairview Cl. Stai 97 D1
enwald Cl. Chert 123 F1	Fairview Dr. Stai 123 C2
eigh Court Dr. Read 87 D4	Fairview Estate. Hen-O-T 35 F4
eigh Court Gdns. Read 87 D4	Fairview Rd. Burn 41 D4
eigh Dene. Newb 104 C1	Fairview Rd. Hung 100 B3
nin Wlk. That 106 A2	Fairview Rd. Slough 21 F1
ington Dr. Wind 67 D3	Fairview Rd. Woki 116 B3
kine Cl. Silc 135 F1	Fairwater Dr. Wood 87 E3
her Cres. Harm 71 F3	Fairway Ave. Read 84 B3
her Rd. Camb 145 D1	Fairway Dr. Char 61 D3
cdale Gdns. Holy 40 A1	Fairway Hts. Camb 152 A3
cdale Rd. Winn 88 A2	Fairway The. Burn 21 E2
cdale Way. Camb 152 B2	Fairway The. Camb 152 A2
kin Cl. Read 85 D4	Fairway The. Fla H 3 E4
sex Ave. Slough 42 A4	Fairway The. Maid 39 D2
sex Cl. Camb 153 F3	Fairway. Chert 124 A1
sex St. Newb 130 B4	Fairways. Ashf 98 A1
sex St. Read 86 A3	Fakenham Cl. Read 114 A4
iel Rd. Ashf 97 F2	Fakenham Way. Crow 143 E1
n Cl. Datch 68 A4	Falaise. Eng G 95 F2
n Ct. Eton 67 E4	Falcon Ave. Read 86 C1
n Pl. Mar 1 B1	Falcon Cl. Camb 152 C4
n Rd. Datch 68 A4	Falcon Dr. Stan 70 C1
n Rd. Harl 71 F4	Falcon Fields. Tad 135 D1
n Sq. Eton 67 E4	Falcon House Gdns. Ball H 129 F1
	Falcon Rd. Shepp 125 F4
	Falcon Way. Woki 115 F3
	Falcon Way. Yate 149 D3

Falcons Croft. Woo G 3 F4	Fernbank. Woki 141 E4
Falconwood. Eng G 95 F2	Fernbrook Rd. Caver 58 C3
Falkland Dr. Newb 130 C4	Ferndale Ave. Read 85 D2
Falkland Garth. Newb 130 B4	Ferndale Cl. Read 57 E2
Falkland Rd. Caver 59 D1	Ferndale Rd. Ashf 97 F2
Falkland Rd. Newb 130 B3	Ferne Cl. Gori 34 B4
Fallowfield Cl. Caver 59 D2	Fernery The. Stai 96 C2
Fallowfield. Yate 149 D4	Fernhill Cl. Black 150 C1
Falmouth Cl. Camb 152 A2	Fernhill Cl. Brac 90 C1
Falmouth Rd. Read 113 C4	Fernhill La. Black 150 C1
Falmouth Rd. Slough 42 A4	Fernhill Rd. Black 150 C1
Falmouth Way. That 106 C2	Fernhill Wlk. Black 150 C1
Falstaff Ave. Read 86 C1	Fernhurst Rd. Ashf 98 B2
Fane Way. Maid 39 E3	Fernhurst Rd. Bur C 84 B2
Fanes Cl. Brac 117 F4	Ferniehurst. Camb 151 F2
Faraday Cl. Arbo 140 C4	Fernley Ct. Maid 19 E1
Faraday Cl. Slough 42 A4	Ferrard Cl. Burl 119 E4
Faraday Rd. Bark 141 D4	Ferrier Gr. Newb 131 D4
Faraday Rd. Newb 105 D2	Ferry Ave. Stai 96 C1
Faraday Rd. Slough 42 A4	Ferry La. Bou E 3 D1
Farcrosse Cl. Sand 150 B4	Ferry La. Gori 34 A3
Fareham Dr. Yate 149 D4	Ferry La. Hamb 16 B3
Faringdon Cl. Sand 143 E1	Ferry La. Medm 17 D3
Faringdon Dr. Brac 118 B2	Ferry La. Shepp 125 D1
Faringdon Wlk. Read 85 D2	Ferry La. Sou S 14 A2
Farleigh Mews. Caver 59 F3	Ferry La. Stai 124 B3
Farley Copse. Brac 117 F4	Ferry La. Warg 36 B1
Farm Cl. Ascot 120 B2	Ferry La. Wray 96 A3
Farm Cl. Brac 117 F4	Ferry Rd. Maid 40 B2
Farm Cl. Brac 143 E4	Ferry Rd. Sou S 14 B2
Farm Cl. Chert 123 D2	Fettiplace Gr She 48 A2
Farm Cl. Gori 34 B3	Fetty Pl. Maid 39 E2
Farm Cl. Holy 40 B1	Fidler's La. East I 30 C4
Farm Cl. Maid 39 D4	Fidlers Wlk. Warg 36 C1
Farm Cl. Pur O T 57 E3	Field Cl. Bur C 111 D1
Farm Cl. Shepp 125 D1	Field Cl. Harl 71 E4
Farm Cl. Stai 96 C2	Field End. West E 153 F3
Farm Cl. Yate 149 E3	Field End. Warg 36 C1
Farm Cres. Slough 43 E4	Field Farm Rd. Bur C 84 C1
Farm Dr. Read 84 A3	Field House Dr. Brac 120 A1
Farm Lea. Woo G 3 F4	Field Hurst. Slough 43 F1
Farm Rd. Bou E 2 C2	Field La. Camb 151 F1
Farm Rd. Burn 41 D3	Field Park. Brac 118 B4
Farm Rd. Camb 151 F1	Field Rd. Black 150 C1
Farm Rd. Hen-O-T 35 F4	Field Rd. Pease 29 E1
Farm Rd. Maid 39 D4	Field Rd. Read 86 A3
Farm Rd. Stai 97 D1	Field View. Caver 59 D2
Farm View. Yate 149 E3	Field View. Felt 98 B2
Farm Way. Stan 69 F1	Field View. Stai 96 B2
Farm Yd. Wind 67 E4	Fielden Pl. Brac 118 B4
Farman Cl. Wood 88 A4	Fieldfare Ave. Yate 149 D3
Farmer's Rd. Stai 96 C2	Fieldhead Gdns. Bou E 3 D2
Farmers Cl. Maid 39 D2	Fieldhouse Ind Est. Mar 1 C1
Farmers Cl. Read 113 E3	Fieldhouse La. Mar 1 C1
Farmers Way. Maid 39 D2	Fieldhouse Way. Mar 1 C1
Farmiloe Cl. Pur O T 57 E2	Fielding Gdns. Crow 143 D2
Farnburn Ave. Slough 42 A4	Fielding Rd. Maid 39 D4
Farnell Rd. Stan 97 D3	Fielding Rd. Sand 150 C3
Farnham Cl. Brac 118 B4	Fieldings The. Holy 65 D4
Farnham Dr. Caver 59 F2	Fieldridge. Newb 105 E3
Farnham La. Slough 21 E1	Fields The. Slough 42 B2
Farnham Park La. Far C 22 B2	Fieldway. Winn 88 B1
Farnham Rd. Slough 42 B4	Fifehead Cl. Ashf 97 F1
Farningham. Brac 118 C2	Fifield La. Holy 65 D1
Farnsfield Cl. Read 114 A4	Fifield Rd. Holy 65 D1
Farrell Cl. Camb 151 E2	Fifth Rd. Newb 104 C1
Farriers Cl. Wood 87 F4	Filbert Dr. Read 84 B4
Farrowdene Rd. Read 113 E4	Filey Rd. Read 86 C4
Farthing Green La. Sto P 23 D2	Filey Spur. Slough 42 A2
Farthingales The. Maid 40 A4	Filmer Rd. Wind 66 B3
Fatherson Rd. Read 86 B4	Finbeck Way. Read 113 F4
Faulkner Pl. Bags 145 F2	Finch Ct. Maid 39 E3
Faversham Rd. Crow 143 E1	Finch Rd. Read 87 E2
Fawcett Cres. Wood 87 E3	Finch Way. Bur C 111 D2
Fawcett Rd. Wind 67 D3	Fincham End Dr. Crow 142 C2
Fawler Mead. Brac 118 C3	Finchampstead Rd. Finch 142 A4
Fawley Bottom La. Faw (Bu) 15 E4	Finchampstead Rd. Woki 142 A4
Fawley Cl. Maid 19 E1	Findhorn Cl. Sand 150 B4
Fawley Rd. Read 85 E3	Finmere. Brac 118 B1
Fawns Manor Cl. Felt 98 B4	Finney Dr. Windl 146 B2
Fawns Manor Rd. Felt 98 B4	Finstock Cl. Winn 87 E1
Fawsley Cl. Stan 69 F4	Finstock Green. Brac 118 C3
Faygate Way. Read 87 D1	Fir Cottage Rd. Bark 141 F4
Feathers La. Wray 96 A3	Fir Cottage Rd. Woki 141 F4
Felbridge Cl. Camb 151 F1	Fir Dr. Black 150 B2
Felix La. Shepp 125 F2	Fir Tree Ave. Sto P 22 C1
Felixstowe Cl. Winn 87 E1	Fir Tree Cl. Ascot 120 A1
Fellow Green Rd. West E 153 F3	Fir Tree La. Newb 105 F2
Fellow Green. West E 153 F3	Fir Tree Paddock. West I 10 A1
Fells The. Read 84 A3	Fir's End. Bur C 111 D1
Felstead Cl. Read 86 C2	Firbank Pl. Eng G 95 D1
Feltham Hill Rd. Ashf 98 A2	Fircroft Cl. Read 57 E1
Feltham Rd. Ashf 98 A2	Fircroft Cl. Sto P 23 D3
Felthorpe Cl. Read 114 A4	Fireball Hill. Sunn 120 B1
Felton Way. Read 84 B4	Firglen Dr. Yate 149 E4
Fencote. Brac 118 B2	Firgrove Rd. Yate 149 D3
Fennel Cl. Newb 105 E3	Firlands Ave. Camb 151 E3
Fennel Cl. Read 86 C1	Firlands. Brac 118 B2
Fenns La. West E 153 F3	Firmstone Cl. Winn 87 E1
Fenton Ave. Stai 97 E2	Firs Ave. Wind 66 C2
Fern Cl. Camb 152 B2	Firs Cl. Woki 141 F4
Fern Cl. Read 84 B3	Firs Dr. Slough 43 F3
Fern Dr. Burn 41 D4	Firs La. Maid 38 C2
Fern Glen. Read 57 E1	Firs Rd. Read 84 B3
Fern La. Lit M 2 C3	Firs The. That 106 A2
Fern Wlk. Ashf 97 E2	First Ave. Mar 2 A1
Fernbank Cres. Burl 119 E4	First Cres. Slough 42 B4
Fernbank Pl. Burl 119 E4	Firtree Cl. Sand 142 C1
Fernbank Rd. Burl 119 E4	Firview Cl. Mar 1 C1

Firwood Dr. Camb 151 E3
Firwood Rd. Went 121 F2
Fisher Green. Binf 90 A1
Fisher's La. Cold A 79 D1
Fisherman's La. Alde 135 D4
Fisherman's Way. Bou E 3 D2
Fishermans Retreat. Mar 1 C1
Fishers Ct. Caver 59 E3
Fishers Wood. Went 121 E1
Fishery Rd. Maid 40 B3
Fishponds Cl. Woki 116 A2
Fishponds Rd. Woki 116 A2
Fitzrobert Pl. Eng G 96 A1
Fitzroy Cres. Wood 88 A3
Five Acre. Read 57 E1
Five Acres. Wo G 3 F4
Flag Staff Sq. That 106 C1
Flambards. Caver 59 E1
Flamborough Cl. Winn 87 F1
Flamborough Spur. Slough 42 A2
Flamingo Cl. Woki 115 F3
Flanders Ct. Stai 96 B2
Flats The. Black 150 B2
Flaxman Cl. Read 86 C1
Flecker Cl. That 106 B3
Fleet Cl. Woki 115 F3
Fleet Hill. Finch 141 E1
Fleet St. Finch 141 D1
Fleetham Gdns. Wood 87 E1
Fleetway. Stai 123 E3
Fleetwood Rd. Slough 42 C3
Fleming Cl. Arbo 140 C4
Fleming Rd. Newb 105 D2
Flemish Fields. Chert 124 A1
Fletcher Gdns. Brac 117 E4
Flexford Green. Brac 117 F2
Flintgrove. Brac 118 B4
Flintlock Cl. Stai 70 A2
Flodden Dr. Bur C 84 B2
Floral Way. That 106 C2
Florence Ave. Maid 39 F4
Florence Ave. Maid 40 A4
Florence Cl. Yate 149 E3
Florence Gdns. Stai 97 D1
Florence Rd. Sand 150 B4
Florence Wlk. Read 86 B4
Florian Gdns. Read 85 D3
Flower's Hill. Pangb 56 B2
Flowers Piece. Asham 54 A3
Fobney St. Read 86 A4
Fokerham Rd. That 106 C1
Folder's La. Brac 91 E1
Foliejohn Way. Whi Wa 38 C1
Folkestone Cl. Slough 44 A1
Follet Cl. Old W 68 A1
Folly La. Bur 110 C3
Folly La. Sulhd 110 C3
Folly Rd. Ink 127 F3
Folly Rd. Lamb 25 D2
Folly The. Newb 105 D1
Fontmell Cl. Ashf 98 A2
Fontmell Park. Ashf 98 A2
Fontwell Cl. Maid 39 D4
Fontwell Dr. Read 84 C3
Fontwell Rd. Newb 105 D1
Forbes Chase. Sand 150 B4
Forbury La. Kint 128 B4
Forbury Rd. Read 86 B4
Forbury The. Read 86 A4
Ford Cl. Ashf 97 F1
Ford Cl. Stai 125 D2
Ford La. Swal 140 A2
Ford Rd. Ashf 97 F2
Ford Rd. Bis 153 F2
Ford Rd. Chert 124 A1
Ford Rd. West E 153 F2
Fordbridge Cl. Chert 124 A1
Fordbridge Rd. Ashf 97 F2
Fordbridge Rd. Shepp 125 F2
Fordham Way. Winn 87 E1
Fordwater Rd. Chert 124 A1
Fordwells Dr. Brac 118 C3
Forehead The. Bee H 137 F2
Forest Cl. Brac 119 E3
Forest Cl. Tad 134 C1
Forest Dr. Stai 98 C1
Forest End Rd. Sand 150 A4
Forest Green Rd. Holy 65 D3
Forest Green. Brac 118 B4
Forest Hill. Read 57 F1
Forest Hills. Camb 151 D2
Forest Rd. Ascot 92 C1
Forest Rd. Binf 90 B2
Forest Rd. Burl 92 C1
Forest Rd. Crow 143 E3
Forest Rd. New G 92 C1
Forest Rd. Wind 66 C3
Foresters Sq. Brac 118 C3
Foresters Way. Crow 143 F2
Forge Cl. Caver 59 E1
Forge Cl. Kint 102 A1
Forge Dr. Far C 22 B3
Forge Hill. Hamp N 53 D3
Forge The. Hung 100 B3
Forlease Cl. Maid 40 A3
Forlease Dr. Maid 40 A3
Forlease Rd. Maid 40 A3
Formby Cl. Winn 87 F2
Forndon Cl. Winn 87 F1

Fortrose Cl. Sand

Fortrose Cl. Sand 150 B4
Fortrose Wlk. Read 84 C2
Forty Green Dr. Mar 1 A1
Fosseway. Crow 143 D3
Fossewood Dr. Camb 151 E4
Foster Ave. Wind 66 C2
Fosters Gr. Windl 146 A3
Fosters La. Wood 87 F3
Fosters Path. Slough 21 F1
Fotherby Ct. Maid 40 A3
Fotheringay Gdns. Slough 42 A3
Foundary Ct. Chert 124 A1
Foundation Park. Maid 38 C2
Foundry La. Hort 69 D2
Fountain Gdns. Wind 67 E2
Fountains Garth. Brac 118 A3
Fourth Ave. Mar 2 A1
Fowler Cl. Read 87 D2
Fowlers La. Brac 118 A4
Fox Cl. Bur C 111 D2
Fox Covert Cl. Ascot 120 B2
Fox Covert. Light 153 D4
Fox Dr. Yate 149 E4
Fox La. Yate 149 D4
Fox Lane N. Chert 123 F1
Fox Lane S. Chert 123 F1
Fox Rd. Slough 43 E1
Foxborough Cl. Slough 44 A1
Foxborough. Swal 139 E3
Foxbury. Lamb 25 D1
Foxcombe Dr. Read 84 B4
Foxcote. Woki 142 A4
Foxdown Cl. Camb 151 E3
Foxes Piece. Mar 1 C2
Foxes Wlk. Char 61 D2
Foxglove Cl. Stan 97 E4
Foxglove Cl. Woki 115 E4
Foxglove Gdns. Read 85 F4
Foxhays Rd. Read 113 E4
Foxherne. Slough 43 E2
Foxhill Cl. Caver 60 A3
Foxhill Cres. Camb 152 A4
Foxhill La. Caver 59 F3
Foxhill Rd. Read 86 C3
Foxhollow Dr. Far C 22 B4
Foxhunt Gr. Read 84 C2
Foxhunter Way. That 105 F2
Foxley Cl. Sand 150 B3
Foxley La. Binf 90 B1
Framewood Rd. Sto P 23 E3
Framlingham Dr. Caver 59 F3
Frampton Cl. Wood 60 C1
France Hill Dr. Camb 151 E3
Frances Ave. Maid 20 B1
Frances Rd. Wind 67 E3
Frances The. That 106 B2
Francis Chichester Cl. Ascot . 120 A2
Francis Cl. Stai 125 D3
Francis Gdns. New G 91 F1
Francis St. Read 86 A3
Francis Way. Slough 41 E3
Frank London Cl. Bou E 3 E2
Franklin Ave. Slough 42 A4
Franklin Ave. Tad 135 D1
Franklin St. Read 85 F4
Franklyn Cres. Wind 66 B2
Frascati Way. Maid 39 F4
Fraser Ave. Caver 59 E3
Fraser Mead. Sand 150 C3
Fraser Rd. Brac 118 A4
Frederick Pl. Woki 116 A3
Free Prae Rd. Chert 124 A1
Freeborn Way. Brac 118 C4
Freeman Cl. Shepp 125 F3
Freemans Cl. Hung 100 B3
Freemans Cl. Sto P 23 D3
Freemantle Rd. Bags 145 F2
Freesia Cl. Woki 115 E4
French Gdns. Black 150 B2
Frenchum Gdns. Slough 41 F3
Frensham Cl. Yate 149 D3
Frensham Green. Read 86 C1
Frensham Rd. Crow 143 D4
Frensham Wlk. Far C 22 B3
Frensham. Brac 118 B2
Freshfield Cl. Winn 87 F2
Freshwater Rd. Read 86 C4
Freshwood Dr. Yate 149 E2
Friar St. Read 86 A4
Friars Keep. Brac 118 A3
Friars Rd. Newb 131 D4
Friars Rd. Vir W 122 B3
Friars Way. Chert 124 A2
Friary Rd. Ascot 120 A2
Friary Rd. Wray 68 B1
Friary Rd. Wray 95 E4
Friary The. Old W 68 B1
Friday St. Hen-O-T 15 F1
Frieth Cl. Read 87 D1
Frilsham Rd. Read 85 D2
Frimley By-Pass. Camb 151 E1
Frimley Cl. Wood 87 E4
Frimley Green Rd. Camb 151 E1
Frimley Grove Gdns. Camb . 151 F1
Frimley Hall Dr. Camb 151 E1
Frimley High St. Camb 151 E1
Frimley Rd. Camb 151 D2
Fringford Cl. Winn 87 E1
Frith Hill Rd. Camb 152 A1

Frithe The. Slough 43 D4
Frithwald Rd. Chert 123 F1
Frobisher Cres. Stan 97 F4
Frobisher Gdns. Stan 97 F4
Frobisher. Brac 118 B1
Frodsham Way. Sand 143 F1
Frog Hall Dr. Woki 116 C3
Frog La. Brac 118 A3
Frogmill. Hurl 17 E2
Frogmore Cl. Slough 42 A2
Frogmore Gr. Black 150 B2
Frogmore Park Dr. Black 150 B2
Frogmore Rd. Sand 150 B3
Frogmore Way. Read 85 D3
Fromer Rd. Bou E 3 E2
Fromont Dr. That 106 B2
Fromow Gdns. Windl 146 B2
Front St. East G 47 E3
Froxfield Ave. Read 85 F3
Froxfield Down. Brac 118 C2
Fruen Rd. Felt 98 C4
Fry Rd. Ashf 97 E2
Fry's La. Bags 145 E1
Fry's La. Yate 149 F4
Frymley View. Wind 66 B3
Fuchia Way. Camb 153 F3
Fuchsia Cl. Read 84 B3
Fullbrook Cl. Maid 40 A4
Fullbrook Cl. Woki 89 D1
Fullbrook Cres. Read 57 E2
Fuller Cl. That 106 C1
Fuller's La. Bur C 112 A2
Fullers La. Ball H 129 E1
Fulmead Rd. Read 85 E4
Fulmer Cl. Read 87 D1
Fulmer Common Rd. Fulm 23 F3
Fulmer Rd. Fulm 23 F4
Furlong Cl. Bou E 3 D2
Furlong Rd. Bou E 3 D2
Furness Sq. Oak G 66 B3
Furness Way. Oak G 66 B3
Furness. Oak G 66 B3
Furnival Ave. Slough 42 A4
Furnival Cl. Went 122 B2
Furrow Way. Maid 39 D2
Furze Hill Cres. Crow 143 E2
Furze Platt Rd. Maid 19 D1
Furze Platt Rd. Maid 19 E1
Furze Rd. Maid 19 E1
Furze Rd. Tad 134 C1
Furzebank. Ascot 120 B3
Furzemoors. Brac 118 A2
Furzen Cl. Slough 22 A1
Fuzzens Wlk. Wind 66 C3
Fydlers Cl. Ascot 93 D1
Fyfield Cl. Black 150 B3
Fyfield Rd. That 106 B1
Fylingdales. That 106 B2

Gables Ave. Ashf 97 F2
Gables Cl. Datch 68 A4
Gables Cl. Maid 40 A4
Gabriels The. Newb 130 B3
Gage Cl. Maid 39 F2
Gainsborough Ave. Kint 102 A1
Gainsborough Cl. Camb 151 F4
Gainsborough Cl. Wood 88 A3
Gainsborough Cres. Hen-O-T . 35 E4
Gainsborough Dr. Ascot 119 E4
Gainsborough Dr. Maid 39 F2
Gainsborough Hill. Hen-O-T . 35 E4
Gainsborough Rd. Hen-O-T . 35 E4
Gainsborough Rd. Read 85 D3
Gainsborough. Brac 118 B2
Gainsborough. Cook 19 F3
Gairn Cl. Read 85 D4
Galahad Cl. Slough 42 A2
Gale Dr. Light 146 A1
Galley La. Head 132 B1
Galleymead Rd. Stan 69 F3
Gallop The. Yate 149 E4
Gallys Rd. Wind 66 B3
Galsworthy Dr. Caver 59 F3
Galsworthy Rd. Chert 124 A1
Galton Rd. Sunn 120 C2
Galvin Rd. Slough 42 B3
Garde Rd. Sonn 60 C2
Garden Cl. Asht 98 B1
Garden Cl. Maid 39 D3
Garden Close La. Newb 130 B2
Gardeners La. Brad 55 E2
Gardens The. Harm 71 E1
Gardens The. Sou S 14 B2
Gardens The. Vir W 122 C2
Gardner Rd. Maid 19 F1
Garfield Rd. Camb 151 E3
Garford Cres. Newb 130 B4
Garlands Cl. Bur C 111 D1
Garnet Cl. Slough 42 A2
Garnet Ct. Mar 1 B1
Garnet Field. Yate 149 D3
Garnet Hill. Read 86 A3
Garnet St. Read 86 A3
Garrard Rd. Slough 21 F1
Garrard St. Read 86 A4
Garrett Rd. Woki 141 F4
Garrick Cl. Stai 97 D1
Garson La. Wray 95 E4
Garson's La. New G 92 A4

Garston Cl. Read 85 D2
Garston Cres. Read 84 A3
Garston Gr. Woki 115 F1
Garswood. Brac 118 B2
Garth Cl. Winn 88 B1
Garth Rd. Mort 137 D3
Garth Sq. Brac 91 D1
Garthlands. Maid 19 E1
Gas Works Rd. Read 86 B4
Gascon's Gr. Slough 22 A1
Gaskell Mews. Newb 131 D4
Gaskells End. Maple 58 B4
Gaston Bridge Rd. Shepp ... 125 E2
Gaston Way. Shepp 125 E2
Gatcombe Cl. Read 84 B2
Gatehampton Rd. Gori 34 B3
Gatewick Cl. Slough 42 C3
Gatward Ave. Maid 39 D2
Gaveston Rd. Slough 21 F1
Gayhurst Cl. Caver 59 E3
Geffers Ride. Ascot 119 F4
Geneva Rd. Read 86 A4
Geneva Cl. Shepp 125 F4
Geoffreyson Rd. Caver 58 C3
George Cl. Mar 1 C2
George Green Rd. Slough 43 F4
George St. Caver 59 D1
George St. Read 85 F4
George St. Stai 96 C2
Georgeham Rd. Crow 143 E1
Georges Dr. Fla H 3 E4
Georgian Cl. Camb 151 F4
Georgian Cl. Stai 97 D2
Gerrards Cross Rd. Sto P 23 D4
Gibbet La. Camb 152 A4
Gibbons Cl. Sand 150 B4
Gibbs Cl. Woki 141 F3
Gibbs Way. Yate 149 D2
Gibraltar La. Cook 2 B1
Gibson Ct. Slough 43 F1
Gibson Pl. Stan 70 B1
Gifford Cl. Caver 59 F3
Gilbert Rd. Camb 151 E1
Gilbey Wlk. Bou E 3 E2
Gilchrist Way. Bish 38 A3
Giles Travers Cl. Stai 123 E3
Gillette Way. Read 86 A1
Gilliat Rd. Slough 42 C3
Gilliatt Cl. Iver 44 C4
Gillott's La. Shipl 35 E4
Gillotts Cl. Hen-O-T 35 D4
Gilman Cres. Wind 66 B2
Gilmore Cl. Slough 43 E2
Gilmore Cres. Ashf 98 A2
Gilpin Way. Harl 71 E4
Gilroy Cl. Newb 130 B3
Gingells Farm Rd. Char 61 D3
Gipsy La. Brac 118 B4
Gipsy La. Hung 100 C4
Gipsy La. Read 57 F1
Gipsy La. Read 87 E2
Gipsy La. Woki 114 B4
Gipsy La. Woki 116 B2
Girton Cl. Crow 143 F1
Glade Rd. Mar 1 C1
Glade The. Ascot 120 B2
Glade The. Newb 130 C4
Glade The. Pur O T 57 E2
Glade The. Stai 97 D1
Gladridge Cl. Read 87 E2
Gladstone Cl. Kint 102 A1
Gladstone Ind Est. Maid 39 F4
Gladstone La. Cold A 106 B4
Gladstone Way. Slough 42 A3
Glaisdale. That 106 B1
Glamis Way. Read 84 A2
Glanmor Rd. Slough 43 D3
Glanty The. Stai 96 A2
Glasgow Rd. Slough 42 A4
Glassonby Wlk. Camb 152 B3
Glebe Cl. Dorn 40 C2
Glebe Cl. Light 146 B1
Glebe Cl. Moul 13 F3
Glebe Gdns. Sonn 60 C2
Glebe La. Sonn 60 C2
Glebe Rd. Maid 40 A3
Glebe Rd. Old W 68 A1
Glebe Rd. Pur O T 57 D3
Glebe Rd. Read 86 B3
Glebe Rd. Stai 96 B1
Glebe Rd. Stai 97 D2
Glebe Ride. Gori 34 A3
Glebe The. Aldw 32 C2
Glebe The. Black 150 C2
Glebefields. Newb 105 D3
Glebeland Gdns. Shepp 125 E2
Glebeland Rd. Sand 150 C2
Glebelands Rd. Woki 116 B4
Glebewood. Brac 118 B2
Glen Ave. Ashf 98 A2
Glen Cl. Stai 125 D3
Glen Innes. Sand 143 F1
Glen The. Silc 135 F1
Glen The. Slough 43 E1
Glenapp Grange. Mort 136 C3
Glenavon Gdns. Slough 43 E2
Glenavon Gdns. Yate 149 E2
Glenbeigh Terr. Read 85 F3
Glendale Ave. Newb 130 B3
Glendale Rd. Tad 135 D1

Glendevon Rd. Wood 87 F4
Gleneagles Cl. Stan 70 B1
Glenfield Rd. Ashf 98 B1
Glenhaven Dr. Stan 70 B1
Glenhurst Cl. Black 150 C2
Glenmore Cl. That 106 B1
Glennon Cl. Read 85 E2
Glenrosa Rd. Read 85 D4
Glentworth Pl. Slough 42 B3
Glenwood Dr. Read 84 B4
Glenwood. Brac 118 B3
Globe Farm La. Black 150 A3
Glory Cl. Woo G 3 F4
Glory Mill La. Woo G 3 F4
Gloucester Ave. Slough 42 B4
Gloucester Cres. Stai 97 E1
Gloucester Ct. Read 85 E4
Gloucester Dr. Stai 96 B3
Gloucester Gdns. Bags 145 E2
Gloucester Pl. Wind 67 E3
Gloucester Rd. Bags 145 F2
Gloucester Rd. Maid 19 F1
Gloucester Rd. Newb 104 C1
Gloucester Rd. Read 85 E4
Glyme Wlk. Read 84 C2
Glynswood. Camb 151 F2
Goaters Rd. Burl 119 E4
Goddard Cl. Shin 113 F3
Goddard Cl. Stai 124 C3
Goddard Ct. Winn 88 A1
Goddards La. Camb 151 D2
Goddington Rd. Bou E 3 D3
Godolphin Rd. Slough 42 B3
Godstow Cl. Wood 87 F4
Goffs Rd. Ashf 98 B2
Gogmore Farm Cl. Chert 123 F1
Gogmore La. Chert 124 A1
Gold Cup La. Burl 119 E4
Goldcrest Cl. Yate 149 D3
Goldcrest Way. Read 84 A3
Golden Ball La. Cook 19 D2
Golden Oak. Far C 22 B3
Golden Orb Wood. Brac 117 E4
Goldfinch La. Newt 131 F2
Golding Cl. That 106 C2
Goldney Rd. Camb 152 B2
Goldsmid Rd. Read 85 F4
Goldsmith Cl. That 106 B3
Goldsmith Way. Crow 143 D2
Goldsworthy Way. Slough 41 E4
Goldthorpe Gdns. Read 113 F4
Goldwell Dr. Newb 104 C2
Golf Dr. Camb 152 A2
Goodboy's La. Bur C 112 A1
Goodboy's La. Mort 112 A1
Goodchild Rd. Woki 116 B3
Goodings Green. Woki 116 C3
Goodliffe Gdns. Pur O T 57 E2
Goodman Park. Slough 43 E3
Goodman Pl. Stai 96 C2
Goodrich Cl. Caver 59 F3
Goodways Dr. Brac 118 B4
Goodwin Cl. Bur C 84 C2
Goodwin Rd. Slough 21 F1
Goodwin Meadows. Woo G .. 3 F3
Goodwin Wlk. Newb 130 B3
Goodwood Cl. Bur C 111 D1
Goodwood Cl. Camb 151 F4
Goodwood Rise. Mar B 1 B4
Goodwood Way. Newb 105 E1
Goose Cnr. New G 91 F2
Goose Green Way. That 106 C2
Goose Green. Far C 22 A2
Goose Green. Lamb 25 D2
Goose La. Leckh 49 F3
Goose Pool. Chert 123 F1
Gordon Ave. Camb 151 E2
Gordon Cl. Stai 97 D1
Gordon Cres. Camb 151 E2
Gordon Cres. Comp 31 F2
Gordon Dr. Shepp 125 E1
Gordon Pl. Read 85 E4
Gordon Rd. Ashf 97 F3
Gordon Rd. Camb 151 E3
Gordon Rd. Crow 143 D2
Gordon Rd. Maid 39 E4
Gordon Rd. Newb 105 D1
Gordon Rd. Shepp 125 E2
Gordon Rd. Stai 96 B2
Gordon Rd. That 106 A3
Gordon Rd. Wind 66 C3
Gordon Wlk. Yate 149 F3
Gore End Rd. Ball H 129 D2
Gore Rd. Burn 21 D1
Goring La. Bur C 111 F2
Goring Rd. Stai 96 C2
Gorrick Sq. Brac 116 A2
Gorse Bank. Light 153 D4
Gorse Dr. Wood 88 A4
Gorse Hill La. Vir W 122 B3
Gorse Hill Rd. Vir W 122 B3
Gorse Meade. Slough 42 A3
Gorse Rd. Cook 19 F3
Gorse Ride N. Woki 141 F4
Gorse Ride S. Woki 141 F3
Gorselands. Caver 59 D3
Gorselands. Newb 130 B3
Gorselands. Tad 135 E1

Gorselands. Yate 149
Gosbrook Rd. Caver 59
Gosden Rd. West E 153
Gosforth Cl. Read 87
Goslar Way. Wind 67
Gosling Green. Slough 43
Gosling Rd. Slough 43
Gosnell Cl. Camb 152
Gossmore Cl. Mar 1
Gossmore La. Mar 1
Goswell Hill. Wind 67
Goswells Rd. Wind 67
Gothic Ct. Harl 71
Gothic Ct. Sand 150
Gough's Barn La. New G 91
Gough's La. New G 91
Gough's Meadow. Sand 150
Gould Rd. Felt 98
Govenor's Rd. Sand 150
Govett Ave. Shepp 125
Govett Gr. Windl 146
Gower Park. Sand 150
Gower St. Read 85
Gower The. Stai 123
Graces La. Chiev 78
Graffham Cl. Read 114
Grafton Cl. Maid 19
Grafton Cl. Slough 43
Grafton Ct. Felt 98
Grafton Rd. Read 84
Graham Cl. Blew 12
Graham Cl. Maid 39
Graham Cl. Read 84
Graham Rd. Cook 19
Graham Rd. Windl 146
Grahame Ave. Pangb 56
Gramp's Hill. Let B 6
Grampian Cl. Harl 71
Grampian Rd. Sand 143
Grampian Way. Slough 44
Granby Ct. Read 86
Granby End. Bur C 111
Granby Gdns. Read 86
Grand Ave. Camb 151
Grange Ave. Crow 143
Grange Ave. Read 87
Grange Cl. Gori 34
Grange Cl. Wray 68
Grange Dr. Bou E 3
Grange Gdns. Far C 22
Grange La. Cook 19
Grange Pl. Stai 124
Grange Rd. Brac 118
Grange Rd. Camb 151
Grange Rd. Cook 19
Grange Rd. Eng G 95
Grange Rd. Hen-O-T 15
Grange The. Burn 21
Grange The. Old W 68
Grange Way. Iver 44
Grangely Cl. Bur C 84
Grangewood. Slough 43
Grant Ave. Slough 42
Grant Cl. Shepp 125
Grant Rd. Crow 143
Grant Wlk. Sunn 120
Grantham Cl. Sand 143
Grantham Rd. Read 84
Granthams The. Lamb 9
Granville Ave. Slough 42
Granville Rd. Read 85
Grasmere Ave. Read 57
Grasmere Ave. Slough 43
Grasmere Cl. Felt 98
Grasmere Cl. Stai 96
Grasmere Par. Slough 43
Grasmere Rd. Light 146
Grass Hill. Caver 58
Grassington Pl. That 106
Grassmead. That 106
Grassmere Cl. Winn 88
Grassy La. Maid 39
Grattan Ct. Mar 2
Gratton Dr. Wind 66
Gratton Rd. Read 113
Gratwicke Rd. Read 84
Gravel Hill. Box 103
Gravel Hill. Caver 59
Gravel Hill. Hen-O-T 15
Gravel Rd. Caver 35
Gravelly Cl. Ball H 129
Graveney Dr. Caver 58
Gravett Cl. Hen-O-T 35
Gray's Pl. Slough 42
Gray's Rd. Slough 42
Grayling Cl. Mar 18
Grays Cres. Wood 87
Grays La. Ashf 98
Grays Park Rd. Sto P 23
Grayshot Dr. Sand 150
Grazeley Rd. Shin 113
Great Hill Cres. Maid 39
Great Hollands Rd. Brac 117
Great Hollands Sq. Brac 117
Great Knollys St. Read 85
Great Severals. Kint 102
Great South West Rd. Felt ... 71
Great South West Rd. Harm .. 71
Green Acre Mount. Read 84

Green Acre Mount. Rea

en Cl. Burn	41	D4
en Cl. Maid	19	F1
en Cres. Fla H	3	E4
en Croft. Woki	116	C4
en Dr. Woki	116	B4
en Dragon La. Fla H	3	D4
en End. Shin	113	D1
en End. Yate	149	E4
en Farm Rd. Bags	145	F2
en Finch Cl. Brac	142	C3
en Hill Cl. Camb	152	B3
en Hill Rd. Camb	152	B3
en La. Ascot	120	C4
en La. Ashf	98	C1
en La. Black	150	C2
en La. Bur C	85	D1
en La. Bur G	38	A3
en La. Burn	21	E2
en La. Caver	35	D1
en La. Far C	22	A3
en La. Hen-O-T	35	E4
en La. Holy	64	A3
en La. Hurst	88	C2
en La. Maid	40	A3
en La. Maid	40	A3
en La. Newb	104	C1
en La. Padw	110	B1
en La. Pangb	56	B2
en La. Sand	150	B3
en La. Sand	150	B4
en La. Shepp	125	E2
en La. Slough	68	A3
en La. Stai	96	A2
en La. Stai	123	F4
en La. That	106	B2
en La. Wind	67	D3
en La. Woki	88	B1
en La. Yate	149	D4
en Lane Cl. Camb	151	D4
en Lane Ct. Burn	21	E1
en Leas Cl. Ashf	98	C1
en Leas. Ashf	98	C1
en Park. Stai	96	C3
en Rd. Read	87	D3
en Rd. Vir W	123	F4
en The. Brac	118	A3
en The. Burn	21	D1
en The. Chil	10	C4
en The. Datch	68	A4
en The. Slough	42	B2
en The. Thea	83	E1
en The. Woki	115	F4
en The. Woo G	3	F3
en The. Wray	68	C1
en Verges. Mar	1	C2
en Way. Burn	21	D2
en Wood. Burl	119	E4
enacre Ct. Eng G	95	E1
enacre. Wind	66	C3
enacres Ave. Winn	88	A2
enacres La. Winn	88	A2
enacres. Ball H	129	F1
encroft Gdns. Read	84	C3
endale Mews. Slough	43	D3
enfell Ave. Maid	39	F3
enfern Ave. Slough	41	E4
enfield Way. Brac	143	D4
enfields Rd. Read	113	D4
enfields. Maid	40	A3
enfinch Cl. Read	84	A3
enham Cl. Wood	88	A3
enham Mill. Newb	105	D2
enham Rd. Newb	105	D1
enham Wood. Brac	118	B2
enhaven. Yate	149	D3
enholme. Camb	152	B3
enhow. Brac	118	A3
enlands Rd. Camb	151	D1
enlands Rd. Newb	105	D1
enlands Rd. Stai	97	D2
enlands. Ball H	129	F1
enlands. Fla H	3	D4
enleas Ave. Caver	59	D4
enleas Cl. Yate	149	E4
enleas. Camb	151	F1
eno Cres. Stai	125	D2
enock Rd. Slough	42	A4
enside. Bou E	3	D3
enside. Crow	142	C3
enside. Slough	42	A4
ensward La. Arbo	114	B1
enway Dr. Stai	124	A4
enway The. Fawl	27	E4
enway The. Slough	41	E3
enways Dr. Maid	39	D4
enways Dr. Sunn	120	C1
enways. Ball H	129	F1
enways. Eng G	95	F2
enways. Lamb	25	D1
enways. Sand	143	D1
enwood Gr. Winn	88	B2
enwood Rd. Crow	143	D3
enwood Rd. Read	84	C3
gory Cl. Winn	114	B4
gory Dr. Old W	68	A1
enfell Pl. Maid	39	F3
enfell Rd. Maid	39	F3

Grenville Cl. Burn	21	D2
Gresham Rd. Slough	42	A4
Gresham Rd. Stai	96	C2
Gresham Rd. Stai	97	D2
Gresham Way. Read	58	A1
Grey's Rd. Hen-O-T	35	E4
Greyberry Copse Rd. Gree	131	E4
Greyfriars Dr. Ascot	120	A2
Greyfriars Rd. Read	86	A4
Greys Ct. Read	86	B4
Greys Hill. Hen-O-T	15	E1
Greystoke Ct. Crow	143	D2
Greystoke Rd. Caver	59	E2
Greystoke Rd. Slough	41	F4
Griffin Cl. Maid	39	F3
Griffin Cl. Slough	42	B2
Griffiths Cl. That	106	C1
Grindle Cl. Cold A	106	B3
Gringer Hill. Maid	39	F4
Grosvenor Ct. Black	150	B2
Grosvenor Dr. Maid	40	B4
Grosvenor Rd. Caver	59	E2
Grosvenor Rd. Stai	97	D1
Grove Cl. Brac	142	C4
Grove Cl. Old W	95	D4
Grove Cl. Slough	43	D2
Grove Cotts. Caver	59	D3
Grove Cross Rd. Camb	151	C1
Grove Ct. Eng G	96	A2
Grove End. Windl	145	F3
Grove Hill. Caver	59	D2
Grove La. Wink	92	A2
Grove Rd. Burn	21	F2
Grove Rd. Camb	151	F3
Grove Rd. Caver	59	D3
Grove Rd. Chert	123	F2
Grove Rd. Hen-O-T	15	F1
Grove Rd. Maid	39	F4
Grove Rd. Newb	104	C3
Grove Rd. Shepp	125	E2
Grove Rd. Wind	67	E3
Grove The. Burl	119	E4
Grove The. Camb	151	E1
Grove The. Eng G	96	A2
Grove The. Read	86	B4
Grove The. Slough	43	D2
Grove The. That	106	B2
Grove The. Twyf	61	E3
Grovefields Ave. Camb	151	E1
Groveland Pl. Read	85	D4
Groveland Rd. Newb	104	C3
Grovelands Ave. Winn	88	B1
Grovelands Cl. Winn	88	B2
Grovelands Rd. Read	85	D4
Grovelands Rd. Shin	113	E1
Groveley Rd. Ashf	98	C2
Groves Lea. Mort	136	C3
Groves Way. Cook	19	F3
Grovestile Waye. Felt	98	B4
Grubwood La. Cook	19	D4
Guards Club Rd. Maid	40	B4
Guards Rd. Oak G	66	B3
Guildford Ave. Felt	98	C3
Guildford Rd. Bags	145	F1
Guildford Rd. Bis	153	F4
Guildford Rd. Light	153	F4
Guildford Rd. West E	153	F4
Guildford St. Chert	124	A1
Guildford St. Stai	97	D1
Gun St. Read	86	A4
Gunthorpe Rd. Mar	2	A2
Gurney Cl. Caver	58	B3
Gurney Dr. Caver	58	B3
Gwendale. Maid	19	E1
Gweneth Ct. Mar	1	B2
Gwent Cl. Maid	39	D2
Gwyn Cl. Newb	130	C4
Gwynne Cl. Read	57	E2
Gwynne Cl. Wind	66	C3
Gwyns Piece. Lamb	25	D2
Gypsy La. Mar	1	C2
Gypsy La. Sto P	22	C4
Habershon Dr. Camb	152	B1
Haddon Dr. Wood	87	F4
Haddon Rd. Maid	39	E3
Hadfield Rd. Stan	70	B1
Hadleigh Rise. Caver	59	F3
Hadlow Cl. Slough	43	B3
Hadrian Cl. Stan	97	F4
Hadrian Way. Stan	97	F4
Hadrian Wlk E. Read	86	B2
Hag Hill La. Burn	41	D4
Hagley Rd. Read	86	A2
Haig Dr. Slough	42	A3
Haig Rd. Sand	150	C3
Hailey La. Beed	29	F1
Hailsham Cl. Crow	143	E1
Halcyon Terr. Read	84	C4
Haldane Rd. Caver	58	C3
Hale End. Brac	118	C3
Hale St. Stai	96	C2
Hale Way. Camb	151	E1
Halewood. Brac	117	F2
Half Mile Rd. Lamb	46	A1
Half Moon St. Bags	145	F2
Halfacre Cl. Shin	113	D2

Halfpenny La. Chol	13	F3
Halfpenny La. Went	121	D1
Halifax Cl. Maid	39	D4
Halifax Rd. Maid	39	D4
Halifax Way. Maid	39	D4
Halkingcroft. Slough	43	E2
Hall Cl. Camb	151	F3
Hall Ct. Datch	68	A4
Hall Farm Cres. Yate	149	E3
Hall La. Harl	71	E4
Hall La. Yate	149	E3
Hall Meadow. Burn	21	E2
Hall Place La. Bur G	38	A4
Hallbrook Gdns. Binf	90	C1
Halldore Hill. Cook	19	F4
Halley Dr. Ascot	119	E4
Hallgrove Bottom. Windl	145	F3
Halliford Cl. Shepp	125	F3
Halliford Rd. Shepp	125	F3
Halls La. Read	86	C1
Halls La. W St L	63	D3
Halls Rd. Read	84	B3
Halpin Cl. Read	84	B2
Halstead Cl. Wood	87	F4
Ham La. Eng G	95	D2
Ham La. Old W	68	B2
Ham Rd. Ham	126	A2
Hamble Ave. Black	150	B3
Hambleden Wlk. Maid	19	F2
Hambledon Cl. Newb	87	F1
Hambleton Cl. Camb	152	A2
Hambridge La. Gree	105	F1
Hambridge Rd. Newb	105	E1
Hamilton Ave. Hen-O-T	15	F1
Hamilton Cl. Chert	123	F1
Hamilton Cl. Felt	98	C2
Hamilton Cl. Black	150	C1
Hamilton Cl. Newb	131	D4
Hamilton Dr. Sunn	120	C1
Hamilton Gdns. Burn	21	D1
Hamilton Rd. Felt	98	C2
Hamilton Rd. Read	86	C3
Hamilton Rd. Slough	42	A4
Hamilton Rd. Warg	36	C1
Hamlet St. Brac	118	C4
Hammond Cl. That	106	C1
Hammond End. Far C	22	B4
Hammond Way. Light	146	A1
Hammonds Heath. Mort	137	D3
Hampden Cl. Sto P	23	D1
Hampden Rd. Caver	59	D1
Hampden Rd. Maid	39	D4
Hampden Rd. Slough	43	F2
Hampdens The. Newb	130	B3
Hampshire Ave. Slough	42	B4
Hampshire Rd. Camb	151	F4
Hampshire Rise. New G	91	F1
Hampshire Way. Woki	115	E3
Hampstead Hill. Caver	60	B4
Hampstead Norreys Rd. Herm	79	D4
Hampton Rd. Newb	104	C1
Hanbury Cl. Burn	41	D4
Hanbury Dr. Bur C	84	B2
Hanbury Way. Camb	151	E2
Hancocks Mount. Ascot	120	B2
Hancombe Rd. Sand	143	D1
Handford La. Yate	149	E3
Hanger Rd. Tad	134	C1
Hangerfield Cl. Yate	149	E3
Hangman's Stone La. Chadd	49	D3
Hanley Cl. Wind	66	B3
Hannibal Rd. Stan	97	F4
Hanover Cl. Camb	151	F1
Hanover Cl. Eng G	95	D1
Hanover Cl. Slough	43	D2
Hanover Cl. Wind	66	C3
Hanover Gdns. Brac	117	F1
Hanover Way. Wind	66	C3
Hanwood Cl. Wood	87	E4
Hanworth Cl. Brac	118	B2
Hanworth La. Chert	123	F1
Hanworth Rd. Brac	118	A1
Harcourt Cl. Dorn	40	C2
Harcourt Cl. Hen-O-T	15	E1
Harcourt Cl. Stai	96	B1
Harcourt Dr. Read	86	C2
Harcourt Rd. Brac	118	A2
Harcourt Rd. Camb	151	D3
Harcourt Rd. Dorn	40	C2
Harcourt Rd. Wind	66	C3
Hardell Cl. Eng G	96	A2
Hardwell Way. Brac	118	C3
Hardwick Cl. Maid	39	D4
Hardwick La. Chert	123	E1
Hardwick Rd. Read	84	C4
Hardwick Rd. Whi-O-T	56	B4
Hardy Ave. Yate	149	E2
Hardy Cl. Caver	59	E1
Hardy Cl. Slough	42	A3
Hardy Cl. That	106	B3
Hardy Green. Crow	143	D2
Hare Shoots. Maid	39	F3
Harefield Cl. Winn	88	B1
Harefield Rd. Maid	39	D4
Harewood Dr. Cold A	106	B4
Harewood Pl. Slough	43	D2
Hargrave Rd. Maid	39	E4
Hargreaves Way. Read	84	C2

Harkness Rd. Burn	41	D4
Harlech Ave. Caver	59	E3
Harlech Rd. Black	150	B2
Harley Rd. Caver	59	D1
Harlington Cl. Harl	71	E4
Harlton Cl. Winn	114	B4
Harmans Water Rd. Brac	118	B2
Harmar Cl. Woki	116	C3
Harmondsworth La. Harm	70	C4
Harness Cl. Read	113	D3
Harold Rd. Kint	102	A1
Harpesford Ave. Went	122	B2
Harpton Cl. Yate	149	E4
Harrier Cl. Wood	88	A3
Harrington Cl. Newb	105	F3
Harrington Cl. Read	87	E1
Harrington Cl. Wind	66	C2
Harris Cl. Lamb	25	D2
Harris Cl. Read	88	A4
Harris Way. Stai	125	F4
Harrison Cl. Twyf	61	F2
Harrison Ct. Stai	125	D2
Harrison Way. Slough	41	E3
Harrogate Ct. Slough	44	A1
Harrogate Rd. Caver	58	C2
Harrow Bottom Rd. Went	122	C2
Harrow Cl. Maid	19	F1
Harrow Ct. Read	85	F3
Harrow La. Maid	19	F1
Harrow Rd. Ashf	98	A3
Harrow Rd. Slough	43	D2
Harrow Way. Stai	125	E4
Hart Cl. Brac	91	D1
Hart Dyke Cl. Brac	116	A1
Hart St. Hen-O-T	15	F1
Hart's La. Sulhd	110	B3
Hartford Rise. Camb	151	E3
Hartigan Pl. Read	88	A4
Hartland Cl. Slough	42	B3
Hartland Rd. Read	86	B1
Hartley Cl. Black	150	A3
Hartley Cl. Sto P	23	E2
Hartley Court Rd. Shin	112	C3
Hartley Way. That	106	C2
Hartmead Rd. That	106	C2
Harts Cl. Arbo	114	C1
Harts Hill Rd. That	106	B2
Harts Leap Cl. Sand	143	D1
Harts Leap Rd. Sand	150	A4
Hartsbourne Rd. Read	87	D2
Hartshill Rd. Tad	134	C1
Hartslock Ct. Pangb	56	A3
Hartslock Way. Read	57	E1
Hartstock View. Upp B	34	C1
Harvard Cl. Wood	88	A4
Harvard Rd. Crow	143	F1
Harvest Cl. Read	84	A3
Harvest Cl. Yate	149	D2
Harvest Ct. Stai	125	D3
Harvest Green. Newb	104	C1
Harvest Hill Rd. Maid	39	F2
Harvest Hill. Bou E	3	E1
Harvest Rd. Eng G	95	E1
Harvest Ride. New G	91	F1
Harvey Rd. Shepp	125	F1
Harvey Rd. Slough	44	A2
Harwich Cl. Winn	87	E1
Harwich Rd. Slough	42	A4
Harwood Gdns. Old W	95	D4
Harwood Rd. Mar	1	B1
Harwood Rise. Ball H	129	F1
Haslemere Cl. Camb	152	B2
Haslemere Rd. Wind	67	D3
Haslett Rd. Shepp	125	F4
Hasting Cl. Maid	40	B1
Hatch Cl. Buck	108	B4
Hatch End. Windl	146	B2
Hatch Gate La. Know H	37	D3
Hatch La. Buck	108	B4
Hatch La. Bur C	111	E3
Hatch La. Harm	70	B4
Hatch La. Wind	67	D3
Hatch Ride. Brac	142	C4
Hatch Ride. Brac	143	D4
Hatch The. Oak G	66	C4
Hatchet La. Ascot	93	D2
Hatchet La. Old W	93	D2
Hatchet La. Wink	93	D2
Hatchets La. Buck	80	B4
Hatchett Rd. Felt	98	B4
Hatchgate Cl. Cold A	106	B4
Hatchgate Copse. Brac	117	F2
Hatchgate Gdns. Burn	21	E1
Hatfield Cl. Maid	39	E3
Hatfield Ct. Bur C	84	A2
Hatfield Rd. Slough	43	D2
Hatford Rd. Read	85	D2
Hatherley Rd. Read	86	C3
Hatherwood. Yate	149	F3
Hatton Ave. Far C	22	B1
Hatton Cl. Wind	67	E3
Hatton Hill. Asham	54	A4
Hatton Hill. Windl	146	B3
Hatton Rd. Felt	98	B4
Hatton Rd. Harm	71	F1
Haughurst Hill. Tad	134	B1
Havelock Cres. Maid	39	D4
Havelock Rd. Maid	39	D4

Havelock Rd. Woki	116	A3
Havelock St. Woki	116	A3
Haven Rd. Ashf	98	A3
Haven The. Kint	102	A1
Haversham Dr. Brac	118	A2
Haw La. Asham	53	F4
Hawkchurch Rd. Read	113	E4
Hawkedon Way. Winn	87	F1
Hawker Way. Wood	88	A4
Hawkes Cl. Woki	116	A4
Hawkes Leap. Windl	146	A3
Hawkesbury Dr. Bur C	84	C2
Hawkesworth Dr. Bags	145	F1
Hawkins Cl. Brac	119	D4
Hawkins Way. Woki	116	C3
Hawks Hill. Bou E	3	E1
Hawkshill Rd. Slough	22	A1
Hawksway. Stai	96	C3
Hawkswood Ave. Camb	151	F1
Hawkswood La. Fulm	23	F4
Hawksworth Rd. Bur C	111	D2
Hawley Cl. Bur C	84	B2
Hawley La. Camb	151	D1
Hawley Rd. Black	150	C2
Hawley Way. Ashf	98	A2
Haws La. Stan	70	A1
Hawthorn Cl. Brac	118	A4
Hawthorn Cl. Mar	1	C2
Hawthorn Gdns. Read	86	C1
Hawthorn La. Burn	22	A3
Hawthorn La. New G	91	F4
Hawthorn Rd. Camb	151	F1
Hawthorn Rd. Newb	105	D2
Hawthorn Way. Shepp	125	E3
Hawthorn Way. Sonn	60	C1
Hawthorne Cres. Black	150	C2
Hawthorne Cres. Slough	42	C4
Hawthorne Rd. Caver	59	F2
Hawthorne Rd. Stai	96	B2
Hawthorne Way. Gr She	48	A2
Hawthorne Way. Stan	97	E4
Hawthornes. Sulh	57	D2
Hawtrey Cl. Slough	43	D2
Hawtrey Rd. Wind	67	E3
Hay La. Fulm	23	E4
Hay Rd. Read	85	F3
Hayes La. Bark	115	E2
Hayes Pl. Mar	1	B1
Hayfield Cl. Read	84	B4
Hayley Green. New G	91	F2
Haymill Rd. Slough	21	E1
Haynes Cl. Slough	43	F1
Hayse Hill. Wind	66	B3
Haywards Cl. Hen-O-T	15	E1
Haywards Mead. Eton	41	F1
Haywards The. That	106	B2
Haywood Cl. Read	86	C4
Haywood Way. Read	84	C3
Haywood. Brac	118	B1
Hazel Cl. Bur C	111	D3
Hazel Cl. Eng G	95	D1
Hazel Cl. Mar B	1	B3
Hazel Cl. Woki	115	F3
Hazel Cres. Read	86	C1
Hazel Dr. Wood	87	E3
Hazel Gr. Stai	97	E1
Hazel Gr. That	106	B3
Hazel Green. Tad	134	B1
Hazel Rd. Pur O T	57	E2
Hazelbank Rd. Chert	124	B1
Hazelbank. Woki	141	F3
Hazeldene. Chiev	51	D1
Hazelhurst Rd. Burn	21	E2
Hazell Cl. Maid	39	F4
Hazell Hill. Brac	118	B3
Hazell Way. Sto P	22	C3
Hazelmere Cl. Harm	71	F1
Hazelwood Cl. Read	57	E1
Hazelwood La. Binf	90	C2
Hazlemere Rd. Slough	43	D3
Heacham Cl. Read	114	A4
Headington Cl. Maid	39	D4
Headington Cl. Woki	116	B4
Headington Dr. Woki	116	B4
Headington Rd. Maid	39	D4
Headley Cl. Wood	88	A4
Headley Park Ind Est. Wood	87	F4
Headley Rd E. Wood	88	A4
Headley Rd. Wood	87	F4
Heads La. Ink	128	A3
Heads La. West W	128	A3
Heardman Cl. That	106	C1
Hearmon Cl. Yate	149	F3
Hearn Rd. Wood	87	F3
Hearn Wlk. Brac	118	C4
Hearne Dr. Holy	40	A1
Hearsey Gdns. Black	150	A3
Heath Cl. Harl	71	E4
Heath Cl. Stan	70	B1
Heath Cl. Vir W	122	B3
Heath Cl. Woki	116	A2
Heath Dr. Caver	35	D1
Heath End Rd. Tad	134	C1
Heath Gr. Ashf	98	C1
Heath Hill Rd N. Crow	143	D2
Heath Hill Rd S. Crow	143	D2
Heath La. That	106	B3

Heath Rd. Bags

Name	Page	Grid
Heath Rd. Bags	145	F2
Heath Rd. Beac	3	F4
Heath Rd. Brad	82	A1
Heath Rd. Read	87	D3
Heath Rd. Silc	135	F1
Heath Ride. Finch	142	B3
Heath Ride. Woki	142	B3
Heath Rise. Camb	151	E3
Heath Rise. Vir W	122	B3
Heathacre. Stan	69	F3
Heathcote Rd. Camb	151	E3
Heathcroft Ave. Ashf	98	C1
Heather Cl. Woki	141	F4
Heather Dr. Tad	134	C1
Heather Dr. Went	121	D1
Heather Mead. Camb	151	F1
Heatherdale Rd. Camb	151	E2
Heatherden Cl. Read	113	E4
Heatherdene Ave. Finch	142	C2
Heatherley Cl. Camb	151	D3
Heatherley Rd. Camb	151	D3
Heathermount Dr. Crow	143	D3
Heathermount. Brac	118	C3
Heathers The. Stan	97	F4
Heatherside Dr. Vir W	122	A2
Heatherway. Crow	143	D3
Heathfield Ave. Ascot	120	C2
Heathfield Ave. Read	84	B3
Heathfield Ave. Shipl	35	D1
Heathfield Cl. Shipl	35	D1
Heathfield Rd. Bou E	20	C4
Heathfield Rd. Tapl	20	C4
Heathlands Dr. Maid	39	D3
Heathlands Rd. Woki	116	C1
Heathlands. Tad	134	C1
Heathmoors. Brac	118	B2
Heathpark Dr. Windl	146	C2
Heathrow Cl. Harm	70	A3
Heathway Cl. Camb	151	E3
Heathway. Burl	119	F4
Heathway. Camb	151	E3
Heathway. Read	84	B4
Heathwood Cl. Yate	149	E4
Heavens Lea. Bou E	3	E1
Hebden Rd. That	106	B1
Hedge Lea. Woo G	3	E4
Hedgeway. Newb	105	E2
Hedingham Mews. Maid	39	E4
Hedley Rd. Fla H	3	D4
Hedsor Hill. Bou E	3	E1
Hedsor La. Bou E	3	F1
Hedsor Rd. Bou E	3	D1
Heelas Rd. Woki	116	A3
Helena Rd. Wind	67	E3
Helgiford Gdns. Ashf	98	C1
Hellyer Way. Bou E	3	E2
Helmsdale Cl. Read	85	D4
Helmsdale. Brac	118	C2
Helston Gdns. Read	86	A1
Helston La. Wind	67	D3
Helvellyn Cl. Stai	96	B1
Hemdean Hill. Caver	59	D2
Hemdean Rd. Caver	59	D2
Hemdean Rise. Caver	59	D2
Hempson Ave. Slough	43	E2
Hemsdale. Maid	19	D1
Hemwood Rd. Wind	66	B2
Hencroft St N. Slough	42	C2
Hencroft St S. Slough	42	C2
Hendon Way. Stan	70	B1
Hendons Way. Holy	40	A1
Hengrave Cl. Winn	87	F1
Hengrove Cres. Ashf	97	E3
Henley Gdns. Yate	149	E3
Henley Rd. Bur G	18	A1
Henley Rd. Caver	60	B4
Henley Rd. Hurl	18	A1
Henley Rd. Maid	18	A1
Henley Rd. Mar	18	A4
Henley Rd. Shipl	60	B4
Henley Rd. Slough	41	F4
Henley Wood Rd. Read	87	E2
Henry Rd. Slough	42	B2
Henry St. Read	86	A3
Henrys The. That	106	B2
Henshaw Cres. Newb	130	B4
Hensworth Rd. Stai	97	E2
Henwick Cl. That	106	A3
Henwick La. That	106	A2
Henwood Copse. Upp B	55	D3
Hepplewhite Cl. Tad	134	C1
Hepworth Croft. Sand	150	B3
Hepworth Way. Shepp	125	F1
Herald Way. Wood	88	A3
Herbert Cl. Brac	118	A2
Hereford Cl. Stan	124	A4
Herewood Cl. Newb	104	C2
Heriot Rd. Chert	124	A1
Hermit's Hill. Bur C	111	E2
Hermitage Cl. Camb	151	F1
Hermitage Cl. Slough	43	E2
Hermitage Cl. Stai	125	D3
Hermitage Dr. Ascot	119	F4
Hermitage Dr. Twyf	61	E3
Hermitage La. Wind	67	D2
Hermitage Rd. Herm	79	D1
Hermitage The. Lamb	25	C1
Hermits Cl. Bur C	111	D2
Herndon Cl. Eng G	96	A2
Heroes Wlk. Read	113	D4
Heron Cl. Burl	119	E4
Heron Dr. Twyf	61	F3
Heron Island. Caver	59	E1
Heron Rd. Woki	115	F3
Heron Shaw. Gori	34	B4
Heron Way. Bur C	85	F2
Heron Way. That	106	A2
Heron's Way. Woki	116	C4
Herondale. Brac	118	B1
Heronfield. Eng G	95	D1
Herongate. Hung	100	B4
Herons Ct. Light	153	E4
Herons Pl. Mar	1	C2
Herrick Cl. Camb	152	B2
Herrings La. Chert	124	A2
Herrings La. Windl	146	B2
Herriot Cl. Yate	149	E2
Herschel Park Dr. Slough	42	C2
Herschel St. Slough	42	C2
Hertford Cl. Caver	59	E3
Hertford Cl. Woki	115	F3
Hetherington Cl. Slough	21	F1
Hetherington Rd. Stai	125	E4
Hever Cl. Maid	39	E3
Hewett Ave. Caver	58	B2
Hewett Cl. Caver	58	B2
Hewlett Pl. Bags	145	F2
Hexham Cl. Crow	143	E1
Hexham Rd. Read	86	B2
Heywood Ave. Whi Wa	39	D1
Heywood Court Cl. Whi Wa	39	D1
Heywood Gdns. Whi Wa	39	D1
Hibbert Rd. Maid	40	A2
Hibbert's Alley. Wind	67	E3
Hicks La. Black	150	A3
Higgs La. Bags	145	E2
High Beech. Brac	118	C3
High Beeches. Camb	151	E1
High Fields. Sunn	120	C2
High Heavens Wood. Mar B	1	B4
High Meadow. Caver	58	B2
High Rd. Cook	19	F3
High St Harlington. Harl	71	E4
High St. Ascot	120	A3
High St. Ascot	120	B2
High St. Bags	145	F2
High St. Box	76	A2
High St. Brac	118	A4
High St. Brac	118	B4
High St. Burn	21	E1
High St. Camb	151	E3
High St. Chiev	51	D1
High St. Comp	31	E2
High St. Cook	20	A4
High St. Crow	143	E2
High St. Datch	68	A3
High St. East I	30	C4
High St. Eng G	96	A2
High St. Eton	67	E4
High St. Felt	98	C3
High St. Gori	34	B3
High St. Harl	71	E4
High St. Harm	70	B4
High St. Hung	100	B3
High St. Iver	44	C4
High St. Iver	69	E4
High St. Kint	102	A1
High St. Lamb	24	C3
High St. Lamb	25	D1
High St. Maid	39	F4
High St. Maid	40	A2
High St. Maid	40	B2
High St. Mar	1	C1
High St. Pangb	56	B3
High St. Read	86	A4
High St. Sand	143	D1
High St. Sand	149	F4
High St. Shepp	125	E2
High St. Slough	42	B2
High St. Slough	42	C2
High St. Slough	44	A1
High St. Sonn	60	B2
High St. Stai	96	C2
High St. Stan	70	B1
High St. Stre	34	A3
High St. Sunn	121	D2
High St. Tapl	20	C1
High St. That	106	B2
High St. Thea	83	F2
High St. Twyf	61	E3
High St. Warg	36	B1
High St. West E	153	F4
High St. Whi-O-T	56	B4
High St. Wick	76	A2
High St. Wind	67	E3
High St. Wray	68	C1
High Town Rd. Maid	39	F3
High Tree Dr. Read	87	D3
High View Cl. Mar B	1	B4
High View Rd. Light	152	C4
Highbeeches. Mar B	1	B4
Highbridge Cl. Caver	59	F2
Highbridge Wharf. Read	86	A4
Highbury Cres. Camb	152	A4
Highbury Rd. Read	84	A4
Highclere Cl. Brac	118	C4
Highclere Dr. Camb	152	A4
Highclere. Ascot	120	B2
Highdown Ave. Caver	59	F4
Highdown Hill Rd. Caver	59	D4
Highdown Hill Rd. Maple	59	D4
Higher Alham. Brac	118	C1
Highfeld Cl. Eng G	95	E1
Highfield Ave. Newb	105	D1
Highfield Cl. Woki	116	A3
Highfield Cl. Bur C	111	D2
Highfield La. Maid	39	D2
Highfield Park. Mar	18	A4
Highfield Park. Warg	36	C1
Highfield Rd. Bou E	3	D2
Highfield Rd. Chert	124	A1
Highfield Rd. Fla H	3	D4
Highfield Rd. Maid	39	D4
Highfield Rd. Newb	104	C1
Highfield Rd. Pur O T	57	E2
Highfield Rd. Shepp	125	F2
Highfield Rd. Wind	66	C3
Highfield. Brac	117	F2
Highfield. Read	87	D1
Highgate Rd. Wood	87	E3
Highgrove Park. Maid	39	F4
Highgrove St. Read	86	B3
Highgrove Terr. Read	86	A3
Highland Ave. Woki	115	F4
Highland Park. Felt	98	C2
Highland Rd. Camb	151	F4
Highlands La. Shipl	35	D4
Highlands. Fla H	3	D4
Highlea Ave. Fla H	3	D4
Highmead Cl. Read	86	C1
Highmoor Rd. Caver	58	C2
Highview Cres. Camb	144	C1
Highview. Read	84	A3
Highway Ave. Maid	39	D3
Highway Rd. Maid	39	D3
Highway. Crow	143	D3
Highwayman's Ridge. Windl	105	E3
Highwood Cl. Newb	105	E3
Highwood Cl. Yate	149	E2
Highwoods Cl. Mar B	1	B4
Highwoods Dr. Mar B	1	B4
Highworth Way. Sulh	57	D1
Hilary Cl. Read	113	E4
Hilborne Way. Bark	115	D1
Hilbury Rd. Read	87	D2
Hilcot Rd. Read	85	E4
Hildens Dr. Read	84	B4
Hilfield. Yate	149	F3
Hill Cl. Newb	130	B4
Hill Cl. Woo G	3	F4
Hill Copse View. Brac	118	C4
Hill Farm App. Woo G	3	F4
Hill Farm Rd. Mar B	1	C2
Hill Farm Rd. Tapl	20	C1
Hill Gdns. Stre	34	A3
Hill Lands. Warg	36	B1
Hill Piece. Chil	10	C4
Hill Rd. Bark	114	C1
Hill Rd. Newb	104	C1
Hill St. Read	86	A3
Hill Top Dr. Mar	1	A1
Hill View Rd. Wray	68	B1
Hillary Dr. Crow	143	D3
Hillary Rd. Slough	43	F2
Hillberry. Brac	118	B1
Hillborn Rd. Bark	140	C4
Hillbrow. Read	86	C1
Hillcrest Ave. Cook	19	F3
Hillcrest Rd. Camb	152	A4
Hillcrest. Tad	135	D1
Hillersdon. Slough	43	D4
Hillgreen La. Pease	50	B4
Hillhouse La. Head	133	E1
Hillingdon Ave. Stan	97	F4
Hillmead Ct. Tapl	40	C4
Hillrise. Slough	69	D4
Hills La. Cook	19	E4
Hillsborough Park. Camb	152	B3
Hillside Dr. Binf	90	B1
Hillside Park. Read	86	C1
Hillside Park. Windl	120	C1
Hillside Rd. Hung	100	B2
Hillside Rd. Mar	1	C2
Hillside Rd. Read	87	E2
Hillside. Bur C	111	E2
Hillside. East G	47	E3
Hillside. Maid	39	E3
Hillside. Sand	150	C4
Hillside. Slough	42	C2
Hillside. Went	122	B2
Hillside. Whi-O-T	56	B4
Hilltop Cl. Ascot	120	C4
Hilltop Rd. Caver	58	B3
Hilltop Rd. Read	87	D4
Hilltop Rd. Twyf	61	F4
Hilltop View. Yate	149	D3
Hillview Cl. Read	57	D1
Hilmanton. Read	113	F4
Hilperton Rd. Slough	42	C2
Hindhead Rd. Read	87	D2
Hinksey Cl. Slough	44	A2
Hinton Cl. Crow	143	D4
Hinton Dr. Crow	143	D4
Hinton Rd. Hurst	62	A1
Hinton Rd. Slough	41	F3
Hintonhatch Cnr. Hurst	62	A1
Hirstwood. Pur O T	57	F1
Hirtes Ave. Shin	113	F3
Hitcham La. Tapl	20	C1
Hitcham Rd. Burn	41	D4
Hitchcock Cl. Stai	124	C3
Hitherhooks Hill. Binf	90	C1
Hitherhooks Hill. Brac	117	F4
Hithermoor Rd. Stan	70	A1
Hobart Ct. Mar	2	A2
Hobbis Dr. Maid	39	D3
Hockett La. Bish	19	D3
Hockett La. Cook	19	D3
Hockford La. Head	134	A2
Hockham Rd. Comp	31	F3
Hockley La. Pur O T	23	D3
Hodgedale La. Warg	37	E3
Hodges Cl. Bags	145	F1
Hodsoll Rd. Read	85	F4
Hoe Benham La. Wick	102	C3
Hogarth Ave. Ashf	98	B1
Hogarth Ave. Read	84	C3
Hogarth Cl. Sand	150	C3
Hogarth Cl. Slough	41	F3
Hogfair La. Burn	21	E1
Hogmoor La. Hurst	61	F1
Hogwood La. Bark	141	D3
Holbeche Cl. Yate	149	D3
Holbeck. Brac	117	F2
Holberton Rd. Read	113	E4
Holborn Hill. Let B	6	B4
Holborne Cl. Newb	130	B3
Holford Cl. Read	84	B4
Holkam Cl. Read	57	F1
Holland Gdns. Stai	123	F4
Holland Pines. Brac	117	F1
Holland Rd. Mar	1	C2
Holland Rd. Read	84	B4
Hollands The. That	106	C2
Hollicombe Cl. Read	84	C4
Hollies The. Newb	130	B3
Hollins Wlk. Read	85	E3
Hollow Hill La. Iver	44	B3
Hollow La. Shin	113	F3
Hollow La. Vir W	122	B3
Holloway La. Harm	70	C4
Holly Ave. Camb	152	A2
Holly Cl. Eng G	95	D1
Holly Cl. Far C	22	B4
Holly Cres. Wind	66	B3
Holly Dr. Maid	39	F4
Holly Dr. Old Wind	67	F1
Holly Hedge Cl. Camb	151	F1
Holly Hedge Rd. Camb	151	F1
Holly La. Asham	54	B3
Holly Rd. Wood	88	A3
Holly Spring La. Brac	118	B4
Holly Way. Black	150	B2
Hollybank. West E	153	F3
Hollybush La. Cook	19	D3
Hollybush La. Iver	44	A3
Hollybush La. Sulhd	110	C2
Hollybush Ride. Brac	142	B3
Hollybush Ride. Finch	142	B3
Hollycombe. Eng G	95	E2
Hollycroft Cl. Harm	71	D4
Hollycroft Gdns. Harm	71	D4
Hollydale Cl. Read	86	C1
Hollyfields Cl. Camb	151	D3
Hollyhook Cl. Brac	143	D3
Hollym Cl. Winn	87	F1
Holmanleaze. Maid	40	A4
Holmbury Ave. Brac	143	D4
Holmdale. Slough	43	E3
Holmdene. Bur C	111	D2
Holme Cl. Brac	143	D4
Holmemoor Dr. Sonn	60	C1
Holmes Cl. Ascot	120	B2
Holmes Cl. Woki	116	A2
Holmes Cres. Woki	116	A2
Holmes Rd. Read	87	D3
Holmewood Cl. Woki	116	A1
Holmlea Rd. Datch	68	B3
Holmlea Rd. Gori	34	B3
Holmlea Wlk. Datch	68	B3
Holmsdale Cl. Iver	44	C4
Holmwood Ave. Read	84	C2
Holmwood Cl. Maid	39	D3
Holsworthy Cl. Winn	87	F2
Holt La. Brig	49	F4
Holt La. Woki	116	A4
Holt Rd. Kint	102	A1
Holt The. Pur O T	57	E2
Holton Heath. Brac	118	C3
Holtspur Ave. Woo G	3	F4
Holtspur La. Woo G	3	F3
Holtwood Rd. Ham M	129	D3
Holybrook Cres. Read	85	D2
Holybrook Rd. Read	85	F3
Holyport St. Holy	65	D4
Holyrood Cl. Caver	59	E3
Holywell Cl. Stan	97	F4
Holywell Way. Stan	97	F4
Hombrook Dr. Brac	117	F4
Home Croft. Sulh	57	D1
Home Farm Cl. Read	86	B3
Home Farm Cl. Shepp	125	F3
Home Farm Way. Sto P	23	
Home Mead. Newb	130	
Home Meadow Dr. Fla H	3	
Home Meadow. Far C	22	
Home Park Farm La. Sonn	60	
Home Park Rd. Yate	149	
Homefield Way. Hung	100	
Homers Rd. Wind	66	
Homestead Rd. Maid	39	
Homestead Rd. Stai	97	
Homewaters Ave. Shepp	125	
Homewood. Slough	43	
Hone Hill. Sand	150	
Honesty Bottom. Brig	28	
Honey End La. Read	85	
Honey Hill. Brac	117	
Honey Hill. Lamb	25	
Honey La. Hurl	17	
Honeybottom Rd. Tad	135	
Honeyfields. Hung	100	
Honeyhill Rd. Brac	118	
Honeysuckle Cl. Brac	143	
Honeysuckle Cl. Yate	149	
Honiton Rd. Read	86	
Honnor Rd. Stai	97	
Hook End La. Upp B	34	
Hook La. West E	153	
Hook Hill La. Light	146	
Hookstone La. West E	153	
Hop Gdns. Hen-O-T	15	
Hope Ave. Brac	118	
Hopeman Cl. Sand	150	
Hopwood Cl. Newb	105	
Horewood Rd. Brac	118	
Hormer Cl. Sand	143	
Horn St. Comp	31	
Hornbeam Cl. Pur O T	57	
Hornbeam Cl. Sand	143	
Hornbeam Cl. Woki	115	
Hornbeam Gdns. Slough	43	
Hornbeams. Swal	139	
Horncastle Dr. Read	84	
Horndean Rd. Brac	118	
Horne Rd. Stai	125	
Horne Rd. That	106	
Hornsea Cl. Read	57	
Horse Cl The. Caver	59	
Horse Gate Ride. Ascot	120	
Horsebrass Dr. Bags	145	
Horseguards Dr. Maid	40	
Horsell Cl. Chert	124	
Horsemoor Cl. Slough	44	
Horseshoe Cl. Camb	151	
Horseshoe Cres. Bur C	111	
Horseshoe Cres. Camb	151	
Horseshoe Hill. Burn	21	
Horseshoe Park. Pangb	56	
Horseshoe Rd. Pangb	56	
Horsham Rd. Crow	143	
Horsham Rd. Felt	71	
Horsnape Gdns. Binf	90	
Horseneile La. Brac	118	
Horton Cl. Maid	20	
Horton Rd. Datch	68	
Horton Rd. Hort	69	
Horton Rd. Stan	69	
Horton Rd. Poyle	69	
Hose Hill. Bur C	111	
Hosier St. Read	86	
Houlton Ct. Bags	145	
Houston Way. Finch	142	
Howard Ave. Slough	42	
Howard Cl. Ashf	98	
Howard Rd. Ashf	97	
Howard Rd. Newb	105	
Howard Rd. Woki	116	
Howard St. Read	85	
Howarth Rd. Maid	40	
Howe La. Holy	63	
Howgate Dr. Gori	34	
Howth Dr. Wood	87	
Hubberholme. Brac	118	
Hubert Rd. Slough	43	
Huckleberry Cl. Pur O T	57	
Huddington Glade. Yate	149	
Hudson Rd. Harl	71	
Hudson Rd. Wood	87	
Hugh Fraser Dr. Read	84	
Hughenden Cl. Maid	39	
Hughenden Rd. Slough	42	
Hughes Rd. Ashf	98	
Hughes Rd. Woki	116	
Hull Cl. Slough	42	
Humber Cl. That	106	
Humber Cl. Woki	115	
Humber Way. Sand	150	
Humber Way. Slough	44	
Hummer Rd. Eng G	96	
Humphrey's La. East G	47	
Hungerford Ave. Slough	42	
Hungerford Cl. Sand	150	
Hungerford Dr. Maid	39	
Hungerford Dr. Read	85	
Hungerford Hill. East G	47	
Hungerford Hill. Lamb	25	
Hungerford La. Hurst	62	
Hungerford La. W St L	62	
Hungerford Rd. Kint	101	
Hunt's La. Tapl	20	

ter's Hill. Bur C 110 C2
tercombe Cl. Burn 41 E4
tercombe Cl. Slough 41 E4
tercombe La N. Slough 41 E4
tercombe La S. Burn 41 E3
tercombe La S. Slough 41 E3
ters Meadow. Gr She 48 A2
ters Mews. Wind 67 E3
ters Way. Shin 113 D1
tingdonshire Cl. Woki 115 E3
tingfield Way. Stai 96 B1
tington Cl. Winn 87 F1
atley Ct. Read 86 C3
tsmans Meadow. Ascot ... 119 F4
tsmoor Rd. Tad 135 D1
tswood La. Burn 20 C2
tswood La. Tapl 20 C2
ey High St. Hurl 17 F2
ey La. Bish 18 A2
ey La. Hurl 18 A2
icane Way. Read 88 A4
icane Way. Wood 88 A4
sley Cl. Read 84 C4
st Gr. Shepp 125 F1
st La. Vir W 123 D4
st Park Rd. Twyf 61 F1
st Rd. Slough 41 E4
st Rd. Twyf 61 F2
stdene Ave. Stai 97 D1
stfield Dr. Burn 41 D4
stwood. Ascot 120 A2
carle Way. Pur O T 57 E2
sons Cl. Woki 116 B4
ton Cl. Newb 105 D2
ton Cl. Read 87 D1
ton Cl. Windl 146 B2
e End La. Brim 133 E3
e End La. Shin 113 E2
e End Rd. Shin 113 E1
e Green. Mar 1 C1
e La. Newt 132 A1
e Terr. Ashf 98 C1
es The. Pur O T 57 E2
e Cl. Wind 66 C3
erion Way. Read 86 A2
e Cl. Brac 118 C2
e End Rd. Wray 96 A3
e Field Ave. Stai 96 B1
e Park Rd. Stai 96 B2
e Rd. Stai 96 B2
e The. Stai 96 C2

Mikardo Way. Caver 59 E1
man Way. Camb 152 A3
ock Cl. Read 85 D4
one Ave. Caver 59 F3
ield Pl. Gori 34 B4
ield Rd. Gori 34 B4
ry Cl. Shin 113 F3
ester Cl. Maid 39 E3
ester Mews. Caver 59 F3
Cl. Eng G 95 D1
Cl. Silc 135 F1
Cl. Yate 149 D3
combe Way. Winn 87 F2
y Rd. Caver 58 C2
y Way. That 106 B1
gworth Ave. Caver 59 F3
gworth Gr. Brac 118 C4
gworth. Wind 66 C2
y Rd. Comp 31 E2
erial Rd. Felt 98 C4
erial Rd. Wind 67 D3
erial Way. Read 113 D4
stone Rd. Silc 135 F1
e Ray. Maid 40 A4
wood. Brac 118 B4
a Rd. Slough 43 D2
e Dell. Camb 151 E2
e Glen. Woki 142 A4
eglen. Far C 22 A4
eside. Stan 69 F3
eton. Brac 118 A3
ewood Ave. Camb 152 B3
ewood Ct. Read 85 E3
ewood Rd. Kint 101 F1
urst Way. Tad 134 C1
erman Rd. Eton 41 F1
en Rd. Read 85 D2
en Rd. Hung 100 C2
en Rd. Kint 102 A1
en Rd. Kint 127 D4
er Ring E. Harm 71 D2
er Ring W. Harm 71 D2
ngs La. Whi Wa 63 E4
itute Rd. Burn 40 C4
itute Rd. Mar 1 C1
itute Rd. Tapl 40 C4
ow Rd. Read 87 D1
ergordon Cl. Read 84 C2
erness Way. Sand 150 B4
ood Cl. Cook 19 D3
a Cres. Slough 41 F4
n Hill Rd. Kint 102 A1
e Pl. Vir W 122 C2
e Way. Winn 114 B4
ac Newton Rd. Bark 115 D1
Cl. Winn 88 A1

Isis Way. Bou E 3 D2
Isis Way. Sand 150 B4
Island Cl. Stai 96 C2
Island Farm Rd. Bur C 110 B1
Island Farm Rd. Bur C 136 C4
Island Farm Rd. Sulhd 110 B1
Island Rd. Bur C 85 F1
Island Rd. Read 85 F1
Islandstone La. Hurst 89 D3
Islet Park Dr. Maid 20 B2
Islet Park. Maid 20 B2
Islet Rd. Maid 20 B2
Ivanhoe Rd. Bark 141 D3
Iver La. Iver 44 C4
Iverdale Cl. Iver 44 B3
Iverna Gdns. Harm 71 E1
Ives Cl. Yate 149 D4
Ives Rd. Slough 44 A2
Ivy Cl. Holy 65 D4
Ivy Cres. Slough 41 F3
Ivy Dr. Light 153 D4
Ivybank. Read 57 E1
Ivydene Rd. Read 58 B1

Jack St. Newb 105 D2
Jackson Cl. Brac 118 A2
Jacob Cl. Brac 117 E4
Jacob Cl. Wind 66 C3
Jacob Rd. Sand 151 D4
James Butcher Dr. Thea 83 F2
James Cl. Mar 1 C2
James Rd. Camb 151 D1
James St. Read 85 F4
James St. Wind 67 E3
James Watt Rd. Bark 140 C4
James Way. Camb 151 D1
James's La. Bur C 111 F2
Jameston. Brac 118 B1
Jamnagar Cl. Stai 96 C1
Janson Ct. Read 85 D3
Japonica Cl. Woki 115 E2
Jaques's La. Sulhd 110 C3
Jarry Ct. Mar 1 C2
Jasmine Cl. Woki 115 E4
Jays Nest Cl. Black 150 B4
Jedburgh Cl. That 106 C2
Jefferson Cl. Slough 44 A1
Jeffries Ct. Bou E 3 D1
Jellicoe Cl. Slough 42 C2
Jenkins Hill. Bags 145 E1
Jennery La. Burn 21 E1
Jennetts Cl. Brad 81 F2
Jennings Field. Fla H 3 E4
Jennings Wharf. Wind 67 E4
Jenny's Wlk. Yate 149 F3
Jerome Cl. Mar 1 C2
Jerome Rd. Wood 87 F3
Jerrymoor Hill. Woki 141 F4
Jesmond Dene. Newb 104 C4
Jesse Cl. Yate 149 F3
Jesse Terr. Read 85 F4
Jessiman Terr. Stai 125 D2
Jevington. Brac 118 B1
Jig's La. New G 91 E1
Job's La. Swal 140 B2
Jock's La. Binf 90 C1
Joel Ct. Read 87 D2
John Childs Cl. Newb 105 D2
John Hunt Cl. That 106 C1
John Nike Way. Binf 117 E4
John Taylor Ct. Slough 42 B3
John's Cl. Ashf 98 B2
Johnson's La. Cold A 106 B4
Jonathan Hill. Newt 131 D2
Jordan Cl. Caver 59 F3
Jordan Cl. Shin 113 E1
Jordan's La. Bur C 110 C1
Jordans Cl. Stan 97 E4
Joseph Ct. New G 91 F1
Josephine Ct. Read 85 F3
Jouldings La. Swal 140 B2
Jourdelay's Pas. Eton 67 E4
Journeys End. Slough 42 C4
Jubilee Ave. Burl 119 F4
Jubilee Ave. Woki 116 A4
Jubilee Cl. Burl 119 F4
Jubilee Cl. Silc 135 F1
Jubilee Cl. Stan 97 E4
Jubilee Rd. Bish 38 A3
Jubilee Rd. Finch 141 F2
Jubilee Rd. Read 87 D3
Jubilee Sq. Read 86 A3
Judy's Pas. Eton 42 B1
Julkes La. Arbo 114 B4
Junction Rd. Ashf 98 B2
Junction Rd. Light 146 A1
Junction Rd. Read 86 C3
Juniper Dr. Maid 40 A4
Juniper Gdns. Ashf 98 C1
Juniper La. Fla H 3 E4
Juniper La. Woo G 3 E4
Juniper Rd. Mar B 1 B3
Juniper Way. Read 57 E1
Juniper. Brac 118 B1
Junnipers The. Woki 115 E2
Jupiter Way. Woki 115 F3
Justice Cl. That 106 C1
Jutland Cl. Woki 115 F3

Jutland Pl. Stai 96 B2

Katesgrove La. Read 86 A3
Kathleen Saunders Ct. Thea ... 83 F2
Kaywood Cl. Slough 43 E2
Keane Cl. Wood 87 F4
Kearsley Rd. Read 85 E3
Keates Green. Brac 118 A4
Keats Cl. Wood 87 F2
Keats La. Eton 67 E4
Keats Rd. Wood 87 F2
Keats Way. Crow 143 D3
Keats Way. Yate 149 D2
Keble Rd. Maid 39 F4
Keble Way. Crow 143 F1
Keel Dr. Slough 42 B2
Keeler Cl. Wind 66 C2
Keepers Combe. Brac 118 B2
Keepers Farm Cl. Wind 66 C2
Keepers Farm Cl. Wind 66 C3
Keepers Wlk. Vir W 122 B2
Keephatch Rd. Woki 116 C4
Keighley Cl. That 106 B1
Kelburne Cl. Winn 88 B2
Kelly Cl. Shepp 125 F4
Kelmscott Cl. Caver 58 C2
Kelpatrick Rd. Slough 41 E4
Kelsey Ave. Woki 141 F3
Kelsey Cl. Maid 39 E2
Kelsey Gr. Yate 149 F3
Kelso Mews. Caver 59 F3
Kelton Cl. Winn 87 F1
Kelvedon Way. Caver 58 C3
Kelvin Cl. Arbo 140 C4
Kelvin Rd. Newb 105 D2
Kemble Ct. Bur C 84 B2
Kemerton Cl. Bur C 84 B2
Kemp Ct. Bags 145 F1
Kempton Cl. Newb 105 E1
Kenavon Dr. Read 86 B4
Kendal Ave. Caver 59 F3
Kendal Ave. Shin 113 F3
Kendal Cl. Felt 98 C4
Kendal Cl. Slough 43 D3
Kendal Cl. That 106 B2
Kendal Dr. Slough 43 D3
Kendal Gr. Camb 152 B2
Kendrick Cl. Woki 116 B3
Kendrick Rd. Newb 130 B3
Kendrick Rd. Read 86 B3
Kendrick Rd. Slough 43 D2
Kenilworth Ave. Brac 118 B4
Kenilworth Ave. Read 85 E3
Kenilworth Ct. Slough 42 C2
Kenilworth Gdns. Stai 97 E2
Kenilworth Rd. Ashf 97 D3
Kenneally. Oak V 66 B3
Kennedy Cl. Far C 22 B3
Kennedy Cl. Maid 39 E3
Kennedy Cl. Mar 1 C2
Kennedy Cl. Newb 130 B3
Kennedy Dr. Pangb 56 C3
Kennedy Gdns. Read 87 D2
Kennel Ave. Ascot 119 F4
Kennel Cl. Ascot 92 C1
Kennel Green. Ascot 119 F4
Kennel La. Brac 91 D1
Kennel La. Cook 19 E4
Kennel La. Windl 146 B3
Kennel Ride. Ascot 92 C1
Kennel Wood. Ascot 119 F4
Kennet Cl. That 106 C2
Kennet Ct. Woki 115 F3
Kennet Pl. Bur C 111 D2
Kennet Rd. Kint 102 A1
Kennet Rd. Maid 39 F4
Kennet Rd. Newb 104 C2
Kennet Side. Newb 105 E2
Kennet Side. Read 86 B4
Kennet St. Read 86 B4
Kennet Way. Hung 100 C4
Kennett Rd. Bou E 3 D2
Kennett Rd. Slough 44 A2
Kensington Rd. Read 85 E4
Kent Ave. Slough 42 B4
Kent Cl. Stai 97 E1
Kent Cl. Woki 115 E3
Kent Rd. Read 85 E4
Kent Rd. Windl 146 B3
Kent Way. Maid 19 F1
Kentigern Dr. Brac 143 D3
Kenton Cl. Brac 118 B4
Kenton Cl. Camb 152 A1
Kenton Cl. Mar 1 C1
Kenton Rd. Read 87 E2
Kenton's La. Warg 36 B4
Kenton's La. Wind 66 C3
Kentwood Cl. Read 57 F1
Kentwood Hill. Read 57 F1
Kenwood Cl. Harm 71 D4
Kenwood Cl. Maid 39 D4
Keppel Spur. Old W 95 D4
Keppel St. Wind 67 E3
Kepple Pl. Bags 145 F2
Kernham Dr. Pur O T 57 E2
Kerria Way. Camb 153 D3
Kerris Way. Read 87 D1
Kersey Cres. Newb 104 C3

Kesteven Way. Woki 115 F3
Keston Cl. Caver 59 E1
Kestrel Ave. Stai 96 C3
Kestrel Cl. That 106 A2
Kestrel Path. Slough 21 F1
Kestrel Way. Read 85 D2
Kestrel Way. Woki 115 F3
Keswick Cl. Camb 152 B2
Keswick Cl. Read 84 B4
Keswick Ct. Slough 42 C3
Keswick Dr. Light 153 D4
Keswick Gdns. Wood 87 F3
Keswick Rd. Stai 96 A1
Ketcher Green. Binf 90 B2
Kettering Cl. Bur C 84 C2
Kevins Dr. Yate 149 F4
Keynsham Way. Crow 143 E1
Keys La. Maid 39 F3
Kibble Green. Brac 118 B2
Kibblewhite Cres. Twyf 61 E3
Kidderminster Rd. Slough 22 A1
Kidmore End Rd. Caver 59 D4
Kidmore End Rd. Maple 59 D4
Kidmore Rd. Caver 58 C3
Kidwells Cl. Maid 39 F4
Kidwells Park Dr. Maid 39 F4
Kier Park. Ascot 120 B3
Kilburn Cl. Bur C 84 B2
Kildare Gdns. Caver 59 E2
Killarney Dr. Maid 39 F4
Kilmartin Gdns. Camb 151 F1
Kilmington Cl. Brac 118 C1
Kilmiston Ave. Shepp 125 E2
Kilmore Dr. Camb 152 A2
Kilmuir Cl. Sand 150 B4
Kiln Cl. Harl 71 E4
Kiln Cl. Herm 79 E4
Kiln Dr. Herm 78 C3
Kiln La. Ascot 93 D1
Kiln La. Bou E 3 E2
Kiln La. Brac 118 A4
Kiln La. Mort 137 E3
Kiln La. Shipl 35 E1
Kiln La. Sulh 84 A4
Kiln La. Sunn 121 D2
Kiln Pl. Maid 19 D2
Kiln Rd. Caver 59 E4
Kiln Rd. Newb 105 E3
Kiln Ride Extension. Woki ... 142 A3
Kiln Ride. Upp B 54 C3
Kiln Ride. Woki 142 A4
Kiln View Rd. Read 86 B1
Kilnsea Dr. Read 87 E1
Kilnsea Dr. Winn 87 E1
Kilowna Cl. Char 61 D2
Kilross Rd. Felt 98 C4
Kimber Cl. Wind 67 D2
Kimber's Cl. Newb 104 C2
Kimber's La. Maid 39 F2
Kimberley Cl. Read 85 F3
Kimberley Cl. Slough 43 F1
Kimberley. Brac 118 B1
Kimbers Dr. Burn 21 E1
Kimbers Dr. Newb 104 B3
Kimmeridge. Brac 118 C2
Kimpton Cl. Read 113 F4
King Edward St. Slough 42 B2
King Edward VII Ave. Wind ... 67 F4
King Edwards Rd. Burl 119 F4
King Edwards Rise. Burl 92 C1
King Edwards Rise. Burl 119 F4
King George Cl. Ashf 98 C2
King James Way. Hen-O-T 35 E4
King John's Cl. Wray 68 B1
King St. Chert 124 A1
King St. Maid 39 F3
King St. Mort 137 D3
King St. Read 86 A4
King Stable St. Eton 67 E4
King Street La. Winn 88 B1
King's Ave. Ashf 98 C1
King's Cl. Stai 97 E1
King's Cres. Camb 151 E4
King's Gr. Maid 39 F3
King's Keep. Sand 143 D1
King's Meadow Rd. Read 86 A4
King's Rd. Ascot 120 B2
King's Rd. Caver 59 E1
King's Rd. Crow 143 E3
King's Rd. Eng G 96 A2
King's Rd. Hen-O-T 15 E1
King's Rd. Read 86 B4
King's Rd. Slough 42 C2
King's Rd. Wind 67 E2
King's Ride. Ascot 119 E3
King's Ride. Brac 119 E3
King's Ride. Camb 151 E4
King's Ride Park. Brac 119 E2
King's Wlk. Sand 150 C3
Kingfisher Ct. Slough 22 A1
Kingfisher Ct. Twyf 61 F2
Kingfisher Dr. Stai 96 C2
Kingfisher Dr. Wood 87 E3
Kingfisher Dr. Yate 149 D3
Kingfisher Pl. Read 86 A4
Kingham Cl. Maid 19 E2
Kingham Park. Maid 19 E2
Kings Cl. Hen-O-T 15 E1
Kings La. Cook 19 D4

Kings La. Eng G 95 D1
Kings La. Windl 146 C3
Kings Mead. Newb 130 B3
Kings Rd W. Newb 105 D1
Kings Rd. Newb 105 D1
Kings Rd. Silc 136 A1
Kings Rd. West E 153 F3
Kings Wlk. Read 86 A4
Kings Wood. Medm 17 E4
Kingsbridge Cotts. Brac 142 C4
Kingsbridge Hill. Swal 139 D3
Kingsbridge Rd. Newb 104 C1
Kingsbridge Rd. Read 86 B1
Kingsbury Cres. Stai 96 B2
Kingsbury Dr. Old W 68 A1
Kingsclear Park. Camb 151 E2
Kingsdown Cl. Read 87 D1
Kingsfield. Wind 66 B3
Kingsford Cl. Wood 88 A3
Kingsgate St. Read 86 B4
Kingsland Grange. Newb 130 C4
Kingsley Ave. Camb 151 E2
Kingsley Ave. Eng G 95 D1
Kingsley Cl. Char 61 D3
Kingsley Cl. Crow 143 D2
Kingsley Cl. Newb 105 D3
Kingsley Cl. Read 113 D3
Kingsley Dr. Mar B 1 B3
Kingsmere Rd. Brac 117 F4
Kingston Ave. Felt 71 F1
Kingston Cres. Stai 97 E2
Kingston Gdns. Read 86 B1
Kingston La. Sulhd 110 B3
Kingston Rd. Camb 152 A4
Kingston Rd. Stai 97 E1
Kingsway. Black 150 C3
Kingsway. Caver 59 F3
Kingsway. Far C 22 B3
Kingsway. Iver 44 C4
Kingsway. Stan 97 E4
Kingsway. That 106 C1
Kingswick Cl. Ascot 120 B3
Kingswick Dr. Ascot 120 B3
Kingswood Cl. Eng G 95 E2
Kingswood Creek. Wray 68 B3
Kingswood Ct. Maid 39 F3
Kingswood Rise. Eng G 95 E2
Kinross Ave. Ascot 119 F2
Kinross Cl. Ashf 98 C2
Kinross Ct. Ascot 119 F2
Kinross Dr. Ashf 98 C2
Kinson Rd. Read 58 A1
Kintbury Rd. Kint 127 E3
Kipling Cl. That 106 B3
Kipling Cl. Yate 149 E2
Kirkfell Cl. Read 57 E1
Kirkham Cl. Caver 59 F3
Kirkham Ct. Crow 143 E1
Kirkstall Ct. Bur C 84 B2
Kirkstone Cl. Camb 152 B2
Kirkwall Spur. Slough 42 C4
Kirkwood Cres. Bur C 110 C4
Kirton Cl. Read 85 D4
Kirtons Farm Rd. Bur C 85 E1
Kitsmead La. Went 122 B1
Kittiwake Cl. Wood 88 A4
Kitwood Dr. Winn 87 F1
Klondyke. Mar 1 B1
Knapp Rd. Ashf 97 F3
Knapp The. Read 85 F4
Knappe Cl. Hen-O-T 35 E4
Knighton Cl. Caver 59 D2
Knights Cl. Stai 96 B1
Knights Cl. Wind 66 B3
Knights La. Ball H 129 E2
Knights Way. Caver 59 D3
Knightsbridge Cres. Stai 97 D1
Knightsbridge Dr. Head 132 A2
Knightsbridge Rd. Camb 151 F4
Knightswood. Brac 118 A1
Knoll Cl. Let B 6 C4
Knoll Rd. Camb 151 E3
Knoll The. Pur O T 57 D1
Knoll Wlk. Camb 151 E3
Knollmead. Bur C 84 B2
Knollys Rd. Silc 135 F1
Knolton Way. Slough 43 E4
Knossington Cl. Read 87 E1
Knott La. Been 109 D2
Knowle Cl. Caver 58 B2
Knowle Gr. Went 122 B1
Knowle Green. Stai 97 D2
Knowle Grove Cl. Went 122 B1
Knowle Hill. Went 122 B1
Knowle Park Ave. Stai 97 D2
Knowle Rd. Wood 87 F2
Knowles Ave. Finch 142 C3
Knowles Ave. Finch 142 C3
Knowsley Cl. Maid 19 D1
Knowsley Rd. Sulh 109 D1
Knox Green. Binf 90 B2
Korda Cl. Stai 124 C3
Krooner Rd. Camb 151 D2
Kybes La. Shin 112 B3
Kyle Cl. Brac 118 A3

La Roche Cl. Slough 43 E2
Laburnam Pl. Eng G 95 D1
Laburnham Rd. Maid 39 F3

Name	Page	Grid
Laburnham Rd. Read	87	D1
Laburnum Cl. Mar	1	C2
Laburnum Gdns. Read	86	C1
Laburnum Gr. Newb	105	D2
Laburnum Gr. Slough	69	D4
Laburnum Rd. Chert	124	A1
Laburnum Way. Stan	97	F4
Laburnums The. Black	150	A3
Lacey Cl. Stai	96	B1
Ladbroke Cl. Wood	87	F3
Ladbrooke Rd. Slough	42	B2
Ladwell Cl. Newb	130	B3
Lady Jane Ct. Caver	59	E2
Lady Margaret Rd. Sunn	120	C1
Ladybank. Brac	118	A1
Ladymask Cl. Read	84	C2
Laffords The. Brad	82	A1
Laggan Rd. Maid	19	F1
Laggan Sq. Maid	19	F1
Laird Ct. Bags	145	F1
Lake Ave. Slough	42	B3
Lake End Rd. Burn	41	D3
Lake End Rd. Dorn	41	D2
Lake End Way. Crow	143	D2
Lake Rd. Vir W	122	A3
Lake Side The. Black	150	B2
Lakeland Dr. Camb	151	F1
Lakeside Dr. Sto P	22	C2
Lakeside Rd. Iver	69	F4
Lakeside. Brac	91	E1
Lakeside. Maid	20	A1
Lakeside. Read	87	D2
Lalande Cl. Woki	115	F3
Laleham Rd. Shepp	125	D2
Laleham Rd. Stai	96	C1
Laleham Rd. Stai	125	D2
Laleys Green. Herm	78	C2
Lamb Cl. That	106	B3
Lambert Ave. Slough	43	F2
Lambert Cres. Black	150	B2
Lambfields. Thea	83	E2
Lambly Hill. Vir W	122	B2
Lambourn Pl. Lamb	25	D2
Lambourn Rd. Newb	104	B3
Lambourne Cl. Read	84	B4
Lambourne Dr. Bags	145	E1
Lambourne Dr. Maid	39	E2
Lambourne Gdns. Read	87	E2
Lambourne Gr. Brac	118	C4
Lambridge La. Hen-O-T	15	E2
Lambridge La. Shipl	15	E2
Lambridge Wood Rd. Hen-O-T	15	D2
Lambs La. Shin	139	D4
Lambwood Hill. Shin	112	B1
Lamerton Rd. Read	86	B1
Lammas Ave. Wind	67	E3
Lammas Ct. Wind	67	E3
Lammas Dr. Wray	96	B2
Lammas Mead. Binf	90	C1
Lammas Rd. Slough	41	E4
Lamorna Cres. Read	57	E1
Lamp Acres. Newb	105	D3
Lamplighters Wlk. Read	84	C2
Lamsden Way. Bur C	111	D2
Lanark Cl. Camb	151	F1
Lanark Cl. Wood	88	A3
Lancashire Hill. New G	91	F1
Lancaster Ave. Slough	22	B1
Lancaster Cl. Hung	100	B2
Lancaster Cl. Read	86	B3
Lancaster Cl. That	106	B2
Lancaster Gdns. Read	87	D2
Lancaster Rd. Maid	39	E4
Lancaster Sq. Hung	100	B2
Lancastria Mews. Maid	39	E4
Lancelot Cl. Slough	42	A2
Lancing Cl. Read	85	E4
Lancing Rd. Felt	98	C3
Landen Ct. Woki	116	A2
Landon Way. Ashf	98	A1
Landrake Cres. Read	86	B1
Landseer Cl. Sand	150	C3
Landsend La. Char	61	D1
Lane End Cl. Shin	113	F3
Lane The. Chert	124	A3
Lane The. Chil	10	C4
Lane The. Silc	136	A1
Lane The. Vir W	122	C3
Lanes Wood. Mort	136	C3
Langborough Rd. Woki	116	B3
Langdale Cl. Maid	40	A3
Langdale Dr. Ascot	119	F4
Langdale Gdns. Read	86	C1
Langdon Cl. Camb	152	B2
Langford Cl. Caver	59	E3
Langham Pl. Eng G	95	F2
Langhams Way. Warg	36	C1
Langley Broom. Slough	43	F1
Langley Common Rd. Arbo	114	C1
Langley Common Rd. Bark	114	C1
Langley Cres. Harl	71	F4
Langley Dr. Camb	151	E3
Langley Hill Cl. Read	84	B3
Langley Hill. Read	84	B3
Langley Park Rd. Iver	44	B3
Langley Park Rd. Slough	44	B3
Langley Rd. Stai	96	C1
Langley Way. Mar	1	B1

Name	Page	Grid
Langton Cl. Maid	39	E4
Langton Way. Stai	96	B1
Langton's Meadow. Far C	22	B3
Langworthy End. Holy	65	D4
Langworthy La. Holy	65	D4
Laniver Cl. Read	87	D1
Lansdowne Ave. Slough	42	C3
Lansdowne Ct. Slough	42	C3
Lansdowne Rd. Read	84	B4
Lansdowne Rd. Stai	97	D1
Lapwing Cl. Read	84	B3
Larch Ave. Ascot	120	C2
Larch Ave. Sunn	120	C2
Larch Ave. Woki	116	A4
Larch Cl. Bur C	111	D2
Larch Cl. Camb	151	F4
Larch Cl. Slough	42	A4
Larch Dr. Wood	87	F3
Larches Way. Black	150	A3
Larchfield Rd. Maid	39	F3
Larchside Cl. Shin	113	D1
Larchwood Dr. Eng G	95	D1
Larchwood Glade. Camb	152	A4
Larges Bridge Dr. Brac	118	B3
Larges La. Brac	118	B4
Larissa Cl. Read	57	F1
Lark Ave. Stai	96	C3
Larkham Cl. Felt	98	C3
Larkings La. Sto P	23	D2
Larks-Meade. Read	87	D1
Larksfield. Eng G	95	E1
Larkspur Cl. Woki	115	E4
Larkswood Cl. Read	57	E3
Larkswood Cl. Sand	143	D1
Larkswood Dr. Crow	143	D3
Lascelles Rd. Slough	43	D2
Lashbrook Mead. Shipl	36	A2
Lashbrook Rd. Shipl	36	A2
Lassell Gdns. Maid	40	A4
Lasswade Rd. Chert	123	F1
Latham Ave. Camb	151	F1
Latimer Dr. Bur C	84	B2
Latimer Rd. Woki	116	A3
Latimer. Brac	118	A1
Latton Cl. Chil	10	C4
Laud Way. Woki	116	C3
Laud's Cl. Hen-O-T	15	E1
Launceston Ave. Caver	59	F3
Launcestone Cl. Read	87	D1
Launder Cl. Camb	151	F1
Laundry La. Sand	150	C3
Lauradale. Brac	118	A3
Laurel Ave. Eng G	95	D2
Laurel Ave. Slough	43	F2
Laurel Cl. Camb	151	E2
Laurel Cl. Stan	69	F4
Laurel Cl. Woki	115	F3
Laurel Dr. Read	57	D3
Laurence Cres. Windl	146	B2
Lauser Rd. Stan	97	E4
Lavenham Dr. Wood	87	F4
Lawford Cres. Yate	149	E3
Lawkland. Far C	22	A1
Lawn Cl. Datch	68	B4
Lawrence Cl. Woki	116	B3
Lawrence Ct. Wind	67	E3
Lawrence Gr. Binf	117	E4
Lawrence Mead. Kint	102	A1
Lawrence Rd. Read	85	D4
Lawrence Way. Sand	150	C3
Lawrence Way. Slough	41	E4
Lawrences La. Cold A	106	B3
Lawson La. Chil	10	B4
Lawson Way. Windl	121	D2
Laxton Green. Maid	39	E2
Layburn Cres. Slough	69	D4
Layland's Green. Kint	102	A1
Laytm Rise. Sulh	57	E2
Layton's La. Shepp	125	F4
Le Marchant Rd. Camb	151	F2
Lea Cl. Mar B	1	B3
Lea Cl. Read	85	D2
Lea Croft. Crow	143	D3
Lea Rd. Camb	151	D1
Lea The. Stai	96	B1
Lea The. Woki	141	F4
Leacroft Cl. Stai	97	D2
Leacroft. Stai	97	D2
Leacroft. Sunn	121	D2
Leafield Copse. Brac	118	C3
Leaholme Gdns. Slough	41	E4
Leas Dr. Iver	44	C4
Leaver Rd. Hen-O-T	15	E1
Leaves Green. Brac	118	B2
Ledbury Cl. Read	58	A1
Ledbury Dr. Bur C	84	B2
Ledger La. Holy	65	E3
Ledger's Rd. Slough	42	B2
Ledran Cl. Winn	87	E1
Lee La. Bish	18	C1
Lee La. Maid	18	C1
Leeds Rd. Slough	42	C3
Lees Cl. Maid	39	D3
Lees Gdns. Maid	39	D3
Lees Wlk. Mar	1	B1
Leeson Gdns. Eton	41	F1
Leicester Cl. Hen-O-T	15	E2
Leicester. Brac	118	C1

Name	Page	Grid
Leigh Field. Mort	136	C3
Leigh Park. Datch	68	B4
Leigh Rd. Slough	42	A3
Leigh Sq. Wind	66	B3
Leighton Gdns. Maid	20	A1
Leiston Cl. Winn	87	E1
Leiston Spur. Slough	42	C4
Leith Cl. Brac	143	D4
Lemart Cl. Read	84	C4
Lemington Gr. Brac	118	A2
Leney Cl. Woki	116	B4
Lenham Cl. Woki	88	C1
Lennox Cl. Bur C	84	A2
Lennox Rd. Read	87	D3
Lent Green La. Burn	21	D1
Lent Rise Rd. Burn	41	D4
Leopold Wlk. Read	86	B4
Leppington. Brac	118	A1
Lerwick Dr. Slough	42	C4
Lesford Rd. Read	85	F3
Leslie Southern Ct. Newb	105	D2
Lesters Rd. Cook	19	D3
Letchworth Ave. Felt	98	C4
Letcombe Sq. Brac	118	C3
Letcombe St. Read	86	A4
Leverton La. Hung	73	D1
Lewendon Rd. Newb	104	C3
Lewins Way. Slough	41	F3
Lewis Wlk. Newb	130	B3
Lewisham Way. Crow	143	E1
Lexington Ave. Maid	39	E3
Lexington Gr. Read	113	E3
Leyburn Cl. Wood	88	A4
Leycester Cl. Windl	146	A3
Leyland Gdns. Shin	113	F3
Leylands La. Stan	69	F2
Leys Gdns. Newb	104	C2
Leyside. Crow	143	D3
Lichfield Cl. Wood	87	E1
Lichfields. Brac	118	C4
Liddel Way. Ascot	119	F2
Liddell Cl. Finch	141	F2
Liddell Sq. Oak G	66	B3
Liddell. Oak G	66	B2
Lido Rd. Chil	9	F4
Lidstone Cl. Winn	114	B4
Liebenrood Rd. Read	85	E3
Lightlands La. Cook	19	F3
Lightwater Meadow. Light	153	D4
Lightwater Rd. Light	153	E4
Lightwood. Brac	118	B2
Lilac Cl. Pur O T	57	E3
Lilacs The. Woki	115	E2
Lillibrooke Cres. Maid	39	D2
Lily Hill Dr. Brac	118	C4
Lily Hill Rd. Brac	118	C4
Lima Ct. Read	85	F3
Lime Ave. Camb	152	A3
Lime Cl. Newb	105	E2
Lime Cl. Woki	115	E2
Lime Tree Rd. Gori	34	A3
Lime Wlk. Brac	118	B3
Lime Wlk. Maid	39	D4
Limecroft. Yate	149	E3
Limefield Cl. Winn	87	F2
Limerick Cl. Brac	118	A4
Limes Cl. Ashf	98	A2
Limes Rd. Eng G	95	F2
Limmer Cl. Woki	115	E2
Limmerhill Rd. Woki	115	F3
Linchfield Rd. Datch	68	B3
Lincoln Cl. Camb	152	A2
Lincoln Cl. Winn	88	A2
Lincoln Gdns. Twyf	61	E3
Lincoln Hatch La. Burn	21	E1
Lincoln Rd. Maid	39	D4
Lincoln Rd. Read	86	B2
Lincoln Way. Slough	41	E3
Lincoln Way. Stai	125	F4
Lind Cl. Read	87	D1
Lindale Cl. Went	121	F3
Lindale Rd. Crow	143	E1
Linden Ave. Maid	19	E1
Linden Cl. Holy	65	D4
Linden Cl. Newb	104	C2
Linden Cl. Woki	115	E2
Linden Ct. Camb	151	F4
Linden Ct. Eng G	95	D1
Linden Dr. Far C	22	B2
Linden Hill La. Warg	37	E1
Linden Rd. Newt	131	F2
Linden Rd. Read	86	C1
Linden Rd. Wood	87	E2
Linden Way. Shepp	125	E2
Lindenhill Rd. Brac	117	F4
Lindores Rd. Holy	65	D4
Lindsay Cl. Stan	70	B1
Lindsay Dr. Shepp	125	E2
Lindsey Cl. Woki	115	F3
Lindsey Gdns. Felt	98	B4
Lines Rd. Hurst	88	C3
Ling Dr. Light	152	C2
Lingfield Rd. Newb	131	E4
Lingholm Cl. Maid	39	E3
Lingholm Cl. Read	84	C3
Lingwood. Brac	118	B2
Link Rd. Datch	68	B3
Link Rd. Felt	98	C4
Link Rd. Newb	105	D1

Name	Page	Grid
Link The. Slough	43	D4
Link The. Yate	149	E4
Link Way. Arbo	114	C1
Link Way. Stai	97	D1
Link Way. That	106	A2
Links App. Fla H	3	D4
Links Dr. Read	85	D4
Links Rd. Ashf	97	F2
Links Rd. Fla H	3	E4
Links The. Burl	119	F4
Links Way. Fla H	3	D4
Linkscroft Ave. Ashf	98	A1
Linkswood Rd. Burn	21	E2
Linkway. Camb	151	E2
Linkway. Crow	142	C3
Linnet Ave. Newt	131	F2
Linnet Cl. Read	84	A3
Lintott Ct. Stan	70	B1
Lion Cl. Stai	124	C3
Lip La. Wick	75	F2
Lipscomb Cl. Herm	79	D3
Lipscombe Cl. Newb	104	C2
Liscombe. Brac	118	A1
Lisle Cl. Newb	104	C3
Lismore Cl. Wood	87	F2
Lisset Rd. Maid	40	A3
Lister Cl. Pur O T	57	E3
Liston Rd. Mar	1	B1
Litcham Spur. Slough	42	B4
Lithgow's Rd. Harm	71	F2
Littington Cl. Winn	114	B4
Little Bowden La. Pangb	55	F2
Little Buntings. Wind	66	C2
Little Cl. Fla H	3	D3
Little Croft Rd. Gori	34	B3
Little Croft. Yate	149	E3
Little Elms. Harl	71	E4
Little Fryth. Woki	142	B3
Little Glebe. Sonn	60	C2
Little Heath Rd. Read	84	A4
Little Hill Rd. Hurst	88	A2
Little John's La. Read	85	E4
Little La. Buck	107	E3
Little London Rd. Silc	136	A1
Little Marlow Rd. Mar	1	C2
Little Moor. Sand	143	E1
Little Oak Dr. Read	84	B4
Little Paddock. Camb	152	A4
Little Ringdale. Brac	118	C3
Little St. Read	85	F4
Little Sutton La. Iver	44	B1
Little Sutton La. Slough	69	D4
Little Vigo. Yate	149	D2
Little Woodlands. Wind	66	C2
Littlebrook Ave. Slough	21	F1
Littlebrook Ave. Slough	41	F4
Littlecote Dr. Read	85	F3
Littlecote Rd. Frox	99	D3
Littlecroft Rd. Eng G	95	F2
Littledale Cl. Brac	118	C3
Littledown Rd. Slough	42	C3
Littlefield Green. Whi Wa	63	F3
Littlejohn's La. Read	58	B1
Littleport Spur. Slough	42	C4
Littlestead Cl. Caver	59	F3
Littleton La. Stai	124	C2
Littleton Rd. Stai	98	B1
Liverpool Rd. Read	86	C4
Liverpool Rd. Slough	42	A4
Livery Cl. Read	86	B4
Livingstone Gdns. Wood	87	F3
Livingstone Rd. Newb	105	D1
Llangar Gr. Crow	143	D3
Llanvair Cl. Ascot	120	A2
Llanvair Dr. Ascot	119	F2
Lochbridge Ct. Maid	40	B4
Lochinvar Cl. Slough	42	A2
Lochinver. Brac	118	A1
Lock Ave. Maid	20	B1
Lock La. Maid	39	E2
Lock Mead. Maid	20	B1
Lock Path. Dorn	66	B4
Lock Pl. Read	86	B4
Lock Rd. Mar	1	C1
Lockbridge Rd. Bou E	3	D2
Locke Gdns. Slough	43	E2
Lockets Cl. Wind	66	B3
Lockram Rd. Bur C	111	E1
Lockram Rd. Mort	111	E1
Locks Ride. Burl	92	B1
Lockstile Mead. Gori	34	B3
Lockstile Way. Gori	34	B3
Lockton Chase. Ascot	119	E3
Loddon Bridge Rd. Winn	87	F3
Loddon Bridge Rd. Wood	87	F3
Loddon Cl. Camb	152	A3
Loddon Dr. Char	61	D4
Loddon Dr. Maid	39	E4
Loddon Hall Rd. Twyf	61	F3
Loddon Rd. Bou E	3	D2
Loddon Spur. Slough	42	C4
Lodge Cl. Eng G	95	E2
Lodge Cl. Mar	1	C1
Lodge Gr. Yate	149	F3
Lodge Rd. Hurst	88	C4
Lodge Way. Ashf	97	F3
Lodge Way. Stai	125	E4
Lodge Way. Wind	66	C2
Logan Cl. Read	84	C4

Name	Page	Grid
Lois Dr. Shepp	125	
Lomond Ave. Caver	59	
London Rd. Ascot	119	
London Rd. Ashf	97	
London Rd. Bags	145	
London Rd. Binf	117	
London Rd. Black	150	
London Rd. Blew	11	
London Rd. Brac	118	
London Rd. Camb	151	
London Rd. Datch	68	
London Rd. Eng G	95	
London Rd. Newb	105	
London Rd. Read	86	
London Rd. Read	87	
London Rd. Slough	43	
London Rd. Stan	97	
London Rd. Sunn	121	
London Rd. That	105	
London Rd. That	106	
London Rd. Twyf	61	
London Rd. Went	121	
London Rd. Windl	146	
London St. Chert	124	
London St. Read	86	
Lone Acre. Windl	146	
Long Barn La. Read	86	
Long Cl. Far C	22	
Long Cl. Kint	102	
Long Dr. Burn	21	
Long Furlong Dr. Slough	21	
Long Gr. Tad	134	
Long Grove. Buck	107	
Long Half Acre. Bish	38	
Long Hedge. Lamb	25	
Long Hill Rd. Burl	119	
Long La. Brig	28	
Long La. Cold A	78	
Long La. Cook	78	
Long La. Herm	78	
Long La. Holy	64	
Long La. Holy	64	
Long La. Pur O T	57	
Long La. Stan	97	
Long La. Sulh	57	
Long La. Wint	78	
Long Mickle. Sand	143	
Long Readings La. Slough	22	
Long's Way. Woki	116	
Longacre. Newb	130	
Longbourne Way. Chert	123	
Longbridge Rd. That	106	
Longcroft Rd. That	106	
Longdon Rd. Winn	88	
Longdown Rd. Sand	143	
Longfield Rd. Twyf	61	
Longford Ave. Felt	71	
Longford Cl. Camb	151	
Longford Way. Stan	97	
Longhurst Cl. Caver	59	
Longlands Way. Camb	152	
Longleat Dr. Sulh	57	
Longleat Gdns. Maid	39	
Longleat Way. Felt	98	
Longmead La. Burn	21	
Longmead. Ball H	106	
Longmead. Wind	66	
Longmeadow. Camb	152	
Longmoor La. Mort	137	
Longmoors. Brac	117	
Longmore Rd. Read	113	
Longridge Cl. Read	85	
Longshot Ind Est. Brac	117	
Longshot La. Brac	117	
Longside Cl. Stai	123	
Longview. Beac	3	
Longwater La. Finch	141	
Longwater Rd. Brac	118	
Longwater Rd. Finch	141	
Longworth Ave. Read	84	
Longworth Dr. Maid	20	
Lonsdale Cl. Maid	40	
Lonsdale Way. Holy	40	
Loosen Dr. Maid	39	
Lord Knyvett Cl. Stan	70	
Loring Rd. Wind	66	
Lorne Cl. Slough	42	
Lorne Pl. Read	85	
Lorne St. Read	85	
Lorraine Rd. Camb	151	
lory Hill La. Beac	3	
Losfield Rd. Wind	66	
Lossie Dr. Iver	44	
Loughborough. Brac	118	
Loundyes Cl. That	106	
Lovatt Cl. Read	84	
Love Green La. Iver	44	
Love Hill La. Slough	44	
Love La. Iver	44	
Love La. Newb	105	
Love La. Yate	149	
Love's Cl. Bur C	111	
Lovedean Ct. Brac	118	
Lovejoy La. Wind	66	
Lovel La. Wink	93	
Lovel Rd. Wink	93	
Lovelace Cl. Hurl	17	
Lovelace Rd. Brac	117	

ell Cl. Hen-O-T 35 E4
ells Cl. Light 146 A1
erock Rd. Read 58 B1
erock Rd. Read 58 B1
es Wood. Mort 136 C3
ett Gdns. Maid 20 B2
ett Rd. Stai 96 B2
rbrook Dr. Maid 39 D2
bury. Brac 118 C3
er Armour Rd. Read 57 E1
er Boyndon Rd. Maid 39 F3
er Britwell Rd. Slough 21 E1
er Broadmoor Rd. Crow . 143 E2
er Brook St. Read 86 A3
er Bungalows. Gori 34 B4
er Canes. Yate 149 D3
er Charles St. Camb 151 E3
er Church Rd. Sand 149 F4
er Cippenham La. Slough . 41 F1
er Common. Finch 140 C1
er Cookham Rd. Maid 20 B1
er Early Way (W). Read 113 F4
er Earley Way. Read 114 B4
er Earley Way. Winn 114 B4
er Early Way (N). Winn 87 F1
er Elmstone Dr. Read 57 E1
er Field Rd. Read 86 A3
er Henley Rd. Caver 59 E2
er Lees Rd. Slough 22 A1
er Meadow Rd. Read 86 B1
er Mill Field. Bags 145 E1
er Nursery. Sunn 121 D2
er Pound La. Mar 18 B4
er Rd. Chil 10 B4
er Rd. Cook 19 F4
er Ridge. Bou E 3 D2
er Sandhurst Rd. Finch . 142 B1
er Sandhurst Rd. Sand 142 B1
er Village Rd. Ascot 120 B2
er Way. That 105 F2
er Way. That 106 A2
er Wokingham Rd. Finch 142 A3
er Wokingham Rd. Finch 142 B3
es Comm. Finch 140 C1
westoft Cl. Winn 87 E1
field Cl. Light 153 E4
field Green. Caver 59 F2
field Rd. Caver 59 E3
lands Rd. Black 150 B2
lands Rd. Stan 70 B1
ry Cl. Sand 150 B3
ther Cl. Woki 115 F4
ther Rd. Woki 115 F4
wood Cl. Felt 98 B4
wood. Read 87 E1
an Dr. Stai 97 E1
as Cl. Yate 149 E3
as Green Rd. West E 153 F2
ey Cl. Sulh 57 D2
le Ave. Ashf 98 A1
kley Rd. Brac 116 A2
kley Wood. Brac 116 A2
kmore Dr. Read 87 D2
ddington Ave. Vir W 122 C4
low Cl. Newb 105 F3
low Rd. Felt 98 C3
low Rd. Maid 39 F3
low. Brac 118 A1
llow. Wind 66 C2
er Ave. Hen-O-T 15 E2
worth Rd. Read 113 E4
ds Farm Rd. Wood 88 A4
dy La. Read 85 E4
in Cl. Bags 145 E1
combe Cl. Caver 59 E2
man's Haven. Know H 37 F3
enworth Dr. Brac 91 E1
on Cl. Read 113 F4
h Gate Cl. Sand 149 F4
roft Cl. Gori 34 B4
bury. Brac 118 C3
ford Ave. Slough 42 B4
ford Rd. Read 86 C3
ney. Brac 118 A1
sey Cl. Slough 22 A1
field Ct. Caver 59 D3
l. Oak G 66 B2
e Gr. Read 57 E1
ington Ave. Yate 149 E3
ington Gate. Caver 58 C3
ch Hill La. Slough 21 F1
ch La. Lamb 25 D1
den Mews. Read 86 A2
dhurst Ave. Black 150 B3
dhurst Ave. Cook 19 F3
dhurst Cl. Brac 119 D3
dhurst Rd. Ascot 120 A3
dhurst Rd. Gori 34 B3
dhurst Rd. Read 58 A1
dwood Dr. Old W 68 A1
e Cl. Went 122 C2
e Crossing Rd. Chert 123 D2
e La. Chert 123 D1
e Rd. Went 122 C2
egrove Ave. Ashf 98 B2
eham Gdns. Maid 19 D1
eham Rd. Crow 143 D3
mouth Rd. Read 59 D1

Lynn Cl. Ashf 98 B2
Lynton Cl. Wood 87 E3
Lynton Ct. Newb 105 D2
Lynton Green. Maid 39 F4
Lynwood Ave. Eng G 95 F1
Lynwood Ave. Slough 43 E2
Lynwood Chase. Brac 91 E1
Lynwood Cres. Sunn 120 C2
Lyon Cl. That 106 C1
Lyon Rd. Crow 143 E3
Lyon Sq. Read 85 D4
Lyon Way. Camb 151 E1
Lysander Cl. Wood 88 A4
Lytham Cl. Read 85 E2
Lytham End. Sulh 57 D2
Lytham Rd. Wood 87 F4
Lytham. Brac 117 F2

Macbeth Ct. Brac 118 C4
Macdonald Rd. Light 153 D4
Mace Cl. Read 87 D1
Mackay Cl. Read 84 C2
Mackenzie St. Slough 42 C2
Macklin Cl. Hung 100 B3
Macphail Cl. Woki 116 C4
Macrae Rd. Yate 149 E3
Maddle Rd. Lamb 24 B4
Madeira Wlk. Wind 67 E3
Madingley. Brac 118 A1
Mafeking Rd. Wray 96 A3
Magdalen Rd. Stai 124 C3
Magdalene Rd. Crow 143 F1
Magill Cl. Shin 113 D1
Magna Carta La. Wray 95 F4
Magna Rd. Eng G 95 D1
Magnolia Cl. Sand 143 E1
Magnolia Gdns. Slough 43 E2
Magnolia Way. Woki 115 F3
Magpie Cl. That 106 A2
Magpie Way. Read 84 A3
Magpie Way. Slough 21 F1
Maguire Dr. Camb 152 B2
Mahonia Cl. Camb 153 D1
Maiden Erlegh Dr. Read ... 87 D2
Maiden Lane Centre. Read 87 E1
Maiden Pl. Read 87 E1
Maidenhead Bsns Cps. Whi Wa38 C1
Maidenhead Court Park. Maid 20 A2
Maidenhead Rd. Binf 89 F2
Maidenhead Rd. Cook 19 F3
Maidenhead Rd. New G 91 D3
Maidenhead Rd. Oak G 66 C4
Maidenhead Rd. Wind 66 C4
Maidens Green. Burl 92 A3
Maidensfield. Winn 88 B1
Main Dr. Burl 119 D4
Main St. Chil 10 B4
Main St. Yate 149 E4
Mainprize Rd. Brac 118 C4
Mainstone Rd. Bis 153 F2
Maise Webster Cl. Stan 97 E4
Maitland Rd. Read 85 F4
Majendie Cl. Newb 104 B3
Major's Farm Rd. Datch 68 C4
Makepeice Rd. Brac 91 D1
Maker Cl. Read 85 D2
Makins Rd. Hen-O-T 35 E4
Malders La. Cook 19 E2
Malders La. Maid 19 E2
Maldon Cl. Read 85 E3
Malet Cl. Stai 96 B1
Malham Fell. Brac 118 A3
Malham Rd. That 106 B2
Mallard Cl. Read 87 D2
Mallard Cl. Twyf 61 F2
Mallard Dr. Slough 41 F3
Mallard Row. Read 86 A4
Mallard Way. Yate 149 D3
Mallards The. Stai 124 A4
Mallards Way. Light 153 D4
Mallory Ave. Caver 59 E3
Mallow Park. Maid 19 E1
Mallowdale Rd. Brac 118 C1
Malone Rd. Wood 87 E3
Malpas Rd. Slough 43 D3
Malt Hill. Eng G 95 F2
Malt Hill. New G 91 F3
Malt House. Old W 95 D4
Malt Shovel La. Lamb 24 C2
Maltby Way. Read 114 A4
Malthouse Cl. That 106 C1
Malthouse La. Read 85 F4
Malthouse La. West E 153 F4
Maltings Pl. Read 86 A4
Maltings The. West I 10 A1
Malton Ave. Slough 42 A3
Malvern Cl. Wood 87 F3
Malvern Ct. Newb 104 C1
Malvern Rd. Harl 71 E4
Malvern Rd. Maid 19 E1
Malvern Way. Twyf 61 F1
Malyons The. Shepp 125 E2
Man's Hill. Bur C 111 E1
Manchester Rd. Read 86 C4
Mandeville Cl. Read 84 C3
Mandeville Ct. Eng G 96 A1
Mandeville Rd. Stai 124 B3
Manea Cl. Winn 114 B4
Manfield Cl. Slough 22 A1

Manners Rd. Wood 87 E4
Mannock Way. Read 88 A4
Manor Cl. Brac 91 D1
Manor Cres. Comp 31 E2
Manor Ct. Mar 1 B2
Manor Farm Ave. Shepp .. 125 D2
Manor Farm Cl. Wind 66 C2
Manor Farm Cotts. Old W .. 68 A1
Manor Farm La. Eng G 96 A2
Manor Farm La. Tidm 56 B1
Manor Farm Rd. Read 86 A1
Manor Gr. Holy 65 E3
Manor House Ct. Shepp .. 125 D1
Manor House Dr. Ascot 93 D1
Manor House La. Slough ... 68 A3
Manor La. Chiev 51 D1
Manor La. Harl 71 E4
Manor La. Herm 79 D4
Manor La. Leckh 49 E3
Manor La. Maid 39 F2
Manor La. Newb 105 F3
Manor La. That 105 F3
Manor Leaze. Stai 96 A2
Manor Park Cl. Read 84 B3
Manor Park Dr. Woki 141 F3
Manor Park Dr. Yate 149 E3
Manor Park. Frox 99 D2
Manor Pl. Newb 104 B3
Manor Pl. Stai 97 D2
Manor Rd. Ashf 98 A2
Manor Rd. Gori 34 A3
Manor Rd. Hen-O-T 35 E4
Manor Rd. Maid 39 F2
Manor Rd. Shepp 125 F1
Manor Rd. Whi-O-T 56 B4
Manor Rd. Wind 66 C3
Manor Rd. Woki 116 A1
Manor Way. Bags 145 F2
Manor Way. Eng G 95 F1
Manor Way. Holy 65 D4
Manor Wood Gate. Shipl ... 36 A2
Manorcrofts Rd. Eng G 96 A1
Manse Cl. Harl 71 E4
Mansel Cl. Slough 43 D4
Mansell Dr. Newb 130 B3
Mansfield Cl. Burl 119 E4
Mansfield Cres. Brac 118 A2
Mansfield Pl. Burl 119 E4
Mansfield Rd. Read 85 F3
Mansfield Rd. Woki 115 F3
Mansion House St. Newb . 105 D2
Mansion La. Iver 44 B3
Manston Dr. Brac 118 B2
Mant Cl. Wick 75 E3
Manygate La. Shepp 125 E2
Maple Cl. Maid 39 E3
Maple Cl. Sand 142 C1
Maple Cl. Sand 150 B3
Maple Cl. Winn 88 B2
Maple Cres. Newb 105 D2
Maple Cres. Slough 43 D3
Maple Ct. Eng G 95 D1
Maple Ct. Gori 34 A3
Maple Dr. Brac 143 E4
Maple Dr. Camb 152 C4
Maple Gdns. Read 86 C1
Maple Gdns. Stan 97 F3
Maple Gdns. Yate 149 E3
Maple La. Upp B 55 D3
Maple Rise. Mar 1 C2
Mapledene. Caver 58 C2
Mapledurham Dr. Pur O T . 57 E3
Mapledurham View. Read .. 57 E1
Mapledurham Wlk. Maid ... 19 F2
Maplin Park. Slough 44 B2
Marathon Cl. Read 88 A4
Marbeck Cl. Wind 66 B3
Marchant Ct. Mar 2 A2
Marchwood Ave. Caver 59 E4
Marconi Rd. Newb 105 D2
Marcus Rd. Read 85 D4
Mardale. Camb 152 B2
Mare La. Whi Wa 63 F2
Marefield Rd. Mar 1 B1
Marefield. Read 87 E1
Marescroft Rd. Slough 41 F4
Marfleet Cl. Winn 87 F1
Margaret Cl. Read 113 E4
Margaret Cl. Stai 97 E1
Marigold Cl. Brac 142 C3
Marina Way. Iver 44 C3
Marina Way. Slough 41 E3
Mariners La. Brad 82 A2
Marion Ave. Shepp 125 D2
Marish Wharf. Slough 43 F2
Markby Way. Winn 87 F1
Market La. Slough 44 B2
Market Pl. Brac 118 A4
Market Pl. Hen-O-T 15 E1
Market Pl. Newb 105 D2
Market Pl. Read 86 A4
Market Pl. Woki 116 B3
Market Sa. Mar 1 B1
Market Sq. Stai 96 C2
Market St. Brac 118 A4
Market St. Gree 105 F1
Market St. Maid 39 F4

Market St. Newb 105 D1
Market St. Wind 67 E3
Markham Centre The. Thea . 83 F1
Marks Rd. Woki 116 A4
Marlborough Ave. Read 86 B3
Marlborough Cl. Maid 39 D3
Marlborough Ct. Read 85 F3
Marlborough Rd. Ashf 97 F2
Marlborough Rd. Maid 39 D3
Marlborough Rd. Slough 43 F1
Marlborough Rise. Camb .. 151 F3
Marlborough Way. Read 84 A2
Marlin Ct. Mar 1 B1
Marling Cl. Read 57 E1
Marlow Bottom. Mar B 18 B2
Marlow Bridge La. Bish 18 C4
Marlow Mill. Mar 1 C1
Marlow Rd. Bish 18 C2
Marlow Rd. Bou E 2 B3
Marlow Rd. Hen-O-T 15 E2
Marlow Rd. Lit M 2 B3
Marlow Rd. Maid 39 F4
Marlow Rd. Mar B 1 A3
Marlowes The. Newb 130 C4
Marlston Rd. Herm 79 E3
Marmion Rd. Hen-O-T 35 F4
Marriott Cl. Harm 71 E1
Mars Cl. Woki 115 F3
Marsack St. Caver 59 E1
Marsh La. Herm 78 B2
Marsh La. Hung 100 A3
Marsh La. Newb 105 D2
Marsh La. Tapl 40 C3
Marsh Rd. That 106 C2
Marshall Cl. Camb 152 B2
Marshall Cl. Read 57 E2
Marshall Rd. Sand 150 B3
Marshfield. Old W 68 B3
Marshland Sq. Caver 59 D3
Marshwood Rd. Light 153 E4
Marston Way. Ascot 119 F4
Marten Pl. Sulh 57 D2
Martin Cl. Wind 66 B3
Martin Cl. Wood 87 F3
Martin Rd. Maid 39 F4
Martin Rd. Slough 42 C2
Martin Way. Camb 151 F1
Martin's Plain. Sto P 22 C2
Martindale Ave. Camb 152 B2
Martineaux La. Hurst 88 C4
Martins Cl. Black 150 B2
Martins Dr. Woki 116 A4
Martins La. Brac 118 C3
Martins The. That 106 C1
Marunden Green. Slough ... 21 F1
Maryland. Woki 141 F4
Mary Mead. New G 91 F1
Maryside. Slough 43 F2
Mascoll Path. Slough 21 F1
Masefield Rd. That 106 B2
Masefield Way. Stan 97 F4
Mason Cl. Yate 149 F3
Mason Pl. Sand 149 F4
Mason St. Read 85 F4
Masonic Hall Rd. Chert ... 123 F2
Masons Rd. Slough 41 F3
Mathisen Way. Stan 69 F3
Matlock Rd. Caver 58 C2
Matson Dr. Rem H 15 F1
Mattewsgreen Rd. Woki .. 116 A4
Matthews La. Stai 96 C2
Matthews Rd. Camb 144 B1
Maultway Cl. Camb 152 A4
Maultway Cres. Camb 152 A4
Maultway N. Camb 145 D1
Maultway The. Camb 152 B3
Mawbray Cl. Read 87 E1
Maxine Cl. Sand 143 D1
Maxwell Cl. Wood 87 F4
Maxwell Rd. Ashf 98 B1
May Cl. Sand 143 E1
May Fields. Woki 115 D4
May Tree Cl. Mar B 1 B3
May's La. Padw 136 A4
Maybrick Cl. Sand 142 C1
Maybury Cl. Slough 41 E4
Mayfair Dr. Newb 104 C1
Mayfair. Read 84 B4
Mayfield Ave. Read 84 A2
Mayfield Cl. Ashf 98 A1
Mayfield Dr. Caver 59 E2
Mayfield Gdns. Stai 96 C1
Mayfield Rd. Camb 151 D1
Mayfield Rd. Woo G 3 F3
Mayflower Dr. Yate 149 D4
Mayflower Way. Far C 22 B4
Maynard Cl. Cold A 106 B3
Mayo Rd. Shepp 125 F1
Mayow Cl. That 106 C1
Maypole Rd. Burn 41 D4
Mays Cl. Read 87 D3
Mays La. Read 87 D3
Mays Rd. Woki 116 C3
Mc Carthy Way. Woki 141 F4
McCrae's Wlk. Warg 36 B1
Mead Ave. Slough 44 A2
Mead Cl. Mar 1 C2

Mead Cl. Pease 50 B4
Mead Cl. Read 84 A3
Mead Cl. Slough 44 A2
Mead Cl. Stai 96 A1
Mead La. Chert 124 A1
Mead La. Upp B 55 F4
Mead The. Gr She 48 A2
Mead Way. Slough 41 E4
Mead Wlk. Slough 44 A2
Meadfield Ave. Slough 44 A2
Meadfield Rd. Slough 44 A2
Meadhurst Rd. Chert 124 A1
Meadow Cl. Black 150 B2
Meadow Cl. Gori 34 B3
Meadow Cl. Mar 1 C1
Meadow Cl. Moul 13 F2
Meadow Cl. Old W 68 A1
Meadow Cl. That 106 B2
Meadow Cres. Comp 31 F3
Meadow Ct. Stai 96 C3
Meadow Gdns. Stai 96 B2
Meadow La. Eton 67 E4
Meadow Rd. Ashf 98 B2
Meadow Rd. Hen-O-T 15 F1
Meadow Rd. Newb 130 C4
Meadow Rd. Read 58 C1
Meadow Rd. Read 87 E2
Meadow Rd. Slough 43 F2
Meadow Rd. Went 121 F2
Meadow Rd. Woki 116 A3
Meadow View La. Holy 64 C4
Meadow View. Mar B 1 C3
Meadow View. Stan 69 F1
Meadow View. Winn 88 B2
Meadow Walk. Woki 116 A3
Meadow Way. Bou E 3 D3
Meadow Way. Brac 91 D1
Meadow Way. Dorn 40 C2
Meadow Way. Holy 65 E3
Meadow Way. Old W 68 A1
Meadow Way. Sand 150 B3
Meadow Way. Thea 83 F2
Meadow Way. West E 153 F2
Meadow Way. Woki 116 A3
Meadowbank Rd. Light 146 B1
Meadowbrook Cl. Stan 69 F3
Meadowcroft Rd. Read 113 E4
Meadows The. Fla H 3 D4
Meadowside Rd. Pangb 56 B3
Meadway Cl. Stai 97 D1
Meadway The. Read 84 C4
Meadway. Ashf 98 A2
Meadway. Camb 151 F1
Meadway. Stai 97 D1
Meare Estate. Woo G 3 F4
Mearings The. Bur C 111 F3
Measham Way. Read 87 E1
Meashill Way. Chil 9 F4
Meavy Gdns. Read 86 A1
Medallion Pl. Maid 40 A4
Medina Cl. Woki 115 F4
Medlake Rd. Stai 96 B1
Medlar Dr. Black 150 C2
Medway Cl. That 106 A3
Medway Cl. Woki 115 F4
Melbourne Ave. Slough 42 B4
Melbourne Ave. Winn 88 B1
Melbury Cl. Chert 124 A1
Meldreth Way. Winn 87 E1
Meldrum Cl. Newb 130 B3
Melford Green. Caver 59 F3
Melksham Cl. Read 113 F4
Melling Cl. Winn 87 F2
Melody Cl. Winn 88 B2
Melrose Ave. Read 87 D3
Melrose Gdns. Arbo 114 C1
Melrose. Brac 118 A1
Melton Ct. Maid 39 F3
Melville Ave. Camb 151 F1
Membury Wlk. Brac 118 C3
Memorial Ave. Shipl 35 F1
Menair Ct. Read 87 D1
Mendip Cl. Char 61 D2
Mendip Cl. Harl 71 E4
Mendip Cl. Slough 44 A1
Mendip Rd. Brac 118 C2
Menpes Rd. Purl 57 E2
Meon Cl. Tad 135 D1
Merchants Pl. Read 86 A4
Mercia Rd. Maid 39 E2
Mercian Way. Slough 41 E3
Mercury Ave. Woki 115 F3
Mere Cl. Mar 1 C1
Mere Rd. Shepp 125 D2
Mere Rd. Slough 42 C2
Mereoak La. Shin 112 C2
Merlewood. Brac 118 B2
Merlin Cl. Slough 69 D4
Merlin Mead. Burl 92 A1
Merrifield Cl. Winn 114 B4
Merrivale Gdns. Read 86 A1
Merron Cl. Yate 149 E3
Merryhill Green Hill. Winn .. 88 B2
Merryhill Rd. Brac 118 A4
Merryman Dr. Brac 143 D3
Merryweather Cl. Woki ... 115 F1
Merrywood Park. Camb ... 151 E3
Mersey Way. That 106 A3
Merton Cl. Maid 39 E2

Merton Rd. Crow 143 F1
Merton Rd. Read 86 A1
Merton Rd. Slough 43 D2
Merton Rd. Slough 43 D2
Mervyn Rd. Shepp 125 E1
Merwin Way. Wind 66 B2
Metcalf Rd. Ashf 98 A2
Meteor Cl. Wood 88 A4
Mews The. Read 86 C3
Mey Cl. Read 84 B3
Meyrick Dr. Newb 130 B3
Michael Cl. Maid 39 E3
Michaelmas Cl. Yate 149 E2
Micheldever Way. Brac 118 C2
Michelet Cl. Light 146 A1
Micklands Rd. Caver 59 F2
Mickle Hill. Sand 143 D1
Midcroft. Slough 22 A1
Middle Cl. Camb 152 B3
Middle Cl. Newb 130 B4
Middle Gordon Rd. Camb .. 151 E3
Middle Green. Slough 43 F3
Middle Hill. Eng G 95 E2
Middle Wlk. Burn 21 E1
Middlefields. Twyf 61 F3
Middlegreen Rd. Slough 43 E3
Middlemoor Rd. Camb 151 F1
Middleton Rd. Camb 151 F4
Midway Ave. Chert 124 A3
Midway Ave. Stai 123 D3
Midwinter Cl. Read 84 C4
Milbanke Ct. Brac 117 F4
Milbanke Way. Brac 117 F4
Mildenhall Cl. Winn 87 E1
Mildenhall Rd. Slough 42 C4
Mile Elm. Mar 2 A2
Miles Pl. Camb 152 C4
Miles Way. Wood 88 A4
Milestone Ave. Char 61 D3
Milestone Cres. Char 61 D2
Milestone Way. Caver 59 E3
Milford Rd. Read 58 C1
Milkhouse Rd. Box 103 E2
Mill Bank. Kint 102 A2
Mill Cl. Woki 115 F4
Mill Farm Ave. Stai 98 C1
Mill Field. Bags 145 E2
Mill Green. Binf 90 C1
Mill Green. Caver 59 E1
Mill House La. Stai 123 D3
Mill La. Ascot 121 D4
Mill La. Brac 117 F3
Mill La. Bur C 84 C2
Mill La. Cook 20 B4
Mill La. Hen-O-T 35 F4
Mill La. Hort 69 D2
Mill La. Lamb 25 E2
Mill La. Newb 105 D2
Mill La. Padw 109 E1
Mill La. Read 86 A4
Mill La. Read 87 F2
Mill La. Sand 149 E4
Mill La. Shipl 36 A1
Mill La. Stai 123 E3
Mill La. Tapl 40 B4
Mill La. Wind 67 D4
Mill La. Winn 87 F1
Mill La. Winn 87 F1
Mill La. Yate 149 E4
Mill Mead. Stai 96 C2
Mill Pl. That 68 B3
Mill Pond Rise. Windl 146 A3
Mill Rd. Bur C 84 C1
Mill Rd. Caver 59 E1
Mill Rd. Gori 34 B4
Mill Rd. Mar 1 C1
Mill Rd. Shipl 36 A2
Mill Reef Cl. That 105 F2
Mill Ride. Burl 119 E4
Mill St. Iver 69 E4
Mill St. Slough 42 C3
Millbank Cres. Wood 87 F3
Millbank. Mar 1 C1
Millboard Rd. Bou E 3 D2
Millbridge Rd. Yate 149 D4
Millbrook Way. Stan 69 F3
Milldown Ave. Gori 34 B4
Milldown Rd. Gori 34 B4
Miller's Field. Gr She 48 A2
Millers Cl. Gori 34 A4
Millers Cl. Stai 97 D2
Millers Gr. Read 84 C2
Millers La. Old W 68 A1
Milley La. Warg 62 A4
Milley Rd. W St L 62 C3
Millfield. Lamb 25 D1
Millfield. Stai 125 E4
Millgreen La. Head 132 C2
Millins Cl. Sand 143 F1
Millmead. Woki 116 A4
Millmere. Yate 149 E4
Mills Spur. Old W 95 D4
Millside. Bou E 3 E2
Millstream La. Slough 41 F3
Millstream Way. Woo G 3 F4
Millworth La. Shin 113 F2
Milman Cl. Brac 119 D4
Milman Rd. Read 86 A3

Milner Rd. Burn 41 D4
Milsom Cl. Shin 113 F3
Milton Cl. Brac 118 A2
Milton Cl. Hen-O-T 15 E1
Milton Cl. Hort 69 D2
Milton Dr. Woki 116 A3
Milton Dr. Stai 124 C3
Milton Gdns. Stan 97 F4
Milton Gdns. Woki 116 A3
Milton Rd. Eng G 95 F2
Milton Rd. Far C 22 B1
Milton Rd. Read 87 D4
Milton Rd. Woki 116 A4
Milton Way. Twyf 61 F3
Milverton Cl. Maid 39 D2
Milward Gdns. Brac 117 E4
Mina Ave. Slough 43 E2
Minchin Green. Binf 90 B2
Minden Cl. Woki 115 F3
Minley Rd. Yate 149 F1
Minniecroft Rd. Burn 21 D1
Minorca Ave. Camb 152 C1
Minorca Rd. Camb 152 C1
Minstead Cl. Brac 118 C3
Minstead Dr. Yate 149 E3
Minster The. Read 86 A4
Minster Way. Slough 43 F2
Minsterley Ave. Shepp 125 F3
Mint Cl. Read 86 C1
Minton Cl. Read 84 C4
Minton Rise. Burn 41 D4
Mirador Cres. Slough 43 E3
Mire La. W St L 62 B2
Misborne Ct. Slough 44 A1
Mistletoe Rd. Yate 149 E2
Mitcham Cl. Read 86 A3
Mitcham Rd. Camb 145 D1
Mitcham Rd. Camb 145 D1
Mitchell Cl. Slough 42 A2
Mitchell Way. Wood 88 A4
Mitford Cl. Read 113 E4
Mitre Cl. Shepp 125 E2
Mixnams La. Chert 124 A3
Moat Dr. Slough 43 E4
Modbury Gdns. Read 86 B1
Moffatts Cl. Sand 150 A4
Moffy Hill. Maid 19 F1
Mohawk Way. Wood 88 A4
Mole Rd. Arbo 114 C3
Moles Cl. Woki 116 B3
Mollison Cl. Wood 88 A4
Molly Millar Bridge. Woki .. 116 A2
Molly Millar's La. Woki 116 A2
Monarch Cl. Felt 98 C4
Mondial Way. Stan 71 E4
Moneyrow Green. Holy 65 D4
Monk's La. Newb 130 C4
Monkey Island La. Holy 40 C1
Monks Cl. Ascot 120 A2
Monks Dr. Ascot 120 A2
Monks Hollow. Mar B 1 C3
Monks Rd. Vir W 122 B3
Monks Rd. Wind 66 B3
Monks Way. Harm 70 C4
Monks Way. Read 85 E3
Monks Way. Stai 97 E1
Monks Wlk. Ascot 120 A2
Monksfield Way. Slough 22 A1
Monkshood Cl. Woki 116 C4
Monkswood Cl. Newb 130 C4
Mons Cl. Woki 115 F3
Mons Wlk. Stai 96 B2
Monsell Gdns. Stai 96 C2
Montacute Dr. That 106 C1
Montagu Rd. Slough 68 A3
Montague Cl. Camb 151 D3
Montague Cl. Light 146 A1
Montague Rd. Slough 42 C3
Montague St. Caver 59 E1
Montague St. Read 86 B4
Montague Terr. Newb 131 D4
Monteagle La. Yate 149 D3
Monteagle La. Yate 149 E3
Montem La. Slough 42 B2
Montgomery Cl. Sand 150 A4
Montgomery Dr. Shin 113 D1
Montgomery Pl. Slough 43 E4
Montgomery Rd. Newb 130 C4
Montpelier Ct. Wind 67 E3
Montpelier Dr. Caver 59 E3
Montrose Ave. Datch 68 B4
Montrose Ave. Slough 42 A4
Montrose Cl. Ashf 98 B2
Montrose Cl. Camb 151 F1
Montrose Cl. Maid 39 D3
Montrose Rd. Felt 71 E1
Montrose Way. Datch 68 B4
Montrose Wlk. Read 84 C2
Monument Cl. Woki 130 B4
Monycrower Dr. Maid 39 F4
Moor Cl. Sand 143 F1
Moor Cl. Woki 141 F4
Moor Copse Cl. Read 87 D2
Moor End. Holy 40 B1
Moor La. Harm 70 B4
Moor La. Maid 19 F1
Moor La. Newb 104 C2
Moor La. Stan 96 B3

Moor Pl. Windl 146 A3
Moorbridge Rd. Maid 40 A4
Moordale Ave. Brac 90 C1
Moore Cl. Slough 42 A2
Moore Grove Cres. Eng G 95 F1
Moores Green. Woki 116 C4
Moores La. Eton 41 F1
Moores Pl. Hung 100 B3
Moorfield Terr. Maid 40 A4
Moorfields Cl. Stai 123 F4
Moorland Rd. Harm 70 B4
Moorlands Pl. Camb 151 D2
Moorlands Dr. Maid 38 C4
Moorlands Rd. Camb 151 D2
Moormede Cres. Stai 96 C2
Moors The. Pangb 56 B3
Moors The. That 106 B1
Moorside Cl. Camb 151 D1
Moorside Cl. Maid 19 F1
Moorside. Woo G 3 F4
Moorstown Ct. Slough 42 C2
Moray Ave. Sand 150 B4
Mordaunt Dr. Crow 143 D2
Morden Cl. Brac 118 C3
Moreau Wlk. Slough 43 F4
Morecambe Ave. Caver 58 C3
Moreland Ave. Iver 69 E4
Moreleigh Cl. Read 113 E4
Morella Cl. Vir W 122 B3
Morello Dr. Slough 43 F3
Moretaine Rd. Ashf 97 E3
Moreton Way. Slough 41 E3
Morgan Rd. Read 86 B3
Moriston Cl. Read 85 D4
Morlands Ave. Read 85 D3
Morley Cl. Slough 43 F2
Morley Cl. Yate 149 D3
Morley Pl. Hung 100 B3
Mornington Ave. Woki 141 F4
Mornington Cl. Tad 134 C1
Mornington Rd. Ashf 98 B2
Morpeth Cl. Read 86 B2
Morrice Cl. Slough 44 A1
Mortimer Cl. Read 113 E4
Mortimer La. Mort 137 E3
Mortimer Rd. Slough 43 E2
Morton Rd. Hort 69 D3
Moss Cl. Caver 59 E2
Mossy Vale. Maid 19 E1
Moulsham Copse La. Yate .. 149 D4
Moulsham La. Yate 149 D4
Mount Cl The. Went 122 B2
Mount Cl. Far C 22 B4
Mount Cl. Newb 105 D1
Mount Felix. Shepp 125 F1
Mount La. Brac 118 B4
Mount La. Chadd 49 D4
Mount Lee. Eng G 95 F2
Mount Pleasant Cl. Light 146 A1
Mount Pleasant Gr. Read 86 A3
Mount Pleasant. Brac 118 B3
Mount Pleasant. Read 86 A3
Mount Pleasant. Sand 143 D1
Mount Pleasant. Tad 135 D1
Mount Pleasant. Woki 116 A3
Mount Rd. That 106 C2
Mount St. Read 86 A3
Mount The. Caver 58 C2
Mount The. Caver 59 D2
Mount The. Read 86 B3
Mount The. Went 122 B2
Mount View. Hen-O-T 15 E1
Mountain Ash. Mar B 1 B3
Mountbatten Cl. Newb 105 E3
Mountbatten Cl. Slough 43 D2
Mountbatten Rise. Sand 142 C1
Mountfield. Gori 34 B4
Mounts Hill. Old W 93 E3
Mounts Hill. Wink 93 E3
Mountsfield Cl. Stan 70 A1
Mowbray Cres. Eng G 96 A2
Mowbray Dr. Read 85 D4
Mower Cl. Woki 116 C4
Moyleen Rise. Mar 1 B1
Muckhatch La. Stai 123 D4
Mud La. Finch 140 C1
Mud La. Pease 50 B3
Muirfield Cl. Read 86 B4
Mulberry Ave. Stan 97 F4
Mulberry Cl. Crow 143 E2
Mulberry Cl. Sand 143 E1
Mulberry Cl. Wood 87 F3
Mulberry Dr. Slough 43 F1
Mulberry Trees. Shepp 125 E1
Mulberry Way. Thea 83 F2
Mulfords Hill. Tad 135 D1
Mullins Rd. Stai 96 B2
Mulroy Dr. Camb 152 A3
Mumbery Hill. Warg 36 C1
Muncaster Cl. Ashf 98 A2
Muncaster Rd. Ashf 98 A2
Munces Rd. Mar B 1 B3
Mundaydean La. Mar 1 A2
Mundesley Spur. Slough 42 C4
Mundesley St. Read 86 A3
Munkle Marsh. That 107 D2
Munnings Dr. Sand 150 C3
Munro Ave. Wood 87 F2

Murdoch Cl. Stai 97 D2
Murdoch Rd. Woki 116 B3
Murray Ct. Ascot 120 B2
Murray Rd. Woki 116 A3
Murrellhill La. Binf 117 E4
Murrells La. Camb 151 D2
Murrin Rd. Maid 39 E4
Mushroom Castle La. Burl 92 A1
Mustard La. Sonn 60 C1
Mustard Mill Rd. Stai 96 C2
Muswell Cl. Thea 83 F2
Mutton Oaks. Brac 117 E4
Myers Way. Camb 152 B1
Myline Sq. Woki 116 B3
Myrke The. Datch 42 C1
Myrke The. Slough 42 C1
Myrtle Ave. Harm 71 F1
Myrtle Cl. Bur C 111 D2
Myrtle Cl. Light 153 D4
Myrtle Cl. Stan 69 F3
Myrtle Cl. Sulh 57 E2
Myrtle Cres. Slough 42 C3
Myrtle Dr. Black 150 B3
Myton Wlk. Thea 83 F2

Nabbs Hill Cl. Read 84 B3
Nairn Cl. Camb 151 F1
Nalderhill Rd. Box 103 D3
Napier Cl. Crow 143 E3
Napier Dr. Camb 152 A4
Napier Rd. Ashf 98 B1
Napier Rd. Crow 143 E2
Napier Rd. Harm 70 B3
Napier Rd. Maid 39 D3
Napier Rd. Read 86 B4
Napier Wlk. Ashf 98 B1
Napper Cl. Burl 119 E4
Narromine Dr. Read 84 C2
Naseby. Brac 118 A1
Nash Cl. Read 87 D2
Nash Gdns. Ascot 119 F4
Nash Grove La. Woki 115 F1
Nash Park. Binf 90 A1
Nash Rd. Slough 44 A1
Nashdom La. Burn 21 D3
Natalie Cl. Felt 98 B4
Neath Gdns. Read 84 C4
Needham Cl. Wind 66 C3
Neil Cl. Ashf 98 B2
Nell Gwynn Ave. Shepp 125 E2
Nell Gwynne Ave. Ascot 120 B3
Nell Gwynne Cl. Ascot 120 B3
Nelson Cl. Brac 118 C4
Nelson Cl. Slough 43 E1
Nelson Rd. Ashf 97 F2
Nelson Rd. Caver 59 E1
Nelson Rd. Harm 70 C3
Nelson Rd. Wind 66 C2
Nelson Way. Sand 150 C2
Nelson's La. Hurst 89 D3
Nene Rd. Harm 71 D3
Neptune Cl. Woki 115 F3
Neptune Rd. Harm 71 E3
Netherton. Brac 118 A3
Netley Cl. Caver 59 E3
Netley Rd (N). Harm 71 E3
Netley Rd. Stan 71 E3
Nettlecombe. Brac 118 C2
Nettleton Rd. Harm 71 D3
Nevelle Cl. Binf 117 E4
Neville Cl. W St L 62 C3
Neville Dr. That 106 C2
Nevis Rd. Read 57 E2
New Bath Rd. Char 61 E3
New Bath Rd. Twyf 61 E3
New Bath Rd. Warg 61 E3
New Bright St. Read 86 A3
New Ct. Mar 1 B1
New Forest Ride. Brac 118 C2
New Forest Ride. Burl 119 D3
New Ham Rd. Harm 71 E3
New Hill. Pur O T 57 E3
New Lane Hill. Read 84 C3
New Meadow. Burl 119 E4
New Mile Rd. Ascot 120 B4
New Mill Rd. Finch 140 C1
New Mill Rd. Bark 140 C2
New Park Rd. Ashf 98 B2
New Rd. Black 150 C2
New Rd. Bou E 3 D2
New Rd. Brac 118 B4
New Rd. Bur C 111 F1
New Rd. Burl 92 C1
New Rd. Cook 19 F4
New Rd. Crow 143 E3
New Rd. Datch 68 B3
New Rd. Felt 71 E1
New Rd. Harl 71 E4
New Rd. Holy 65 D4
New Rd. Hurl 17 F2
New Rd. Mar B 1 B3
New Rd. Mort 111 F1
New Rd. Newb 105 E1
New Rd. Read 86 B3
New Rd. Sand 150 A4
New Rd. Shipl 36 A2
New Rd. Slough 44 A2
New Rd. Stai 96 B2

New Rd. Stai 125
New Rd. Twyf 61
New Rd. Twyf 61
New Rd. Windl 146
New Rd. Woki 115
New Square. Felt 98
New St. Bee H 138
New St. Hen-O-T 15
New St. Stai 97
New Way. Brad 82
New Wickham La. Eng G 96
New Wickham La. Stai 96
New Wokingham Rd. Crow 143
New Zealand Ave. Shepp 125
Newall Rd. Harm 71
Newalls Rise. Warg 36
Newark Rd. Windl 146
Newark St. Read 86
Newber Way. Slough 42
Newbery Cl. Read 57
Newbewrry Cres. Wind 66
Newbold Rd. Newb 104
Newbolt Cl. That 106
Newbury Dr. Maid 40
Newbury Hill. Hamp N 52
Newbury La. Comp 31
Newbury Rd. Gr She 48
Newbury Rd. Harm 70
Newbury Rd. Herm 79
Newbury Rd. Lamb 25
Newbury Rd. Stan 71
Newbury St. Kint 102
Newbury St. Lamb 25
Newcastle Rd. Read 86
Newchurch Rd. Slough 41
Newchurch Rd. Tad 135
Newfield Gdns. Mar 1
Newfield Rd. Mar 1
Newfield Way. Mar 1
Newhaven Cres. Ashf 98
Newhaven Spur. Slough 42
Newhurst Gdns. New G 91
Newlands Ave. Caver 59
Newlands Cl. Yate 149
Newlands Dr. Maid 39
Newlands Dr. Stan 69
Newlyn Gdns. Read 86
Newlyn Rd. Harm 71
Newman Rd. Harm 71
Newmarket Cl. Winn 87
Newport Cl. Newb 105
Newport Rd. Harm 71
Newport Rd. Newb 105
Newport Rd. Read 59
Newport Rd. Slough 21
Newquay Dr. Read 87
Newton Ave. Caver 59
Newton Cl. Slough 43
Newton Ct. Old W 68
Newton La. Old W 68
Newton Rd. Harm 70
Newton Rd. Hen-O-T 35
Newton Rd. Newb 131
Newtonside Orch. Old W 68
Newtown Gdns. Hen-O-T 35
Newtown Rd. Hen-O-T 35
Newtown Rd. Newb 131
Newtown Rd. Sand 150
Newtown. Tad 87
Niagara Rd. Hen-O-T 35
Nicholas Rd. Hen-O-T 15
Nicholls. Oak G 66
Nicholson Wlk. Eng G 96
Nicholsons La. Maid 39
Nideggen Cl. That 106
Nightingale Cres. Brac 118
Nightingale Gdns. Sand 150
Nightingale La. Mort 137
Nightingale Park. Burn 21
Nightingale Rd. Wood 88
Nightingales The. Newb 131
Nightingales The. Stan 97
Nimrod Cl. Wood 88
Nimrod Rd. Harm 71
Nimrod Way. Harm 71
Nimrod Way. Read 86
Nine Mile Ride. Bark 142
Nine Mile Ride. Brac 142
Nine Mile Ride. Woki 142
Nixey Cl. Slough 43
Noakes Hill. Asham 54
Nobel Dr. Stan 71
Nobles Way. Eng G 95
Norcot Rd. Read 84
Norden Cl. Maid 39
Norden Rd. Maid 39
Norelands Dr. Burn 21
Nores Rd. Read 113
Norfolk Ave. Slough 42
Norfolk Cl. Woki 115
Norfolk Park Cotts. Maid 39
Norfolk Rd. Maid 39
Norlands La. Stai 123
Norlands. That 106
Norman Ave. Hen-O-T 15
Norman Rd. Ashf 98
Norman Rd. Caver 59
Normandy Wlk. Stai 96
Normanhurst. Ashf 98

Normans The. Slough 43 D4
Normanstead Rd. Read 84 B4
Normay Rise. Newb 130 B3
Normoor Rd. Bur C 110 C1
Norreys Ave. Woki 116 B4
Norreys Dr. Maid 39 E2
Norris Field. Chadd 49 D4
Norris La. Chadd 49 D4
Norris Rd. Read 87 D3
Norris Rd. Stai 96 C2
North Burnham Cl. Burn 21 D2
North Cl. Felt 71 E1
North Cl. Medm 17 E4
North Cl. Wind 66 C3
North Croft. Woo G 3 F3
North Dr. Sulhd 110 B4
North Dr. Went 121 F2
North End La. Went 121 D1
North Fryerne. Yate 149 E4
North Gr. Chert 123 F2
North Green. Brac 118 B4
North Green. Maid 19 F1
North Green. Slough 42 C3
North Hatton Rd. Harm 71 E3
North Links Rd. Fla H 3 D4
North Lodge Dr. Burl 119 E4
North Park. Iver 44 B2
North Rd. Burl 119 D4
North Rd. Felt 71 E1
North Rd. Maid 39 F4
North Rd. Moul 13 F2
North St. Caver 59 D1
North St. Eng G 95 F1
North St. Read 85 F4
North St. Wink 93 D3
North Standen Rd. Hung 100 A2
North Star La. Maid 39 E3
North Town Cl. Maid 19 F1
North Town Mead. Maid 19 F1
North Town Moor. Maid 19 F1
North Town Rd. Maid 19 F1
North Wlk. Thea 83 F2
Northam Cl. Winn 87 F2
Northampton Ave. Slough 42 B4
Northampton Cl. Brac 118 C3
Northborough Rd. Slough 22 A1
Northbourne Cl. Read 87 D1
Northbrook Copse. Brac 118 C2
Northbrook Rd. Caver 59 E3
Northbrook St. Newb 105 D2
Northbury Ave. Twyf 61 F3
Northbury La. Twyf 61 F3
Northcott. Brac 118 A1
Northcourt Ave. Read 86 B2
Northcroft Cl. Eng G 95 D2
Northcroft Gdns. Eng G 95 D2
Northcroft La. Newb 104 C2
Northcroft Rd. Eng G 95 D2
Northcroft Villas. Eng G 95 D2
Northcroft. Slough 22 A1
Northdean. Maid 19 F1
Northern Ave. Newb 105 D3
Northern Hts. Bou E 3 D3
Northern Perimeter Rd W. Harm70 C3
Northern Perimeter Rd. Harm . 71 E3
Northern Rd. Slough 22 B1
Northfield Ave. Shipl 36 A2
Northfield Ct. Chert 124 A4
Northfield Ct. Hen-O-T 15 E2
Northfield End. Hen-O-T 15 E2
Northfield Rd. Eton 41 F1
Northfield Rd. Maid 19 F1
Northfield Rd. Read 59 D1
Northfield Rd. Shipl 36 A2
Northfield Rd. Stai 124 A4
Northfield Rd. That 106 A2
Northfield. Light 153 D4
Northfields. Chiev 51 D2
Northfields. Lamb 25 D2
Northgate Dr. Camb 152 A4
Northington Cl. Brac 118 C2
Northmead Rd. Slough 41 F4
Northolt Rd. Harm 70 C3
Northrop Rd. Harm 70 C3
Northumberland Ave. Read 86 B2
Northumberland Cl. Stan 70 C1
Northumberland Cres. Felt ... 71 F1
Northumbria Rd. Maid 39 D2
Northview. Hung 100 B3
Northway. Newb 105 D1
Northway. That 106 B3
Northway. Woki 115 F4
Northwood Dr. Newb 105 E2
Northwood Rd. Harm 70 B3
Norton Cl. Newb 130 B3
Norton Park. Ascot 120 B2
Norton Rd. Camb 152 B3
Norton Rd. Read 86 C2
Norton Rd. Swal 139 E2
Norton Rd. Woki 116 B3
Norton Rd. Wood 87 F3
Norway Dr. Slough 43 D4
Norwich Ave. Camb 151 F2
Norwich Dr. Wood 87 E4
Norwood Cres. Harm 71 E3
Norwood Rd. Read 86 C4
Notley End. Eng G 95 E1

Notton Way. Read 113 F4
Nuffield Dr. Crow 143 F1
Nuffield Rd. Bark 140 C4
Nugee Ct. Crow 143 D3
Nugent Cl. Mar 1 C2
Nun's Acre. Gori 34 A4
Nuneaton. Brac 118 C2
Nunhide La. Sulh 83 F3
Nuns Wlk. Vir W 122 B2
Nuptown La. Burl 91 F4
Nursery Gdns. Purl 57 D3
Nursery Gdns. Shepp 125 F4
Nursery Gdns. Stai 97 D1
Nursery La. Burl 119 F4
Nursery La. Slough 43 E3
Nursery Rd. Burn 41 D4
Nursery Rd. Shepp 125 F4
Nursery Way. Wray 68 B1
Nursery Wlk. Mar 1 A1
Nut La. W St L 62 C3
Nutbean La. Swal 139 F3
Nuthatch Dr. Read 87 D2
Nuthurst. Brac 118 C2
Nutley Cl. Yate 149 E3
Nutley. Brac 118 A1
Nutmatch Cl. Stan 97 F4
Nutmeg Cl. Read 86 C1
Nutter's Hill. Swal 140 A4
Nutty La. Stai 125 E3

Oak Ave. Sand 143 E1
Oak Ave. Stai 96 B1
Oak Dr. Bur C 110 C1
Oak Dr. Wood 88 A3
Oak End Way. Padw 109 E2
Oak Farm Cl. Sand 150 B3
Oak Grove Cres. Sand 150 C3
Oak Hill. Frox 99 E2
Oak La. Eng G 95 F4
Oak La. Wind 67 D3
Oak Stubbs La. Dorn 40 C2
Oak Tree Ave. Mar 1 C2
Oak Tree Cl. Mar 1 B2
Oak Tree Cl. Tad 135 D1
Oak Tree Cl. Went 122 B2
Oak Tree Copse. Read 57 F2
Oak Tree Dr. Eng G 95 E2
Oak Tree Mews. Brac 118 B3
Oak Tree Rd. Mar 1 B2
Oak Tree Rd. Read 57 E1
Oak Tree Rd. That 106 C1
Oak Tree Wlk. Pur O T 57 E3
Oak View. Read 84 B4
Oak Way. Felt 98 C4
Oak Way. Wood 87 E2
Oakdale Cl. Read 84 B4
Oakdale Wlk. Wood 88 A4
Oakdale. Brac 118 B2
Oakdene. Bur C 111 D1
Oakdene. Sunn 120 C2
Oaken Cl. Maid 19 E1
Oaken Gr. Newb 130 B4
Oakengates. Brac 118 A1
Oakfield Ave. Slough 42 A3
Oakfield Rd. Ashf 98 A2
Oakfield Rd. Black 150 C2
Oakfield Rd. Bou E 3 D2
Oakfield Rd. Silc 135 F1
Oakhall Dr. Ashf 98 C2
Oakham Cl. Read 57 E1
Oakhurst. Maid 20 A2
Oaklands Cl. Ascot 92 C1
Oaklands Dr. Woki 116 A3
Oaklands La. Crow 143 D4
Oaklands Park. Woki 116 A2
Oaklands. Yate 149 E3
Oaklea Dr. Finch 140 C1
Oakley Cres. Slough 42 C3
Oakley Green Rd. Holy 66 A3
Oakley Green Rd. Oak G 66 A3
Oakley Rd. Camb 151 D2
Oakley Rd. Caver 58 C2
Oakley Rd. Newb 105 E2
Oakridge. West E 153 F3
Oaks Rd. Shipl 36 A2
Oaks Rd. Stan 70 B1
Oaks The. Brac 118 B4
Oaks The. Yate 149 E3
Oakside Way. Read 113 F4
Oaktree Way. Sand 143 D1
Oakway Dr. Camb 151 F1
Oakwood Rd. Brac 118 C4
Oakwood Rd. Vir W 122 B2
Oakwood Rd. Windl 146 C2
Oareborough. Brac 118 C3
Oast House Cl. Wray 95 F4
Oatlands Dr. Shepp 125 F1
Oatlands Dr. Slough 42 B4
Oatlands Rd. Shin 113 F3
Oban Ct. Slough 42 B2
Oban Gdns. Wood 87 F2
Obelisk Way. Camb 151 E2
Oberon Way. Stai 124 C3
Ockwells Rd. Maid 39 E2
Octavia Dr. Stai 97 D1
Octavia. Brac 118 A1
Oddfellows Rd. Newb 104 C1
Odell Cl. Read 114 A4

Odencroft Rd. Slough 22 A1
Odiham Ave. Caver 59 F3
Odiham Rd. Swal 139 E1
Odney La. Cook 20 A4
Ogmore Cl. Read 84 C4
Okingham Cl. Sand 143 E1
Old Barn Cl. Caver 59 D3
Old Bath Rd. Char 61 D3
Old Bath Rd. Newb 104 C2
Old Bath Rd. Sonn 60 B1
Old Bisley Rd. Camb 152 B2
Old Bracknell Cl. Brac 118 A3
Old Bracknell La E. Brac 118 A3
Old Bracknell La W. Brac 118 A3
Old Charlton Rd. Shepp 125 E2
Old Court Cl. Maid 39 D2
Old Dean Rd. Camb 151 E4
Old Elm Dr. Read 84 B4
Old Farm Cres. Read 57 E1
Old Farm Dr. Brac 91 E1
Old Ferry Dr. Wray 68 B1
Old Fives Ct. Burn 21 D1
Old Forest Rd. Read 88 C1
Old Forge Cl. Maid 40 A2
Old Forge Cres. Shepp 125 D2
Old Green La. Camb 151 E4
Old Hayward La. Hung 73 E2
Old Kiln Rd. Fla H 3 D4
Old La The. Read 85 F3
Old La. Ham M 102 C1
Old La. Head 133 F1
Old Lands Hill. Brac 118 B4
Old Marsh La. Dorn 40 C2
Old Mill La. Maid 40 B2
Old Newtown Rd. Newb 104 C1
Old Orchard The. Bur C 84 C1
Old Pasture Rd. Camb 151 F2
Old Pond Cl. Camb 151 E1
Old Portsmouth Rd. Camb 152 A3
Old Post Office La. Maid 39 F4
Old Sawmill La. Crow 143 E3
Old School Ct. Wray 95 F4
Old School La. Yate 149 E3
Old Slade La. Iver 44 C1
Old St. Chiev 51 E3
Old St. Chiev 51 F1
Old St. Herm 78 C4
Old Station La. Wray 69 D1
Old Station Way. Bou E 3 F1
Old Vicarage Way. Bou E 3 E2
Old Watery La. Woo G 3 F4
Old Welmore. Yate 149 F3
Old Whitley Wood. Read 113 E3
Old Wokingham Rd. Brac 143 E3
Oldacre. West E 153 D4
Oldacres. Maid 40 A4
Oldbury Rd. Chert 123 F1
Oldbury. Brac 117 F3
Oldcorne Hollow. Yate 149 D3
Olde Farm Dr. Black 150 A3
Oldershaw Mews. Maid 39 D4
Oldfield Cl. Read 87 D4
Oldfield Rd. Maid 40 A4
Oldhouse La. Light 146 B1
Oldmoor La. Woo G 3 F4
Oldstead. Brac 118 B2
Oldway La. Slough 41 E3
Oleander Cl. Brac 143 D4
Oliver Dr. Read 84 B3
Oliver Rd. Ascot 120 A3
Oliver's Paddock. Mar B 1 B3
Ollerton. Brac 118 A1
Omega Way. Stai 123 E4
Omer's Rise. Bur C 110 C2
One Pin La. Far C 22 B4
Onslow Dr. Ascot 93 D1
Onslow Gdns. Caver 59 E2
Onslow Mews. Chert 124 A2
Onslow Rd. Went 121 D1
Opal Way. Woki 115 F4
Opendale Rd. Burn 41 D4
Opladen Way. Brac 118 C2
Orbit Cl. Woki 141 F3
Orchard Ave. Ashf 98 B1
Orchard Ave. Harm 71 E1
Orchard Ave. Slough 41 E4
Orchard Ave. Wind 67 D3
Orchard Chase. Hurst 88 C4
Orchard Cl. Ashf 98 B1
Orchard Cl. Black 150 C1
Orchard Cl. Hen-O-T 15 F1
Orchard Cl. Herm 79 E4
Orchard Cl. Maid 40 A2
Orchard Cl. Newb 105 E3
Orchard Cl. Pur O T 57 E2
Orchard Cl. Shin 113 D1
Orchard Cl. Shipl 35 F1
Orchard Cl. West E 153 E3
Orchard Cl. Woki 116 B3
Orchard Cl. Wool 108 B1
Orchard Cl. Harm 70 B4
Orchard Ct. Read 113 E4
Orchard Dr. Bou E 3 E2
Orchard Est. Twyf 61 F3
Orchard Gate. Far C 22 B4
Orchard Gate. Sand 150 A4
Orchard Gr. Maid 39 E4
Orchard Gr. Fla H 3 D4
Orchard Hill. Windl 146 B2

Orchard Park Cl. Hung 100 B2
Orchard Pl. Woki 116 B3
Orchard Rd. Hurst 88 C4
Orchard Rd. Mort 137 D3
Orchard Rd. Old W 68 A1
Orchard St. Read 86 A3
Orchard The. Eng G 96 A2
Orchard The. Fla H 3 D4
Orchard The. Light 153 D4
Orchard The. Mar 1 C2
Orchard The. Thea 83 F2
Orchard The. Vir W 122 C2
Orchard Way. Ashf 97 F3
Orchard Way. Camb 151 D1
Orchard Way. Slough 43 F3
Orchardene. Newb 105 D2
Orchardville. Burn 21 D1
Orchids The. Chil 10 B4
Oregon Ave. Read 57 D2
Oregon Wlk. Woki 141 F4
Oriel Hill. Camb 151 E2
Oriental Rd. Ascot 120 B3
Orion. Brac 118 A1
Orkney Cl. Bur C 84 C2
Ormonde Rd. Woki 116 A3
Ormsby St. Read 85 F4
Orrin Cl. Read 85 D4
Orts Rd. Newb 105 D1
Orts Rd. Read 86 B4
Orville Cl. Wood 88 A4
Orwell Cl. Caver 58 C2
Orwell Cl. Wind 67 E2
Osborne Ave. Stan 97 F4
Osborne Dr. Light 153 D4
Osborne La. New G 91 E2
Osborne Mews. Wind 67 E3
Osborne Rd. Eng G 95 F1
Osborne Rd. Read 85 D4
Osborne Rd. Wind 67 E2
Osborne Rd. Woki 116 B3
Osborne St. Slough 42 C2
Osbourne Ct. Wind 67 E3
Osman's Cl. Burl 92 A1
Osnaburgh Hill. Camb 151 D3
Osney Rd. Maid 19 F1
Osterley Cl. Woki 116 C3
Osterley Dr. Caver 59 F3
Ostler Gate. Maid 19 E1
Oswald Cl. New G 91 F1
Otter Cl. Brac 143 D4
Ouseley Rd. Old W 95 E4
Overbury Ave. Woki 88 C1
Overdale Rise. Camb 151 F2
Overdown Rd. Read 57 E1
Overlanders End. Read 57 F2
Overlord Cl. Camb 151 E4
Owen Rd. Newb 105 D3
Owen Rd. Windl 146 B3
Owl Cl. Woki 115 F3
Owlsmoor Rd. Sand 143 E1
Owston. Read 87 E1
Oxenhope. Brac 118 A3
Oxford Ave. Burn 21 D2
Oxford Ave. Harl 71 F4
Oxford Ave. Slough 41 F4
Oxford Cl. Stai 98 B1
Oxford Rd E. Wind 67 E3
Oxford Rd. Mar 1 B1
Oxford Rd. Newb 104 B3
Oxford Rd. Read 58 A1
Oxford Rd. Sand 143 F1
Oxford Rd. Wind 67 D3
Oxford Rd. Woki 116 A3
Oxford St. Caver 59 D1
Oxford St. Hung 100 C4
Oxford St. Lamb 25 D2
Oxford St. Newb 104 C2

Pack and Prime La. Hen-O-T .. 15 E1
Padbury Cl. Felt 98 C4
Paddick Cl. Sonn 60 C2
Paddock Cl. Camb 152 A3
Paddock Cl. Whi Wa 39 D1
Paddock Hts. Twyf 61 F2
Paddock Rd. Caver 59 D1
Paddock Rd. Newb 130 C4
Paddock The. Crow 143 D3
Paddock The. Maid 19 E1
Paddock The. Newb 105 E1
Paddock The. Slough 68 A3
Paddocks The. Fla H 3 D4
Paddocks Way. Chert 124 A1
Padstow Cl. Slough 43 F2
Padstow Gdns. Read 86 A1
Padworth Rd. Mort 136 B4
Padworth Rd. Silc 136 B4
Page Rd. Felt 98 B4
Page's Croft. Woki 116 B3
Paget Dr. Mar 1 C2
Paget Rd. Maid 39 D2
Paget Rd. Slough 43 F1
Pagoda The. Maid 20 A1
Paice Green. Woki 116 B4
Paices Hill. Alde 135 D3
Paley St. Holy 64 A3
Palmer Cl. Brac 143 D4
Palmer Park Ave. Read 87 D3
Palmer School Rd. Woki 116 B3
Palmer's Hill. Asham 54 B3

Palmer's La. Bur C 111 D1
Palmer's La. Bur C 112 A2
Palmera Ave. Bur C 84 B2
Palmers Cl. Maid 39 D2
Palmerston Ave. Slough 43 D2
Palmerstone Rd. Read 87 D3
Pamber Heath Rd. Silc 135 F1
Pamela Row. Holy 65 D4
Pan's Gdns. Camb 151 F2
Panbourne Hill. Pangb 56 B3
Pangbourne Rd. Upp B 55 E2
Pangbourne St. Read 58 A1
Pankhurst Dr. Brac 118 B2
Pantile Row. Slough 44 A1
Papist Way. Chol 14 A4
Paprika Cl. Read 86 C1
Parade The. Ashf 98 C1
Parade The. Bou E 3 F2
Parade The. Wood 87 F4
Paradise Rd. Hen-O-T 15 E1
Paradise Way. Buck 108 B4
Park Ave. Camb 151 E2
Park Ave. Stai 96 B1
Park Ave. Stai 97 D1
Park Ave. That 106 B2
Park Ave. Woki 116 A3
Park Ave. Wray 68 B2
Park Cl. Wind 67 E3
Park Cres. Read 85 D3
Park Cres. Sunn 120 C2
Park Crnr. Wind 66 C2
Park Dr. Sunn 120 C2
Park End. Newb 105 D2
Park Gr. Read 85 D3
Park La. Bark 141 D3
Park La. Bee H 137 E1
Park La. Box 103 D1
Park La. Burn 21 F4
Park La. Camb 151 E3
Park La. Char 61 D2
Park La. Hort 69 D2
Park La. Newb 105 D2
Park La. Read 84 B4
Park La. Slough 43 D2
Park La. That 106 B2
Park Rd. Ashf 98 A2
Park Rd. Brac 118 B4
Park Rd. Camb 151 E2
Park Rd. Eng G 96 A2
Park Rd. Far C 22 B2
Park Rd. Hen-O-T 15 F1
Park Rd. Sand 150 B4
Park Rd. Shepp 125 D1
Park Rd. Stan 70 B1
Park Rd. Sto P 22 B2
Park Rd. Woki 116 A3
Park St. Bags 145 F2
Park St. Camb 151 E3
Park St. Hung 100 B3
Park St. Maid 39 F4
Park St. Newb 105 D2
Park St. Slough 42 C2
Park St. Stan 69 E3
Park St. Wind 67 E3
Park The. Lamb 25 D2
Park View Dr N. Char 61 D3
Park View Dr S. Char 61 D2
Park View. Bags 145 F2
Park Wall La. Upp B 34 B1
Park Way. Hung 100 C2
Park Way. Newb 105 D2
Park Wlk. Pur O T 57 E3
Parkcorner La. Arbo 114 C3
Parkgate. Burn 21 E1
Parkhill Cl. Black 150 B2
Parkhill Dr. Read 57 E1
Parkhill Rd. Black 150 B2
Parkhouse La. Read 85 E3
Parkland Ave. Slough 43 E1
Parkland Dr. Brac 118 C4
Parkland Gr. Ashf 98 A2
Parkland Rd. Ashf 98 A2
Parkside Rd. Read 85 E3
Parkside Rd. Sunn 121 D2
Parkside Rd. That 106 B3
Parkside. Hen-O-T 15 E1
Parkside. Maid 19 E1
Parkstone Dr. Camb 151 E2
Parkview Chase. Slough 41 F4
Parkview. Fla H 3 D4
Parkway Dr. Sonn 60 C2
Parkway. Camb 151 E2
Parkway. Crow 143 D3
Parkway. Mar 2 A2
Parlaunt Rd. Slough 44 A1
Parliament La. Burn 20 C3
Parnham Ave. Light 153 E4
Parry Green N. Slough 43 F1
Parry Green S. Slough 44 A1
Parsley Cl. Read 86 C1
Parson's Wood La. Far C 22 B3
Parsonage Gdns. Mar 1 C1
Parsonage La. Far C 22 B2
Parsonage La. Hung 100 B3
Parsonage La. Lamb 25 D1
Parsonage La. Wind 67 D3
Parsonage Pl. Lamb 25 D1
Parsonage Rd. Eng G 95 D2
Parsons Cl. Bark 141 D4

Parsons Cl. Newb

Parsons Cl. Newb 104 C1
Parsons Field. Sand 150 A4
Part La. Swal 139 F2
Parthia Cl. Read 86 A3
Partridge Ave. Yate 149 D3
Partridge Dr. Read 84 B3
Partridge Mead. Maid 19 F1
Paschal Cl. Camb 151 F4
Pasture Cl. Read 114 A4
Patches Field. Mar B 1 C3
Paterson Cl. Camb 152 B2
Paterson Rd. Ashf 97 E2
Pates Manor Dr. Felt 98 B4
Patricia Cl. Slough 41 F3
Patrick Rd. Caver 59 D1
Patriot Pl. Read 86 B4
Patten Ash Dr. Woki 116 C4
Patten Ave. Yate 149 E3
Pavenham Cl. Read 114 A4
Pavilion Gdns. Stai 97 D1
Pavy Cl. That 106 C1
Paxton Ave. Slough 42 B2
Payley Dr. Woki 116 C4
Paynesdown Rd. That 106 A2
Peace La. Cook 19 F3
Peach St. Woki 116 B3
Peachy Dr. That 106 C1
Peacock Ave. Felt 98 B4
Peacock La. Brac 117 E3
Peacock Rd. Mar 2 A2
Pear Tree La. Newb 105 E3
Pear Tree Rd. Ashf 98 B2
Pearce Cl. Maid 19 F1
Pearce Rd. Maid 19 F1
Pearces Orch. Hen-O-T 15 E2
Pearl Gdns. Slough 42 A3
Pearmain Cl. Shepp 125 D2
Pearman's Glade. Read 113 F4
Pearson Rd. Sonn 60 B2
Pearson Way. Wood 87 F3
Peascod Pl. Wind 67 E3
Peascod St. Wind 67 E3
Pease Hill. Buck 107 F4
Peasemore Hill. Pease 50 A4
Pebble Hill. Kint 128 A3
Peddlars Gr. Yate 149 F3
Peel Cl. Caver 59 E1
Peel Cl. Wind 67 D2
Peel Ct. Slough 42 A4
Peg's Green Cl. Read 85 D3
Pegasus Cl. That 106 A2
Pegasus Ct. Read 84 B4
Peggotty Pl. Crow 143 F1
Peket Cl. Stai 123 F4
Pelican La. Newb 105 D2
Pelican Rd. Alde 135 F1
Pell St. Read 86 A3
Pelling Hill. Old W 95 D4
Pemberton Gdns. Bur C 84 B2
Pemberton Rd. Slough 21 F1
Pembroke Broadway. Camb . 151 E3
Pembroke Cl. Ascot 120 B2
Pembroke Cl. Bur C 111 E2
Pembroke Pl. Caver 59 E2
Pembroke Rd. Newb 105 D2
Pembroke. Brac 118 A1
Pembury Ct. Harl 71 E4
Pendals Cl. Hamp N 52 C3
Pendell Ave. Harl 71 F4
Pendennis Ave. Caver 59 F3
Pendine Pl. Brac 118 A2
Pendlebury. Brac 118 A1
Pendragon Way. Camb 152 B2
Pendred Rd. Read 113 E3
Peninsular Cl. Felt 71 F1
Penling Cl. Cook 19 F3
Penn Cl. Caver 59 D3
Penn Meadow. Sto P 22 C2
Penn Rd. Datch 68 B3
Penn Rd. Farc 22 B1
Penn Rd. Newb 104 B3
Pennfields. Twyf 61 F3
Pennine Cl. Read 84 A3
Pennine Rd. Slough 42 A4
Pennine Way. Char 61 D2
Pennine Way. Harl 71 E4
Pennylets Green. Sto P 23 D3
Pennypiece. Gori 34 B4
Pennyroyal Ct. Read 86 A3
Penroath Ave. Read 85 E3
Penrose Ave. Wood 87 F3
Penrose Cl. Newb 104 C3
Penrose. Eng G 95 E1
Penry La. Shepp 125 F1
Pensford Ct. Crow 143 D4
Penshurst Rd. Maid 39 E3
Pentland Ave. Stai 125 D2
Pentland Cl. Read 84 C3
Pentland Pl. That 106 B1
Pentland Rd. Slough 42 A4
Pentlands The. Kint 102 B1
Penton Ave. Stai 123 F4
Penton Hall Dr. Stai 124 A4
Penton Rd. Stai 96 C1
Penwood Ct. Maid 39 D4
Penwood Gdns. Brac 117 E2
Penwood La. Mar 1 B1
Penwood Rd. Ball H 130 B2

Penyston Rd. Maid 39 E4
Penzance Spur. Slough 22 A1
Peppard La. Hen-O-T 35 F4
Peppard Rd. Caver 59 E3
Pepper La. Read 86 B2
Pepys Cl. Slough 69 D4
Perch Cl. Mar 18 B4
Percival Rd. Felt 98 C3
Percy Ave. Ashf 98 A2
Percy Bryant Rd. Stai 98 C1
Percy Pl. Slough 68 A3
Peregrine Cl. Brac 118 A2
Peregrine Cl. Woki 115 F3
Peregrine Rd. Shepp 125 F4
Periam Cl. Hen-O-T 35 E4
Perkins Way. Woki 116 A3
Perrin Cl. Ashf 97 F2
Perry Oaks Dr. Harm 70 B3
Perry Oaks. Brac 118 C4
Perry Way. Brac 118 C4
Perry Way. Camb 152 C4
Perrycroft. Wind 66 C2
Perryhill Dr. Sand 142 C1
Perryman Way. Slough 21 F1
Perserverance Hill. Hen-O-T ... 15 D3
Perth Ave. Slough 42 A4
Perth Cl. Wood 61 D1
Perth Trad Est. Slough 42 A4
Peterhouse Cl. Crow 143 F1
Petersfield Ave. Slough 43 D3
Petersfield Ave. Stai 97 E1
Petersfield Rd. Stai 97 E2
Petrel Cl. Woki 115 F3
Petts La. Stai 125 D3
Petworth Ave. Read 84 C2
Petworth Ct. Wind 67 D3
Pevensey Ave. Caver 59 F3
Pevensey Rd. Slough 42 A4
Pewsey Vale. Brac 118 C2
Pheasant Cl. Winn 88 B1
Pheasants Croft. Maid 39 D3
Philip Dr. Fla H 3 E4
Philip Rd. Stai 97 E1
Phillimore Rd. Caver 59 E4
Phipps Cl. Whi Wa 39 D1
Phipps Rd. Burn 41 F4
Phoebe Ct. Read 86 A3
Phoenix Cl. Woki 115 F3
Phoenix Wlk. Newb 130 B3
Phyllis Court Dr. Faw (Bu) 15 F2
Pickering. Brac 118 A3
Picket Post Cl. Brac 118 C3
Picketts La. Pangb 55 F2
Pickford Dr. Slough 43 F3
Pickins Piece. Hort 69 D3
Pickwell Cl. Wood 87 E1
Picton Way. Caver 59 D2
Pierce's Hill. Read 57 E1
Piercefield. Bur C 84 B2
Pierson Rd. Wind 66 B3
Pigeonhouse La. Wink 92 C2
Pigeons Farm Rd. Gree 131 E4
Piggott's Rd. Caver 59 E1
Pigott Rd. Woki 116 C4
Pike La. Mar 18 B4
Pike St. Newb 105 D2
Pikeshaw Way. Read 57 E1
Pimento Dr. Read 86 C1
Pincents La. Sulh 84 A3
Pinchcut. Bur C 111 D2
Pinchington La. Gree 131 D4
Pine Ave. Camb 151 E2
Pine Cl. Maid 39 D4
Pine Cl. Sand 150 C4
Pine Croft Rd. Woki 116 A1
Pine Dr. Black 150 C2
Pine Dr. Mort 136 C3
Pine Dr. Woki 142 A4
Pine Gr. Twyf 61 E3
Pine Gr. Windl 146 B2
Pine Mount Rd. Camb 151 E2
Pine Ridge. Bur C 111 D2
Pine Ridge. Newb 105 E3
Pine Way. Eng G 95 D1
Pinecote Dr. Sunn 120 C1
Pinecroft. Mar 1 B2
Pinefields Cl. Crow 143 D2
Pinehill Rd. Crow 143 E2
Pinehill Rise. Sand 150 B4
Pinehurst. Ascot 120 B2
Pinetree Ct. Caver 59 D3
Pinewood Ave. Crow 143 E3
Pinewood Cl. Tad 134 B1
Pinewood Dr. Stai 97 D2
Pinewood Gdns. Bags 145 E2
Pinewood Rd. Vir W 122 A3
Pinewood Rd. Went 122 A3
Pingewood Rd S. Bur C 112 B4
Pingewood Rd S. Shin 112 B4
Pingewood Rd. Bur C 85 D2
Pinglestone Cl. Harm 70 C4
Pink La. Burn 21 D2
Pinkneys Dr. Maid 38 C4
Pinkneys Rd. Maid 39 D4
Pinks La. Tad 134 C1
Pipers Cl. Burn 21 E1
Pipers Ct. That 107 D1
Pipers End. Vir W 122 B3
Pipers Way. That 107 D1

Pipit Cl. That 106 A2
Pippins Ct. Ashf 98 A1
Pippins The. Slough 43 F3
Pipsons Cl. Yate 149 E3
Pitch Pl. Binf 90 B2
Pitcroft Ave. Read 87 D3
Pitfield La. Mort 137 E2
Pitfield La. Silc 137 E2
Pitford Rd. Wood 88 A4
Pitt's La. Read 87 D4
Pitts Cl. Binf 90 B1
Pitts Rd. Slough 42 B3
Plackett Way. Slough 41 E3
Plaitinson Rd. Read 113 E3
Planes The. Chert 124 B1
Plantation Cl. Herm 78 C3
Plantation Rd. Camb 151 D3
Plantation Rd. Chil 9 F4
Plantation Rd. Tad 134 C1
Plantation Row. Camb 151 D3
Platt La. Lamb 45 E3
Play Platt. Thea 83 F2
Players Green. Wood 87 F3
Playhatch Rd. Caver 60 A3
Plough La. Sto P 23 D2
Plough La. Woki 116 C3
Plough Rd. Yate 149 F4
Ploughlands. Brac 117 F4
Ploughlands. Brac 117 F4
Ploughlees La. Slough 42 C3
Plover Cl. Stai 96 C3
Plover Cl. Woki 115 F3
Plowden Way. Shipl 35 F1
Plumpton Rd. Newb 105 E1
Plumtrees. Read 87 D1
Pluto Rd. Chil 9 F4
Plymouth Ave. Wood 87 E3
Plymouth Rd. Slough 41 F4
Plympton Cl. Winn 87 F2
Pococks La. Eton 42 C1
Poffley Pl. That 107 D2
Pointers Cl. Chiev 51 D1
Points The. Maid 39 D2
Polehampton Cl. Twyf 61 E2
Pollard Cl. Old W 68 A1
Pollard Gr. Camb 152 B2
Pollardrow Ave. Brac 117 F4
Polsted Rd. Read 57 E1
Pond Cl. Newb 130 B4
Pond Croft. Yate 149 F3
Pond Head La. Read 87 E2
Pond La. Herm 79 E4
Pond La. Maple 57 F4
Pond Moor Rd. Brac 118 A2
Pond Rd. Stai 96 B1
Pondside Cl. Harl 71 E4
Pool La. Slough 42 C3
Pool La. W St L 63 D3
Poole Cl. Read 85 D4
Pooley Ave. Stai 96 A2
Pooley Green Cl. Stai 96 B2
Pooley Green Rd. Stai 96 B2
Poolmans Rd. Wind 66 B2
Pope Cl. Felt 98 C4
Popes Cl. Iver 69 E4
Popes La. Cook 19 E4
Popeswood Rd. Binf 117 E4
Popham Cl. Brac 118 C2
Poplar Ave. Read 84 C3
Poplar Ave. Windl 146 A3
Poplar Cl. Stan 69 F3
Poplar Gdns. Read 86 C1
Poplar La. Hurst 62 A1
Poplar La. Winn 88 B2
Poplar Rd. Ashf 98 B2
Poplars Gr. Maid 20 A1
Poplars The. Ascot 120 A2
Poppy Dr. That 106 C2
Poppy Way. Read 84 B3
Poppyhills Rd. Camb 151 F4
Porchester Rd. Newb 105 D1
Porchester. Ascot 120 A3
Porchfield Cl. Read 87 D1
Porlock Cl. That 106 B1
Porlock Pl. Bur C 84 B2
Porter Cl. Winn 114 B4
Porter End. Newb 131 D4
Portesbery Hill Dr. Camb 151 F3
Portesbury Rd. Camb 151 F3
Portland Cl. Slough 21 E1
Portland Cres. Felt 98 B2
Portland Gdns. Read 84 B4
Portland Rd. Ashf 97 F3
Portlands. Mar 1 B1
Portlock Rd. Maid 39 E4
Portman Cl. Brac 118 A4
Portman Rd. Read 58 B1
Portnall Dr. Went 121 F2
Portnall Rd. Went 121 F2
Portrush Rd. Wood 87 E3
Portsmouth Rd. Camb 152 A4
Portway Cl. Read 85 F3
Portway. Swal 139 E1
Portway. Tad 134 C1
Post Horn Pl. Read 84 C2
Post Office La. Slough 43 E4
Post Office Rd. Ink 127 F3
Posting House Mews. Newb . 104 C2

Potley Hill Rd. Yate 149 F3
Pottery La. Ink 127 F3
Pottery Rd. Read 57 F1
Potts Pl. Mar 1 B1
Poulcott. Wray 68 C1
Pound Cres. Mar 1 B1
Pound La. Hurst 89 D3
Pound La. Lit M 2 B2
Pound La. Mar 1 B1
Pound La. Newb 104 B2
Pound La. Sonn 60 C1
Pound La. That 106 A2
Pound La. Windl 146 B2
Pound Piece. Hung 100 B3
Pound Rd. Chert 124 A1
Pound St. Newb 104 C1
Poundfield La. Cook 19 F4
Powis Cl. Maid 39 D2
Powney Rd. Maid 39 E4
Poyle La. Burn 21 D2
Poyle Rd. Stan 69 F3
Poynings. Iver 44 C1
Precincts The. Burn 21 E1
Prescott Rd. Stan 69 F3
Prescott. Brac 117 F1
Preston Rd. Read 86 A3
Preston Rd. Slough 43 E3
Preston Rd. Stai 125 D2
Prestwood. Slough 43 D4
Pretoria Rd. Chert 123 F1
Priest Ave. Woki 116 C3
Priest Hill. Caver 59 D2
Priest Hill. Eng G 95 E3
Priest La. West E 153 E3
Priestwood Ave. Brac 117 F4
Priestwood Court Rd. Brac ... 118 A4
Primrose Cl. Pur O T 57 E3
Primrose La. Winn 88 B2
Primrose Lea. Mar 1 B1
Primrose Way. Sand 143 D1
Primrose Wlk. Brac 118 A2
Prince Albert Dr. Brac 119 E2
Prince Andrew Cl. Maid 20 A1
Prince Andrew Rd. Maid 20 A1
Prince Andrew Way. Burl 119 E4
Prince Consort Cotts. Wind 67 E3
Prince Consort Dr. Brac 119 E3
Prince Dr. Sand 143 D1
Prince Hold Rd. That 106 A2
Prince of Wales Ave. Read 85 E4
Prince William Dr. Read 57 E1
Prince's La. Pease 50 B3
Prince's St. Read 86 B4
Princes Cl. Eton 41 F1
Princes Rd. Ashf 97 F2
Princes Rd. Bou E 3 E2
Princes Rd. Eng G 95 F1
Princes Rd. Felt 98 C3
Princes St. Slough 43 D2
Princess Ave. Wind 67 D2
Princess Marina Dr. Bark 115 D1
Princess Marina Dr. Bark 140 C4
Princess St. Maid 39 F3
Princess Way. Camb 151 E3
Prior Croft Cl. Camb 152 A2
Prior End. Camb 152 A3
Prior Rd. Camb 152 A3
Prior's La. Black 150 A3
Priors Cl. Maid 40 A1
Priors Cl. Slough 43 D2
Priors Court Rd. Chiev 78 C4
Priors Rd. Tad 135 D1
Priors Rd. Wind 66 B2
Priors Way. Maid 40 A1
Priors Wood. Woki 142 B3
Priory Ave. Caver 59 D4
Priory Ave. Hung 100 B2
Priory Cl. Hung 100 B2
Priory Cl. Went 121 D1
Priory Green. Stai 97 D2
Priory La. New G 91 E1
Priory Mews. Stai 97 D2
Priory Rd. Burl 119 D4
Priory Rd. Hung 100 B2
Priory Rd. Newb 105 D1
Priory Rd. Slough 41 E4
Priory Rd. Went 121 D1
Priory The. Winn 88 B2
Priory Way. Datch 68 A4
Priory Way. Harm 70 C4
Priory Wlk. Brac 118 C3
Proctors Rd. Woki 116 C3
Promenade Rd. Caver 59 D1
Promenade. Wind 67 E4
Prospect Ct. Read 85 D3
Prospect La. Eng G 95 D2
Prospect Pl. Hurl 17 F2
Prospect Pl. Newb 105 D1
Prospect Pl. Stai 96 C2
Prospect Rd. Hung 100 B3
Prospect Rd. Mar 1 B1
Prospect St. Caver 59 D1
Prospect St. Read 85 F4
Providence La. Harl 71 E4
Providence Pl. Maid 39 F4
Prune Hill. Eng G 95 E1

Radnor Rd. Rea

Prunus Cl. Camb .... 153 F
Pudding Hill. Know H .... 37 C
Pudding La. Brig .... 28 C
Puffers Way. Newb .... 104 C
Pump La N. Lit M .... 1 C
Pump La s. Lit M .... 2 A
Pump La. Shin .... 112 B
Pump La. Wink .... 120 C
Pumpkin Hill. Burn .... 21 F
Pundles La. Whi Wa .... 63 E
Purbrook Ct. Brac .... 118 C
Purcell Rd. Crow .... 143 C
Purfield Dr. Warg .... 36 C
Purley La. Pur O T .... 57 E
Purley Rise. Pur O T .... 56 C
Purley Village. Pur O T .... 57 E
Purley Way. Pangb .... 56 C
Purssell Cl. Maid .... 39 D
Purton Ct. Far C .... 22 B
Purton La. Far C .... 22 B
Putman Pl. Hen-O-T .... 15 F
Pyegrove Chase. Brac .... 118 C
Pyke's Hill. Asham .... 54 B
Pyle Hill. Newb .... 105 D
Pyrcroft Rd. Chert .... 123 F

Quadrant Ct. Brac .... 118 C
Quadrant The. Maid .... 40 A
Qualitas. Brac .... 117 F
Quantock Ave. Caver .... 59 E
Quantock Cl. Char .... 61 D
Quantock Cl. Harl .... 71 E
Quantock Cl. Slough .... 44 A
Quantocks The. That .... 106 B
Quarrington Cl. That .... 106 C
Quarry Bank. Light .... 153 D
Quarry La. Yate .... 149 F
Quarrydale Dr. Mar .... 1 C
Quartz Cl. Woki .... 115 E
Quaves Rd. Slough .... 43 E
Quebec Gdns. Black .... 150 B
Quebec Rd. Hen-O-T .... 35 F
Queen Anne's Cl. Old W .... 94 A
Queen Anne's Rd. Wind .... 67 E
Queen Annes Gate. Caver ...... 59 E
Queen Charlotte St. Wind ...... 67 E
Queen Cl. Hen-O-T .... 15 F
Queen Elizabeth Rd. Camb .. 144 B
Queen Mary Ave. Camb ...... 151 D
Queen Mary Rd. Stai .... 125 D
Queen St. Caver .... 59 D
Queen St. Chert .... 124 A
Queen St. Hen-O-T .... 15 F
Queen St. Maid .... 39 F
Queen Victoria St. Read .... 86 A
Queen's Cl. Old W .... 68 A
Queen's Cotts. Read .... 86 B
Queen's Cl. Slough .... 42 C
Queen's Dr The. Read .... 86 B
Queen's La. Maid .... 39 F
Queen's Mead. Datch .... 68 A
Queen's Pl. Ascot .... 120 A
Queen's Rd. Ascot .... 120 B
Queen's Rd. Bis .... 153 E
Queen's Rd. Caver .... 59 E
Queen's Rd. Datch .... 68 A
Queen's Rd. Eng G .... 95 F
Queen's Rd. Mar .... 1 B
Queen's Rd. Newb .... 105 D
Queen's Rd. Read .... 86 B
Queen's Rd. Slough .... 42 C
Queen's Rd. Wind .... 67 E
Queens Acre. Wind .... 67 E
Queens Cl. Burl .... 119 F
Queens Gate. Wind .... 67 E
Queens Hill Rise. Ascot .... 120 B
Queens Park Gdns. Felt .... 98 C
Queens Park Gdns. Felt .... 98 C
Queens Pine. Brac .... 118 C
Queens Rd. Camb .... 151 D
Queens Rd. Eton .... 41 F
Queens Way. Kint .... 102 A
Queens Wlk. Ashf .... 97 E
Queensborough Dr. Caver ...... 58 C
Queensbury Pl. Black .... 150 B
Queenshill Lodge. Ascot ...... 120 A
Queensmere Rd. Slough .... 43 D
Queensway. Caver .... 59 E
Queensway. Read .... 19 F
Quentin Rd. Wood .... 87 E
Quentin Way. Vir W .... 122 A
Quinbrookes. Slough .... 43 E
Quince Cl. Ascot .... 120 A
Quincy Rd. Eng G .... 96 A
Quintilis. Brac .... 117 F
Quoiting Sq. Mar .... 1 B
Quoitings Dr. Mar .... 1 B

Rackstraw Rd. Crow .... 143 E
Radbourne Rd. Bur C .... 84 B
Radcliffe Way. Brac .... 117 F
Radcot Ave. Slough .... 44 A
Radcot Cl. Maid .... 19 F
Radcot Cl. Wood .... 87 F
Radical Ride. Woki .... 141 F
Radley Bottom. Wick .... 101 E
Radnor Cl. Hen-O-T .... 15 F
Radnor Rd. Brac .... 118 C
Radnor Rd. Read .... 87 E

Radnor Way. Slough

Radnor Way. Slough 43 F1
adstock La. Read 87 D1
aedstock Rd. Read 86 C4
aeburn Way. Sand 150 B3
aeburn Way. Sand 150 B4
agdale. Bur C 111 D2
aggleswood Cl. Read 87 E2
aghill. Alde 135 E3
aglan Gdns. Caver 59 E2
agley Mews. Caver 59 E3
agmans Cl. Mar B 1 B4
agstone Rd. Slough 42 C2
ailside. Wool 108 C1
ailton Cl. Read 113 E4
ailway App. Chert 123 F1
ailway Rd. Newb 105 D1
ailway Terr. Slough 42 C3
ailway Terr. Stai 96 B2
ailways Cotts. Gori 34 B3
ainsworth Cl. Read 114 A4
ainsborough Chase. Maid 39 D2
aleigh Cl. Slough 42 A3
aleigh Cl. Wood 87 F3
aleigh Cl. Stai 97 D2
aleigh Rd. Felt 98 C3
alphs Ride. Brac 118 C3
ambler Cl. Burn 41 D4
ambler La. Slough 43 E2
ambury Cl. Brac 117 F2
amptons La. Silc 136 A3
amsay Rd. Windl 146 C3
amsbury Dr. Read 87 D2
amsey Cl. Winn 87 F1
ances La. Woki 116 C3
andall Cl. Slough 43 F1
andall Mead. Binf 90 A1
andall Cl. Black 150 C1
andolph Rd. Read 59 D1
andolph Rd. Slough 43 F2
anelagh Cres. Burl 119 E4
anelagh Dr. Brac 118 B3
ange Rd. Brac 142 A4
ange Ride. Sand 150 C4
ange View. Sand 150 C4
angewood Ave. Read 84 C2
apley Cl. Camb 151 F4
apley Green. Brac 118 B2
atby Cl. Read 87 E1
aven Cl. Yate 149 D3
avendale Mews. Stai 97 D1
avendale Rd. Shepp 125 F4
avenglass Cl. Read 87 E2
avens Field. Slough 43 E2
avensbourne Ave. Stan 97 F4
avensbourne Dr. Wood 87 F4
avenscourt. Shepp 125 F4
avenscroft Rd. Hen-O-T 15 E1
avensdale Rd. Ascot 120 A2
avensfield. Eng G 95 E1
avenshoe Cl. Bou E 3 D2
avenstone Rd. Camb 152 B3
avenswood Ave. Crow 142 C3
avenswood Ave. Finch 142 C3
avenswood Dr. Camb 152 A3
avensworth Rd. Slough 22 A1
awlinson Rd. Camb 151 D3
ay Cl. Maid 40 A4
ay Lea Cl. Maid 40 A4
ay Lea Rd. Maid 40 A4
ay Lodge Mews. Maid 40 A4
ay Mead Ct. Maid 20 B1
ay Mead Rd. Maid 40 A4
ay Mill Rd E. Maid 20 A1
ay Mill Rd W. Maid 40 A4
ay Park Ave. Maid 40 A4
ay Park La. Maid 40 A4
ay Park Rd. Maid 40 A4
ay St. Maid 40 A4
aymond Cl. Stan 69 F3
aymond Rd. Maid 39 E4
aymond Rd. Slough 44 A2
ayners Cl. Iver 69 E4
ays Ave. Wind 66 C4
aywood Cl. Harl 71 E4
eading Bridge. Read 86 A4
eading Rd. Aldw 33 D1
eading Rd. Arbo 114 B2
eading Rd. Bark 140 C2
eading Rd. Black 150 A2
eading Rd. Bur C 111 E2
eading Rd. Chol 14 A4
eading Rd. Finch 140 C2
eading Rd. Gori 34 C3
eading Rd. Hen-O-T 15 F1
eading Rd. Moul 14 A4
eading Rd. Pangb 56 B3
eading Rd. Stre 34 A3
eading Rd. Woki 115 F4
eading Rd. Wood 87 E4
ecreation La. Shin 113 D1
ecreation Rd. Bou E 3 D2
ecreation Rd. Bur C 111 D1
ecreation Rd. Read 84 C4
ecreation Rd. Warg 36 C1
ectory Cl. Brac 118 B3
ectory Cl. Far C 22 A1
ectory Cl. Newb 104 C1

Rectory Cl. Sand 149 F4
Rectory Cl. Stai 125 D3
Rectory Cl. Wind 67 D3
Rectory Cl. Woki 116 B3
Rectory La. Blew 12 C4
Rectory La. Brac 118 A3
Rectory La. Windl 146 B2
Rectory Rd. Caver 59 D1
Rectory Rd. Padw 135 F4
Rectory Rd. Stre 33 E4
Rectory Rd. Tapl 20 C1
Rectory Rd. Woki 116 B3
Red Cottage Mews. Slough 43 E2
Red Cross Rd. Gori 34 B3
Red Ct. Slough 42 C3
Red Hill. Shipl 35 D3
Red House Cl. Read 114 A4
Red La. Alde 135 E3
Red Leaf Cl. Slough 43 F3
Red Lion Way. Woo G 3 F3
Red Rd. West E 152 C4
Red Rose. Binf 90 B2
Red Shute Hill. Herm 79 D2
Redberry Cl. Caver 59 E3
Redcrest Gdns. Camb 151 F3
Reddington Dr. Slough 43 F1
Redditch. Brac 118 B1
Redfield Ct. Newb 105 E2
Redford Rd. Wind 66 B3
Redhatch Dr. Read 87 D1
Redlands Rd. Read 86 B3
Redlane Hill. Alde 135 E3
Redleaves Ave. Ashf 98 A1
Redmayne. Camb 152 B2
Redriff Cl. Maid 39 E3
Redruth Gdns. Read 86 A1
Redshots Cl. Mar 1 C2
Redvers Rd. Brac 118 A2
Redwood Ave. Wood 88 A3
Redwood Dr. Camb 152 B2
Redwood Dr. Windl 121 D2
Redwood Gdns. Slough 42 B3
Redwood Way. Read 57 E2
Redwood. Burn 21 D2
Redwood. Stai 123 F4
Reed Cl. Iver 44 C4
Reed Wlk. Newb 105 E2
Reed's Hill. Brac 118 A2
Reeds Ave. Read 86 C2
Reedsfield Rd. Ashf 98 A2
Reeve Rd. Holy 65 D4
Reeves Way. Woki 116 A2
Reform Rd. Maid 40 A4
Regency Hts. Caver 58 C2
Regent Cl. Hung 100 B3
Regent Cl. Read 87 E1
Regent Ct. Bags 145 F1
Regent Ct. Maid 39 F4
Regent Ct. Read 86 A4
Regent Ct. Wind 67 E3
Regent St. Read 86 C4
Regent Way. Camb 152 A1
Regents Pl. Sand 150 B4
Regents Wlk. Ascot 120 B1
Regis Cl. Read 113 E4
Regnum Dr. Newb 105 D3
Reid Ave. Maid 39 F3
Rembrandt Way. Read 85 F3
Rembrant Cl. Woki 115 E3
Remembrance Rd. Newb 104 C1
Remenham Church La. Rem H 16 A2
Remenham La. RemH 15 F2
Renault Rd. Wood 88 A3
Renfrew Way. Shepp 125 D1
Rennie Cl. Ashf 97 E3
Repton Cl. Maid 39 E2
Repton Rd. Read 87 E2
Restwold Cl. Read 85 E2
Retford Cl. Wood 60 C1
Retreat The. Eng G 95 F2
Retreat The. Holy 65 E4
Revel Rd. Woo G 3 E4
Revesby Cl. Maid 39 E2
Revesby Cl. West E 153 E3
Rex Ave. Ashf 98 A2
Reynards Cl. Winn 88 B1
Reynolds Green. Sand 150 B3
Rhodes Cl. Eng G 96 A2
Rhodes Cl. Winn 87 F2
Rhododendron Cl. Burl 92 C1
Rhododendron Rd. Camb 152 A1
Rhododendron Wlk. Burl 92 C1
Ribbleton Cl. Winn 87 F2
Ribstone Rd. Maid 39 D2
Ricard Rd. Old W 68 A1
Richards Cl. Harl 71 E4
Richborough Cl. Read 87 D1
Richfield Ave. Read 58 C1
Richings Way. Iver 44 C2
Richmond Ave. Felt 71 F1
Richmond Ave. Felt 98 C4
Richmond Cl. Camb 151 F1
Richmond Cres. Slough 43 D3
Richmond Cres. Stai 96 C2
Richmond Dr. Shepp 125 E2
Richmond Rd. Caver 58 C2
Richmond Rd. Read 85 E4
Richmond Rd. Sand 150 C4
Richmond Rd. Stai 96 C2

Richmond Rise. Woki 115 F4
Richmondwood. Went 121 D1
Rickman Cl. Arbo 114 C1
Rickman Cl. Brac 118 B2
Rickman Cl. Wood 87 E3
Rickman's La. Sto P 22 C3
Riddings La. Head 133 E1
Rider's La. Bur C 112 A2
Rideway Cl. Camb 151 D2
Ridge Hall Cl. Caver 58 C2
Ridge Mount Rd. Windl 121 D1
Ridge The. Cold A 106 B4
Ridge The. Upp B 55 F4
Ridge Way. Iver 44 C3
Ridge Way. Warg 36 C1
Ridgebank. Slough 41 F3
Ridgemead Rd. Eng G 95 D3
Ridgemount Cl. Sulh 57 D1
Ridgeway Cl. Light 153 D4
Ridgeway Cl. Mar 1 C2
Ridgeway The. Brac 118 B3
Ridgeway The. Caver 59 D2
Ridgeway The. Light 146 A1
Ridgeway The. Mar 1 C2
Ridgeway The. Wood 87 F3
Ridgeway. Iver 44 C3
Ridgeway. Shepp 125 F1
Riding Court Rd. Datch 68 C4
Riding Way. Woki 115 F3
Ridings The. Camb 152 A2
Ridings The. Caver 59 E4
Ridings The. Iver 44 C1
Ridings The. Maid 39 D3
Ridlington Cl. Winn 87 F1
Riley Rd. Mar 1 B1
Riley Rd. Read 84 C4
Ring The. Brac 118 B4
Ringmead. Brac 117 F2
Ringwood Cl. Ascot 120 A3
Ringwood Rd. Black 150 B3
Ringwood Rd. Read 58 A1
Ringwood. Brac 117 F1
Ripley Ave. Eng G 95 F1
Ripley Cl. Slough 43 F1
Ripley Rd. Read 58 A1
Ripon Cl. Camb 152 B2
Ripplesmere. Brac 118 B3
Ripplesmore Cl. Sand 150 A4
Ripston Rd. Ashf 98 B2
Risborough Rd. Maid 39 F4
Rise Rd. Sunn 120 C2
Rise The. Caver 59 D2
Rise The. Cold A 106 B4
Rise The. Crow 142 C3
Rise The. Crow 143 D3
Rise The. Finch 141 D1
Rise The. Woki 116 A4
Riseley Rd. Maid 39 E4
Rissington Cl. Read 57 F2
River Gdns. Maid 40 B2
River Gdns. Pur O T 57 E3
River Mount. Shepp 125 F1
River Park Ave. Stai 96 B2
River Park. Newb 105 D2
River Rd. Caver 58 B2
River Rd. Read 86 A3
River Rd. Stai 123 F4
River Rd. Tapl 40 B4
River Rd. Yate 149 D4
River St. Wind 67 E4
River View. Fla H 3 D4
River Wlk. Newb 105 E2
Riverbank. Stai 96 C1
Riverdene Dr. Winn 88 A2
Riverfield Rd. Stai 96 C1
Rivermead Ct. Bish 18 C4
Rivermead Rd. Camb 151 D1
Rivermead Rd. Wood 87 F3
Riverpark Dr. Mar 1 C1
Riversdale Rd. Read 86 C4
Riversdell Cl. Chert 123 F1
Riverside Ave. Light 153 E4
Riverside Dr. Stai 96 C2
Riverside Dr. Stai 123 F4
Riverside Pl. Stan 70 C1
Riverside Rd. Stai 96 C1
Riverside Rd. Stan 70 B1
Riverside Rd. Stan 70 C1
Riverside. Bou E 3 E2
Riverside. Eng G 96 A3
Riverside. Shepp 125 F1
Riverside. Wray 95 E4
Riverview Rd. Pangb 56 B3
Riverway. Stai 124 A4
Riverwoods Ave. Mar 2 A1
Riverwoods Dr. Mar 2 A1
Rixman Cl. Maid 39 E3
Rixon Cl. Slough 43 F4
Road Hill. Box 76 B2
Roashill La. Dorn 41 E1
Roberts Cl. Stan 70 B1
Roberts Rd. Camb 151 D3
Roberts Rd. Sand 151 D3
Roberts Way. Eng G 95 E1
Robertsfield. That 105 F2
Robertson Cl. Newb 131 D4
Robin Cl. Bur C 111 D2

Robin Cl. Bur C 111 D2
Robin Hill Dr. Camb 152 A2
Robin Hood Cl. Slough 41 F3
Robin Hood Way. Winn 88 B2
Robin La. Sand 143 E1
Robin Way. Read 84 A3
Robin Way. Stai 96 C3
Robin's Bow. Camb 151 D2
Robindale Ave. Read 87 E2
Robinhood La. Winn 88 B2
Robins Cl. Newb 130 C4
Robins Grove Cres. Yate 149 D3
Robins Hill. Ink 127 F3
Robinson Ct. Read 87 D1
Rochester Ave. Felt 98 C3
Rochester Ave. Wood 60 C1
Rochford Way. Burn 41 D4
Rochfords Gdns. Slough 43 E3
Rockbourne Gdns. Read 58 A1
Rockfield Way. Sand 150 B4
Rockfield. Lamb 25 D1
Rockingham Rd. Newb 104 C1
Rockmoor La. Link 147 D1
Rodney Way. Stan 69 F3
Rodway Rd. Read 57 F1
Routh Ct. Felt 98 B4
Routh La. Read 84 C3
Row La. Caver 59 F4
Rowallan Cl. Caver 59 E3
Rowan Ave. Stai 96 B2
Rowan Cl. Camb 151 F4
Rowan Cl. Woki 115 F3
Rowan Dr. Brac 143 E4
Rowan Dr. Crow 143 E3
Rowan Dr. Newb 105 D3
Rowan Dr. Wood 87 F4
Rowan Way. Bur C 111 D3
Rowan Way. Slough 42 A4
Rowanhurst Dr. Far C 22 B4
Rowans Cl. Black 150 C1
Rowans The. Ashf 98 C2
Rowcroft Rd. Arbo 140 C4
Rowe Ct. Read 85 D4
Rowland Cl. Wind 66 B2
Rowland Way. Stai 98 B1
Rowley Cl. Brac 118 C3
Rowley La. Sto P 23 E2
Rowley Rd. Read 86 A2
Roxburgh Cl. Camb 152 B2
Roxford Cl. Shepp 125 F2
Roxwell Cl. Slough 41 F3
Roy Cl. Herm 78 C3
Royal Ave. Read 84 B3
Royal Victoria Gdns. Ascot 120 A2
Roycroft La. Woki 141 F4
Royston Cl. Read 84 C4
Royston Way. Slough 41 E4
Ruby Cl. Slough 42 A2
Ruby Cl. Woki 115 F4
Rudd Hall Rise. Camb 151 F2
Ruddlesway. Wind 66 B3
Rudland Cl. That 106 B1
Rudsworth Cl. Iver 69 E4
Rugby Cl. Sand 143 F1
Ruggles-Brise Rd. Ashf 97 E2
Rumsey's La. Blew 12 A4
Runnemede Rd. Eng G 96 A2
Runnymede Ct. Eng G 96 A2
Rupert Cl. Hen-O-T 15 F2
Rupert Rd. Newb 130 C4
Rupert St. Read 86 B4
Rupert's La. Hen-O-T 15 F2
Ruscombe Gdns. Datch 68 A4
Ruscombe Park. Twyf 61 F3
Ruscombe Rd. Twyf 61 F3
Ruscombe Way. Felt 98 C4
Rushall Cl. Read 113 F4
Rusham Park Ave. Eng G 95 F1
Rusham Rd. Eng G 95 F1
Rushbrook Rd. Wood 87 E4
Rushburn. Woo G 3 F3
Rushden Dr. Read 86 C1
Rushes The. Maid 40 A3
Rushes The. Mar 18 B4
Rushey Way. Read 87 E1
Rushington Ave. Maid 39 F3
Rushmoor Gdns. Bur C 84 A2
Ruskin Ave. Felt 71 F1
Ruskin Rd. Stai 96 C1
Ruskin Way. Woki 115 F3
Russell Cl. Maid 39 F4
Russell Dr. Stan 70 B1
Russell Rd. Maple 58 B4
Russell Rd. Newb 104 C1
Russell Rd. Shepp 125 E1
Russell St. Read 85 F4
Russell St. Wind 67 E3
Russell Way. Winn 88 A1
Russet Cl. Stan 69 F1
Russet Gdns. Camb 151 E2
Russet Glade. Bur C 111 D1
Russet Glade. Caver 59 E4
Russet Rd. Maid 39 E2
Russington Rd. Shepp 125 E2
Russley Green. Woki 116 A1
Rustington Cl. Read 87 D1
Ruston Way. Ascot 119 F4
Rutherford Wlk. Read 84 A4

Rutherford Wlk. Read

Rossett Cl. Brac 118 A3
Rossey Pl. Eton 42 B1
Rossington Pl. Read 113 E4
Rossiter Cl. Slough 43 F1
Rosslyn Cl. Ashf 98 C1
Rother Cl. Sand 150 B4
Rotherfield Ave. Woki 116 A4
Rotherfield Cl. Thea 83 F2
Rotherfield Rd. Hen-O-T 35 F4
Rotherfield Rd. Caver 59 D2
Rothwell Gdns. Wood 61 D1
Rothwell Wlk. Caver 59 E1
Rotton Row Hill. Brad 81 F2
Roughgrove Copse. Binf 90 A1
Rounce La. West E 153 E3
Round Cl. Yate 149 F3
Round End. Newb 130 B3
Roundabout La. Woki 115 E4
Roundfield. Buck 107 D3
Roundhead Rd. Thea 83 D2
Roundway Cl. Camb 152 B3
Roundway. Camb 152 B3
Roundway. Stai 96 B2

Rutherwyk Rd. Chert 123 F1
Rutland Pl. Maid 39 E3
Rutland Rd. Maid 39 E3
Rutland Rd. Read 85 E4
Ruxbury Rd. Chert 123 E2
Ryan Mount. Sand 150 A4
Ryans Mount. Mar 1 B1
Rycroft. Wind 66 C2
Rydal Ave. Read 57 F1
Rydal Cl. Camb 152 B3
Rydal Dr. That 106 A2
Rydal Pl. Light 153 D4
Rydal Way. Stai 96 A1
Ryde The. Stai 124 A4
Rydings. Wind 66 C2
Rye Cl. Brac 118 B4
Rye Cl. Maid 39 D2
Rye Cl. New G 91 F1
Rye Ct. Slough 43 D2
Rye Gr. Light 146 C1
Ryecroft Cl. Warg 36 C1
Ryecroft Cl. Wood 60 C1
Ryecroft Gdns. Black 150 C2
Ryehurst La. Binf 90 C3
Ryeish La. Shin 113 E2
Ryemead La. Wink 92 B3
Ryhill Way. Read 113 F4
Ryland Cl. Felt 98 C2
Rylstone Cl. Maid 39 E2
Rylstone Rd. Read 85 E4
Ryvers Rd. Slough 43 F2
Ryves Ave. Yate 149 D3

Sackville St. Read 86 A4
Saddleback Rd. Camb 151 E4
Saddlewood. Camb 151 E2
Sadler's La. Woki 115 E4
Sadlers Ct. Woki 88 B1
Sadlers Rd. Ink 127 D3
Saffron Cl. Datch 68 A3
Saffron Cl. Newb 104 C2
Saffron Cl. Read 87 E2
Saffron Rd. Brac 118 A3
Sage Cl. Read 87 D1
Sage Rd. Sulh 57 E2
Sagecroft Rd. That 106 B3
St Adrian's Cl. Maid 39 D2
St Agnes Terr. Lamb 25 D1
St Albans St. Wind 67 E3
St Andrew's Ave. Wind 66 C3
St Andrew's Cl. Old W 68 A1
St Andrew's Cl. Shepp 125 E3
St Andrew's Cl. Wray 68 C1
St Andrew's Cres. Wind 66 C3
St Andrew's Rd. Caver 58 C2
St Andrew's Rd. Hen-O-T 35 E4
St Andrew's Way. Slough 41 E3
St Andrews Cl. Woki 142 C4
St Andrews. Brac 117 F2
St Ann's Cl. Chert 123 F2
St Ann's Hill Rd. Chert 123 E2
St Ann's Rd. Chert 123 F2
St Anne's Cl. Hen-O-T 15 E1
St Anne's Rd. Caver 59 D1
St Annes Ave. Stan 97 E4
St Annes Glade. Bags 145 E2
St Anthony's Way. Harm 71 F2
St Anthonys Cl. Brac 118 A4
St Barnabas Rd. Caver 59 D3
St Barnabas Rd. Read 86 C1
St Bartholomews Rd. Read 86 C4
St Bernards Rd. Slough 43 E2
St Birinus Rd. Read 84 B3
St Catherine's Cl. Woki 88 A1
St Catherines Rd. Camb 151 F1
St Chad's Rd. Maid 39 D2
St Christophers Gdns. Burl 119 E4
St Clements Cl. Wood 87 E1
St Columba's Cl. Maid 39 D2
St David's Cl. Caver 58 C3
St David's Cl. Maid 39 D2
St David's Rd. Newb 104 C1
St Donats Pl. Newb 105 D1
St Dunstan's Rd. Felt 98 C3
St Edward's Rd. Read 87 D3
St Elizabeth Cl. Read 113 D4
St Elmo Cres. Far C 22 B1
St George's Ave. Newb 104 C1
St George's Cl. Wind 66 C3
St George's Cres. Slough 41 E3
St George's La. Ascot 120 A3
St George's La. Ascot 120 A3
St George's Rd. Caver 85 E4
St George's Terr. Read 85 D4
St Georges Rd. Camb 151 E3
St Giles Cl. Read 86 A3
St Helens Cres. Sand 150 A4
St Helier Cl. Read 116 A2
St Hilda's Ave. Ashf 97 F2
St Ives Cl. Thea 83 E1
St Ives Rd. Maid 40 A4
St James Cl. Pangb 56 B3
St James Cl. Twyf 61 F3
St James Rd. Woki 141 F4
St James Wlk. Iver 44 C2
St John's Hill. Read 86 B4
St John's Rd. Ascot 92 C1
St John's Rd. Caver 59 E1
St John's Rd. Mort 137 D3

St John's Rd. Newb 105 D1
St John's Rd. Read 86 B4
St John's Rd. Sand 150 B4
St John's Rd. That 106 B2
St John's St. Read 86 B4
St Johns Ct. Eng G 96 A2
St Johns Dr. Wind 67 D3
St Johns Rd. Slough 43 D3
St Johns Rd. Wind 67 D3
St Jude's Cl. Eng G 95 E2
St Jude's Rd. Eng G 95 E2
St Katherine's Rd. Hen-O-T 35 E4
St Laurence Way. Slough 43 D2
St Leonard's Ave. Wind 67 E3
St Leonard's Hill. Wind 66 C2
St Leonard's Rd. Wind 67 E2
St Leonards Rd. Wind 66 B1
St Leonards Wlk. Iver 44 C2
St Luke's Rd. Maid 39 F4
St Luke's Rd. Old W 68 A1
St Lukes Way. Caver 59 D2
St Margaret's Rd. Maid 39 D4
St Margarets Rd. Ashf 98 A2
St Mark's Cl. Brad 83 D3
St Mark's Pl. Wind 67 E3
St Mark's Rd. Binf 117 E4
St Mark's Rd. Hen-O-T 35 E4
St Mark's Rd. Maid 39 E4
St Mark's Rd. Wind 67 E3
St Marks Cl. That 106 B2
St Marks Cres. Maid 39 D4
St Marks Rd. Binf 90 B1
St Martin's Ct. Stai 97 E2
St Martins Cl. Wood 87 E1
St Mary's Ave. Pur O T 57 E3
St Mary's Ave. Stan 97 E4
St Mary's Butts. Read 86 A4
St Mary's Cl. Hen-O-T 35 D4
St Mary's Cl. Maid 40 A4
St Mary's Cl. Stan 97 E4
St Mary's Cres. Stan 97 E4
St Mary's Dr. Felt 98 B4
St Mary's Gdns. Bags 145 F2
St Mary's Gdns. Bags 145 F2
St Mary's Hill. Ascot 120 B2
St Mary's Rd. Ascot 120 A2
St Mary's Rd. Camb 151 E3
St Mary's Rd. Mort 137 D3
St Mary's Rd. Newb 105 D2
St Mary's Rd. Newb 105 D2
St Mary's Rd. Slough 43 E2
St Mary's Rd. Woki 88 A1
St Mary's Way. Bur C 111 D2
St Mary's Wlk. Maid 39 F4
St Marys Cl. Sand 150 B4
St Marys La. Wink 92 B3
St Michael's Ct. Slough 21 E1
St Michael's Rd. Newb 104 C1
St Michael's Rd. Read 84 B4
St Michael's Rd. Sand 149 F4
St Michaels Cl. Lamb 25 D1
St Michaels Ct. Twyf 61 F3
St Michaels Rd. Camb 151 D3
St Micheals Rd. Ashf 98 A2
St Nazaire Cl. Stai 96 B2
St Nicholas Dr. Shepp 125 D1
St Nicholas' Rd. Newb 104 C1
St Olave's Cl. Slough 96 C1
St Patrick's Ave. Char 61 D3
St Patrick's Cl. Maid 39 D2
St Paul's Cl. Ashf 98 B2
St Paul's Ct. Read 86 A3
St Paul's Gate. Woki 116 A3
St Paul's Rd. Stai 96 B1
St Pauls Ave. Slough 43 D3
St Peter St. Mar 1 C1
St Peter's Ave. Caver 58 C2
St Peter's Cl. Burn 21 D1
St Peter's Cl. Old W 68 A1
St Peter's Cl. Stai 96 C1
St Peter's Gdns. Yate 149 E3
St Peter's Hill. Caver 58 C2
St Peter's Rd. Maid 19 E1
St Peter's Rd. Read 87 D3
St Pinnock Ave. Stai 124 A4
St Ronan's Rd. Read 85 D4
St Saviour's Rd. Read 85 F3
St Sebastians Cl. Woki 142 C4
St Stephens Cl. Caver 59 D1
St Swithins Cl. Wick 75 E2
St Theresa's Rd. Harm 71 F2
St Thomas Ct. That 106 C2
Saint Catherine's Hill. Silc ... 136 C3
Saint-Cloud Way. Maid 40 A4
Salamanca. Finch 142 C3
Salcombe Dr. Read 87 D2
Salcombe Rd. Ashf 97 F3
Salcombe Rd. Newb 104 C1
Salcombe Rd. Read 86 B2
Sale Garden Cotts. Woki 116 B3
Saleby Cl. Winn 87 F1
Salford Cl. Read 113 E4
Salisbury Ave. Slough 42 B4
Salisbury Cl. Woki 116 A1
Salisbury Rd. Harm 71 E1
Salisbury Rd. Hung 100 B2
Salisbury Rd. Read 85 F4
Salisbury Rd. Sand 150 B3
Salmon Cl. Shin 113 D1

Salmond Rd. Read 113 E3
Salt Hill Ave. Slough 42 B3
Salt Hill Dr. Slough 42 B3
Salt Hill Way. Slough 42 B3
Salters' Rd. Maid 40 A4
Saltersgate Cl. Winn 87 E1
Salwey Cl. Brac 118 A2
Samarkand Cl. Camb 152 A2
Samian Pl. Binf 90 C1
Sampage Cl. Read 113 E3
Sampson Park. Brac 117 E4
Sampsons Green. Slough 21 F1
Sanctuary Cl. Read 84 C4
Sanctuary Rd. Stan 71 D1
Sandcroft Rd. Caver 58 C3
Sandell's Ave. Ashf 98 B2
Sanden Cl. Hung 100 B3
Sandford Down. Brac 118 C2
Sandford Dr. Wood 60 C1
Sandford La. Hurst 88 B3
Sandgate Ave. Read 57 F1
Sandhills. St. Vir W 122 C2
Sandhills La. Vir W 122 C2
Sandhills Way. Read 84 C2
Sandhurst La. Black 150 A3
Sandhurst Rd. Brac 142 A4
Sandhurst Rd. Crow 143 D2
Sandhurst Rd. Yate 149 F4
Sandisplatt Rd. Maid 39 D3
Sandleford Cl. Read 113 E3
Sandleford Rise. Newb 131 D4
Sandlers End. Slough 22 A1
Sandown Ave. Read 84 A2
Sandown Cl. Black 150 B3
Sandown Dr. Camb 151 F1
Sandown Rd. Slough 41 F4
Sandown Way. Newb 105 E1
Sandpit Hill. Newb 130 B2
Sandpit La. Swal 140 A3
Sandringham Ct. Slough 41 E4
Sandringham Dr. Ashf 97 E2
Sandringham Rd. Maid 19 F1
Sandringham Rd. Stan 70 C1
Sandringham Way. Read 84 A2
Sands Farm Dr. Burn 21 E1
Sandstone Cl. Winn 88 B1
Sandy Cl. Herm 79 D2
Sandy Dr. Felt 98 C4
Sandy La. Brac 118 B4
Sandy La. Camb 151 F3
Sandy La. Herm 78 C2
Sandy La. Sand 143 D1
Sandy La. Sunn 121 D2
Sandy La. Vir W 122 C3
Sandy La. Woki 115 E2
Sandy Mead. Holy 40 B1
Sandy Way. Shepp 125 F1
Sandygate Cl. Mar 1 B2
Sandygate Rd. Mar 1 B2
Sapgood Cl. That 106 C1
Sapphire Cl. Woki 115 F4
Sarsby Dr. Wray 96 A3
Sarum Cres. Woki 116 B4
Sarum Rd. Tad 135 D1
Sarum Way. Hung 100 B2
Sarum. Brac 117 F1
Saturn Cl. Woki 115 F3
Saunton Ave. Harl 71 F4
Savernake Cl. Read 84 C4
Savernake Way. Brac 118 C2
Savill Way. Mar 1 C1
Saville Cres. Ashf 98 B1
Saville Gdns. Camb 152 A3
Savory Wlk. Binf 90 B1
Savoy Gr. Black 150 B2
Sawmill Rd. Herm 79 D2
Sawpit Rd. Hurst 88 C4
Sawtry Cl. Winn 87 F1
Sawyer's Cl. Wind 66 C4
Sawyers Cres. Whi Wa 39 D1
Sawyers Cres. Whi Wa 39 D1
Saxe Cl. Bur C 111 D2
Saxon Cl. Slough 43 F2
Saxon Gdns. Tapl 20 B1
Saxon Rd. Ashf 98 B1
Saxon Way. Harm 70 B4
Saxon Way. Old W 68 A1
Sayers Cl. Gree 131 D4
Scafell Cl. Read 57 E1
Scafell Rd. Slough 41 F4
Scampton Rd. Stan 70 C1
Scania Wlk. Burl 92 A1
Scarborough Rd. Stan 71 E1
Scarborough Way. Slough 42 A2
Scarletts La. Warg 37 E1
Scholars Cl. Caver 58 C2
School Green. Shin 113 F2
School Hill. Crow 143 E2
School Hill. Sand 143 D1
School Hill. Warg 36 B1
School La. Bags 145 F1
School La. Bish 38 A2
School La. Box 76 C2
School La. Bur C 111 D1
School La. Caver 59 D1
School La. Caver 59 D3
School La. Cook 19 D4
School La. Cook 20 A4
School La. East G 47 E3

School La. Eng G 96 A2
School La. Frox 99 D1
School La. Lit M 2 B3
School La. Maid 19 F1
School La. Medm 17 D3
School La. Padw 109 F1
School La. Shepp 125 D2
School La. Sto P 23 D2
School La. W St L 62 C2
School La. Warg 36 B1
School La. Windl 146 B2
School La. Yate 149 D3
School Rd. Ascot 120 B2
School Rd. Ashf 98 A1
School Rd. Bark 114 C1
School Rd. Bis 153 F2
School Rd. Bur C 111 E3
School Rd. Chiev 78 A4
School Rd. Comp 31 F2
School Rd. Harm 70 B4
School Rd. Hurst 88 C4
School Rd. Read 84 B4
School Rd. Read 114 C1
School Rd. Swal 139 F2
School Rd. Windl 146 A3
School Rd. Woki 116 B3
School Rd. Woo G 3 F3
School Terr. Read 86 C4
Schroder Ct. Eng G 95 D2
Scotland Hill. Sand 143 D1
Scotlands Dr. Far C 22 A3
Scots Cl. Stan 97 E4
Scots Dr. Woki 115 F4
Scott Cl. Caver 59 D3
Scott Cl. Far C 22 B4
Scott Cl. Wood 88 A4
Scott Terr. Brac 118 C4
Scott's Ave. Ashf 98 C1
Scott's Way. Ashf 98 C1
Scottalls La. Hamp N 52 C3
Scours La. Read 58 A1
Scratchface La. Brad 81 F3
Scrivens Mead. That 106 C2
Scylla Cres. Felt 98 A4
Scylla Rd. Felt 71 D1
Seacourt Rd. Slough 44 A1
Seaford Gdns. Wood 87 F3
Seaford Rd. Stan 70 B1
Seaford Rd. Woki 116 B3
Sealand Rd. Stan 71 D1
Searles Farm La. Bur C 85 D1
Seaton Dr. Ashf 97 F3
Seaton Gdns. Read 86 B1
Seaton Rd. Camb 151 D3
Second Cres. Slough 42 B4
Sedgefield Rd. Newb 131 E4
Sedgmoor Gdns. Fla H 3 D4
Sedgmoor La. Fla H 3 D4
Sedgmoor Rd. Fla H 3 D4
Seebys Oak. Sand 150 B3
Sefton Cl. Sto P 22 C2
Sefton Cl. West E 153 F3
Sefton Paddock. Sto P 23 D3
Segsbury Gr. Brac 118 C3
Selborne Gdns. Read 58 A1
Selbourne Cl. Black 150 B3
Selby Rd. Ashf 98 B1
Selcourt Cl. Wood 87 E4
Sellafield Way. Read 87 E1
Selsdon Ave. Wood 87 F4
Selsey Way. Read 114 A4
Selwood Cl. Stan 70 B1
Selwood Gdns. Stan 70 B1
Selwyn Dr. Yate 149 D3
Send Rd. Caver 59 E1
Setley Way. Brac 119 D3
Seton Dr. Read 84 C3
Sett The. Yate 149 D3
Sevenoaks Rd. Read 87 D2
Severn Cl. Sand 150 B4
Severn Cl. That 106 A3
Severn Cres. Slough 69 D4
Severn Way. Read 84 C3
Sewell Ave. Woki 116 A4
Sewell Cl. Cold A 79 D1
Seymour Ave. Shin 113 F3
Seymour Cl. Maid 39 D2
Seymour Court Rd. Mar 1 B2
Seymour Ct Rd. Mar B 1 B2
Seymour Ct La. Mar B 1 A3
Seymour Park Rd. Mar 1 B2
Seymour Plain. Mar 1 B3
Seymour Plain. Mar B 1 B3
Seymour Rd. Slough 42 B2
Seymour Way. Ashf 98 C1
Shackleton Rd. Slough 42 C3
Shackleton Way. Wood 88 A4
Shaftesbury Cres. Stai 97 E1
Shaftesbury Mount. Black 150 B2
Shaftesbury Rd. Bis 153 F2
Shaftesbury Rd. Read 58 A1
Shaftsbury Cl. Brac 118 B2
Shaggy Cal. La. Slough 43 D3
Shakespeare Cl. Caver 59 E3
Shakespeare Rd. That 106 B2
Shakespeare Way. Brac 118 C4
Shalbourne Cl. Hung 100 A3
Shalbourne Rise. Camb 151 E3
Sharney Ave. Slough 44 A2

Sharnwood Dr. Read .... 84 C
Sharpethorpe Cl. Read .... 87 D
Shaw Farm Rd. Newb .... 105 D
Shaw Hill. Newb .... 105 D
Shaw Park. Crow .... 143 D
Shaw Rd. Newb .... 105 D
Shaw Rd. Read .... 85 F
Shaw The. Cook .... 19 F
Sheehy Way. Slough .... 43 D
Sheep Leaze La. Pease .... 29 E
Sheep Wlk. Caver .... 59 D
Sheepcote La. Bou E 3
Sheepcote La. Holy .... 64 B
Sheepcote Rd. Eton .... 42 A
Sheepcote Rd. Wind .... 66 A
Sheepdrove Rd. Lamb .... 25 E
Sheephouse Rd. Maid .... 20 A
Sheephouse Way. Chadd .... 49 D
Sheepridge La. Bou E 2
Sheepridge La. Fla H .... 2 C
Sheepwalk. Shepp .... 124 C
Sheepwalk. Stai .... 124 C
Sheepwash. Newt .... 131 D
Sheepways La. Maple .... 58 A
Sheerlands Rd. Arbo .... 140 C
Sheerlands Rd. Bark .... 140 C
Sheerlands Rd. Bark .... 140 C
Sheet St. Wind .... 67 E
Sheet Street Rd. Old W .... 94 A
Sheet Street Rd. Wind .... 67 E
Sheet Street Rd. Wind .... 94 A
Sheffield Rd. Harm .... 71 E
Sheffield Way. Harm .... 71 E
Shefford Cres. Woki .... 116 B
Sheldon Gdns. Read .... 86 B
Shelgate Wlk. Wood .... 87 E
Shelley Ave. Brac .... 118 C
Shelley Cl. Medm .... 17 E
Shelley Cl. Slough .... 43 F
Shelley Cl. Wood .... 87 F
Shelley Rd. Mar .... 1 C
Shelley Rd. That .... 106 B
Shelley Walk. Yate .... 149 E
Shelson Ave. Felt .... 98 C
Shelton Ct. Slough .... 43 E
Shenstone Cl. Woki .... 142 A
Shenstone Dr. Burn .... 21 E
Shenstone Park. Ascot .... 120 C
Shenstone Rd. Read .... 86 A
Shephards La. Brac .... 91 D
Shepherd's House La. Read .... 87 D
Shepherds Ave. Read .... 87 D
Shepherds Chase. Bags .... 145 E
Shepherds Cl. Hurl .... 17 E
Shepherds Cl. Shepp .... 125 D
Shepherds Hill. Brac .... 118 B
Shepherds Hill. Comp .... 31 F
Shepherds Hill. Wood .... 87 E
Shepherds La. Caver .... 58 E
Shepherds La. Hurl .... 17 E
Shepherds Mount. Comp .... 31 F
Shepherds Rise. Comp .... 31 F
Shepherds Way. Crow .... 142 C
Shepherds Wlk. Wood .... 87 E
Shepley Dr. Read .... 85 E
Shepley Dr. Went .... 121 E
Shepley End. Went .... 121 E
Shepperton Court Dr. Shepp .. 125 D
Shepperton Rd. Stai .... 124 B
Sheraton Cl. Black .... 150 C
Sheraton Dr. Read .... 57 E
Sherborne Cl. Stan .... 69 F
Sherborne Rd. Felt .... 98 B
Sherbourne Dr. Went .... 121 E
Sherbourne Dr. Wind .... 66 C
Sherbourne Dr. Wood .... 87 F
Sherbourne Wlk. Far C .... 22 B
Shergold Way. Cook .... 19 F
Sheridan Ave. Caver .... 59 D
Sheridan Cres. Tad .... 134 C
Sheridan Way. Woki .... 115 F
Sherman Rd. Read .... 86 A
Sherman Rd. Slough .... 42 C
Sherrardmead. Newb .... 105 D
Sherring Cl. Brac .... 91 E
Sherwood Cl. Brac .... 119 E
Sherwood Cl. Slough .... 43 F
Sherwood Dr. Maid .... 39 D
Sherwood Gdns. Hen-O-T ...... 35 E
Sherwood Rd. Winn .... 88 B
Sherwood Rise. Purl .... 57 D
Sherwood St. Read .... 85 E
Shield Rd. Felt .... 98 B
Shifford Cres. Maid .... 19 F
Shildon Cl. Camb .... 152 B
Shinfield Rd. Read .... 86 C
Shinfield Rise. Read .... 86 C
Shipley Cl. Wood .... 61 E
Shipton Cl. Read .... 57 E
Shire Cl. Bags .... 145 F
Shire's Head Cl. Read .... 85 E
Shires The. Woki .... 115 F
Shires Way. Yate .... 149 E
Shirley Ave. Read .... 113 E
Shirley Ave. Wind .... 66 C
Shirley Rd. Maid .... 39 E
Shirley Rd. Stan .... 97 F
Shooter's Hill. Pangb .... 56 B
Shop La. Leckh .... 49 F

Shop La. Newb 104 C3
Shoppenhanger's Rd. Maid 39 F2
Shoreham Rd (E). Stan 70 C1
Shoreham Rd (W). Stan 70 C1
Short La. Stan 97 F4
Short Rd. Stan 70 C1
Short St. Caver 59 D1
Short St. Pangb 56 B3
Short St. Read 86 A3
Short The. Pur O T 57 E3
Shortfern. Slough 43 E4
Shortheath La. Sulhd 110 C2
Shortland. Harl 71 E4
Shortlands Hill. Moul 13 E2
Shortwood Ave. Ashf 97 D2
Shrewsbury Rd. Harm 71 E1
Shrivenham Cl. Sand 150 B4
Shrubbs Hill La. Went 121 D1
Shrubland Dr. Read 85 D2
Shrublands Dr. Light 153 D4
Shute End. Woki 116 A3
Shyshack La. Tad 134 C1
Sibley Park Rd. Read 87 D1
Sibson. Read 87 E1
Sidbury Cl. Sunn 121 D2
Sidestrand Rd. Newb 130 C4
Sidmouth Grange Cl. Read 87 D4
Sidmouth Grange Rd. Read 87 D4
Sidmouth St. Read 86 B4
Sidney Rd. Stai 97 D2
Silbury Cl. Bur C 84 A2
Silchester Rd. Read 85 E2
Silco Dr. Maid 39 F3
Silver Birches. Woki 115 E2
Silver Cl. Maid 39 D3
Silver Dr. Camb 152 B2
Silver Fox Cres. Wood 87 E3
Silver Hill. Sand 150 C4
Silver La. Padw 136 A4
Silver St. Read 86 A3
Silverdale Rd. Read 87 E2
Silverdale Rd. Tad 135 D1
Silverdale Rd. Warg 36 C1
Silverglades. Yate 149 E2
Silverthorne Dr. Caver 58 C3
Silvertrees Dr. Maid 39 D3
Silverwood Dr. Camb 152 A4
Silwood Cl. Ascot 120 B4
Silwood Rd. Sunn 120 C3
Silwood. Brac 117 F1
Simkins Cl. Burl 92 A1
Simmonds Cl. Brac 117 F4
Simmonds St. Read 86 A4
Simmons Cl. Slough 44 A1
Simmons Rd. Hen-O-T 15 E2
Simms Farm La. Silc 136 C3
Simon's La. Woki 115 E4
Simons Cl. Pur O T 57 E2
Simons Wlk. Eng G 95 E1
Simpson Cl. Maid 40 A4
Sindlesham Rd. Arbo 114 C2
Singer La. Hen-O-T 15 F1
Singers Cl. Hen-O-T 35 F4
Sinhurst Rd. Camb 151 D2
Sirius Cl. Woki 115 F3
Six Acre La. Ham 126 A3
Skeffling Cl. Winn 87 F1
Skelmerdale Way. Winn 87 F2
Skerritt Way. Read 57 E2
Skilton Rd. That 106 C2
Skilton Rd. Read 57 E2
Skimpedhill La. Brac 118 A4
Skinners Green La. Ham M ... 130 A4
Skippons Cl. Newb 130 B3
Skomer Path. Slough 21 F1
Skye Cl. Read 84 C2
Skyes Dr. Stai 97 D2
Skylings. Newb 105 E2
Skyport Dr. Harm 70 B4
Sladburn Green. Brac 118 C1
Slanting Hill. Herm 79 D3
Slaughterhouse Rd. Felt 98 C4
Slim Rd. Camb 151 D3
Sloan Ct. Gori 34 B3
Slopes. The. Caver 59 E1
Slough Rd. Datch 68 A4
Slough Rd. Eton 42 C1
Slough Rd. Slough 42 C1
Slumburgh Way. Slough 42 C4
Smallmead Rd. Bur C 85 E1
Smallmead Rd. Read 86 A1
Smith's Green. Windl 146 B2
Smith Sq. Brac 118 B4
Smith's Hill. Let B 6 C3
Smith's La. Wind 66 C3
Smitham Bridge Rd. Hung 100 B3
Smithfield Cl. Whi Wa 39 D2
Smithfield Rd. Maid 39 D2
Smithy's Green. Windl 146 B2
Snape Spur. Slough 42 C4
Snipe La. Newt 131 F1
Snow's Paddock. Windl 146 A4
Snowball Hill. Whi Wa 64 A4
Snowberry Cl. Woki 115 F3
Snowden Cl. Wind 66 B2

Snowden Dr. Read 84 A3
Snowdon Cl. That 106 B1
Snowdon Rd W. Harm 71 E1
Snowdon Rd. Harm 71 E1
Snowdrop Gr. Winn 88 B2
Snows Ride. Windl 146 A3
Soham Cl. Winn 114 B4
Soho Cres. Bou E 3 E2
Soke Rd. Alde 135 F2
Soke Rd. Silc 135 F2
Soldiers Rise. Brac 142 B4
Solent Rd. Stan 70 C1
Somerford Cl. Maid 40 A4
Somersby Cres. Maid 39 F2
Somerset Cl. Hung 100 B3
Somerset Cl. Woki 115 E3
Somerset Way. Iver 44 C2
Somerset Wlk. Read 84 A3
Somerton Gdns. Read 87 D1
Somerton Gr. That 106 B1
Somerville Cres. Yate 149 F3
Somerville Cl. Woki 115 E2
Somerville Rd. Eton 42 B1
Sonning La. Sonn 60 B1
Sonning Meadows. Sonn 60 B1
Sonninge Cl. Sand 150 B4
Sopwith Cl. Wood 88 A4
Sorrel Cl. Bur C 111 D2
Sorrel Cl. Newb 105 E3
Sorrel Cl. Woki 116 C4
Sorrel Dr. Light 152 C4
Sospel Ct. Far C 22 B2
South Ave. Hen-O-T 35 F4
South Ave. Stai 96 B1
South Cl. Medm 17 E4
South Cl. Slough 41 E3
South Cl. Woki 116 B2
South Dr. Read 86 C1
South Dr. Sonn 60 B1
South Dr. Sulhd 110 B4
South Dr. Went 122 A1
South Dr. Woki 116 B3
South End Rd. Brad 82 A1
South Gate Ave. Felt 98 B2
South Gr. Chert 123 F2
South Green. Slough 42 C3
South Hill Rd. Brac 118 A2
South Lake. Wood 87 F3
South Lynn Cres. Brac 118 A2
South Meadow La. Eton 67 E4
South Meadow. Crow 143 D4
South Path. Wind 67 E3
South Pl. Mar 117 F3
South Rd. Bis 153 F2
South Rd. Crow 143 F2
South Rd. Eng G 95 E1
South Rd. Maid 39 F3
South Row. Chil 10 B4
South St. Blew 12 A4
South St. Caver 59 D1
South St. Read 86 B4
South St. Stai 96 C2
South View Ave. Caver 59 E1
South View Park. Caver 59 E1
South View. Hung 100 B3
Southampton Cl. Black 150 B3
Southampton Rd. Stan 70 C1
Southampton St. Read 86 A3
Southampton Way. Stan 70 C1
Southbourne Dr. Bou E 3 D2
Southbury Cl. Twyf 61 F3
Southcote Ave. Felt 98 C3
Southcote Dr. Camb 152 A3
Southcote Farm La. Read 85 E2
Southcote La. Read 85 E2
Southcote Rd. Read 85 E3
Southcroft. Slough 22 A1
Southdown Rd. Caver 59 D3
Southdown Rd. Tad 135 D1
Southdown Rd. That 105 F2
Southend. That 106 B3
Southern Hill. Read 86 B3
Southern Perimeter Rd. Harm 71 E1
Southern Perimeter Rd. Stan .. 70 B1
Southern Rd. Camb 151 E3
Southerndene Cl. Read 57 E1
Southfield Gdns. Burn 41 D4
Southfields Ave. Ashf 98 A1
Southlands Cl. Woki 116 B3
Southlands Rd. Woki 116 B2
Southlea Rd. Datch 68 A3
Southside. Chert 124 A3
Southview Cl. Twyf 61 F3
Southview Rd. Mar 1 C2
Southville Cl. Felt 98 C4
Southville Cres. Felt 98 C4
Southville Rd. Felt 98 C4
Southwark Cl. Yate 149 E3
Southway. Camb 151 D2
Southwell Park Rd. Camb 151 E3
Southwick Ct. Brac 118 C2
Southwick. Bags 145 F1
Southwold Cl. Winn 87 E1
Southwold Spur. Slough 44 B2
Southwold. Brac 117 F1
Southwood Gdns. Bur C 111 D2
Southwood Gdns. Cook 19 F3
Southwood Rd. Cook 19 F3

Southwood. Woki 116 B2
Spackman Cl. That 106 B1
Spackmans Way. Slough 42 B2
Spade Oak Meadows. Bou E ... 2 C2
Span Hill. Caver 60 B4
Sparrow Cl. Woki 115 F3
Sparrowbill. Brig 28 C1
Sparvell Way. Camb 151 E3
Speedwell Way. That 106 C2
Speen Hill Cl. Newb 104 C2
Speen La. Newb 104 B2
Speen Lodge Ct. Newb 104 C2
Speen Pl. Newb 104 C2
Spelthorne Gr. Stai 98 C1
Spelthorne La. Stai 125 E4
Spencer Cl. Silc 135 F1
Spencer Cl. Woki 115 E3
Spencer Gdns. Eng G 95 E2
Spencer Rd. Brac 117 F4
Spencer Rd. Newb 130 B3
Spencer Rd. Read 113 D4
Spencer Rd. Slough 43 F2
Spencers Cl. Maid 39 E4
Spencers La. Cook 19 F3
Spencers Rd. Maid 39 E4
Spenwood Cl. Shin 113 D1
Sperling Rd. Maid 19 F1
Spey Rd. Read 85 D4
Spinfield La W. Mar 1 B1
Spinfield La. Mar 1 A1
Spinfield Mount. Mar 1 A1
Spinfield Park. Mar 1 B1
Spinis. Brac 117 F1
Spinner Green. Brac 118 A2
Spinners Wlk. Mar 1 B1
Spinners Wlk. Wind 67 E3
Spinney Cl. Caver 59 D4
Spinney Dr. Felt 98 B4
Spinney The. Camb 152 B3
Spinney The. Read 84 C2
Spinney The. Sunn 120 C2
Spinney The. Woki 141 F4
Spinney The. Yate 149 E4
Spinney. Slough 42 A3
Spinningwheel La. Binf 90 B4
Spitfire Way. Wood 88 A4
Spittal St. Mar 1 B1
Spode Cl. Read 84 C4
Spout La N. Stan 70 A2
Spout La. Stan 70 A2
Spray La. Brig 28 B1
Spray Rd. Ham 126 C2
Spray Rd. Ink 127 D2
Spriggs Cl. That 106 B1
Spring Ave. Eng G 95 F1
Spring Cl. Maid 19 F1
Spring Cl. Pangb 55 E3
Spring Gdns. Ascot 120 A3
Spring Gdns. Bou E 3 D2
Spring Gdns. Burl 92 C1
Spring Gdns. Camb 152 A3
Spring Gdns. Mar 1 C2
Spring Gdns. Shin 113 D1
Spring Gdns. Woo G 3 F4
Spring Gr. Read 86 A3
Spring Hill. Maid 39 F2
Spring La. Alde 135 E4
Spring La. Ast T 12 C4
Spring La. Caver 60 A3
Spring La. Cold A 106 B4
Spring La. Cook 19 E3
Spring La. Far C 22 B3
Spring La. Mort 137 D3
Spring La. Slough 41 F3
Spring La. Swal 139 D2
Spring Meadow. Brac 118 B4
Spring Meadows. Gr She 48 A2
Spring Rd. Felt 98 C3
Spring Rise. Eng G 95 F1
Spring Wlk. Warg 36 B1
Spring Wood La. Bur C 111 D1
Spring Woods. Sand 143 E1
Spring Woods. Vir W 122 A3
Springate Field. Slough 43 F2
Springcross Ave. Black 150 B2
Springdale. Read 87 D1
Springdale. Woki 141 F4
Springfield Cl. Wind 67 D3
Springfield End. Gori 34 B4
Springfield Gr. Shepp 125 F4
Springfield La. Newb 131 D4
Springfield Park. Holy 40 B1
Springfield Park. Twyf 61 F2
Springfield Rd. Ashf 97 F2
Springfield Rd. Binf 117 E4
Springfield Rd. Camb 152 A3
Springfield Rd. Silc 135 F1
Springfield Rd. Slough 69 D4
Springfield Rd. Wind 67 D3
Springfield. Light 153 E4
Springhill Rd. Gori 34 B4
Spruce Dr. Light 153 D4
Spruce Rd. Wood 88 A3
Spur The. Slough 41 E4
Spur The. Warg 36 C2
Spurcroft Rd. That 106 C1
Square The. Bags 145 F2
Square The. Harm 70 C4
Square The. Pangb 56 B3

Square The. Shin 113 D1
Squire's Bridge Rd. Stai 124 C3
Squires Rd. Stai 125 D3
Squires Wlk. Ashf 98 B1
Squirrel Cl. Sand 150 A4
Squirrel Rise. Mar B 1 B3
Squirrels Drey. Crow 142 C3
Squirrels Way. Read 87 D1
Stable Cl. Bur C 111 D2
Stable Croft. Bags 145 E1
Stable Cl. Newb 105 D3
Stable View. Yate 149 E4
Stables Ct. Mar 1 A1
Staddlestone Cl. Read 57 E1
Stadium Way. Read 58 A1
Staff College Rd. Camb 151 D3
Staff College Rd. Sand 151 D3
Stafferton Way. Maid 40 A3
Stafford Ave. Slough 22 B1
Stafford Cl. Burn 41 D4
Stafford Cl. Wood 87 F4
Stafford Lake. Bis 153 F1
Staffordshire Cl. Read 57 F1
Staffordshire Croft. New G 91 F1
Stag Hill. Chil F 73 D1
Stainash Cres. Stai 97 D2
Staines By-Pass. Stai 97 E2
Staines La. Chert 124 A2
Staines Lane Cl. Chert 123 F2
Staines Rd W. Ashf 98 B1
Staines Rd. Felt 98 B4
Staines Rd. Stai 123 F2
Staines Rd. Wray 95 F4
Stainford Cl. Ashf 98 B2
Stamford Ave. Camb 151 F1
Stamford Rd. Maid 39 E3
Stanbrook Cl. Brad 82 A1
Stanfield. Tad 135 D1
Stanham Rd. Read 84 C4
Stanhope Heath. Stan 70 B1
Stanhope Rd. Read 86 B2
Stanhope Rd. Sand 150 C2
Stanhope Rd. Slough 41 E4
Stanhope Way. Stan 70 B1
Stanlake La. Twyf 61 F2
Stanley Cl. Mar 1 C2
Stanley Cotts. Slough 42 C3
Stanley Gr. Read 85 F4
Stanley Green E. Slough 43 F1
Stanley Green W. Slough 43 F1
Stanley Rd. Ashf 97 F2
Stanley Rd. Newb 105 D1
Stanley Rd. Woki 116 C3
Stanley St. Read 85 F4
Stanmore Cl. Ascot 120 A3
Stanmore Gdns. Mort 136 C3
Stanmore Rd. Beed 30 B1
Stanmore Rd. East I 30 C4
Stanshawe Rd. Read 86 A4
Stanstead Rd. Stan 70 C1
Stanton Cl. Read 87 E2
Stanton Way. Slough 43 F1
Stanwell Cl. Stan 70 B1
Stanwell Gdns. Stan 70 B1
Stanwell Moor Rd. Harm 70 A2
Stanwell Moor Rd. Stan 70 A2
Stanwell New Rd. Stai 97 D3
Stanwell Rd. Ashf 97 F2
Stanwell Rd. Felt 71 D1
Stanwell Rd. Felt 98 A4
Stanwell Rd. Hort 69 E2
Stanwell Rd. Stan 69 E2
Stapleford Rd. Read 85 E2
Staplehurst. Brac 117 F1
Stapleton Cl. Mar 1 C2
Stapleton Cl. Newb 130 B3
Star La. Know H 37 F2
Star La. Read 86 A4
Star Post Rd. Camb 151 F4
Star Rd. Caver 59 E1
Starling Cl. Woki 115 F3
Starlings Dr. Read 84 A3
Starmead Dr. Woki 116 C3
Starting Gates. Newb 105 E1
Startins La. Cook 19 E4
Starwood Ct. Slough 43 E2
Statham Ct. Brac 117 F4
Station App. Ashf 97 F2
Station App. Mar 1 C1
Station App. Read 86 A4
Station App. Shepp 125 E2
Station App. Stai 97 D2
Station App. Vir W 122 B3
Station Cres. Ashf 97 F2
Station Hill. Ascot 120 A3
Station Hill. Cook 19 F4
Station Hill. Read 86 A4
Station Par. Vir W 122 B3
Station Rd. Ashf 97 F2
Station Rd. Bags 145 F2
Station Rd. Ball H 130 A2
Station Rd. Bou E 3 D2
Station Rd. Brac 118 A4
Station Rd. Camb 151 E1
Station Rd. Chert 124 A1
Station Rd. Cook 19 F4
Station Rd. East G 47 E3
Station Rd. Eng G 96 A2
Station Rd. Gori 34 B3

Station Rd. Gr She 48 A2
Station Rd. Hen-O-T 15 F1
Station Rd. Hung 100 B3
Station Rd. Kint 102 A1
Station Rd. Lamb 25 D1
Station Rd. Mar 1 C1
Station Rd. Newb 104 B3
Station Rd. Newb 105 D1
Station Rd. Pangb 56 B3
Station Rd. Read 86 A4
Station Rd. Read 87 E2
Station Rd. Shepp 125 E2
Station Rd. Shipl 36 A2
Station Rd. Slough 41 F4
Station Rd. Slough 44 A2
Station Rd. Sunn 121 D2
Station Rd. Tapl 40 C4
Station Rd. That 106 C1
Station Rd. Twyf 61 E2
Station Rd. Warg 36 B1
Station Rd. Woki 116 A3
Station Rd. Wool 108 B1
Station Rd. Wray 69 D1
Station Rise. Mar 117 F3
Staunton Rd. Slough 42 B4
Staveley Rd. Ashf 98 B1
Staverton Cl. Brac 91 D1
Staverton Cl. Woki 116 C3
Staverton Rd. Read 86 B2
Stayne End. Went 122 A3
Steam Farm La. Harm 71 F2
Steeple Wlk. Read 113 F4
Steerforth Copse. Crow 143 F1
Stepgates. Chert 124 A1
Stephen Cl. Stai 96 B1
Stephen's Cl. Mort 136 C3
Stephens Firs. Mort 136 C3
Stephenson Cl. That 106 B2
Stephenson Rd. Bark 141 D4
Stephenson Rd. Wind 67 D4
Sterling Way. Read 58 A1
Stevens Hill. Yate 149 F3
Stevenson Dr. Binf 90 B2
Stewart Ave. Slough 42 C4
Stewart Ave. Stai 125 D3
Stewart Cl. Holy 65 E3
Stewarts Dr. Far C 22 A4
Stewarts Way. Mar B 1 B4
Stile Rd. Slough 43 E2
Stilton Cl. Winn 87 F1
Stilwell Cl. Yate 149 F3
Stirling Cl. Camb 151 F1
Stirling Cl. Caver 59 E3
Stirling Cl. Wind 66 B3
Stirling Rd. Slough 42 A4
Stirling Rd. Stan 70 C1
Stockbridge Way. Yate 149 E2
Stockbury Cl. Read 87 D1
Stockdales Rd. Eton 41 F1
Stockton Rd. Read 86 B1
Stockwells. Tapl 20 B1
Stockwood Rise. Camb 151 F3
Stoke Common Rd. Fulm 23 D4
Stoke Common Rd. Sto P 23 D4
Stoke Court Dr. Sto P 22 C2
Stoke Gdns. Slough 42 C3
Stoke Green. Sto P 23 D1
Stoke Park Ave. Far C 22 A1
Stoke Poges La. Slough 42 C4
Stoke Rd. Slough 42 C4
Stoke Wood. Sto P 22 C2
Stokeford Cl. Brac 118 C2
Stokes View. Pangb 56 B3
Stokesay. Slough 42 C3
Stokesley Rise. Woo G 3 F4
Stomp Rd. Burn 21 E1
Stomp Rd. Burn 41 D4
Stomp Rd. Slough 41 D4
Stompits Rd. Holy 65 E4
Stone Cres. Felt 98 C4
Stone House La. Cook 2 B1
Stone St. Read 58 A1
Stonea Cl. Winn 114 B4
Stonecroft Ave. Iver 44 C4
Stonefield Park. Maid 39 E4
Stonegate. Camb 152 B3
Stoneham Cl. Read 85 D3
Stonehaven Dr. Wood 88 A3
Stonehill Rd. Light 146 A1
Stonehouse Rise. Camb 151 F1
Stoneleigh Ct. Camb 151 F1
Stoney Cl. Yate 149 E2
Stoney La. Burn 22 A2
Stoney La. Cold A 105 E3
Stoney La. Newb 105 E3
Stoney La. That 106 C2
Stoney Meade. Slough 42 A3
Stoney Rd. Brac 118 A4
Stoney Ware Cl. Bish 18 C4
Stoney Ware. Bish 18 C4
Stoneyfield. Been 109 D3
Stoneyland Cl. Eng G 95 F2
Stoneylands Rd. Eng G 95 F2
Stookes Way. Yate 149 D2
Stour Cl. Read 85 D4
Stour Cl. Slough 42 A4
Stovell Rd. Wind 67 D4
Stowe Rd. Slough 41 F3

Straight Bit. Fla H 3 D4
Straight La. Lamb 46 C3
Straight Mile The. Hurst 89 E3
Straight Mile The. W St L 62 C1
Straight Rd. Old W 68 A1
Strand La. Cook 19 F3
Strand Way. Wood 87 E1
Stranraer Cl. Stan 70 C1
Stratfield Rd. Slough 43 D2
Stratfield. Brac 117 F1
Stratford Cl. Slough 21 E1
Stratford Dr. Bou E 3 E2
Stratford Gdns. Maid 39 E2
Stratford Rd. Harm 71 E1
Stratford Way. Read 84 A3
Strathcona Cl. Fla H 3 E4
Strathcona Way. Fla H 3 E4
Strathearn Ave. Harl 71 F4
Stratheden Pl. Read 85 F4
Strathmore Dr. Char 61 D2
Strathy Cl. Read 85 D4
Stratton Gdns. Read 86 B1
Stratton Rd. Shepp 125 F4
Strawberry Hill. New G 91 F1
Strawberry Hill. Newb 104 C2
Streatley & Goring Bridge. Gori 34 A3
Streatley Hill. Stre 33 F3
Street The. Alde 135 D4
Street The. Brad 83 D3
Street The. Mort 137 E3
Street The. Moul 14 A3
Street The. Sou S 14 A2
Street The. Swal 139 E4
Street The. Tidm 56 B1
Street The. W St L 63 D3
Streets Heath. West E 153 F4
Stretton Cl. Brad 82 A1
Strode St. Eng G 96 A2
Stroller Cl. That 105 F2
Strongrove Hill. Hung 100 B3
Stroud Cl. Wind 66 B2
Stroud Farm Rd. Holy 65 D4
Stroud Way. Ashf 98 A1
Stroude Rd. Vir W 122 C3
Stroude Rd. Vir W 123 D4
Strouds Meadow. Cold A 106 B4
Strouds The. Been 108 C3
Stuart Cl. Caver 59 D3
Stuart Cl. Wind 66 C3
Stuart Rd. Newb 130 B3
Stuart Way. Stai 97 D1
Stuart Way. Vir W 122 A3
Stuart Way. Wind 66 C3
Stubbles La. Cook 19 D3
Stubbs Folly. Sand 150 B4
Studios Rd. Stai 124 C3
Studland Cl. Read 113 E4
Sturbridge Cl. Wood 87 E1
Sturdee Cl. Camb 151 F1
Sturges Rd. Woki 116 B3
Sturt Green. Holy 64 C4
Styventon Pl. Chert 123 F1
Suck's La. Asham 54 B2
Suffolk Cl. Slough 41 F4
Suffolk Cl. Woki 115 E3
Suffolk Rd. Maid 39 E2
Suffolk Rd. Read 85 E4
Suffork Cl. Bags 145 F1
Sulham Cl. Pangb 56 C2
Sulham La. Pur O T 56 C2
Sulham La. Sulh 56 C2
Sulham Wlk. Read 85 D2
Sulhamstead Hill. Sulhd 110 B3
Sulhamstead La. Sulhd 110 B2
Sulhamstead Rd. Bur 111 D3
Sulhamstead Rd. Sulhd 111 D3
Sullivan Rd. Camb 151 D3
Summer Gdns. Camb 152 B2
Summerfield Cl. Woki 88 C1
Summerfield Rise. Gori 34 B4
Summerhouse La. Harm 70 B4
Summerlea. Slough 42 A3
Summerleaze Rd. Maid 20 A1
Summers Rd. Burn 21 E1
Summit Cl. Woki 141 F4
Sun Gdns. Bur C 111 D1
Sun La. Maid 39 F4
Sun La. Swal 139 D1
Sun Pas. Wind 67 E3
Sun Ray Estate. Sand 150 A4
Sun St. Read 86 B4
Sunbury Cres. Felt 98 C3
Sunbury Rd. Eton 67 E4
Sunbury Rd. Felt 98 C3
Sunderland Cl. Wood 88 A4
Sunderland Rd. Maid 39 D4
Sundew Cl. Camb 153 E4
Sundew Cl. Woki 116 C4
Sundon Cres. Went 122 B2
Sundown Rd. Ashf 98 B2
Sunley Cl. Newb 130 B3
Sunmead Rd. Shepp 125 F3
Sunning Ave. Sunn 120 C1
Sunninghill Cl. Ascot 120 B3
Sunninghill Rd. Ascot 120 B3
Sunninghill Rd. Windl 146 A4
Sunninghill Rd. Wink 93 E1
Sunnybank. Mar 1 B2

Sunnyside. Newb 104 C3
Surbiton Rd. Camb 145 D1
Surley Row. Caver 59 D3
Surly Hall Wlk. Wind 66 C3
Surrey Ave. Camb 151 D2
Surrey Ave. Slough 22 B1
Surrey Rd. Read 86 A2
Surridge Ct. Bags 145 F1
Sussex Cl. Slough 43 D2
Sussex Gdns. Wood 87 F4
Sussex La. Shin 113 E1
Sussex Pl. Slough 43 D2
Sutcliffe Ave. Read 87 E2
Sutherland Ave. Shepp 125 F4
Sutherland Chase. Ascot 119 F4
Sutherland Gdns. Shepp 125 F4
Sutherland Gr. Read 84 C2
Sutherlands Ave. Read 86 B3
Sutherlands. Newb 130 C4
Sutton Ave. Slough 43 E2
Sutton Cl. Cook 20 A4
Sutton Cl. Maid 39 E3
Sutton La. Slough 44 B1
Sutton Pl. Slough 69 D4
Sutton Rd. Camb 145 D1
Sutton Rd. Cook 20 A3
Sutton Rd. Newb 104 B3
Sutton Wlk. Read 86 B3
Suttons Park Ave. Read 86 C4
Swabey Rd. Slough 44 A1
Swainstone Rd. Read 86 A3
Swaledale. Brac 118 A2
Swallow Cl. Read 84 B3
Swallow Cl. Stai 96 C3
Swallow Cl. Yate 149 D3
Swallow St. Iver 44 B4
Swallow Way. Woki 115 F3
Swallowfield Dr. Read 113 E3
Swallowfield Gdns. Thea 83 F2
Swallowfield Rd. Arbo 114 B1
Swallowfield. Eng G 95 D1
Swan La. Sand 150 A4
Swan Pl. Read 86 A4
Swan Rd. Iver 44 C4
Swancote Green. Brac 118 A2
Swangate. Hung 100 B4
Swanholm Gdns. Read 84 C2
Swanmore Cl. Winn 87 F1
Swanscourt. Twyf 61 F2
Swansdown Wlk. That 106 A2
Swansea Rd. Harm 71 E1
Swansea Rd. Read 86 A3
Swansea Terr. Read 57 E1
Swanston Field. Whi-O-T 56 B4
Sweeps La. Eng G 95 F2
Sweet Briar Dr. Bur C 84 B2
Sweetbriar. Brac 143 D4
Sweetzer's Piece. Silc 136 C3
Swepstone Cl. Read 87 E1
Swift Cl. Woki 115 F3
Swift La. Windl 145 F2
Swinbrook Cl. Read 57 E2
Swindon Rd. Harm 71 E1
Swinley Rd. Brac 119 E2
Swiss Cottage Cl. Read 84 B4
Switchback Cl. Maid 19 E1
Switchback Rd N. Cook 19 F2
Switchback Rd N. Maid 19 F2
Switchback Rd S. Maid 19 F1
Switchback Rd. Cook 19 F2
Switchback The. Maid 19 E1
Sycamore Cl. Bur C 111 D2
Sycamore Cl. Camb 151 F1
Sycamore Cl. Sand 150 A4
Sycamore Cl. Wood 87 E3
Sycamore Ct. Wind 67 E2
Sycamore Dr. Camb 151 F1
Sycamore Dr. Mar B 1 B3
Sycamore Dr. Twyf 61 E3
Sycamore Rd. Read 86 C1
Sycamore Rise. Brac 118 B3
Sycamore Rise. Newb 105 E3
Sycamore Wlk. Eng G 95 D1
Sycamore Wlk. Slough 43 F4
Sycamores The. Black 150 A3
Sydings The. Newb 104 B3
Sydney Cl. Brac 143 E4
Sydney Cres. Ashf 98 A1
Sydney Gr. Slough 42 B4
Syke Cluan. Iver 44 C2
Syke Ings. Iver 44 C2
Sykes Rd. Slough 42 A4
Sylvan Ridge. Sand 143 D1
Sylvan Wlk. Read 85 E2
Sylvanus. Brac 117 F1
Sylverns Ct. New G 91 F1
Sylvester Cl. Newb 104 C3
Sylvester Rd. Maid 19 F1
Symondson Mews. Binf 90 B2
Sympson Rd. Tad 135 E1

Tachbrook Rd. Felt 98 C4
Tadcroft Wlk. Read 84 C2
Tadham Pl. That 106 B1
Tadley Common Rd. Tad 135 E1
Tadmor Cl. Shepp 125 F3
Taff Way. Read 85 D2
Tag La. Warg 37 D1
Talbot Ave. Slough 43 F2

Talbot Cl. Caver 59 E1
Talbot Cl. Newb 104 C3
Talbot Ct. Read 86 A4
Talbot Pl. Bags 145 F2
Talbot Pl. Datch 68 B3
Talbot Rd. Ashf 97 F2
Talbot Way. Sulh 57 E2
Talbots Dr. Maid 39 D3
Talfourd Ave. Read 87 D3
Talisman Cl. Woki 142 B3
Tall Trees. Stan 69 F3
Tallis La. Read 85 E2
Tamar Gdns. Read 86 B2
Tamar Way. Slough 44 A1
Tamar Way. Woki 115 F4
Tamarind Way. Read 86 C1
Tamarisk Ave. Read 86 C1
Tamarisk Rise. Woki 116 B4
Tamarisk Way. Slough 42 A2
Tamworth Cl. Wood 87 E1
Tamworth. Brac 118 B1
Tandem. Brac 117 E4
Tangier La. Eton 67 E4
Tanglewood Ride. West E 153 F4
Tanglewood. Woki 142 A4
Tangley Dr. Brac 116 A2
Tanglyn Ave. Stai 125 D2
Tanhouse La. Woki 116 A3
Tank Rd. Sand 150 C3
Tanner Ct. Newb 105 D2
Tanners La. Maple 58 C4
Tanners Yd. Bags 145 F2
Tape La. Hurst 88 C4
Taplow Common Rd. Burn 21 D2
Taplow Common Rd. Tapl 21 D2
Taplow Rd. Burn 41 D4
Tarbat Ct. Sand 150 B4
Tarbay La. Oak G 66 B2
Target Cl. Felt 71 F1
Targett Cl. Winn 88 A1
Tarlton Ct. Read 84 C3
Tarmac Way. Harm 70 A4
Tarn La. Newb 130 C4
Tarnbrook Way. Brac 118 C3
Tarragon Cl. Read 86 C1
Tarragon Way. Bur C 111 D2
Tarrants Hill. Hung 100 B3
Tasker Cl. Harl 71 E4
Tatchbrook Cl. Maid 40 A4
Tattersall Cl. Woki 116 C3
Tavistock Cl. Maid 39 D4
Tavistock Cl. Stai 97 E1
Tavistock Rd. Read 86 A2
Tawfield. Brac 117 F1
Tay Rd. Read 85 D4
Taylor's Cl. Mar 1 C1
Tazewell Cl. Read 85 F3
Tebbit Cl. Brac 118 B4
Teesdale Rd. Slough 41 F4
Tekels Ave. Camb 151 E2
Tekels Way. Camb 151 F2
Telford Cres. Wood 60 C1
Telford Dr. Slough 42 A2
Telston Cl. Bou E 3 D3
Tempest Rd. Stai 96 B1
Templar Cl. Sand 150 A4
Templars Pl. Mar 1 C1
Temple Gdns. Stai 123 F4
Temple La. Bish 18 B3
Temple Mill Island. Bish 18 B3
Temple Park. Hurl 17 F2
Temple Pl. Read 86 A3
Temple Rd. Wind 67 E3
Temple Way. Binf 90 C1
Temple Way. Far C 22 B4
Templecroft. Ashf 98 B1
Templedene Ave. Stai 97 E1
Templeton Gdns. Read 86 B1
Templewood La. Far C 22 B4
Ten Acre La. Stai 123 E4
Tenaplas Dr. Upp B 54 C3
Tenby Ave. Caver 59 E3
Tenby Dr. Ascot 120 B2
Tennyson Rd. Ashf 97 F2
Tennyson Rd. That 106 B2
Tennyson Way. Slough 21 F1
Tern Cl. Read 85 D3
Terrace Rd N. Binf 90 B2
Terrace Rd S. Binf 90 B1
Terrace The. Ascot 120 B2
Terrace The. Crow 143 E3
Terrace The. Maid 40 B2
Terrace The. Woki 116 A3
Terrington Hill. Mar 1 B1
Terry's La. Cook 19 F4
Tesimond Dr. Yate 149 D3
Tessa Rd. Read 58 C1
Test Cl. Read 85 D4
Testwood Rd. Wind 66 B3
Teviot Rd. Read 84 C4
Thakerays The. That 106 B1
Thames Ave. Chert 124 A3
Thames Ave. Pangb 56 B3
Thames Ave. Read 59 D1
Thames Cl. Bou E 3 D2
Thames Cl. Chert 124 B1

Thames Cres. Maid 20 A1
Thames Dr. Char 60 C4
Thames Ind Est. Mar 1 C1
Thames Mead. Wind 66 C3
Thames Rd. Gori 34 A3
Thames Rd. Slough 44 A2
Thames Rd. That 106 A3
Thames Reach. Medm 17 E4
Thames Reach. Pur O T 55 E3
Thames Side Prom. Read 59 D1
Thames Side. Chert 124 B1
Thames Side. Hen-O-T 15 F1
Thames Side. Read 59 D1
Thames Side. Stai 96 C1
Thames Side. Wind 67 E4
Thames St. Shepp 125 F1
Thames St. Sonn 60 B2
Thames St. Stai 96 C2
Thames St. Wind 67 E4
Thamesfield Ct. Shepp 125 E1
Thamesfield Gdns. Mar 1 C1
Thanington Way. Read 87 D1
Thatchers Dr. Maid 39 D3
Theal Cl. Sand 150 B4
Theale Rd. Bur C 111 E3
Theobald Rd. Read 57 E2
Theobalds Way. Camb 152 B2
Thetford Mews. Caver 59 E3
Thetford Rd. Ashf 97 F3
Thibet Rd. Sand 150 B4
Thicket Gr. Maid 38 C4
Thicket Rd. Read 84 C4
Thickthorne La. Stai 97 E1
Third Ave. Mar 1 C1
Third Cres. Slough 42 B4
Thirkleby Cl. Slough 42 B3
Thirlmere Ave. Read 57 F1
Thirlmere Cl. Stai 96 A1
Thirtover. Cold A 79 D1
Thistledown. Read 57 E1
Thistleton Way. Winn 87 F1
Thomas Dr. New G 91 F1
Thomas La. Woki 141 F4
Thomas Rd. Bou E 3 E2
Thompkins La. Burn 22 A3
Thompson Cl. Herm 78 C3
Thompson Cl. Slough 44 A1
Thompson Dr. That 106 C1
Thomson Wlk. Bur C 84 C2
Thone Cl. Brac 143 D4
Thorburn Chase. Sand 150 B3
Thorn Dr. Slough 43 F4
Thorn La. Read 86 A4
Thorn St. Read 86 A4
Thornaby Pl. Woo G 3 F4
Thornbank Cl. Stan 70 A1
Thornbers Way. Char 61 D3
Thornbridge Rd. Read 113 D4
Thornbury Cl. Crow 143 D3
Thorncroft. Eng G 95 E1
Thorndike. Slough 42 A1
Thorndown La. Windl 146 B2
Thorndown La. Windl 146 B2
Thorne Cl. Stai 98 B1
Thorne Cl. Woki 115 E2
Thorney Cl. Winn 87 F1
Thorney La N. Iver 44 C3
Thorney La S. Iver 44 C3
Thornfield Green. Black 150 C2
Thornfield. Head 132 B2
Thornford Rd. Gree 132 B2
Thornford Rd. Head 132 C2
Thornford Rd. That 132 B2
Thornhill Way. Stai 125 D2
Thornhill. Brac 118 C3
Thorningdown. Chil 10 B4
Thornton Mews. Read 85 E4
Thornton Rd. Read 85 E4
Thorp Cl. Binf 90 B2
Thorpe By Pass. Stai 123 D3
Thorpe Cl. Woki 116 A2
Thorpe Lea Rd. Stai 96 A1
Thorpe Rd. Chert 123 E2
Thorpe Rd. Stai 96 B2
Thorpe Rd. Stai 123 E2
Thrale Mews. Read 85 D4
Three Acre Rd. Newb 130 C4
Three Firs Way. Bur C 110 C1
Three Gables La. Stre 34 A4
Three Post La. Lamb 25 D1
Threshfield. Brac 118 A2
Thrift La. Holy 64 B4
Throgmorton Rd. Yate 149 D3
Thrush Cl. Bur C 111 D2
Thurlby Way. Maid 39 E2
Thurlestone Cl. Shepp 125 E2
Thurlestone Gdns. Read 86 B1
Thurnscoe Cl. Read 113 F4
Thurso Cl. Read 85 D4
Thurston Rd. Slough 42 C4
Thyme Cl. Read 87 D1
Tichborne Cl. Black 150 B3
Tichbourne Cl. Camb 151 F2
Tickenor Dr. Woki 141 F4
Tickhill Cl. Read 113 F4
Tidmarsh La. Pangb 56 A1
Tidmarsh La. Tidm 56 A1
Tidmarsh Rd. Pangb 56 B2

Tidmarsh Rd. Tidm .... 56 B
Tidmarsh St. Read .... 58 A
Tiffany Cl. Woki .... 115 E
Tiger Cl. Wood .... 88 A
Tigerseye Cl. Woki .... 115 E
Tilbury Cl. Caver .... 59 E
Tile Barn Row. Ball H .... 129 F
Tilecotes Cl. Mar .... 1 E
Tilehurst La. Binf .... 90 E
Tilehurst Rd. Read .... 85 E
Tilling Cl. Read .... 57 F
Tilly's La. Stai .... 96 C
Tilney Way. Read .... 113 F
Tilstone Ave. Eton .... 41 F
Tilstone Cl. Eton .... 41 F
Timbers Wlk. Maid .... 39 F
Timline Green. Brac .... 118 C
Timsway. Stai .... 96 C
Tindal Cl. Yate .... 149 E
Tinkers La. Wind .... 66 E
Tinkers La. Windl .... 121 E
Tinsey Cl. Stai .... 96 A
Tinsley Cl. Read .... 113 F
Tintagel Dr. Camb .... 151 F
Tintagel Rd. Brac .... 142 A
Tintern Cl. Slough .... 42 C
Tintern Cres. Read .... 58 A
Tinwell Cl. Winn .... 87 F
Tippett Rise. Read .... 86 A
Tippings La. Wood .... 88 A
Tippits Mead. Brac .... 117 E
Tiptree Cl. Read .... 113 F
Titcombe Way. Kint .... 102 A
Tite Hill. Eng G .... 95 E
Tithe Barn Dr. Holy .... 40 E
Tithe Cl. Holy .... 40 E
Tithe Ct. Slough .... 44 E
Tithe La. Wray .... 69 E
Tithe Meadows. Went .... 122 E
Tithebarn Gr. Read .... 86 A
Titlarks Hill Rd. Went .... 121 E
Tiverton Cl. Wood .... 88 A
Toad La. Black .... 150 E
Tockley Rd. Burn .... 21 E
Tofrek Terr. Read .... 85 E
Tokers Green Rd. Maple .... 58 E
Tokersgreen La. Caver .... 58 E
Tokersgreen La. Maple .... 58 E
Toll Gdns. Brac .... 118 E
Tollgate. Maid .... 39 E
Tolpuddle Way. Yate .... 149 E
Tomlin Cl. That .... 106 E
Tomlin Rd. Slough .... 21 E
Tomlins Ave. Camb .... 151 E
Tomlinson Dr. Brac .... 142 E
Top Common. New G .... 91 E
Topaz Cl. Slough .... 42 E
Topaz Cl. Woki .... 115 E
Tope Cres. Bark .... 140 E
Tope Rd. Bark .... 140 E
Torcross Gr. Bur C .... 84 E
Torin Ct. Eng G .... 95 E
Torquay Spur. Slough .... 22 E
Torridge Rd. Slough .... 69 E
Torrington Rd. Read .... 86 E
Toseland Way. Winn .... 87 E
Totnes Rd. Read .... 113 E
Tottenham Wlk. Crow .... 143 E
Totterdown. Bur C .... 110 E
Toutley Cl. Woki .... 88 E
Toutley Rd. Woki .... 89 E
Tower Cl. Caver .... 59 E
Tower Cl. Fla H .... 3 E
Tower Hill. Chadd .... 49 E
Towers Dr. Crow .... 143 E
Town Farm Way. Stan .... 97 E
Town La. Bou E .... 3 E
Town La. Stan .... 70 E
Town La. Stan .... 97 E
Town Sq. Brac .... 118 E
Town Square. Camb .... 151 E
Town Tree Rd. Ashf .... 98 E
Townsend Cl. Brac .... 118 E
Townsend Rd. Aldw .... 32 E
Townsend Rd. Read .... 58 E
Townsend Rd. Stre .... 34 E
Towpath. Shepp .... 124 E
Tozer Wlk. Wind .... 66 E
Trafalgar Cl. Woki .... 115 E
Trafalgar Ct. Read .... 85 E
Trafalgar Way. Sand .... 150 E
Trafford Rd. Read .... 58 E
Travic Rd. Slough .... 21 E
Travis Ct. Slough .... 22 E
Travis La. Sand .... 150 E
Tredegar Rd. Caver .... 59 E
Tree Cl. Read .... 84 E
Tree Tops Ave. Camb .... 152 E
Trees Rd. Bou E .... 3 E
Treesmill Dr. Maid .... 39 E
Treeton Cl. Read .... 113 E
Trefoil Cl. Woki .... 116 E
Trelawney Ave. Slough .... 43 E
Trelawney Dr. Read .... 57 E
Trelleck Rd. Read .... 58 E
Tremayne Wlk. Camb .... 152 E
Trenchard Rd. Holy .... 65 E
Trenches La. Slough .... 22 E
Trent Cl. Woki .... 115 E

ent Cres. That 106 A3
ent Rd. Slough 69 D4
nton Cl. Camb 152 A1
esham Cres. Yate 149 D3
evelyan. Brac 117 F1
angle The. Read 84 B4
ndledown. Brac 91 D1
ng Rd. Read 57 E1
nity Ave. Mar 1 B2
nity Cl. Stan 70 B1
nity Cl. Sunn 121 D2
nity Pl. Read 85 F4
nity Pl. Wind 67 E3
nity Rd. Mar 1 B1
nity. Crow 143 F1
umph Cl. Harl 71 E3
tsworth Ave. Vir W 122 C3
etwood Cl. Crow 143 F1
ut Cl. Mar 18 B4
ut Wlk. Newb 105 E2
utbeck Cl. Twyf 61 E3
awe's La. Bee H 138 B2
awe's La. Swal 139 E3
mbull Rd. Brac 91 D1
mps Green Cl. Vir W 122 C2
mps Mill La. Went 122 C2
mpsgreen Ave. Went 122 B2
mpsgreen Rd. Went 122 B2
ro Cl. Maid 39 D4
ss Hill Rd. Ascot 120 B2
st Cnr. Hen-O-T 35 F4
sthorpe Cl. Winn 87 F1
obbs Farm Cl. Lamb 25 D1
owell Rd. Sto P 23 D2
dor Cl. Ashf 97 F2
dor Cl. Woki 116 C3
dor Dr. Woo G 3 E4
dor Cl. Yate 149 E2
dor Gdns. Slough 41 E4
dor Rd. Old W 95 E4
dor Rd. Ashf 98 B1
dor Rd. Newb 105 D1
dor Rd. Read 86 A4
dor Way. Wind 66 C3
nel Link Rd. Stan 71 D1
nel Rd E. Harm 71 D3
nel Rd W. Harm 71 D3
ns Hill Cotts. Read 87 D3
ns La. Hen-O-T 15 F1
ns La. Slough 42 B2
osley Rd. Read 85 F3
f Hill Rd. Camb 151 F4
k's La. Silc 137 D2
meric Cl. Read 86 C1
mberry. Brac 117 F1
nbridge Cl. Read 114 A4
ner Pl. Sand 150 B3
ner Rd. Slough 43 E2
ners Cl. Stai 97 D2
ners Dr. That 106 C1
nery The. That 106 B2
nfields. That 106 B2
rnoak Park. Wind 66 C2
npike Rd. Brac 117 F4
npike Rd. Newb 105 F2
npike Rd. That 105 F2
nstone Cl. Winn 88 A2
nton End. Yate 149 D3
nville Cl. Light 146 A1
pin Rd. Felt 71 F1
pins Gr. Maid 39 D3
pins Rise. Windl 146 A3
nton Way. Slough 42 B2
scam Way. Sand 150 C2
scan Cl. Read 57 F1
xford Mews. Read 85 D4
eed Ct. Read 85 D4
eed Rd. Slough 69 D4
n Oaks. Caver 59 D3
nches La. Slough 42 A3
o Tree Hill. Hen-O-T 35 D4
yford Rd. Binf 89 D1
yford Cl. Binf 90 B4
yford Rd. W St L 62 C3
ynham Rd. Maid 39 D4
erton Pl. Read 85 F3
dehams. Newb 130 C4
r. Pl. Old W 68 A1
e Rd. Read 84 B4
er Cl. Caver 58 C3
er's La. Buck 80 A1
ers Pl. Read 84 C4
e Way. That 106 A3
ell Gdns. Wind 66 C2
erton. Brac 118 B4

ngton Cl. Read 84 B4
don Dr. Brac 118 C3
cott Cl. Read 113 F4
swater Cl. Light 146 A1
swater Cl. Slough 41 E4
swater Cl. That 106 A2
swater Dr. Read 57 E2
swater Rd. Light 146 A1
swater. Brac 117 F1
ter Cl. Caver 59 E3
berville Way. Slough 21 F1
derhill Cl. Maid 39 F3
derhill. Moul 14 A2

Underwood Rd. Read 85 D2
Underwood. Brac 117 F2
Union Cl. Sand 143 F1
Union Rd. Brad 82 B2
Union St. Read 86 A4
Unity Cl. Caver 59 D3
Unwin Ave. Harm 71 E1
Upavon Dr. Read 85 F3
Upavon Gdns. Brac 118 C2
Upcroft. Wind 67 D2
Updown Hill. Windl 146 B2
Upland Rd. Camb 151 E4
Uplands Cl. Sand 150 A4
Uplands Rd. Caver 58 C3
Uplands. Hung 100 B3
Uplands. Mar B 1 B3
Upper Bray Rd. Maid 40 B2
Upper Broadmoor Rd. Crow . 143 E3
Upper Charles St. Camb 151 E3
Upper Chobham Rd. Camb .. 152 A2
Upper College Ride. Camb .. 151 F4
Upper Crown St. Read 86 A3
Upper End. Chadd 49 D4
Upper Gordon Rd. Camb 151 E3
Upper Halliford Rd. Shepp .. 125 F3
Upper Lambourn Rd. Lamb .. 25 D2
Upper Lees Rd. Slough 22 A1
Upper Meadow Rd. Read 86 B1
Upper Nursery. Sunn 121 D2
Upper Park Rd. Camb 151 F3
Upper Red Cross Rd. Gori .. 34 B3
Upper Redlands Rd. Read .. 86 C3
Upper Village Rd. Ascot 120 B2
Upper Warren Ave. Caver 58 B2
Upper Woodcote Rd. Caver .. 58 B3
Uppingham Dr. Wood 60 C1
Uppingham Gdns. Caver 59 E3
Upshire Gdns. Brac 118 C3
Upton Cl. Hen-O-T 15 F1
Upton Cl. Slough 42 C2
Upton Court Rd. Slough 43 D1
Upton Lea Par. Slough 43 D3
Upton Park. Slough 42 C2
Upton Rd. Read 85 D4
Upton Rd. Slough 43 D2
Urquhart Rd. That 106 C1
Usk Rd. Read 84 C3
Uxbridge Rd. Slough 43 E3

Vachel Rd. Read 86 A4
Vale Cres. Read 57 F1
Vale Gr. Slough 42 C2
Vale Rd. Camb 151 D2
Vale Rd. Wind 66 C3
Valentia Rd. Read 85 E4
Valentine Cres. Caver 59 E2
Valeview Dr. Bee H 138 B3
Valley Cl. Caver 59 D2
Valley Cl. Gori 34 B3
Valley Cres. Woki 116 A4
Valley End. Iver H 23 E1
Valley Rd. Bur C 111 D2
Valley Rd. Camb 152 B1
Valley Rd. Hen-O-T 35 D4
Valley Rd. Newb 130 C4
Valley Way. Silc 135 F1
Valon Rd. Arbo 140 C4
Valpy St. Read 86 A4
Valroy Cl. Camb 151 E3
Vandyke. Brac 117 F2
Vanloree Way. Read 84 B3
Vanners La. Ham M 129 E3
Vansittart Rd. Bish 18 C4
Vansittart Rd. Wind 67 D3
Vantage Rd. Slough 42 A3
Vanwall Bsns Park. Maid 39 E3
Vanwall Rd. Maid 39 E2
Vastern Rd. Caver 59 D1
Vaughan Copse. Eton 42 B1
Vaughan Way. Slough 21 F1
Vauxhall Dr. Wood 88 A3
Vegal Cres. Eng G 95 E2
Venetia Cl. Caver 59 E4
Venning Rd. Bark 140 C4
Ventnor Rd. Read 57 E1
Venus Cl. Woki 115 F3
Verey Cl. Twyf 61 F2
Vermont Rd. Slough 21 F1
Vermont Woods. Woki 141 F4
Verney Cl. Mar 1 B1
Verney Mews. Read 85 E4
Verney Rd. Slough 44 A1
Vernon Cres. Read 113 D4
Vernon Dr. Ascot 119 F4
Vernon Rd. Felt 98 C3
Verran Rd. Camb 151 E2
Viburnum St. Camb 153 F3
Vicarage Ave. Stai 96 A2
Vicarage Cl. Cook 20 A4
Vicarage Cres. Stai 96 A2
Vicarage Ct. Felt 98 B4
Vicarage Ct. Stai 96 A1
Vicarage Dr. Maid 40 B2
Vicarage Gdns. Ascot 120 A2
Vicarage La. Cold A 106 B4
Vicarage La. Stai 124 B3
Vicarage La. Wray 95 F4
Vicarage La. Yate 149 E4
Vicarage Rd. Ashf 98 C1

Vicarage Rd. Bags 145 E2
Vicarage Rd. Black 150 C2
Vicarage Rd. Hen-O-T 35 F4
Vicarage Rd. Maid 39 F4
Vicarage Rd. Read 86 B3
Vicarage Rd. Stai 96 A1
Vicarage Rd. Stai 96 C3
Vicarage Rd. Yate 149 E4
Vicarage Way. Iver 69 E4
Vicarage Wlk. Maid 40 B2
Vickers Cl. Shin 113 F2
Vickers Cl. Wood 88 A4
Victor Rd. That 106 C2
Victor Rd. Wind 67 E2
Victor Way. Wood 88 A4
Victoria Ave. Camb 151 D3
Victoria Cres. Iver 44 C3
Victoria Cl. Bags 145 F1
Victoria Dr. Black 150 B2
Victoria Gdns. Newb 105 D2
Victoria La. Harl 71 E4
Victoria Rd. Ascot 120 A2
Victoria Rd. Caver 59 D2
Victoria Rd. Eton 41 F1
Victoria Rd. Far C 22 B3
Victoria Rd. Mar 1 C1
Victoria Rd. Mort 136 C3
Victoria Rd. Read 84 B4
Victoria Rd. Sand 143 F1
Victoria Rd. Slough 43 D3
Victoria Rd. Stai 96 C3
Victoria Rd. Warg 36 C1
Victoria St. Eng G 95 E1
Victoria St. Read 86 B4
Victoria St. Slough 42 C2
Victoria St. Wind 67 E3
Victory Rd. Chert 124 A1
Vigo La. Yate 149 E2
Vigo La. Yate 149 E3
Viking. Brac 117 F2
Village Cl. Read 113 D3
Village Rd. Dorn 41 E2
Village Rd. Stai 123 E3
Village The. Finch 141 F2
Village The. Old W 94 A3
Village Way. Ashf 98 A2
Village Way. Yate 149 E4
Villiers Mead. Woki 116 A3
Villiers Rd. Slough 42 B4
Villiers Way. Newb 130 B3
Villiers Wlk. Newb 130 B3
Vincent Cl. Chert 123 F1
Vincent Cl. Harm 71 D4
Vincent Cl. Wood 87 F3
Vincent Dr. Shepp 125 F3
Vincent Rd. Chert 123 F1
Vincent Rise. Brac 118 C3
Vine Cl. Stan 70 A1
Vine Cres. Read 85 D2
Vine Rd. Sto P 22 C3
Vineries Cl. Harm 71 D4
Vinery The. Warg 36 B1
Vines The. Woki 115 E2
Vineyard Dr. Bou E 3 D3
Viola Ave. Stan 97 F4
Virginia Ave. Vir W 122 B2
Virginia Beeches. Vir W 122 A1
Virginia Cl. Stai 124 B3
Virginia Dr. Vir W 122 B3
Virginia Way. Read 85 D3
Viscount Rd. Stan 97 F4
Viscount Way. Harm 71 F2
Viscount Way. Wood 88 A4
Vivien Cl. Cook 19 F3
Voller Dr. Read 84 B3
Volunteer Rd. Thea 83 E1
Vulcan Cl. Sand 150 A4
Vulcan Way. Sand 150 A4

Wabone Rd. Bou E 3 D2
Wade Dr. Slough 42 A3
Wadham Cl. Shepp 125 E1
Wadham. Crow 143 F1
Wagbullock Rise. Brac 118 B2
Waggoners Hollow. Bags 145 F1
Wagner Cl. Whi Wa 38 C2
Wagtail Cl. Twyf 61 F2
Waingels Cl. Char 61 D1
Waingels Rd. Wood 61 D1
Wakefield Cres. Sto P 22 C3
Wakeford Cl. Silc 135 F1
Wakelins End. Cook 19 F4
Wakeman Rd. Bou E 3 D2
Wakemans. Pangb 55 E2
Walbury. Brac 118 C3
Waldeck Rd. Maid 40 A4
Waldeck St. Read 86 A3
Waldegrave Pl. Newb 105 D2
Walden Ave. Arbo 114 B2
Waldens Cl. Bou E 3 D2
Waldorf Hts. Black 150 B2
Waldron Hill. Brac 118 C4
Walgrove Gdns. Whi Wa 63 F4
Walk The. Ashf 98 C1
Walk The. Eton 42 A1
Walker Rd. Maid 40 A2
Walker's La. Lamb 25 D2
Walker's Ridge. Camb 151 F3

Walkers Pl. Read 85 E4
Wall La. Silc 136 B1
Wallace Cl. Mar 1 C2
Wallace Cl. Shepp 125 E3
Wallace Cl. Wood 87 E3
Walled Gdn The. Warg 36 B1
Waller Dr. Newb 105 F3
Wallingford Cl. Brac 118 C3
Wallingford Rd. Comp 31 F3
Wallingford Rd. Gori 14 B3
Wallingford Rd. Sou S 14 B3
Wallington Rd. Camb 145 D1
Wallington's Rd. Kint 101 F1
Wallis Ct. Slough 43 D2
Wallner Way. Woki 116 C3
Walmer Cl. Crow 143 E3
Walmer Cl. Read 85 D3
Walmer Rd. Wood 60 C1
Walnut Cl. Woki 115 F3
Walnut Cl. Yate 149 E2
Walnut Tree Cl. Bou E 3 D1
Walnut Tree Cl. Twyf 61 F3
Walnut Tree Ct. Stai 34 B3
Walnut Tree Rd. Stai 125 E3
Walnut Tree Rd. Stai 125 E4
Walnut Way. Bou E 3 D1
Walnut Way. Read 84 B4
Walpole Rd. Old W 95 D4
Walpole Rd. Slough 41 E4
Walrus Cl. Wood 88 A4
Walter Rd. Woki 115 F4
Walters Cl. Cold A 106 B4
Waltham Cl. Crow 143 E1
Waltham Cl. Whi Wa 38 C1
Waltham Rd. Twyf 61 F2
Waltham Rd. Twyf 62 A3
Waltham Rd. Whi Wa 38 C1
Walton Ave. Hen-O-T 35 F4
Walton Bridge Rd. Shepp 125 F1
Walton Cl. Wood 87 E4
Walton Dr. Ascot 119 F4
Walton Gdns. Felt 98 C2
Walton La. Burn 21 F2
Walton La. Shepp 125 F1
Walton Way. Newb 105 E2
Wandhope Way. Read 57 E1
Wanstraw Gr. Brac 118 C1
Wantage Cl. Brac 118 C2
Wantage Rd. Gr She 48 B3
Wantage Rd. Lamb 25 D2
Wantage Rd. Read 85 E4
Wantage Rd. Sand 150 B4
Wantage Rd. Stre 33 F4
Wapshott Rd. Stai 96 C2
War Memorial Pl. Hen-O-T 35 F4
Waram Cl. Hung 100 C4
Warbler Cl. Read 84 A3
Warborough Ave. Read 84 A4
Warborough Rd. Let B 7 D4
Warbreck Dr. Sulh 57 D2
Warbrook La. Finch 141 D1
Ward Cl. Iver 44 C3
Ward Cl. Woki 116 B4
Ward Gdns. Slough 41 F3
Ward Royal. Wind 67 D3
Ward Stone Park. Brac 118 C1
Wardle Ave. Read 57 E1
Wardle Cl. Bags 145 F2
Wareham Rd. Brac 118 C2
Warfield Rd. Brac 91 E1
Warfield Rd. Felt 98 C4
Warfield St. New G 91 E2
Wargrave Hill. Warg 36 B1
Wargrave Rd. Rem H 36 A4
Wargrave Rd. Twyf 61 E3
Wargrove Dr. Sand 150 B4
Waring Cl. Winn 114 B4
Warley Rise. Sulh 57 E2
Warner Cl. Harl 71 E4
Warner Cl. Slough 41 F3
Warners Hill. Cook 19 E4
Warnford Rd. Read 84 C4
Warnsham Cl. Read 87 D1
Warren Cl. Bur C 111 D2
Warren Cl. Sand 150 A4
Warren Cl. Slough 43 F2
Warren La. Woki 141 F1
Warren Rd. Ashf 98 C1
Warren Rd. Wood 60 B1
Warren Rise. Camb 151 D2
Warren Row Rd. Know H 37 E3
Warren Row. Burl 119 E4
Warren The. Caver 58 C2
Warrington Ave. Slough 42 B4
Warrington Spur. Old W 95 D4
Warwick Ave. Slough 22 B1
Warwick Ave. Stai 97 E1
Warwick Cl. Camb 152 A2
Warwick Cl. Maid 39 D2
Warwick Dr. Newb 105 D1
Warwick Rd. Ashf 97 F2
Warwick Rd. Read 86 B2
Warwick. Brac 118 C2

Wasdale Cl. Crow 143 E1
Wash Hill Lea. Bou E 3 E2
Wash Hill. Bou E 3 F2
Wash Water. Ham M 130 A2
Wash Water. Newb 130 A2
Washing La. Brim 134 B3
Washington Cl. Mar 2 A2
Washington Dr. Slough 41 E3
Washington Dr. Wind 66 C2
Washington Gdns. Woki 142 A4
Washington Rd. Caver 59 D1
Watchetts Dr. Camb 151 E1
Watchetts Lake Cl. Camb 151 E2
Watchetts Rd. Camb 151 D2
Watchmoor Rd. Camb 151 D2
Water La. Gree 131 E4
Water Rd. Read 85 D4
Water St. Hamp N 52 C3
Waterbeach Rd. Slough 42 B4
Waterfall Cl. Vir W 122 A3
Waterford Way. Woki 116 B3
Waterham Rd. Brac 118 A2
Waterhouse Mead. Sand 150 C4
Waterloo Cres. Woki 116 C3
Waterloo Rd. Crow 143 D2
Waterloo Rd. Read 86 A3
Waterloo Rd. Woki 116 C3
Waterloo Rise. Read 86 A2
Waterman Pl. Read 59 D1
Waterman's Rd. Hen-O-T 35 F4
Waterman's Way. Warg 36 B1
Watermead. Felt 98 C4
Watermill Ct. Wool 108 B1
Waters Dr. Stai 96 C2
Watersfield Cl. Read 87 D1
Waterside Cl. Newb 105 D2
Waterside Dr. Pur O T 57 E3
Waterside Dr. Slough 44 A2
Wareside Dr. Thea 83 F2
Waterside Gdns. Read 86 A4
Waterside Park Ind Est. Brac 117 F4
Waterside. Woo G 3 F4
Watersplash La. Ascot 120 C4
Watersplash La. Wink 120 C4
Watersplash Rd. Stai 125 D3
Watery La. Chert 123 E1
Watery La. Kint 128 C3
Watery La. Woo G 3 F4
Watkins Cl. Woki 141 F4
Watlington St. Read 86 B4
Watmore La. Winn 88 B1
Watson Cl. Woki 115 F1
Watt's La. Blew 12 A4
Wavell Cl. Read 86 C1
Wavell Gdns. Slough 21 F1
Wavell Rd. Maid 39 D3
Wavendene Ave. Stai 96 B1
Waverley Cl. Camb 151 F2
Waverley Dr. Camb 151 F3
Waverley Dr. Vir W 122 A3
Waverley Rd. Bags 145 F2
Waverley Rd. Read 85 E4
Waverley Rd. Slough 42 B4
Waverley Way. Woki 115 F1
Waverley Way. Woki 141 F4
Waverley. Brac 117 F2
Waverleys The. That 106 B2
Waybrook Cres. Read 86 C3
Wayland Cl. Brac 118 C3
Waylen St. Read 85 F4
Ways End. Camb 151 F2
Wayside Mews. Maid 39 F4
Weald Rise. Read 57 F1
Wealden Way. Read 57 F1
Wealden Way. Read 84 C4
Weavers La. Ink 127 E3
Weavers Wlk. Newb 105 D2
Webb Cl. Bags 145 F1
Webb Cl. Binf 90 C1
Webb Cl. Slough 43 E1
Webb Ct. Woki 116 C4
Webbs Acre. That 106 C1
Webbs La. Been 109 D4
Webster Cl. Maid 39 D3
Wedderburn Cl. Winn 88 B1
Wedgewood Way. Read 57 F1
Weekes Dr. Slough 42 A2
Weighbridge Row. Read 58 C1
Weir Cl. Read 84 C2
Weir Pl. Stai 123 F4
Weir Rd. Chert 124 A1
Welbeck Rd. Maid 39 E3
Welbeck. Brac 117 F2
Welby Cl. Maid 39 D2
Welby Cres. Winn 88 A1
Weldale St. Read 85 F4
Welford Rd. Wood 88 A4
Well Cl. Camb 151 D2
Well House Cl. Swal 140 B2
Well Meadow. Newb 105 D3
Welland Cl. Read 57 E1
Welland Cl. Slough 69 D4
Wellbank. Tapl 20 C1
Wellcroft Rd. Slough 42 A3
Weller Dr. Brac 141 D3
Weller Dr. Camb 151 E2
Weller's La. New G 91 E4
Wellesley Ave. Iver 44 C2
Wellesley Cl. Bags 145 E2

Wellesley Dr. Brac 142 C3
Wellesley Dr. Finch 142 C3
Wellesley Rd. Slough 43 D2
Welley Ave. Wray 68 C2
Welley Rd. Hort 68 C1
Welley Rd. Wray 68 C1
Wellfield Cl. Read 84 B4
Wellhill Rd. Fawl 27 E3
Wellhouse La. Buck 79 F3
Wellhouse La. Herm 79 F3
Wellhouse Rd. Maid 19 F1
Wellington Ave. Read 86 B2
Wellington Ave. Vir W 122 A2
Wellington Ave. Went 122 A2
Wellington Busn Park. Woki .. 142 C2
Wellington Cl. Newb 105 E3
Wellington Cl. Sand 150 B4
Wellington Cl. Shepp 125 F1
Wellington Cres. Tad 134 B1
Wellington Dr. Brac 118 C2
Wellington Rd. Ashf 97 F2
Wellington Rd. Crow 143 E2
Wellington Rd. Harm 71 F1
Wellington Rd. Maid 39 E4
Wellington Rd. Sand 150 B4
Wellington Rd. Woki 116 A3
Wellington St. Slough 43 D2
Wellingtonia Ave. Finch 142 B2
Wells Cl. Wind 67 D4
Wells La. Ascot 120 A3
Welsh La. Swal 139 D1
Welshman's Rd. Silc 136 A3
Welwick Cl. Winn 87 F1
Welwyn Ave. Felt 71 F1
Wendan Rd. Newb 130 C4
Wendover Dr. Camb 152 B2
Wendover Pl. Stai 96 B2
Wendover Rd. Bou E 3 D3
Wendover Rd. Burn 41 D4
Wendover Rd. Slough 41 D4
Wendover Rd. Stai 96 B2
Wendover Way. Read 84 B4
Wenlock Edge. Char 61 D2
Wenlock Way. That 106 B1
Wensley Cl. Twyf 61 E3
Wensley Rd. Read 85 F3
Wensleydale Dr. Camb 152 B3
Wentworth Ave. Burl 119 E4
Wentworth Ave. Read 113 E4
Wentworth Ave. Slough 22 A1
Wentworth Cl. Ashf 98 A2
Wentworth Cl. Brac 142 C3
Wentworth Cl. Yate 149 E3
Wentworth Cres. Maid 39 E3
Wentworth Ct. Newb 105 D1
Wentworth Dr. Vir W 122 A2
Wentworth Way. Burl 119 E4
Wescott Rd. Woki 116 B3
Wesley Dr. Eng G 96 A1
Wessex Cl. Hung 100 B3
Wessex Gdns. Twyf 61 F2
Wessex Rd. Bou E 3 D1
Wessex Rd. Harn 70 C2
Wessex Way. Maid 39 D2
Wessons Hill. Cook 19 E4
West Cl. Ashf 97 F2
West Cl. Medm 17 E4
West Cres. Wind 66 C3
West Dean. Maid 39 F4
West Dr. Read 84 C3
West Dr. Sonn 60 C1
West Dr. Went 121 F1
West Dr. Went 122 A1
West End Ct. Sto P 22 C2
West End La. Hart 71 E4
West End La. Sto P 22 C2
West End Rd. Silc 136 C3
West Fryerne. Yate 149 E4
West Green Ct. Read 85 F3
West Green. Yate 149 D4
West Hill. Read 86 A3
West Mead. Maid 19 F1
West Mills. Newb 104 C2
West Point. Slough 41 E3
West Ramp. Harm 71 D3
West Rd. Camb 151 E3
West Rd. Felt 98 B4
West Rd. Maid 39 F4
West Ridge. Bou E 3 D2
West Sq. Iver 44 C4
West St. Hen-O-T 15 E1
West St. Maid 39 F4
West St. Mar 1 B1
West St. Newb 104 C2
West St. Read 86 A4
West View. Felt 98 B4
West View. Pease 50 B4
West Way. Shepp 125 E2
Westacott Way. Bur G 38 B2
Westborough Ct. Maid 39 E3
Westborough Rd. Maid 39 E3
Westbourne Rd. Felt 98 C3
Westbourne Rd. Sand 150 C4
Westbourne Rd. Stai 97 D1
Westbourne Terr. Read 85 E4
Westbrook Cl. Hung 100 B3
Westbrook Gdns. Brac 118 B4
Westbrook Green. Blew 11 F4
Westbrook Rd. Read 58 B1

Westbrook Rd. Stai 96 C2
Westbrook St. Blew 11 F4
Westbrook. Holy 40 C1
Westbury Cl. Crow 143 D3
Westbury Cl. Shepp 125 D2
Westbury La. Pur O T 57 D3
Westcombe Cl. Brac 118 C1
Westcote Rd. Read 85 E3
Westcotts Green. New G 91 F1
Westcroft. Slough 22 A1
Westdene Cres. Caver 58 C2
Westerdale Dr. Camb 152 A2
Westerdale. That 106 B2
Western Ave. Chert 124 A3
Western Ave. Hen-O-T 35 F4
Western Ave. Newb 104 C2
Western Ave. Stai 123 D3
Western Ave. Wood 60 C1
Western Cl. Chert 124 A3
Western Dr. Bou E 3 F3
Western Dr. Shepp 125 E2
Western Elms Ave. Read 85 F4
Western End. Newb 104 C1
Western Oaks. Read 57 F1
Western Perimeter Rd. Harm . 70 A2
Western Perimeter Rd. Stan .. 70 A2
Western Rd. Brac 117 F4
Western Rd. Hen-O-T 35 F4
Western Rd. Read 85 F3
Westfield Cotts. Medm 16 C3
Westfield Cres. Shipl 36 A2
Westfield Cres. That 106 A2
Westfield Rd. Camb 151 D1
Westfield Rd. Caver 59 D1
Westfield Rd. Chol 13 E4
Westfield Rd. Maid 39 D4
Westfield Rd. Slough 22 A1
Westfield Rd. That 106 A3
Westfield Rd. Winn 88 A1
Westfield Way. Newb 104 C1
Westfields. Comp 31 E2
Westgate Cres. Slough 41 F3
Westgate Rd. Newb 104 C1
Westhatch Cnr. New G 91 E3
Westhatch La. New G 91 E3
Westhope Rd. Mar 1 C2
Westland Cl. Stan 70 C1
Westland. That 106 A2
Westlands Ave. Read 86 C1
Westlands Ave. Slough 41 E4
Westlands Cl. Slough 41 E4
Westlands Rd. Newb 131 D4
Westley Mill. Binf 90 C4
Westley Mill. Holy 63 F1
Westlyn Rd. Silc 135 F1
Westmacott Dr. Felt 98 C4
Westmead Dr. Newb 130 C4
Westmead. Wind 67 D2
Westminster Way. Wood 87 E1
Westmorland Cl. Woki 115 E3
Westmorland Dr. Camb 152 A2
Westmorland Dr. New G 91 F1
Westmorland Rd. Maid 39 E3
Weston Gr. Bags 145 F1
Weston Rd. Slough 41 F4
Westonbirt Dr. Caver 58 C2
Westons. Beed 51 E4
Westridge Ave. Pur O T 57 E3
Westview Dr. Twyf 61 F3
Westward Rd. Woki 115 F4
Westwates Cl. Brac 118 B4
Westway. Gori 34 B4
Westwood Glen. Read 57 E1
Westwood Green. Cook 19 F3
Westwood Rd. Mar 1 B1
Westwood Rd. Newb 105 E1
Westwood Rd. Read 57 E1
Westwood Rd. Windl 146 C3
Westwood Row. Read 57 E1
Wetherby Cl. Caver 59 E3
Wethered Dr. Burn 41 D4
Wethered Rd. Mar 1 B1
Wetton Pl. Eng G 96 A2
Wexham Park La. Iver H 23 E1
Wexham Park La. Sto P 23 E1
Wexham Rd. Slough 43 D3
Wexham St. Sto P 23 D2
Wexham Woods. Slough 43 E4
Wey Ave. Chert 124 A1
Wey Cl. Camb 151 D3
Weybridge Mead. Yate 149 F4
Weycrofts. Brac 90 C1
Weymead Cl. Chert 124 B1
Whaley Rd. Woki 116 B4
Wharf La. Bou E 3 D2
Wharf La. Hen-O-T 15 F1
Wharf Rd. Newb 105 D2
Wharf Rd. Wray 95 E4
Wharf St. Newb 105 D2
Wharf The. Newb 105 D2
Wharfdale Rd. Winn 88 A2
Wharfside. Padw 109 E2
Whatley Green. Brac 118 A2
Whatmore Cl. Stan 70 A1
Wheatash Rd. Chert 124 A1
Wheatbutts Meadow. Eton ... 41 F1
Wheatfield Cl. Maid 39 D2
Wheatfields Rd. Shin 113 F3
Wheatlands Cl. Read 84 C2

Wheatlands La. Ham M 130 A3
Wheatlands Rd. Slough 43 E2
Wheatley Cl. Read 86 C1
Wheatley. Brac 117 F2
Wheatsheaf La. Newb 105 D2
Wheatsheaf La. Stai 96 C1
Wheble Dr. Wood 87 E4
Wheeler Cl. Bur C 111 D2
Wheelers Green Way. That .. 106 C1
Wheelton Cl. Winn 87 F2
Whins Cl. Camb 151 D2
Whins Dr. Camb 151 D2
Whinshill Ct. Went 121 D1
Whistler Gr. Sand 150 B3
Whistley Cl. Brac 118 C3
Whitamore Row. Hen-O-T 35 F4
Whitby Dr. Read 86 B3
Whitby Green. Caver 59 E3
Whitby Rd. Slough 42 B3
Whitchurch Cl. Maid 19 F2
Whitchurch Rd. Pangb 56 B3
White Bridge Cl. Felt 71 F1
White City. Crow 143 E3
White Cl. Herm 78 C3
White Cl. Slough 42 B3
White Gates. Wick 75 E3
White Hart Rd. Maid 39 F4
White Hart Rd. Slough 42 B2
White Hart Row. Chert 124 A1
White Hill. Beac 3 F4
White Hill. Rem H 16 A1
White Hill. Shipl 35 D3
White Hill. Windl 146 A3
White Hill. Woo G 3 F4
White Horse La. Finch 141 E3
White Horse Rd. Wind 66 B3
White House Gdns. Yate 149 E4
White Lilies Island. Wind 67 D4
White Lion Way. Yate 149 E4
White Lodge Cl. Suth 57 D2
White Lodge. Mar B 1 B3
White Paddock. Whi Wa 39 D1
White Rd. Chil 10 B4
White Rd. Sand 150 C3
White Rock. Maid 20 A1
White Shoot. Blew 12 A3
White's La. Been 109 D4
Whitebeam Cl. Woki 115 E2
Whiteford Rd. Slough 42 C4
Whitegates La. Read 87 D4
Whitehall Dr. Arbo 140 C4
Whitehall Farm La. Vir W 122 C3
Whitehall La. Eng G 95 F1
Whitehall La. Wray 69 D1
Whitehill Cl. Mar B 1 B3
Whitehill Pl. Vir W 122 C2
Whitehill Rd. Camb 151 E4
Whitehills Green. Gori 34 B3
Whiteknights Rd. Read 86 C3
Whitelands Dr. Burl 119 E4
Whitelands Rd. That 106 B2
Whiteley. Wind 66 C4
Whitemoor La. Upp B 54 C3
Whitepit La. Fla H 3 E4
Whites Hill. Sulhd 110 C3
Whites La. Datch 68 A4
Whitestone Cl. Winn 87 F2
Whitewalls Cl. Comp 31 F3
Whiteways Ct. Stai 97 D1
Whitley Cl. Stan 70 C1
Whitley Park La. Read 86 B2
Whitley Rd. Yate 149 E2
Whitley St. Read 86 A3
Whitley Wood La. Read 113 E4
Whitley Wood Rd. Read 113 E4
Whitmoor Rd. Bags 145 F1
Whitmore Cl. Sand 143 E1
Whitmore La. Sunn 121 D2
Whitstone Gdns. Read 86 B1
Whittaker Rd. Slough 21 F1
Whittenham Cl. Slough 43 D3
Whittle Cl. Crow 143 D1
Whittle Cl. Woki 141 F4
Whittle Parkway. Slough 41 E4
Whitton Cl. Brac 118 C3
Whitton Cl. Winn 87 E1
Whitworth Rd. Bark 141 D4
Whurley Way. Maid 19 F1
Whynstones Rd. Ascot 120 A2
Whyteladyes La. Cook 19 F3
Wick Hill La. Woki 142 A3
Wick La. Eng G 94 C1
Wick Rd. Eng G 95 D1
Wick's Green. Binf 90 A2
Wickford Way. Read 113 F4
Wickham Cl. Bags 145 F3
Wickham La. Eng G 96 A1
Wickham Rd. Camb 151 F4
Wickham Rd. Winn 87 F1
Wickham Vale. Brac 117 F2
Widbrook Rd. Maid 20 A2
Widecombe Pl. Read 86 A1
Widecroft Rd. Iver 44 C4
Widmere La. Mar B 1 A4
Wield Ct. Winn 87 F1
Wiggett Gr. Binf 90 B1
Wigmore La. Read 58 A1
Wigmore La. Read 58 B1
Wigmore La. Thea 83 E1

Wigmore Rd. Tad 134 C1
Wilberforce Way. Brac 118 B2
Wilcox Gdns. Stai 124 C3
Wild Briar. Woki 141 F4
Wild Cl. Winn 114 B4
Wildcroft Dr. Woki 116 A1
Wilder Ave. Pangb 56 C3
Wilderness Ct. Read 87 D2
Wilderness Rd. Camb 151 F1
Wilderness Rd. Read 87 D2
Wilders Cl. Brac 91 D1
Wilders Cl. Camb 151 F2
Wildgreen N. Slough 44 A1
Wildgreen S. Slough 44 A1
Wildridings Rd. Brac 118 A3
Wildridings Sq. Brac 118 A3
Wildwood Dr. Tad 134 B1
Wildwood Gdns. Yate 149 E2
Wilford Rd. Slough 43 F1
Wilfred Way. That 107 D2
Wilfrids Wood Cl. Bou E 3 D3
Willats Cl. Chert 124 A2
William Cl. That 106 B1
William Ellis Cl. Old W 68 A1
William Slim Wood. Burl 92 A1
William St. Read 85 F4
William St. Slough 42 C3
William St. Wind 67 E3
Williant Cl. Whi Wa 38 C1
Willington Cl. Camb 151 D3
Willoners. Slough 42 A4
Willoughby Rd. Brac 117 F3
Willoughby Rd. Slough 44 A2
Willow Cl. Bur C 111 D3
Willow Cl. Fla H 3 E3
Willow Cl. Iver 69 E4
Willow Cl. Newb 104 C1
Willow Cl. Camb 151 E1
Willow Dr. Brac 118 B4
Willow Dr. Maid 40 A1
Willow Dr. Twyf 61 E3
Willow Gdns. Read 86 C1
Willow Green. West E 153 F3
Willow La. Black 150 B2
Willow La. Wray 36 B2
Willow Park. Sto P 23 D3
Willow Pl. Eton 67 E4
Willow Rd. Newt 131 F1
Willow Rd. Stan 69 F3
Willow St. Read 86 A3
Willow Tree Glade. Bur C 84 B2
Willow Way. Sand 142 C1
Willow Wlk. Chert 124 A1
Willow Wlk. Eng G 95 E2
Willowbrook Rd. Stan 97 F3
Willowbrook. Eton 42 B1
Willowdale. Woki 141 F4
Willowford. Yate 149 E3
Willowmead Cl. Mar 1 C2
Willowmead Cl. Newb 130 B3
Willowmead Gdns. Mar 1 C2
Willowmead Rd. Mar 1 C2
Willowmead Sq. Mar 1 C2
Willowmead. Stai 124 A4
Willows End. Sand 150 A4
Willows Rd. Bou E 3 D2
Willows The. Caver 59 D1
Willows The. Light 146 B1
Willowside. Wood 60 C1
Willson Rd. Eng G 95 D2
Wilmington Cl. Wood 87 F4
Wilmot Cl. Binf 90 B1
Wilmot Rd. Burn 21 D1
Wilmot Way. Camb 151 F2
Wilmot Wlk. Newb 130 B3
Wilmott Cl. Winn 88 A1
Wilsford Cl. Read 113 E4
Wilson Ave. Hen-O-T 35 F4
Wilson Cl. Comp 31 F2
Wilson Cl. Winn 88 A1
Wilson Rd. Read 85 E4
Wilton Cl. Harm 70 B4
Wilton Cres. Wind 66 B2
Wilton Rd. Camb 151 D2
Wilton Rd. Read 85 E4
Wiltshire Ave. Crow 143 D3
Wiltshire Ave. Slough 22 B1
Wiltshire Dr. Woki 116 B4
Wiltshire Gr. New G 91 F1
Wiltshire Rd. Mar 1 C2
Wiltshire Rd. Woki 116 B4
Wiltshire Wlk. Read 84 A3
Wilwood Rd. Brac 117 F4
Wilwyne Cl. Caver 59 E2
Wimbledon Cl. Camb 144 C1
Wimbledon Rd. Camb 144 C1
Wimblington Dr. Winn 114 B4
Wimborne Gdns. Read 58 A1
Wimbushes. Woki 141 E3
Winbury Ct. Maid 39 F4
Wincanton Rd. Read 113 E4
Winch Cl. Binf 90 B2
Winchbottom La. Lit M 2 A3
Winchcombe Rd. Newb 105 D1
Winchcombe Rd. Twyf 61 F2
Winchester Cl. Stan 69 F3
Winchester Dr. Maid 39 D2
Winchester Rd. Harl 71 F4
Winchester Rd. Read 86 A2

Winchester Way. Black 150
Winchgrove Rd. Brac 91
Winchstone Cl. Stai 124
Wincroft Rd. Caver 58
Windermere Cl. Felt 98
Windermere Cl. Read 88
Windermere Cl. Stai 98
Windermere Rd. Light 146
Windermere Rd. Read 86
Windermere Way. Slough 41
Windermere Way. That 106
Winding Wood Dr. Camb 152
Windle Cl. Windl 146
Windlebrook Green. Brac ... 118
Windlesham Cl. Windl 146
Windlesham Rd. Brac 117
Windlesham Rd. West E 153
Windmill Ave. Woki 115
Windmill Cl. Stai 98
Windmill Cl. Wind 67
Windmill Cl. Woki 115
Windmill Cnr. Mort 137
Windmill Field. Windl 146
Windmill La. Buck 108
Windmill La. Wool 108
Windmill Rd W. Stai 125
Windmill Rd. Brac 118
Windmill Rd. Cook 19
Windmill Rd. Fulm 23
Windmill Rd. Mort 137
Windmill Rd. Slough 42
Windmill Rd. Stai 125
Windrush Ave. Slough 42
Windrush Hts. Sand 150
Windrush Way. Maid 39
Windrush Way. Read 85
Windsor Dr. Ashf 97
Windsor Hill. Bou E 3
Windsor La. Burn 21
Windsor Park Rd. Harl 71
Windsor Rd. Ascot 120
Windsor Rd. Datch 68
Windsor Rd. Eng G 95
Windsor Rd. Holy 40
Windsor Rd. Maid 40
Windsor Rd. Oak G 40
Windsor Rd. Oak G 40
Windsor Rd. Slough 42
Windsor Rd. Sto P 23
Windsor Rd. Wray 68
Windsor Ride. Sand 151
Windsor Ride. Woki 142
Windsor Rise. Newb 131
Windsor St. Chert 124
Windsor Way. Read 84
Wing Cl. Mar 1
Wingate Rd. Wood 87
Wingfield Gdns. Camb 152
Wingrove Rd. Read 85
Winkfield Cl. Woki 116
Winkfield La. Wink 92
Winkfield Rd. Ascot 120
Winkfield Row. Burl 92
Winkfield St. Burl 92
Winnersh Gate. Winn 88
Winnersh Gr. Winn 88
Winscombe. Brac 117
Winser Dr. Read 85
Winston Cl. Shin 113
Winston Way. Pur O T 57
Winston Way. That 106
Winter Hill. Cook 2
Winter Hill. Cook 19
Winter Hill. Cook 19
Winter Hill. Maid 19
Winterbourne Rd. Box 8
Winterbourne Rd. Wint 76
Winterton Dr. Newb 104
Winton Cres. Yate 149
Winton Rd. Read 113
Wintoun Path. Slough 21
Wintringham Way. Pur O T .. 57
Winvale. Slough 42
Winwood. Slough 43
Wise's Firs. Sulhd 110
Wishmoor Cl. Camb 151
Wishmoor Rd. Camb 151
Wispington Cl. Winn 87
Wistaria La. Yate 149
Wisteria Cl. Woki 115
Wiston Terr. Read 86
Witcham Cl. Winn 114
Withey Cl. Wind 66
Witheygate Ave. Stai 97
Withy Cl. Light 146
Withy Cl. Read 84
Withy Croft. Slough 43
Withybed La. Kint 101
Wittenham Ave. Read 85
Wittenham Rd. Brac 118
Woburn Cl. Camb 152
Woburn Cl. Caver 58
Wokingham Rd. Brac 117
Wokingham Rd. Hurst 88
Wokingham Rd. Read 87
Wokingham Rd. Sand 143
Wolf La. Wind 66
Wolseley St. Read 86
Wolsey Rd. Ashf 97

olsey Rd. Caver 59 D1
olsingham Way. That 106 B1
ondesford Dale. Binf 90 B2
ooburn Manor Park. Bou E 3 F3
ooburn Mews. Bou E 3 F3
ood Cl. Wind 67 E2
ood End. Crow 142 C2
ood Green Cl. Read 85 F4
ood La. Arbo 114 C2
ood La. Binf 90 B1
ood La. Iver 44 B4
ood La. Slough 42 A2
ood Moor. Finch 141 F1
ood Rd. Camb 151 D1
ood Rd. Stai 125 D3
ood Ridge. Newb 130 C4
oodberry Cl. Caver 59 D2
oodbine Cl. Sand 150 B4
oodbine Cl. Winn 87 E1
oodbine La. Newt 130 C1
oodbourne Cl. Yate 149 E3
oodbridge Rd. Black 150 A3
oodbridge Rd. Read 84 A3
oodbury. Lamb 25 E1
oodby Dr. Sunn 120 C1
oodcote Rd. Caver 58 C2
oodcote Rd. Sou S 14 B2
oodcote Way. Caver 58 B3
oodcote. Maid 39 E3
oodend Cl. Burl 119 F4
oodend Dr. Ascot 120 A2
oodenhill. Brac 117 F1
oodfield Dr. Maid 39 D3
oodfield Way. Thea 83 F2
oodford Cl. Caver 58 C2
oodford Green. Brac 118 C3
oodford Way. Slough 22 A1
oodhall La. Windl 146 C4
oodhaw. Stai 96 A2
oodhouse La. Head 133 E1
oodhouse St. Binf 90 C1
oodhouse St. Brac 117 F4
oodhurst La. Woki 115 F4
oodhurst Rd. Maid 20 A1
oodies Cl. Binf 90 B1
oodland Ave. Slough 42 B3
oodland Ave. Wind 66 C2
oodland Ave. Woki 115 F4
oodland Cl. Mar 1 C2

Woodland Cres. Brac 91 E1
Woodland Dr. Read 84 B4
Woodland Way. Mar 1 C2
Woodlands Ave. Bur C 111 D2
Woodlands Ave. Wood 87 E4
Woodlands Busn Park. Maid ... 39 D1
Woodlands Cl. Ascot 119 F2
Woodlands Cl. Black 150 C1
Woodlands Cl. Herm 78 C3
Woodlands Cl. Crow 143 F1
Woodlands Gr. Caver 59 F2
Woodlands La. Windl 146 C2
Woodlands Parade. Ashf 98 B1
Woodlands Park Ave. Whi Wa 39 D1
Woodlands Park Rd. Maid 39 D2
Woodlands Park Rd. Whi Wa . 39 D2
Woodlands Rd E. Vir W 122 B3
Woodlands Rd W. Vir W 122 B3
Woodlands Rd. Camb 151 D3
Woodlands Rd. Shipl 35 F2
Woodlands Rd. Tad 134 B1
Woodlands Rd. Vir W 122 B3
Woodlands Ride. Ascot 120 A2
Woodlands The. Woki 115 E2
Woodlands Wlk. Black 150 C1
Woodlands. Yate 149 E2
Woodlee Cl. Vir W 122 B4
Woodley Green. Wood 87 F4
Woodman Cl. Read 113 E3
Woodman's La. Bur C 110 C2
Woodmancott Cl. Brac 118 C2
Woodmere Cl. Read 87 D1
Woodmere. Brac 118 C3
Woodmoor End. Cook 20 A4
Woodpecker Cl. Twyf 61 F2
Woodridge Cl. Brac 118 B3
Woodrow Dr. Woki 116 C3
Woods Rd. Caver 59 F2
Woodsend Cl. Read 113 E4
Woodshore Cl. Vir W 122 A2
Woodside Ave. Fla H 3 E4
Woodside Cl. Buck 107 E3
Woodside Cl. Woki 141 F4
Woodside La. Wink 93 E2
Woodside Rd. Ascot 93 D1
Woodside Way. Read 113 E4
Woodside Way. Vir W 122 A3
Woodside. Black 150 B2
Woodside. Fla H 3 E3

Woodside. Newb 130 B4
Woodside. Sand 150 C4
Woodstock Ave. Slough 43 E1
Woodstock Cl. Maid 19 F1
Woodstock St. Read 86 C4
Woodthorpe Rd. Ashf 97 E2
Woodthorpe Rd. Stai 97 E2
Woodview Rd. Pangb 56 B3
Woodville Cl. Black 150 A3
Woodward Cl. Winn 88 B1
Woodway Rd. Blew 12 A4
Woodway. Camb 151 D3
Woodwaye. Wood 87 E4
Woodyer Cl. Wood 87 F3
Woolacombe Dr. Read 86 C1
Woolford Cl. Burl 92 B1
Woolhampton Hill. Wool 108 B2
Woolhampton Way. Brac 118 B2
Woosehill La. Woki 115 F3
Woosehill La. Woki 115 F4
Woosehill. Woki 115 F3
Wootton Cl. Read 84 B4
Wootton Dr. Woo G 3 F4
Wootton Rd. Hen-O-T 35 E4
Wootton Way. Maid 39 E3
Worcester Cl. Maid 39 E2
Worcester Cl. Read 85 D3
Worcester Dr. Ashf 98 A2
Wordsworth Ave. Yate 149 D2
Wordsworth Ct. Caver 59 E4
Wordsworth Rd. Slough 21 E1
Wordsworth Rd. That 106 B2
Wordsworth. Brac 117 F2
Worlds End Hill. Brac 118 C2
Worple Cl. Ashf 97 D1
Worple Rd. Stai 97 D1
Worple The. Wray 68 C1
Worrall Way. Read 113 F4
Worster Rd. Cook 19 F3
Worton Dr. Read 113 D4
Wrabness Way. Stai 124 A4
Wraysbury Rd. Stai 96 B3
Wraysbury Rd. Wray 96 B3
Wren Cl. Bur C 111 D2
Wren Cl. Woki 115 F3
Wren Cl. Yate 149 D3
Wren Ct. Slough 44 A2
Wren's Ave. Ashf 98 B2
Wrenfield Dr. Caver 58 C3

Wrensfield. Mar 1 B1
Wrenswood Cl. Read 113 D4
Wright Cl. Wood 88 A4
Wright. Oak G 66 B2
Wroxham Rd. Wood 87 E4
Wroxham. Brac 117 F2
Wurford Dr. That 106 C2
Wyatt Rd. Stai 97 D2
Wyatt Rd. Wind 66 B2
Wychcotes. Caver 58 C2
Wychelm Rd. Light 153 E4
Wychelm Rd. Shin 113 F3
Wychwood Ave. Brac 118 C3
Wychwood Cl. Read 86 C1
Wychwood Cres. Read 86 C2
Wychwood Pl. Camb 145 D1
Wychwood Pl. Camb 152 A4
Wycombe La. Woo G 3 E4
Wycombe Rd. Mar 1 C2
Wycombe Rd. Mar B 1 C3
Wye Cl. Ashf 98 A2
Wye Cl. Read 84 C3
Wye Rd. Woo G 3 E4
Wykeham Cl. Harm 71 D4
Wykeham Rd. Read 87 D3
Wylam. Brac 117 F2
Wylands Rd. Slough 44 A1
Wyld Court Hill. Hamp N 53 E3
Wymers Cl. Burn 21 D2
Wymers Wood Rd. Burn 21 D2
Wyncote Cl. Read 86 C1
Wyndale Cl. Hen-O-T 15 F1
Wyndham Cl. Yate 149 E4
Wyndham Cres. Burn 21 D2
Wyndham Cres. Wood 60 B1
Wyndham Rd. Newb 105 E3
Wynford Cl. Read 85 E2
Wynnstay Gdns. Mar B 1 C3
Wynsham Way. Windl 146 A3
Wyre Ct. Sulh 57 E2
Wyres Dale. Brac 118 C1
Wythe Mead. Binf 90 A1
Wyvern Cl. Brac 118 A3

Yale Cl. Crow 143 F1
Yard Mead. Eng G 96 A3
Yardley. Brac 117 F2
Yarnold Cl. Woki 116 C4
Yarnton Cl. Caver 59 E3

Yateley Dr. Yate 149 D1
Yateley Rd. Sand 149 F4
Yattendon La. Asham 54 B1
Yattendon La. Yatt 54 B1
Yattendon Rd. Herm 79 D4
Yaverland Dr. Bags 145 E1
Ye Meads. Tapl 40 C3
Yelverton Rd. Read 86 B2
Yeomans La. Newt 131 D1
Yeomans Way. Camb 151 F3
Yeosfield. Swal 139 E2
Yeoveney Cl. Stan 96 B3
Yeovil Rd. Burn 41 F4
Yeovil Rd. Sand 143 F1
Yew Cl. Woki 115 F3
Yew Gate. Newb 104 C3
Yew La. Read 85 F3
Yew Tree Cl. Maid 39 F4
Yew Tree Ct. Gori 34 B3
Yew Tree Rd. Slough 43 D2
Yew Tree Rise. Read 84 B3
Yew Tree Wlk. Camb 151 F1
Yewhurst Cl. Twyf 61 E3
Yewtrees. Stai 123 E3
Yield Hall La. Read 86 A4
Yield Hall Pl. Read 86 A4
Yockley Cl. Camb 152 B2
Yoreham Cl. Winn 87 F1
York Ave. Slough 42 B4
York Ave. Wind 67 D3
York Cl. Newb 105 D1
York Rd. Binf 90 B2
York Rd. Camb 151 E4
York Rd. Hen-O-T 15 E1
York Rd. Hung 100 B2
York Rd. Maid 40 A4
York Rd. Mar 1 B1
York Rd. Newb 105 D1
York Rd. Read 59 D1
York Rd. Wind 67 D3
York Way. Sand 150 A4
Yorktown Rd. Sand 150 B4
Youlden Cl. Camb 152 A3
Youlden Dr. Camb 152 A3

Zealand Ave. Harm 70 C4
Zinnia Cl. Woki 115 E4
Zinzan St. Read 85 F4

ORDNANCE SURVEY
STREET ATLASES

The Ordnance Survey / Philip's County Street Atlases provide unique and definitive mapping of entire counties

Counties available
- Berkshire
- Buckinghamshire
- East Essex
- West Essex
- North Hampshire
- South Hampshire
- Hertfordshire
- East Kent
- West Kent
- Nottinghamshire
- Oxfordshire
- Surrey
- East Sussex
- West Sussex
- Warwickshire

The County Street Atlases are revised and updated on a regular basis and new titles are added to the series. Many counties are now available in full-size hardback and softback editions as well as handy pocket-size versions.

The series is available from all good bookshops or by mail order direct from the publisher. However, the order form opposite may not reflect the complete range of titles available so it is advisable to check by telephone before placing your order. Payment can be made by credit card or cheque/postal order in the following ways:

By phone *Phone your order through on our special Credit Card Hotline on 0933 410511. Speak to our customer service team during office hours (9am to 5pm) or leave a message on the answering machine, quoting CSA94, your full credit card number plus expiry date and your full name and address*

By post *Simply fill out the order form opposite (you may photocopy it) and send it to: Cash Sales Department, Reed Book Services, PO Box 5, Rushden, Northants, NN10 6YX*

STREET ATLASES

CSA94

	Hardback	Softback	Pocket	
	£12.99	£8.99	£4.99	
Berkshire	£ ___ . ___ ISBN 0-540-05992-7	£ ___ . ___ ISBN 0-540-05993-5	£ ___ . ___ ISBN 0-540-05994-3	► £ ___ . ___
Buckinghamshire	£ ___ . ___ ISBN 0-540-05989-7	£ ___ . ___ ISBN 0-540-05990-0	£ ___ . ___ ISBN 0-540-05991-9	► £ ___ . ___
East Essex	£ ___ . ___ ISBN 0-540-05848-3	£ ___ . ___ ISBN 0-540-05866-1	£ ___ . ___ ISBN 0-540-05850-5	► £ ___ . ___
West Essex	£ ___ . ___ ISBN 0-540-05849-1	£ ___ . ___ ISBN 0-540-05867-X	£ ___ . ___ ISBN 0-540-05851-3	► £ ___ . ___
North Hampshire	£ ___ . ___ ISBN 0-540-05852-1	£ ___ . ___ ISBN 0-540-05853-X	£ ___ . ___ ISBN 0-540-05854-8	► £ ___ . ___
South Hampshire	£ ___ . ___ ISBN 0-540-05855-6	£ ___ . ___ ISBN 0-540-05856-4	£ ___ . ___ ISBN 0-540-05857-2	► £ ___ . ___
Hertfordshire	£ ___ . ___ ISBN 0-540-05995-1	£ ___ . ___ ISBN 0-540-05996-X	£ ___ . ___ ISBN 0-540-05997-8	► £ ___ . ___
East Kent	£ ___ . ___ ISBN 0-540-06026-7	£ ___ . ___ ISBN 0-540-06027-5	£ ___ . ___ ISBN 0-540-06028-3	► £ ___ . ___
West Kent	£ ___ . ___ ISBN 0-540-06029-1	£ ___ . ___ ISBN 0-540-06031-3	£ ___ . ___ ISBN 0-540-06030-5	► £ ___ . ___
Nottinghamshire	£ ___ . ___ ISBN 0-540-05858-0	£ ___ . ___ ISBN 0-540-05859-9	£ ___ . ___ ISBN 0-540-05860-2	► £ ___ . ___
Oxfordshire	£ ___ . ___ ISBN 0-540-05986-2	£ ___ . ___ ISBN 0-540-05987-0	£ ___ . ___ ISBN 0-540-05988-9	► £ ___ . ___
Surrey	£ ___ . ___ ISBN 0-540-05983-8	£ ___ . ___ ISBN 0-540-05984-6	£ ___ . ___ ISBN 0-540-05985-4	► £ ___ . ___
East Sussex	£ ___ . ___ ISBN 0-540-05875-0	£ ___ . ___ ISBN 0-540-05874-2	£ ___ . ___ ISBN 0-540-05873-4	► £ ___ . ___
West Sussex	£ ___ . ___ ISBN 0-540-05876-9	£ ___ . ___ ISBN 0-540-05877-7	£ ___ . ___ ISBN 0-540-05878-5	► £ ___ . ___
	£10.99			
Warwickshire	£ ___ . ___ ISBN 0-540-05642-1			► £ ___ . ___

Name _____

Address _____

Postcode _____

Account number ⬤⬤⬤⬤⬤ ⬤⬤⬤⬤ ⬤⬤⬤⬤ ⬤⬤⬤⬤

Expiry date ⬤⬤ ⬤⬤

Signature _____

I enclose a cheque/postal order for £ ___ made payable to **Reed Book Services** or please debit my ◄Access ◄American Express ◄Visa account by £ ___

⬤ Please tick this box if you do not wish your name to be used by other carefully selected organisations that may wish to send you information about other products and services

◆ **Free postage and packing** ◆ All available titles will normally be dispatched within 5 working days of receipt of order, but please allow up to 28 days for delivery.

Registered office: Michelin House, 81 Fulham Road, London SW3 6RB. Registered in England No 1974080